# ROUTLEDGE HANDBOOK OF BORDERS AND TOURISM

The *Routledge Handbook of Borders and Tourism* examines the multiple and diverse relationships between global tourism and political boundaries. With contributions from international, leading thinkers, this book offers theoretical frameworks for understanding borders and tourism and empirical examples from borderlands throughout the world.

This handbook provides a comprehensive overview of historical and contemporary thinking about evolving national frontiers and tourism. Tourism, by definition, entails people crossing borders of various scales and is manifested in a wide range of conceptualizations of human mobility. Borders significantly influence tourism and determine how the industry grows, is managed, and manifests on the ground. Simultaneously, tourism strongly affects borders, border laws, border policies, and international relations. This book highlights the traditional relationships between borders and tourism, including borders as attractions, barriers, transit spaces, and determiners of tourism landscapes. It offers deeper insights into current thinking about space and place, mobilities, globalization, citizenship, conflict and peace, trans-frontier cooperation, geopolitics, "otherness" and here versus there, the heritagization of borders and memory-making, biodiversity, and bordering, debordering, and rebordering processes.

Offering an unparalleled interdisciplinary glimpse at political boundaries and tourism, this handbook will be an essential resource for all students and researchers of tourism, geopolitics and border studies, geography, anthropology, sociology, history, international relations, and global studies.

**Dallen J. Timothy** is Professor of Community Resources and Development at Arizona State University and Senior Sustainability Scientist at the Julie Anne Wrigley Global Institute of Sustainability. He is also Senior Research Associate at the University of Johannesburg, South Africa; Visiting Professor at Hunan Normal University, Guangxi University, and Luoyang Normal University, China; and Guest Professor in the Erasmus Mundus European Master in Tourism Management programme based at the University of Girona, Spain. He is the founding editor of the *Journal of Heritage Tourism* and currently serves on the editorial boards of 24 international journals. He is a commissioning or co-commissioning editor for four book series with Routledge and other publishers. He has ongoing research projects in North America, Asia, Europe, the Middle East, and Africa on topics related to borders and tourism, religious tourism, heritage, and community empowerment.

**Alon Gelbman** is Senior Lecturer in the Department of Tourism and Hotel Management at Kinneret College on the Sea of Galilee, Israel. He is a cultural geographer and his research interests include international tourism and geopolitical borders, tourism and peace, urban/rural tourism, and host–guest relationships. His research papers have been published in leading academic journals, and he has conducted empirical field studies, developed theories, presented frequently at international conferences, taught, and received invitations regularly to speak at conferences and seminars abroad. A major thrust of his research in the tourism area is developing a theoretical foundation for tourism–geopolitical border relations between countries around the world and developing global models and theories about it, with significant connections to the topic of tourism and peace.

# ROUTLEDGE HANDBOOK OF BORDERS AND TOURISM

Edited by
*Dallen J. Timothy and Alon Gelbman*

Cover image: © Getty Images

First published 2023
by Routledge
4 Park Square, Milton Park, Abingdon, Oxon OX14 4RN

and by Routledge
605 Third Avenue, New York, NY 10158

*Routledge is an imprint of the Taylor & Francis Group, an informa business*

© 2023 selection and editorial matter, by Dallen J. Timothy and Alon Gelbman; individual chapters, the contributors

The right of Dallen J. Timothy and Alon Gelbman to be identified as the authors of the editorial material, and of the authors for their individual chapters, has been asserted in accordance with sections 77 and 78 of the Copyright, Designs and Patents Act 1988.

All rights reserved. No part of this book may be reprinted or reproduced or utilized in any form or by any electronic, mechanical, or other means, now known or hereafter invented, including photocopying and recording, or in any information storage or retrieval system, without permission in writing from the publishers.

*Trademark notice*: Product or corporate names may be trademarks or registered trademarks, and are used only for identification and explanation without intent to infringe.

*British Library Cataloguing-in-Publication Data*
A catalogue record for this book is available from the British Library

ISBN: 978-0-367-48277-0 (hbk)
ISBN: 978-1-032-38662-1 (pbk)
ISBN: 978-1-003-03899-3 (ebk)

DOI: 10.4324/9781003038993

Typeset in Bembo
by SPi Technologies India Pvt Ltd (Straive)

# CONTENTS

*List of Figures* ix
*List of Tables* xi
*Contributors* xii

1 Understanding Borders and Tourism: Complex Relationships and Evolving Patterns 1
  *Dallen J. Timothy and Alon Gelbman*

**PART I**
**Past and Present Perspectives on Borders, Tourism, and Mobility** 15

2 Travellers' Tales: How Human Stories Portray "Elsewhere" 17
  *Noel Parker*

3 Borderlands and Commensality 32
  *Thomas M. Wilson*

4 New Borders and Mobility in the Age of Globalization: De-bordering, Re-bordering, and Beyond 47
  *Anssi Paasi and Md Azmeary Ferdoush*

5 *Aurea Mediocritas*: Cross-border Cooperation between Materiality and Relationality 61
  *Sylwia Dołzbłasz and Katarzyna Szmigiel-Rawska*

6 Tourism, Citizenship and Border Governance: Past Dynamics and New Reconfigurations 73
  *Raoul V. Bianchi and Marcus L. Stephenson*

7  How Space, Borders and Boundaries Shape Biodiversity Values         87
    *Martin Dallimer and Niels Strange*

**PART II**
**Borders, Barriers, Access, and (Im)mobilities**                       **99**

 8  Migration and Borders                                               101
    *Sascha Krannich*

 9  Physical Access and Perceived Constraints: Borders as Barriers to Travel
    Mobilities and Tourism Development                                  112
    *Olga Hannonen and Eeva-Kaisa Prokkola*

10  Enclave Tourism: Bounded Spaces and Social Exclusion                126
    *Adam Weaver*

11  Globalization, Mobility, and Border Restrictions: Tourism Perspectives  134
    *Aharon Kellerman*

12  Military Occupations and Tourism                                    145
    *Jack Shepherd and Daniel Laven*

13  Cultural Boundaries and Ethnic Representation in Cross-border Tourism
    Destinations                                                        161
    *Min (Lucy) Zhang and Jaume Guia*

**PART III**
**The Anomalous Border Landscape: Tourism Values and Assets**          **175**

14  Borderlines: Linear Tourist Attractions in Liminal Space            177
    *Marek Więckowski*

15  Borders of Conflict as Tourist Attractions                          195
    *Alon Gelbman*

16  Borders as Dark Tourism Spaces                                      205
    *Richard Sharpley*

17  Borders, Heritage, and Memory                                       219
    *Dallen J. Timothy and Marek Więckowski*

18  Tour Guiding in Contested Geopolitical Borderlands: Narratives
    and Approaches    241
    *Alon Gelbman and Rachel Schweitzer*

19  Tourists' Performances at Border Landmarks in the Era of Social Media    253
    *Alix Varnajot*

## PART IV
## The Competitive Advantage of the Border    267

20  Outshopping Abroad: Cross-border Shopping Tourism and
    the Competitive Advantage of Borders    269
    *Teemu Makkonen*

21  Borders and Healthcare: Medical Mobility, Globalization and
    Borderland Tourism    281
    *Tomás Cuevas Contreras and Isabel Zizaldra Hernández*

22  Crossing Borders and Border Crossings: Sex, Tourism, and
    Travelling in the Sensual Spaces of Borderlands    296
    *C. Michael Hall and Kimberley J. Wood*

23  Transboundary Second-home Tourism    310
    *Olga Hannonen*

24  Merchants, Smugglers, and Wanglers: Non-conventional Tourism and
    Trade across Political Borders    324
    *Gábor Michalkó, Mihály Tömöri, and Noémi Ilyés*

## PART V
## Contemporary Change: Transfrontier Cooperation and Collaboration    339

25  Planning and Managing Tourism in Transborder Areas    341
    *Arie Stoffelen*

26  Cross-border Tourism Initiatives in the European Union    353
    *Eeva-Kaisa Prokkola*

27  Tourism in Protected Areas and Transboundary Parks for Peace    366
    *Alon Gelbman and Rachel Schweitzer*

28 Transfrontier Routes and Trails: Cooperation and Scalar Considerations 379
*Arie Stoffelen*

29 Tourism Cluster Management in Cross-border Destinations: Blind Spots and Invisible Lines 391
*Jaume Guia, Dani Blasco, and Natàlia Ferrer-Roca*

30 Tourism and Political Borders: Past–present Dynamics and the Age of Globalization 403
*Dallen J. Timothy and Alon Gelbman*

*Index* 419

# FIGURES

| | | |
|---|---|---|
| 1.1 | The attractiveness factors of border tourism | 6 |
| 7.1 | People may hold non-use values for conservation in countries far away | 91 |
| 7.2 | International collaboration is crucial for conservation of migratory species such as the Montagu's Harrier. However, public support may be greater for local conservation initiatives than global ones | 93 |
| 12.1 | "Les touristes allemands au Maroc" ("The German tourists in Morocco"). Front cover of Free French Newspaper, *Le Courrier de l'Air*, March 10, 1941 | 147 |
| 12.2 | Entrance to Shuhada Street, Hebron | 156 |
| 12.3 | Divergent pathways—an example of apartheid infrastructure in Hebron. While Israelis and tourists can walk on the left side of the barrier, Palestinians must walk on the right | 157 |
| 14.1 | Checkpoint Charlie, one of Berlin's top tourist attractions | 183 |
| 14.2 | The Haskell Free Library and Opera House is divided by the USA–Canada border | 185 |
| 14.3 | The tripoint where Belgium, Germany, and the Netherlands meet has been developed into a tourist attraction and amusement park | 186 |
| 14.4 | The Iron Curtain Trail (*EuroVelo* 13) near the Czech–Austria border | 189 |
| 15.1 | Bental Mountain Observatory view of Syria, Lebanon, and Israel | 198 |
| 15.2 | The Dorasan train station is located just inside South Korea near the border of the contentious Demilitarized Zone between the North and the South | 199 |
| 16.1 | View towards Varosha | 206 |
| 16.2 | UN Buffer zone in Nicosia, Cyprus | 212 |
| 17.1 | The extraordinarily large Turkish Republic of Northern Cyprus flag visible from the Republic of Cyprus | 224 |
| 17.2 | The authors working on this chapter astride an historic border marker in the Krkonise-Karkonisze Transfrontier Biosphere Reserve. Marek is in Poland. Dallen is in the Czech Republic | 227 |
| 17.3 | Reconstructed Dodendraad (Wire of Death) on the Dutch–Belgian border from WWI with interpretive signs | 229 |
| 17.4 | This boundary obelisk inside the Roman ruins of Panissars demarcates the French–Spanish border | 235 |
| 18.1 | Selected tour guiding approaches at contested border tourism destinations | 245 |
| 18.2 | Tour guiding at the 'Island of Peace' on the Israeli-Jordanian border | 247 |

| | | |
|---|---|---|
| 18.3 | Tour guiding narrative and freedom at conflict and contested border tourism attractions | 250 |
| 19.1 | Approaching the restricted area of the Finnish–Russian border, in Näränkä, south of Kuusamo, Finland | 255 |
| 19.2 | The state of Alaska welcoming us on the Klondike Highway, on our way to Skagway | 256 |
| 19.3 | One foot here, one foot there at the Arctic Circle in Rovaniemi, Finland | 258 |
| 19.4 | Leaving the mundane world for the unfamiliar Arctic | 259 |
| 19.5 | A passport stamp from the Arctic Circle in Rovaniemi, Finland | 261 |
| 20.1 | Cross-border shopping tourism: preconditions, rationales, impact, and reactions | 276 |
| 21.1 | Most requested treatments in medical tourism | 283 |
| 21.2 | Medical tourism, health, and wellness market | 286 |
| 21.3 | Part of the medical tourism landscape of Mexicali, a 'medical tourism lane' enables American medical tourists a quicker return to the US border crossing. Note the US border fence on the right | 289 |
| 21.4 | The medical landscape of Los Aldgodones is dominated by dental services but is also comprised of many other healthcare services | 290 |
| 23.1 | German and other foreign-owned second homes on the island of Gran Canaria, Spain | 314 |
| 23.2 | A Russian-owned second home in the Finnish countryside | 317 |
| 24.1 | The Corozal Free Trade Zone lies just inside Belize before Belizean customs. Here, Mexican consumers shop at much lower prices for merchandise for their own use, as well as to re-sell at home. This commercial zone provides retail opportunities for legal and illegal trade | 327 |
| 24.2 | Hegyeshalom—former border checkpoint between Austria and Hungary, where smuggling was common. Nowadays, as both countries are EU and Schengen states, it is no longer used and sits deserted | 330 |
| 27.1 | Three spatial types of international parks | 370 |
| 27.2 | An ecosystem exhibition of the Russian–Norwegian transboundary cooperation in the Barents region as part of the European Green Belt along the former Iron Curtain | 374 |
| 27.3 | The interaction between sustainable tourism and community, environment and peace diplomacy | 376 |
| 28.1 | Examples of existing transboundary trails on different continents and at different scales. Top left: EuroVelo cycling routes in Europe (EuroVelo, 2020). Top right: transboundary hiking and cycling trails in the borderlands between the states of Bavaria, Thuringia and Saxony in Germany, and the Czech Republic. Bottom left: interstate routes of the US National Trail System (National Park Service, 2021) and interstate recreational trails in Canada. Bottom right: Existing and proposed ecotourism and cultural tourism trails and corridors in the Himalayas by ICIMOD (2019). Note that these maps do not include all existing tourism routes and trails in the highlighted regions | 383 |
| 29.1 | Phases in cross-border tourism cluster evolution | 394 |
| 29.2 | The cross-border Cerdanya Valley region, including the enclave Llívia | 396 |
| 30.1 | This Egyptian casino only 150 meters from the Israeli border was built at this site to capitalize on its close proximity to Israel | 404 |
| 30.2 | Though clearly demarcated, the Colombia-Brazil border at Tabatinga and Leticia is open and facilitates a truly transfrontier lived action space for borderlanders and tourists | 412 |
| 30.3 | The editors agreeing to edit this book together across the Dutch–Belgian border! | 414 |

# TABLES

| | | |
|---|---|---|
| 9.1 | Physical and mental barriers | 113 |
| 17.1 | UNESCO World Heritage List, transboundary properties | 232 |
| 17.2 | Examples of divided or twin heritage towns and cities | 236 |
| 21.1 | Top ten medical tourism destinations, 2021 | 284 |
| 21.2 | Important variables that promote medical tourism mobility | 286 |
| 27.1 | Examples of recently established nature-based transboundary protected areas | 368 |
| 27.2 | Examples of international peace parks established to commemorate or encourage peaceful relations and nature conservation | 373 |
| 28.1 | Share of tourism investments and route and trail investments as part of the 2007–2014 INTERREG IV-a programme in Europe | 382 |

# CONTRIBUTORS

**Raoul V. Bianchi** is Reader in Political Economy in the Future Economies Research Centre and Department of Economics, Policy and International Business at Manchester Metropolitan University. His main research interests include the political economy of international tourism and visitor economies, tourism geopolitics and citizenship, tourism work and labour relations, and the transition to tourism economies beyond capitalism. His principal geographical focus is southern Europe and the Mediterranean. He is currently an Associate Editor of *Annals of Tourism Research: Empirical Insights* and sits on the editorial board of *Tourism Planning and Development* and the *Journal of Balkan and Near Eastern Studies*. He previously served on the executive council of the UK-based NGO, Tourism Concern.

**Dani Blasco** is a tenure-track lecturer in the Faculty of Tourism, University of Girona, Catalonia. He is also Senior Research Associate at the University of Johannesburg, South Africa. His PhD thesis was titled *Tourism Destination Zoning and Governance in Border Regions*. His research interests are organizational networks and governance in tourism, tourism destinations as complex systems, tourism destination planning and development, and human capital in tourism destinations and organizations. He has published in tourism journals, such as *Annals of Tourism Research*, the *Journal of Sustainable Tourism*, *Tourism Geographies*, *Tourism Review*, the *Journal of Heritage Tourism*, *Tourism Planning & Development*, and the *European Journal of Tourism Research*. He has also reviewed for many international journals in the field of tourism.

**Tomás Cuevas Contreras** is Research Professor in the Administrative Sciences Department in the Universidad Autónoma de Ciudad Juárez, Mexico. He is a member of the National System of Researchers (SNI), level 1, and the Professional Development Program for Teachers (PRODEP). His research analyses social networks, creativity, innovation and competitiveness, culture in tourism, and the USA–Mexico border and its implications for medical, health, and well-being tourism. He has organized the International Seminar on Tourism, Administration and Finance and held the Sergio Molina International Heritage Chair in Tourism since 2006. He has recently received several awards, including the National Prize for Tourism Education in 2018; a Research Recognition Award from the Center for Applied Research in 2018; and the Making a Difference award presented by the Tom Lea Foundation. Dr Cuevas is also Visiting Professor with the International Visitor Leadership Program, Economic Development through Tourism, sponsored by the US Department of State.

*Contributors*

**Martin Dallimer** is affiliated with the Sustainability Research Institute in the School of Earth and Environment at the University of Leeds. He is interested in applying and integrating research techniques from across different disciplines to better understand the sustainable management of natural environments, biodiversity, and ecosystems in a human-dominated world. His research falls into three broad areas: (i) land degradation, sustainable agriculture, land-use, and development; (ii) urbanization, urban greenspaces, and sustainable cities; and (iii) ecosystem services and biodiversity conservation. His work centres on applying and developing methods to understand the multiple values (including in monetary and non-monetary terms, as well as the metrics of ecological "quality") of ecosystems and natural environments. He is particularly interested in how values differ between sectors of society, such as across borders and cultures, whether values might be linked to biodiversity and ecosystem properties, and the implications for how we manage, conserve, and restore the natural world.

**Sylwia Dołzbłasz** is Associate Professor in the Department of Spatial Management in the Institute of Geography and Regional Development at the University of Wrocław, Poland,. Her main research interests include border studies and regional development. Recent publications include "Bilateral Relations at the Subnational Level: Transborder Cooperation Networks in the Polish–German Borderlands" with Andrzej Raczyk (2021), "From Service Areas to Empty Transport Corridors? The Impact of Border Openings on Service and Retail Facilities at Polish–Czech Border Crossings" with Marek Furmankiewicz and Krzysztof Buryło (2020), and "Border-city Pairs in Europe and North America: Spatial Dimensions of Integration and Separation" with Francisco Lara-Valencia (2019).

**Md Azmeary Ferdoush** is a postdoctoral researcher at the Karelian Institute in the University of Eastern Finland. Azmeary specializes in the study of borders, (im)mobilities, (non-)citizenship, states, territories, sovereignty, and geopolitics with a regional focus on South Asia and the Finnish Arctic. Specifically, by analysing interrelations between global, national, and domestic (f)actors, Azmeary questions the complex and multilayered (re)production of artificially created categories such as nations, migrants, boundaries, and "(il)legals". An author of many academic journal articles and book chapters, he is also co-editor of *Borders and Mobility in South Asia and Beyond*, which was published in 2018.

**Natàlia Ferrer-Roca** is Adjunct Lecturer at the University of Girona (PhD, Victoria University of Wellington, New Zealand; MA, Westminster University, UK; and BA, Autonomous University of Barcelona). Her research focuses on the intersection between media and communication studies, and tourism and destination branding, with a special focus on political economy. She is also an independent trainer, researcher, and advisor, having worked for the European Broadcasting Union (EBU, Geneva), the Government of Catalonia, and Diputació de Barcelona, among others.

**Alon Gelbman** is Senior Lecturer in the Department of Tourism and Hotel Management at Kinneret College on the Sea of Galilee, Israel. He is a cultural geographer and his research interests include international tourism and geopolitical borders, tourism and peace, urban/rural tourism and host–guest relationships. His research papers have been published in leading academic journals, and he has conducted empirical field studies, developed theories, presented frequently at international conferences, taught, and received invitations regularly to speak at conferences and seminars abroad. A major thrust of his research in the tourism area is developing a theoretical foundation for tourism–geopolitical border relations between countries around the world and developing global models and theories about it, with significant connections to the topic of tourism and peace.

**Jaume Guia** is Associate Professor at the University of Girona and Senior Research Associate at the University of Johannesburg, South Africa and has been involved in the design, coordination, and delivery of international innovative joint master's degree programmes of excellence in the field of tourism management. Over the years he has led academic exchange programmes with partner universities in Ghana, Ethiopia, Kenya, Madagascar, South Africa, Botswana, Mauritius, Seychelles, Malaysia, India, China, USA, Canada, Mexico, Iran, Mongolia, and Fiji. He has supervised over 20 PhD dissertations, has led research and consultancy projects, and has published academic papers in internationally reputed journals on a variety of topics in the field of tourism destination management, including cross-border destinations, as well as in tourism and place-making, understanding travellers' experiences, new mobilities and forms of tourism, and tourism, sustainability, and justice.

**C. Michael Hall** is Professor in Marketing and Tourism at the University of Canterbury, Christchurch, New Zealand. He is also: Docent in Geography, Oulu University, Finland; Visiting Professor in tourism, Linneaus University, Kalmar, Sweden; and Guest Professor in the Department of Service Management, Lund University Helsingborg, Sweden. He is Co-editor of *Current Issues in Tourism*, and has published widely on tourism, regional development, sustainability, global environmental change, and world heritage.

**Olga Hannonen** is a post-doctoral researcher in the Business School at the University of Eastern Finland. Her expertise focuses largely on transborder tourism and mobilities. She has conducted research on: Russian transborder tourism and second-home ownership in Finland; intra-European residential tourism and digital nomadism on Gran Canaria, Spain; residential mobility in the Turkish Republic of Northern Cyprus; and digital nomadic mobilities. Thematically, she has been working with the socio-political implications of international mobilities and property ownership, travel motivations and constraints, and bordering mobilities in various forms.

**Noémi Ilyés** is an innovation program director at the CheckINN Tourism Innovation Hub in Hungary and a tourism analyst expert at the Hungarian Tourism Association. She graduated from the Corvinus University of Budapest as a tourism economist. Her nearly ten years of professional experience was mostly related to the management of tourism projects and international tourism organizations, which she used in the field of tourism diplomacy at the Ministry of Foreign Affairs and Trade in Hungary before joining the Hungarian Tourism Association. Her specialization is domestic and international tourism economics. She has been involved in several research projects and is currently working in the area of global tourism innovation. She works with her team at CheckINN to foster various tourism ideas and implement a talent development programme specialized in tourism in Hungary.

**Aharon Kellerman** is Professor Emeritus in the Department of Geography and Environmental Studies at the University of Haifa, Israel. He currently serves as President of Zefat Academic College in Israel. His specialities include the geography of information, the Internet, and personal mobilities. He has published widely on these and other topics.

**Sascha Krannich** is a researcher at Giessen University, Germany, with a focus on migration, transnationalism, development, and global health. He studied political science, sociology, and economics, and received his PhD as a scholar of the Friedrich Ebert Foundation at the Graduate School of Politics at Munster University, Germany. Within the frame of his research projects, he undertook several research stays abroad, including at the University of Oxford, Princeton University, the University of California, Los Angeles, as well as the Universidad de Guadalajara in Mexico and the Universidad Javeriana in Bogotá, Colombia. Currently, he is conducting a research project on the health of the Tamil diaspora in Germany and the United Kingdom in post-war Sri Lanka (funded by the Fritz Thyssen Foundation).

**Daniel Laven** is Associate Professor of Human Geography and currently serves as the head of the Department of Economics, Geography, Law, and Tourism at Mid Sweden University. Daniel's research is conducted under the auspices of the university's ETOUR Research Centre and focuses on issues of heritage.

**Teemu Makkonen** is Professor of Regional Studies and Economic Geography at the Karelian Institute (University of Eastern Finland). He also holds the title of Docent in Economic Geography (University of Helsinki) and Cross-border Economic Development (University of Eastern Finland). Among other duties, he has previously worked as Assistant Professor at the Department of Border Region Studies (University of Southern Denmark) and as a Post-doctoral Marie Curie fellow at the School of Hospitality and Tourism Management (University of Surrey). His research interests include regional innovativeness and development, tourism, and cross-border regions. Concerning tourism and borders, he has particularly focused on studying knowledge transfer processes in cross-border cooperation projects and cross-border shopping. He has published in leading tourism journals including *Annals of Tourism Research*, the *Journal of Travel Research*, and *Tourism Management*.

**Gábor Michalkó** is a scientific advisor at the CSFK Geographical Institute, and is Professor of Tourism at Corvinus University of Budapest, Hungary, where he is head of the Doctoral School of Business and Management. He was awarded a PhD in Geography from the University of Debrecen in 1998, and a DSc (academic doctor of sciences) from the Hungarian Academy of Sciences in 2009, for his contribution to tourism geography. His recent research interests include urban tourism, shopping tourism, health tourism, human ecology of tourism, and the relationship between tourism and the quality of life. He has published 8 books and 150 scientific articles. He has presented at many international conferences (e.g., the American Association of Geographers (AAG), the Association of Geographical Societies in Europe (EUGEO), and the International Geographical Union (IGU)). He is a member of the steering committee of the Commission on Global Change and Human Mobility (IGU GLOBILITY), as well as a member of the editorial boards of the *Hungarian Geographical Bulletin* and *Regional Statistics*.

**Anssi Paasi** was Professor of Geography at the University of Oulu, Finland, from 1989; he has been Professor Emeritus since February 2022. He has published widely on spatial/political geographic theory, concepts, and processes in various geography and political science/international relations (IR) journals and edited collections. He has also been interested in power–knowledge relations in contemporary neoliberal academia. He is the author of *Territories, Boundaries and Consciousness* (1996). His most recent co-edited books are *Handbook on the Geographies of Regions and Territories* and *Borderless Worlds for Whom? Ethics, Moralities and Mobilities* (Routledge, 2019).

**Noel Parker** is Associate Professor Emeritus of Political Theory in the Department of Political Science at the University of Copenhagen. Over the years, he has contributed to the theory of

*Contributors*

margins—starting with *Margins in European Integration* (2000). *The Geopolitics of Europe's Identity* (2008) and "From Borders to Margins" (in *Alternatives* 2009) followed. A recent item was "Borderwork and its Contraries" in Cooper and Tinning's (2021) *Debating and Defining Borders*. Other publications have addressed the global history of revolutions and of empires. He is currently working on a memoir of Britain's foreign-policy identity and Europe, entitled *British Post-imperialism from Below*.

**Eeva-Kaisa Prokkola** is Professor of Geography at the University of Oulu and holds the title of Docent in Human Geography and Border Studies at the University of Eastern Finland. She has extensive experience in the conceptual and empirical studies of borders, border regions, and communities and their tourism development. She has published widely about European internal and external border regions in internationally acclaimed journals and book volumes and has served as an expert on several international panels and journals. Prokkola has co-edited several anthologies, such as *Borderlands Resilience: Transitions, Adaptation and Resistance at Borders* (Routledge, Border Region Series, 2022). She is currently leading a Eudaimonia Institute spearheaded project on "Cross-border region resilience" at the University of Oulu.

**Rachel Schweitzer** holds a master's degree with honours in Geography and the Environment from Bar-Ilan University, Israel, in the programme "Planning, Conservation and Development of Landscape and Cultural Assets". Her research focuses on the development of conservation concepts and conservation policy in connection with built heritage in Israel during the twentieth and early twenty-first centuries. Her interests are in cultural heritage, family history, tourism, and photography.

**Richard Sharpley** is Professor of Tourism and Development at the University of Central Lancashire, Preston, UK. His principal research interests fall under the broad areas of tourism, development and sustainability, and the sociology of tourism, and he has published widely in both. His books include *Tourism and Development: Concepts and Issues* (2002; 2015, with David Telfer), *The Darker Side of Travel: The Theory and Practice of Dark Tourism* (2009, with Philip Stone), and *Tourism, Tourists & Society, Fifth Edition* (2018). His most recent book is the *Routledge Handbook of the Tourist Experience* (2021).

**Jack Shepherd** is a doctoral candidate at the European Tourism Research Institute at Mid Sweden University, Östersund, Sweden, and Visiting Research Fellow at the University of Wakayama, Japan. His research bridges insights from both tourism and peace studies in order to explore the relationship between tourism and peacebuilding, with most of his work focusing on the Israeli-Palestinian conflict. Jack's research often employs creative forms of narrative inquiry.

**Marcus L. Stephenson** is Professor of Tourism and Hospitality Management and Dean of the School of Hospitality and Service Management at Sunway University (Malaysia). Prior to his appointment in October 2017, he was Professor and Head of the School of Tourism and Hospitality Management at the University of the South Pacific, Fiji. He also worked at Middlesex University Dubai, United Arab Emirates, as Chair of Research and Associate Professor from 2005 to 2014. He is a co-author of *Tourism and Citizenship: Rights, Freedoms and Responsibilities in the Global Order* (2014, Routledge) and a co-editor of *International Tourism Development and the Gulf Cooperation Council States: Challenges and Opportunities* (2017, Routledge). He has consulted significantly in the education and tourism and hospitality sectors, as well as publishing extensively on the sociology of tourism, especially concerning nationality, culture, race, ethnicity, and religion.

**Arie Stoffelen** is Assistant Professor at the Department of Earth and Environmental Sciences, Division of Geography and Tourism, at the University of Leuven (KU Leuven), Belgium. Previously, he was affiliated with the Faculty of Spatial Sciences at the University of Groningen, the Netherlands. His research revolves around regional development processes and contestations in a globalizing world characterized by increasing cross-border mobility and place-based development strategies. In particular, he is interested in tourism-related sustainable regional development processes, spatial identity analysis, and the political-economic geography and geopolitics of cross-border (im)mobilities. Currently, he is an associate editor of the international academic journal *Annals of Tourism Research*.

**Niels Strange** (PhD, Dr.agro) is Professor in Management Planning of Forest and Nature at the Department of Food and Resource Economics, University of Copenhagen. He is also affiliated with the Center for Macroecology, Evolution and Climate at the GLOBE Institute, University of Copenhagen. Niels Strange's research interests focus on forestry, biodiversity conservation, environmental economics and planning, environmental behaviour, and economics under uncertainty. He is involved in a number of research projects concerning payments for environmental services, conservation finance, conservation planning, landowner behaviour and contract design, multi-criteria analysis, environmental economics, and spatial planning under risk of calamities.

**Katarzyna Szmigiel-Rawska** is Associate Professor in the Department of Local Development and Policy at the Faculty of Geography and Regional Studies at the University of Warsaw. Her theoretical work is focused on inter-organisational collaboration and coordination mechanisms in local government. She takes a theoretical perspective of new institutional economics. She is also a coordinator of, and participant in, national and international research projects and consulting projects for government organizations and local authorities. She is the principal investigator of the project 'Institutions, Local Governance and Land-use Changes: A Comparative Study of Selected European Countries' financed by the Polish National Science Centre. Katarzyna is the author of numerous articles and book chapters, and is author or editor of seven books on local government and strategic public management.

**Dallen J. Timothy** is Professor of Community Resources and Development at Arizona State University and Senior Sustainability Scientist at the Julie Anne Wrigley Global Institute of Sustainability. He is also a Senior Research Associate at the University of Johannesburg, South Africa; Visiting Professor at Hunan Normal University, Guangxi University, and Luoyang Normal University, China; and Guest Professor in the Erasmus Mundus European Master in Tourism Management programme based at the University of Girona, Spain. He is the founding editor of the *Journal of Heritage Tourism* and currently serves on the editorial boards of 24 international journals. He is commissioning or co-commissioning editor for four book series with Routledge and other publishers. He has ongoing research projects in North America, Asia, Europe, the Middle East, and Africa on topics related to borders and tourism, religious tourism, heritage, and community empowerment.

**Mihály Tömöri** is College Associate Professor in the Institute of Tourism and Geography at the University of Nyíregyháza, Hungary. He holds an MSc degree in geography, an MA in

English language and literature, and a PhD in earth sciences from the University of Debrecen (Hungary). His research interests include shopping tourism, cross-border shopping, geography of consumption, retailing, and shopping malls.

**Alix Varnajot** is a postdoctoral researcher at the University of Oulu, Finland. He earned his PhD in Human Geography from the University of Oulu in 2020. His PhD dissertation explored conceptual and theoretical developments in Arctic tourism, including place-meaning, place representations, and place-making of the Arctic in tourism. His research interests encompass tourism at borders, tourists' performances, as well as the development of tourism in polar regions. More recently, Varnajot's work has focused on the implications of global warming and a thawing cryosphere to the future of Arctic tourism, exploring novel and innovative adaptation strategies to climate change for the tourism industry.

**Adam Weaver** is Professor in the School of Hospitality, Tourism and Sport at Niagara College Canada. Prior to his return to Canada, he taught at Victoria University of Wellington in New Zealand for over a decade. His research interests include tourism marketing, cruise tourism, and the history of academic programmes in the fields of hospitality and tourism. The intersection between tourism and commerce is the focus of much of his work. Recent publications have appeared in academic journals such as *Annals of Tourism Research*, *Tourism Geographies*, the *Journal of Vacation Marketing*, and the *Journal of Teaching in Travel and Tourism*. Over the course of his career in post-secondary education, Adam has served in a variety of administrative roles.

**Marek Więckowski** is Professor in the Institute of Geography and Spatial Organization at the Polish Academy of Sciences. He is the Vice Chairman of the Scientific Council at the institute and is editor-in-chief of the journal *Geographia Polonica*. He was a member of the IGU Commission for the Geography of Tourism, Recreation and Global Change (2012–2020). His field of research is political geography (borders, cross-border collaboration), tourism geography, transport geography (accessibility), and regional marketing. He has been the primary investigator (PI) of many international and national scientific projects (the most recent is about "Polish Borders as Resources—Between Heritage and Tourism Products", funded by the National Scientific Center in Poland). He has published his research results in many books and leading international journals, including *Tourism Geographies*, the *Journal of Destination Marketing and Management*, and the *Scandinavian Journal of Hospitality and Tourism*.

**Thomas M. Wilson** is Professor of Anthropology at Binghamton University, State University of New York. In 2022 he became a Fulbright Research Professor at the Maynooth University Social Sciences Institute, Republic of Ireland, while he researches changes in rural and suburban Irish political culture. A political anthropologist, he formerly was a faculty member at the Queens University Belfast's Institute of European Studies, where he co-founded the Centre for International Borders Research. Following a stint as Visiting Fellow, he is now a Visiting Scholar in Queens University Belfast's School of History, Anthropology, Politics and Philosophy, while continuing ethnographic research on Brexit's impact on the Northern Ireland borderlands.

**Kimberley J. Wood** is currently undertaking a doctorate about musicians' experiences of performance spaces in the Department of Management, Marketing and Entrepreneurship at the University of Canterbury, Christchurch, New Zealand. A tutor at the New Zealand National Academy of Singing and Dramatic Arts, she completed a masters on the marketing of music education in 2020. Her research interests include: performance, experiencescapes, and eventscapes; dance as practical and symbolic performity; music education; online relationship marketing; and demarketing.

**Min (Lucy) Zhang** was Assistant Professor in the School of Hospitality and Tourism Management, Yunnan University of Finance and Economics, Kunming, China. Her research interests included border tourism governance, community-based tourism, cultural heritage, and sociocultural sustainability in tourism destinations. She has consulted for the United Nations Development Programme (UNDP) on various ethnic tourism projects in the border regions of China and surrounding countries. Sadly, Lucy passed away in June 2022. We are grateful for her contribution to this book.

**Isabel Zizaldra Hernández** is Research Professor in the Administrative Sciences Department at the Universidad Autónoma de Ciudad Juárez, Mexico. She is a faculty member in the Department of Tourism and Leisure Studies. She is also a member of Programa para el Desarrollo Profesional Docente (Program for the Professional Development of Teachers—PRODEP) and the National System of Researchers (SNI) Level 1. Isabel's research topics include managing tourism and recreation operations and cultural tourism. She has delivered many addresses and invited presentations, and has undertaken research stints at the Universidad Nacional Autónoma de México, the Autonomous University of Aguascalientes (Mexico), the Technological University of the Coast (Mexico), the University of Girona (Spain), the University of Carabobo (Venezuela), and the University of Quilmes (Argentina). She is a member of, or partner with: the Research Center for Creativity, Innovation, and Competitiveness; the National College of Tourism, Hotel Management, and Gastronomy; the Paso del Norte Society for the Culture of History; and the American Association of Geographers. She has published many journal articles, book chapters, and broadcasts.

Throughout this long history of border and territorial evolution, humans have had to grapple with the constraints and opportunities that such conditions produce. In some cases, even in very recent history, shifting boundaries have meant that people have gone to bed at night in one country and awoken in another. There are many cases of homes, farms, and neighbourhoods being divided by a new international boundary seemingly overnight with the swish of a pen or an act of aggression. One of the most recent examples of this happening with a transfrontier treaty was the exchange of territory between India and Bangladesh in 2015 in which nearly 200 small enclaved pieces of each country were transferred to the other, and with it the country of residence for most of the area's 52,000 people, although many of them chose to relocate to maintain their current citizenship (Ferdoush & Jones, 2018). With the collapse of the Soviet Union in 1991, other examples dominated headlines at the Belarus–Lithuania boundary, the Azerbaijan–Armenia frontier, as well as in the Central Asian republics (Vinokurov, 2007; Borthakur, 2017), but history is replete with examples of border changes that affect the lives of people and the character of places.

For centuries, borders have kept people apart, and with the division of the earth through colonialism and the seventeenth-century-onward legal definitions of state borders, they have become increasingly fixed as states assert their lines of sovereign control. Nonetheless, evidence suggests debordering occurred as early as the Middle Ages through various peace treaties and resource sharing (e.g., fishing) agreements (Timothy, 2021). In 1834, a customs union was ratified among the German states (Keller & Shiue, 2014), and in 1922, the Common Travel Area between Ireland and the United Kingdom diminished their shared border by ensuring free movement between the two countries, which came to include the right to live, work, gain an education, and share social benefits (Butler & Barrett, 2018).

Following the Second World War, in response to the devastation and the need to collaborate across borders for recovery and growth, supranationalism grew to include the Benelux customs union in 1944 and the Benelux Economic Union in 1958. The European Coal and Steel Community (1951) was enacted to regulate the coal and steel industries among its original six members: West Germany, Italy, France, the Netherlands, Belgium, and Luxembourg (Timothy, 2019, 2021). These early forerunners to the European Economic Community, later the European Union (EU), saw the greatest level of debordering the world had known until that time. Since the 1970s, supranationalism and other manifestations of debordering (e.g., cross-border cooperation, economic globalization, transportation innovations, and communications technology) have ushered in an age of increased trade, greater human mobility, global marketplaces, greater merchandise selection in shopping malls and supermarkets, and more diverse tourism destinations, products, and experiences.

Borders and borderlands, therefore, have been increasingly characterized since the mid-twentieth century as integrated meeting grounds, no longer functioning simply as isolators but also as unifiers, spaces of connectivity and facilitators of the exchange of ideas, the trade in goods and services, business development, and travel (Timothy, 2001, 2002; Brunet-Jailly, 2005, 2022; Paasi, 2012; Parker & Vaughan-Williams, 2014). The history of the state dictates that frontiers are lines of conflict, barriers to interaction, and exclusion, whereas the history of human connectedness changes borders to places of exchange, socialization, and inclusion through the process of "borderwork"—the ways in which ordinary people make or unmake borders (Rumford, 2006, 2009). Many borders today are dynamic and relational, and are constituted or deconstructed through border practices and policies, as well as encounters and how they perform or are performed (Timothy & Teye, 2009; Donnan & Wilson, 2010; Timothy et al., 2016). State frontiers perform through passport inspections, visa controls, and securityscapes. Borders are performed by crossing, straddling, transiting, and being used as tools for economic

# 1
# UNDERSTANDING BORDERS AND TOURISM
## Complex Relationships and Evolving Patterns

*Dallen J. Timothy and Alon Gelbman*

The very nature of political boundaries and their functions have long determined human spatial and socioeconomic activities, including tourism. In fact, the very existence of borders constitutes "international tourism … as something measurable" (Timothy et al., 2016, p. 1), and borders simultaneously deter and stimulate travel. Not too long ago, borders in most cases were considered marginal to national economic and social interests, other than security or levying taxes. This drove many scholars to examine borderlands from the perspective of core–periphery relationships, examining the position of borders as peripheries that had little value or interest to state power brokers, business elites, or economic developers (Prescott, 1987; Paasi, 1996; Sofield, 2006; Pelc, 2007; Nagy et al., 2012). Today, however, borders are regarded by scholars and governments as zones of social and economic exchange that are now worthy of more development attention and better management (Timothy, 2001, 2002; Sohn, 2014; Timothy et al., 2016).

Tourism entails the temporary movement of people away from their home environments for any purpose, including leisure and pleasure, education, business, medical services and healthcare, sport, religion and spirituality, and visiting friends and relatives. The World Tourism Organization includes the parameters of staying at least one night away from home but less than a year. Nonetheless, even same-day trips are part of the larger tourism system, as they entail people utilizing services and contributing to the visitor economy. Day trips, as well as overnight visits, often take place across national boundaries, and are nowadays a salient part of performing borders.

Since the beginning of the Anthropocene, humans have defined space in different ways. Embryonic forms of the modern state emerged thousands of years ago with inter-tribal warfare in response to spatial incursions by unwelcomed others, fixed human settlements during the Neolithic period, the Roman limes in Europe, the territorialization of crown lands and fiefdoms, the fuzzy frontiers (marches) that separated geopolitical entities in the Middle Ages, and the securely bounded state of the modern era. The modern-day notion of legally defined states and boundaries began in the mid-seventeenth century or slightly earlier. Since that time, many sovereign states have appeared and disappeared from the world map, and defined national boundaries have undergone momentous changes as wars, acts of secession, transfer of ownership and sovereignty, and natural accretion have changed the shapes and sizes of sovereign states.

development (Timothy, 1995b, 1998; Varnajot, 2019). Tourism is a pervasive manifestation of border performance and plays a critical role in debordering processes (Timothy et al., 2016; Więckowski & Timothy, 2021).

In the last several years, actions of rebordering have received significant media and academic attention with the processes involved in remaking boundaries where boundaries had in many ways previously diminished (Newman, 2003, 2006; Rumford, 2006; Yuval-Davis et al., 2019). Although much of the world has undergone a course of debordering since the mid-twentieth century, certain events have brought about a widespread rebordering process. This is especially the case in relation to security concerns since the 9/11 terror attacks in the United States and terrorist events elsewhere since that time. With the 2001 event, borders in many localities, including the external borders of the EU, were remade and reinforced in an effort to repel people with extremist and violent tendencies. Likewise, masses of undocumented immigrants entering the United States from the early 2000s until now and in Europe from 2014 until now have also drawn a dramatic response in rebordering. This manifested clearly in the erection of fences and "walls" along several EU borders, both internal and external, as well as along the USA–Mexico frontier (Koca, 2019; Mutz & Simmons, 2022). During the early 2000s, dozens of borders in Europe, Asia, Africa, and the Americas have been fortified with defensive structures for the purpose of quelling illegal immigration, drug smuggling, and terrorism. The outbreak of the novel coronavirus saw many border closures in 2020 and 2021, some of which gradually opened toward the end of 2021 but in early 2022 are in danger of closing once again due to new variants of the disease.

With security an overwhelmingly greater border concern since 2001, large waves of migrants who are escaping civil unrest and poverty in their home countries, and the COVID-19 pandemic, the past 22 years have been a time of serious rebordering. Many communities located at once-open borders have now been cut off from one another with heavy restrictions, reimposed border formalities, and physical barriers. Permitted pedestrian traffic in several towns on the USA–Canada border that were once open to informal crossings has now been suppressed, with fences and gates blockading the sidewalks and residential streets once used by locals and tourists. The twin towns of Stanstead, Quebec, and Derby Line, Vermont, on the USA–Canada border are home to the famous Haskell Free Library and Opera House, which straddles the borderline. Since 2001, heavy border restrictions have limited some use of the library by non-residents, and all transfrontier movements are now heavily monitored, and the library was closed during the pandemic.

In the face of mass illegal immigration and asylum seeking in Europe, even friendly and intra-EU and intra-Schengen border barricades were erected between 2015 and 2018 to stem the flow of mass border crossings. The most notable examples include Austria's new barricade on its borders with Italy and Slovenia, and Hungary's barrier on its border with Croatia. The latest in these border-making trends is the "wall" on the border of Poland and Belarus, which commenced construction in late 2021.

With the rapid spread of COVID-19 in 2020, most countries obstructed their borders to contain the number of cases of the disease and to keep it from spreading. Most national borders in the EU and the Schengen Zone were blockaded with fences, rock piles, tyres, bricks, or metal barricades, and most had a strong police presence, at least at major road crossings. The USA–Canada border was closed for all but very essential travel, and Australia locked down its borders for nearly two years, until in February 2022, when it began to allow vaccinated travellers to return home or to visit. The global lockdown was a disaster for tourism, with many businesses declaring bankruptcy, billions of dollars of revenue lost, and millions of people losing their jobs. Destination communities suffered a great deal, although some tourism-dependent countries remained open throughout the pandemic, including several in the Caribbean, which required quarantines, proof of vaccinations, and a negative PCR test. Travel warnings by tourists' home country governments dissuaded many people from visiting the Caribbean and other regions, but other intrepid tourists spent their island holidays in these far-less-crowded island destinations.

Borders have direct impacts on the ordinary lives of ordinary people who live in their shadows, as well as indirect impacts on the lives of people who live far away and those wishing to visit. During the past decade, scholars have concentrated on understanding many aspects of border life, borderwork, and bordering processes. The most prevalent themes in border studies include, but are not limited to, security (e.g., Brandell, 2006; Kinnvall & Svensson, 2015; Woosnam et al., 2015; Longo, 2018; Laine et al., 2021), gender and ethnicity in borderlands (e.g., Naples & Mendez, 2015; Hoy, 2021), culture, society and citizenship (e.g., Bianchi & Stephenson, 2014; Konrad & Kelly, 2021; Stoffelen, 2022), territorial politics and identity (e.g., Brandell, 2006; Staudt, 2018; Yuval-Davis et al., 2019; Espejo, 2020), resilience and change (e.g., Andersen & Prokkola, 2022), and tourism and economic development (e.g., Timothy, 2001; Krakover & Gradus, 2002; Wachowiak, 2006). Although most early studies on borders and bordering were undertaken by geographers and law professionals, border studies is now a multidisciplinary field that encapsulates critical theory perspectives (Wastl-Walter, 2011; Wilson & Donnan, 2012a; Parker & Vaughan-Williams, 2014), as well as applied studies that may help policymakers and tourism industry professionals navigate the challenges of performing state frontiers (e.g., Timothy & Butler, 1995; Chan, 2006; Tömöri, 2010; del Río et al., 2017; Gao et al., 2019; Zhang et al., 2019; Boonchai & Freathy, 2020).

In summary, borders are now seen not simply as stagnant lines of separation but dynamic lines of integration where people, places, histories, and economies meet (Brunet-Jailly, 2005) through processes of debordering (Paasi, 2012; Wilson & Donnan, 2012b). This long history of bordering, debordering, and rebordering affects tourism in many ways and is profoundly affected by tourism.

## Borders and Tourism

Because of its desirable economic impacts (e.g., jobs, taxes, regional income, and entrepreneurial growth), tourism is a major focus of economic development in all parts of the world. Tourism destinations may grow organically through a natural development process from discovery to maturation where both positive and negative social, environmental, and economic outcomes are observable (Butler, 1980; Mathieson & Wall, 1982), or they may be purposely planned to become tourism engines of growth.

Bordering processes and the associated state functions and boundary mechanisms associated with border areas have traditionally hindered mainstream tourism development, although some unconventional types of "tourism" have thrived, including smuggling, petty trade, illicit gambling, and prostitution. Debordering has led to the growth of more legitimized, mainstream types of tourism in border areas, such as heritage tourism, ecotourism, shopping tourism, pilgrimage, sport tourism, medical tourism, and beach tourism—activities that might not have been feasible in some frontier localities prior to recent physical and administrative changes and in accordance with transborder differences that provide an impetus for tourism growth (e.g., lower taxes, different scenery, or lower consumer prices), or a unique competitive advantage that causes people to want to cross (Michalkó & Váradi, 2004; Timothy & Canally, 2008; Michalkó et al., 2014; Hannonen et al., 2015; Prokkola & Lois, 2016). Although, we should point out that the touristic activities of dubious legality and morality continue to exist, even in so-called debordered frontier spaces, such as along inner-EU borders where tobacco and alcohol smuggling continue to thrive and where prostitution remains in many cases.

In addition to these borderland forms of tourism, the borderline itself can be a major draw for tourists and function as an "anchor attraction" that draws people specifically to see and experience it. This was certainly the case along the former Iron Curtain before 1990, where people would gather in the West to observe life in the foreboding East. Today, the remnants of the Iron Curtain and other borders remain important assets for tourism, particularly those of a conflicted nature, including the Korean DMZ, Israel's borders with its neighbours, the UN buffer zone in Cyprus, and the Line of Control between India and Pakistan (Timothy, 2006; Webster & Timothy, 2006; Gelbman, 2010, 2016, 2019; Chhabra, 2018). However, even ordinary borders exude an appeal as they demarcate the differences between "here" and "there": distinctive landscapes, foreign languages, different currencies and monetary policies, and extraordinary cultures (Timothy, 2001; Gelbman & Timothy, 2011, 2019; Więckowski & Timothy, 2021; Więckowski, 2010, in press). Indeed, the psychological functions of borders create an imagined other that appeals to potential visitors (Brandell, 2006).

Studies have identified people's motivations for visiting and crossing borders (Askew & Cohen, 2004; Timothy & Canally, 2008; Park et al., 2019). For some people, crossing is more practical, such as for shopping or medical care, whereas for others, crossings may reflect a romantic nostalgia for the mystique about what awaits on the other side, and the border formalities and different landscapes can make the experience more foreign and exciting (Medvedev, 1999, p. 43). The actual demarcation of borders is an unusual and interesting heritage feature that attracts some tourists. People's fascination with borders is sometimes ascribed to lifestyle differences between two adjacent places (Ryden, 1993, p.1).

In line with this conceptualization of the appeal of borders, Gelbman and Timothy (2010) suggest the following typology for border tourism attractions: the border as a subject of tourism, the border location and environment as the subject of tourism, and the development of the borderlands as a tourism asset (Figure 1.1). Various types of attractions exist near borders associated with both natural phenomena and elements of the human and geopolitical landscapes. In many cases, borderlines constitute a focal point for hostilities and disputes between countries. Such a phenomenon may also arouse curiosity and interest among visitors and tourists, as can be seen in tourist visits to hostile border areas (Timothy, 2001).

Despite their apparent appeal, borders continue to separate people and places. The same borderline can be a non-barrier for one person and a significant barrier for another, depending on where the crossers are from or where they were born (Bianchi & Stephenson, 2014). Thus, global citizenship is not standard for everyone: some citizenships are more global and welcome than others, and border performances make these mobility inequalities quite obvious with differential policies and visa requirements for different nationalities (Paasi et al., 2019; Stoffelen, 2022). This is a perfect example of the simultaneity of borders as spaces of belonging and spaces of exclusion. Borders function both as psychological constraints and physical barriers to travel, with the psychological perspectives often being more of a barrier than the physical borderscape (Timothy & Tosun, 2003; Canally & Timothy, 2007). Fears, phobias, and misinformation frequently keep people from crossing who have the freedom to do so, whereas restrictions placed upon certain citizens and physical barricades keep many people from travelling who desire to do so (Canally & Timothy, 2007).

Two additional relationships between borders and tourism are frontiers as simple lines of transit, and tourism and borders as modifiers of the landscape. From a transit perspective, people usually pass by as quickly as possible in pursuit of a "better" place to be. In this sense, borders (including airport transit spaces) are often viewed as non-places and rarely valued by

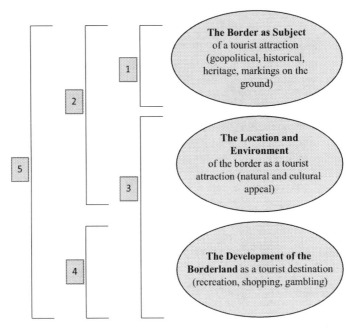

Examples: 1. the Great Wall, China; 2. the Golden Triangle, Thailand-Laos-Myanmar; 3. La Amistad International Peace Park, Costa Rica-Panama; 4. Macau-PR China; 5. Niagara Falls, USA-Canada

*Figure 1.1* The Attractiveness Factors of Border Tourism (after Gelbman & Timothy, 2010).

the travelling public as spaces of importance. In a sense, they have nothing to offer except a point of entry, a place to exchange currency, buy insurance, or fill up the tank with petrol. Secondly, the development of tourism in border communities frequently creates a unique urban morphology defined by clusters of services and agencies built to cater to the needs of borderland tourists (Arreola & Curtis, 1993; Timothy, 2020). Arreola and Curtis (1993) outline how Mexican border cities evolved because of "tourisms of vice", especially prostitution, gambling, and drinking in the early twentieth century, and how these activities generated unique urban border landscapes to satisfy the needs of visitors. Today, common activities on the same border include dental and medical services, which also have recreated a tourism-induced urban landscape of most of Mexico's norther border towns.

To enhance the tourism competitive advantages of borders, to mitigate the negative effects of tourism, to market regions more holistically, and to bring down the barrier effects of borders for tourism, cross-border cooperation is essential. However, even in frontier areas that have undergone significant debordering, many border related obstacles persist. The most common obstacles are a lack of political will, nationalism and one-sided protective measures, cultural clashes, legal and policy differences, distinctive and often incompatible management traditions, financial difficulties, unbalanced participation, different levels of economic development, and contradictory approaches to participatory planning, community empowerment, and grassroots decision-making (Timothy, 1999, 2002; Prokkola, 2007, 2008; Blasco et al., 2014; Stoffelen et al., 2017; Stoffelen & Vanneste, 2018).

Where success is found, the areas of most common concern in transfrontier collaboration are natural resource protection, joint infrastructure development, transboundary human mobility, trade in goods and services, and regional tourism marketing (Timothy, 1999; Dallimer &

and war history buffs. Carrying on from Gelbman's overview of border conflicts, Chapter 16 (Richard Sharpley) draws attention to border spaces as dark places owing to the multiple types of dark events that take shape at national borders. Sharpley provides a useful typology of dark border spaces that can be utilized in any border region of the world. Following the three preceding chapters, Dallen Timothy and Marek Więckowski (Chapter 17) continue the discussion of borders as tourist attractions by framing the phenomenon within a broader heritage. They argue that borders are salient heritage sites in many current and former border regions that help reaffirm individual and/or national identity and which are often commemorated as places of memory and thereby become heritage attractions worth saving, interpreting, and selling to tourists. Alon Gelbman and Rachel Schweitzer (Chapter 18) provide insight into guiding and the role of guides in border areas as mediators of history and narrators of conflict. In particular, they highlight several guiding approaches and strategies that dominate border areas, including official narratives, personal beliefs, adapted narratives, and the dialogue-promoting approach. Finally, Chapter 19 (Alix Varnajot) provides a unique perspective on borderlines as attractions, things to be straddled, photographed, and shared on social media. Varnajot explains various performances associated with crossing the Arctic Circle and other borders, be they political, temporal, or purely geodetic. The senses of otherness, hereness, and thereness are encapsulated by the experiences of crossing or straddling these real or imagined lines of separation.

The fourth part of the book—The Competitive Advantage of the Border—plays off the previous section, acknowledging that although the borderline itself may exude a sense of mystique, curiosity, or intrigue, the regions adjacent to state borders (borderlands) are home to certain types of tourism because of the advantages the borderline provides in terms of taxes, merchandising, greater levels of permissiveness, and other distinctive differences. Teemu Makkonen (Chapter 20) describes the borderland conditions that promote the development of cross-border shopping and retail. These include boundary permeability, knowledge of consumers about what lies on the other side, and border laws and regulations (e.g., taxes, import limitations, and duties) that provide competitive advantages for border locations in retail. In Chapter 21, Tomás Cuevas Contreras and Isabel Zizaldra Hernández draw attention to the increasingly popular phenomenon of medical tourism, which is growing in many parts of the world, but especially in border areas. They describe the experiences and services sought in cross-border medical mobility and the advantages that borders have in stimulating transfrontier travel for healthcare and medical treatment. Like the chapters before it in this Part IV, Chapter 22 (Michael Hall and Kim Wood) investigates the role of borders and their permissive environments in the development of sex tourism and prostitution. The authors emphasize the importance of borderlands as spaces of sexual practices that might be frowned upon, ridiculed, or judged negatively at home, but which may be undertaken in a more clandestine manner abroad. The spaces of borders are also venues in which people can explore their sexualities and play out their sexual fantasies as men, women, or other gender. Cross-border second-home tourism is the focus of Chapter 23 by Olga Hannonen. She looks at many perspectives of second-home tourism, including retirement migration, which is a growing phenomenon in Europe and elsewhere where national borders determine the advantage of moving abroad in retirement and owning summer cottages or other second homes. Borders provide tax incentives and price differentials but also foreign-feeling environments that are different but somehow familiar. Chapter 24 (Gábor Michalkó, Mihály Tömöri, and Noémi Ilyés) describes a unique and non-conventional form of tourism: petty trade, smuggling, and border business travel. Although participants in these activities do not fit the normative definition of tourists in most respects, their activities are important local forms of tourism that have significant implications for local socioeconomic development and involve other economic activities that exist because of their proximity to a border. In fact, these activities would not be possible in non-border locations.

The book's fifth part addresses contemporary issues and changes in traditional ways of thinking about borders and tourism, focusing largely on debordering processes. In particular, it focuses on cross-border cooperation in managing, planning, and policy-making in tourism. Chapter 25 (Arie Stoffelen) emphasizes the importance of sound tourism planning in border regions, particularly with reference to principles of sustainability, including participatory actions, cross-border collaboration for equity and inclusion, and integrative planning. Stoffelen argues that planning is needed to enhance the positive effects of tourism in borderlands and to mitigate the negative elements, although there are a number of sociopolitical constraints to effective transfrontier tourism planning. The EU is perhaps the best example of debordering and transboundary collaboration in tourism development through its various regional programmes and initiatives. Eeva-Kaisa Prokkola (Chapter 26) addresses the EU's efforts to develop cross-boundary regions through policy and funding initiatives and how EU enlargement affects those policies. She supports the idea that engaging transfrontier stakeholders is essential but challenging, and she examines the ways in which cross-border heritage and other tourism assets may be developed. Alon Gelbman and Rachel Schweitzer (Chapter 27) shed light on transfrontier protected areas and peace parks. They briefly review the history of transborder nature reserves and note the importance of the human element by way of resident communities whose livelihoods are impacted by the designation of these parks. The authors discuss the multiple roles of transfrontier parks as nature protectors, promoters of peaceful relations, and providers of livelihood for local residents. Spinning off from his previous chapter on planning and managing transborder tourism, Arie Stoffelen (Chapter 28) describes the development potential of transfrontier routes and trails as manifestations of common resources and cross-border cooperation. This increasingly popular linear tourism product is rife with challenges to, and opportunities for, collaboration and economic development in border regions. In Chapter 29, Jaume Guia, Dani Blasco, and Natàlia Ferrer-Roca dissect the notion of cross-border tourism clusters, or transborder governance structures. These are networks of stakeholders that deal with matters of a transfrontier nature to enhance regional products beyond local interests. They provide an empirical example of the Cerdanya Valley on the border of France and Spain to illustrate transfrontier managerial structures that have regional interests rather than only one-sided interest and territory-based identities. In the concluding chapter (Chapter 30) Dallen Timothy and Alon Gelbman highlight many of the prominent themes that appear in this tome and suggest areas for additional research that will shed light on gaps in our current knowledge about borders and tourism.

As readers will see in this volume, borders are far more complex than simply lines on a map or on the ground. Although technically, literally, and legally, borders have no width (they are simply the vertical planes where two polities meet), they do have depth—impacts, perceptions, performances, and experiences. The crossover between political boundaries and tourism is multidimensional, complex, and extremely dynamic. The following chapters provide key insights from a multi-disciplinary perspective into barriers and constraints, opportunities for development, transfrontier networks and collaboration, and a wide range of other concepts that are in desperate need of additional academic attention. Our purpose in putting this collection of essays together was to provide a theoretical and applied foundation for understanding as many issues in the border and tourism relationship as possible and to encourage additional work in these ever-changing subfields of tourism and geopolitics.

Strange, 2015). With careful cross-border planning and collaboration, transfrontier areas can move closer from spaces of division to places of sharing (Dołzbłasz, 2017)—shared knowledge, shared trust, shared governance, and shared responsibility both for successes and failures (Prokkola, 2007, 2008; Blasco et al., 2014; Makkonen et al., 2018).

Borderlands are, perhaps, one of the best laboratories for understanding the dynamics of tourism, and tourism is one of the best frameworks for understanding the workings of borders. The two concepts are entirely interdependent and have received considerable research attention since the 1990s (Timothy, 1995a, 1995b, 2001; Krakover & Gradus, 2002; Wachowiak, 2006). Tourism is a key force in bordering, debordering, and rebordering at global, regional, and even very local scales (see Xu et al., 2018), and these border-making or unmaking processes have direct effects on tourism. Tourism, in fact, often gives borderlands meaning and helps create a sense of place in frontier areas.

The very functions of borders include monitoring the flows of transfrontier traffic, including tourists and, as noted earlier, crossing borders is the very essence of international tourism. By the same token, borders and borderlands play an important part in tourism and its development. It is these multiple and complex relationships that form the foundations of this book. The chapters that follow examine current thinking in border studies and tourism studies, and highlight the diverse relationships between these two inseparable phenomena.

## Contents of the Book

The book's first part provides a strong theoretical and conceptual foundation by drawing on current multidisciplinary thinking about the meanings and manifestations of borders, boundedness, scale, territory, place, here and there, belonging, exclusion, and the familiar and the "other"—all foundational elements of tourism (Timothy, 2018). It introduces historical and contemporary thinking about human mobilities, the importance of borders, citizenship and the global order, increasing movements towards borderlessness, border imaginaries, border social spaces, border cultures, and borderland dynamics. In his historico-political treatise on "Here" and "Elsewhere", Noel Parker (Chapter 2) examines the notion of being away, beyond the boundaries of home. He uses historical evidence to suggest that transborder travel is not only a challenge, but also an opportunity for discovery, a reconfiguration of Here and Elsewhere, and a bordered experience of otherness. In Chapter 3, Tom Wilson scrutinizes identity production and reproduction through national and local bordering. He examines the emotional and social connections among borderland people through the prisms of border space and place, transfrontier cultures, as well as tourism and tourists as agents of cultural change in frontier regions. Chapter 4 (Anssi Paasi and Md Azmeary Ferdoush) revisits the relevant and interrelated notions of debordering, rebordering, changes in the meaning of borders, and globalization. The authors speculate on the "unbounded world" of mobility through tourism and other globalization forces. Paasi and Ferdoush argue that border, sovereignty, and globalization may have different meanings in different national contexts. Sylwia Dołzbłasz and Katarzyna Szmigiel-Rawska (Chapter 5) investigate the notion of scaling and rescaling borders and territory. They hone in on the value of cross-border cooperation, its relational approaches, and global integration as a strong manifestation of transfrontier collaboration. Cooperation, they argue, is the foundation for interconnectedness throughout the world and builds a foundation of transnational trust and institution-building. The focus of Chapter 6 (Raoul Bianchi and Marcus Stephenson) is global citizenship and the right to travel, or "mobility justice". They elaborate on the rights of tourists as global citizens and suggest that borders in fact are constraints to the rights of (global) citizenship. Finally, Martin Dallimer and Niels Strange (Chapter 7) examine the relationships between political borders and ecosystems management. They elucidate the connections between borders and protective legislation, looking at different policies and practices on opposite sides of borders, scales of borders, and the policy implications of scale, and they highlight how different state administrations and populations value biodiversity differently. In the context of nature-based tourism, knowledge sharing and capacity building, financing conservation, and enacting international agreements are key in protecting transfrontier ecosystems.

The chapters in Part II—Borders, Barriers, Access, and (Im)mobilities—examine the multifarious ways in which state boundaries restrict humankind's mobile behaviours and shape people's lived experiences. In tourism terms, this includes tourists' action spaces, limits on their transfrontier mobilities, and limits to the potential of cross-border regions to develop cohesive tourism products. Chapter 8 (Sascha Krannich) focuses on issues related to borders and migration in general and specifically in relation to tourism. Krannich examines migration policies, barriers, and mobility rights. He draws particular attention to migrants' transnational networks and how these relate to the tourism sector. In Chapter 9, Olga Hannonen and Eeva-Kaisa Prokkola deconstruct the permeability and impermeability of national borders for tourist mobility and tourism development. They frame these issues in terms of physical access and perceived constraints, suggesting that physical barriers, legal constraints, and mental perceptions of borders constrain tourist mobilities and the potential for developing tourism in border regions. Adam Weaver (Chapter 10) writes about the bounded spaces of tourism enclaves, particularly in the contexts of cruise ships, resorts, and backpacker enclaves. Although these tourist bubbles are not bounded politically, they are in fact bordered by reaffirmations of social hierarchies and exclusion between the haves and the have-nots in destination communities. The boundaries of enclaved tourism spaces reflect bordered spaces of power, exclusion, and wealth versus poverty. Aharon Kellerman (Chapter 11) discusses the main implications of globalization with regard to global mobility and tourism as a manifestation of globalization. Borders as controllers of mobility are discussed from the perspective of transportation, accessibility, governance, economic ability to travel, and the right to travel. We often do not think about military occupations as having any other effect on tourism than quelling its development, but in Chapter 12, Jack Shepherd and Daniel Laven hone in on the effects of military occupations on tourism, including the associated border-related hardships and restrictions on movement, but they also examine different ways in which occupations enable certain unusual types of tourism to develop, such as soldiers as tourists. They provide many empirical examples to show how military occupations affect mobility and tourism growth but also how tourism can be an instrument in normalizing occupations. The focus of Chapter 13 (Lucy Zhang and Jaume Guia) is cultural and ethnic boundaries, which may in some cases be political on their own, but this essay deals more with ethnic borderlands, mobilities, ethnic heritage, cultural representation, and performativity in borderlands, as well as the fact that ethnic and state identity do not always correspond with one another.

The focus of Part III is the borderline and its adjacent territories as tourism assets. From borderlines themselves, to landscapes of border conflict, as well as numerous tourism types in between, borders can be salient tourist attractions, and borderlands are known to be important destinations, even if they are sometimes ignored by national authorities and discounted as less worthy of planning, policy, and funding attention than other areas in the state. Chapter 14 (Marek Więckowski) describes the role of borders as tourist attractions, including the multitude of ways borders manifest in the landscape and exude a sense of exoticness or intrigue that appeal to tourists. Alon Gelbman (Chapter 15) reports on the importance of border conflicts, particularly former war zones and areas of active confrontations, as attractions for adventurous tourists

## References

Andersen, D.J., & Prokkola, E-K. (Eds.) (2022). *Borderlands resilience: Transitions, adaptation and resistance at borders*. London: Routledge.

Arreola, D.D., & Curtis, J.R. (1993). *The Mexican border cities: Landscape anatomy and place personality*. Tucson: University of Arizona Press.

Askew, M., & Cohen, E. (2004). Pilgrimage and prostitution: Contrasting modes of border tourism in lower south Thailand. *Tourism Recreation Research, 29*(2), 89–104.

Bianchi, R., & Stephenson, M. (2014). *Tourism and citizenship: Rights, freedoms and responsibilities in the global order*. London: Routledge.

Blasco, D., Guia, J., & Prats, L. (2014). Emergence of governance in cross-border destinations. *Annals of Tourism Research, 49*, 159–173.

Boonchai, P., & Freathy, P. (2020). Cross-border tourism and the regional economy: A typology of the ignored shopper. *Current Issues in Tourism, 23*(5), 626–640.

Borthakur, A. (2017). An analysis of the conflict in the Ferghana Valley. *Asian Affairs, 48*(2), 334–350.

Brandell, I. (2006). *State frontiers: Borders and boundaries in the Middle East*. New York: Bloomsbury.

Brunet-Jailly, E. (2005). Theorizing borders: An interdisciplinary perspective. *Geopolitics, 10*, 633–649.

Brunet-Jailly, E. (2022). Cross-border cooperation: A global overview. *Alternatives, 47*(1), 3–17.

Butler, G., & Barrett, G. (2018). Europe's 'Other' open-border zone: The Common Travel Area under the shadow of Brexit. *Cambridge Yearbook of European Legal Studies, 20*, 252–286.

Butler, R.W. (1980). The concept of a tourist area cycle of evolution: Implications for management of resources. *Canadian Geographer, 24*(1), 5–12.

Canally, C., & Timothy, D.J. (2007). Perceived constraints to travel across the US-Mexico border among American university students. *International Journal of Tourism Research, 9*(6), 423–437.

Chan, Y.W. (2006). Coming of age of the Chinese tourists: The emergence of non-Western tourism and host-guest interactions in Vietnam's border tourism. *Tourist Studies, 6*(3), 187–213.

Chhabra, D. (2018). Soft power analysis in alienated borderline tourism. *Journal of Heritage Tourism, 13*(4), 289–304.

Dallimer, M., & Strange, N. (2015). Why socio-political borders and boundaries matter in conservation. *Trends in Ecology & Evolution, 30*(3), 132–139.

del Río, J.A.J., Agüera, F.O., Cuadra, S.M., & Morales, P.C. (2017). Satisfaction in border tourism: An analysis with structural equations. *European Research on Management and Business Economics, 23*(2), 103–112.

Dołzbłasz, S. (2017). From divided to shared spaces: Transborder tourism in the Polish–Czech borderlands. In D. Hall (Ed.), *Tourism and geopolitics: issues and concepts from Central and Eastern Europe*, pp. 163–177. Wallingford: CABI.

Donnan, H., & Wilson, T.M. (Eds.) (2010). *Borderlands: Ethnographic approaches to security, power, and identity*. Plymouth: University Press of America.

Espejo, P.O. (2020). *On borders: Territories, legitimacy, & the rights of place*. Oxford: Oxford University Press.

Ferdoush, M. A., & Jones, R. (2018). The decision to move: Post-exchange experiences in the former Bangladesh-India border enclaves. In A. Horstmann, M. Saxer, & A. Rippa (Eds.) *Routledge handbook of Asian borderlands*, pp. 255–265. London: Routledge.

Gao, J., Ryan, C., Cave, J., & Zhang, C. (2019). Tourism border-making: A political economy of China's border tourism. *Annals of Tourism Research, 76*, 1–13.

Gelbman, A. (2010). Border tourism attractions as a space for presenting and symbolizing peace. In O. Moufakkir, & I. Kelly (Eds.), *Tourism, progress and peace*, pp. 83–98. Wallingford: CABI.

Gelbman, A. (2016). Tourism along the geopolitical barrier: implications of the Holy Land fence. *GeoJournal, 81*(5), 671–680.

Gelbman, A. (2019). Tourism, peace, and global stability. In D.J. Timothy (Ed.), *Handbook of globalisation and tourism*, pp. 149–160. Cheltenham: Edward Elgar.

Gelbman, A., & Timothy, D.J. (2010). From hostile boundaries to tourist attractions. *Current Issues in Tourism, 13*(3), 239–259.

Gelbman, A., & Timothy, D.J. (2011). Border complexity, tourism and international exclaves: A case study. *Annals of Tourism Research, 38*(1), 110–131.

Gelbman, A., & Timothy, D. J. (2019). Differential tourism zones on the western Canada–US border. *Current Issues in Tourism, 22*(6), 682–704.

Hannonen, O., Tuulentie, S., & Pitkänen, K. (2015). Borders and second home tourism: Norwegian and Russian second home owners in Finnish border areas. *Journal of Borderlands Studies*, *30*(1), 53–67.

Hoy, B. (2021). *Creating the Canada-United States border across indigenous lands*. Oxford: Oxford University Press.

Keller, W., & Shiue, C.H. (2014). Endogenous formation of free trade agreements: Evidence from the Zollverein's impact on market integration. *Journal of Economic History*, *74*(4), 1168–1204.

Kinnvall, C., & Svensson, T. (Eds.) (2015). *Governing borders and security: The politics of connectivity and dispersal*. London: Routledge.

Koca, B.T. (2019). Bordering practices across Europe: The rise of "walls" and "fences". *Migration Letters*, *16*(2), 183–194.

Konrad, V., & Kelly, M. (Eds.) (2021). *Borders, culture, and globalization*. Ottawa: University of Ottawa Press.

Krakover, S., & Gradus, Y. (Eds.) (2002). *Tourism in frontier areas*. Lanham, MD: Lexington Books.

Laine, J.P., Liikanen, I., & Scott, J.W. (Eds.) (2021). *Remapping security on Europe's northern borders*. London: Routledge.

Longo, M. (2018). *The politics of borders: Sovereignty, security and the citizen after 9/11*. Cambridge: Cambridge University Press.

Makkonen, T., Williams, A.M., Weidenfeld, A., & Kaisto, V. (2018). Cross-border knowledge transfer and innovation in the European neighbourhood: Tourism cooperation at the Finnish-Russian border. *Tourism Management*, *68*, 140–151.

Mathieson, A., & Wall, G. (1982). *Tourism: Economic, physical and social impacts*. London: Longman.

Medvedev, S. (1999). Across the line: Borders in post-Westphalian landscapes. In H. Eskelinen, I. Liikanen, & J. Oksa (Eds.), *Curtains of iron and gold: Reconstructing borders and scales of interaction*, pp. 43–56. Aldershot: Ashgate.

Michalkó, G., & Váradi, Z. (2004). Croatian shopping tourism in Hungary: The case study of Barcs. *Tourism*, *52*(4), 351–359.

Michalkó, G., Rátz, T., Hinek, M., & Tömöri, M. (2014). Shopping tourism in Hungary during the period of the economic crisis. *Tourism Economics*, *20*(6), 1319–1336.

Mutz, D.C., & Simmons, B.A. (2022). The psychology of separation: Border walls, soft power, and international neighborliness. *Proceedings of the National Academy of Sciences*, *119*(4), e2117797119.

Nagy, G., Nagy, E., & Timár, J. (2012). The changing meaning of core–periphery relations in a non-metropolitan "urban region" at the Hungarian–Romanian border. *DISP-The Planning Review*, *48*(2), 93–105.

Naples, N.A., & Mendez, J.B. (Eds.) (2015). *Border politics: Social movements, collective identities, and globalization*. New York: New York University Press.

Newman, D. (2003). On borders and power: A theoretical framework. *Journal of Borderlands Studies*, *18*(1), 13–25.

Newman, D. (2006). Borders and bordering: Towards an interdisciplinary dialogue. *European Journal of Social Theory*, *9*(2), 171–186.

Paasi, A. (1996). *Territories, boundaries and consciousness*. Chester: Wiley.

Paasi, A. (2012). Border studies reanimated: Going beyond the territorial/relational divide. *Environment and Planning A*, *44*, 2303–2309.

Paasi, A., Prokkola, E-K., Saarinen, J., & Zimmerbauer, K. (Eds.) (2019). *Borderless worlds for whom? Ethics, moralities and mobilities*. London: Routledge.

Park, J., Musa, G., Moghavvemi, S., Thirumoorthi, T., Taha, A.Z., Mohtar, M., & Sarker, M.M. (2019). Travel motivation among cross border tourists: Case study of Langkawi. *Tourism Management Perspectives*, *31*, 63–71.

Parker, N., & Vaughan-Williams, N. (Eds.) (2014). *Critical border studies: Broadening and deepening the 'lines in the sand' agenda*. London: Routledge.

Pelc, S. (2007). Traces of marginality in Slovenian border areas. In G. Jones, W. Leimgruber, & E. Nel (Eds.), *Issues in Geographical Marginality*, pp. 11–19. Grahamstown, South Africa: Rhodes University.

Prescott, J.V.R. (1987). *Political frontiers and boundaries*. London: Unwin Hyman.

Prokkola, E-K. (2007). Cross-border regionalization and tourism development at the Swedish-Finnish border: "Destination Arctic Circle". *Scandinavian Journal of Hospitality and Tourism*, *7*(2), 120–138.

Prokkola, E-K. (2008). Resources and barriers in tourism development: Cross-border cooperation, regionalization and destination building at the Finnish-Swedish border. *Fennia-International Journal of Geography*, *186*(1), 31–46.

Prokkola, E-K., & Lois, M. (2016). Scalar politics of border heritage: An examination of the EU's northern and southern border areas. *Scandinavian Journal of Hospitality and Tourism*, *16*(1), 14–35.

Rumford, C. (2006). Borders and rebordering. In *Europe and Asia beyond east and west* (pp. 195–206). Routledge.

Rumford, C. (Ed.) (2009). *Citizens and borderwork in contemporary Europe*. London: Routledge.

Ryden, K.C. (1993). *Mapping the invisible landscape: Folklore, writing, and the sense of place*. Iowa City: University of Iowa Press.

Sofield, T. H. (2006). Border tourism and border communities: An overview. *Tourism Geographies*, 8(2), 102–121.

Sohn, C. (2014). Modelling cross-border integration: The role of borders as a resource. *Geopolitics*, 19(3), 587–608.

Staudt, K. (2018). *Border politics in a global era: Comparative perspectives*. Lanham, MD: Rowman & Littlefield.

Stoffelen, A. (2022). Managing people's (in)ability to be mobile: Geopolitics and the selective opening and closing of borders. *Transactions of the Institute of British Geographers*, 47(1), 243–256.

Stoffelen, A., Ioannides, D., & Vanneste, D. (2017). Obstacles to achieving cross-border tourism governance: A multi-scalar approach focusing on the German-Czech borderlands. *Annals of Tourism Research*, 64, 126–138.

Stoffelen, A., & Vanneste, D. (2018). The role of history and identity discourses in cross-border tourism destination development: A Vogtland case study. *Journal of Destination Marketing & Management*, 8, 204–213.

Timothy, D.J. (1995a). International boundaries: New frontiers for tourism research. *Progress in Tourism and Hospitality Research*, 1(2), 141–152.

Timothy, D.J. (1995b). Political boundaries and tourism: Borders as tourist attractions. *Tourism Management*, 16(7), 525–532.

Timothy, D.J. (1998). Collecting places: Geodetic lines in tourist space. *Journal of Travel and Tourism Marketing*, 7(4), 123–129.

Timothy, D.J. (1999). Cross-border partnership in tourism resource management: International parks along the US-Canada border. *Journal of Sustainable Tourism*, 7(3/4), 182–205.

Timothy, D.J. (2001). *Tourism and political boundaries*. London: Routledge.

Timothy, D.J. (2002). Tourism in borderlands: Competition, complementarity, and cross-frontier cooperation. In S. Krakover, & Y. Gradus (Eds.), *Tourism in frontier areas*, pp. 233–258. Lanham: Lexington Books.

Timothy, D.J. (2006). Relationships between tourism and international boundaries. In H. Wachowiak (Ed.), *Tourism and Borders: Contemporary issues, policies and international research*, pp. 9–18. Aldershot: Ashgate.

Timothy, D. J. (2018). Geography: The substance of tourism. *Tourism Geographies*, 20(1), 166–169.

Timothy, D.J. (2019). Supranationalism and tourism: Free trade, customs unions, and single markets in an era of geopolitical change. In D.J. Timothy (Ed.) *Handbook of globalisation and tourism*, pp. 100–113. Cheltenham: Edward Elgar.

Timothy, D.J. (2020). Borderscapes and tourismscapes: The place of postcards in Mexican border town tourism. *Geographia Polonica*, 93(4), 553–568.

Timothy, D.J. (2021). *Tourism in European microstates and dependencies: Geopolitics, scale and resource limitations*. Wallingford: CABI.

Timothy, D.J., & Butler, R.W. (1995). Cross-border shopping: A North American perspective. *Annals of Tourism Research*, 22(1), 16–34.

Timothy, D.J., & Canally, C. (2008). The role of the US-Mexico border as a destination: student traveler perceptions. *Tourism Analysis*, 13(3), 259–269.

Timothy, D.J., Saarinen, J., & Viken, A. (2016). Tourism issues and international borders in the Nordic region. *Scandinavian Journal of Hospitality and Tourism*, 16(1), 1–13.

Timothy, D.J., & Teye, V.B. (2009). Regional alliances and cross-border tourism in Africa: Border implications and the Economic Community of West African States. *Tourism Review International*, 12(3/4), 203–214.

Timothy, D.J., & Tosun, C. (2003). Tourists' perception of the Canada-USA border as a barrier to tourism at the International Peace Garden. *Tourism Management*, 24(4), 411–421.

Tömöri, M. (2010). Investigating shopping tourism along the borders of Hungary – a theoretical perspective. *GeoJournal of Tourism and Geosites*, 6(2), 202–210.

Varnajot, A. (2019). "Walk the line": An ethnographic study of the ritual of crossing the Arctic Circle—Case Rovaniemi. *Tourist Studies*, 19(4), 434–452.

Vinokurov, E. (2007). *A theory of enclaves*. Lanham, MD: Lexington Books.

Wachowiak, H. (Ed.) (2006). *Tourism and borders: Contemporary issues, policies and international research*. Aldershot: Ashgate.

Wastl-Walter, D. (Ed.) (2011). *The Ashgate research companion to border studies*. Farnham: Ashgate.

Webster, C., & Timothy, D.J. (2006). Traveling to the 'Other Side': The occupied zone and Greek Cypriot views of crossing the Green Line. *Tourism Geographies*, *8*(2), 162–181.

Więckowski, M. (2010). Tourism development in the borderlands of Poland. *Geographia Polonica*, *83*(2), 67–81.

Więckowski, M. (in press) How border tripoints offer opportunities for transboundary tourism development. *Tourism Geographies*, https://doi.org/10.1080/14616688.2021.1878268

Więckowski, M., & Timothy, D.J. (2021). Tourism and an evolving international boundary: Bordering, debordering and rebordering on Usedom Island, Poland-Germany. *Journal of Destination Marketing & Management*, *22*, 100647.

Wilson, T.M., & Donnan, H. (Eds.) (2012a). *A companion to border studies*. Oxford: Blackwell.

Wilson, T.M., & Donnan, H. (2012b). Borders and border studies. In T.M. Wilson, & H. Donnan (Eds.), *A companion to border studies*, pp. 1–25. Oxford: Blackwell.

Woosnam, K.M., Shafer, K.S., Scott, D., & Timothy, D.J. (2015). Tourists' perceived safety through emotional solidarity with residents in two Mexico-United States border regions. *Tourism Management*, *46*, 263–273.

Xu, H., Huang, X., & Zhang, Q. (2018). Tourism development and local borders in ancient villages in China. *Journal of Destination Marketing & Management*, *9*, 330–339.

Yuval-Davis, N., Wemyss, G., & Cassidy, K. (2019). *Bordering*. Cambridge: Polity Press.

Zhang, S., Zhong, L., Ju, H., & Wang, Y. (2019). Land border tourism resources in China: Spatial patterns and tourism management. *Sustainability*, *11*(1), 1–20.

# PART I

# Past and Present Perspectives on Borders, Tourism, and Mobility

# 2
# TRAVELLERS' TALES
## How Human Stories Portray "Elsewhere"

*Noel Parker*

### Introduction

Human beings have always spent time on the move. Since hunter-gatherers learned to follow the seasonal movement of game, pastoral groups learned to move their herds, and settled groups found better places to settle, mobility has been a part of the human experience. In the abstract, however, it is easy to imagine that human beings are primarily conscious of their own existence in one location, their "home", and that is also the starting point that many philosophical accounts of human consciousness have often resorted to.

The *ne plus ultra* of this strategy is the philosopher Heidegger,[1] for whom embedding the sense of feeling at home is the theme running through his phenomenology of human life (Escudero, 2019). In his influential lecture "Building, Dwelling, Thinking",[2] he grounds the best of human life in staying put. Humans' *building* constructs a *dwelling place* from meaningless three-dimensional space, where human life can flourish: "Building and thinking are able to listen if both, belonging to *dwelling*, remain within their limits and know that one, as much as the other, comes from the workshop of long experience and continual practice" (Heidegger, 1951, p. 15).

However, the oldest of human stories reveal a wanderlust at odds with any definite home or dwelling-place. Whereas humans may well ground their perception of the world from a "Here", they are always conscious of the pull of "Elsewhere". Humans' own narratives often deal with the passage between Here and Elsewhere. This chapter groups human narratives, both ancient and modern, under five headings, each with an associated ontology of the world of Here and of There, and the possibility of moving between the one and the other.

Many narratives are organized around a journey (real or imaginary) between Here and There. This is the basic trope of what is known as a "travelogue", but these narrative forms embrace much more than the illustrated lecture or documentary film. Many narratives, of which Homer's *Odyssey* is the paradigm instance, are organized around movement from Here/home/the starting point to Elsewhere, or vice versa. Alongside any story of mere travel, there lies a deeper ontology that imagines the possibilities, negative or positive, of journeying to Elsewhere: whether that be a place of challenge, of triumph, of pleasure, of maturation, of a meeting with the sacred, or a place of discovery for commentary and comparison. Each

DOI: 10.4324/9781003038993-3

narrative trope implies claims about the character of Here and of Elsewhere. This can range from a place of dragons and devils, to the Eldorado myth,[3] to stories of descending to the underworld.

The chapter proceeds through critical readings of narratives of human movement, grouping them in terms of their evocation of the character of the Here and the Elsewhere. What is Elsewhere like? What can the traveller expect? What is to be won or lost? Is Elsewhere a place of evil or good? How does Elsewhere resemble Here? What priority does each possess in the order of the world? The layers of meaning that these narratives build up still contribute to the continuing significance of stories of travel today. Finally, the narratives contribute to the politics of bordering, in so far as the political border can be construed as anything from a meeting point (Luhman, 1982) to an existential security threat. Political processes, political actors, and the wider public determine which narratives come into play.

## Travelling as Challenge

The oldest travel narratives begin with heroes. What is being suggested when kings (such as Agamemnon, Menelaus, or Gilgamesh), demi-gods (such as Achilles), or heroes (such as Odysseus or Beowulf) people these narratives? The world of Elsewhere appears to be one that only the great, the heroic, or demi-gods can confront.

Homer's *Odyssey*, the epitome of difficult journeys home, and the *Epic of Gilgamesh*, probably the oldest surviving story in history, construct a world of the imagination, where Elsewhere is a space for action by larger-than-life figures. The challenges of being Elsewhere are frequently the weft of the action of these figures. Furthermore, the supernatural world frequently takes a hand in the successes or the setbacks of the eponymous heroes. Their journeys are undertaken in pursuit of glory, revenge, repute, or treasure to capture from cities laid waste[4] over the course of their travels. In Homer's two epics, the *Iliad* and the *Odyssey*, the goal of Menelaus is to recover his wife, Helen, abducted by a son of Troy. But Agamemnon, Greece's premier king, aims to confirm his dominance, and many accompanying warriors take the journey far from home in pursuit of enhanced repute in battle and of booty. Elsewhere is inhabited by gods and feuding warriors competing for glory and bounty.

The most famous travel narrative in Western history begins after Troy was captured by the Greek forces following Odysseus' trickery with the Trojan Horse. Although the journey from Greece to lay siege to Troy does not appear in either saga, Odysseus' journey home is a narrative in its own right because the god Poseidon impedes his return home at every stage. Thus it is that Odysseus has to use all his determination, his guile, his bravery, his charm, and, from time to time, the direct intervention of another god, Athene, to negotiate his way around the many obstacles that Poseidon's bitterness puts in his path. So the most famous of all travel narratives pits the human hero's powers against the will of one of the most powerful gods on Olympus.

Hence, there is a topography suggested by the *Odyssey*. Elsewhere presents opportunities and challenges. Odysseus can only re-establish the right to his home by matching guile, determination, and blood-letting. Going Elsewhere and returning to the starting point calls on all the human capacities of a heroic man, plus the good fortune of having some gods on one's side. The qualities required are courage, strength, physical beauty (both Calypso and Circe fall for Odysseus), cunning (e.g., in killing the Cyclops), and determination (to break away from the attractions of Calypso, or to resist the temptations of the Sirens). In short, the world beyond home requires the wanderer to rise to challenges and resist temptations; but, conversely, it offers the opportunity of enhanced repute and a more solidly based possession of the home.

There are no complete texts of the *Epic of Gilgamesh*, and those that have survived are at odds with each other at various points. But the best preserved one dates from not less than 1000 years BCE. In this version, Gilgamesh is a cruel leader of his people for whose improvement the gods create a wild man, Ediku. After Ediku has been tamed by the courtesan Shamat, Gilgamesh confronts him in a wrestling match which leads to a close friendship. The two travel together to the Cedar Forest to defeat the monster who guards it and slay the Bull of Heaven who is sent to attack them in revenge. After the fight, Ediku sickens and dies, and Gilgamesh travels to the underworld in a futile attempt to bring him back to the land of the living. Familiar themes run through this narrative: the need for heroic men to demonstrate their courage, test their strength, find a fitting place for the sensual in their dealings with the female sex, journey to confront the supernatural forces, and confront mortality.

Many of these features recur in a narrative of Norsk origin, written down by Anglo-Saxon monks around the year 1000: *Beowulf*. Again we find a journey to confront the forces of evil, protect against them, and to secure the right to a home by brave deeds. Beowulf sets sail from his home amongst the Geats (possibly the Goths) with a band of retainers to travel to the seat of the king of the Danes at Heorot (probably located in Northern Jutland) in order to offer it protection from a marauding monster called Grendel. Beowulf kills Grendel, a descendent of Cain, the eternal outcast, but Grendel's mother seeks revenge for his death. After Beowulf has pursued her all the way to her home at the bottom of a lake, he returns home laden with gifts from the grateful king. But, even though Beowulf seems to have earned the right to his home, the struggle is not yet over. A dragon attacks Beowulf in his home territory on behalf of Grendel and his mother. After this third battle, Beowulf, though he kills the dragon, sickens and dies, poisoned.

As Stuart Eldon points out (Elden, 2013, pp. 123–128), there is a tension in the story regarding entitlement to home territory. The story is tragic insofar as Beowulf cannot ultimately secure his home; heroic deeds alone appear not to be sufficient to ensure legitimate possession.

In these narratives, Elsewhere is dominated by the risk of death and supernatural forces that the travelling hero challenges. The confrontation is not decisive, but the hero forces recognition from the supernatural order. We will find this relationship between the human and the supernatural again in quest narratives and in pilgrimage. In the latter case, however, the relationship between the god(s) and man is somewhat reversed: pilgrims seek out the supernatural for what it may teach them, rather than to attempt to overcome it.

## Travelling as Discovery

Mythical narratives of travel pre-date the purportedly realistic conception of the world where the ostensible purpose of the journey is to find out about what exists Elsewhere. In Herodotus' *Histories* from early the fourth century BCE, he himself appears as a traveller who is not going to war, but seeking to discover conditions on the ground, and retelling the attitudes and even the speeches of the different parties in the outside world. The supernatural is not wholly absent: not only in the form of ethnography (such as peoples' origin myths), but in peoples' belief in the role of the gods in their successes or their setbacks, and in lending weight to stories of the gods' direct intervention from time to time. There are frequent instances of reference being made to oracles and omens. As Sean Sheehan (2018, pp. 7–12) points out, though, the distinction between myth and empirical fact in pre-Socratic writing was not at all clear. Thus, stories that might be regarded in the modern world as *mere* stories were not excluded from explaining events in a world where signs and portents were influential accompaniments to human action.

Reading from *The Histories* was included in religious festivals (Flory, 1980). In that light, we should not consider *The Histories* as turning from myth to discovery of a simple factuality, but as broadening the scope of agents from gods and heroes, to add soldiers, military technologies, social systems, and ethnological particularities amongst various peoples. This melange survives into nationalist narratives of human mobility to this day wherever the peculiar capacities of a nation are paired with the blessings of heaven.

There are two threads running through *The Histories*. One seemingly, a "comparative studies" thread, arises from travels that Herodotus probably undertook himself in the southern Mediterranean, especially Egypt (Books II & III), and to the north and west of the Grecian mainland, especially in the area of the Scythians (Book IV), almost certainly supplemented by unacknowledged debts to other Greek travellers, such as Dionysius of Miletus and Hellenacus of Lesbos (Herodotus, 2003, p. xix). In the former, he relates the physical features of the Nile and considers at length explanations of its yearly flood (II. 5–28[5]): "What I particularly wished to know was why the water begins to rise at the summer solstice and continues to do so for a hundred days, and falls again" (II. 19). But he "could get no information from the priests [though he did ask them!], or anyone else" (II. 19).

In Book IV, he seems to have visited places and gleaned second-hand what he could, some of it far-fetched, about the practices of the locals as far afield as the Persians and the Indians. Regarding the origin of the Scythians, for example, he begins by giving what "The Scythians say" (IV: 5): their story according to the Greeks of Pontus (IV: 8–10), which involves Herakles' inseminating a viper-woman; and then the story that he considers "the most likely of the three"(!) (IV: 11) about the inter-rivalries between nomadic tribes in the region. Herodotus seems to become more assertive in the course of his fourth book, pouring scorn on rivals in the business of map-making[6] before setting out to describe in detail the eight rivers of Asia (IV: 47–59) and thereafter, with equal confidence, the habits of the Scythians and the nature of their terrain (IV: 64–82)—some of the evidence of which "[t]hey did actually show me" (IV: 81). Notwithstanding his claim to have visited places and heard witnesses relating their stories, the accounts that Herodotus gives of the more remote parts of Scythian society and customs are difficult to credit, notably their blood-thirstiness.

The second thread, the historical, concerns the rise of the Persian dynasty, its invasion of territory held by the Scythians, and, later, the Greeks' expulsion of the Persians from Europe. That narrative increasingly dominates in the course of Book IV[7] and thereafter, embracing not only accounts of particular battles, but the supposed speeches of participants.

So in Herodotus, there exist two styles of writing about the world of Elsewhere. In one, the outside world appears to be an object of curiosity and reflection, with a wide variety of sources and a high degree of permissible uncertainty. In the other, there is a chronological narrative of battles, tactical gains, and strategic advantage, where human military heroism—stopping short of the direct intervention of the gods—is called upon.

A more benign version of the world of Elsewhere emerges over time in a Greek and Greco-Roman culture where the struggle to dominate militarily had *already* been successful. It becomes strong after the short-lived conquest of Persia and the Punjab by Alexander the Great, over the decade beginning in 323 BCE. Even though the empire of Alexander rapidly dissolved into numerous satrapies, a space had been opened up for inquiry, diplomatic (as against warlike) relations between equals, and comparative ethnography (Stoneman 2019, ch. 8). Many influential accounts of travel were circulated by Greek and Greco-Roman *public servants*.

First amongst these was Megasthenes (*c*.350 BCE–*c*.290 BCE). In the course of his work as an ambassador of one of Alexander's successors, the Greek Satrap of Babylon, Seleucus, to the

> All the degrees of retribution are necessary for this reason, that the seeking of salvation from the fetters of matter frequently does not proceed on a straight line which leads to absolute [that is, Islamic] knowledge, but on lines chosen by guessing or by guessing because others had chosen them.
>
> *(Al-Biruni, 1910, p. 62)*

In other words, even if it supports an erroneous, non-Islamic theology, the ignorance of Hindus can be considered in sympathetic terms because it maintains morality via the system of rewards and punishments. So confident is Islam of its own universal truth that it can tolerate whatever non-Islamic social structures ensure social peace. Al-Biruni evinces the same tolerance when it comes to Indian forms of knowledge. He is perfectly able to learn from Hindu mathematics, pharmacology, mineralogy, and the like. The second half of the collection assembled by Edward Sachau pursues questions prompted by Al-Biruni's scientific speculations, such as measurements of time, which he learnt from Indian scholarship. The existence of non-Islamic parts of the world is no threat to the truth of Islam. He believes that proper scholars will be able to winnow worthwhile knowledge from the chaff of non-Islamic witchcraft and the like. He confidently condemns proponents of witchcraft and alchemy who seek to shelter behind recondite practices for the sake of money: "The scholars [who 'flock to the door of the rich'] are well aware of the use of money, but the rich are ignorant of the nobility of science" (Al-Biruni, 1910, p. 188).

The supreme confidence of (in this case, Islamic) universality lies behind Al-Biruni's capacity to contemplate, or even admire, social mores in the non-Islamic world. People Elsewhere are as much subject to Allah as those who believe in him, so there is nothing to fear. The same can be said of belief in Rome's universal empire and, as will be argued below, belief in the universal truth of European Christianity. Untroubled consideration of places travelled to appears following displays of military might and the associated confidence in the universality of the traveller's/discoverer's position.

The same can be argued regarding Chinese universalism, built on Buddhism and imperial sovereignty. David Abulafia (2019) describes how Ming emperors sought *tribute*, as against opportunities for trade, from voyages beyond mainland China. To the Chinese authorities collecting tribute from the outside world meant an acknowledgement of the emperor's supremacy in the world order. Indeed, the voyages initiated by the Ming emperor Yong-le (ruled 1402–1424) were so costly that they could only have been undertaken to impress and obtain confirmation of that supremacy, rather than with the aim of commercial profit.

According to Abulafia (2019), Luo Mao-Deng, the collective name for the keepers of the official imperial record, subsequently published a "novel" about the expedition under the title *The Grand Director Goes Down to the Western Ocean* (Abulafia, 2019, p. 254). Its language can be imagined from the declaration that the emperor required the Sinhalese rulers to display[15]:

> His Imperial Majesty, Emperor of the Great Ming, has dispatched ... Zheng He ... and others, to set forth his utterances before the Lord Buddha, the World-Honored One, as follows: ... Of late we dispatched missions to announce our Mandate to foreign nations and during their voyages they have been favored by your beneficent protection ... Wherefore according to the Rites we bestow offerings in recompense ... obligations of gold and silver, gold-embroidered jeweled banners of variegated silk [etc., etc.] ... with other gifts to manifest the high honor of the Lord Buddha.

The purpose of this narration was confirmation that the Ming emperors' claim of supremacy was valid.

Edward Said's (1978) *Orientalism* introduced a classic, though much disputed, thesis on the nineteenth/twentieth-century attitudes in European/Western literature and thinking regarding the non-Western world—then firmly under colonial rule. The nineteenth/twentieth-century imaginary expressed, as Said points out, a presumed comparison between modern/Christian Europe/the West and the "Orient": advanced versus undeveloped, civilized versus primitive, open for improvement versus passive recipients of improvement. Orientalism fitted with a relationship of dominance of the West over the East:

> Orientalism is a Western style for dominating, restructuring, and having authority over the Orient … [W]ithout examining Orientalism as a discourse one cannot possibly understand the enormously systematic discipline by which European culture was able to manage – and even produce – the Orient politically, sociologically, militarily, scientifically, and imaginatively during the post-Enlightenment period … In brief, because of Orientalism the Orient was not (and is not) a free subject of thought or action.
>
> *(Said, 1978, p. 3)*

Said's book is rich in examples of European/Western travellers, conquerors, governors, and modernizers who have seen "the Orient" as a passive subject to be moulded in keeping with the passivity that Orientalism presupposes. European/Western travellers and the rest had already *pacified* the East in their imagination before dealing with its reality.

It is my contention that the dynamic of Orientalism is analogous to that of the Roman Empire, the Caliphate, and the Chinese Imperial Throne: if "Elsewhere" is not to be dominated by terrors, the fates, or the gods, some kind of universal predominance needs to be installed in thought in advance of venturing forth to experience whether the world beyond is safe. That is the role of Orientalism fulfilled for Europe/the West, together with the other universalisms produced by earlier forms of dominance. Long before Napoleon installed his army in Egypt, European travellers sought to tame their fears of the unknown beyond Europe. Marco Polo's late medieval travel narrative does its best with his insistence that there is a civilized and organized society in Cathay (China) whose emperor is deeply impressed by Catholic Christianity. The discussion will return to that below.

## Travel as Pilgrimage

There is evidence that, in the ancient world, pilgrimage meant travel to other cities to discover their rituals and their cultures (Anghel, 2016; Elsner & Rutherford, 2005). This sociable/cultural side of pilgrimage, though often present, is not often to the fore in presenting the practice.[16] That is easily forgotten, although it is entirely consistent with Victor and Edith Turner's classic account of pilgrimage as a "liminal" experience (Turner & Turner, 1978). Furthermore, that liminality is present in fictional travel narrations, for example, in Chaucer's *Canterbury Tales* (around 1390), where the pilgrims swap stories, often ribald or disrespectful ones, as they go their way to Canterbury.[17] Their absence from home has seemingly liberated them from normal constraints. This is an effect of what Foucault refers to as heterotopia, a place apart, beyond society's practices and norms (Foucault, 1986).

Undertaking a pilgrimage presupposes that the Elsewhere is not fearful and/or that it is under the sway of a universal—be it the Christian, Islamic, or Buddhist god, or the spreading forces of modernity. In travelling for religious pilgrimage, the aim is to get closer to God or the gods, so that the god(s) the pilgrim aims to get closer to has/have to be present all over Elsewhere. In the case of universalistic religions, God is, of course, everywhere, though especially present in certain historic locations.

A significant Chinese pilgrimage is the journey that Faxian (or Fa-Hien or Fa-Hsien) undertook into India at the start of the fourth century BCE in pursuit of a purer Buddhism. In the 1886 translation by James Legge, Faxian (1886, ch. I) states his purpose plainly:

> Deploring the mutilated and imperfect state of the collection of the [Buddhist] Books of Discipline … he entered into an engagement with [four named companions] that they should go to India to seek for the Disciplinary Rules … [C]rossing the desert, in which there are many evil demons and hot winds.

The nearer Faxian approaches to the Indian sub-continent, the more he is impressed by others' admiration and practices of Buddhism (Faxian, 1886, ch. XVI).

Faxian returned to northern China, bearing texts that he had acquired, and continued translating them for the remainder of this life. His strategy, therefore, was to attain a greater spiritual purity by travelling *away* from his starting point and conveying that *back* to home to China. This entails that that there is more worth Elsewhere than back home where he started, and thus his efforts to improve China's Buddhism. This Buddhist universalism was in use in the hands of the Ming imperial house: Chinese supremacy was reinforced by Buddhism, and the legitimation was mutual. *Mutatis mutandis*, the same can be said of pilgrimage in general.

The presupposition of pilgrimage is that the supernatural/the divine is to be found in the Elsewhere, usually more eminently than at home. The pilgrim returns a better person and/or is the instrument for conveying a better spirit to his starting location (Gothóni, 1993). The Muslim practice of hajj is the paradigm instance in the contemporary world, because it is a primary obligation on all Muslims to join their fellow believers once in their lifetime at various ceremonies at historic sites in the founding of their faith. The rituals of purification that they share (e.g., shedding the signs of material life, foregoing physical indulgences, and symbolically joining Mohammed in his struggle against the Devil) partake of the divine in the very location where the original events of the faith occurred. The hajjis return better people with a stronger faith, which they spread in the environment to which they return.

Naturally, it is also possible to undertake a *fictional* pilgrimage, following the same narrative trope without stirring from home. Two influential *fictional* pilgrimages realize that possibility: Dante's *Divine Comedy*[18] (completed 1320) and Bunyan's *Pilgrim's Progress*[19] (1678 and 1684). These two instances observe the same dynamic as the practice of religious pilgrimage: through his journey, the pilgrim attains a greater knowledge and/or belief in relation to the faith.

In the first, the pilgrim in the story, Dante himself,[20] undertakes (like Odysseus) a journey through Hell. In Dante's case, though, it is not heroism that guides him out the other side to pursue his journey toward Paradise, but the guidance of that epitome of Latin poetry, Virgil, whose guidance he follows through Hell and Purgatory. Hell and Purgatory are divided according to the Catholic categorization of sin, which categorization Virgil, or the inhabitants themselves (for all the world like a good Catholic) carefully explains. Dante meets many acquaintances and adversaries along the way, supplying the poet with numerous opportunities to make judgements on the behaviour of individuals, express his regret about the condition of Florence (his native city, from which he was banished for political reasons for the last two decades of his life), and to state political positions regarding Italian politics.[21] The poem is rich in imagery, but the narrative of the traveller's journey is often, after the manner that Robert Cioffi points out in the *Aeneid*, discursive. It suggests a compatibility of Catholic teaching and the classical literature that Italian humanists were exploring, *inter alia* explaining away the theological anomaly that those born before the Revelation of Christ (including Virgil!) could not aspire to enjoy the Christian Paradise.

An analogous theological discourse can be found in the *Pilgrim's Progress*. In that narrative, the central figure, Christian, troubled with his burden of sin and his hope of eternal life, sets out to pursue the straight and narrow path to salvation, leaving many fainter hearts behind[22] and surviving many tests of his faith. He passes through numerous places with allegoric names, such as the Slough of Despond, the Valley of Humiliation, Vanity Fair, or the Valley of the Shadow of Death, and meets many allegorically named persons such as the giant Despair and his wife Diffidence,[23] the Interpreter, Hopeful, Atheist (who derides Christian's faith), the Flatterer (who leads them to follow an easier path than "the Way"), and others. The attitude to the good life is puritanical, to say the least. In keeping with Puritan Protestant sermonizing, there are numerous biblical references, such as the Celestial City or the lesson of Lot's wife. As in the *Divine Comedy*, debates between pilgrims and those they meet along their way, resolve many tricky points of theology, such as the so-called Great Heart's explanation to Christian's wife regarding good deeds and the grace of Jesus Christ. Having survived his many trials and been corrected in his errors along the way, Christian ultimately comes to the Celestial City.

## Travelling as Commentary

With that, I return to Marco Polo, whose status amongst a number of eastward travel writers in the late Middle Ages[24] represents the first step to modern European travel writing. His journey with his father and brother was undertaken during the last three decades of the twelfth century to seek out commercial opportunities. Polo was a merchant who had travelled to furthest Asia and back, and then found himself imprisoned by the Genoese, then at war with his native Venice. He had every reason to promote his own abilities as an intermediary between Europe and the East. But Polo (or Rustichello da Pisa, his cell-mate, who ostensibly took down faithfully his recollections) knew the right picture to present to the literate commercial classes of Christian Europe. In the years following the last of the Crusades in the Eastern Mediterranean, Polo told of a peaceful and orderly Tartar Empire beyond the Muslim Near East, under the authority of Kubla Khan. What is more, Marco Polo himself had seen the civilizing effects of Kubla Khan's regime.

Thus, Polo describes how the Khan presides over a benign, though pagan, empire, but is often impressed by the decency and discipline of his Christian subjects, and therefore eager to know more about the faith they profess. Polo makes clear his family's position in the Khan's court and the faith that the latter had shown to them in entrusting them with a mission to obtain from the Papacy a mission of Catholic scholars (Polo, 1926, chs 2–4). Polo also recounts hearsay stories about the successes of Christianity, such as the story of Chagatai's, or Zakotin's, conversion (ch. 31). Those Muslims who are not subject to the civilizing influence of the Khan get a bad press: often condemned as dishonest, unreliable, or even murderous. Conversely, there are titillating stories about access to sexual services on the way east, such as the practice of Szechuan men to make their wives and daughters available to passing guests—a tradition that the Khan had seemingly chosen to tolerate as it accorded with time-honoured practice, in spite of his distaste for it (chs 34, 36).

Written in gaol, Marco Polo needed his *Travels* to succeed with its potential readership of Christian burgers. As Simon Gaunt (2013) suggests, Polo is a teller of tall tales—not especially reliable on matters of fact, but conveying an agreeable and partially accurate impression to his readers. Hence, the confirmation of their negative views about the Muslims of the Near East matched with a seductive picture of a Far East under the Kubla Khan, where Polo himself was an able intermediary, but also confirmation of a universalistic Christian God's benign power in the world outside Europe.

In the centuries following Polo's travels, Europeans continued to travel eastward to deal with, or to skirt around, the Islamic Near East (Darwin, 2007).[25] From the fifteenth century, conquerors, missionaries, traders, and carpetbaggers of all sorts travelled also to the Americas and met native populations, whom they oftentimes exploited, enslaved, and/or forcefully converted to Christianity. From the earliest days, these travellers' accounts raised numerous challenges to established assumptions about the status of European society (Prieto, 2011). Notably, a Dominican missionary called Bartolomé de Las Casas was instrumental in promoting new legislation in the mid-sixteenth century alleviating the conditions suffered by native populations under Spanish governance. In short, as in the case of much modern European travel, discovery was accompanied by critical commentary.

A later instance is the Enlightenment controversy aroused by the 1771 publication of Louis-Antoine de Bougainville's *Voyage autour du monde par la frégate du roi La Boudeuse et la flûte L'Étoile* (*Voyage round the world on the frigate "La Boudeuse" and trading ship "L'Étoile"*), which was the occasion of much speculation around themes of the oppression of native populations by Christianity, especially the Catholic Church, as against the innocent pleasures of their simple lives (Bougainville, 1771). The progressive side of the controversy promoted images of the peaceability, innocence, and sensual freedoms of native populations which cast the oppressed condition of European societies in a sombre light (Diderot, 1796; Rousseau, 1755).

Over the same period, a genre sprung up of ostensibly autobiographical texts written by those low in the social order revealing conditions in contemporary societies: the picaresque novel. Fictional journeys into the lower levels of European societies exposed critical truths at home, as well as overseas. This made the life of such books difficult: what some regard as the classic (Garrido Ardila 2015), *Lazarillo de Tormes* (1554), originally published anonymously in Spain, was rapidly censored. Better known examples in the English-speaking world include Daniel Defoe's *Moll Flanders*, Henry Fielding's *Tom Jones*, and Tobias Smollet's *Humphrey Clinker*. The degree of direct social comment varies. Voltaire's *Candide* represents an extreme; it takes a purported philosophical position and subjects it to merciless contradiction in the life of an innocent devotee.

In this fashion, European fictional or real travel narrative has fully exploited the potential for comment in travel writing, negative as well as positive. Over and above the many detailed real or fictional travels in Said's *Orientalism*, there are those that had a more or less explicit political purpose. The most influential instance in the nineteenth century has to be de Tocqueville's account of his travels in the United States, *Democracy in America* (1835 and 1840), which shaped modern European liberalism. Others with political implications would include Fanny Trollope's *Domestic Manners of the Americans* (1832), which blends observation of the lack of polite manners amongst Americans with slightly half-hearted praise of the equality amongst them.

In the twentieth century, fictional travels, such as Joseph Conrad's (1899) *Heart of Darkness*, have been used to explore the realities of European empires. Actual experience in the British Empire has been behind the writings of, for example, George Orwell's (1934) *Burmese Days*, and journeys undertaken by colonial civil servants, such as Margery Perham,[26] have been the basis for domestic reforms to colonialism.

In sum, although modern Western/European travel stories have partaken of other narrative forms, the degree to which they *comment* and even *judge* whatever is discovered in the course of travelling has been a predominant, though not exclusive, quality of modern European narratives.

## Concluding Remarks

One thing is evident following this survey of narratives in stories of travel: mobility in life is equally present to the human imagination as *im*mobility. Elsewhere appears to be as much present as Here in humans' understanding of the world. However, just like the Here, according to the philosopher Gaston Bachelard (1957), there are diverse notions of Elsewhere.

Over the course of this brief survey, I have identified five underlying notions of Elsewhere in narratives of travel: challenge, discovery, reconfiguration, pilgrimage, and commentary. I have presented them in a roughly historical sequence, but that is not to say they are discrete from one another. In practice, narratives of travel entertain various notions of the world that the traveller ventures into. There is much commentary in Herodotus or Faxian, even though they appear under two different headings, neither of which is "commentary". Travel narrative continues to feed off earlier tropes today: quest stories such as *The Lord of the Rings* continue to be settings for heroes to test their mettle; holiday brochures continue to sell the promise of degrees of indulgence unavailable at home; and *Game of Thrones* continues to haunt the contemporary imagination with the danger of Elsewhere.

The *Game of Thrones* imagery of the danger of any Elsewhere beyond the Ice Wall suggests how much borders (such as that Wall) are "political" in the sense that narratives about Elsewhere are constitutive of the politics of bordering. If the Elsewhere on the far side of the border is felt to be familiar, benign or subject to some degree of common order, the political field/political actors are able to constitute an Elsewhere not requiring defensive barriers. If Elsewhere is felt to be none of these things, the political field (often with the help of opportunistic politicians and media) will propose building "Ice Walls" against the unknown.

Instead of more obvious examples in US politics, I choose to illustrate this possibility with the politics of my own small country, Denmark. Here there is a broad consensus amongst established political parties on a so-called "strict" policy as regards immigration and refugees. Hence, the current Danish government has jumped through hoops to avoid bringing a couple of dozen Danish wives and widows of ISIS fighters and their children back onto Danish territory. The rhetoric employed makes these few young women and their children appear as an imminent danger, of a "terror on the streets of Danish cities". That rhetoric is the side-product of a view of Islam as radically Other. Mirroring that view of the Otherness of the Islamic Elsewhere, there has grown up an image of Denmark as a country that the whole world envies and would, at the drop of a hat, seek to migrate to in order to exploit our welfare state. Thus, the imagery of Elsewhere shapes the politics of bordering between Here and Elsewhere.

Still avoiding the obvious in recent US politics, I can illustrate the evolution of Elsewhere in the books of an apolitical figure, the novelist Cormac McCarthy. In his first widely read novel (and the first of what is known as his Border Trilogy), *All the Pretty Horses* (1992), his young cowboy hero, John Grady, wanders over the Mexican border. There he confronts and survives many challenges—often provoked by the youngest of his two companions, one Jimmy Blevins. On the other hand, he also finds love and learns the rules of honour within Mexican society. Grady has been partly brought up in a Mexican family and speaks fluent Spanish, so the Mexican Elsewhere is far from unknown to him. This is a story where danger and treasure are to be found in the Mexican Elsewhere. By contrast, in McCarthy's *No Country for Old Men* (2005), the same Elsewhere appears to the narrator, a middle-aged Texan sheriff policing a border county, to be the hotbed of dangers that defy all understanding—as does much of the criminality in contemporary America. An analogous figure to John Grady, the free-booting Vietnam vet, Lewellyn Moss, is pursued and killed by the mysterious bogeyman hailing from

Mexico, Anton Chigurh. By this time, the Mexican border appears as a terrain of threat. This is the stuff of which the "immigrant caravans" of Donald Trump and Fox News are made.

I have argued that much depends on the ontology of the whole. A crucial development, I claim, is that towards a monotheistic or universalist perception of the world, such that the entirety of Elsewhere is embraced by the one deity or one ontological dynamic. But a universalism that has lost its self-belief is no longer sure of its hold on Elsewhere. As the USA and the West more broadly inevitably surrenders its hold over the rest of the world, it is especially important to hang on to, or nurture, what we do share with other parts of the globe, so that the loss of direct control does not necessarily produce anger and aggressiveness towards what would consequently be experienced as a threatening Elsewhere.

## Notes

1. Debating with Heidegger's phenomenological approach to human self-consciousness is widespread in thinking about space and territory. See, *inter alia*, Casey, 1997; Debray, 2010; Cooper & Tinning, 2019, chs 4 & 7.
2. For discussion of Heidegger's wider influence on, for example, architecture see Woessner (2003) and Sharr (2007).
3. Or the inappropriately named Greenland, widely supposed to have been named 'green' by Eric Thorvaldsson (c.950-c.1003), or 'Eric the Red', in the hope of attracting others to join him on his travels to its snow-bound coasts.
4. Amongst the many epithets routinely used to refer to Odysseus is that of "layer of waste to cities".
5. References to Herodotus' text are to book and page of the original text.
6. "I cannot help laughing at the absurdity of all the map-makers who show Ocean running like a river around a perfectly circular earth" (IV: 36).
7. IV: 44ff. concerning Darius' ambition to conquer the Scythians and their natural military advantages in their own territory.
8. "The Indians all live frugally … They dislike a great undisciplined multitude, and consequently they observe good order. Theft is of very rare occurrence" (McCrindle, 1877, p. 69).
9. "Of the great officers of state, some have charge of the market, others of the city, others of the soldiers. Some supervise the rivers, as is done in Egypt, and inspect the sluices by which water is let out from the main canals to their branches" (McCrindle, 1877, p. 86).
10. E.g. regarding "fantastical tribes" (McCrindle, 1877, pp. 74–79).
11. At that point of the story, Roman readers might have relished comparing the triumph of Aeneas over Dido with the Roman victory in the Punic Wars against Carthage.
12. A pseudo-biblical parallel narrative appeared in mid-nineteenth century with the British–Israel movement, which contended that the Lost Tribe of Israel was the race that seeded the British (John Wilson (1840). *Our Israelitish Origin: Lectures on Ancient Israel, and the Israelitish Origin of the Modern Nations of Europe*. London: J. Nisbet). The British-Israel-World Federation, promoting a similar doctrine, exists to this day (www.britishisrael.co.uk). See Cottrell-Boyce (2020) for a history of the movement.
13. Ghazni lies to the east in present-day Afghanistan.
14. Although he did not have much good to say of his new master (Biruni, 1910, pp. x–xiii).
15. Quoted in Levathes (1994, p. 82). The story had an unexpected outcome as the Sinhalese king refused the tribute and was subsequently dragged back to Nanking for the Emperor's judgment and, ultimately, reprieve.
16. Contemporary Hindus undertake pilgrimages in groups, often walking from sacred site to sacred site, as do groups of Irish Catholics to Knock and European Catholics to Lourdes. There must be numerous other instances.
17. Liminality is also in evidence in the text that greatly influenced Chaucer, Boccaccio's *Decameron* (from around 1353), in which the storytellers escape from the Black Death in Florence to a garden where they tell stories to each other, one of which concerns a pilgrimage to Rome where the pilgrim is deeply disappointed by the corrupt practices of the Roman Church!
18. See Havely (1998) for Dante's literary influence.

19 During the seventeenth and eighteenth centuries, the family Bible was frequently accompanied by a family copy of *Pilgrim's Progress*. See Rasmussen (2018) for the impact of *Pilgrim's Progress* on American thinking.
20 Dante is frequently referred to as a "pilgrim" in the text.
21 Notably, to judge from the position assigned to Frederik the Holy Roman Emperor, he seems to favour the Holy Roman Empire's meeting its responsibilities in Italy, which gives it its Catholic legitimacy, rather than pursuing dynastic goals in Germany.
22 Including his family, who, in the event, reconsider and join him later.
23 At that time, meaning "distrust".
24 Others include: Odoric of Pordenone, Giovanni da Pian del Carpine, Sir John Mandeville. All are shadowy figures about whom it is difficult to know what actual travels they undertook, as is the case with Polo, though less so.
25 A striking instance is the Englishman Anthony Jenkinson, who reached Aleppo in 1553 (Brotton, 2017), and made four trips into Russia and further east to establish trading networks.
26 Whose *African Apprenticeship: An Autobiographical Journey in Southern Africa 1929* and *West African Passage* were actually published in respectively 1974 and 1983, and which informed her influential work at Oxford University in the 1930s and 1940s and her 1961 Reith Lectures.

# References

Abulafia, D. (2019). *The boundless sea: A human history of the oceans*. London: Allen Lane.
Al-Biruni, M. Ibn Ahmad (1910). *Alberuni's India, Vol. 1* (E.C. Sachau, Trans.). New York: Kegan Paul, Trench & Trubner.
Anghel, S. (2016). Ancient tourism: Can modern concepts be applied to modern contexts? *Journal of Tourism Challenges and Trends*, *9*(1), 9–29.
Bachelard, G. (1957). *La poétique de l'espace (The poetics of space)*. Paris: Quadriges/PUF.
Bang, P.F. (2005, 18 June). *Universal empire - the state, heterogeneous power and hegemony in the Roman and Mughal worlds*. Presented at the *Historical Sociology and Universal Empire*, Faculty of Arts, University of Copenhagen.
Bang, P.F., & Kolodziejczyk, D. (2012). *Universal Empire: A comparative approach to imperial culture and representation in Eurasian history*. Cambridge: Cambridge University Press.
Berry, J., & Laurence, R. (1998). *Cultural identity in the Roman Empire*. London: Routledge.
Bougainville, L.-A. de (1771). *Voyage autour du monde par la frégate du roi La Boudeuse et la flûte L'Étoile*.
Brotton, J. (2017). *This Orient isle: Elizabethan England and the Islamic world*. Milton Keynes: Allen Lane.
Casey, E.S. (1997). *The fate of place: A philosophical history*. Berkeley: University of California Press.
Conrad, J. (1899). *The heart of darkness*. London: William Blackwood & Sons.
Cioffi, R.L. (2016). *Travel in the Roman world*. Oxford: Oxford Handbooks Online.
Cooper, A., & Tinning, S. (2019). *Debating and defining borders: Philosophical and theoretical perspectives*. London: Taylor & Francis.
Cottrell-Boyce, A. (2020). *Israelism in modern Britain*. London: Routledge.
Darwin, J. (2007). *After Tamerlane: The global history of empire*. London: Allen Lane.
Debray, R. (2010). *Eloge des frontières (In praise of frontiers)*. Paris: Gallimard.
Diderot (1796). *Supplément au voyage de Bougainville, ou dialogue entre A et B sur l'inconvénient d'attacher des idées morales à certaines actions physiques qui n'en comportent pas (Supplement to the voyage of Bougainville, or dialogue between A and B on the difficulty of attaching moral ideas to certain physical actions that do not entail them)*. Paris: Librarie Générale Française.
Elden, S. (2013). *The birth of territory*. Chicago: Chicago University Press.
Elsner, J., & Rutherford, I. (2005). *Pilgrimage in Graeco-Roman antiquity: Seeing the gods*. Oxford: Oxford University Press.
Escudero, J.A. (2019). Homeland and politics of space. In A. Cooper, & S. Tinning (Eds.) *Debating and defining borders: Philosophical and theoretical perspectives*, pp. 112–123. London: Taylor & Francis.
Faxian (1886). *A record of the Buddhistic kingdoms: Being an account by the Chinese monk Fa-Hsien* (J. Legge, Trans.). Oxford: The Clarendon Press.
Flory, S. (1980). Who reads Herodotus' histories? *The American Journal of Philology*, *101*(1), 12–28.
Foucault, M. (1986). Of other spaces. *Diacritics*, *16*(1), 22–27.

Garrido Ardila, J. (2015). *The picaresque novel in western literature: From the sixteenth century to the neopicaresque.* Cambridge: Cambridge University Press.

Gaunt, S. (2013). *Marco Polo's Le Devisement du Monde: Narrative voice, language and diversity.* Cambridge: Boydell & Brewer.

Gothóni, R. (1993). Pilgrimage = transformation journey. *Scripta Instituti Donneriani Aboensis, 15*, 101–116.

Havely, N. (1998). *Dante's modern afterlife: Reception and response from Blake to Heaney.* New York: St Martin's Press.

Heidegger, M. (1951). *Building, dwelling, thinking* (A. Bobeck, Ed. & Trans). Adam Bobeck - Academia.edu – accessed September 2020.

Herodotus. (2003). *The Histories* (J. Marincola, Ed.; A. de Sélincourt, Trans.). London: Penguin.

Jansari, S. (2020). From geography to paradoxography: The use, transmission and survival of Megasthenes' Indica. *Journal of Ancient History, 8*(1), 26–49.

Levathes, L. (1994). *When China ruled the seas: The treasure fleet of the Dragon Throne, 1405-1433.* New York: Oxford University Press.

Luhman, N. (1982). Territorial borders as system boundaries. In R. Strassoldo, & G. delli Zoti (Eds.), *Cooperation and conflict in border areas*, pp. 235–245. Milan: Franco Angeli.

McCarthy, C. (1992). *All the pretty horses.* New York: Alfred Knopf.

McCarthy, C. (2005). *No country for old men.* New York: Alfred Knopf.

McCrindle, J. (1877). *Megasthenes and Arrian: Being a translation of the fragments of the Indika of Megasthenes collected by Dr. Schwanbeck, and the first part of the Indika of Arrian.* London: Trübner & Co.

Nicolet, C. (1991). *Space, geography, and politics in the early Roman Empire.* Ann Arbor: University of Michigan Press.

Orwell, G. (1934). *Burmese days.* New York: Harper & Brothers.

Polo, M. (1926). *The travels of Marco Polo.* (W. Marsden, Trans., 2001). New York: The Modern Library.

Pretzler, M. (2007). *Pausanias: Travel writing in ancient Greece.* London: Duckworth.

Prieto, A.I. (2011). *Missionary scientists: Jesuit science in Spanish South America, 1570-1810.* Nashville: Vanderbilt University Press.

Rawlinson, H. (1916). *Intercourse between India and the Western World: From earliest times to the fall of Rome.* Cambridge: Cambridge University Press.

Rousseau, J.-J. (1755). *Discours sur l'origine et les fondemens de l'inégalité parmi les hommes (Discourse on the origin and foundations of inequality amongst human beings).* Amsterdam: Marc Michel Rey.

Said, E.W. (1978). *Orientalism.* London: Routledge and Kegan Paul.

Sharr, A. (2007). *Thinkers for architects.* London: Routledge.

Sheehan, S. (2018). *A guide to reading Herodotus' Histories.* London: Bloomsbury.

Stoneman, R. (2019). *The Greek experience of India from Alexander to the Indo-Greeks.* Princeton, NJ: Princeton University Press.

Turner, V., & Turner, E. (1978). *Image and pilgrimage in Christian culture: Anthropological perspectives.* Oxford: Blackwell.

Woessner, M. (2003). Ethics, architecture and Heidegger. *City: Analysis of Urban Change, Theory, Action, 7*(1), 23–44.

# 3
# BORDERLANDS AND COMMENSALITY

*Thomas M. Wilson*

## Introduction

In the summer of 2019, I interviewed a local businessman in the principal market town at the eastern end of the Northern Ireland land border between the Republic of Ireland and the United Kingdom about the potential impact of Brexit, the impending departure of the UK from the European Union (EU). He had a lot to say about the threat Brexit posed for his livelihood, which was overwhelmingly tied to the provision of hospitality services in food, drink and lodging. Of worry to him was the effect Brexit was going to have on cross-border tourism, which had literally been wholly revitalized after the agreements between the warring parties in 1998 to end hostilities in the Northern Ireland war, known locally as "The Troubles". As this entrepreneur saw it in 2019, two years before Brexit in fact was completed, at least in its first stage,[1] the situation represented a disaster for him and his family, one that in all likelihood would destroy most, if not all, of his businesses and investments.

In particular he worried that Brexit would establish a "hard" border—a borderline with a returned security army, police and customs presence, a hardening that would kickstart the return of violence and cut off the lively consumer and tourist trade that had flowed into the town, with its newly refurbished central square complete with modern hotel, a trade mainly from the Republic of Ireland just a few miles south of town, across what had become an open and "soft" border over the last 20 years between two fellow member states of the EU:

> How are we going to attract the punters from the Republic, who stopped coming to the North during the Troubles? Of course, we always had a small trade in petrol sales and drink [alcohol] from the people just over the border that saw X____ as their market town. But the tourists from deep down in the Republic took their sweet time getting up the nerve and the curiosity to look around up here. Now they are here, along with the Yanks and the Germans and the French, but all of that will go away if the border goes back to the way it was.
>
> *(Respondent, 22 August 2019)*

He was referencing the decades when the security forces blocked all but a few approved road links between his town and its neighbors to the south, but he also knew that the town had been a regional center for the secret war waged against the British security forces by the Irish Republican Army. This made the town famous to some and infamous to others, and clearly one that would suffer again if the border hardened after Brexit. But in response to my efforts to get my respondent to consider further the ramifications of Brexit in his community, he indicated one concern, which he said was shared by many people in town, not just business people. He reminded me of the ties that bound local people to their friends, kin and neighbors across the borderline, in what I concluded was the shared sense of *communitas* that has sustained many people during the Troubles, in the face of particular and significant dangers. But he opined beyond that:

> Over the last ten years or so you can see, you can feel, a different mentality hereabouts, a sense of so much we share with Irish we haven't seen here for donkey's years. And I don't just mean nationalism and republicanism. Sure, we share a lot of that. I mean we share a sense of history, or being Irish, maybe even of being European, and when they come here to visit us or when we go south to Dublin, Cork and Galway, we are doing the same. Enjoying life together, enjoying the peace, and enjoying so much that we share being Irish.
>
> *(Respondent, 22 August 2019)*

Elsewhere I have suggested that sentiments such as this may be the basis of a new form of European identity, a type of "Banal Europeanism" (Wilson, 2020), but I was struck that day by the emotional dimensions my respondent displayed, and introduced as a wider phenomenon, to cross-border travel, tourism and social interactions. He certainly left me with the impression that, perhaps for the first time in their adult lives or perhaps for the first time in a generation or more, many people were free to just revel in their own and shared notions of community and commensality.

I returned to this theme, of what was being shared over the last 20 years with the people on the other side of the borderline, with the same respondent in later discussions, and I introduced it to other people with whom I interacted in the Northern Ireland borderlands in that and subsequent summers. As the research has progressed, it seems that the respondent that summer, who worried about the barriers that might be reinstated to make cross-border communality and commensality more difficult than they had been over the last 20 years, was not alone. It is commonly held today in these borderlands that the barriers that would come back with a hardened border would represent a return to the bad days of the Troubles, in a so-called post-Brexit "return to the future".[2]

This pessimism was evidence of what most Northern Ireland borderlanders in my experience have acknowledged, that they and their communities have suffered a longstanding marginality, in a general condition of finding themselves "in-between" so much that is mainstream in the UK and the Republic of Ireland. This state of liminality, experienced in like manner by many other borderland peoples beyond Ireland, is widely recognized in Northern Ireland as a sad but inescapable dimension of border life. What seemed significant to me, and was expressed often to me as new and worthy of note in my current ethnographic project in the borderlands, was the identification of the generalized and normalized cross-border relations, the attractions and comforts of the actual and metaphorical "breaking bread" with the people of the other side of the borderline, which many of my respondents felt was most in jeopardy. As one community activist concluded, in an interview in summer 2018 (Respondent, 27 August 2018), the "greatest loss" border communities might experience if a "hard" border returned would be to be separated yet again from their "neighbors, friends and relations just across the border".

In this chapter I move beyond the roles that borders play as institutions and processes of state power, sovereignty and citizenship, and the processes of national and local bordering and identity production and reproduction (Newman, 2006), that have been so soundly explored in each of the social sciences over the last few decades, to consider more closely the emotional and other social connections among borderland peoples and communities on either side of, and across, international borderlines.[3] While border peoples, communities and cultures are often portrayed as peripheral, at the edge of national territory and on the margins of state sovereignty, in an in-between condition that suggests a lingering if not constant liminality, they are also interlinked, on their side of the border but also, and sometimes more so, with those across the borderline. However, the cross-border flows that have so vitalized comparative border studies have increasingly ignored or obscured the moments, institutions and events that slow these flows and make them points of spatial and temporal punctuation, realized social meanings and relations that anchor aspects of border life. It is these points and moments of contact that should make border scholars retain their perspective on what borderlanders perceive and remember as relatively fixed or stationary in border life. In the sections that follow I review some of these issues by considering scholarly attention, mainly by ethnographers but not exclusively, to matters of space and place in the social, political, and discursive landscapes of borderlands. This perspective, while acknowledging the shifting roles that international borders play in bounding nations, states and border communities, also leads to a consideration of the border as a social field, in which issues of cross-border sociality are tied up with varying degrees of liminality and commensality, which are evidenced in borderland and cross-border tourism.

## Border Space and Place

It is widely recognized by border scholars across the social sciences and humanities that borders must be seen as more than normative frames and fixed facts of the social and political life of (their) nations. Borders should also be seen in their roles as institutions, agents and processes that help "enhance or restrict the pursuit of a decent life" (Agnew, 2008, p. 183, quoted in Megoran, 2012, p. 475). Over the last few decades border scholars have provided case studies not only of people and communities on one or both sides of a borderline, but also of the historical context to contemporary borders, as ways to problematize the historical forces that in some cases predated the nations and states which borders are seen to contain today. These "boundary biographies" allow scholars to explore how borders "materialize, rematerialize and dematerialize in different ways, in different contexts, at different scales and at different times" (Megoran, 2012, pp. 475–476).

Border studies as a field has pursued some recognizable themes across the many scholarly disciplines in which borders have captured the imagination of researchers and authors (van Houtum & Strüver, 2002, p. 144). As Henk van Houtum (2000) has indicated, in his overview of geographical research on borders in Europe, there have been at least three different methodological or theoretical approaches that have resulted in major tropes in European border studies: "the flow approach, the cross-border co-operation approach and the people approach". Accepting van Houtum's mastery of the multidisciplinary field of border studies 20 years ago, and through my reading of how it has evolved since, I suggest that this summary still holds for global border studies today. Within the rubrics of contemporary cross-border flows may be found all manner of trade, work, shopping, migration, refugees and tourism, along with the day to day matters of cross-border cooperation in the economics and politics of security, government, governance, public welfare and public sector services. In their approaches to these cross-border relations and relationships, scholars have employed metaphors of walls, doors, court of the Indian monarch, Chandragupta Maurya, Megasthenes gathered his *Indika* about the geography (physical and human), fauna, social structures, and political administration of India. These include an explanation of the fertility of the land (McCrindle, 1877, pp. 54–55), an at-times admiring account of Indian manners,[8] the strict application of justice and punishment by the king (ibid., pp. 71–73), the comparative administration of public affairs,[9] their schools of philosophy (ibid., pp. 104–105), and their Brahmin (or *Brahman*) sect (ibid., pp. 120–122). Even though his accounts do stray into the fantastical,[10] there is a serious effort being made to travel and report back coolly on what the writer observes. Furthermore, Megasthenes feels free to openly praise aspects of Indian society: its absence of slavery, the probity of its subjects, the freedom of its women (Rawlinson, 1916, p. 58f.). The moral of this story may be that consideration of an external world already made safe by conquest (even if short-lived) permits factual inquiry, comparison, and even praise.

What can be properly called Greek "travel-writing", notably that of Pausanias (Pretzler, 2007), arose in the first two centuries CE for a market of cosmopolitan Greek speakers. A striking feature of these writings is that Elsewhere is the world of other Greek speakers, who can be relied upon to share certain beliefs, values, and, of course, forms of expression. Maria Pretzler writes that "[l]ike most ancient Greek writers Pausanias generally shows little interest in spatial relationships between the places he describes" because he "may have assumed that any reader who needed exact directions could consult local people" (Pretzler, 2007, pp. 69–70). In short, this kind of travel writing resembles the modern forms of guidebook in assuming that there is an Elsewhere that is comprehensible in the same terms as home.

The text of Megasthenes' writing has been lost (see Jansari, 2020), but we can reconstruct it via the writings of Arrian, a Greek from modern-day Anatolia, who gravitated to Rome, attained a Senate seat under the Roman Emperor Hadrian, and, around 132 CE, an appointment as governor further east in Anatolia. This is not accidental. After Alexander, ambitious Greeks were gravitating towards the rising power centre of Rome and identifying their world with that of Rome: a "Greco-Roman" world was developing (Stoneman, 2019). On the Roman side, generals and emperors sought the mantel of Alexander, the conqueror of Asia, to drive home their claim to rule the known world (Bang, 2005; Bang & Kolodziejczyk, 2012). The claim to a "universal" power needed, and got, the backing of progressive Greek figures who were instrumental in preserving and extending the approach to the wider world that diplomacy-following-conquest made possible.

## Travel as Reconfiguration—and Claims to the Universal

In parallel with the fusion of the Greek world with the Greco-Roman one, poetic fiction laid claim to the Greek heritage. The dominant work of Latin epic, Virgil's *Aeneid* (written between 29 and 19 BCE), is manifestly an effort to reshape the world so as to reconfigure Rome as its most important location. In the *Odyssey*, *Gilgamesh*, and *Beowulf*, it is clear where home, the journey's starting point, lies. The overarching theme is how the hero earns a return home. But in the *Aeneid*, the final goal lies in the Elsewhere, and the narrative concerns how he will fulfil his destiny to earn his entitlement to a *different* home. Effectively, the *Aeneid* moves the centre of the world from the Greek-speaking portion to Rome.

The trials of Aeneas shadow those of Odysseus except that the final destination of Aeneas' god-given destiny lies elsewhere than his original home. Escaping Troy with a small band of followers, Aeneas wanders on the sea towards Carthage, where he is royally received by the young Queen Dido. But, wresting himself free of the feminine temptations of Dido, who goes on to commit dramatic suicide,[11] Aeneas abandons her to seek the greater glory of establishing his sovereignty in a new location amongst the Latins. As Robert Cioffi (2016, p. 21), amongst others, points out:

> The teleology of the Aeneid's travels establishes a clear sense of center, but … the poem imagines Rome's periphery to be a (literally) boundless one, "an empire without an end" … The connection between travel and state foundation in the *Aeneid* is indicative of a broader trend for the poetics of travel and space to invite and frame discussion of the political, the social, and the moral in the poetry of Virgil and his contemporaries … In Roman poetry, travel therefore offers a space to discuss a range of other issues, such as political power, imperial ambitions, and Roman urbanism.

As in the *Odyssey*, so it is in the *Aeneid*. The supernatural world is frequently on hand to make a timely intervention in our hero's actions: Poseidon against Athene in Odysseus' case, Neptune against Venus in Aeneas' case. It is in this sense that Aeneas' ultimate destiny is "god-given". Elsewhere is ultimately ruled over by the gods, and the intercession of the gods is needed if even an heroic figure is going to survive and establish an alternative centre of the globe out in the unknown.[12]

A founding father of the discipline of geography, Strabo (63 BCE–24 CE), is another instance of reconfiguration. He was another Greek-speaking scholar and traveller who hailed from what is now Anatolia, and who advanced his career under the patronage of Rome. He assembled from his travels his own observations and those of many predecessors, including Megasthenes and Arrian, with his reflections on the nature of the entire globe in a comprehensive *Geography*. The work dates from the reign of the first two Roman emperors, and was an element in the empire's hegemonic cultural identity (Berry & Laurence, 1998). It is clear that Strabo's intentions are political; the geography is, as Claude Nicolet (1991, p. 47) observes, "constructed so as to lead to Rome's pretended universal domination".

When, in 1017, the Muslim scholar, Al-Biruni, was brought to his capital, Ghazni,[13] by Mahmud, the first Ghaznavid ruler in the eastern of part of the Persian Empire, he was already an established scholar and polymath. He continued his scholarship under Mahmud.[14] But Al-Biruni's studies and travels, especially in India, continued for at least a decade after the accession of the next sultan, Mas'ud, whose patronage he appears to have welcomed (Biruni, 1910, pp. xiii–xvi). Although it is not clear whether Al-Biruni held any official position under the sultans, his situation can be compared to that of Greek speakers in the early years of the Roman Empire: encouraged and patronized (or perhaps employed) in the course of their travels to far-flung places, and implicitly supportive of the reach of that power which made their travels possible.

Al-Biruni is known as a founding father of "Indology", the systematic study of the society and culture of the Indian sub-continent. But in his voluminous writings, Al-Biruni was primarily interested in universal questions: geodesy (the nature of the globe), astronomy, mathematics, linguistics, astrology, and so on, as befits a commentator from the Caliphate of a universal religion. It is in a spirit of an anthropologist that Al-Biruni examines, for example, the rigour of the moral-theological teachings of the Hindu religion. Thus, following a long account of the elements of Hindu eschatology, he adds: "We have given this enumeration only in order to show what kinds of deeds the Hindu abhors as sins" (Al-Biruni, 1910, p. 61). Thereafter, having learnt what counts as sins, the question at hand is the social effect of that eschatology:

windows, bridges, tunnels and all sorts of conduits and barriers to explicate the nature of borders as institutions, events and processes. The "people" approach is also still central in border studies, in respect of the myriad ways in which borders matter in people's lives, particularly in terms of personal and group identities and identifications. It is apparent too that the three approaches are not mutually exclusive, for borders as economic facts, political realities, social formations and cultural symbols are all constitutive of each other.

Rather than simply seen as a borderline that marks and contains the territory and institutions of the nation and state, a border today is also variously perceived as "a spatially binding power, which is objectified in everyday sociopolitical practices … differentiators of socially constructed mindscapes, identities and meanings" (van Houtum, 2012, p. 406). The emphasis on bordering and ordering processes have made borders "more of a verb, a practice, a relation, and also importantly a part of imagination and desire, than they are a noun or an object" (Green, 2012, p. 579; see also van Houtum, 2010). Borders are geopolitical facts, not only socially constructed and reproduced presentations of state power and national sovereignty, but representations of different meanings in the often widely various and disparate lives of borderland residents, crossers, workers and observers. As such, a border must be seen as both a thing and an idea, both something signified and a signifier (van Houtum & Strüver, 2002).

Borders as boundaries are arenas for political action, frames of reference for many interactions within a nation-state and across the international borderline, and emotionally charged narratives at the disposal of disparate national groups. Thus, borders can be alternatively and simultaneously the cause and effect of the logics and the politics of fear, for example of threats from outside the body politic, and the logics and politics of hospitality, in welcoming new ideas, people and goods. These border-related notions of fear, loathing, serenity, and welcoming are dynamic, products of an almost incessant social redrawing of the culturally contoured maps of borders and borderlands, even when the actual borderline may not have shifted for generations. Thus, borders, which often are marked by varying degrees of *phobophilia*, a morbid love of fear that certainly seems to have captured the imagination of many politicians in today's world (Andersson, 2019, p. 18), must also be seen as a point, or a series of points composing a line of greeting and hospitality. While many elites and other populations, in metropolitan centers and in borderlands alike, see the border as a key ingredient in their *xenophobia*, borders are also often the first contacts in a people's and a state's *xenophilia*.

It is thus not surprising that the negotiable, contestable and contextual dimensions of borders, borderlands and frontiers are almost always significant in any examination of an international border, mainly because their volatile dimensions bring so much attention to such borders. It is also not surprising that scholars are just as immersed in contesting and negotiating their definitions of borders as are the people who daily deal with geopolitical and cultural borders. In this chapter, I present borders in the first instance as the borderline that demarcates the national territory of a state and which is identifiable and accessible in most instances with precise geographic accuracy. Borders are also simultaneously the geographical and social zones that stretch both away from the borderline into the state and across the borderline into the other state. This latter notion of border, though, is not as precise as the former, because it reflects various social, cultural, economic and political constructions. These delineate social space and place framed by such things as local communities tied together by kinship, marriage, work and play; by agreements between governments to have cross-border relations, bodies and regions; and by trade and production treaties, which, for example, create tax-free border shopping and manufacturing zones. Thus, it is clear too that international borders, and their related border zones, must also be seen in various ways as "frontiers", the places and spaces of mixing international culture, of transnationalism at diverse social and political levels, where the stuff of both quotidian and longstanding historical life is, and often has long been, contested, negotiated and agreed in practice.[4]

While border crossing is a prominent feature of much postmodern theorizing in the social science of such things as cultural flows, movement, mobility, hybridization, integration and globalization, relatively little attention has been paid in anthropology and its cognate disciplines to border-crossers, other than refugees and migrants, and the emotional response to the borders and border peoples. Of particular interest in this relative disregard are three sorts of border-crossing people: daily and seasonal workers; shoppers and those who seek to enjoy the economic and social benefits of personal, consumer economic exchanges across borderlines; and tourists, people who are also consumers but who have goals related to matters of leisure, enjoyment, social and cultural interaction, and the recognition, realization and appreciation of history and culture.

Bordering as a dynamic process and as an approach in border studies allows scholars to get away from seeing borders as fixed boundaries, historical institutions and a space of precise places, and to see the nations and states that are simultaneously joined and divided at borderlines as "fluid manifestations of power and culture in both spatial and temporal dimensions" (Linde-Laursen, 2010; see also Wilson & Donnan, 1998; Donnan & Wilson, 1999, p. 9). While it has become commonplace in the postmodern age over the last few decades to view borders as sites and tropes of displacement, of shifting local, national and global boundaries, and as spaces of new forms of culture and identity (as summarized and stimulated by works such as Gupta and Ferguson, 1997), borders and borderlands are also sites and tropes of emplacement, continuity and the reproduction of welcome sociality and traditional boundaries. These tensions, between, on the one hand, the institutions and forces of movement and mobility, most often perceived as displacement and disjuncture, and, on the other hand, those of embeddedness, emplacement and fixity, often seen in terms of tradition and community, are at the heart of the integrating and differentiating multiple logics of "borderness" (Green, 2012; Roitman, 2005).

Thus, over the last few decades, in their attempt to identify and chronicle ethnographically the dynamics of borders, borderness and border cultures (Donnan & Wilson, 1999), anthropologists, among other scholars in the broad field of border studies, have contributed to the continuing problematization and theorizing of the related concepts of place and space. Although the definitions and the concepts in use often vary by scholar and academic discipline, it is widely accepted in social science that space refers to the precise points and locations where people live, work and play, to the factual, determinable and demonstrable actual physical geography of peoples' daily lives. Place, on the other hand, refers to the meanings people attach to these locations, and to the relations and relationships connected, framed, inspired, inhibited and perhaps even caused, in their minds, by these same spaces.[5] The concepts, although often discussed as separate and distinct, are inextricably linked in human experience. Engaged with and experienced both as a physical and ambient dimension, as distance, location or topography, space is recognized as an important cultural medium, an idiom through which individuals can think and can produce practices that are social, aesthetic, political, religious or economic. Place is a framed or contained space that is meaningful to people, a presence that comes into being through human experience, dreaming, perception, imaginings and sensation, and within which a sense of being in the world can develop (Aucoin, 2017, p. 397). And the space that is framed operates at many levels, such as natural (geophysical) space, physical space (including the social paraphernalia that control movement at and across the borderline), mental space (the perspectives people hold regarding physical space) and political space (including the practices and instruments of state control).[6]

It is important to recognize, however, that the places and spaces of borderland life do not end at the borderline, except in the most severe conditions of geographical and political constraint. Ethnographic studies, along with macro-level analyses of international borders, have consistently addressed the many ways that the people on both sides of a borderline are tied to each other, as well as to other peoples more distant within their own country and those on the other side. But these ties are variable, in that not all people have them, and the links themselves may be many or few, strong or weak, waxing or waning, old or new, legal or illegal, calm or tense, comfortable or stressful.

Amid the often heavy, sometimes surprising, but always voluminous literature in border studies it is somewhat rare for scholars to query why people want or sometimes even bother to cross international borders. When this is asked, it is often as a rhetorical question by those who see an international borderline as a marked cleavage between widely divergent national trajectories, in which national experiences, cultures and societies are defined much more by their differences from the other side of the border than their similarities. This hegemonic narrative is a pervasive one among the nation-states of the world, despite the social realities that many nations, as self- and other-identified ethnic entities with notions of a shared history, contemporary experience and future, often straddle international borders, due largely to the arbitrariness of state-established borderlines (Wilson & Donnan, 1998). But if the question is not rhetorical, then social scientists must be charged with finding out both general and specific answers to it. The answer is abundantly clear for many people, such as refugees and economic migrants, who are pushed to move across the boundaries of physical landscapes, time zones and state borders, seeking something better and avoiding something worse. But other people cross borders on a daily or other regular schedule, for employment, leisure activities or to avail themselves of public services—yet in the wide and still growing field of border studies true cross-border case studies of these regular border-crossings are in short supply.

One reason for the relative dearth of cross-border ethnographic studies, where a relatively balanced portrait is sketched of people and communities on both sides of an international divide, is the difficulties in getting the permissions, funding and local contacts to facilitate such research, which in many instances is in regions seen by governments as areas of particular concern in terms of political and economic security (Donnan & Wilson, 1994, pp. 6–7). Even when cross-border studies have been conducted, such as in ethnographic analyses of borderland culture where it is clear that the people and relations of work, life and kinship on one side of the border cannot be isolated from those on the other side, there are often too many "fundamental differences of context" to be included in any one publication or presentation (Heyman, 1991, p. 213).

But another cause of the relative ethnographic inattention to both sides of a border has been the impetus in recent decades for anthropologists and other scholars to theorize mobility, hybridity, displacement and disjuncture, hallmarks of postmodernity and globalization, and key themes in academic production since the 1990s. In the initial rush and now longstanding effort to recognize and narrate the metaphorical qualities of borders, as zones of liminality, ambiguity and transition, border scholars have emphasized the processes of "becoming", particularly in regard to personal and social identities, to the relative neglect of what "is". This myopia is particularly surprising in anthropology because it has resulted in a relative inattention to issues of political economy, especially regarding the state (a position argued at greater length in Wilson and Donnan, 1998; Donnan & Wilson, 1999). But all of the clever theorizing regarding variable notions of being and belonging cannot make the institutions and agents of the state disappear, for they are the omnipresent realizations of the state's sovereignty and territory that mark and substantiate international borders. The border, like the state, exists.

> The border is *there* – in the line of barbed wire, in the separation wall, in the security fence, in the checkpoint, in the no-man's land that people anxiously wait to cross. The state is *there* – visible and material, in the border guards, the customs officers, the legislation making some crossings legal and others illegal, in the technological apparatus of control or punishment.
>
> *(Reeves, 2014, p. 52; italics in original)*

In the general trend to show the incoherence of borders and borderlands, in disputing realist models of state and international relations, scholars have often ignored those aspects of coherence and cohesion that bind border people to each other, within and across borderlines.[7] In the everyday lives of border peoples and communities, in the everyday workings of border cultures, the border is not "a singular object in a singular location" (Reeves, 2014, p. 54), but is multisemic and multisomatic, where each and every borderline and borderland is its own "multiple" (for anthropological views on the "border multiple", see Andersen et al., 2012; Reeves, 2014).

The multiplicity of border lives, in the wide range of meanings attached to and signifying border institutions, events and people, and in the ways of doing and being in borderlands, is simultaneously coherent and incoherent, depending on the observer's viewpoint. While ethnographers have promulgated the perspective on border lives that suggests displacement and disjuncture, another seemingly contradictory perspective—though here I argue instead for its complementarity—is the emplacement and fixity of many dimensions of border places and space. There is no doubt that some of this relative permanence and stability at international borders is related to the institutions of the state, established to manage the flow of people, goods, services and all items and ideas that may be beneficial or detrimental to the national body politic. But there are other forms of emplaced local border culture, some internal to border communities but also some that sustain ties to their counterparts across the borderline. While borders may be sites and symbols of the time-space compression that is a hallmark of postmodernity, as discussed by Harvey (1990), they are also moments and places where things begin and end. In this vein, borders should be viewed as punctuation points, wherein at some precise points along the continuum of points that make up a borderline in time and space some things come to a complete stop, some are paused and some flow freely on (Smart & Smart, 2008).

The fact that borders are constructed social space, like so many other bounded entities in social relations, does not make them any less real. Being imagined does not make them figments of imagination. But the emphasis on cross-border relations often maximizes the importance of the border and minimizes the relations themselves. This occludes the oft-recognized fact that the border in many cases may be seen as the intrusion, the perturbation, of older and more significant social structures and political organizations formed around webs of kinship and community that predate the division caused by the borderline. In this sense, along with seeing the border as a "bridge" that connects people by over-coming and over-going the "border as obstacle", as a "door" that stops or permits entry to the other side (van Houtum & Strüver, 2002, p. 143), or as a wall of indeterminate size and scale with a capacity to interdict communication and stop movement (Arslan et al., 2021; Janz, 2005), borders may be viewed as the "commons" or the "field", in which the relatively normal relations of border life are constituted. The border in this perspective does not divide, interdict or bound separate social spaces and separated social places, but is a central feature of a sometimes coherent, sometimes incoherent, borderland, a place with its own history, its own story to tell, its own "borderlands genre" (Alvarez, 1995). It must be remembered too, however, that borders identify and delimit spaces of power, including the issues of state and national power that mark all geopolitical international borders (Donnan & Wilson, 1999, pp. 40–41). But in addition to these perspectives, which Paasi (2013, p. 484) has labeled the "discursive landscapes of social power" and the "technical landscapes of social control", must be appended the symbolic landscape of sociality, which involves the seemingly contradictory dimensions of border liminality and commensality.

## Border Liminality and Border Commensality

Borders are places and spaces "in-between". This notion of borders as being the limit of the national territory, a place apart from mainstream national life, is found in most grand national narratives of borders as borderlines. In this view, people and goods leave one nation and enter another, but to do so they must cross, as in cross-over, placing them if only for a short period not quite in either jurisdiction. As part of this perspective, borderlands often are portrayed as "out of touch and out of synch" with mainstream and hegemonic institutions, peoples and cultures of the nation and state (Donnan & Wilson, 1999, p. 74). However, these borderlands are home to peoples and social institutions that persist, and sometimes thrive, often playing major roles in the lives of the nation, by securing the state, for example. The abiding importance of borders in national consciousness alone demonstrates that borderlands must be in synch and in touch in significant ways with some entities. Because of the centrality of borders and frontiers to so many versions of the history and contemporary configuration of nations, some anthropologists have examined the everyday lives of the people who reside and work, regularly if not permanently, in this in-between border zone. One of the ways they have provided a fuller picture of borderland life has been by interrogating what has often been asserted about border people, namely that they are in a relatively permanent liminal state.

Liminality is a concept that has long been a core interest of both social and cultural anthropologists, who have since the 1950s investigated the "interstitial spaces" of non-institutional social life, in those areas that played at the margins of the normative.[8] In this processual approach to social and cultural relations, anthropologists easily turned to borderlands as arenas of national culture-mixing and societal acculturation. Borderlands were seen as interstitial spaces between the relatively fixed zones of national sovereignty and social approbation, wherein states and other structures of power attempted to secure territory, emplace people and inscribe the master symbols and other cultural stuff associated with nations. Thus, by definition, and wide common assertion and acceptance, borderlands often have been seen as zones of transition and peripherality, areas of ambiguity and liminality, in which all participants must struggle to slow down if not fix the conditions of their everyday life. "Fix" here may be seen as having two meanings: to both make the transitory permanent, and to repair what is presumed to be broken in the social disarray and cultural anomie of border life. Borderlands in this view are in a permanent disorienting mix, in "a constant state of transition" (Anzaldúa, 1987, p. 3).

However, despite what scholars and other observers have concluded about the constant impermanency of border life, and the permanent transitions of living at the margins of supposedly more important social entities, ethnographic and other studies have demonstrated that border people live and work with an expectation of relative continuity and security. Their daily lives are often much like those of people elsewhere, in the sense that all social life has some degrees of predictability and precarity. In this sense, border people often live normal lives as far as they are concerned, and do so with the assurances that derive from longstanding social, economic and political institutions, networks and relations that are the hallmarks of any community, anywhere.

Thus, it is not surprising that many ethnographic studies of border people, border communities, borderlands and border cultures demonstrate a wide range of legal and illicit, normative and idiosyncratic, and widespread and minority relations, relationships and intermittent interactions between and among individuals and groups intra-nationally, internationally, and transnationally, at and across borderlines. Many of these relations and relationships are based on clearly recognized shared social institutions and cultural meanings, making borderland commensality of like order and significance to borderland liminality. Nonetheless, because of the focus on borders as divisive and differentiating, the commensal nature of border life is often rendered obscure in social science case studies of everyday border life. This is regrettable, because without a balanced portrait of shared border culture, apparent in many features of commensal border relations and relationships, the fuller picture of border spaces and places is impossible.

A commensal relationship denotes, in the first instance, sharing food, as in sharing the same table. "Commensality, in its literal sense, means eating at the same table (*mensa*)" (Fischler, 2011, p. 529). The root word is the Latin for table, *mensa*, but that can also be understood as a reference to visitors and guests, in other words those who are welcome to the hospitality of the house and home. Thus, a related meaning of commensality is the quality or state of interaction and relationship between hosts and guests, and of sharing resources in a manner in which all parties benefit. In this sense, "commensal behavior is a metaphor for the acceptance and rejection of others" (Hamer, 1994, p. 141), and commensality provides the means and situation for social bonding and intimacy (Fischler, 2011, p. 533). Commensality "is thus one of the most powerful operators of the social process" because it "will cause, or at least maintain, a common substance among those who commune together" (Bloch, 1999, p. 133). Although most ethnographers who examine commensality do so in terms of the sharing of food and the acts of dining together, I use the commensal metaphor to encompass, and as a motoring force in, communality and communal interaction. While commensality might be most readily recognized as providing the substance and sustenance, literal and metaphorical, for communal sharing, in borderlands it also substantiates the totality of intercommunity and intercultural relationships. *Border commensality* is about the sharing of place and space within border areas, in a manner that accepts, if not welcomes, relations that straddle, penetrate and crisscross the borderline, infusing the border zone with various expressions, means and symbols of borderland mutuality.

The particular dimensions of border commensality, of explicit ways that culture is transnationally shared, produced, reproduced, negotiated and changed, can be found in most, if not all, ethnographies of border regions. These case studies contribute to the wider anthropology of borders by demonstrating that, while borderlands are sites of constant transition, they are also sites of dynamic social consistency. One need only look at the range of patterns in borderland and cross-border social life, as, for example, may be seen in international sport (Klein, 1997), cross-border shopping and consumerism (Timothy & Butler, 1995; Wilson, 1995), tourism and military heritage (Prokkola, 2010), transnational marriage and kinship (Amster, 2010), town and region twinning (Darian-Smith, 1999; Dürrschmidt, 2002) and many other borderland ties of affinity, affiliation and hospitality. These and so many more transnational relationships in border regions fit into the continuum in cross-border relations offered by Webster and Timothy (2006, pp. 164–165), including alienation, co-existence, cooperation, collaboration and integration. Almost all of these cross-border relations involve specific acts of sharing food and other forms of culture. They are also shaped by the type of border set up by the state, in terms of security and other forms of policing (Arslan et al., 2021), and by the historical and other cultural ties between like or disparate borderland societies (Timothy, 1995). Acts of sharing and modes of engendering social ties, that build fields of cooperation if not trust, contribute to the commensality of border life, which as a process is often in evidence in border tourism.

## Border Tourism

There have been many significant overviews of the interplay between international borders and tourism in both tourism studies and border studies, but these perspectives in the main have had more of an impact in the former. As Eeva-Kaisa Prokkola (2010, p. 223) concludes, "the relationship between tourism and international borders is a fundamental one: travel almost always involves crossing some political or other border, and borderlands are often the first or last areas of a state that travelers see". This assertion is particularly trenchant if one substitutes social and cultural boundaries for the "other border" in her statement, thus making the fundamental relationship even more significant for those individuals, groups and communities living and working at an international border, which for some also entails daily or otherwise regular border crossing.

Overviews of borders and tourism have highlighted the various border institutions and activities which draw tourists to state and other political boundaries (Timothy, 1995). While border studies within and across scholarly disciplines might be forgiven for reifying borders, and sometimes confusing borders, borderlands, borderlines and frontiers as to whether they are the subjects or objects of research, it is also clear that some things which happen elsewhere in a country happen in sharpest relief in a state's borderlands, and some other things happen most, best and/or only in the borderlands (Donnan & Wilson, 1999, p. 4). Some borderland activities of note that act as draws for cross-border travel, tourism and consumption include cross-border shopping, bordertown gambling, public and private tourist welcome centers, and national territorial enclaves and exclaves (Timothy, 1995, pp. 529–530).

Still other inducements would attract people to regularly travel to the "other side" (Webster & Timothy, 2006) of an international border. Some of these are matters of everyday border life, because they are regular, commonplace and banal, aspects of what was introduced above as forms of common cross-border culture, shared mainly between the people proximate to the borderline, within a recognized borderland of often fluctuating depth and width. Among these inducements are: work and employment, both legal and illicit; maintaining one's cross-border business, commerce and farm; religious and other social practices; and kinship, marriage and sociality of all sorts, including eating, dining, drinking and all manner of commensality.

Not surprisingly, metaphors applied to borders and borderland peoples also have figured prominently in the scholarly study of tourists. Thus, tourists have been perceived as liminoid, often out of their place and out of their time, participating in the meta-social processes often associated with rituals and other social performances (Crick, 1989, p. 332). Tourists have been likened at times to pilgrims, electing to take themselves out of their own safe zones of culture and identity to move into new ones, sometimes permanently, sometimes temporarily, from a structured to a liminal state and back again (Nash & Smith, 1991, p. 17). And although there has been some significant attention paid to tourists and tourism through the lens of "hosts" and "guests" (Smith, 1989), the metaphors of hospitality in the tourist experience often prove unsustainable (Crick, 1989, p. 331).

In the borderlands of Northern Ireland, changes in border culture, in the daily attitudes and actions in regard to outsiders of all sorts, including tourists and academic researchers, have changed almost beyond recognition over the last 20 years, at least as far as my own perceptions and experiences go.[9] In 1990, when I first traveled to the market town that is at the political and social heart of the eastern end of the Northern Ireland side of the border, in one of the first steps in my new ethnographic project on cross-border economic relations, I had the feeling that I had entered a time-space warp, being catapulted back to the Wild West of Hollywood films. On a weekday in late afternoon I had entered a pub on the market square, picked by me because of the conversation and laughter that I heard from the footpath, to get a soft drink and some directions. But at the moment I entered all conversation died, and the silence continued as I proceeded to the bar, accompanied only by the tune of my own shoe leather striking the wooden floorboards (more likely shoe rubber squeaking). I immediately decided to forego the drink, I asked my question, received directions to the local tourist office, and quickly retraced my steps to the front door, which once crossed led to the resumption of conversation and laughter within, now perhaps at my expense. Fast forward to summer 2017, at the beginning of a new ethnographic project, where, when I relayed the same story to regular customers in that same pub, and to others in the market square's newly modernized hotel, I elicited various responses, which converged around four themes:

> Those were the days of war, [death, violence, informers, spies, etc.] with the army barracks just across the square: what did you expect?
>
> We were never that inhospitable [afraid, worried, anxious]; you must be mistaken [Yank].
>
> That was then and this is now. We have all come a long way and we do not want to go back.
>
> Now we have Brexit, so tell that [how the border communities are faring] to the Brits [Unionists, Yanks, EU]. The future is going back to where we were.

Tourism had become a symbol to these borderland people of the return to a more integrated Ireland, one where cross-border relations were not problematic. Brexit now threatened tourism, and threatened a revitalized cross-border commensality. As part of the new tourism culture in the borderlands, or as part of new border cultural values that were infusing attitudes about tourism, aspects of the recent past were forgotten or reinterpreted. But most of my respondents in this research are members of the Nationalist and Republican communities in Northern Ireland. The few Unionists I interviewed on these subjects did not lament the loss of cross-border solidarity as much as they regretted the impact Brexit would have on their businesses and livelihoods. But for the Nationalists, tourism had become a sign and symbol of wider border commensality, and its loss was having a knock-on effect in other areas of border life.

## Conclusion

Extrapolating from these brief examples of the state of tourism in the Northern Ireland borderlands, in what was once a location of intense ethno-nationalist conflict, where the fear of the return to violence due to state national machinations seemingly beyond the control of local people has affected both tourism and border commensality, tourists and tourism are agents and agencies of local cultural change. Tourism is also an element in the banal culture of the borderlands, in that border people also cross the borderline regularly to share bread, history, modes of governance and matters of identity with each other. Just as it is difficult if not impossible to understand tourism anywhere without reference to commensality, the same is true of borders. The questions for ethnographers remain regarding border commensality, what is shared, how often, by whom and for what reasons: what roles do borders play in enabling the commensality and what part does commensality play in shaping border place and space?

These are also the sort of questions I ask of university students when introducing an anthropological sensibility as applied to real-world, real-life border problems, or problems of nation and state related to borders. When teaching undergraduates about the comparative study of international borders my first task is to get them to perceive the human dimensions of border life, including the day to day activities of those who live, work and cross the borderline on a permanent or a regular basis. My intention is to complement the institutional, and mainly historical, political, legal and economic frames that seem to structure most peoples' notions of why national borders are so significant. I try too to make the point that these perspectives, while influencing all sorts of policies and practices at borders, and regarding borders, are incomplete without consideration of their impact on border peoples, border cultures and border societies. Ignoring these border lives adds to their marginalization, and while many, some would argue most, borderlands are seen as peripheral in the daily concerns of the nation and state, they often play significant roles in grand national and international narratives, as Brexit has shown in Northern Ireland and continues to be seen in the borderlands of Israel and Palestine. International borders have many more human, communal and commensal dimensions, given the multitude of social and cultural boundaries that crisscross state borderlines, than is suggested by a strict adherence to the geopolitical positioning implied by the borderline.

Thus, border communities have more than one border to consider in their makeup. While the institutional and geopolitical aspects of borderlines are clearly part of the story of border communities, I also stress in my teaching that borderland cultures and societies, which often transcend the borderline in significant ways, have their own logics, dynamics, histories and goals. This borderland milieu (Martinez, 1994) is an essential ingredient in borderland genres (Alvarez, 1995), and they cohere to some degree to attract visitors who want to experience the expected difference and otherness of border regions, often making tourism both a welcome and a tolerated aspect of border life.

While it is clear to most scholars if not most national leaders that international borders are not permanent, no matter how timeless they seem and how much they are memorialized, marked and remarked upon, it is still surprising how many people consider state borders as permanent fixtures, as solid and as old as the nation and state. This is at least partly due to the familiarity many people have with the facts and ideas of a borderline, an easy blueprint for the binary opposition implied by the association of nation with state (Popescu, 2012, p. 86). But the bordering approach in current border studies shows how borders come and go, advance and retreat, proliferate and diminish, and are variously and simultaneously hard and soft, sharp and blunt. It is also true that borders, in their roles as political and social boundaries, do not simply, or even mainly, divide the world, as much as they construct the world in their roles as key elements in social place and space. As such it is worth viewing borders with "a new spatial thinking that identifies fields of relation rather than discontinuous points and lines" (Mezzadra & Neilson, 2012, p. 60). However, in focusing on the dynamics of bordering, on processes of flows and hybridization, border scholars are in danger of losing sight of what is perceived, by borderlanders as much as by others, to be fixed, stationary, permanent and/or durable in border life. In emphasizing what is fixed and longstanding, on the one hand, and in flux on the other hand, modes of perception, reception, representation, and the dialectics of meaning, symbolization and lived experiences can be overlooked, masqueraded and forgotten.

The focus in this chapter and in much anthropological attention to international borders has been on border cultures. In anthropological terms it is all but impossible to study borders and border peoples without reference to culture. National cultures frame all geopolitical state decisions regarding its borders. The cultures that have evolved at and across borderlines are both reactions to wider political, economic and social forces, and proactive forces in their own right. Border cultures are elements in the creation and maintenance of social boundaries in border regions themselves, creating conditions of multiple "border cultures" within and sometimes in spite of what their related nations and states construct as their overarching "border culture".[10]

As has become increasingly apparent in the anthropology of transnationalism over the last few decades, while social and cultural belonging still adhere to particular places and spaces, they also adhere to particular interactions and expressions of sociality and commensality. In the case of borderlands in general, and in the specific case of the evolving Northern Ireland border, borders, whether hard or soft, closed or open, can frame, constrict, enhance and create forms of cross-border culture. Given this importance of border culture to national culture, and the significance of border cultures in the lives of border peoples, this chapter has examined some of the ways in which tourism culture contributes to the liminality and commensality that are inescapable aspects of border culture, writ large and writ small.

## Notes

1. In 2022, Brexit, while now a matter of agreed treaty between the UK and the EU, has left Northern Ireland in its well-known liminal state, because it is still *de facto* within the EU's customs union and single market, linking it closely with the Republic of Ireland in an all-island economy, and separating it, at least temporarily, from the rest of the UK, with the border between Great Britain and the EU afloat in the middle of the Irish Sea. This chapter is based in part on research I have conducted in Northern Ireland on the first and continuing responses to Brexit in the Northern Ireland borderlands. I would like to acknowledge with thanks the financial support of Binghamton University's Mileur Fellowship of Harpur College, in summer 2016, and the Wenner Gren Foundation for Anthropological Research, in summer 2019. See Wilson (2019, 2020) for initial research results on this matter.
2. The "return to the future" was a slogan used in a poster and billboard campaign sponsored by a political party in Northern Ireland in opposition to the Brexit result.
3. While almost all border studies problematize the nature of social and political boundaries, there is no separate or generally recognized field of boundary studies, and many scholarly approaches to social boundaries freely and predictably use the metaphor of geopolitical borders to make their point (for a review of the state of boundary studies within border studies, see Jones 2009). In this chapter I use the term "borders" mainly in reference to international, state borders, but in a few instances also to community boundaries in borderlands.
4. The evolution of the scholarship in anthropology that has offered, sometimes contradictory but mostly complementary, definitions of borders, as places, spaces, institutions and zones, may be traced in Donnan and Wilson (1994, 1999, 2010a, 2012) and Wilson and Donnan (1998, 2012).
5. This section of the chapter relies on work I jointly authored with Hastings Donnan (see, e.g., Wilson & Donnan, 1998, 2012; Donnan & Wilson, 1999, 2010b). The definitions I use regarding space and place in this chapter reflect some changes from these earlier publications.
6. This list of variable spaces is my modification of the perspective offered in Sofield (2006).
7. In her fine ethnographic study of borders in Central Asia, Madeline Reeves (2014, p. 54) examines the notion of the "production of singularity", which as a process, and as a frame for analysis, seeks to establish coherence. Reeves suggests that, despite the intention, some objects do not and perhaps cannot or should not cohere. I have borrowed from her insight, but on a different tack, to apply it to border studies.
8. For a review of the history of anthropological attention to the interstitial and liminal, with a particular focus on the anthropology of borders, see Wilson and Donnan (2005).
9. The changes in the Northern Ireland borderlands over the last 20 years have been well-documented, including from historical, macro-sociological and comparative perspectives, as may be seen, for example, in Hayward (2017); O'Dowd (2010); McCall (2011, 2012, 2014).
10. An excellent example of the interplay among border cultures is offered by Alvarez (2012), who shows how the USA–Mexico border, perhaps the most studied border in the world, is connected, through various vertical and horizontal ties, to many people and institutions within the nation-states, and beyond, as a conduit to the Americas, Asia and the Global South.

## References

Agnew, J. (2008). Borders on the mind: Re-framing border thinking. *Ethics and Global Politics* 1(4), 175–191.

Alvarez, Jr., R.R. (1995). The Mexican-US border: The making of an anthropology of borderlands. *Annual Review of Anthropology*, 24, 447–470.

Alvarez, Jr., R.R. (2012). Reconceptualizing the space of the Mexico-US borderline. In T.M. Wilson, & H. Donnan (eds) *Companion to border studies*, pp. 538–556. Oxford: Wiley-Blackwell.

Amster, M.H. (2010). Borderland tactics: Cross-border marriage in the highlands of Borneo. In H. Donnan, & T.M. Wilson (eds) *Borderlands: Ethnographic approaches to security, power and identity*, pp. 93–107. Lanham, MD: University Press of America.

Andersen, D.J., Klatt, M., & Sandberg, M. (eds) (2012). *The border multiple: The practicing of borders between public policy and everyday life in a re-scaling Europe*. Aldershot: Ashgate.

Andersson, R. (2019). *No go world: How fear is redrawing our maps and infecting our politics*. Berkeley, CA: University of California Press.

Anzaldúa, G. (1987). *Borderlands/la frontera: The new mestiza*. San Francisco, CA: Aunt Lute Books.

Arslan, Z., Can, Ş., & Wilson, T.M. (2021). Do border walls work? Security, insecurity and everyday economy in the Turkish-Syrian borderlands. *Turkish Studies*, 22(5), 744–772.

Aucoin, P.M. (2017). Toward an anthropological understanding of space and place. In B.B. Janze (ed.) *Place, space and hermeneutics*, pp. 395–412. Cham, Switzerland: Springer.

Bloch, M. (1999). Commensality and poisoning. *Social Research*, 66(1), 133–149.

Crick, M. (1989). Representations of international tourism in the social sciences: Sun, sex, sights, savings, and servility. *Annual Review of Anthropology*, 18, 307–344.

Darian-Smith, E. (1999). *Bridging divides: The Channel Tunnel and English legal identity in the New Europe*. Berkeley: University of California Press.

Donnan, H., & Wilson, T.M. (1994). An anthropology of frontiers. In H. Donnan, & T.M. Wilson (eds) *Border approaches: Anthropological perspectives on frontiers*, pp. 1–14. Lanham, MD: University Press of America.

Donnan, H., & Wilson, T.M. (1999). *Borders: Frontiers of identity, nation and state*. Oxford: Berg/Bloomsbury Academic.

Donnan, H., & Wilson, T.M. (2010a). Ethnography, security and the 'Frontier Effect' in borderlands. In H. Donnan, & T.M. Wilson (eds) *Borderlands: Ethnographic approaches to security, power and identity*, pp. 1–20. Lanham, MD: University Press of America.

Donnan, H., & Wilson, T.M. (2010b). Symbols of security and contest along the Irish border. In H. Donnan, & T.M. Wilson (eds) *Borderlands: Ethnographic approaches to security, power and identity*, pp. 73–91. Lanham, MD: University Press of America.

Dürrschmidt, J. (2002). 'They're worse off than us.' The social construction of European space and boundaries in the German/Polish twin-city Guben-Gubin. *Identities: Global Studies in Culture and Power*, 9(2), 123–150.

Fischler, C. (2011). Commensality, society and culture. *Social Science Information*, 50(3–4), 528–548.

Green, S. (2012). A sense of border. In T.M. Wilson, & H. Donnan (eds) *A companion to border studies*, pp. 573–592. Oxford: Wiley-Blackwell.

Gupta, A., & Ferguson, J. (eds) (1997). *Culture, power, and place: Explorations in critical anthropology*. Durham: Duke University Press.

Hamer, J. (1994). Commensality, process and the moral order: An example from southern Ethiopia. *Africa: Journal of the International African Institute*, 64(1), 126–144.

Harvey, D. (1990). *The condition of postmodernity: An enquiry into the origins of cultural change*. Oxford: Blackwell.

Hayward, K. (2017). *Bordering on Brexit: Views from local communities in the central border region of Ireland/Northern Ireland*. Belfast: Irish Central Borders Study Network and Centre for International Borders Research, Queens University.

Heyman, J.M. (1991). *Life and labor on the border: Working people of northeastern Sonora, Mexico, 1886-1986*. Tucson: The University of Arizona Press.

Janz, B. (2005). Walls and borders: The range of place. *City and Community*, 4(1), 87–94.

Jones, R. (2009). Categories, borders and boundaries. *Progress in Human Geography*, 33(2), 174–189.

Klein, A.M. (1997). *Baseball on the border: A tale of two Laredos*. Princeton: Princeton University Press.

Linde-Laursen, A. (2010). *Bordering: Identity processes between the national and personal*. Farnham: Ashgate.

McCall, C. (2011). Culture and the Irish border: Spaces for conflict transformation. *Cooperation and Conflict*, 46(2), 201–221.

McCall, C. (2012). Debordering and rebordering the United Kingdom. In T.M. Wilson, & H. Donnan (eds) *A companion to border studies*, pp. 214–229. Oxford: Wiley-Blackwell.

McCall, C. (2014). European Union cross-border cooperation and conflict amelioration. *Space and Polity*, 17(2), 197–216.

Martinez, O.J. (1994). *Border people: Life and society in the US-Mexico borderlands*. Tucson: University of Arizona Press.

Megoran, N. (2012). 'B/ordering' and biopolitics in Central Asia. In T.M. Wilson, & D. Hastings (eds) *A companion to border studies*, pp. 473–491. Oxford: Wiley-Blackwell.

Mezzadra, S., & Neilson, B. (2012). Between inclusion and exclusion: On the topology of global space and borders. *Theory, Culture and Society*, 29(4/5), 58–75.

Nash, D., & Smith, V.L. (1991). Anthropology and tourism. *Annals of Tourism Research*, 18(1), 12–25.

Newman, D. (2006). The lines that continue to separate us: Borders in our 'borderless' world. *Progress in Human Geography*, 30, 143–161.

O'Dowd, L. (2010). From a 'borderless world' to a 'world of borders': Bringing history back in. *Environment and Planning D: Society and Space*, 28, 1031–1050.

Paasi, A. (2013). Borders and border-crossings. In N.C. Johnson, R.H. Schein, & J. Winders (eds) *The Wiley-Blackwell companion to cultural geography*, pp. 478–493. Oxford: Wiley-Blackwell.

Popescu, G. (2012). *Bordering and ordering the twenty-first century: Understanding borders*. Lanham, MD: Rowman and Littlefield.

Prokkola, E-K. (2010). Borders in tourism: The transformation of the Swedish-Finnish border landscape. *Current Issues in Tourism*, 13(3), 223–238.

Reeves, M. (2014). *Border work: Spatial lives of the state in rural Central Asia*. Ithaca, NY: Cornell University Press.

Roitman, J.L. (2005). *Fiscal disobedience: An anthropology of economic regulation in Central Africa*. Princeton: Princeton University Press.

Smart, A., & Smart, J. (2008). Time-space punctuation: Hong Kong's border regime and limits on mobility. *Pacific Affairs*, 8(2), 175–193.

Smith, V.L. (ed.) (1989). *Hosts and guests: The anthropology of tourism*, 2nd ed. Philadelphia: University of Pennsylvania Press.

Sofield, T.H.B. (2006). Border tourism and border communities: An overview. *Tourism Geographies*, 8(2), 102–121.

Timothy, D.J. (1995). Political boundaries and tourism: Borders as tourist attractions. *Tourism Management*, 16(7), 525–532.

Timothy, D.J., & Butler, R.W. (1995). Cross-border shopping: A North American perspective. *Annals of Tourism Research*, 22(1), 16–34.

van Houtum, H. (2000). An overview of European geographical research on borders and border regions. *Journal of Borderland Studies*, 15(1), 57–83.

van Houtum, H. (2010). Waiting before the law: Kafka on the border. *Social and Legal Studies*, 19, 285–298.

van Houtum, H. (2012). Remapping borders. In T.M. Wilson, & H. Donnan (eds) *A companion to border studies*, pp. 405–418. Oxford: Wiley-Blackwell.

van Houtum, H., & Strüver, A. (2002). Borders, strangers, doors and bridges. *Space and Polity*, 6(2), 141–146.

Webster, C., & Timothy, D.J. (2006). Travelling to the 'other side': The Occupied Zone and Greek Cypriot views of crossing the Green Line. *Tourism Geographies*, 8(2), 162–181.

Wilson, T.M. (1995). Blurred borders: Local and global consumer culture in Northern Ireland. In J.A. Costa, & G.J. Bamossy (eds) *Marketing in a multicultural world: Ethnicity, nationalism and cultural identity*, pp. 231–256. London: Sage.

Wilson, T.M. (2019). Old and new nationalisms in the Brexit borderlands of Northern Ireland. In K.C. Donahue, & P. Heck (eds) *Cycles of hatred and rage: What right wing extremists in Europe and their parties tell us about the U.S.*, pp. 25–51. London: Palgrave MacMillan.

Wilson, T.M. (2020). Fearing Brexit: The changing face of Europeanization in the borderlands of Northern Ireland. *Ethnologia Europaea*, 50(2), 32–48.

Wilson, T.M., & Donnan, H. (1998). Nation, state and identity at international borders. In T.M. Wilson, & H. Donnan (eds) *Border identities: Nation and state at international frontiers*, pp. 1–30. Cambridge: Cambridge University Press.

Wilson, T.M., & Donnan, H. (2005). Territory, identity and the places in-between: Culture and power in European borderlands. In T.M. Wilson, & H. Donnan (eds) *Culture and power at the edges of the state: National support and subversion in European border regions*, pp. 1–31. Munster: Lit Verlag.

Wilson, T.M., & Donnan, H. (2012). Borders and border studies. In T.M. Wilson, & H. Donnan (eds) *A companion to border studies*, pp. 1–25. Oxford: Wiley-Blackwell.

# 4
# NEW BORDERS AND MOBILITY IN THE AGE OF GLOBALIZATION
## De-bordering, Re-bordering, and Beyond

*Anssi Paasi and Md Azmeary Ferdoush*

### Introduction

This book focuses on the relations between political borders and tourism from a variety of societal viewpoints, such as politics, culture, nationalism, and sustainability. Borders and border regions have been, for a long time, significant in tourism research. Attractions such as relict boundaries, boundary parks and monuments or certain natural attractions located at international borders have been studied by tourism scholars (Timothy, 1995). Later tourism studies have taken steps towards other disciplines in reassessing the general roles of borders in the globalizing world (Sofield, 2006).

The present chapter scrutinizes borders in the context of globalization, another crucial but equally complex topic. We critically examine the progress and status of borders and border studies in various narratives related to globalization. Both "border" and "globalization" are contested and historically contingent categories. While it is typical to think that globalization is a unidirectional process that leads to a gradual opening of borders (and territories) and to an increasing interaction and collaboration between and across them, the currently raging COVID-19 pandemic has provided a useful reminder of such historical and spatial contingencies and the power of the state. In 2019, 1.5 billion travelers crossed international borders as tourists and at the same time almost 272 million people were living outside the country where they were born (United Nations, 2019; UNWTO, 2020). When the microbial virus ostensibly began its journey from a Chinese wet-market to virtually every corner of the globe at the end of 2019, a number of states restricted or banned travel and migration across their borders. Within a very short period of time, by spring 2020, numerous borders had been closed, which essentially put a stop to business travel and tourism. More than 90 percent of the world's population lived in countries that had imposed travel restrictions (Connor, 2020). Acknowledging the gravity of the pandemic, ordinary people have generally accepted new regulations. However, in some states, like Germany and the USA, public demonstrations emerged against the new restricted "normal". Today, two years later, the situation is still dire and mobilities, not least in the tourism sector, are effectively controlled. A number of flight operators, tourist resorts, and travel agencies have ended up in serious trouble, warranting states to step in with economic relief.

Instead of focusing explicitly on the issues of tourism, the emphasis of this chapter is threefold. First, we scrutinize how globalization became topical in research from the 1990s. Tourism has been recognized as an important force in the process of globalization (Timothy, 2019), owing largely to its contribution to creating modern transportation systems and infrastructure that support traveling, such as airports, hotels, and resorts. Expanding tourism also forced governments to simplify formal procedures related to travel and adopt innovative technologies, such as self-check-in kiosks, which enable the processing of an escalating number of tourists (Cohen, 2012). Second, we examine how borders became a keyword in the age of globalization, and how the meaning of borders has been gradually shifting. Tourism, along with other forms of mobilities, both corporeal and imaginative travel, has contributed to the touristic vision of the world as "un-bounded", often drawing on the metaphors of "networks" and "fluids" (Urry, 2000).

Globalization is characteristically associated with numerous forms of mobility that occur at and across various spatial scales, from the local to the global. These cover the movement of not only tourists but also various modalities of capital, ideas, immigrants, and refugees, for example. Globalization does not inevitably suggest a homogenization of the world in the matrix of such interactions (Agnew, 1994). Rather it may lead to territorial transformation, fragmentation, and variation. As Julio Aramberri (2009) has reminded, tourism is an activity practiced all over the world; it is one of the clearest manifestations of globalization. Respectively, visions of global links between richer parts of the world with poorer pleasure peripheries are a figment of "post-romantic collective imagination that dominates much of tourism research" (Aramberri, 2009, p. 367). Cultural and economic flows and the mobility of human beings are indicators of structural changes, uneven development, and spatial differentiation. Hence, our third aim is to problematize the relations between territories, borders, and (tourism) mobilities. Much of the debate on state borders and mobility today focuses on immigration and its ethical dimensions. This has given rise to such questions as whether state borders should be controlled more effectively, or whether they should be more open, or even totally removed. This is a critical issue that differs with various forms of mobility. While people are increasingly active in deciding where to live, work, or study, simultaneously we see contradicting and increasingly stronger opinions about building more border walls and fences to control immigration and opening up borders to attract more tourists. Territoriality is mobilized mainly to prevent immigration but, at the same time, overtourism in certain destinations, such as Barcelona, has given rise to opinions that numbers of tourists must be effectively controlled to protect the built environment and biodiversity, and to respect local communities and their ways of life (Mustafa, 2010). Borders and mobilities are becoming increasingly two sides of the same coin, but mobility itself is divided.

## When Was/Is Globalization?

While being keywords in contemporary social sciences, "globalization" and "border" have different genealogies. Border research and the term "border" have a long history in political geography, whereas the use of the term "globalization" has exploded in the social sciences quite recently. While borders are processes that relate to regional transformation and the geo-historical institutionalization of territories, globalization refers to the "compression" of global reality (Harvey, 1989), to the expanding social, economic, and political networks, to the intensification of the flows of goods, capital, information, cultural objects and people, as well as to the expanding social consciousness of the world as a whole (Castells, 1989; Robertson, 1992; Scholte, 2005, Sparke, 2013).

Globalization, hence, is a contested subject, and disagreements exist over its definition, measurement, chronology, and explanation (Scholte, 2005). Although the term has become widespread recently, scholars often use it in the spirit of presentism to denote various historical or temporal scales. For Robertson (1992), the roots of globalization are to be found in the fifteenth century. Hirst and Thompson (1996) write that internationalization developed during the last decades of the nineteenth century. If globalization denotes, as some believe, the spread of supra-territoriality, it has unfolded relatively recently. The largest expansion of pan-global relations occurred from the 1960s (Scholte, 2005). One way of viewing this is to consider the unprecedented tension between the forces of particularism and universalism resulting from interdependent connections between the local and the global (Stegar, 2003). Appadurai (2020) notes that many historians, political scientists, sociologists, and economists have made a career out of resisting the newness of globalization. He demonstrates the way globalization seems to provoke "a distinct anxiety about its own not-newness" (p. 1). Appadurai's suggested method to historicize globalization combines the study of connections and connectivities. This strategy helps us, he argues, to think globally without sacrificing contingency and context. However, when it comes to answering the question "When was/is globalization?" we believe the most productive way to look at it is to scrutinize the context. Thus, we suggest that the process of globalization started to unfold gradually with the Industrial Revolution and the condition of modernity. However, with the postmodern turn from the 1950s and 1960s, globalization has gained pace and become more visible. Finally, the process continues and has yet to reach its pinnacle (Stegar, 2003, p. 8).

There are a number of driving forces of globalization that deeply influence tourism, travel, and the hospitality industries. Mairna Mustafa (2010) observes several features that have contributed to the continuous expansion of tourism, such as the liberalization of air transport and trade in services, the spread of information communications technologies, and the use of the internet in selling and marketing travel and tourism packages. The expanding tourism industry has been in a critical position in the diffusion of the Western consumerist ethos across national borders into increasingly distant parts of the non-Western world. It has also contributed to the commodification of tourist attractions in non-Western contexts (Cohen, 2012). This makes numerous destinations in the Global South exclusively dependent on the socioeconomic well-being of the Global North, making less-developed destinations extremely fragile, especially as the ongoing COVID-19 pandemic has poignantly shown.

To take the arguments related to borders and globalization further, it is useful to consider strong and weak varieties of globalization, as they offer different interpretations of borders (Anderson & O'Dowd, 1999). Strong interpretations typically focus on economy and technology, with culture being secondary. Similarly, state sovereignty is understood to be eroded by transnational businesses or social movements and groups that think little of national borders. For strong supporters of globalization, borders are static and outdated. Similarly, territoriality and sovereignty are recognized in essentialist terms, in the spirit of the modernist language of traditional international relations studies and political geography. Borders are thus understood as lines separating social entities, not as contested discursive formations and processes that are embedded in the social and cultural practices constitutive of these entities. Japanese business scholar Kenichi Ohmae (1990, 1995) used the term "borderless world", but instead of discussing concrete state boundaries, he referred to borders metaphorically to denote the condition of economic liberalism and intensifying capitalism (Green & Gruhleder, 1995). "Big metaphors" (Barnes & Duncan, 1992) are often powerful and change the rhetoric and conceptual apparatuses used in research. Ohmae's forthcoming borderless world was characterized by cross-border regions or regional states (Paasi, 2019). In reality, borders always combine both the material and the conceptual/symbolic, and Sofield (2006) suggests that tourism is interrelated intimately with both of these elements.

Globalization sceptics or supporters of weaker versions of it perceive internationalization to be more significant than globalization (Anderson & O'Dowd, 1999; Held et al., 1999). For them, the state is the foremost context where people run their everyday lives, even if a state's functions and bordering practices fluctuate constantly (Hirst & Thompson, 1996). From this vantage point, territorial states are not waning but simply having to operate in a dynamic global context. Hence, globalization does not epitomize the end of territorial distinctions and distinctiveness, rather new dynamics influence local (economic) identities and development capacities (Amin & Thrift, 1995; Massey & Clark, 2008). The eventual question, then, is: How has globalization affected our practices and understandings of borders?

## Globalization, Borders, and Border Studies

Although it is a mammoth task to answer the question posed above, we undertake a brief attempt in the discussion below, mostly focusing on an analysis of the changes that have taken place in our perceptions of borders and practices of bordering since the process of globalization gained pace. Globalization has been closely associated with the idea of opening borders or debordering, and border-crossings. Several core forces behind globalization, such as rationalist knowledge, capitalist production, automated technology, and bureaucratic governance (Scholte, 2005), seem to both de-border (with capitalist accumulation, neoliberalization, and internationalization as new rationalities) and re-border (border control bureaucracy and novel security technologies). Although studied much earlier as outer membranes of the state, borders became significant in research from the 1990s as part of the globalizing world. Firstly, scholars suggested that borders have to be understood more dynamically. The key background for this was that borders were challenged by major global transformations, such as the collapse of the dividing line between the capitalist and socialist blocks and the subsequent rise of new states from the ruins of the former European socialist regime. The second significant background was the revival of "old" nations and ethnic groups, which led to horrible wars in the former Yugoslavia and elsewhere. Events like these suggest that globalization and ethno-territorial identities can be an explosive mixture.

On the other hand, the tourism industry capitalized on the opportunity by focusing on the opening of the former socialist states. The nature of some formerly strictly controlled borders, such as the Berlin Wall, changed dramatically and quickly became a favored tourist attraction where tourists could buy pieces of the concrete wall as souvenirs and return home with memories of the isolated socialist "East Germany". In some former eastern European states like Poland, Lithuania, Hungary, and Georgia, former communist symbolisms have been forcefully rejected. In Georgia, a Freedom Charter accepted in 2011 required the removal of the symbols of the communist era, such as place names, memorials, statues, and buildings (Paasi, 2013). Russia, in contrast, continues to celebrate such symbols as tourist attractions and public memorials.

People's consciousness of global flows has triggered efforts to affirm old borders and a search for ontological security, solid orientation points, and frames for action. It may also lead to efforts to produce new borders (Meyer & Geschiere, 1999). Among the first scholars to reflect the relations between the purportedly "old" spatial patterns and "new" ones was Manuel Castells (1989, p. 349). He argues that the dominant space of places will be superseded by a space of flows, which expresses the disarticulation of place-based societies and cultures from the organizations of power and culture that remain to dominate society without succumbing to its control. This inescapably resonates with the questions of identity and the old and new dividing lines bounding or opening social communities at various spatial scales. Massey and Clark (2008, p. 3) provided a nuanced, probably very realistic, view on this complex subject:

> One of the ways in which a "globalized world" is frequently characterized is in terms of a planet in which all borders and boundaries have dissolved and in which flows of people, money, cultural influence, communications and so on flow freely. It is this feature of globalization that can give rise to feelings of being bombarded from all directions ... Yet, even as this image of a globalized world becomes ever more powerful, it is clear that the world does still have its borders and distances, that it is still in many ways divided up into territories; indeed, that new enclosures are being erected in the very midst of the production of powerful new flows. Nation states still exist; there are fierce debates over international migration; the rich may try to seal themselves off against the poverty outside; and aboriginal peoples may fight to protect their lands from invasion by multinational corporations. It may even be that the very process of opening up which is implied in so many stories (and realities) of globalization itself encourages a need to build protective boundaries, to define areas of privacy – territories which can be controlled in some way or other.

The globalizing world thus manifests itself at and across spatial scales concurrently with an endless process of re-bordering, the construction of new territories, and de-bordering, reflecting the power and speed of flows (ibid.). In addition to this interchange, there is one serious question that needs to be asked: Why is there a tendency to think that regional or territorial spaces should be almost self-evidently bounded and distinct from the wider world? We know that territorial transformation is a continuous process, and that the institutionalization of territories occurs through the emergence of borders, institutions, and symbolisms. Yet bordering is a relational rather than strictly territorial phenomenon, and the significance of each border is more of an empirical rather than theoretical issue. Further, relational borders are always characterized by a certain porousness. Even before relational thinking on space emerged (Massey, 1993), researchers were reminded that there is no need to think of place in terms of a (bounded) area but as a network, or a space of interaction between what is global, national, and local. Similarly, when we understand social relations as spatial, it does not require the existence of a contiguous or meaningful territory (Berdoulay, 1989; Pratt, 1991).

Yet, it is a paradox that globalization depends on lines that separate states, regions, and cities. Capital can circulate only between competing legal spaces formed within states and/or regions and with the support of their guarantees (Laine, 2016). While the territorial authority of the state still is dominant, the mechanisms of sovereign authority are less absolute than they used to be (Sassen, 2009; Paasi, 2020). Transnational and external geopolitical relations have at all times diluted the sovereignty of states. Such a relational view is obvious in the efforts to promote and manage international tourism across relatively strictly guarded borders even if other forms of human mobilities are prohibited.

In such a context, especially during the last two or three decades, border research has become one of the most energized fields in political geography, international relations, political science, security studies, sociology, anthropology, history, literature theory, and tourism studies. Interdisciplinary approaches in critical border studies have emerged and borders are understood as dynamic and contested social constructs, processes, social institutions, discourses, and manifestations of power relations (e.g., Paasi, 1996; Newman & Paasi, 1998; Kolossov, 2005; Parker & Vaughan-Williams, 2009; Popescu, 2011; Cohen, 2012; Burridge et al., 2017; Ferdoush, 2018; Brambilla & Jones, 2020). Correspondingly, the conceptual foundation of border studies has expanded, which echoes the major transformations that have occurred around the globe, particularly the processes of globalization in the domains of economy, culture, and social consciousness. Consciousness is an oft-neglected element even though it is critically related to borders. A border may be constitutive of national and other identities but it also has negative effects. As Agnew (2008, p. 176) observes, borders often tend to limit the exercise of "intellect, imagination and political will", and in the same spirit Balibar (2008, p. 216) observes that what can be "demarcated, defined, and determined has a constitutive relation with what can be thought". These statements contend that methodological nationalism is an invisible escort of state borders. Borders limit not only socio-spatial entities but also human minds, often faraway from physical manifestations of themselves. These domains regularly become fused in and, at times, polarize debates regarding the economic, political, and cultural costs and benefits of immigration (see Jones, 2019; Sager, 2020).

The 1990s not only entailed a rapid increase in border research but also the enlargement of its terminology. Terms such as "boundary producing practices" (Ó Tuathail & Dalby, 1998), bordering (Linde-Laursen, 2010; Yuval-Davis et al., 2019), and de-bordering and re-bordering (Albert & Brock, 1996) became widespread slogans. Rapid conceptual development echoed many dramatic societal events that took place at that time. The most significant changes were the downfall of the political dividing line between the capitalist West and the socialist East, the gradual evolution of information technology, and the invention of cyberspace and the internet, which accelerated emerging globalization. Such changes motivated researchers to develop fancy utopian views of the new, brave, borderless world that would witness the vanishing of the nation state and borders (Paasi, 2019).

Besides such general expressions as "borderless world" or re-bordering and de-bordering, more theoretically sophisticated examples of a new lexis were perhaps de- and re-territorialization, which Deleuze and Guattari (1984) outlined to reflect the effects of capitalism on preceding alleged static orders of class, kinship, and space. Despite their original yet abstract ambiguous usage, scholars have applied these terms later in more concrete senses. Both de- and re-territorialization express economic, cultural, and political power relations and take place in numerous institutional practices and discourses. The majority of border scholars have been somewhat straightforward when referring to these terms but, at times, use them in a metaphoric sense, similarly to how the slogan "borderless world" has been used. For instance, in discussions regarding the "re-location" of borders to airports or shopping centers deep inside states, or in the debates on dispersed surveillance systems in cities, or when reflecting on the future of borders in the globalizing post-national world, borders often denote the process of bordering (i.e., a verb) rather than referring to specific borders. The same places, though, may bear completely different commercial meanings in the context of tourism.

The development of technology and the invention of cyberspace are viewed as critical for the de-territorialization of existing spatializations and in realizing the metaphor of "border crossings" in social activities. For Sassen (1999), new electronic spaces were crucial in capital accumulation. This has undoubtedly been the case in the internationalization of the banking and finance sectors, for example (Christophers, 2013). Cyberspace allows the formation of identity groups that are not territorially limited and may challenge the state-bound territorial traps. Electronic spaces have been important for social movements and indigenous groupings that operate both inside and across state borders. They have also helped the rise of new approaches modifying earlier perspectives that were embedded in the notion of de-territorialization. A fitting example are translocal geographies where, for instance, migrant experiences are seen to be situated within and across various localities, so that the territorial boundedness of states does not dominate the setting (Brickell & Datta, 2011).

De- and re-territorialization have also been critical concepts in interpreting border developments in the context of the European Union (EU). The EU's key economic and political motivation has been, for a long time, to make goods and people mobile—but only a certain group of people. As a result of such a preference, immigrants struggle against the inherent violence and injustice of external EU borders (Jones, 2012). Hence, the border becomes a gateway for EU citizens, often rich tourists, businesspeople, and academics, but it remains an ever-hardening barrier for migrants.

The case of de- and re-territorialization demonstrates that there are, at once, two conflicting tendencies: one, a move towards economic globalization and a globalized "borderless world" and two, securitization discourses and practices acting to close borders and harden them through bordering processes. Respectively, some borders are opening or becoming softer (de-territorialized), whereas some others are closing or becoming harder (re-territorialized). This tension gives rise to uneven and fragile border regimes (Vradis et al., 2018). Border studies itself struggles to comprehend this binary, and in response many have suggested a shift in focus. As mentioned above, instead of just focusing on the physical border at the edge of the state, scholars have productively understood borders from numerous vantage points. Thus, contemporary border studies remains a dynamic and fast-paced field of study. Such work, for instance, ranges from a focus on the *motion* of both human and nonhuman agents (Konrad, 2015; Nail, 2016, 2019) to the *place* of the border (Jones & Johnson, 2014; Johnson et al., 2011), the practice of *bordering* and *borderity* (Amilhat-Szary & Giraut, 2015), the role of ordinary people in *borderwork* (Rumford, 2006, 2009), and different *borderscapes* (Rajaram & Grundy-Warr, 2007; Brambilla, 2015).

## Territories, Borders, and Mobilization

Instead of fixity, borders in the age of globalization are often seen as mobile and stretching in space in the form of diverse social and political practices and discourses. Hence, not only people, goods, and capital are seen as mobile and crossing borders but also borders themselves are mobile. The dissociation of border functions and their locations has become an issue of strong scholarly interest (Amilhat-Szary & Giraut, 2015). Borders may be mobile because they are manifested in the biometric features of mobile human bodies and in their travel documents (e.g., passports and visas) (Häkli, 2015). In the field of tourism, the mobility of borders is at present the order of the day (e.g., Więckowski & Timothy, 2021). New technologies may further be used to establish new borders, that is in the re-territorialization and in the construction of dividing lines between "our community" and our "rivals". This has been evident in a number of conflicts, civil wars, and in response to terrorist attacks. Probably more than any other event during the last few decades, the 9/11 terrorist attacks on US soil and the subsequent war on terror, led to practices of re-bordering (not just in North America) and multiplied security-related border studies that were characterized by keywords like biopolitics, circulation, and technology (Dillon & Lobo-Guerrero, 2008). Louise Amoore's (2006) suggestion of the term "biometric borders" captures such features. Biometric borders are mobilized in risk profiling, in governing mobility, in the representations of biometrics and the body, and in the practices of authorization. Travelers are further strictly classified according to their backgrounds and motives for mobilizing.

Similar re-bordering has continued, as witnessed by the construction of physical walls and fences around the world. These fortifications accelerated after the 9/11 events. Following the Second World War, only seven such walls existed, but at the turn of the 1990s, the number had doubled, and by 2018 approximately 80 border walls were in operation (Hjelmgaard, 2018;

Vallet, 2016). According to the Transnational Institute (2020), boundary walls can be found on every continent, and their significance becomes obvious in the fact that six out of ten people in the world live in a nation with a border wall. One of the most prominent examples is in South Asia along the border of Bangladesh and India. These two countries share a 4,096 kilometer land border, and almost all of it was unfenced until the 1990s. Although the central government of India authorized border fencing along the Bangladeshi border in 1986, it faced resistance from the Indian state of West Bengal. By the end of 2000, only 5 percent of the entire border between India and Bangladesh was fenced (Van Schendel, 2005). However, after the 9/11 attack on the USA, Indian leaders took an active role in "securing" the nation from external terrorist attacks and started to depict neighboring Bangladesh as a source of potential threat. India also passed the Prevention of Terrorism Act in 2002, which was modeled on the USA's PATRIOT Act. Gaining traction with the United States "war on terror", such laws and narratives added wind to the sails of re-bordering, and the fencing of the border with Bangladesh lunged forward at an unprecedented pace. The dominant narrative from India described Bangladesh as a state that could not control its borders and prevent extremists from operating within its territory. As a result, Bangladesh was depicted as the adversarial "other"—a neighbor that harbors separatist leaders who frequently cross into India to carry out attacks. Bangladesh was also depicted as a source of millions of illegal immigrants who "snuck" into India to find work. With such narratives, India was able to successfully pacify the initial resistance against fencing the border. By 2011, India had completed fencing 2,734 kilometers of its eastern border and constructed 3,528 kilometers of roads to facilitate the movement of its border guards (Jones, 2012). By the end of 2020, India had completed almost 3,120 kilometers of fencing and aims to finish the remaining sections in the near future (Chowdhury, 2020).

One major problem in thinking through the relations between borders and globalization is that our understanding of both of these phenomena is colored by our fixity on the almost self-evident framework of states as bounded spaces. Scholars in various academic fields have criticized the taken-for-granted views of borders as simple lines. In international relations and security studies, Walker (1993) challenged the sharp division between inside and outside, and clear borders. Agnew's (1994) concept of the territorial trap has become a widely accepted critique of the concept of state-centric territory embedded in international relations. At the same time, Peter Taylor (1995) discussed the problematics of "embedded statism". Subsequent debates on methodological nationalism (Wimmer & Glick Schiller, 2002) have challenged the assumption that the nation/state/society is the natural social and political form of the modern world. Similarly, the role of tourism as a tool to open closed national spaces has been reflected in various forms and places (Cohen, 2012). The shutting of open borders with fences and barriers turned border regions into places of tourist attraction boosting tourism operations centered around borders and border walls, for instance along the borders of the USA and Mexico, the USA and Canada, Israel and its neighbors, and Vietnam's borders with its neighbors (Timothy, 1999; Chan, 2006; Sofield, 2006; Gelbman, 2008; Berdell & Ghoshal, 2015).

More normative approaches to borders claim that state boundaries are illusions created by power-wielding actors to maintain their power and to control citizens (Ohmae, 1990, 1995). The rise of globalization raised opinion about the impact of this phenomenon on state systems. Rudolph (2005, p. 2) rhetorically questioned, "Does globalization threaten the core institutions of world order, including sovereignty and the nation-state? Are we moving into a borderless world?" He argues that the short answers to these central questions are "probably not, certainly not, and quite the opposite".

In the context of contemporary (labor) migration, borders are ever more often seen as topologically constituted devices that states use to select, filter, and channel labor which often has tragic consequences for migrants who are forced to travel under dangerous conditions (Mezzadra & Neilson, 2012). This reflects an emphasis on the time-spaces of labor mobilities, or the way time and space work through one another and transform established views of inside and outside at the border (Allen & Axelsson, 2019).

These days, scholars and social movements forward normative, deeply ethically grounded claims that accentuate the need for free mobility and migration. Advocates for open borders have demanded that society abandon bounded spaces as self-evidently imagined frames for social life (see Anderson et al., 2009; Jones, 2019; Sager, 2020; Sharma, 2020). More radical voices have been raised by the supporters and activists of the "no borders" movement, which claims, at times in the spirit of anarchism, the rejection of borders, nations, and states, and emphasizes free movement (King, 2016; Walia, 2013). Free movement, of course, emphasizes the mobility of migrants and refugees, rather than tourists, since tourism has not suffered from border controls the same way immigration has. Concurrently, diverging right-wing movements claim that borders should be closed, and their management and control should be hardened to prevent the mobility of immigrants and refugees. A certain fixity associated with borders and the perpetual power of the state to control mobilities is obviously not just a pure illusion created by leaders who are greedy for power, even if we recognize that as the foundation of sovereignty. There are some major institutional factors behind such understandings. One key player is the United Nations, an organization representing independent, sovereign states rather than nations. A major important legal framework is provided by international laws, which determine the rules, norms, and standards that regulate the relations between states and international organizations. The number of sovereign states has gradually increased, which means that the number of borders is also growing.

Scholars have paid increasing attention to the processes of border*ing* (Linde-Laursen, 2010; Van Houtum & Van Naerssen, 2002; Yuval-Davis et al. 2019), perhaps reflecting the fact that more and more walls have been constructed to prevent immigration and lessen terrorist threats and smuggling. In fact, research demonstrates that the top three justifications for wall-building are controlling immigration, fighting terrorism, and preventing smuggling (Benedicto et al., 2020). As Van Houtum and Van Naerssen (2002) suggested at the turn of the millennium, semantically, the word "border" unnecessarily indicates that places are fixed in space and time, and "should rather be understood in terms of bordering, as an ongoing strategic effort to make a difference in space among the movements of people, money or products" (Van Houtum & Van Naerssen, 2002, p. 126). Likewise, attention has recently focused on "mobile borders", or the dissociation between border functions and the locations of borders (Amilhat-Szary & Giraut, 2015; Paasi, 2013).

Saskia Sassen (2009) argues that the governance of state borders is increasingly characterized by multi-layered, dispersed, and segmented modes of regulation and governance. These new assemblages of political, legal, and territorial practices suggest continuing pressures between new global relationships, national identity, and state security. This demands original conceptual tools for understanding these relationships, and Sassen (2009) suggests these vary from institutions that neutralize the border (for instance, free trade alliances) to those that weaponize it (for instance, the deployment of extraordinarily high numbers of armed guards and weaponry). Along with these tendencies, bordering is becoming a practice and a capability that can be disconnected from traditional border geographies (e.g., international airports and consular offices). Correspondingly, some scholars have grown increasingly interested in what Sassen (2013) calls "transversally bordered spaces", wherein a state border is not simply a legal boundary line but rather a mix of regimes with variable content, geographic and institutional locations, and arrangements. She argues that various flows (capital, information, professional or undocumented migrants) constitute bordering through a particular arrangement of interventions, with diverse institutional and geographic locations. The actual state borders matter in some of these flows but not in all of them.

As Furedi (2020) has observed, the attempt to change or eradicate conventional borders coexists with the imperative of constructing new ones. Thus, de-bordering and re-bordering are parallel, context-bound, socio-spatial processes that have a material basis but are also related to diverging ideological struggles. The extremes in such ideologies are critical cosmopolitan thinking that calls for opening or even rejecting borders, on one axis, while on the other ethnonationalism. Ethnonationalism represents ethnonational communities and their ability to separate themselves from one another within the framework of the sovereign state, accentuating ethnic heritage and social boundaries in the making of nations.

## Concluding Thoughts

The preceding examination demonstrates the varied views of the contemporary roles of borders. Such interpretations arise from diverging conceptual agendas that reflect what globalization, territory, mobility, and sovereignty mean. They also display that borders have many concrete functions. They are apparatuses to organize and manage international governance and tools that states mobilize to police and control their territories. Elden (2005) suggests that territory is dependent on a specific way of grasping space as calculable and that seeing space in this way not only makes bounded territories possible but also underlies new global configurations. Accordingly, he argues, globalization is a reconfiguration of prevailing understandings rather than a radical break. Further, borders are often mobilized as constituents and challengers of existing social identities and related narratives that may fuse individual experience with wider, geohistorical, and state-centric ideologies (Meyer & Geschiere, 1999; Paasi & Prokkola, 2008). Moreover, diverse perspectives on borders show that knowledge and understandings are situated phenomena. Politico-economic and cultural contexts critically impact how borders and related terms are used to interpret territorial transformations. Borders and their roles, globalization, and sovereignty often produce dissimilar meanings to researchers working in different countries. They also have different functions to legislators, military leaders, international capitalists, economists, immigrants, refugees, and ordinary citizens. A major difference is, however, related to various forms of mobilities, especially tourism and immigration.

"Truths" regarding borders or states are therefore themselves also products of contested discourses and manifestations of various ideologies and the rhetoric of power. The political, cultural, and economic elites may have incompatible motives with regard to borders. For example, economic actors often aim to encourage cross-border activities, whereas politicians and the military struggle to preserve the state, its devices of violence and narratives of "the nation under threat" in operation, as well as to control mobilities (Paasi, 2019). However, despite globalization and the general opening of borders, each state aims to control its territory, borders, "national identity", and loyalties. Examples of such controls are incessantly evident around the world. In a few European states (e.g., Hungary and Poland), leaders aim fervently to regulate national identity narratives by mobilizing ideologies and bordering practices based on anti-immigration. In Spain, let alone explicit anti-state activities, one can end up in prison for simply joking about themes that challenge national integrity (Jokinen, 2018, cited in Paasi, 2020). Suppressive state violence is also used to control the Catalans' struggle for national independence. In India, possessing unsanctioned detailed maps of borders and queries into border issues, both academic and journalistic, may land a person in prison (Cons, 2016). These are signs of broader questions that will be substantial also for the future of borders; for example, why do some states disintegrate often along ethnic lines, while others are held together over long periods, decades, and centuries, even if their inhabitants are diverse (Wimmer, 2018)? Consequently, national memory and understanding of the past are not innocent; they have strategic, political, and ethical consequences (Ferdoush, 2019). Therefore, queries into struggles over the past are crucial in understanding the present and the future of a territory (Hodgkin & Radstone, 2012; Paasi, 2020). Correspondingly, political integration and national identification form two sides of the same "nation-building coin" (Wimmer, 2018, p. 229).

These issues and many other *glocal* themes, themes that bring together the local and global, will provide border and tourism scholars with a number of future challenges. Many of them will likely be related to human mobilities and uneven global development but most potentially to climate change, one of the major future reasons for migration and refuge. This simply means that borders and mobilities are ever more often two sides of the same coin.

## References

Agnew, J. (1994). The territorial trap: The geographical assumptions in international relations theory. *Review of International Political Economy*, 1(1), 53–80.
Agnew, J. (2008). Borders on the mind: Re-framing border thinking. *Ethics & Global Politics*, 1(4), 175–191.
Albert, M., & Brock, L. (1996). Debordering the world of states: New spaces in international relations. *New Political Science*, 18(1), 69–106.
Allen, J., & Axelsson, L. (2019). Border topologies: The time-spaces of labour migrant regulation. *Political Geography*, 72, 116–123.
Amilhat-Szary, A-L., & Giraut, F. (eds) (2015). *Borderities and the politics of contemporary mobile borders*. Basingstoke: Palgrave-Macmillan.
Amin, A., & Thrift, N. (1995). Territoriality in the global political economy. *Nordisk Samhällsgeografisk Tidskrift*, 20, 3–16.
Amoore, L. (2006). Biometric borders: governing mobilities in the war on terror. *Political Geography*, 25(3), 336–351.
Anderson, B., Sharma, N., & Wright, C. (2009). Editorial: Why no borders? *Refuge*, 26(2), 5–18.
Anderson, J., & O'Dowd, L. (1999). Border, border-regions and territoriality: Contradictionary meanings, changing significance. *Regional Studies*, 33(7), 593–604.
Appadurai, A. (2020). Globalization and the rush to history. *Global Perspectives*, 1(1), 1–7.
Aramberri, J. (2009). The future of tourism and globalization: Some critical remarks. *Futures* 41(6), 367–376.
Balibar, E. (2008). The borders of Europe. In P. Cheah, & B. Robbins (eds) *Cosmopolitics*, pp. 216–229. Minneapolis, MN: University of Minnesota Press.
Barnes, T., & Duncan, J. (eds) (1992). *Writing worlds*. London: Routledge.
Benedicto, A.R., Akkerman, M., & Brunet, P. (2020). *A walled world towards a global apartheid*. Barcelona: Centre Delàs d'Estudis per la Pau.
Berdell, J., & Ghoshal, A. (2015). US–Mexico border tourism and day trips: An aberration in globalization? *Latin American Economic Review*, 24(1), 1–18.
Berdoulay, V. (1989). Place, meaning, and discourse in French language geography. In J.A. Agnew, & J.N. Duncan (eds) *The power of place*, pp. 124–139. Boston: Unwin Hyman.
Brambilla, C. (2015). Exploring the critical potential of the borderscapes concept. *Geopolitics*, 20(1), 14–34.
Brambilla, C., & Jones, R. (2020). Rethinking borders, violence, and conflict: From sovereign power to borderscapes as sites of struggles. *Environment and planning D: Society and space*, 38(2), 189–208.
Brickell, K., & Datta A. (2011). *Translocal geographies: Spaces, places, connections*. London: Routledge.
Burridge, A., Gill, N., Kocher, A., & Martin, L. (2017). Polymorphic borders. *Territory, Politics, Governance*, 5(3), 239–251.
Castells, M. (1989). *The informational city*. Oxford: Blackwell.
Chan, Y.W. (2006). Coming of age of the Chinese tourists: The emergence of non-Western tourism and host—guest interactions in Vietnam's border tourism. *Tourist Studies*, 6(3), 187–213.

Chowdhury, S. (2020, September 23). India completes fencing. *The New Age*. https://www.newagebd.net/article/117038/india-completes-fencing-three-fourths-of-border#:~:text=The%20Indian%20government%20has%20completed,total%20international%20border%20with%20Bangladesh

Christophers, B. (2013). *Banking across boundaries: Placing finance in capitalism*. London: Wiley.

Cohen, E. (2012). Globalization, global crises and tourism. *Tourism Recreation Research*, 37(2),103–111.

Connor, P. (2020, April 1). More than nine-in-ten people worldwide live in countries with travel restrictions amid COVID-19. *Pew Research Center*. https://www.pewresearch.org/fact-tank/2020/04/01/more-than-nine-in-ten-people-worldwide-live-in-countries-with-travel-restrictions-amid-covid-19/

Cons, J. (2016). *Sensitive space: Fragmented territory at the India-Bangladesh border*. Seattle: University of Washington Press.

Deleuze, G., & Guattari, F. (1984). *Anti-Oedipus*. London: Athlone.

Dillon, M., & Lobo-Guerrero, L. (2008). Biopolitics of security in the 21st century: An introduction. *Review of International Studies*, 34(2), 265–292.

Elden, S. (2005). Missing the point: Globalization, deterritorialization and the space of the world. *Transactions of the Institute of British Geographers*, 30(1), 8–19.

Ferdoush, M.A. (2018). Seeing borders through the lens of structuration: A theoretical framework. *Geopolitics*, 23(1), 180–200.

Ferdoush, M.A. (2019). Acts of belonging: The choice of citizenship in the former border enclaves of Bangladesh and India. *Political Geography*, 70, 83–91.

Furedi, F. (2020). *Why borders matter: Why humanity must relearn the art of drawing boundaries*. London: Routledge.

Gelbman, A., (2008). Border tourism in Israel: Conflict, peace, fear and hope. *Tourism Geographies*, 10(2), 193–213.

Green, C., & Gruhleder, K. (1995). Globalization, borderless worlds, and the Tower of Babel: Metaphors gone awry. *Journal of Organizational Change Management*, 8(4), 55–68.

Häkli, J. (2015). The border in the pocket: The passport as a boundary object. In A.L. Amilhat-Szary & F. Giraut (eds) *Borderities and the politics of contemporary mobile borders*, pp. 85–99. London: Palgrave Macmillan.

Harvey, D. (1989). *The condition of post-modernity: An enquiry into the origins of cultural change*. Oxford: Blackwell.

Held, D., McGrew, A., Goldblatt, D., & Perraton, J. (1999). *Global transformations*. Cambridge: Polity Press.

Hirst, P., & Thompson, P. (1996). *Globalization in question*. Cambridge: Polity Press.

Hjelmgaard, K. (2018, May 24). From 7 to 77: There's been an explosion in building border walls since World War II. *US Today*. https://www.abc10.com/article/news/nation-now/from-7-to-77-theres-been-an-explosion-in-building-border-walls-since-world-war-ii/465-35423df4-3515-40e6-8eb8-1267f4db8184

Hodgkin, K., & Radstone, S. (eds) (2012). *Memory, history, nation: Contested pasts*. London: Transaction Publishers.

Johnson, C., Jones, R., Paasi, A., Amoore, L., Mountz, A., Salter, M., & Rumford, C. (2011). Interventions on rethinking "the border'" in border studies. *Political Geography*, 30(2), 61–69.

Jokinen, M. (2018, August 5). Ei voi puhua ja vitsailla kuin 1980- ja 1990-luvuilla – mielipide ja huumori vievät vankilaan myös Euroopassa. *Suomen Kuvalehti*. https://suomenkuvalehti.fi/jutut/ulkomaat/eurooppa/enaa-ei-voi-puhua-ja-vitsailla-kuin-1980-ja-1990-luvuilla-mielipide-ja-huumori-vievat-vankilaan-myos-euroopassa/

Jones, R. (2012). *Border walls: Security and the war on terror in the United States, India, and Israel*. London: Zed Books.

Jones, R. (ed) (2019). *Open borders: In defense of free movement*. Athens, GA: The University of Georgia Press.

Jones, R., & Johnson, C. (eds) (2014). *Placing the border in everyday life*. Aldershot: Ashgate.

King, N. (2016). *No borders: The politics of immigration control and resistance*. London: Zed Books.

Kolossov, V. (2005). Border studies: Changing perspectives and theoretical approaches. *Geopolitics* 10(4), 602–632.

Konrad, V. (2015). Toward a theory of borders in motion. *Journal of Borderlands Studies*, 30(1), 1–17.

Laine, J. (2016). The multiscalar production of borders. *Geopolitics*, 21(3), 465–482.

Linde-Laursen, A. (2010). *Bordering: Identity processes between the national and personal*. Aldershot: Ashgate.

Massey, D. (1993). Power-geometry and a progressive sense of place. In J. Bird, B. Curtis, & T. Putnam (eds) *Mapping the futures: Local cultures, global change*, pp. 75–85. London: Routledge.

Massey, D., & Clark, N. (2008). Introduction. In N. Clark, D. Massey, & P. Sarre (eds) *Material Geographies*, pp. 1–6. London: Sage.

Meyer, B. & Geschiere, P. (eds) (1999). *Globalization and identity: Dialectics of flow and closure*. Oxford: Blackwell.

Mezzadra, S., & Neilson, B. (2012). Between inclusion and exclusion: On the topology of global space and borders. *Theory, Culture & Society*, 29(4–5), 58–75.

Mustafa, M.H. (2010). Tourism and globalization in the Arab world. *International Journal of Business and Social Science*, 1(1), 37–48.

Nail, T. (2016). *Theory of the border*. Oxford: Oxford University Press.

Nail, T. (2019). *Being and motion*. Oxford: Oxford University Press.

Newman, D., & Paasi, A. (1998). Fences and neighbours in the postmodern world: Boundary narratives in political geography. *Progress in Human Geography*, 22(2), 186–207.

Ó Tuathail, G. & Dalby, S. (1998). Introduction: Rethinking geopolitics: Towards critical geopolitics. In G. Ó. Tuathail & S. Dalby (eds) *Rethinking geopolitics*, pp. 1–15. London: Routledge.

Ohmae, K. (1990). *Borderless world*. London: Harper Collins.

Ohmae, K. (1995). *The end of the nation-state*. New York: Free Press.

Paasi, A. (1996). Inclusion, exclusion and territorial identities: The meanings of boundaries in the globalizing geopolitical landscape. *Nordisk Samhallsgeografisk Tidskrift*, 23(3), 3–17.

Paasi, A. (2013). Borders and border crossings. In N. Johnson, R. Schein, & J. Winders (eds) *A New companion to cultural geography*, pp. 478–493. London: Wiley-Blackwell.

Paasi, A. (2019). Borderless worlds and beyond: Challenging state-centric cartographies. In A. Paasi, E-K. Prokkola, J. Saarinen, & K. Zimmerbauer (eds) *Borderless worlds for whom? Ethics, moralities, mobilities*, pp. 21–36. London: Routledge.

Paasi, A. (2020). Nation, territory and memory: Making state-space meaningful. In D. Storey (ed) *A research agenda for territory and territoriality*, pp. 61–82. Cheltenham: Edward Elgar.

Paasi, A., & Prokkola, E-K. (2008). Territorial dynamics, cross-border work and everyday life in the Finnish-Swedish border. *Space and Polity*, 12(1), 13–29.

Parker, N., & Vaughan-Williams, N. (2009). Lines in the sand? Toward an agenda for critical border studies. *Geopolitics*, 14(3), 582–587.

Popescu, G. (2011). *Bordering and ordering the twenty-first century: Understanding borders*. Lanham, MD: Rowman & Littlefield.

Pratt, A.C. (1991). Discourses of locality. *Environment and Planning A*, 23(2), 257–266.

Rajaram, P.K., & Grundy-Warr, C. (eds) (2007). *Borderscapes: Hidden geographies and politics of territory's edge*. Minneapolis: University of Minnesota Press.

Robertson, R. (1992). *Globalization: Social theory and global culture*. London: Sage.

Rudolph, C. (2005). Sovereignty and territorial borders in a global age. *International Studies Review*, 7(1), 1–20.

Rumford, C. (2006). Theorizing borders. *European Journal of Social Theory*, 9(2), 155–169.

Rumford, C. (ed) (2009). *Citizens and borderwork in contemporary Europe*. London: Routledge.

Sager, A. (2020). *Against borders: Why the world needs free movement*. London: Rowman & Littlefield.

Sassen, S. (1999). Beyond sovereignty: De-facto transnationalism in immigration policy. *European Journal of Migration and Law*, 1, 177–198.

Sassen, S. (2009). Bordering capabilities versus borders: Implications for national borders. *Michigan Journal of International Law*, 30(3), 567–597.

Sassen, S. (2013). When territory deborders territoriality. *Territory, politics, governance*, 1, 41–45.

Scholte, A. (2005). *Globalization: A critical introduction*. Basingstoke: Palgrave-Macmillan.

Sharma, N. (2020). *Home rules: National sovereignty and the separation of natives and migrants*. Durham, NC: Duke University Press.

Sofield, T.H.B. (2006). Border tourism and border communities: An overview. *Tourism Geographies*, 8(2), 102–121.

Sparke, M. (2013). *Introducing globalization: Ties, tensions, and uneven integration*. Chichester: Wiley-Blackwell.

Stegar, M.B. (2003). *Globalization: A very short introduction*. London: Routledge.

Taylor, P.J. (1995). Embedded statism and the social sciences: Opening up to new spaces. *Environment and Planning A*, 28(11), 1917–28.

The Transnational Institute (TNI). (2020, November 18). 6 out of 10 people worldwide live in a country that has built border walls. *The Transnational Institute*. https://www.tni.org/en/article/6-out-of-10-people-worldwide-live-in-a-country-that-has-built-border-walls

Timothy, D.J. (1995). Political boundaries and tourism: Borders as tourist attractions. *Tourism Management*, 16(7), 525–532.

Timothy, D.J. (1999). Cross-border partnership in tourism resource management: International parks along the US-Canada border. *Journal of Sustainable Tourism*, 7(3-4), 182–205.

Timothy, D.J. (ed) (2019). *Handbook of globalisation and tourism*. Cheltenham: Edward Elgar.

United Nations. (2019, September 17). The number of international migrants reaches 272 million, continuing an upward trend in all world regions, says UN. *Department of Economic and Social Affairs*. https://www.un.org/development/desa/en/news/population/international-migrant-stock-2019.html

UNWTO. (2020, January 20). International tourism growth continues to outpace the global economy. *UNWTO*. https://www.unwto.org/international-tourism-growth-continues-to-outpace-the-economy

Urry, J. (2000). Mobile sociology. *British Journal of Sociology*, 51(1), 185–203.

Vallet, E. (2016). *Borders, fences and walls: State of insecurity?* London: Routledge.

Van Houtum, H., & Van Naerssen, T. (2002). Bordering, ordering and othering. *Tijdscrift voor Economische en Sociale Geografie*, 93(2), 125–136.

Van Schendel, W. (2005). *The Bengal borderland: Beyond state and nation in South Asia*. Delhi: Anthem Press.

Vradis, A., Papada, E. Painter, J., & Papousti, A. (eds) (2018). *New borders: Hotspots and the European migration regime*. London: Pluto Press.

Walia, H. (2013). *Undoing border imperialism*. Chico, CA: AK Press.

Walker, R.B.J. (1993). *Inside/outside: International relations as political theory*. Cambridge: Cambridge University Press.

Więckowski, M., & Timothy, D.J. (2021). Tourism and an evolving international boundary: Bordering, debordering and rebordering on Usedom Island, Poland-Germany. *Journal of Destination Marketing & Management*, 22, 100647.

Wimmer, A. (2018). *Nation-building*. Princeton, NJ. Princeton University Press.

Wimmer, A., & Glick Schiller, N. (2002). Methodological nationalism and beyond: nation–state building, migration and the social sciences. *Global Networks*, 2(4), 301–334.

Yuval-Davis, N., Wemyss, G., & Cassidy, K. (2019). *Bordering*. Cambridge: Polity.

# 5
# *AUREA MEDIOCRITAS*
## Cross-border Cooperation between Materiality and Relationality

*Sylwia Dołzbłasz and Katarzyna Szmigiel-Rawska*

### Introduction

One of the biggest challenges of human socioeconomic activity is to find its optimal scale—desired or correct in such a way that it makes human actions as effective and efficient as possible. In the setting of democratic states, this scalar correctness is also related to transparency and representation. Scale is defined by the size of territories, organizations and institutions people design to manage and govern, but also by the permeability of borders between those territories, organizations and institutions, since permeability establishes the grounds for cooperation. Cooperation itself is yet another way of finding the desired scale: a way to overcome borders while retaining at least some control over resources.

Scale, cooperation, effectiveness, efficiency, transparency and representation underscore the concept of rescaling. The conceptual development at the turn of century in the social sciences, especially in geography, is a result of the conviction that process and movement have more explanatory power than the status quo and more stability in contemporary societies. Rescaling processes are understood as continuous re-creations of embedded scalar configurations through sociopolitical struggles (Brenner, 2001).

The description of the processes of rescaling entails the relativization of the scale in question in relation to other scales. The description or designation of a geographical unit (e.g., state or province) is gained by identifying its distinctiveness from other units, hence the need to define a geographical hierarchy together with processes of scalar sociopolitical changes and differentiations. According to this paradigm, geographical scales are intertwined and created through the interrelationships of different dimensions and functions (Brenner, 2001). In this sense, a thorough scrutiny of a geographical realm requires an interpretation of boundaries, overlapping spaces and clear edges between scales. Politics- and practice-driven studies based on this paradigm focus largely on the notions of globalization and political integration.

Recent views on territoriality have privileged spatiality over materiality, with extreme notions in this paradigm creating a world of spaces that is completely detached from physical space— "supraterritoriality" (Scholte, 2008), "non-place" (Hardt & Negri, 2001), software instead of soil (Tuathail, 1999) and other related terms and concepts (see Usher, 2020). Even if mainstream views entangle space, network and the physical world together, the emphasis is on territory, understood as a social concept rather than a physical quality (Usher, 2020). Obviously, there can be no return to pure environmental determinism in viewing space, place, territory and boundaries in contemporary sciences. That notion was long ago deemed inadequate for developing knowledge and government policies and practices (Usher, 2020). However, ongoing crises related to the COVID-19 pandemic, climate change, social media's influence on politics as well as issues on a smaller geographical scale but nonetheless significant, such as the war in Syria and a lack of adequate policies regarding refugees, the rise of populist regimes, the construction of a wall on the USA–Mexico border and Brexit, prove that one of the most significant challenges of science with regard to territory, space and boundaries is to identify a universal concept that encapsulates unbounded, immaterial space and the resource-driven world of physical areas. This missing link creates the need for a redefinition of concepts like scale, border, border area and supranationalism but also a redefinition of cooperation as an abstract notion, its drivers and expected gains.

In this chapter we define the notion of cross-border cooperation, considering the relational definition of territory and space jointly with a socio-ecological framework defining grounds for self-organization to cooperate over common resources. The aim is to add to the understanding of contemporary challenges of cooperation over state administrative borders by defining a conceptual path between materialism and a relational approach.

## Theoretical Underpinnings of Cooperation: The Socio-ecological Framework

The socio-ecological framework proposed by Elinor Ostrom (2009) provides a theoretical context in which cooperation is defined and analysed as an institution embedded both in social relations and in natural resources. The concept conditions cooperation and decision making with regard to common goods—resources that can be worn out or depleted, although excluding any members from using the common resources is costly.

The commons have had good and bad times in the history of civilization (De Moor, 2015), but as a scientific notion, it is currently the most comprehensive analytical concept to describe the significance of transactions and relations in the development of people and systems. The concept was proposed by Olson (1965) and developed since 1970 by scholars such as Ostrom and Ostrom (1971) and many others. The most important message of the commons framework is that people and organizations can self-organize for resource use. The breakthrough element of the common pool concept is empirical proof that hierarchies are not needed to govern common resources—one government is not necessary (Ostrom, 2009). This is a game-changing assertion, especially for international relations and border studies in which a lack of a singular, encompassing governing body is a key feature of analysis. Recognizing the importance of the socio-ecological framework for supranational studies requires recognition of both the social and physical conditions for defining borders and territories.

According to Ostrom (2009, p. 42), social self-organization around common resources depends on ten different variables that describe social systems and managed resources. These variables are: the size of the resource system, the productivity of the system, predictability of system dynamics, collective-choice rules, resource unit mobility, number of users, leadership/entrepreneurship, norms/social capital, knowledge of socio-ecological system/mental models and the importance of resources. Although a detailed explanation of these is beyond the scope of this chapter, the key message is that the important premises of self-organization are preliminarily recognized and can be implemented in research and practice in different border regions and social systems of different levels. These variables can be viewed as facilitators of cross-border cooperation and institution-building processes.

To explain this view in more detail, we refer to the management of European macro-regions or supra-regions (both terms are currently in use) as an analytical example. The macro-regions of Europe cross state borders and are defined by large ecosystems or resources, such as the Baltic Sea Region or the Danube Region. Zimmerbauer and Paasi (2020, p. 772) write of these regions as being "mobilized soft spaces that have gradually 'hardened' through planning and governance". They are an illustration of a path between what we are defining here. We claim that "hardening" occurs practically and conceptually through policy and management activities but also intentionally by efforts to harvest resources sustainably. The institutional patterns of such regions are very complex, involving central governments, regional and local authorities, the European Union (EU), business organizations and non-governmental organizations of different kinds, who all have interests in harvesting different elements of the macro-regions' resources. The size of said resources is large, which usually makes self-organization difficult, but the management of most macro-regions is supported by EU leadership, which makes the definition of the resource boundaries and their monitoring less costly and more efficient.

Self-organisation is more likely to happen when cooperating actors recognize the scarcity of the resource at the centre of their cooperation (Ostrom, 2009). In European macro-regions, the aims of cooperation and the scarcity of resources are usually well defined by the development strategies assembled by the stakeholders involved in enacting regional cooperation. Still, implementing those cooperative strategies (e.g., the EU Strategy for the Baltic Sea Region) and disseminating knowledge about the scarcity of resources and the need to protect them is crucial for cooperation. These established regions support the predictability of cooperation and its fruition. Predictability is an important feature of cooperation and distinguishes it from free-market, non-intervened relationships. As Axelrod's (1984) concept of "shadow of the future" describes it, cooperation is something that occurs through the long-term effects of present activities. The EU's defining development strategies in Europe's macro-regions plays an "umbrella" role (Baldersheim & Ståhlberg, 1999) in supporting cooperation. Hence, European integration can be seen as a facilitator of predictability and collective-choice rules.

In this role, one important limitation is that the EU or any other supranational organization cannot create rules that are not embedded in local conditions. According to the rules of the socio-ecological framework, support for cooperation needs to be locally grounded at the grassroots level, in this example regionally. However, the EU and other international alliances can play the role of rulemaking facilitator by providing knowledge and disseminating information. According to the socio-ecological framework, in the international context, the largest challenges related to self-organization stem from a lack of common norms and lack of social capital. Often, there is an absence of shared values between collaborating parties from different geographical areas. These manifest in language barriers, religious and cultural differences, and diverging management and planning approaches (Timothy, 2006). In the context of self-organization, shared moral and ethical standards are key variables to successful cooperation (Ostrom, 2009). Given the degree of European integration, recent research by Capello et al. (2018) suggests that lack of trust is the only major barrier to regional growth for the border regions of Europe. A deficit of trust makes exploiting resources in borderlands more difficult than in other parts of Europe (Capello et al., 2018). The significance of trust for cooperation is largely recognized in the literature. It constitutes the foundations of interpersonal relationships and extends to a larger scale with social institutions and social constructs (Cook et al., 2005). Trust at all levels and stable social institutions on local, regional and cross-border scales form the foundations of sustainable cross-border cooperation (Szmigiel-Rawska, 2016).

## Conceptualizing Cross-border Cooperation

Cross-border cooperation has emerged as a common strategy to overcome the dividing function of borders through the closer integration of border areas at national, but especially regional and local, levels. Collaboration affects border areas and can lead to the formation of transfrontier regions that stretch across more than one state border, forming strong ties of various kinds on many levels and involving local authorities, inhabitants and businesses, reflecting expressions of changes in "border territoriality" (Popescu, 2012, pp. 5–6).

To describe cross-boundary cooperation, the general term "international cooperation" was initially used most often, as only states are subjects of international law (Nye & Welch, 2013). Therefore, terms such as external cooperation, interregional cooperation, territorial cooperation, transborder cooperation, paradiplomacy and similar others are used to label these transfrontier relations in the literature and in organizations, such as the EU and the Council of Europe, with the aim of supporting cooperation at the regional and local level in Europe. This regional and local cross-frontier collaboration is carried out mainly by the authorities of subnational territorial units, as well as by associations, cultural and scientific institutions, local development agencies, and technology and innovation transfer agencies. That the EU programmes (e.g., Interreg) have dominated this type of cooperation since the 1990s has led to the popularity of the term "territorial cooperation". This consists of transfrontier (often at a local level), transnational (usually carried out by polities and other regional and local institutions at macro- or supra-regional levels) and interregional cooperation between state entities and other regional and local actors in areas that are not necessarily adjacent to one another and do not form a larger regional cooperation area.

The concept of cross-border or transborder cooperation is the most precisely defined and widespread, characterized by direct neighbours across national borders working together to achieve common goals. The Madrid Outline Convention of 1980 laid down the first and basic formal provisions on cross-border cooperation in Europe, which entails any joint activities designed to strengthen and further develop neighbourly relations between the geo-territorial entities and authorities of two or more states but which may be limited by the ability of adjacent communities and authorities to work together according to the domestic laws of each state.

The definition of borders is changing in accordance with the redefinition of territory, space and place. In recent decades, border discourse has shifted from a narrow, one-dimensional understanding where the border is viewed as a definitive line, a barrier and feature of state territory, to a multidimensional perspective with a broader understanding that addresses mobilities, flows, cooperation and networks. The dual character of borders as dividing lines and spaces of contact is still present in the literature. Borders simultaneously separate and bring into contact different political, social and economic systems (Popescu, 2012; Prescott & Triggs, 2008). On one hand, political boundaries allow states to close themselves off from others (i.e., "Fortress Europe"), whereas on the other hand they are "windows to the world" enabling contact with others (Anderson & O'Dowd, 1999). Borders are spaces for making connections and effecting cooperation. They continue to be studied as lines but also now as zones (e.g., borderlands and cross-border areas) with depth, breadth and networks. "Border" is an ambiguous concept used in many different contexts. It is deeply rooted in social consciousness and, even when it is physically distant, it has an impact on people's lives.

Despite recent physical securitization of state borders throughout the world, with the increasingly relational conceptualization of space and territory, borders are progressively defined as "fuzzy", meaning that they are now being seen as soft spaces—more social than physical without clear-cut distinctions about what should be "in" and what should be "out"

(Zimmerbauer & Paasi, 2020). In their efforts to analyse regional planning processes and summarize recent literature on theoretical representations of regions, Zimmerbauer and Paasi (2020) conclude that the world consists of both soft spaces and hard spaces. Hence, political and management activities can be best accomplished by navigating between these two types of spaces. This conclusion is based on two premises. First, well-established polities with solid borders and firm administrative controls co-exist beside regions or polities with softer borders that are spaces of cooperation, negotiation and framing through visual representations, marketing and strategic planning. In this case, both regions affect one another and political and management practices can transform one type of region into the other (Zimmerbauer & Paasi, 2020).

The second premise relates to the definition of borders in which borders are not only solid or porous; in a sense they are both—a condition which Zimmerbauer and Paasi (2020) define as "penumbral" borders, which are multi-layered, with certain layers at times being more solidified or blurred than at other times, representing a half-shadowed effect. Thus, borders are multi-layered constructs that are both impermeable and open at different times. This conceptualization adds significantly to research on cooperation. Cooperation, as defined by Ostrom (2009), is a social practice rooted in a need for the sustainable use of resources. When cross-frontier cooperation is identified in the world of penumbral borders, significant details need to be added to the basic rules of self-organization. At the core is the need to define the permeability of layers of the areas that are cooperating: the permeability of social manifestations of borders (i.e., administrative, political, organizational and linguistic) but also of the material manifestation of the same borders (i.e., transportation availability, infrastructure gaps and divisions, and resource locations and limits). The socio-ecological approach to cross-border cooperation in a world of penumbral borders requires a description of resources (water bodies, forest, rivers, seas) while considering them one territory within which there are layered borders that do not influence ecological processes, while at the same time certain border layers cut them into smaller segments—administrative, political, infrastructure and others. The integration of knowledge on different layers present in both dimensions—material and social—in cross-border cooperation is a contemporary challenge for understanding cross-border cooperation emerging from new world crises.

## Cross-border Cooperation in the Multi-layered Hierarchy of Geographical Units

Cross-border cooperation is a direct outcome of global integration processes (Timothy, 2019). Due to the dynamics of these processes, many parts of the world have seen a growth in transfrontier collaboration and regional integration. This is particularly true in Europe, where the period after the Second World War saw an increasingly closer integration of countries, which eventually led to the creation of the EU in its present form: the most integrated supranational alliance in the world today.

At the beginning of the 1990s, it appeared that due to globalization and democratization in Central and Eastern Europe, political borders began losing their traditional importance in that part of the world. The so-called "disappearance" of borders, or rather the diminishing of their dividing role (debordering) (Newman & Paasi, 1998), became the norm in the 1990s. The catchphrase a "borderless world" even emerged at that time (Ohmae, 1990). In Europe, although many barriers disappeared with the fall of the Berlin Wall and the Iron Curtain, borders have continued to strengthen (Amilhat-Szary, 2007) and the emergence of new barriers, such as limited access to the EU through its external border (Agnew et al., 2003), has become more pronounced. Into the twenty-first century, the re-emergence of this traditional role of borders gained prominence in a process known as "rebordering" (Newman, 2006), especially since 2015 with mass immigration from Africa and the Middle East, security concerns in the EU and the COVID-19 pandemic (Więckowski & Timothy, 2021). Many researchers emphasize that the 2001 terrorist attacks in the United States were a watershed moment for understanding borders (e.g., Newman, 2006). In the shadow of this event and other happenings and the intensity of cross-border flows (people, goods, diseases), much more attention was devoted to security issues, particularly at state borders. While ostensibly allowing greater mobility, borders have a second role of providing security for the states they surround, and even within Europe's "borderless" Schengen Zone, barriers have been re-erected to deter refugees and to prevent the spread of the Coronavirus (Vaughan-Williams, 2015; Kovras & Robins, 2016; Böhm, 2021).

The recent dynamics of change in geopolitical conditions are associated with the coexistence of strong integration and disintegration processes. A visible expression of the latter is the emergence of new walls along many of the world's borders. Contrary to predictions right after the fall of the Berlin Wall, wall-building has accelerated in the modern era. Prominent examples include the Trump administration's construction of a new wall on many parts of the USA–Mexico border, the introduction of barrier fences on state boundaries in Southeastern Europe, even between EU and Schengen states, and the current plans (November 2021) of the Polish government to erect a wall along its border with Belarus to prevent unlawful influxes of Asian and Middle Eastern refugees from entering the EU. The new walls reflect problems in managing the forces and processes unleashed by globalization and the "new colonialism" (Till et al., 2013). With the scramble towards rebordering and the securitization of national frontiers in Europe, North America and elsewhere, borders as lines of sovereignty and security spaces will remain.

The need to redefine state borders after the Second World War stems primarily from two types of changes in the global social order. The first is the unique rise of economic flows and interconnections between national markets and the creation of the global market. The second is the rise in the number of supranational organizations that emerged to control the global market and to prevent global political conflicts. These processes are encompassed in the concept of supranationalism, which at its narrowest can be defined as the creation and functioning of supranational (multinational) organizations to which states delegate some of their powers. In a broader sense, however, the term is understood as a collection of different unions, organizations, associations and networks established to deal with issues that are beyond any individual state (Gagnon & Fleuss, 2020).

In line with the framework of rescaling, which gives a theoretical context for the processes of supranationalism, the latter may occur at a number of geographical scales: regional, macro-regional and global (Timothy et al., 2016; Gagnon & Fleuss, 2020). Nye and Welch (2013), among others, use the term "intergovernmental organizations" to describe the UN, OPEC and the Arab League, and point out that "supranational" is also sometimes understood as a regional organization, agreement or cooperative arrangement that brings together countries from a larger part of a continent, which implies some sort of territorial proximity or contiguity as opposed to intergovernmental organizations. The main argument behind supranationalism as a distinct concept describing relations in the international arena is an acknowledgement that states are not the only actors in supranational relations and that there are structural results of these relations that may affect entities besides states (Tsebelis & Garrett, 2001).

Broadly defined, supranationalism interrelates both types of global processes which change the understanding of borders, both economic and political. From this perspective, inter-state political alliances aim to decrease trade barriers and increase human mobilities. The ultimate aim in these endeavours is to enhance connectivity on a global scale to effect peace and a higher quality of life for Earth's inhabitants (Timothy et al., 2016).

The dynamic changes of recent years are affecting many spheres of state functions, including their borders and cooperation at different levels. Today, the progressive process of globalization manifests itself in an increase in the number and intensity of connections between different entities in all areas of socioeconomic life. The interdependence of countries, societies, enterprises, non-commercial institutions as well as regions and cities is increasing, creating a worldwide network of interdependence in different spheres. At the same time, globalization faces responses like the growth of nationalism and populism, both of which challenge supranationalism and many forms of cooperation as populists oppose giving up any degree of sovereignty in favour of multilateral organizations; they also focus on national borders, bordering practices and the securitization of state boundaries (Nye & Welch, 2013; Casaglia et al., 2020).

Although supranationalist alliances exist in all parts of the world (e.g., SAARC, ASEAN, MERCOSUR, ECOWAS, SADC), the EU is by far the most developed and integrated of these, and Europe is the most common geographical context for understanding supranationalization and its broader implications. European integration permeates all areas of life, crossing political and institutional boundaries. The EU's institutional structures provide the backbone for formal and informal cooperative initiatives, top-down and bottom-up. These activities intersect across scales, from local to multinational, which contributes to the proliferation of cross-border regions and transfrontier socioeconomic activities as a result of political commitments to regional integration. Cross-border regions are seen as innovations in relation to scale, place and space resulting from the rescaling process (Jessop, 2002).

The issue of integration can be considered in relation to borderlands, and although researchers agree that each border region is unique (Anderson & O'Dowd, 1999; Prescott & Triggs, 2008), there have been attempts to provide a model description of integration processes in the borderlands. Jessop (2002, pp. 38–41), for instance, defines nine ways in which cross-border regions emerge: (1) the solidifying of space organized around the exchange of goods disapproved by states (liminal forms); (2) through previously suppressed historical economic interdependence; (3) as a spillover of a metropolitan centre; (4) through intentionally created new functional economic space (e.g., innovation clusters); (5) as a top-down creation to restabilize the national scale (by the states); (6) as top-down construction to undermine national scale (by supranational bodies); (7) as a reaction to uneven development—thus, they become a means of improving the competitiveness of border regions; (8) as nation-building projects in multi-national states; and (9) as career- and institution-building initiatives. These strategies are not mutually exclusive but may overlap and reinforce one another. The list shows how analytically complex studying cross-border cooperation can be and how the emergence of cross-border regions depends on the reinforcement or weakening of national, supranational and regional integration, centralization and disintegration among the most globally important political and economic actors.

Significant scholarly attention has been devoted to cross-border cooperation in metropolitan regions (Decoville et al. 2013; Nelles & Durand, 2014; Durand et al., 2017). These studies show different models of cross-border integration and different layers of borders impacting the integration process. Decoville et al. (2013) analyse spatial integration in ten European cross-border metropolitan regions by comparing three indicators: flows of cross-border commuters, differentials of gross domestic product per capita and residents' citizenship. Their results led to a typology based on three modes of cross-border integration: by specialization, by polarization and by osmosis. According to this line of thinking, the greater the economic disparities between two sides of a boundary, the greater the level of interactions measured by cross-border commuting; economic exchanges will also have an impact on the cross-border integration of communities.

## Tourism and the Fuzziness of Cross-border Cooperation

Originally, cross-border cooperation was perceived as a means of helping to overcome the peripheral characteristics of most border regions (Blatter & Clement, 2000). Over time, however, it has started to be seen also as a way to exploit the potential of border areas (borderlands as a whole), and to create transfrontier regions (Blatter & Clement, 2000; Lara-Valencia, 2011; Dörry & Decoville, 2012; Durand & Nelles, 2012; Knotter, 2014; Dołzbłasz & Raczyk, 2015).

One of the capacities of borderland areas is their considerable appeal to tourists and their potential as venues for tourism development. Many borderlands are home to significant natural assets because borders are often based in rivers or mountain ranges, and because the physical peripherality of borderlands often favours the survival of valuable natural areas. As a result, transboundary environmental protection in borderlands fosters cooperation between countries, and the presence of transboundary protected areas can be an important element shaping regional ties (Więckowski, 2013).

Transboundary tourism is an important development tool on the margins of many states and can develop organically through differential pricing, tax structures and rules and regulations, as well as the cultural and natural appeal of peripheral regions as noted above. Likewise, tourism may be developed intentionally in borderlands through planned efforts to provide jobs and income for marginal regions and people who are frequently the poorest in the country (Timothy, 2001; Timothy & Gelbman, 2015). The organic approach to tourism development in border zones resembles the self-organization reflected on earlier, while the purposive planning of tourism is more intentional but nonetheless requires collaboration and trust from both sides of the border.

It is worth noting that initially cross-border cooperation focuses on institutional dimensions, and in Europe it was particularly related to the processes of integration. Hence, its key foci were legal matters, cooperation structures and their instruments and activities (Blasco et al., 2014a). Over time, European cooperation has expanded well beyond mere formal ties. For example, the role of cooperation between firms and other institutions outside the public sector, as well as private connections and networks, and informal relationships based on friendship and private acquaintances (social capital), have been emphasized (Krätke & Borst, 2007; Lara-Valencia, 2011; Dołzbłasz & Raczyk, 2017). Sometimes these informal approaches are favoured over government-to-government approaches owing to the difficulties (or even impossibilities) in establishing effective, formal, cross-border institutions (Hooper & Kramsch, 2007; Szmigiel-Rawska, 2016). Tourism is one such area that often spurs informal collaboration between local communities and service enterprises (Blasco et al., 2014a; Villa Zamorano, 2022).

Social, political and economic networks and cross-border cooperation are essential in tourism contexts to uphold principles of equity, community empowerment and sustainable growth. Transfrontier collaboration in tourism is becoming more commonplace and complex, and deals primarily with nature and culture conservation, common infrastructure development, joint marketing and promotional efforts, increased freedom of mobility, and regional identity and branding (Timothy, 2001, 2019; Prokkola, 2010).

Blatter and Clement (2000, p. 31) note the paradigm shift in studies of cross-border cooperation in Europe and North America. They identify "networking" as the main feature of cooperation in the border regions they studied. The concept of networks is nowadays used in many contexts and describes various cross-border phenomena (Blasco et al., 2014b), and the great generality of the term causes it to be understood in very different ways. It is a fact, however, that an increase in connections and various types of relations in many spheres of life is what makes a network approach useful in learning, describing and explaining them better.

Castells (1996), who is often quoted in this context, notes that due to the dynamic growth of information technology, a "network society" has developed, and the flow of information, goods, capital, services and, to a lesser extent, people crossing borders creates "spaces of flows", which have replaced the traditional "spaces of places" in the organization of societies. This is truer today than it was when Castells asserted it 25 years ago.

As a result, networking at different levels in the context of spaces of flows marks a new methodological approach to borderlands research (Blatter, 2004; Leick, 2012; Blasco et al., 2014a; Dołzbłasz, 2018; Ferrer-Roca et al., 2022). As Strihan (2008) points out, the network approach helps create an understanding of borders, not as areas separating homogeneous groups of social units, but as areas characterized by specific patterns of interaction, which may exclude or integrate these groups. In this context, border regions are understood to be areas of interpenetration, not division, where borders function more as bridges than barriers. The functional approach emphasizes the functional links and the need to see the borderland (and its management) as dynamic spaces of flows as opposed to the dominant approach of spaces of places and hierarchical government. Looking for an answer in-between the spaces of flows and the spaces of places, between the networked blurry world and bounded state territories, a path is being delineated on which the state *sensu stricto* does not change (its material conditions, its administrative range) due to the development of cross-border cooperation, but what changes dynamically are cross-border connections—their scope, nature and intensity.

## Conclusion

Awareness of the need for integrating the material and social dimensions of borders within areas of cooperation, along with strengthening trust and institution-building practices, seems to be the most important challenge for theory and practice in cross-border cooperation, stemming both from theoretical reconceptualizations and the recent geopolitical and humanitarian events of the past two decades, including Russia's 2022 invasion of Ukraine.

Although we observe contradictory signals and tendencies throughout the world, as well as in individual countries and regions (and across different scales), and the existing logic of centuries-old divisions and conflicts will probably continue, it seems that the world is reaching a turning point. This may require revaluating and redefining notions, both in the political dimension (e.g., state sovereignty as understood today) and in the economic dimension, mainly in relation to capitalism and neoliberalism and especially within the realm of tourism. The twenty-first century has ushered in significant changes in state functions, the role of sovereignty and the meaning of borders. It seems that, despite everything, cooperation at various levels, including globally, is necessary because of the multiplicity and multifaceted nature of interconnectedness, not least of which comes through global travel. The COVID-19 pandemic showed both the power and weaknesses of globalization, and it drew considerable attention to borders and their primary role: to protect the state. Since March 2020, what we have observed is both a normative urge to close borders and lock societies and nations within the membranes of their sovereign states, yet such actions have been shown to be pointless in many respects, because countries simply cannot function in isolation and the world is now far too connected to be segmented solely into sovereign states without considering what goes on beyond state borders.

Cross-border cooperation is a laboratory in which important contemporary social and political challenges can be recognized and may be mediated and addressed. Cross-border cooperation in theory and practice derives from the social capital practices of cooperation, negotiation and compromise; at the same time these processes are often rooted in natural resource protection or natural barrier management. Hence it is the grounds for further development of an integrative approach between materialist and relational views of territories and borders and, at the same time, it is a referent point for states to define borders and understand their role in a new global reality.

## Acknowledgement

This chapter was written within the framework of the project 'Stability of transborder cooperation in the example of Polish borderlands' (2018/31/B/HS4/00550) financed by the National Science Centre, Krakow, Poland.

## References

Agnew, J., Mitchell, K., & Toal, G. (2003). Introduction. In J. Agnew, K. Mitchell, & G. Toal (Eds.) *A companion to political geography*, pp. 1–9. Oxford: Blackwell.
Amilhat-Szary, A-M. (2007). Are borders more easily crossed today? The paradox of contemporary trans-border mobility in the Andes. *Geopolitics*, 12, 1–18.
Anderson, J., & O'Dowd, L. (1999). Borders, border regions and territoriality: Contradictory meanings, changing significance. *Regional Studies*, 33(7), 593–604.
Axelrod, R.M. (1984). *The evolution of cooperation*. New York: Basic Books.
Baldersheim, H., & Ståhlberg, K. (1999). *Nordic region-building in a European perspective*. Aldershot: Ashgate.
Blasco, D., Guia, J., & Prats, L. (2014a). Emergence of governance in cross-border destinations. *Annals of Tourism Research*, 49, 159–173.
Blasco, D., Guia, J., & Prats, L. (2014b). Heritage tourism clusters along the borders of Mexico. *Journal of Heritage Tourism*, 9(1), 51–67.
Blatter, J. (2004). "From spaces of place" to "spaces of flows"? Territorial and functional governance in cross-border regions in Europe and North America. *International Journal of Urban and Regional Research*, 28(3), 530–548.
Blatter, J., & Clement, N. (2000). Cross-border cooperation in Europe: Historical development, institutionalization, and contrasts with North America. *Journal of Borderlands Studies*, 15(1), 14–53.
Böhm, H. (2021). The influence of the Covid-19 pandemic on Czech-Polish cross-border cooperation: From debordering to re-bordering? *Moravian Geographical Reports*, 29(2), 137–148.
Brenner, N. (2001). The limits to scale? Methodological reflections on scalar structuration. *Progress in Human Geography*, 25(4), 591–614.
Capello, R., Caragliu, A., & Fratesi, U. (2018). Measuring border effects in European cross-border regions. *Regional Studies*, 52(7), 986–996.
Casaglia, A., Coletti, R., Lizotte, C., Agnew, J., Mamadouh, V., & Minca, C. (2020). Interventions on European nationalist populism and bordering in time of emergencies. *Political Geography*, 82, 102238.
Castells, M. (1996). *The information age: Economy, society and culture, Vol 1: The rise of the network society*. Malden, MA: Blackwell.
Cook, K.S., Hardin, R., & Levi, M. (2005). *Cooperation without trust?* New York: Russell Sage Foundation.
De Moor, T. (2015). *The dilemma of the commoners: Understanding the use of common-pool resources in long-term perspective*. Cambridge: Cambridge University Press.
Decoville, A., Durand, F., Sohn, C., & Walther, O. (2013). Comparing cross-border metropolitan integration in Europe: Towards a functional typology. *Journal of Borderlands Studies*, 28(2), 221–237.
Dołzbłasz, S. (2018). A network approach to transborder cooperation studies as exemplified by Poland's eastern border. *Geographia Polonica*, 91(1), 63–76.
Dołzbłasz, S., & Raczyk, A. (2015). Different borders–different co-operation? Transborder co-operation in Poland. *Geographical Review*, 105(3), 360–376.
Dołzbłasz, S., & Raczyk, A. (2017). Transborder co-operation and competition among firms in the Polish–German borderland. *Tijdschrift voor Economische en Sociale Geografie*, 108(2), 141–156.
Dörry, S., & Decoville, A. (2012). *Transportation policy networks in cross-border regions: First results from a social network analysis in Luxembourg and the Greater Region*. Esch-sur-Alzette, Luxembourg: CEPS/INSTEAD.
Durand, F., Decoville, A., & Knippschild, R. (2017). Everything all right at the internal EU borders? The ambivalent effects of cross-border integration and the rise of Euroscepticism. *Geopolitics*, 25(3), 587–608.

Durand, F., & Nelles, J. (2012). *Cross-border governance within the Eurometropolis Lille-Kortrijk-Tournai (ELKT) through the example of crossborder public transportation*. Esch-sur-Alzette, Luxembourg: CEPS/INSTEAD.

Ferrer-Roca, N., Guia, J., & Blasco, D. (2022). Partnerships and the SDGs in a cross-border destination: The case of the Cerdanya Valley. *Journal of Sustainable Tourism*, 30(10), 2410–2427.

Gagnon, J.-P., & Fleuss, D. (2020). The case for extending measures of democracy in the world "Beneath", "Above", and "Outside" the national level. *Political Geography*, 83, 102276.

Hardt, M., & Negri, A. (2001). *Empire*. Cambridge, MA: Harvard University Press.

Hooper, O., & Kramsch, O. (2007). Post-colonising Europe: The geopolitics of globalisation, empire and borders: Here and there, now and then. *Tijdschrift voor Economische en Sociale Geografie*, 98(4), 526–534.

Jessop, B. (2002). The political economy of scale. In M. Perkmann, & N-L. Sum (Eds.) *Globalization, regionalization, and cross-border regions*, pp. 25–49. Basingstoke: Palgrave.

Knotter, A. (2014). Perspectives on cross-border labor in Europe: "(Un)familiarity" or "push-and-pull"? *Journal of Borderlands Studies*, 29(3), 319–326.

Kovras, I., & Robins, S. (2016). Death as the border: Managing missing migrants and unidentified bodies at the EU's Mediterranean frontier. *Political Geography*, 55, 40–49.

Krätke, S., & Borst, R. (2007). EU eastern enlargement and the configuration of German–Polish inter-firm linkages. *Tijdschrift voor Economische en Sociale Geografie*, 98(5), 621–640.

Lara-Valencia, F. (2011). The "thickening" of the US-Mexico border: Prospects for cross-border networking and cooperation. *Journal of Borderlands Studies*, 26(3), 251–264.

Leick, B. (2012). Business networks in the cross-border regions of the enlarged EU: What do we know in the post-enlargement era? *Journal of Borderlands Studies*, 27(3), 299–314.

Nelles, J., & Durand, F. (2014). Political rescaling and metropolitan governance in cross-border regions: Comparing the cross-border metropolitan areas of Lille and Luxembourg. *European Urban and Regional Studies*, 21(1), 104–122.

Newman, D. (2006). Borders and bordering. Towards an interdisciplinary dialogue. *European Journal of Social Theory*, 9(2), 171–186.

Newman, D., & Paasi, A. (1998). Fences and neighbours in the postmodern world: Boundary narratives in political geography. *Progress in Human Geography*, 22(2), 186–207.

Nye, J.S., & Welch, D.A. (2013). *Understanding global conflict and cooperation: An introduction to theory and history*. London: Pearson.

Ohmae, K. (1990). The borderless world. *McKinsey Quarterly*, 3, 3–19.

Olson, M. (1965). *The logic of collective action: Public goods and the theory of groups*. Cambridge, MA: Harvard University Press.

Ostrom, E. (2009). A general framework for analyzing sustainability of social-ecological systems. *Science*, 325(5939), 419–422.

Ostrom, V., & Ostrom, E. (1971). Public choice: A different approach to the study of public administration. *Public Administration Review*, 31(2), 203–216.

Popescu, G. (2012). *Bordering and ordering in the twenty-first century: Understanding borders*. Lanham, MD: Rowman & Littlefield.

Prescott, V., & Triggs, G.D. (2008). *International frontiers and boundaries: Law, politics and geography*. Leiden: Martinus Nijhoff Publishers.

Prokkola, E-K. (2010). Borders in tourism: The transformation of the Swedish-Finnish border landscape. *Current Issues in Tourism*, 13(3), 223–238.

Scholte, J.A. (2008). Defining globalisation. *World Economy*, 31(11), 1471–1502.

Strihan, A. (2008). A network-based approach to regional borders: The case of Belgium. *Regional Studies*, 42(4), 539–554.

Szmigiel-Rawska, K. (2016). Sustainability of cross-border cooperation: PHARE CBC partnership development paths. *European Urban and Regional Studies*, 23(3), 513–526.

Till, K.E., Sundberg, J., Pullan, W., Psaltis, C., Makriyianni, C., Celal, R.Z., Samani, M.O., & Dowler, L. (2013). Interventions in the political geographies of walls. *Political Geography*, 33(1), 52–62.

Timothy, D.J. (2001). *Tourism and political boundaries*. London: Routledge.

Timothy, D.J. (2006). Tourism and conservation in border regions. In K. Hoffman (ed.) *The U.S. Mexican border environment: Transboundary ecosystem management*, pp. 225–242. San Diego: San Diego State University Press.

Timothy, D.J. (2019). Supranationalism and tourism: Free trade, customs unions, and single markets in an era of geopolitical change. In D.J. Timothy (ed.) *Handbook of globalisation and tourism*, pp. 100–113. Cheltenham: Edward Elgar.

Timothy, D.J., & Gelbman, A. (2015). Tourist lodging, spatial relations, and the cultural heritage of borderlands. *Journal of Heritage Tourism*, 10(2), 202–212.

Timothy, D.J., Saarinen, J., & Viken, A. (2016). Tourism issues and international borders in the Nordic region. *Scandinavian Journal of Hospitality and Tourism*, 16(1), 1–13.

Tsebelis, G., & Garrett, G. (2001). The institutional foundations of intergovernmentalism and supranationalism in the European Union. *International Organization*, 55(2), 357–390.

Tuathail, G.Ó. (1999). Borderless worlds? Problematising discourses of deterritorialization. *Geopolitics*, 4(2), 139–154.

Usher, M. (2020). Territory incognita. *Progress in Human Geography*, 44(6), 1019–1046.

Vaughan-Williams, N. (2015). "We are not animals!" Humanitarian border security and zoopolitical spaces in Europe. *Political Geography*, 45, 1–10.

Villa Zamorano, Z.M. (2022). *Cross-border cooperation and competitiveness strategies of the lodging sector in Ciudad Juárez, Chihuahua and El Paso, Texas*. Unpublished doctoral dissertation, Autonomous University of Ciudad Juárez, Mexico.

Więckowski, M. (2013). Eco-frontier in the mountainous borderlands of Central Europe: The case of Polish border parks. *Journal of Alpine Research*, 101(3), 1–12.

Więckowski, M., & Timothy, D.J. (2021). Tourism and an evolving international boundary: Bordering, debordering and rebordering on Usedom Island, Poland-Germany. *Journal of Destination Marketing & Management*, 22, 100647.

Zimmerbauer, K., & Paasi, A. (2020). Hard work with soft spaces (and vice versa): Problematizing the transforming planning spaces. *European Planning Studies*, 28(4), 771–789.

# 6

# TOURISM, CITIZENSHIP AND BORDER GOVERNANCE

## Past Dynamics and New Reconfigurations

*Raoul V. Bianchi and Marcus L. Stephenson*

### Introduction

International tourism and the concomitant freedom of movement on which it depends are profoundly shaped by an ideologically contested and often conflictual politics of mobility. International tourism is one of the most powerful expressions of the individual freedoms and consumerist ideologies associated with neoliberal capitalism. The foregrounding of tourist mobilities at the expense of other less privileged mobilities serves to reveal the continuing contradictions within twenty-first-century notions of mobility rights and citizenship, incongruities which cannot be ignored by tourism scholars.

The comprehensive disruption to travel and the collapse of global tourism brought about by the outbreak of the COVID-19 pandemic in early 2020 has also forcefully underlined the vital importance of tourism to the economic fabric and livelihoods of many states (Behsudi, 2020). Despite resistance to the state-sanctioned abrogation of free movement in certain quarters and the evasion of local quarantine restrictions by small numbers of tourists (Hilliar, 2020), for the most part a strong global consensus has emerged around the need for states to impose draconian border restrictions and domestic "lockdowns" to suppress the virus.

We aim to revisit some of the central ideas and arguments presented elsewhere by us (see Bianchi et al., 2020; Bianchi & Stephenson, 2013, 2014, 2019; Stephenson, 2006), and to present a critical reflection on the diverse intersections between international travel and citizenship, encompassing questions concerning the right to travel, border politics and mobility justice. We also consider the implications of the pandemic and disruption to global travel and other mobilities on the emergent power dynamics governing the relationship between travel, rights and borders.

### Tourism and Citizenship in the Modern Interstate System

Modern citizenship and its corollary, national identity, coalesced around the sovereign-territorial state and the stabilization of interstate relations following the 1815 Congress of Vienna (Torpey, 2000). Modern citizenship rights were subsequently consolidated under the auspices of the nation-state, which acted as a mechanism for mitigating the inequalities produced by capitalist development and the containment of the attendant class conflict (Marshall, 1950 [1992]).

The status of citizenship also encompassed the growing demands of the labour movement for better pay and working conditions, as well as social rights to leisure and paid holidays (Clarke & Critcher, 1985).

The zenith of European colonialism in the late nineteenth century marked the birth of a new era of leisure travel, especially as the cost of maritime transport fell and colonized territories became integrated into an expanding network of settler societies linked by trade. Notwithstanding the reality of European imperialism, Thomas Cook was a firm supporter of free trade and the emancipatory potential of travel (Brendon, 1991, p. 36). A commercial travel industry subsequently emerged on the back of steamship trade and the construction of colonial hotels in major ports-of-call, eclipsing an earlier era of genteel "cosmopolitan" travel undertaken predominantly by aristocratic men for the purposes of adventure and attaining social status that was nevertheless marked by a strong sense of European superiority (Pratt, 1992).

In the early twentieth century, mobility became synonymous with modernity as technological advances in transport technologies, particularly automobility and aviation, accelerated and expanded the geographic scope of travel. During the interwar period, writers and artists congregated in a series of cosmopolitan enclaves along the Mediterranean Riviera and across North Africa, epitomized by Tangier's International Zone (1924–1956). The "emancipated lifestyles and bohemianism" associated with these cosmopolitan (elite) spaces of leisure and artistic culture became "critical counterpoints to the restrictions of nationalist citizenship" in the conformist European and North American societies from where the majority of these "tourists" originated (Rojek, 1998, p. 303). However, following the Second World War, as states entered an era of peace and international diplomacy underpinned by the newly established United Nations system, mass tourism and its corollary, the right to travel, emerged as both a marker of status and citizenship as well as an essential driver of capitalist growth and labour markets. The extension of the right to leisure and subsequently access to tourism was partly facilitated through the legislative provision for paid holidays in the late 1930s, which became the cornerstone of a post-war social contract in many West European societies and in parts of the Global South (e.g., Argentina).

Support for the freedom of movement also became intertwined with the geopolitical interests of the major powers, principally the USA, for whom tourism was embraced as an ideological tool to promote the virtues of free market capitalism (Endy, 2004). While overseas travel and internal freedom of movement remained heavily restricted in the Soviet Union, domestic tourism was presented as "purposeful and patriotic" and harnessed to the construction of the ideal Soviet citizen (Gorsuch, 2013, p. 42). By the mid-1950s, the need for hard currency accompanied by an ideological shift towards a more open foreign policy under Khrushchev led to a loosening of restrictions on overseas travel. Travel was initially permitted to the Soviet Republics, not least Estonia, and other communist bloc states, followed later by some allowances made for travel to capitalist countries (Gorsuch, 2013, p. 11).

Of all the rights enshrined in law, the right to the freedom of movement, while perhaps not seen as the most critical of citizenship rights, is arguably one of the most politicized of rights enshrined in the 1948 Universal Declaration of Human Rights. By this time most states only began to fully consolidate their rights and the capacity to monopolize the authority to regulate international cross-border movement, namely through the issuance of passports and visas (Torpey, 2000). Although the passport is often synonymous with state sovereignty and national citizenship, during the early nineteenth century, passports were often issued to nationals of one state by another state (Lloyd, 2003, p. 10). It was not until the issuance of passports had come firmly under the control of states that the issuance of travel documents became more closely associated with the political rights of national citizenship. State sovereignty and the control of borders were further extended into the skies through bilateral agreements and legislation regulating international air travel and demarcating airspace in accordance with the overlapping demands of commercial aviation and national security (Pascoe 2001). Throughout the post-war period a global network of tourism, resorts and hotels were increasingly drawn into regional and global geopolitical rivalries and "connected to broader architectures of security and insecurity, war and peacemaking" (Fregonese & Ramadan, 2015, p. 793). Moreover, the growth of US aviation corporations and the concomitant expansion of international US hotel chains into the Middle East were closely intertwined with the US strategic control of oil supplies in the region and thus became integral to the projection of US power overseas (Hazbun, forthcoming).

Holiday-making was transformed from an elite pursuit to an instrument of economic development in "developing countries", becoming a driver of capital accumulation for a widening array of global hotel, tourism and leisure corporations by the end of the twentieth century (Britton, 1991). Tourism's growing importance in international trade and economic development was bolstered by a discourse concerning individual rights to tourism, promoted by such organizations as the World Tourism Organization (UNWTO) (1999, 2017). This signalled an important ideological turn indicating that "freedom of travel is synonymous with freedom of trade" (O'Byrne, 2001, p. 409). The right to the freedom of movement is clearly set out in Article 13 of the Universal Declaration of Human Rights (1948), while the 1966 International Covenant on Economic, Social and Cultural Rights sets out the right to leisure and holidays within a legally binding political framework (Breakey & Breakey, 2013, p. 741).

Although the moral, political and legal foundations of the "right" to tourism lack a solid legal foundation, the idea that "tourists must be allowed freedom of movement in the destination countries" enjoys a broad consensus (Nkyi & Hashimoto, 2015, p. 397). Any hindrance to the freedom of travel and restrictions on the growth of tourism is often regarded by some as a violation of human freedom, tantamount to a "war on tourism" (Butcher, 2020). Nonetheless, while the right to tourism is one which has received considerable institutional support—albeit not in law—this is not reciprocated in terms of support for development rights (Higgins-Desbiolles, 2007) nor the safeguarding of labour rights (Gascón, 2019).

The abrogation of the rights of destination hosts to travel and experience being tourists implicates that they only have the economic right, if permitted, to serve the interests and needs of tourists. Tourism scholars too have been complicit in this way of thinking, through largely ignoring the tourism needs and tourist experiences of local communities. Although there is a growing recognition that tourism is not principally a Western phenomenon (Cohen & Cohen 2014), "Western epistemologies" continue to be favoured at the expense of perceiving people from the Global South as "producers of tourism knowledge" but rather "as objects of tourism research" (Chambers & Buzinde, 2015, p. 3). This position is disquieting in so far as it suggests that tourism destination authorities should ensure that tourists are protected and pampered, as evidenced by frequent crackdowns on begging and other forms of local behaviour deemed distressing or threatening to tourists (García Gallo, 2015).

## Tourism, Neoliberalism and the Contradictions of Global Citizenship

Following the collapse of the Soviet Union and its "satellite" states in the early 1990s, the eastward expansion of tourism provided a further catalyst for the integration of Eastern Bloc countries into the expanding dynamics of neoliberal capitalism and tourist flows. This brought a plethora of new spaces into the global economy of tourism. Ironically, the new democratic rights of citizenship that were constructed in the ruins of Soviet communism, including the right to freedom of travel, were increasingly subsumed by neoliberal capitalism and commercialization of social life by market forces, ensuring that citizenship was becoming conflated with consumerism (Streeck, 2012).

The processes of democratization and market reform which followed the Soviet Union's disintegration marked a major turning point in the embrace of the freedom of movement and expansion of travel in Europe. Shortly thereafter, John Urry (1995, p. 165) wrote that "the right to travel has become a marker of citizenship", foregrounding how such "rights" implied "claims to consume other cultures and places throughout the world" and which were distinct from struggles over representation and resources more typically associated with the political rights of citizenship. As neoliberalism eroded the social-democratic state and globalization undermined the attachment of citizens to states (Isin & Wood, 1999, p. 7), tourism powerfully expressed mobility freedoms and epitomized marketized (and neoliberal) conceptions of citizenship.

Together with globalization and the emergence of increasingly cosmopolitan (multi-ethnic) societies, new stratifications of extreme wealth inequality have accentuated unequal mobility empowerments (see Hannam et al., 2006), giving rise to a "denationalized global elite" (Falk, 1994, p. 135). The hypermobility of this elite "class" of global "citizens" has been enabled by an increased accumulation of wealth at the top (Keeley, 2015), affording them access to new forms of investor-citizenship which can be purchased for a hefty sum (see Abrahamian, 2015). These privileged mobilities render borders, for some, all but a thing of the past. Meanwhile, the growth of ostensibly ethical, responsible and philanthropic forms of travel, motivated by a shared "ethic of care" for the planet and cultures threatened by globalization and mass tourism, expresses more solidaristic readings of global citizenship (Falk, 1994) or, for others, what has been described as "planetary citizenship" (see Thompson, 2001).

"Ethical" travellers are interpreted by some as part of the vanguard of "thoughtful travellers, campaigning NGOs, farsighted tour operators and radical organizers" who have become increasingly "aware of our responsibilities as global citizens" (Pattullo, 2006, p. 13). Discourses of global citizenship and cosmopolitanism are attributed to new and diverse forms of travel marked by an openness to cultural difference, such as "round-the-world" travel (Germann Molz, 2005), while more politically engaged forms of justice tourism (Kassis, 2005) are rooted in a cosmopolitan "politics of morality" (Hirst & Thomson, 1991, p. 263).

Butcher (2017, p. 129) challenges global citizenship's "inadequate moral and political framework". Global citizenship as expressed in volunteer tourism, for instance, aligns more readily with contemporary forms of "lifestyle politics" in which ostensibly ethical lifestyle choices (e.g., travel) become detached from struggles for political rights of citizenship within nation-states. Nevertheless, the global reach of tourism capital and the mobility of tourists implicate them in a web of transnational practices and issues that go beyond the capacity of any one state to address in a fair and equitable manner. However, the lack of an adequate framework of global governance means that the question of how to judiciously balance such complex rights and duties between tourists and locals is effectively harnessed to the growth of tourism, whose "externalities" are largely borne by host states.

While the development of tourism, particularly in poorer parts of the world, has long been accompanied by degrees of segregation from impoverished local communities and by dedicated security in the form of "tourist police", the heightened threat of global terrorism and concern over the recent upsurge in migration has further drawn tourism into the orbit of a complex and variable matrix of securitization and border governance strategies. Normative ideas of "security management" permeate the tourism industries and its institutional apparatuses whose priority is to ensure the security of tourists and the smooth running of the tourism industries in the face of diverse and varied threats. Thus, given its almost universal significance as an item of trade worldwide, "touristic security" is integral to the logics and practices of border governance that are "central to the functioning of global neoliberal capitalism" (Becklake, 2020, p. 77). Such forms of security can be perceived as a "mobile form of consumer protection" in contrast to other "less favourable" forms of human mobility whose value is not reducible to a monetary calculus (Becklake, 2020, pp. 80–81).

## Geopolitics, Travel and Border Governance

Irrespective of moves to liberalize cross-border formalities and introduce multilateral mobility arrangements in certain parts of the world during the 1990s, Ohmae's (1990) vision of a "borderless world" bears little resemblance to a world increasingly shaped by resurgent nationalisms, geopolitical tensions and the proliferation of restrictive bordering practices and securitization strategies. Meanwhile, the current disruption of tourism and economic crisis triggered by the COVID-19 pandemic, while challenging certain neoliberal orthodoxies associated with the freedom of movement and flexible borders, underscores the continued power of the nation-state to regulate mobility and the importance of political rights of citizenship.

International tourism is arguably marked by a fundamental paradox: tourism demands open borders and a minimum of hindrances to the right to travel and freely move across borders, while simultaneously calling for strong security measures to uphold and protect these very same rights. As Almeida (2020, p. 71) notes, "one of the indispensable requirements of the tourism industry is the control of security, so as to generate a space of absolute tranquillity in the tourist destination". Meanwhile, those without "legitimate" credentials for travel enjoy no such rights. Hence, the intersection between tourism, citizenship and mobility rights is at its sharpest at borders and within the often contested and shifting spaces of borderlands. As discussed elsewhere (Bianchi *et al.*, 2020), it is not merely a case of tourism being a consequence of such discrepant mobilities, rather that tourist mobilities are implicated in the very bordering practices and securitization strategies put in place to literally "make the world safe for travel" (Goldstone, 2001).

Consequently, tourism's association with the production of global citizenship is undermined by the unequal mobility rights and unresolved injustices bound up within the process of global touristification at all stages (Jamal & Higham, 2021). In her recent work on mobility justice, Sheller (2018, p. 14) deepens the theorization of the dynamics and inequality that shape contemporary mobilities and travel, linking "governance and control of movement" to interconnected struggles for environmental, economic and social justice at multiple scales. In this way, mobility inequalities can be understood not just in terms of unequal political citizenship rights but, rather, as constituted out of the intersecting axes of inequality and injustice born out of the global structural inequalities and resource conflicts associated with extractive capitalism, political instability and climate-induced ecological disruptions (see Mann, 2020).

In spite of the worldwide economic significance of tourism and the continual lobbying by such organizations as the World Travel and Tourism Council (WTTC) to remove any encumbrances to travel (e.g., restrictive visa regimes and taxes), the "fixity" of "borders, institutions and territories of nation-states" (Favell, 2001, pp. 391–392) continue to shape the political geographies of tourism and travel. This is particularly so where geopolitical tensions result in the citizens of one country being denied entry by another (Bianchi & Stephenson, 2014, pp. 100–107). While restrictive border regimes often draw the ire of such organizations as the WTTC (*Travel Weekly*, 2017), borders themselves may "invoke a unique type of fascination" for tourists (Timothy, 2000, p. 57). Additionally, the right to travel may serve as a powerful "de-bordering" discourse, as witnessed during the struggle to overthrow the East German communist regime and bring down the Berlin Wall in 1989 (Burstein, 1991, pp. 54–55).

While states retain considerable power and authority over their borders and the regulation of cross-border movements, geopolitics scholars have challenged the "territorialist epistemology" that shapes state-centric conceptions of borders (Vaughan-Williams, 2012). The border does more than simply delineate the geographic boundaries of the sovereign political authority, it is the "primary site where contemporary inequalities and injustices, hegemony and repression are created and reproduced" (Bauder, 2012, p. 1). The neoliberal era brought forth a new rationality of bordering practices where states seek to manage "contradictory spatialities inherent in borders" (Prokkola, 2012, p. 1320). These spatialities are marked by tensions arising from attempts to reconcile national security with the imperative of maintaining frictionless trade and the movement of capital (Tuathail, 1999) – indeed, tourism. Contemporary border regimes, notwithstanding variances resulting from distinctive state ideologies and regional governance systems, are mobile and diffuse, and constituted out of "coexisting networks and partnerships at diverse spatial scales" (Prokkola, 2012, p. 1321). Neoliberal border governance regimes thus involve simultaneous processes of rescaling and out-sourcing (or "off-shoring") to often nebulous networks of private contractors, as well as pre-emptive forms of bordering using sophisticated tracking and surveillance technologies to deter the movement of "risky" subjects prior to their arrival at the border (Vaughan-Williams, 2012, p. 24). These changes illustrate an important shift in the function of borders and the securitization of society in so far as border control has increasingly become a major instrument for the policing of "dangerous mobilities" (Walters, 2006, p. 199).

During this period, migration and the threat of terrorism increasingly began to be conflated by states in the Global North, especially as security threats and suspect forms of mobility necessitate new and more sophisticated forms of border control. However, borders are not mere entry/exit points of varying degrees of permeability and managed according to the severity of threats, rather they act as a vector of power relations through which differentially empowered categories of mobility are in fact constituted.[1] The very "legitimacy" of travel is often determined before one reaches the physical border (Torabian & Miller, 2017), where visa applicants can find travel requests denied on questionable grounds, often linked to their ethnicity (Addley & Holpuch, 2015) and nationality.

Nowhere perhaps is the "collective fiction of universal rights" (Calori, 2015, n.p.) more starkly revealed than at the frontiers of Europe and the Mediterranean where mobility injustices are starkly revealed. Notwithstanding Russell's (2003, p. 834) observation that "tourists and refugees have become the fastest growing social and economic phenomena in the 21st century", tourism and migration are often treated as entirely different categories of analysis. However, as the spread of refugee and migrant detention centres and "buffer zones" along Europe's southern and eastern border clearly demonstrates, what were once considered spaces of leisure, governed by relatively open mobility regimes (i.e., the Mediterranean), are increasingly at the centre of complex, intersecting regimes of mobility and border governance (Vergnano, 2019). In Tunisia, a country often hailed for building a successful tourism economy, but suffering from rising poverty and chronic unemployment, the injustices faced by young Tunisians desperate to improve their lives are expressed in relation to the freedoms commonly enjoyed by tourists: "Nearly everyone dreams of going to Italy, to escape the feeling of being shut in, and exercise what they claim is a right to travel like that enjoyed by Europeans" (Brésillon, 2021, n.p.).

The discriminatory logics of bordering practices have in recent years been shaped and reinforced by the deployment of sophisticated digital bordering technologies and surveillance apparatuses. Border security is not merely a state concern but is one that intersects with the desire of private corporations who are increasingly "involved in every aspect of the national security state" (Engelhardt, 2015, p. 6) to exploit a growing and profitable market for security technologies. The market size for facial recognition systems alone in 2019 was USD3.54 billion, and this is anticipated to reach USD9.99 billion by 2025 (Cision PR Newswire, 2020a). The integrity of such surveillance technologies is also highly questionable. The facial recognition systems used for tracking people's movements and identifying "suspect travellers" in the USA has caused some travellers to undergo lengthy interrogations, resulting in false arrests and harassment from border agents (Holmes, 2019). The use of digital surveillance technologies is set to intensify in the wake of the pandemic, ostensibly to "restore trust" and to ensure "seamless" travel (see Serra & Leong, 2020). While this may "facilitate better services for mobile, affluent citizens" it should be juxtaposed with the potential "worsening of the position of more marginalized groups" (Graham & Wood, 2003, p. 229), who may find their mobility and other freedoms curtailed though the deployment of digital tools. Digital technologies powerfully reconfigure new modes of mobile and deterritorialized border governance as citizens and travellers are engaged as active agents in the diffusion of mobile surveillance technologies (Weaver, 2008).

## Tourism, Racism and the Politics of Space

The increasing pervasiveness and severity of bordering practices in which differential mobility rights are becoming more marked and borders less porous, reaffirms Mau's (2010, p. 344) contention that "borders are rarely open or closed per se, but only with regards to specific persons and types of mobility". The strengthening of external borders has occurred in tandem with the diffusion of diverse internal bordering practices and the racialization of "suspect communities" (Hickman et al., 2011). Bordering processes increasingly align with and accentuate discriminatory immigration policies, as illustrated by the "Muslim travel ban" imposed by former US President Trump in January 2017 (Withnall, 2017). This has induced a state of "permanxiety" amongst Muslim travellers (not just in the USA), who constantly fear being turned back or detained by border agents (Ali, 2017). Since the implementation of the travel ban more than 41,000 travel visa requests have been blocked, though US President Joe Biden lifted the ban within the first week of his presidency and formally announced that he will aim to submit to congress the U.S. Citizenship Act, in order to legally restrict future presidents from being able to ratify discriminatory travel bans (Khan, 2021). The US travel ban thus exposes contradictions in the US Constitution's emphasis on human rights and democratic freedoms. The so-called "Trump ban" indicated a move away from the kind of borderless global economy envisaged by Ohmae (1990), towards a new era of realpolitik, involving intense interstate rivalry and power politics. It can also be interpreted as a rejection of "liberal values", namely "equality of opportunity", "individual life chances" and "freedom of choice" (Mau, 2010, p. 342), potentially expressed in the freedom of movement and travel itself.

Travel rights may also be "weaponized" by states. Political tensions between the USA and China brought about the cancellations of numerous visas for Chinese students intending to study in the USA. The alleged ties that Chinese students have with the Chinese military and their perceived motive to access technologies and intellectual property in the USA were pursued by the former Trump government (Mittelmeir et al., 2020). According to a Pew Research Centre survey in 2020, negative views of China in the USA rose nearly 20 percentage points during Trump's presidency (Silver et al., 2020). Acts of aggression against ethnic and religious people in public spaces may also be inflamed by a media-fuelled climate of perpetual insecurity and fear implicating such groups in various alleged threats, be it migration, terrorism or the COVID-19 virus. The positioning of refugees and migrants as interlopers in "hospitable" spaces, which often includes the squares and streets of major cities with a major tourist presence, has increasingly marked those of different appearance and habits as targets. For example, following the Nice terror attack of July 2016, French resort towns controversially banned the "burkini" (subsequently overturned) on the grounds that it represented a threat to public order (AFP, 2016).

The conflation of "Islamic terrorism" with Muslims provided the pretext for both discriminatory state policies and random acts of micro-aggression against individuals. In March 2020, 8,000 followers of Tablighi Jamaat, a transnational Islamic missionary movement, travelled to an Islamic event in New Delhi and were attacked on social media with such hashtags as "corona jihad" and "corona terror", accusing the group of purposefully spreading the virus (Nortajuddin, 2020). These acts of racial discrimination, however, should be framed within a wider political context in which ethnonationalists have consistently demonized Muslims (Shaban, 2018).

The alleged Chinese origins of the COVID-19 virus and its subsequent spread across the globe is invoked in the name of virus suppression and public safety (Reidy, 2020), while being implicated in the racialization of leisure spaces and the concomitant escalation of racist hate crimes, such as the attack on a Singaporean student in Oxford Street in London on 24 February 2020. A 15-year-old boy, who was part of a group of five teenagers, was convicted of racially aggravated bodily harm, where it was alleged that the perpetrator had also shouted: "I don't want your coronavirus in my country" (Yong, 2021, n.p.). Consequently, the nationalistic and xenophobic sentiment towards Chinese people has spilled over to all those of Asian descent. The European Union Agency for Fundamental Rights has documented that people of Asian descent in such places as Denmark, Estonia, Finland, France, Germany and Italy have encountered various forms of racial intolerance (e.g., name calling and physical violence) (Wang, 2021).

Such forms of internal bordering are premised upon the dehumanization and "othering" of racialized citizens and can be expressed through cultural, social and religious stereotypes in public and tourism spaces (Balibar, 1991, p. 18). Although the intention is to connote the racial superiority of one group more than another, it also reflects a celebration of "civic belonging" by the perpetrators, underpinning the dominant group's conceptions of their "own normality" (Gover et al., 2020). The current strengthening of external borders is inextricably tied to the heightened securitization of societies through which more diffuse forms of exclusion and internal bordering operate. Sundstrom and Kim (2014) emphasize that civil exclusion is the core meaning of xenophobia. Accordingly, as societal inclusion and relations are "social goods" which encourage individuals to participate in a modern polity, acts of intentional or unintentional exclusionism prevent equitable access to such goods, and also to economic forms of consumption. Individuals are thus denied "political agency" and are not able to experience "the full complement of rights that protect or enable fulfillment within the polity" (Sundstrom & Kim, 2014, p. 24).

## COVID-19 and the New Dynamics of Borders and Travel

The global coronavirus pandemic transforms and reconfigures the dynamic interrelationship between tourism, borders and the politics of space in new and unforeseen ways. The pandemic has challenged the core tenets of the contemporary neoliberal order as states drastically curtailed the freedom of movement and reasserted almost complete control over the lives and movement of citizens in an endeavour to suppress the virus. While it may be argued that trust in government decision-making is higher in such eastern states as South Korea and Taiwan, whose successful deployment of digital technologies and other tools to suppress the virus has been rightly hailed, the effectiveness of such strategies is also the result of a strong civil society, high levels of social cohesion and a commitment to human rights and democracy (Eyres, 2021).

Moreover, given the face-to-face nature of the tourism and hospitality industries and their dependence on cross-border mobility, these industries have been hard hit and some sectors will have to confront an uncertain future (de Bellaigue, 2020).

In severely disrupting travel mobilities the coronavirus pandemic has accentuated existing mobility inequalities and border injustices. Accordingly, some states invoked the need to suppress viral transmission by suspending asylum protocols and imposing further punitive restrictions on migration (Mann, 2020), while other states have neglected the plight of hundreds of thousands of cruise ship and other maritime workers from the Global South left stranded at sea (Kaji, 2020). Moreover, while significant numbers of tourism and hospitality workers in rich nations have been able to survive due to state-backed furlough schemes, thousands of resort workers in such destinations as the Maldives, many of whom are also migrants from other parts of South Asia, were forced to take unpaid leave or have been cut adrift, while up to one thousand tourists remained "marooned" by choice in the luxury resorts (Sharma, 2020). The pandemic has in fact witnessed a boom in luxury travel, including private jet purchases (Cision PR Newswire, 2020b), while a number of destinations (e.g., Thailand) announced plans to focus on upmarket luxury tourism as part of their recovery (Luxus Plus, 2020), potentially reinforcing the exclusionary logics of travel under the guise of creating sanitized resort environments.

The pandemic has not merely accentuated mobility inequalities, it has partly upended the pre-existing hierarchy of value attached to "essential" versus "non-essential" mobilities (Salazar, 2021). While digital technologies enabled many professionals to continue working remotely, others (e.g., health workers, delivery drivers and those working in public transport, logistics and supermarkets) did not have the choice to work online. Moreover, the pandemic laid bare the socioeconomic fragilities of tourism dependence. Reliant as they are upon the tourism and hospitality industries to create jobs, low-income states (particularly small island developing states) were faced with a difficult choice between economic survival and ensuring the health of their citizens, a choice further aggravated by the inequality of global vaccine distribution. This resulted in proposals which emphasized that tourists should pay a premium for travel to such destinations once borders reopen, as a way of partly compensating them for lost revenue during the pandemic (South Pacific Travel Organisation, 2021). Better still, a global mobility tax or levy could generate the financial resources to assist cash-strapped, tourism-dependent nations in the event of such a crisis (see Isin & Turner, 2007, p. 15).

The pandemic also exposed hitherto relatively hidden inequalities of class, race and power, determining access to and use of natural spaces. The easing of the lockdown in the UK (and the USA) in the spring of 2020 led to media outcry over public littering and poor behaviour of visitors to natural beauty spots. However, what these responses seemed to largely ignore are the unresolved contradictions and inequalities related to access to nature and the "right to roam". In the UK, as a result of massively unequal structures of land tenure, a majority of the countryside and waterways remain off-limits to the public (Evans, 2019).

Most notably, the pandemic galvanized the power of states as they have reinforced and extended powers to close borders and impose national lockdowns. In addition, governments stepped up efforts to harness the expertise of digital tech companies to deploy data analytics and "'smart" technologies in the management of tourist mobility—including the use of drones to monitor and control the movement of people in natural areas—and border crossings in the interest of "public safety". The further rollout of digital technologies through the use of virus tracking apps and digital vaccine passports has raised serious questions concerning the erosion of civil liberties, as well as reinforcing structures of corporate-managed "surveillance capitalism" (Zuboff, 2019). Moreover, vaccine passports risked accentuating racialized mobility injustices given the unequal availability of vaccines within and across countries (Thrasher, 2021).

Such digital tracking and monitoring systems indicate a further shift in the dynamic relationship between mobility, borders and security; the intention is not merely to "make the world safe for tourism" but to ensure that citizens themselves can be deemed "safe for travel".

## Conclusion

Tourism mobility is intrinsic to modern citizenship and closely intertwined with the accumulation of political, civil, social and economic citizenship rights. In the Global North, tourism mobility is commonly conceived as involving the right to travel and the freedom of movement, synonymous with freedom of choice and the right to consume. Crucially, the rights and freedoms of mobility enjoyed by tourists are not commensurate with the rights of development and are thus contrary to discourses of "borderless worlds" and those proclaiming the benefits of globalization. Subsequently, the era of neoliberal globalization has witnessed increased demarcations between "desirable" and "undesirable" mobilities—as migration, once seen by rich nations as essential to economic growth, is now being perceived as a prevailing threat. Consequently, unequal mobilities have continued to transpire despite the rise of so-called "global citizens" and their worldly attempts to ensure more emancipated forms of tourism and travel. Globalization, which has seen the emergence of increasingly cosmopolitan and multi-ethnic societies, along with new stratifications of extreme wealth inequality, have heightened unequal mobility empowerments.

Restrictive and digitally enhanced bordering practices and securitization strategies are increasingly implicated in governing tourism mobilities. Moreover, a panoply of new, enhanced bordering technologies has been introduced in the wake of the pandemic, ostensibly to ensure seamless and "COVID-secure" forms of travel and sanitized destination business models. However, while border governance has become more technologically sophisticated, it has also become more discriminatory and politically motivated. Such technical forms of border management, introduced for the purpose of ensuring efficient travel and seamless border crossings (for some), may come at the expense of racialized and socially marginalized communities who may seek to enact their universal right to travel and freedom of movement but yet are confronted with movements that are fraught with fear and further restrictions on mobility. As this chapter affirms, the dehumanization involved at external and internal borders for politically vulnerable individuals and groups, equates to wider forms of exclusion from civic society. Bordering processes are also intrinsic to the production and reproduction of global tourism capitalism, implicating citizens and travellers into the tentacles of surveillance capitalism. As bordering becomes literally encoded into the movement of "safe" and "unsafe" bodies, the biopolitical economy of post-pandemic border governance will continue to accentuate and reconfigure the discursive framing and material geographies of travel and mobility injustice.

## Note

1 Not only are such terms as "migrant", "refugee" and "asylum seeker" used interchangeably by many media commentators, the precise political status of people seeking to cross international borders is not fixed and cannot be known *a priori*.

## References

Abrahamian, A. A. (2015). *The cosmopolites: The coming of the global citizen*. New York: Columbia Global Reports.
Addley, E., & Holpuch, A. (2015, December 22). US stops British Muslim family from boarding flight to visit Disneyland. *The Guardian*. https://www.theguardian.com/us-news/2015/dec/22/us-stops-british-muslim-family-flight-disneyland-david-cameron

AFP (Agence France Presse) (2016, August 19). Nice becomes latest French city to impose burkini ban. *The Guardian*. https://www.theguardian.com/world/2016/aug/19/nice-becomes-latest-french-city-to-impose-burkini-ban.

Ali, R. (2017, October 23). The anxieties of a Muslim traveller. *Skift*. https://skift.com/2017/10/23/the-anxieties-of-a-muslim-traveler/

Almeida, F. (2020). Security, terrorism and tourism in the Mediterranean. In E. Cañada (ed.) *Tourism in the geopolitics of the Mediterranean*, pp. 70–75. Barcelona: Alba Sud.

Balibar, E. (1991). Is there a "neo-racism"? In E. Balibar, & I. Wallerstein (eds.) *Race, nation and class: Ambiguous identities*, pp. 17–28. London: Verso.

Bauder, H. (2012). Open borders: A utopia? *Justice Spatiale – Spatial Justice*, 5. Online at: https://halshs.archives-ouvertes.fr/halshs-01518746/

Becklake, S. (2020). Touristic security: Interrogating an emerging security practice. In E. Cañada (ed.) *Tourism in the geopolitics of the Mediterranean*, pp. 76–81. Barcelona: Alba Sud.

Behsudi, A. (2020, April 9). Wish you were here. *IMF Finance and Development*. https://www.imf.org/external/pubs/ft/fandd/2020/12/impact-of-the-pandemic-on-tourism-behsudi.htm?utm_medium=email&utm_source=govdelivery#.X_98Xa8bHyU. linkedin.

Bianchi, R. V., & Stephenson, M. L. (2013). Deciphering tourism and citizenship in a globalized world. *Tourism Management*, 39, 10–20.

Bianchi, R. V., & Stephenson, M. L. (2014). *Tourism and citizenship: Rights, freedoms and responsibilities in the global order*. London: Routledge.

Bianchi, R. V., & Stephenson, M. L. (2019). Tourism, mobility rights and the fault-lines of global citizenship. In A. Paasi, E. Prokkola, J. Saarinen, & K. Zimmerbauer (eds.) *Borderless worlds – for whom? Ethics, moralities and (in)justices in mobilities*, pp. 123–138. London: Routledge.

Bianchi, R. V., Stephenson, M. L., & Hannam, K. (2020). The contradictory politics of the right to travel: Mobilities, borders and tourism. *Mobilities*, 15(2), 290–306.

Breakey, N., & Breakey, H. (2013). Is there a right to tourism? *Tourism Analysis*, 18(6), 739–748.

Brendon, P. (1991). *Thomas Cook: 150 years of popular tourism*. London: Secker & Warburg.

Brésillon, T. (2021, March 19). Tunis youth's lost future. *Le Monde Diplomatique*. https://mondediplo.com/2021/01/02tunisia

Britton, S.G. (1991). Tourism, capital and place: Towards a critical geography of tourism. *Environment and Planning D: Society and Space*, 9, 451–478.

Burstein, D. (1991). *Euroquake: Europe's explosive economic challenge will change the world*. New York: Simon and Schuster.

Butcher, J. (2017). Citizenship, global citizenship and volunteer tourism: A critical analysis. *Tourism Recreation Research*, 42(2), 129–138.

Butcher, J. (2020, May 4). The war on tourism. *Spiked*. https://www.spiked-online.com/2020/05/04/the-war-on-tourism/

Calori, A. (2015, October 12). From mare nostrum to triton, Europe's response to the Mediterranean crisis is little more than another budget cut. https://www.opendemocracy.net/en/can-europe-make-it/from-mare-nostrum-to-triton-europes-response-to-mediterranean-crisis/

Chambers, D., & Buzinde, C. (2015). Tourism and decolonisation: Locating research and self. *Annals of Tourism Research*, 51, 1–16.

Cision PR Newswire (2020a, June 8). Facial recognition market size to reach USD 9.99 billion by 2025: Valuates reports. https://www.prnewswire.com/news-releases/facial-recognition-market-size-to-reach-usd-9-99-billion-by-2025--valuates-reports-301071952.html

Cision PR Newswire (2020b, August 18). Demand for private aviation surges in response to COVID-19. https://www.prnewswire.com/news-releases/demand-for-private-aviation-surges-in-response-to-covid-19-301114071.html

Clarke, J., & Critcher, C. (1985). *The devil makes work: Leisure in capitalist Britain*. London: Macmillan.

Cohen, E., & Cohen, S. A. (2014). A mobilities approach to tourism from emerging world regions. *Current Issues in Tourism*, (18 April 6–7)(1), 11–43.

de Bellaigue, C. (2020, June 18). The end of tourism? *The Guardian*. https://www.theguardian.com/travel/2020/jun/18/end-of-tourism-coronavirus-pandemic-travel-industry?CMP=Share_iOSApp_Other

Endy, C. (2004). *Cold war holidays: American tourism in France*. Chapel Hill: University of North Carolina Press.

Engelhardt, T. (2015). We didn't ordain this constitution. *Le Monde Diplomatique*. https://mondediplo.com/2015/04/11usa

Evans, R. (2019, May 17). Half of England is owned by less than 1%'. *The Guardian*. https://www.theguardian.com/money/2019/apr/17/who-owns-england-thousand-secret-landowners-author

Eyres, H. (2021, February 24). Why Taiwan matters. *New Statesman*. https://www.newstatesman.com/world/asia/2021/02/why-taiwan-matters

Falk, R. (1994). The making of global citizenship. In B. Steenbergen (ed.) *The condition of citizenship*, pp.127–140. London: Sage.

Favell, A. (2001). Migration, mobility and globaloney: Metaphors and rhetoric in the sociology of globalization. *Global Networks*, 1(4), 389–98.

Fregonese, S., & Ramadan, A. (2015). Hotel geopolitics: A research agenda. *Geopolitics*, 20, 793–813.

García Gallo, B. (2015, April 27). Aguirre quiere sacar a los 'sin hogar' de la calle para impulsar el turismo. https://elpais.com/ccaa/2015/04/27/madrid/1430144657_879791.html

Gascón, J. (2019). Tourism as a right: A "frivolous claim" against degrowth? *Journal of Sustainable Tourism*, 27(12), 1825–1838.

Germann Molz, J. (2005). Getting a "flexible eye": Round-the-world travel and scales of cosmopolitan citizenship. *Citizenship Studies*, 9(5), 517–531.

Goldstone, P. (2001). *Making the world safe for travel*. New Haven: Yale University Press.

Gorsuch, A. E. (2013). *All this is your world: Soviet tourism at home and abroad after Stalin*. Oxford: Oxford University Press.

Gover, A. R., Harper, S. B., & Langton, L. (2020). Anti-Asian hate crime during the COVID-19 pandemic: Exploring the reproduction of inequality. *American Journal of Criminal Justice*, 45, 647–667.

Graham, S., & Wood, D. (2003). Digitizing surveillance: Categorization, space, inequality. *Critical Social Policy*, 23(2), 227–248.

Hannam, K., Sheller, M., & Urry. J. (2006). Editorial: Mobilities, immobilities and moorings. *Mobilities*, 1(1), 1–22.

Hazbun, W. (Forthcoming). Aviation, hijackings, and the eclipse of the 'American century' in the Middle East. In D. Bertrand Monk, & M. Sorkin (eds.) *Between catastrophe and revolution: Essays in honor of Mike Davis*. New York: Urban Research/OR Books.

Hickman, M., Thomas, L., Silvestri, S., & Nickels, H. (2011). *Suspect communities? Counter-terrorism policy, the press, and the impact on Irish and Muslim communities in Britain*. London: London Metropolitan University.

Higgins-Desbiolles. F. (2007). Hostile meeting grounds: Encounters between the wretched of the earth and the tourist through tourism and terrorism in the 21st century. In P. Burns, & M. Novelli (eds.) *Tourism and politics: Global frameworks and local realities*, pp. 309–332. Oxford: Elsevier.

Hilliar, A. (2020, December 28). Hundreds of British tourists escape quarantine in Swiss ski resort. *France24*. https://www.france24.com/en/europe/20201228-hundreds-of-british-tourists-escape-quarantine-in-swiss-ski-resort

Hirst, P., & Thomson, G. (1991). *Globalization in question* (2nd ed.). Cambridge: Polity.

Holmes, A. (2019, December 20). Facial-recognition technology has a racial-bias problem, according to a new landmark federal study. *Business Insider*. https://www.businessinsider.com/facial-recognition-racial-bias-federal-study-2019-12.

Isin, E.F., & Turner, B. S. (2007). Investigating citizenship: An agenda for citizenship studies. *Citizenship Studies*, 11(1), 5–17.

Isin, E. F., & Wood, P. (1999). *Citizenship and identity*. London: Sage.

Jamal, T., & Higham, J. (2021). Justice and ethics: Towards a new platform for tourism and sustainability. *Journal of Sustainable Tourism*, 29(2-3), 143–157.

Kaji, M. (2020, September 11). 300,000 seafarers still stuck on ships: We feel like hostages. *ABC News*. https://abcnews.go.com/Politics/300000-seafarers-stuck-ships-feel-hostages/story?id=72948111

Kassis, R. (2005). The Palestinians and justice tourism. In R. Solomon (ed.) *Pilgrimages for transformation. Proceedings of a Study Workshop on Interfaith Cooperation for Justice in the Occupied Territories – Human encounters for peace and reconciliation through tourism*, 21–24 October (31–36), Alexandria, Egypt.

Keeley, B. (2015). *Income inequality: The gap between rich and poor*. Paris: OECD Publishing.

Khan, A. (2021, January 22). American Muslims welcome the end of Trump's travel ban. *The Washington Post*. https://www.washingtonpost.com/gdprconsent/?next_url=https%3a%2f%2fwww.washingtonpost.com%2freligion%2fmuslim-travel-ban-end-trump-biden%2f2021%2f01%2f22%2fd09b42de-5c10-11eb-b8bd-ee36b1cd18bf_story.html

Lloyd, M. (2003). *The passport: The history of man's most travelled document*. Stroud: Sutton.

Luxus plus (2020, June 23). Economy: How Thailand plans to boost luxury tourism. https://luxus-plus.com/en/economy-how-thailand-plans-to-boost-luxury-tourism/

Mann, I. (2020, August 21). Border justice in the age of the pandemic. *Just Security*. https://www.justsecurity.org/72078/border-justice-in-the-age-of-pandemic/

Marshall, T.H. (1950 [1992]). Citizenship and social class. In T.H. Marshall, & T. Bottomore (eds.) *Citizenship and social class*, pp. 1–51. London: Pluto Press.

Mau, S. (2010). Mobility citizenship, inequality, and the liberal state: The case of visa policies. *International Political Sociology*, 4, 339–361.

Mittelmeir, J., Lim, M. A., & Lomer, S. (2020, October 6). Why international students are choosing the UK – despite coronavirus. *The Conversation*. https://theconversation.com/why-international-students-are-choosing-the-uk-despite-coronavirus-147064

Nkyi, E., & Hashimoto, A. (2015). Human rights issues in tourism development. In R. Sharpley, & D. J. Telfer (eds.) *Tourism and development: Concepts and issues* (2nd ed.), pp. 378–399. Bristol: Channel View Publications.

Nortajuddin, A. (2020, May 12). Hate and discrimination in a pandemic world. *The Asian Post*. https://theaseanpost.com/article/hate-and-discrimination-pandemic-world

O'Byrne, D.J. (2001). On passports and border controls. *Annals of Tourism Research*, 28(2), 399–416.

Ohmae, K. (1990). *The borderless world*. London: Collins.

Pattullo, P. (2006). *The ethical travel guide: Your passport to exciting alternative holidays*. London: Earthscan.

Pascoe, D. (2001). *Airspaces*. London: Reaktion Books.

Pratt, M.L. (1992). *Imperial eyes: Travel writing and transculturation*. London: Routledge.

Prokkola, E-K (2012). Neoliberalizing border management in Finland and Schengen. *Antipode*, 45(5), 1318–1336.

Reidy, M. (2020, June 29). Briefing: Coronavirus and the halting of asylum at the US-Mexico border. *The New Humanitarian*. https://www.thenewhumanitarian.org/news/2020/06/29/Mexico-US-coronavirus-mass-expulsions-asylum-halt

Rojek, C. (1998). Tourism and citizenship. *International Journal of Cultural Policy*, 4(2), 291–310.

Russell, R. V. (2003). Tourists and refugees: Coinciding sociocultural impacts. *Annals of Tourism Research*, 30(4), 833–846.

Salazar, N. (2021). Existential vs. essential mobilities: Insights from before, during and after a crisis. *Mobilities*, 16(1), 20–34.

Serra, A., & Leong, C. (2020, May 6). Here's what travelling could be like after COVID-19'. *World Economic Forum*. https://www.weforum.org/agenda/2020/05/this-is-what-travelling-will-be-like-after-covid-19/

Shaban, A. (ed.) (2018). *Lives of Muslims in India: Politics, exclusion and violence*. London: Taylor & Francis.

Sharma, A. (2020, April 15). Coronavirus hits Maldivesà lucrative tourism industry. https://www.dw.com/en/coronavirus-hits-maldives-lucrative-tourism-industry/a-53131198

Sheller, M. (2018). *Mobility justice: The politics of movement in an age of extremes*. London: Verso.

Silver, L., Delvin K., & Huang, C. (2020, October 6). Unfavourable views of China reach historic highs in many countries: Majorities say China has handled COVID-19 outbreak poorly. *Pew Research Centre: Global Attitudes and Trends*. https://www.pewresearch.org/global/2020/10/06/unfavorable-views-of-china-reach-historic-highs-in-many-countries/

South Pacific Travel Organisation (2021, February 26). Covid-19: Kiwis should expect to pay more for Pacific travel when borders reopen – experts. https://corporate.southpacificislands.travel/covid-19-kiwis-should-expect-to-pay-more-for-pacific-travel-when-borders-reopen-experts/

Stephenson, M.L. (2006). Travel and the freedom of movement: Racialised encounters and experiences amongst ethnic minority tourists in the EU. *Mobilities*, 1(2), 285–306.

Streeck, W. (2012). Citizens as consumers: Consideration of the new politics of consumption. *New Left Review*, 76, 27–47.

Sundstrom, R.R., & Kim, D. H. (2014). Xenophobia and racism. *Critical Philosophy of Race*, 2(1), 20–45.

Thompson, J. (2001). Planetary citizenship: The definition and defence of an ideal. In J. Thompson (ed.) *Governing for the environment*, pp. 135–146. London: Palgrave Macmillan.

Thrasher, S. W. (2021, April 7). Global vaccine equity is much more important than 'vaccine passports'. *Scientific American*. https://www.scientificamerican.com/article/global-vaccine-equity-is-much-more-important-than-vaccine-passports/

Timothy, D. J. (2000). Borderlands: An unlikely tourist destination? *IBRU Boundary and Security Bulletin*, 8(1), 57–65.

Torabian, P., & Miller, M. C. (2017). Freedom of movement for all? Unpacking racialized travel experiences. *Current Issues in Tourism*, 20(9), 931–945.

Torpey, J. (2000). *The invention of the passport: Surveillance citizenship and the state.* Cambridge: Cambridge University Press.

*Travel Weekly* (2017, February 16). Closing borders risks jobs. World Travel & Tourism Council. https://www.travelweekly.com.au/article/closing-borders-risks-jobs-world-travel-tourism-council/

Tuathail, G.Ó. (1999). Borderless worlds? Problematising discourses of deterritorialisation. *Geopolitics*, 4(2), 139–154.

UNWTO (2017, September 20). *Framework convention on tourism ethics.* Madrid: World Tourism Organization. https://www.unwto.org/ethics-convention

UNWTO (WTO) (1999). *Global code of ethics for tourism.* Madrid: World Tourism Organization.

Urry, J. (1995). *Consuming places.* London: Routledge.

Vaughan-Williams, N. (2012). *Border politics: The limits of sovereign power.* Edinburgh: Edinburgh University Press.

Vergnano, C. (2019). Refugees and tourist: The two faces of Mediterranean geopolitics. In Cañada, E. (ed.) *Tourism in the geopolitics of the Mediterranean*, pp. 82–85. Barcelona: Alba Sud.

Walters, W. (2006). Border/control. *European Journal of Social Theory*, 92, 187–203.

Wang, Z. (2021). From crisis to nationalism? The conditioned effects of the COVID-19 crisis on neo-nationalism in Europe. *Chinese Political Science Review*, 6, 20–39.

Weaver, A. (2008). When tourists become data: Consumption surveillance and commerce. *Current Issues in Tourism*, 11(1), 1–23.

Withnall, A. (2017, January 30). UN denounces Trump's travel ban as 'mean-spirited' and illegal under human rights law. *The Independent.* http://www.independent.co.uk/news/world/americas/donald-trump-muslim-travel-ban-illegal-un-rights-chief-a7552991.html

Yong, C. (2021, January 5). S'porean student punched in London: Attach by 15-year-old was racially motivated, says British court. *The Straits Times.* https://www.straitstimes.com/singapore/15-year-olds-attack-on-singaporean-student-in-london-a-racially-motivated-one-says-british

Zuboff, S. (2019). *The age of surveillance capitalism.* London: Profile Books.

# 7
# HOW SPACE, BORDERS AND BOUNDARIES SHAPE BIODIVERSITY VALUES

*Martin Dallimer and Niels Strange*

## Introduction

Nature-based tourism relies on high-quality natural environments, well-functioning ecosystems that are aesthetically pleasing and which support rare, charismatic or particularly abundant species. Such phenomena attract visitors locally, regionally within a country and internationally. Nature-based tourism is a major generator of regional income, and the fact that visitors are often willing to pay substantial amounts to experience natural phenomena indicates that the use values people hold for the natural world can be substantial and can transcend socio-political borders and boundaries. Indeed, for many people, travelling across borders is the only way to see particular species, habitats or ecosystems. Further, even those who will never experience certain species directly, often hold substantial non-use values associated with simply knowing that a species or national park exists.

Paralleling the cross-border values people hold for biodiversity, managing the ecosystems that support diverse species assemblages, or indeed individual species themselves, through effective conservation efforts, is also intimately linked with the presence and type of borders and boundaries. Biodiversity, natural resources and ecosystems rarely respect, or coincide with, human-imposed political boundaries (Dallimer & Strange, 2015; but see Arrondo et al., 2018 for counter examples). Nevertheless, these boundaries can have a profound impact on biodiversity conservation. This is true for boundaries at increasing spatial scales (e.g., land management decisions by private individuals, protected area designation and regional or international political borders).

The actions and decisions of private individuals are central to the persistence of many species (e.g., Dallimer et al., 2009; Reeson et al., 2011). Species of conservation concern are frequently found on privately owned land (Groves et al., 2000; Hanley et al., 2012), much of which is managed for reasons other than protecting biodiversity. Establishing protected areas is a tool that is frequently used to help address some of the unpredictability associated with how individuals manage their own parcels of land (Gaston et al., 2008; Myers et al., 2000; Rodrigues et al., 2004). Protected areas have become central to biodiversity conservation and often form the backbone of tourist activities associated with the natural world and how humankind values ecosystems. Indeed, the fiscal value of human benefits from ecosystems has been estimated to be more than USD125 trillion per year, greater than the total global gross domestic product (Costanza et al., 2014). A substantial part of this value is related to recreational and cultural services in protected areas. For instance, between 2009 and 2019, 100 million visits were made to national parks in England (Natural England, 2019). Similarly, the Great Barrier Reef in Australia, one the world's largest coral reef ecosystems, is not only an important marine hotspot of biodiversity but also has the highest per hectare use value for tourism and recreation (Costanza et al., 2014; see Farr et al. 2014 for a review of estimates). Global coverage by protected areas is impressive, at over 20 million km$^2$ (Gaston et al., 2008), and recent efforts to meet the Aichi Biodiversity Targets means that around 15% of the global land area is covered by protected areas (Visconti et al., 2019).

Although protected areas offer many benefits for biodiversity conservation, drawbacks remain and their overall effectiveness in terms of shielding species and habitats that are at risk from extinction or human exploitation is debated (Maxwell et al., 2020). One particular challenge is that protected areas are fixed in space and time (Rayfield et al., 2008). Where the targets of conservation are not stationary, it is unlikely that the protected area will be effective. Species movements, for example, are generally not considered in the design of protected areas (Powell & Bjork, 2004). Similarly, both international (Opermanis et al., 2012) and domestic provincial borders (Opermanis et al., 2013) can affect the coherence of a network of protected areas if the designation of sites on either side of a border is not coordinated at a larger scale. Most assessments of threats to biodiversity are not carried out in a coordinated manner. This can result in conflicting prioritizations at different spatial scales. Across the Carpathian region many species have been assigned to high threat categories within each country, but at the biogeographical level, they were assigned to lower risk categories, while in the European Alps, certain plant species have been assigned to different risk categories in neighbouring countries (Gentili et al. 2011), and a similar situation exists on the USA–Canada border with regard to certain fish and mammal species (Timothy, 1999). In these situations, a high priority may be given to a species that is atypical and rare in a certain country, even if the species is widespread and common in neighbouring countries. Differing cross-border treatments of species may therefore play a disproportionately strong role in choosing which areas to protect (Erasmus et al., 1999). Scholars agree that increased cooperation on biodiversity conservation across international borders within the EU would enhance the region's conservation outcomes (Opermanis et al., 2012, 2013).

Some species, such as those that are highly mobile or migratory, require coordinated management across properties and habitats. In some cases, coordination may only be needed across spatially adjacent habitats or properties (e.g., Dallimer et al., 2012), but frequently coordination will be required in areas that are separated by large distances and dispersed across many owners, regions or nation states. Long-distance migratory species can be seen as a special case of mobile animals. Migrants are crucially dependent on international collaboration for their protection, and it is perhaps for that reason that many migratory species are endangered (Wilcove & Wikelski, 2008).

The habitats that migratory species require throughout their annual cycles expose them to varied environmental conditions and threats (Norris et al., 2004; Sanderson et al., 2006; Wilson et al., 2011). This means that their management can be particularly challenging (Runge et al., 2017). Where species are highly mobile, such as long-distance migrants, protecting their entire range is not feasible owing to costs, competing land uses and the constraints of geopolitical boundaries (Milner-Gulland et al., 2011). Migratory animals are similarly at risk, even when they attract large numbers of visitors, including wildebeest in the Maasai Mara in Kenya and Tanzania, monarch butterflies in Mexico and North America, and the passage of raptors in southern Europe.

In this chapter we describe why economics and values are important for biodiversity. We go on to examine how the presence of boundaries and physical distance can help us understand the values that people hold for biodiversity. Finally, we present some conclusions regarding the role of trans-boundary tourism in biodiversity conservation.

## How Can Understanding Economics and Values Help Biodiversity Conservation?

Economics is recognized as an important part of environmental decision-making and is therefore particularly relevant given that motivations for promoting tourism activities are usually based on financial gain. Environmental threats and human behaviour are closely linked to economic interests (Shogren et al., 1999). The degradation of ecosystems and loss of biodiversity have a measurable adverse impact on human well-being. Designing policies and creating incentives for promoting the protection of environmental and biodiversity values requires economic considerations and an understanding of human behaviour. Frequently, policies are bounded by limited budgets, and decisions need to compare the costs and benefits of intervention.

Although there are pluralistic views on the values and benefits (e.g., utilitarian, relational, ethical) people obtain from ecosystems (MEA, 2005; Pascual et al., 2017), environmental valuation is frequently applied in order to allow for comparison with other goods. Such values, and associated perceptions, often then frame policies and allocations of conservation investments. Spatial heterogeneity and patterns of values may play an important role in understanding incentives for local and global support for conservation, including in transboundary contexts, not least because how people value biodiversity may vary or change across borders and boundaries.

Biodiversity, habitats and ecosystem conservation is generally considered as a public good (Deke, 2008). In most contexts, consumptive or non-consumptive values held for biodiversity are non-excludable and non-rivalrous. This means that individuals cannot be excluded from using or receiving benefits from nature without paying for it, and use by one individual does not reduce availability to others. In some situations, benefits can be experienced independently of where the biodiversity itself is located. For instance, people living at considerable distances from where particularly charismatic species are found can value the preservation of those species from afar (Wang et al., 2018). In contrast, geographical distance may matter, in that people might value local biodiversity more highly than that found elsewhere (Dallimer et al., 2015). In such cases, biodiversity is not a pure public good but a rather impure, or quasi-private, public good (Perrings & Gadgil, 2003). In such cases, people are likely to hold use values, such as those derived from visiting biodiverse local landscapes.

## Spatial Variation in Biodiversity Values

Given the central role of economic value, it is important to have a more complete understanding of how people's values for biodiversity vary spatially. For instance, we know that biodiversity can have local use value (i.e., important to those living near, or with, particular species), as well as global value, which may have a non-use value, such as the value placed on the existence of rare, charismatic or threatened species, even if those species will never be experienced directly. These values are not merely reflected as a continuum from local to global but are framed by a range of spatially and socio-culturally constructed spaces and boundaries.

Use values might be expected to depend on the spatial context and the geographical distance to the site of biodiversity, such as a national park or nature-based tourism location

(Bateman et al., 2006). The question is if geographical distance would also impact non-use values, from which utility may be derived even without being present at, or living nearby, the site. International borders may also impact people's values of a particular site, either by limiting access or by socially or culturally representing it as part of their national identity. Here we describe some exemplar studies on distance decay and the importance of borders in our understanding of how values vary.

## International Borders Can Determine Values Held for Biodiversity

Managing ecosystem services frequently requires coordination across international borders, which often delivers greater conservation gains than countries acting alone. However, evidence regarding whether the public supports such an international approach remains mixed. For instance, the public does have strong preferences regarding where investments for conservation should take place, perhaps especially when those investments are at least in part aimed at increasing recreational and tourist visits to a particular area, such as through the establishment of new national parks (Jacobsen & Thorsen, 2010). In contrast, using the same questionnaire in three countries, public preferences for ecosystem service delivered in home countries and across international borders were quantified by Dallimer et al. (2015). In all three countries, Denmark, Poland and Estonia, respondents were generally willing to pay for improved ecosystem service delivery. However, ecosystem services with a use element, such that respondents might reasonably expect that they might themselves visit a site and experience the result of any improvements, such as habitat conservation and landscape preservation, attracted a patriotic premium. In other words, people were willing to pay significantly more for locally delivered services. This suggests that there is a limit to which the efficiency gains associated with managing ecosystem services at supranational levels would be supported by the general public (Dallimer et al., 2015). This study was based on a little-known habitat (semi-natural grasslands) within a relatively constrained region (northern Europe) that shares several common institutions and many cultural similarities. However, evidence regarding the value that people have for conservation across borders can span huge distances and bridge substantial cultural differences. For instance, according to one study, residents of China were willing to pay up to USD23.88 per household per year for hypothetical projects aimed at conserving the African elephant thousands of kilometres distant from where they live (Wang et al., 2018) (see Figure 7.1).

In all these cases, there is no requirement for conservation efforts to be coordinated internationally, as the environmental goods themselves were not directly shared between the study countries. Thus, management efforts elsewhere do not directly influence the quality of public goods available in the respondents' home country. However, for some elements of the natural world, such as migratory species, or tracts of habitat and river catchments (e.g. Allan et al., 2019) that span borders, the opposite is true in that coordination is almost a prerequisite of successful environmental management.

Transboundary protected areas are now a common and widespread tool that is used to protect and manage tracts of land that span international boundaries. Although these protected areas do generate conservation benefits, there is still only a limited understanding of how people living on either side of those international borders might value, and therefore experience an economic benefit from, such transboundary protected areas. For instance, Bialowieza Forest is shared by Poland and Belarus. In Poland in particular, the presence of what is described as the last remnant of primeval undisturbed forest in Europe draws substantial numbers of tourists. A discrete choice experiment in both countries (Valasiuk et al., 2017) demonstrated that there was a near universal preference for conserving the forest land within respondents' own country. However, while

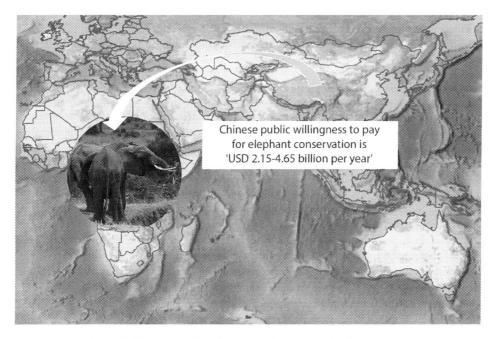

*Figure 7.1* People may hold non-use values for conservation in countries far away.

(adapted from Wang et al. 2018) (inserted Elephant picture: Neil D. Burgess)

Polish respondents were willing to pay to increase the area under conservation management, those in Belarus were happy with the current area under protection. Further, evidence showed that some respondents were not willing to pay for collaborative or coordinated conservation efforts spanning the two countries. This finding suggested that perhaps residents did not view the forest as a shared, bilateral public good. Therefore, despite the clear conservation benefits that would accrue if the forest were managed as a single, cross-border habitat, the strict division of the forest by the international boundary perhaps better reflects a lack of support for a more coordinated approach to managing and protecting this important natural asset.

The persistence of migratory species depends on the appropriate management of habitat quality across a large area, inevitably involving several different countries. Ensuring the long-term conservation of the monarch butterfly (*Danaus plexippus*) is complex because its migratory behaviour crosses international boundaries and depends on multiple regions and habitat types within the countries the species occupies. In the United States, through which the butterfly passes, residents were willing to pay significant amounts, equivalent to one-time payments totalling USD4.78–6.64 billion on growing plant species that were beneficial for the butterfly (Diffendorfer et al., 2014), demonstrating considerable support for conserving this lepidopteran. However, people's conservation interests seem to be centred only on conservation actions in their home country. Given the dependence of the monarch on vulnerable roosting sites in Mexico, even considerable investments in butterfly habitats and plants might not result in increased population sizes. Further work on the value of the butterfly does, however, suggest that a large proportion of residents in Canada and the United States are willing to pay for conservation efforts that take place outside of their own countries, suggesting that transnational conservation initiatives for this iconic and culturally important species would likely garner considerable support (Solis-Sosa et al., 2019).

A similar pattern emerges for another migratory species in North America, the northern pintail duck. This migratory waterfowl provides human and environmental benefits, such as recreational hunting and nutrient transfer, and its habitat spans the borders of Mexico, the United States and Canada. One study demonstrates that across all three countries, willingness to pay to protect pintail habitats is highest in the respondents' own country, but that respondents also attach a substantial value to the pintail's habitat in the other two countries (Haefele et al., 2019). Willingness to pay also varied substantially between the three countries. This theme of difference between countries was mirrored by work carried out on the migratory raptor, Montagu's harrier (*Circus pygargus*), which moves between West Africa and northern Europe. In an economic lab experiment Vogdrup-Schmidt et al. (2019) revealed the complexity of how donations for conservation varied between different countries. In Denmark and Ghana, participants in the experiment contributed more when pre-donation information stressed that transnational collaboration is needed, and when they were told that a portion of their donation would be forwarded to participants in other countries. In Spain, participants donated less overall and were insensitive to the information provided to them (Figure 7.2). What these studies share in common is that citizens generally value conservation efforts beyond their national borders, even if those values are lower than for conservation closer to home. The concept of a "patriotic premium" and the role of borders in shaping how people value the natural world is, therefore, likely to be universal.

## How Important Is Physical Distance in Determining Values for Biodiversity?

As mentioned above, conservation biodiversity and habitats may contribute co-benefits (e.g., cultural or regulating ecosystem services) to beneficiaries who live nearby. Several studies have found values of biodiversity conservation and other environmental goods to be distance-dependent (Bateman et al. 2006; Hanley et al. 2003; Nielsen et al. 2016; Schaafsma et al. 2013). However, distance and the effects of national borders may influence people's values simultaneously. Bakhtiari et al. (2018) disentangled these two separate effects and estimated individuals' marginal willingness to pay for comparable biodiversity conservation measures and outcomes across state borders, and with different distances from their place of residence to comparable conservation locations in Denmark and in southern Sweden. The locations are similar in terms of climate, geology, vegetation and biodiversity, thereby allowing this study to distinguish the effect of distance from the effect of country of residence versus country where the biodiversity is located. The study finds a clear and distinguishable effect of both country of residence and where the biodiversity is located. Even though Swedes and Danes share similar distance and transport costs to the conservation sites, and in principle should be indifferent, they clearly prefer biodiversity protection within their own countries.

Distance effects are not always straightforward to interpret, and simple patterns may be confounded by the availability of substitute sites, which are locations that provide similar benefits but are in closer proximity. For instance, in a study of public willingness to pay for rural landscape improvement measures in Ireland, Campbell et al. (2009) found a significantly lower level of support for protecting "mountain land", "stonewalls", "farm tidiness" and "cultural heritage" in rural western Ireland, compared to urban people's support. Similarly, Schaafsma et al. (2013) investigated people's willingness to pay for water-based recreation activities. They were able to distinguish distance decay effects but found that the strength of these effects varied among sites and between participants, with individuals who regularly undertook water recreation being willing to pay more than those who did not. These studies suggest that proximity to, and use of, high quality natural environments are both important determinants of likely

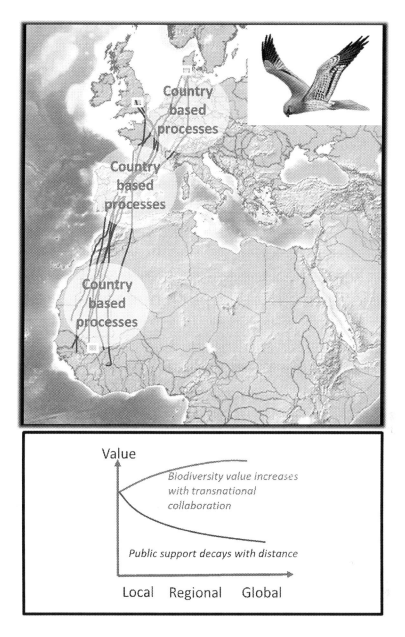

*Figure 7.2* International collaboration is crucial for conservation of migratory species such as the Montagu's Harrier. However, public support may be greater for local conservation initiatives than global ones.

(Adapted from Vogdrup-Schmidt et al. 2019)

public support for biodiversity conservation. Given that most high-quality natural environments are at some distance from the towns and cities where people live, public support for protecting these areas might be lower than support for the retention and conservation of nearby sites and potentially of lower conservation value.

## Implications for Biodiversity Conservation and Nature-based Tourism

Biodiversity values clearly demonstrate spatial variability. We can go some way to understanding these variations by ensuring that any approach to measuring and modelling value explicitly considers the key concept of distance decay and the important role of socio-political boundaries. However, if we wish in some way to operationalize these values to enhance ecological conservation, or the provision of protected areas by, for example, leveraging additional funding and financing, then certain core principles should be considered.

### *Knowledge Sharing and Capacity Building*

A first step in establishing transboundary policies at larger spatial scales may be to increase knowledge and capacity building to highlight the need for transboundary collaboration, not least to identify the mutual benefits stakeholders may gain from such collaboration. This may spur discussions between countries, or other geopolitical units, regarding potential benefits and associated mechanisms for collaboration. Indeed, recent assessments of the importance of biodiversity and ecosystem services (IPBES, 2019) emphasize that value is multi-dimensional, and that the importance of different dimensions of value will alter between countries, regions and human populations. To date, however, most decisions regarding implementing transboundary policies are made without the inclusion, or awareness, of the consequences for economic and non-economic values. The studies presented in this chapter have largely been carried out for research purposes. Moving this type of knowledge and expertise into the early stages of transboundary policy development may improve the likelihood that such policies are successful.

### *Finance and Payments*

In many cases, the costs of biodiversity conservation and establishing and managing protected areas are borne locally, while the benefits accrue internationally. Recreational and tourism benefits from migratory species represent one such case. The benefits people may receive from a migratory species at any location depends not only on suitable environmental conditions at a given location but also along its entire migratory route. A framework around spatial subsidies has been suggested to quantify the difference between the socioeconomic benefits supported by a location but received elsewhere and the socioeconomic benefits received at a specific location but supported by other areas (Bagstad et al., 2019; López-Hoffman et al., 2017; Semmens et al., 2018). A mismatch in the spatial distribution of costs and benefits can mean that conservation initiatives are not supported by local populations and can fail, or be less effective than originally envisaged. Transboundary incentive schemes and foundations may promote collaboration. International and neutral NGOs may be suitable handling institutions for collecting donations and allocating funds for conservation projects at the local level along the entire migratory route (e.g., BirdLife International Flyway programmes) or international institutions such as the EU Natura 2000 network of conservation areas.

There can, however, still be mismatches between locations that provide biodiversity conservation and the beneficiaries of that conservation. These mismatches can potentially exacerbate existing human–wildlife conflicts. One such example is large predator conservation. The protection of large predators is often supported by urban populations, but in most cases these supporters live some distance from the centres of conflict and where costs are borne. Recent returns of the wolf after 200 years to northern and western Europe (e.g., Denmark, Germany and the Netherlands) has created divergent public opinions (Drenthen, 2015). Wolves killing livestock have left farmers frustrated and the general public split between whether they should welcome the wolf or not. Differences in perceptions may reflect differences between urban and rural notions of environmental identity and views of the human–nature relationship (Drenthen, 2015). Designing spatial incentive schemes on the basis of quantified costs and benefits seems appealing for the conservation of charismatic species such as lions, leopards, elephants and rhinos, which are also important for tourism and the economy (Naidoo & Adamowicz, 2005; Okello et al., 2008).

## *International Agreements*

There is a need to develop strong international agreements that bind countries to protect diverse ecosystems and their associated biodiversity, even when doing so requires potentially complex multinational compacts. Transboundary governance can be motivated by presenting win–win arguments, such as protecting wide-ranging charismatic species that inhabit more than one country, or an intact habitat straddling national borders that attract tourists to multiple countries. These agreements may prioritize the protection of threatened species and habitats and establish special areas of interest for tourism. This would require multi-level governance and vertical coordination at supranational levels, as well as horizontal coordination at the subnational level. Examples of related supranational agreements include the EU's Birds Directive, which coordinates the protection of listed threatened and migratory ornithological species across EU member states. Bilateral or multilateral agreements require national conservation legislation within individual state borders to ensure compliance with the transboundary agreements. However, signing and enforcing agreements may be compromised by national interests, such as natural resource exploitation (Timothy, 1999, 2006). Setting up international biodiversity credit systems or some kind of economic transfer system between coordinating countries may be a pathway to building stronger international agreements.

## Conclusions

High quality natural environments and the biodiversity they support offer many human benefits, including both use and non-use values associated with their conservation and preservation. These values vary spatially, and the reasons for this variation are complex and include the effects of distance decay, the availability of substitutes and the presence of international or other socio-political borders and boundaries. Nevertheless, it is clear that the benefits from conserving biodiversity are experienced far more widely than are any associated costs, such as loss of livelihood options or conflicts. What is less clear is the extent to which it might be possible to utilize our understanding of how values for biodiversity vary geographically in designing and implementing mechanisms to support biodiversity protection.

Although the benefits of international tourism for biodiversity conservation have been debated (e.g., Hausmann et al., 2017; Wei et al., 2018), there is clearly an opportunity to transfer revenue from international and domestic tourism to those responsible for, or who bear the costs of, nature conservation. However, tourism may not be a reliable way of transferring "value" from the global marketplace to local places that rely on a tourism economy. In such cases, when tourists leave, the financial support for local communities is no longer in place. Tourism and values are volatile. Changes in travel patterns and demand, as well as perceptions of local versus global values, are unreliable. Ensuring that other mechanisms, such as formal international agreements, are in place makes biodiversity conservation management more robust and less subject to shocks.

## References

Allan, J.R., Levin, N., Jones, K.R., Abdullah, S., Hongoh, J., Hermoso, V., & Kark, S. (2019). Navigating the complexities of coordinated conservation along the river Nile. *Science Advances*, *5*(4), eaau7668.

Arrondo, E., Moleón, M., Cortés-Avizanda, A., Jiménez, J., Beja, P., Sánchez-Zapata, J.A., & Donázar, J. A. (2018). Invisible barriers: Differential sanitary regulations constrain vulture movements across country borders. *Biological Conservation*, *219*, 46–52.

Bagstad, K.J., Semmens, D.J., Diffendorfer, J.E., Mattsson, B.J., Dubovsky, J., Thogmartin, W.E., Wiederholt, R., Loomis, J., Bieri, J.A., Sample, C., Goldstein, J., & Lopez-Hoffman, L. (2019). Ecosystem service flows from a migratory species: Spatial subsidies of the northern pintail. *Ambio*, *48*, 61–73.

Bakhtiari, F., Jacobsen, J.B., Thorsen, B.J., Lundhede, T.H., Strange, N., & Boman, M. (2018). Disentangling distance and country effects on the value of conservation across national borders. *Ecological Economics*, *147*, 11–20.

Bateman, I.J., Day, B.H., Georgiou, S., & Lake, I. (2006). The aggregation of environmental benefit values: Welfare measures, distance decay and total WTP. *Ecological Economics*, *60*(2), 450–460.

Campbell, D., Hutchinson, W.G., & Scarpa, R. (2009). Using choice experiments to explore the spatial distribution of willingness to pay for rural landscape improvements. *Environment and Planning A*, *41*(1), 97–111.

Costanza, R., De Groot, R., Sutton, P., Van der Ploeg, S., Anderson, S. J., Kubiszewski, I., … Turner, R. K. (2014). Changes in the global value of ecosystem services. *Global Environmental Change*, *26*, 152–158.

Dallimer, M., Acs, S., Hanley, N., Wilson, P., Gaston, K.J., & Armsworth, P.R. (2009). What explains property-level variation in avian diversity? An inter-disciplinary approach. *Journal of Applied Ecology*, *46*(3), 647–656.

Dallimer, M., Skinner, A.M., Davies, Z.G., Armsworth, P.R., & Gaston, K.J. (2012). Multiple habitat associations: The role of offsite habitat in determining onsite avian density and species richness. *Ecography*, *35*(2), 134–145.

Dallimer, M., Jacobsen, J.B., Lundhede, T.H., Takkis, K., Giergiczny, M., & Thorsen, B.J. (2015). Patriotic values for public goods: Transnational trade-offs for biodiversity and ecosystem services? *Bioscience*, *65*(1), 33–42.

Dallimer, M., & Strange, N. (2015). Why socio-political borders and boundaries matter in conservation. *Trends in Ecology & Evolution*, *30*(3), 132–139.

Deke, O. (2008). *Environmental policy instruments for conserving global biodiversity*. Berlin: Springer Science & Business Media.

Diffendorfer, J.E., Loomis, J.B., Ries, L., Oberhauser, K., Lopez-Hoffman, L., Semmens, D., & Thogmartin, W. E. (2014). National valuation of monarch butterflies indicates an untapped potential for incentive-based conservation. *Conservation Letters*, *7*(3), 253–262.

Drenthen, M. (2015). The return of the wild in the Anthropocene: Wolf resurgence in the Netherlands. *Ethics, Policy & Environment*, *18*(3), 318–337.

Erasmus, B.F., Freitag, S., Gaston, K.J., Erasmus, B.H., & Jaarsveld, A.S.V. (1999). Scale and conservation planning in the real world. *Proceedings of the Royal Society of London. Series B: Biological Sciences*, *266*(1417), 315–319.

Farr, M., Stoeckl, N., & Beg, R.A. (2014). The non-consumptive (tourism) 'value' of marine species in the northern section of the Great Barrier Reef. *Marine Policy*, *43*, 89–103.

Gaston, K.J., Jackson, S.F., Nagy, A., Cantú-Salazar, L., & Johnson, M. (2008). Protected areas in Europe: Principle and practice. *Annals of the New York Academy of Sciences*, *1134*(1), 97–119.

Gentili, R., Rossi, G., Abeli, T., Bedini, G., & Foggi, B. (2011). Assessing extinction risk across borders: Integration of a biogeographical approach into regional IUCN assessment? *Journal for Nature Conservation*, *19*(2), 69–71.

Groves, C.R., Kutner, L.S., Stoms, D.M., Murray, M.P., Scott, J.M., Schafale, M., Weakley, A.S., & Pressey, R.L. (2000). Owning up to our responsibilities: Who owns lands important for biodiversity? In B. Stein, L.S. Kutner, & J.S. Adams (eds) *Precious heritage*, pp. 275–300. New York: Oxford University Press.

Haefele, M.A., Loomis, J.B., Lien, A.M., Dubovsky, J.A., Merideth, R.W., Bagstad, K.J., Huang, T.K., Mattsson, B.J., Semmens, D.J., Thogmartin, W.E., Wiederholt, R., Diffendorfer, J.E., & Lopez-Hoffman, L. (2019). Multi-country willingness to pay for transborder migratory species conservation: A case study of northern pintails. *Ecological Economics*, *157*, 321–331.

Hanley, N., MacMillan, D., Patterson, I., & Wright, R.E. (2003). Economics and the design of nature conservation policy: A case study of wild goose conservation in Scotland using choice experiments. *Animal Conservation Forum*, *6*(2), 123–129.

Hanley, N., Banerjee, S., Lennox, G.D., & Armsworth, P.R. (2012). How should we incentivize private landowners to 'produce' more biodiversity? *Oxford Review of Economic Policy*, *28*(1), 93–113.

Hausmann, A., Slotow, R., Fraser, I., & Di Minin, E. (2017). Ecotourism marketing alternative to charismatic megafauna can also support biodiversity conservation. *Animal Conservation*, *20*(1), 91–100.

IPBES (2019). *Global assessment report on biodiversity and ecosystem services*. Bonn: Intergovernmental Science-Policy Platform on Biodiversity and Ecosystem Services.

Jacobsen, J.B., & Thorsen, B.J. (2010). Preferences for site and environmental functions when selecting forthcoming national parks. *Ecological Economics*, *69*(7), 1532–1544.

López-Hoffman, L., Chester, C.C., Semmens, D.J., Thogmartin, W.E., Rodríguez-McGoffin, M.S., Merideth, R., & Diffendorfer, J.E. (2017). Ecosystem services from transborder migratory species: Implications for conservation governance. *Annual Review of Environment and Resources*, *42*, 509–539.

Maxwell, S.L., Cazalis, V., Dudley, N., Hoffmann, M., Rodrigues, A.S., Stolton, S., Visconti, P., Woodley, S., Kingston, N., Lewis, E., Maron, M., Strassburg, B.B.N., Wenger, A., Jonas, H.D., Venter, O., & Watson, J.E.M. (2020). Area-based conservation in the twenty-first century. *Nature*, *586*(7828), 217–227.

MEA (2005). *Ecosystems and human well-being: Synthesis report*. Washington, DC: Island Press.

Milner-Gulland, E.J., Fryxell, J.M., & Sinclair, A.R.E.E. (2011). *Animal migration: A synthesis*. Oxford: Oxford University Press.

Myers, N., Mittermeier, R.A., Mittermeier, C.G., Da Fonseca, G.A., & Kent, J. (2000). Biodiversity hotspots for conservation priorities. *Nature*, *403*(6772), 853–858.

Naidoo, R., & Adamowicz, W.L. (2005). Economic benefits of biodiversity exceed costs of conservation at an African rainforest reserve. *Proceedings of the National Academy of Sciences*, *102*(46), 16712–16716.

Natural England (2019). *Monitor of engagement with the natural environment – The national survey on people and the natural environment headline report 2019*. Peterborough: Natural England.

Nielsen, A.S.E., Lundhede, T.H., & Jacobsen, J.B. (2016). Local consequences of national policies: A spatial analysis of preferences for forest access reduction. *Forest Policy and Economics*, *73*, 68–77.

Norris, D.R., Marra, P.P., Kyser, T.K., Sherry, T.W., & Ratcliffe, L.M. (2004). Tropical winter habitat limits reproductive success on the temperate breeding grounds in a migratory bird. *Proceedings of the Royal Society of London. Series B: Biological Sciences*, *271*(1534), 59–64.

Okello, M.M., Manka, S.G., & D'Amour, D.E. (2008). The relative importance of large mammal species for tourism in Amboseli National Park, Kenya. *Tourism Management*, *29*(4), 751–760.

Opermanis, O., MacSharry, B., Aunins, A., & Sipkova, Z. (2012). Connectedness and connectivity of the Natura 2000 network of protected areas across country borders in the European Union. *Biological Conservation*, *153*, 227–238.

Opermanis, O., MacSharry, B., Evans, D., & Sipkova, Z. (2013). Is the connectivity of the Natura 2000 network better across internal or external administrative borders? *Biological Conservation*, *166*, 170–174.

Pascual, U., Balvanera, P., Díaz, S., Pataki, G., Roth, E., Stenseke, M., & Yagi, N. (2017). Valuing nature's contributions to people: The IPBES approach. *Current Opinion in Environmental Sustainability*, *26*, 7–16.

Perrings C., & Gadgil M. (2003). Conserving biodiversity: Reconciling local and global public benefits. In I. Kaul (ed) *Providing global public goods*, pp. 532–555. Oxford: Oxford University Press.

Powell, G.V., & Bjork, R.D. (2004). Habitat linkages and the conservation of tropical biodiversity as indicated by seasonal migrations of Three-wattled Bellbirds. *Conservation Biology*, *18*(2), 500–509.

Rayfield, B., James, P.M., Fall, A., & Fortin, M.J. (2008). Comparing static versus dynamic protected areas in the Quebec boreal forest. *Biological Conservation*, *141*(2), 438–449.

Reeson, A., Williams, K., & Whitten, S. (2011, September). Targeting enhanced spatial configuration in biodiversity conservation incentive payment programs. In *13th BIOECON Annual Conference: Resource Economics, Biodiversity Conservation and Development, Geneve, Switzerland, 11–13 September 2011*, pp. 1–23.

Rodrigues, A.S.L., Andelman, S.J., Bakarr, M.I., Boitani, L., Brooks, T.M., Cowling, R.M., Fishpool, L.D.C., da Fonseca, G.A.B., Gaston, K.J., Hoffmann, M., Long, J.S., Marquet, P.A., Pilgrim, J.D., Pressey, R.L., Schipper, J., Sechrest, W., Stuart, S.N., Underhill, L.G., Waller, R.W., Watts, M.E.J., & Yan, X. (2004). Effectiveness of the global protected area network in representing species diversity. *Nature*, *428*(6983), 640–643.

Runge, C.A., Gallo-Cajiao, E., Carey, M.J., Garnett, S.T., Fuller, R.A., & McCormack, P.C. (2017). Coordinating domestic legislation and international agreements to conserve migratory species: A case study from Australia. *Conservation Letters*, *10*(6), 765–772.

Sanderson, F.J., Donald, P.F., Pain, D.J., Burfield, I.J., & Van Bommel, F.P. (2006). Long-term population declines in Afro-Palearctic migrant birds. *Biological Conservation*, *131*(1), 93–105.

Schaafsma, M., Brouwer, R., Gilbert, A., Van Den Bergh, J., & Wagtendonk, A. (2013). Estimation of distance-decay functions to account for substitution and spatial heterogeneity in stated preference research. *Land Economics*, *89*(3), 514–537.

Semmens, D.J., Diffendorfer, J.E., Bagstad, K.J., Wiederholt, R., Oberhauser, K., Ries, L., Semmens, B.X., Goldstein, J., Loomis, J., Thogmartin, W.E., Mattsson, B.J., & López-Hoffman, L. (2018). Quantifying ecosystem service flows at multiple scales across the range of a long-distance migratory species. *Ecosystem Services*, *31*, 255–264.

Shogren, J.F., Tschirhart, J., Anderson, T., Ando, A.W., Beissinger, S.R., Brookshire, D., … Polasky, S. (1999). Why economics matters for endangered species protection. *Conservation Biology*, *13*(6), 1257–1261.

Solis-Sosa, R., Semeniuk, C.A., Fernandez-Lozada, S., Dabrowska, K., Cox, S., & Haider, W. (2019). Monarch butterfly conservation through the social lens: Eliciting public preferences for management strategies across transboundary nations. *Frontiers in Ecology and Evolution*, *7*, 316.

Timothy, D.J. (1999). Cross-border partnership in tourism resource management: International parks along the US-Canada border. *Journal of Sustainable Tourism*, *7*(3-4), 182–205.

Timothy, D.J. (2006). Tourism and conservation in border regions. In K. Hoffman (Ed.), *The U.S. Mexican border environment: Transboundary ecosystem management*, pp. 225–242. San Diego: San Diego State University Press.

Valasiuk, S., Czajkowski, M., Giergiczny, M., Żylicz, T., Veisten, K., Elbakidze, M., & Angelstam, P. (2017). Are bilateral conservation policies for the Białowieża Forest unattainable? Analysis of stated preferences of Polish and Belarusian public. *Journal of Forest Economics*, *27*, 70–79.

Visconti, P., Butchart, S.H., Brooks, T.M., Langhammer, P.F., Marnewick, D., Vergara, S., Yanosky, A., & Watson, J.E. (2019). Protected area targets post-2020. *Science*, *364*(6437), 239–241.

Vogdrup-Schmidt, M., Abatayo, A.L., Shogren, J.F., Strange, N., & Thorsen, B.J. (2019). Factors affecting support for transnational conservation targeting migratory species. *Ecological Economics*, *157*, 156–164.

Wang, Z., Gong, Y., & Mao, X. (2018). Exploring the value of overseas biodiversity to Chinese netizens based on willingness to pay for the African elephants' protection. *Science of the Total Environment*, *637*, 600–608.

Wei, F., Wang, S., Fu, B., Zhang, L., Fu, C., & Kanga, E.M. (2018). Balancing community livelihoods and biodiversity conservation of protected areas in East Africa. *Current Opinion in Environmental Sustainability*, *33*, 26–33.

Wilcove, D.S., & Wikelski, M. (2008). Going, going, gone: Is animal migration disappearing. *PLoS Biology*, *6*(7), e188.

Wilson, S., LaDeau, S.L., Tøttrup, A.P., & Marra, P.P. (2011). Range-wide effects of breeding-and non-breeding-season climate on the abundance of a Neotropical migrant songbird. *Ecology*, *92*(9), 1789–1798.

# PART II

# Borders, Barriers, Access, and (Im)mobilities

# 8
# MIGRATION AND BORDERS

*Sascha Krannich*

## Introduction: Historical and Political Considerations

This chapter deals with the relationship between migration and borders. First, I briefly describe the history of this relationship and define the political linkages. Second, I illustrate current trends in international migration and immigration policies, and then move on to the current challenges of migration in relation to state borders, particularly transnational migration and circular mobility. Last, I hone in on future perspectives on migration, borders, and global governance.

Migration, meaning the movement of humans from one place to another, is as old as humankind itself, starting with the first humans migrating out of Africa. International migration in the modern sense started with the establishment of states and their borders, which began after the Thirty Years' War with the Peace of Westphalia in 1648. At that time, the aristocratic heads of the European Great Powers agreed to establish a state order in Europe for the first time. This international state order was based on the principle of interior and exterior sovereignty, of territorially divided and formally equal states. In this sense, states are entities based on the congruency of state power, state territory, and a state population; or in Weberian terms, the monopoly of a government to use legitimate force within a certain bordered territory (Weber, 1984 [1921]). In this regard, states are defined by geographical borders, which are meant to protect against invaders and other unwanted entrants (e.g., certain immigrants).

Belonging to a state is connected to citizenship with certain rights and responsibilities.[1] However, civic rights were not always granted to all people living inside the borders of a country. This kind of unequal treatment, as well as oppression and violence against particular ethnic and religious groups by the state, often led to emigration. Historically well-known examples are the escape of Jews from almost all European countries because of pogroms and other forms of persecution over the centuries, and the emigration of religiously suppressed Protestant Huguenots in France in the seventeenth century, who found refuge in the Protestant states of England and Prussia (Sassen, 1996).[2] While it was still relatively easy to cross state borders in Europe in the seventeenth and eighteenth centuries, this became increasingly more difficult due to rising levels of unwanted migration and increased border controls in the nineteenth century.

The territorial state was the basis of the nation-state, which evolved in Europe during the long nineteenth century (Hobsbawm, 1987). The central idea of the nation-state is that a state should ideally consist of a single nation, or a people who share a common history, culture, language, and identity. State borders mark the membranes of a state's territory and serve to exclude people who do not belong to that specific nation, particularly by preventing people from abroad from entering the state territory without permission from the destination state.[3] Since the creation of the nation-state, the regulation of migration has been one of its most urgent interests. National governments decide who is allowed to migrate across state borders and who is not. Theoretically, in democratic states, these decisions are the result of public discourse and should reflect the common interests of the people.

In some respects, states have established international regulations that transcend state borders and determine under which circumstances states must receive immigrants, even if a state is against it, and how refugees should be treated. From the tragic experiences of two world wars and the consequentially enormous waves of refugee migrants, the international community of states created new frameworks for accepting refugees and granting them protection after the Second World War. For this purpose, the Geneva Refugee Convention was ratified at the UN Convention Relating to the Status of Refugees in 1951. This convention marks the foundation of international refugee law which is still in effect today. It defines who can be considered a refugee and what guarantees of protection a state should grant to refugees and asylum seekers. Furthermore, the refugee convention codifies the rights of refugees and emergency measures. In contrast to citizenship rights for citizens of a state, rights for refugees are based on human rights, which should apply to all human beings independent of their national, ethnic, or religious origins.

There are institutions and organizations in the system of the United Nations that (should) work and advocate for the rights of migrants. This includes the International Labor Organization (ILO) which, in addition to representatives of states and employers and employees, advocates for the global basic work conditions of labor migrants.[4] The International Organization for Migration (IOM) also aims to support the management of all forms of migration worldwide, in cooperation with individual states.[5] The internationalization of migration and border management is particularly advanced in the European Union with free movement of labor for EU citizens, as well as a common border regime to protect external borders and a collective asylum policy. However, many states, as in other policy fields, try to surrender as little as possible of their sovereignty to international border regimes and supranational organizations, which can be seen in the current dispute over asylum policies among EU member states.[6]

## Global Trends in Migration and Immigration Policies

To operationalize and clarify who is an international migrant, the previously noted institutions, organizations, and supranational alliances (e.g., the European Union) refer to the definition established by the United Nations. International migrants are persons who live at least one year in a foreign country, regardless of the reasons for migrating (UN, 1998, p. 10). According to this definition, there are about 272 million international migrants worldwide, which is approximately 3.5 percent of the entire world population (UN, 2019).[7] International migration almost doubled in the last 30 years. However, it is difficult to record the exact numbers of global migrants and forms of migration, because they are registered and measured differently by international organizations and national institutions. So far, there is no central and permanent data gathering by the United Nations. People who migrate inside their own countries (internal migrants) are not included in these numbers. It is estimated that there are an additional 763 million internal migrants (IOM, 2019), with most internal migration taking place in China and India. Thus, there are over one billion people "on the move" in total worldwide.

More than half of these migrants live in developed countries of the Global North, while migration in regions of the Global South is also continuing to increase. The country with the largest intake of immigrants is the United States (about 1 million net immigrants on average per year in the last ten years), followed by Germany (about 500,000 immigrants per year), and Turkey (about 320,000 immigrants per year, most of which are refugees). Other prominent receiving countries include Russia, the United Kingdom, Canada, Saudi Arabia, Italy, and South Africa. In recent years, the countries with the highest emigration rates are Syria, India, Bangladesh, China, Pakistan, and Myanmar (UN, 2019).

The largest trend in international migration is by far labor migration. The ILO estimates that there are about 164 million labor migrants worldwide (ILO, 2019). These people migrate to another country because of job opportunities and the expectation of socioeconomic upward mobility. The second largest cohort of migrants is comprised of refugees. It is difficult to identify precise numbers, but according to the United Nations High Commissioner for Refugees (UNHCR, 2021), there are more than 80 million forcibly displaced people worldwide (45.7 million of them are internally displaced people). Most of these left their home countries owing to political oppression, discrimination, violence, or environmental disasters. Other large migrant groups are classified as education migrants (to pursue a better education), family migrants (with the aim of reuniting with previously departed family members), and increasing forms of global short-term mobility, including tourism.

These forms of migration are all subject to the different immigration and border policies of the receiving states (Hollifield et al., 2014). In most cases, states have drafted immigration and integration laws and policies that differ between *wanted* and *unwanted* immigration. For the most part, countries enable easier entry for immigrants they deem beneficial to the state. For instance, most countries have established liberal immigration laws and policies that make relocating easier for highly skilled and other trained labor migrants who are in demand in the national labor market and are, therefore, expected to contribute to the welfare of the state through their labor and tax contributions. Education-related immigrants, such as secondary and post-secondary students, scholars, and volunteers, can be also regarded as desirable migrants, because they are expected to become skilled workers in the future, already socially well-integrated and possessing excellent language, cultural, and professional skills. The easing of immigration requirements for these groups appears in visa policies, such as specific long-term visas for labor migrants who already have a job agreement before they actual arrive, or students who have already been accepted into a university, preferably with a scholarship (Krannich & Hunger, 2020). The United States has traditionally practiced such liberal immigration policies for highly skilled migrants, symbolized by the "green card", which allows newcomers permanent residence in the country. Other Western countries have also made immigration easier for skilled workers and students. For instance, Germany recently allowed foreign academics and skilled workers to immigrate to seek employment for up to six months (Krannich & Hunger, 2020). Tourists and cash-rich short-term migrants are also desirable forms of mobility. They are expected to help create new jobs and sources of revenue in destination countries. In particular, poor countries in the Global South expect more development from rising tourism and mobility and have eased many visa policies for foreign visitors (Brown & Hall, 2008).[8]

On the other hand, restrictive immigration and integration policies usually preclude migrants who are less in demand in the labor market, and therefore are likely to cost more than they benefit the state, for instance in the form of social services. Borders are meant to prevent unwanted immigration (or even make it impossible), including undocumented migrants and unregulated refugees.[9] While most labor migrants and tourists enter a country by airplane with passports and proper visas, many undocumented migrants and refugees enter a country over land or sea borders. Borders are usually strongly controlled or, if necessary, additionally secured with fences or walls where unwanted border crossings are common or where many waves of immigrants are expected. This can be observed most commonly where relatively poor countries are adjacent to rich countries.

Highly controversial is the situation at the 3,145 km USA–Mexico border, where more than 400,000 undocumented migrants from Latin American countries try to enter the United States each year. Most of them are fleeing violence and state oppression in their homelands and are seeking refuge and work opportunities in the United States or Canada. Many of them die in the US or Mexican desert during their attempts to cross the border. Although they contribute to the development of the US economy, they are unwelcomed by many segments of the host society due in part to negative stereotypes and racism (Krannich, 2017).

The EU border between Greece and Turkey illustrates another case of tough border controls. EU member states want to prevent migrants—mainly refugees fleeing conflicts in the Middle East or Africa—from entering European territory unregulated overland or via Mediterranean water routes. The European Border and Coast Guard Agency (Frontex) is the central organization of the EU border regime and is in charge of controlling the European Schengen Area borders in cooperation with state border police forces. Many NGOs have criticized Frontex because of its support for the Greek coast guard in pushing back refugees who have reached Greek territorial waters. These pushbacks are illegal under international human rights laws and the Geneva Refugee Convention. It is technically the obligation of Frontex to rescue these migrants. More than 3,000 people died in the Mediterranean during the 2015 European refugee crisis, and during the COVID-19 pandemic at least 550 people died up to September 2020 (BBC, 2020).

## Transnational Challenges for State Borders

The regulation of forms of migration by the state is made more difficult by new links and practices of migrants across national borders, which migration researchers call transnational migration (Faist et al., 2013; Portes & Martinez, 2019; Pries, 2015). Globalization, cheaper travel costs, and faster communication via the internet have made it easier for people to make permanent and long-term connections and create transnational networks. These migrants' ties are manifold and link countries of residence with countries of origin. To understand these transborder occurrences better, researchers have developed different theoretical approaches. The two most prominent approaches are the "transnational field approach" (Levitt & Glick Schiller, 2004) and the "transnational space approach" (Faist et al., 2013). The first approach applies Pierre Bourdieu's theory of social fields to explore the social, cultural, economic, and political activities of migrants and non-migrants who cross state borders (Amelina & Horvath, 2017; Levitt & Glick Schiller, 2004). The second approach frames these cross-border activities as short-term configurations, including private activities and mass actions and kinship groups, as well as long-term configurations, such as organizations, networks, and communities, which are sustained in social, economic, or political transnational spaces (Faist, 2000; Faist et al., 2013). In addition, these processes are even strengthened by "circular migration" or "mobility" (Portes & Fernandez-Kelly, 2015). In these situations, migrants move regularly back and forth between countries, either privately because they have two residences or family members living in another country, or for job reasons. These approaches help to overcome "methodological nationalism" (Wimmer & Glick Schiller, 2003), which sees migration only as a one-time border crossing from a specific state's perspective, usually from the perspective of the receiving state (Glick Schiller, Basch & Szanton Blanc, 1995).

National borders represent insignificant obstacles in these transnational processes. This can be observed worldwide as many empirical examples demonstrate. A famous example of strong transnational social networks are Mexican immigrants in the United States, who founded "hometown associations" (HTAs) to support development in their hometowns in Mexico as early as the 1960s and 1970s (Massey & Durand, 2004; Massey et al., 2016). In this process, some members of HTAs frequently travel back to Mexico to help build schools and hospitals, or to fund the restoration of churches and town parks. Some of them live in the USA without proper papers, so they sometimes cross the US–Mexican border through the Sonoran Desert as undocumented travelers to accomplish these aims. They also use transnational networks to support local businesses in their home regions, or to send money back to their family members or friends, which is sorely needed to pay for daily living expenses and the education of their children (Krannich, 2017). In 2019, Mexican immigrants in the United States sent more than USD35 billion in private remittances back to Mexico (World Bank, 2020).[10]

In contrast, highly skilled Indian migrants in the United States have created strong transnational economic networks. In the 1980s and 1990s, many Indian students studied in the science, technology, engineering, and mathematics (STEM) fields in California and eventually became successful employees at leading technology companies in Silicon Valley and other parts of the United States. They contributed to building the Indian economy through transnational networks, know-how transfers, and re-migration. Almost half of the IT companies in India were founded by returning migrants, who contributed to the software boom and the rise of India into one of the leading technology regions of the world (Hunger, 2004). Indian return migrants and entrepreneurs usually continue to use their strong networks in the United States, which they built during their time studying and working there, to develop their companies and to find cooperation partners (Argawala, 2015).

The cases of Kurdish and Tamil diasporas in Western Europe and North America illustrate vital transnational political activities across national borders. Neither of these two ethnic groups has its own nation-state, and both are engaged in political movements in their original homelands from abroad, struggling for the creation of a Kurdish or Tamil state with its own sovereignty and defined borders. Kurdish migrant organizations abroad support Kurdish-related parties and organize demonstrations and other political activities in Germany as well as in northern Iraq and Turkey (Candan, 2018). Overseas Tamil migrant organizations had an accelerating impact on the war in Sri Lanka by supporting the 1983–2009 fight of the militant Tamil organization the Liberation Tigers of Tamil Eelam (LTTE) against the Sri Lankan government for an independent Tamil state (Fair, 2007). In the end, they were unsuccessful in achieving their aim, but they clearly articulated their longing for an independent homeland. After the defeat of the LTTE, Tamils worldwide founded the Global Tamil Forum (GTF) in 2009 to support the self-determination of Sri Lanka's Tamil population and support their claims of war crimes against Tamils (Van Hear & Cohen, 2017). Emigrants can contribute to the creation of new nation-states through their transnational political activities, which were originally intended to overcome state borders in one way or another.

Similar patterns of political influence can be observed among larger migrant groups located in all Western countries, who are able to transfer knowledge and capital across international borders, and therefore detract from state regulations. This includes, for example, Chinese migrants in Canada and the United States (Zhou & Lee, 2015), Kenyan, Ghanaian, Congolese, and Surinamese migrant organizations in Great Britain and the Netherlands (Nijenhuis & Zoomers, 2015; Portes & Fernandez-Kelly, 2015), Turks in Germany (Pries & Sezgin, 2012), and Moroccans in France (Lacroix & Dumont, 2015) and Germany (Metzger, 2017).[11]

Transnationality and cross-border networks also affect tourism. Migration leads to more tourism, and tourism often leads to more migration across state frontiers. For instance, Krannich and Hunger's (2020) study of international students in Germany showed that many Indonesians who studied engineering, business, and tourism in Berlin moved back to Jakarta after completing their studies to create their own tourism enterprises by collaborating with famous hotel chains in Bali. In their business operations, they use their strong social and economic networks in Germany to reach European tourists and to advertise their seaside resorts in Indonesia. They work closely with German tour companies and travel agencies. Indonesians who stayed in Germany after their studies also contribute to the tourism industry in Indonesia. One Indonesian alumna working for a tourist company in Cologne is in charge of tourist destinations in Indonesia. In doing so, she applies her Indonesian cultural knowledge and language skills to work with Indonesian partners, which is important for her German employer to succeed in the Indonesian tourism industry.

Other examples of the migration–tourism nexus are the notions of migrant workers in hospitality and tourism, "return visits", "diaspora visits", and "solidarity tourism". In many countries, tourism services are staffed largely by migrant workers, some of whom are recruited directly from abroad or who are already in a country and are hired by tourism establishments for their less-expensive labor costs, willingness to work in the services sector, and language abilities (Kopnina, 2007). Return travel indicates diasporic people traveling back to their homelands to visit relatives, participate in festivals and religious ceremonies, or simply to visit their original homeland. Vice versa, people in countries of origin visit their relatives or family members in the diaspora abroad, many times in connection with holidays and sightseeing in famous tourist destinations (Timothy, 2002). Famous ethnic neighborhoods, such as Chinatown, Koreatown, or Little India in global cities like New York, Los Angeles, Chicago, or London, also attract tourists from all parts of the world, including from the diasporic homeland.

Likewise, a type of political tourism—solidarity tourism—has become a salient mechanism for helping support national independence or at least for forwarding a national cause. Many emigrants are heavily involved in return travel and solidarity tourism, with many examples in the literature focusing on the Palestinian, the Jewish (Israeli), and the Croatian diasporas (Carter, 2004; Guia, 2021; Huang, Haller & Ramshaw, 2013; Kassis, Solomon & Higgins-Desbiolles, 2015). Here, borders can play a crucial role and even contribute to peace developments as in the case of the Berlin Wall or the Israeli-Palestinian border, where border tourism was organized by political peace organizations (Gelbman, 2019).

In addition, the travel habits and retirement migration of older people in Europe and North America show how tourism can lead to long-term migration across national borders. Many studies have shown how short-term vacations in Spain, Greece, or Mexico have led to people's decisions to migrate to these countries on a more permanent basis and spend their retirement in warmer climates, less expensive places, and fascinating environments (Hall & Müller, 2018; Kuentzel & Ramaswamy, 2005; Zasada et al., 2010).

Some countries realize the potential benefits of these transnational migrations, particularly the advantages for the economies in the countries of origin (Faist et al., 2013; Portes, 2015; Portes & Fernandez-Kelly, 2015), as noted previously with regard to remittances and other support. To tap into these benefits, emigration states have established specific institutions for cross-border and long-distance cooperation with their diasporas abroad. For instance, Mexico created a so-called *tres por uno* state program, which adds three dollars to every dollar sent back by Mexican migrant organizations abroad to help realize development projects like road building or renovating schools and hospitals. In doing so, the Mexican state expects important contributions to the development of rural areas by Mexicans abroad (Krannich, 2017).

In India, the government created the Ministry of Overseas Indian Affairs (MOIA) to support Indians living abroad. India's idea is to profit from social networks, knowledge transfer, and financial remittances from successful Indians abroad (Naujoks, 2013). Georgia established a diaspora ministry (in 2016 it merged with the Ministry of Foreign Affairs), which also addresses tourist-related issues to generate more tourism in the country with the support of its diaspora in Europe and the United States (Georgian Ministry of Foreign Affairs, 2017). Nevertheless, attempts to work closely with emigrants abroad are often not as successful as homeland states expect, because many emigrants are suspicious of their home governments based on their experiences of oppression, unequal treatment, and corruption. This has been observed, for instance, in the cases of the relationships between the Mexican state and its diaspora (Krannich, 2017), as well as the Moroccan state and its diaspora (Metzger, 2017).

## Conclusion: Migration without Borders—Utopia or Dystopia?

Although many states realize the potential of migration for new countries of residence, as well as for countries of origin, political decision-makers in receiving countries still differ strongly between *desired* and *undesired* migrants. As a result, strong borders continue to be used as state protection measures. However, increasing transnational networks and circular migration and mobility show the need to rethink the meaning of national borders. If increasing numbers of people decide to live and work in more than one country, and even share transnational identities and citizenship, states may be forced to adapt their policies to facilitate better living conditions for all migrants, including low-skilled labor migrants and refugees.

Opponents of strict border regimes argue that preventing people from migrating is a violation of human rights. Researchers, politicians, and activists who prefer the free movement of people across state borders have noted Immanuel Kant's idea of *Weltbürgerrecht* (world civil law or cosmopolitan rights). A utopian idea that all people should have the right to freely and peacefully stay on the land in possession of other people or of another state. However, Kant (2005 [1795]) also makes it clear that there is no permanent right to hospitality or right of residence, but only a right to visit.

This leads to the question of whether or not borders are necessary to grant the right to visit or asylum to refugees and other migrants. Theoretically, only sovereign states with functioning borders are able to grant protection to immigrants, because only through secured borders can they guarantee the functioning of a state polity and internal security and public order. Abolishing state borders would probably lead to a destruction of the international state order and jeopardize global peace. However, the free movement of people in the European Union indicates that policy instruments do exist to regulate migration and tourism more liberally, including residence, labor, and tax regulations. These policy instruments could also be applicable in other regions of the world.

To address the challenges of international migration and transnational migrant networks adequately and ethically, states need to pursue global agreements and border regimes that maintain their state sovereignty and protect their borders. Here, they have to include the needs and perspectives of the Global South. Complete isolation of the Global North from problems of the Global South would only increase forced migration and create more pressure on national borders in the Global North, as we saw during the 2015 refugee crisis at the EU's borders. Migration to the Global North holds not only economic prospects for individual migrants, but also for the countries of the Global South, if their former citizens have opportunities to participate in social programs, and are able to transfer their newly gained capital, know-how, and contacts back to their countries of origin. In some places this happens only after many years, sometimes even after centuries, but in the long run, migration can play a stabilizing role in international relations and local development.

A better solution to migration and border challenges, particularly to reduce undocumented and refugee migration, would be the creation of more legal ways for the labor and educational migration of people from Africa and other parts from the Global South to the more affluent countries. This could potentially relieve the stresses of high birthrates in emigrant countries and help to rejuvenate the low birthrates of immigrant countries. Therefore, a proactive, farsighted, and orderly immigration policy would not only be based on humanitarian precepts, but also on the economic interests of the Global South and North (Hunger & Krannich, 2019).

The Global Compact on Migration,[12] signed by all UN member states, except the United States, in the UN General Assembly in December 2018, is a step in the direction of more globalized visions of migration, even though it is non-binding under international law. This international treaty is an attempt to understand migration as an opportunity and refers to the significant potential for countries of the Global South. Its goals could be realized by the creation of legal migration opportunities and the prevention of illegal state border crossings (UN, 2018). This compact in connection with the establishment of the UNHCR, IOM, Global Forum on Migration and Development (GFMD),[13] and other international institutions and organizations, suggests that the regulation of international migration can be seen as an effort to build global migration governance (Betts, 2010), which has so far not fully developed its potential structures and decision-making processes. New global migration governance would be helpful in managing international migration and other forms of human mobility in fair, sustainable, and human-rights-based ways. Such a framework would support migrants not only during the time before and during their mobilities, but also following their migration, to help them become more integrated into the host society as well as during re-migration and re-integration into their countries of origin should they choose to return. Integration and re-integration bear the biggest challenges for migrants, including finding work and a place to live, as well as navigating infrastructure and new culture (Krannich & Hunger, 2020). Due to the close link between migration and tourism, which has been described above, global governance structures should also consider tourist mobility, including visa agreements, travel regulations, and opportunities, to change status more easily from a tourist to a student or labor immigrant. Here, the problem of illegal visa overstayers—people who stay longer in the country than their legal tourist or other visa status allows—should be also addressed. According to these considerations, states would be required to hand over certain responsibilities and authorities to international institutions that create a migration and border regime, much the way the European Union and the Schengen Agreement have done in Europe, to generalize and harmonize rights of migrants to cross national borders legally and independently from their countries of origin, and reduce restrictions on transnational migration networks and circular mobility.

## Notes

1 The idea of citizenship, according to Aristotle, is to endow members of a political entity with certain political rights. Later, it also formed the basis of several migration theories, including theories about the connections of integration, identity, and belonging, as well as development (Faist et al. 2013).
2 At that time, they did not use the term *refugee*. This term was mentioned for the first time in the *Encyclopaedia Britannica* in 1796 (Marrus, 1985).
3 Even ongoing social conflicts in modern immigration states can be traced back to the classic idea of a nation-state with one people, because immigrants from different national backgrounds are oftentimes not perceived as full members of the national host society. This form of national and social exclusion can be expressed in legal disadvantages and even racial and ethnic discrimination.

4 The ILO is a UN agency founded in 1919 under the League of Nations in Geneva. Its mandate is to set international labor standards, including for migrants.
5 However, the IOM, founded in 1951, is also criticized for its attempts to prevent migrants from unlawful border crossings instead of helping to regulate migration in a humane way. For instance, the involvement of the IOM in Australia's "Pacific Solution". In cooperation with the Australian government, the IOM operated the Nauru Detention Center on the Pacific island of Nauru from 2002 to 2006, where Afghan boat refugees were imprisoned in degrading conditions. Several human rights organizations adverted to the occurrences there, including Human Rights Watch (2003).
6 This dispute is in particular about a fairly shared distribution of asylum seekers and refugees in the European Union. This became dramatically evident during the refugee crisis in 2015 and 2016 (Hunger & Krannich, 2019).
7 More than half of international migrants are males (about 53 percent); the median age is about 39 years (UN, 2019).
8 For instance, the economy in Thailand earned more than USD60 billion from international tourists in 2019 (before the COVID-19 pandemic broke out in 2020). That was the highest of all countries in the Global South, and ranking fourth behind the United States (1), Spain (2), and France (3) (World Tourism Organization, 2020).
9 I prefer the terms *undocumented* or *irregular* migration instead of *illegal* migration, because the term *illegal* is a discriminating term (expressed in the slogan "No Human Being Is Illegal", used by Elie Wiesel for the first time in 1988, which also became the title of an international network in 1997). Migrants from Latin American countries in the United States often use the term *undocumented* to describe their own situation, and therefore call themselves *indocumentados* (Krannich, 2017).
10 The total amount of international remittances worldwide exceeded USD466 billion in 2017 (KNOMAD, 2018), while state investments for the developmental cooperation of OECD donor countries amounted to USD146.6 billion (OECD, 2018).
11 These numerous empirical cases led to the induction of further theories based on transnationalism, including "brain drain, brain gain" and "brain circulation" theories (Hunger, 2004) and "migration and development" theories, which help to explain relationships between migrants abroad and their countries of origin (Portes, 2015; Pries, 2015).
12 The entire and official name of the global compact is Global Compact for Safe, Orderly, and Regular Migration (GCM). The GCM includes 23 objectives and commitments regarding, among others, data usage for migration policies, improvement of safe migration, better access of migrants to basic social services, risk education of migrants, improving life-saving measures, and inclusion of more relevant international actors in the field of migration (UN, 2018).
13 The GFMD, formed in 2007, is a state-led and non-binding forum based on regular meetings of the relevant actors (states, international organizations, NGOs, businesses, etc.) to discuss global issues on migration and development (GFMD, 2021).

# References

Amelina, A., & Horvath, K. (2017). Sociology of migration. In K.O. Korgen (ed.) *The Cambridge handbook of sociology: Core areas in sociology and the development of the discipline* (Volume 1), pp. 455–464. Cambridge: Cambridge University Press.

Argawala, R. (2015). Tapping the Indian diaspora for Indian development. In A. Portes, & P. Fernandez-Kelly (eds.) *The state and the grassroots: Immigrant transnational organizations in four continents*, pp. 84–110. Oxford: Berghahn.

BBC (British Broadcasting Corporation) (2020). Hundreds of migrants still dying in Med five years since 2015. Online https://www.bbc.com/news/world-europe-53764449.amp (03/30/2021).

Betts, A. (2010). Global migration governance – the emergence of a new debate. Global economic governance programme briefing paper. Online: https://www.imi.ox.ac.uk/files/news/global-migration-governance_paper_2010.pdf (03/30/2021).

Brown, F., & Hall, D. (2008). Tourism and development in the Global South. *Third World Quarterly*, 29(5), 839–849.

Candan, M. (2018). *Die Rolle der irakischen Diaspora beim Wiederaufbau im Irak nach 2003*. Eschborn: Deutsche Gesellschaft für Internationale Zusammenarbeit.

Carter, S. (2004). Mobilizing *Hrvatsko*: Tourism and politics in the Croatian diaspora. In T. Coles, & D.J. Timothy (eds.) *Tourism, diasporas and space*, pp. 188–201. London: Routledge.

Fair, C. (2007). The Sri Lankan Tamil diaspora: Sustaining conflict and pushing for peace. In H. Smith, & P. Stares (eds.) *Diasporas in conflict: Peace-makers or peace-wreckers?*, pp. 172–195. Tokyo: United Nations University Press.

Faist, T. (2000). *The volume and dynamics of international migration and transnational social spaces*. Oxford: Oxford University Press.

Faist, T., Fauser, M., & Reisenauer, E. (2013). *Transnational migration*. Cambridge: Polity Press.

Gelbman, A. (2019). Tourism, peace, and global stability. In D.J. Timothy (ed) *Handbook of globalisation and tourism*, pp. 149–160. Cheltenham: Edward Elgar.

Georgian Ministry of Foreign Affairs (2017). *Georgia and the Georgian diaspora*. Tbilisi: Ministry of Foreign Affairs.

GFMD (Global Forum on Migration and Development) (2021). About the GFMD. Online https://www.gfmd.org (03/31/2021).

Glick Schiller, N., Basch, L., & Szanton Blanc, C. (1995). From immigrant to transmigrant: Theorizing transnational migration. *Anthropological Quarterly* 68, 48–63.

Guia, J. (2021). Conceptualizing justice tourism and the promise of posthumanism. *Journal of Sustainable Tourism*, 29(2–3), 503–520.

Hall, C.M., & Müller, D. (eds.) (2018). *The Routledge handbook of second home tourism and mobilities*. London: Routledge.

Hobsbawm, E. (1987). *The age of empire: 1875-1914*. London: Weidenfeld and Nicolson.

Hollifield, J., Martin, P., & Orrenius, P. (eds.) (2014). *Controlling immigration: A global perspective*. Stanford: Stanford University Press.

Huang, W.J., Haller, W.J., & Ramshaw, G.P. (2013). Diaspora tourism and homeland attachment: An exploratory analysis. *Tourism Analysis*, 18(3), 285–296.

Human Rights Watch (2003). The International Organization for Migration (IOM) and human rights protection in the field: Current concerns, submitted by Human Rights Watch, IOM Governing Council Meeting, 86th session, November 18-21, 2003, Geneva. Online https://www.hrw.org/legacy/backgrounder/migrants/iom-submission-1103.htm (03/30/2021).

Hunger, U. (2004). Indian IT-entrepreneurs in the US and India: An illustration of the "brain gain hypothesi". *Journal of Comparative Policy Analysis*, 6(2), 99–109.

Hunger, U., & Krannich, S. (2019). Internationale Migration und Migrationspolitik 2018: Wo kommen wir her, wo stehen wir und wie geht es weiter? *Zeitschrift für Außen- und Sicherheitspolitik*, 11(4), 167–176.

ILO (International Labor Organization) (2019). *New developments of international labor migration*. Geneva: ILO.

IOM (International Organization for Migration) (2019). *World migration report 2019*. Geneva: IOM.

Kant, I. (2005 [1795]). *Zum ewigen Frieden*. Darmstadt: Wissenschaftliche Buchgesellschaft.

Kassis, R., Solomon, R., & Higgins-Desbiolles, F. (2015). Solidarity Tourism in Palestine: the Alternative Tourism Group of Palestine as a catalyzing instrument of resistance. In R.K. Isaac, C.M. Hall, & Higgins-Desbiolles, F. (eds) *The politics and power of tourism in Palestine*, pp. 37–52. London: Routledge.

KNOMAD (Global Knowledge Partnership on Migration and Development) (2018). Migration and remittances: Recent developments and outlook. Migration and Development Brief, 29. Online https://www.knomad.org/sites/default/files/2018-04/Migration%20and%20Development%20Brief%2029.pdf (03/30/2021).

Kopnina, H. (2007). *Migration and tourism: Formation of new social classes*. New York: Cognizant.

Krannich, S. (2017). *The reconquest of paradise? How indigenous migrants construct community in the United States and Mexico*. Münster: LIT Verlag.

Krannich, S., & Hunger, U. (2020). *Internationale Studierendenmigration und Entwicklung: Eine Fallstudie am Beispiel des KAAD*. Wiesbaden: Springer VS Verlag.

Kuentzel, W. F., & Ramaswamy, V. M. (2005). Tourism and amenity migration: A longitudinal analysis. *Annals of Tourism Research*, 32(2), 419–438.

Lacroix, T., & Dumont, A. (2015). Moroccans in France: Their organizations and activities back home. In A. Portes & P. Fernandez-Kelly (eds.) *The state and the grassroots: Immigrant transnational organizations in four continents*, pp. 212–235. Oxford: Berghahn.

Levitt, P., & Glick Schiller, N. (2004). Conceptualizing simultaneity: A transnational social field perspective on society. *International Migration Review*, 38, 1002–1039.

Marrus, M. (1985). *The unwanted: European refugees in the twentieth century*. Oxford: Oxford University Press.

Massey, D., & Durand, J. (2004). *Behind the smokes and mirrors: Research from the Mexican Migration Project*. New York: Russel Sage Foundation.

Massey, D., Durand, J., & Pren, K. (2016). Why border enforcement backfired. *American Journal of Sociology*, 121(5), 1557–1600.

Metzger, S. (2017). *Entwicklungspolitisches Engagement marokkanischer Migrantenorganisationen in Deutschland*. Eschborn: Deutsche Gesellschaft für Internationale Zusammenarbeit.

Naujoks, D. (2013). *Migration, citizenship, and development: Diasporic membership policies and overseas Indians in the United States*. Oxford: Oxford University Press.

Nijenhuis, G., & Zoomers, A. (2015). Transnational activities of immigrants in the Netherlands: Do Ghanaian, Moroccan, and Surinamese diaspora organizations enhance development? In A. Portes, & P. Fernandez-Kelly (eds.) *The state and the grassroots: Immigrant transnational organizations in four continents*, pp. 236–263. Oxford: Berghahn.

OECD (Organisation for Economic Co-operation and Development) (2018). Mittel für Entwicklungszusammenarbeit 2017 leicht gesunken. Online http://www.oecd.org/berlin/presse/mittel-fuer-entwicklungszusammenarbeit-2017-leicht-gesunken-09042018.htm (03/30/2021).

Portes, A. (2015). Immigration, transnationalism, and development: The state of the question. In A. Portes, & P. Fernandez-Kelly (eds.) *The state and the grassroots: Immigrant transnational organizations in four continents*, pp. 1–26. Oxford: Berghahn.

Portes, A., & Fernandez-Kelly, P. (eds.) (2015). *The state and the grassroots: Immigrant transnational organizations in four continents*. Oxford: Berghahn.

Portes, A., & Martinez, B. (2019). They are not all the same: Immigrant enterprises, transnationalism, and development. *Journal of Ethnic and Migration Studies*, 46(10), 1991–2007.

Pries, L. (2015). *Die Transnationalisierung der sozialen Welt: Sozialräume jenseits von Nationalgesellschaften*. Frankfurt: Suhrkamp.

Pries, L., & Sezgin, Z. (eds.) (2012). *Cross-border migrant organisations in comparative perspective*. Houndmills: Palgrave.

Sassen, S. (1996). *Guests and aliens*. New York: New Press.

Timothy, D.J. (2002). Tourism and the growth of urban ethnic islands. In C.M. Hall, & A.M. Williams (eds.), *Tourism and migration: New relationships between production and consumption*, pp. 135–151. Dordrecht: Kluwer.

UN (United Nations) (1998). *Recommendations on statistics of international migration*. New York: United Nations.

UN (United Nations) (2018). Global compact for safe, orderly and regular migration: Final draft. Online: https://refugeesmigrants.un.org/sites/default/files/180711_final_draft_0.pdf (03/30/2021).

UN (United Nations) (2019). *International migration report 2019*. New York: United Nations.

UNHCR (United Nations High Commissioner for Refugees) (2021). Refugee data finder. Online https://www.unhcr.org/refugee-statistics/ (03/30/2021).

Van Hear, N., & Cohen, R. (2017). Diasporas and conflict: Distance, contiguity and spheres of engagement. *Oxford Development Studies*, 45(2), 171–184.

Weber, M. (1984 [1921]). *Soziologische Begriffe*. Tübingen: Mohr Siebeck.

Wimmer, A., & Glick Schiller, N. (2003). Methodological nationalism, the social sciences, and the study of migration: An essay in historical epistemology. *International Migration Review* 37, 576–610.

World Bank (2020). Personal remittances, received (current US$) – Mexico. Online https://data.worldbank.org/indicator/BX.TRF.PWKR.CD.DT?locations=MX (03/30/2021).

World Tourism Organization (2020). UNWTO world tourism barometer and statistical annex. Online https://www.e-unwto.org/doi/abs/10.18111/wtobarometereng.2020.18.1.7 (03/30/2021).

Zasada, I., Alves, S., Müller, F.C., Piorr, A., Berges, R., & Bell, S. (2010). International retirement migration in the Alicante region, Spain: Process, spatial pattern and environmental impacts. *Journal of Environmental Planning and Management*, 53(1), 125–141.

Zhou, M., & Lee, R. (2015). Traversing ancestral and new homelands: Chinese immigrant transnational organizations in the United States. In A. Portes, & P. Fernandez-Kelly (eds.) *The state and the grassroots: Immigrant transnational organizations in four continents*, pp. 27–59. Oxford: Berghahn.

# 9
# PHYSICAL ACCESS AND PERCEIVED CONSTRAINTS
## Borders as Barriers to Travel Mobilities and Tourism Development

*Olga Hannonen and Eeva-Kaisa Prokkola*

### Introduction

Between 1945 and 1991, 19 border walls and barriers were built. From 1991 to 2012, 30 more structures were built or announced (Vallet & Charles-Philippe, 2012), and several countries in Europe (e.g., Hungary, Slovenia, Greece, and Bulgaria) built barbed-wire fences on their southern and eastern borders between 2015 and 2019, some even between fellow EU member states. In July 2021, Lithuania began erecting strong border barriers on its boundary with Belarus, and borders as physical barriers continue to be erected in many places of the world. The building of border walls impacts international travel which, by definition, involves crossing a political boundary. The literature on travel mobilities is rich with references to borders and border crossings. However, academic interest in the multifaceted relationships between tourism and borders started to grow only in the late 1990s and early 2000s (Fors, 2018; Hartman, 2006; Ioannides, Nielsen & Billing, 2006; Leimgruber, 1998; Paasi & Raivo, 1998; Prokkola, 2007; Timothy, 1995, 2001). This increased research interest mirrors the fact that increasing border permeability and the easing of geopolitical tensions, such as the disappearance of the Berlin Wall and the East–West European divide, have strongly impacted travel mobilities worldwide.

The ground-breaking research thoroughly bridging the concepts of tourism and borders came along with the work of Dallen Timothy (Gelbman & Timothy, 2011; Timothy, 1995, 2001; Timothy & Tosun, 2003; Timothy & Teye, 2004). Timothy's research provides a theoretical and conceptual framework that has inspired scholars worldwide to proceed and extend the study of the fundamental and complex relationships between international travel and political borders, and how borders manifest as both barriers and attractions. The current interdisciplinary interest in the relationships between borders and travel mobilities brings together scholars from tourism studies, border studies, human geography, anthropology, political and planning studies, among others.

Border permeability and the barrier effects caused by the border directly influence tourism mobilities and development. It is common in the literature to differentiate between two types of border barriers: physical and mental (or real and perceived) (Schack, 2000; Timothy, 2001; Timothy & Tosun, 2003; Van der Velde & Spierings, 2010). Physical barriers are the typical fortifications, walls, and fences visible in the landscape. As a concrete barrier, many borders also impose requirements for crossing (e.g., travel documents), limitations on the crossers' length of stay, restrictions on the types and amounts of goods that can be transported, and strict rules for customs and taxation. Mental barriers are manifested in different geopolitical, economic, and socio-cultural circumstances and attitudes, influencing travel behavior in many ways (Timothy, 2001; Timothy & Tosun, 2003) (see Table 9.1). Physical and mental barriers are not separate: they are interconnected in many ways (Sofield, 2006). Physical barriers often influence mental ones, and vice versa. Mental and psychological barriers aimed at "the other side" can help explain some efforts toward building massive border walls (Brown, 2010).

During the last few decades, academic interest has turned towards the legal-political, infrastructural, economic, and socio-cultural construction of borders and everyday bordering practices, instead of focusing on the physical or natural features of borderlines (Timothy, Saarinen & Viken, 2016; Newman, 2006; Timothy, 2001). Thus, in addition to border barriers per se, and border formalities, an important aspect in understanding borders is the process of bordering, or the way the border is perceived and maintained (Hannonen, 2019; Newman, 2006; Schack, 2000).

Borders as barriers to tourism are unstable. A border which forms a barrier to travel mobility in one period may represent a cross-border destination at another time. The barrier effects that borders create for international travel and tourism development are usually entangled with geopolitical turbulence (Mostafanezhad & Norum, 2016; Rowen, 2016), natural hazards, and, as has been recently seen, with other events, such as an outbreak of a pandemic. Not all geopolitical borders form a similar kind of barrier to travel mobilities and peoples, however. The permeability of a single border often varies between adjacent countries and on each side of the border (Timothy, 2001, pp. 12–17). This is clear on the USA–Mexico border, where the same frontier is permeable for US citizens but much less so for Mexicans. A border that is seen as a threat by one state and its citizens may simultaneously represent an attractive destination and a land of opportunity in the neighboring country (Matznetter, 1978, p. 66). Even within the same country a border and the act of crossing it will not be the same phenomenon for all people but can be experienced differently by different groups of people (see Webster & Timothy, 2006).

This chapter presents the current conceptual and empirical facets of borders as barriers to travel and tourism. The discussion starts by introducing borders as real physical barriers and moves to an overview of visa regimes, sanctions, and case-specific regulations that act as extensions of border infrastructure and its barrier functions on the margins of the state. The discussion continues with different ways of mental bordering and borders as psychological barriers to tourism development. The final section presents contemporary and future perspectives on tourism and borders.

*Table 9.1* Physical and mental barriers

| Real/physical barrier | Mental/perceived barrier |
| --- | --- |
| Physical border fortifications | Language differences |
| Pre-border: paper borders, e-borders, visa regimes | Cultural differences |
| Economic borders: travel costs, price differences, tax and custom regulations | Administrative, legislative and political differences |
| Nonpharmaceutical interventions: health screening and testing at borders, travel restrictions, quarantine requirements, and border closures | Border-crossing formalities: encounters with border officials, lack of information and experience |
| Sanctions | Religious differences |
| Case-specific regulations and temporary travel | Perceptions of risk and safety |

## Borders and Physical Access

Borders as barriers to travel mobilities are often approached in terms of a discontinuity. Borders may form an almost impermeable barrier for certain cross-border activities and mobilities, or they can simply discourage interaction across the line (Nijkamp, Rietveld & Salomon 1990; Spierings & van der Velde, 2013). Timothy (2001) and Gelbman and Timothy (2011) show how, in terms of accessibility, borders can be categorized as a continuum from functionally closed, or strong, borders with almost no trans-boundary interaction to integrated, soft borders that are highly stable and present almost no obstacles to the movement of people and goods. The level of interaction between people across the border depends on the type of border: interactions are high across soft borders and low when the border is strong and less permeable (Hannonen, 2019; Schack 2001). Borders create discontinuities, yet they may simultaneously stimulate communication and interaction in one or both directions.

A physical border can form a barrier to tourism flows, or it can be crossed almost unnoticed. The physical existence of an international border usually results from its demarcation in the landscape, yet the physical materializing of a border can vary considerably—from nearly invisible EU internal borders to kilometers-long walls and barriers on the USA–Mexico, India–Pakistan, Israel–Lebanon, and North–South Korean borders, for example (Fors, 2018; Gelbman, 2008; Jones, 2012). The construction of infrastructure such as buildings and defense apparatuses are the material manifestations of state operations. Borders and borderlands are often less developed margins of the state and lack basic infrastructure to access borders and to cross them.

Border crossing can be time-consuming, which itself creates both physical and mental barriers. Physical access across a border can vary considerably and is interlinked with the type of border crossing in question. The experiences, time requirements, and practices of short-distance, cross-border land travel, or water crossings by ferry boat are different from the experience of long-distance air travel, for example. Transportation networks in border areas and on the opposite side are frequently poor, unsafe, and uncomfortable (Bätzner & Stephenson, 2017). International air travel always involves crossing borders, but the experience of departing, entering, and security checks at airports, where the most innovative surveillance methods have been introduced (Adey, 2009), are usually quite different than at land crossings.

Borders are multilayered, complex structures (Schack, 2000) that are also crossed by severing different layers. Thus, some barriers are easier to pass through than others. Economic factors create barriers to human mobility and tourism activities across national borders. Difference in the purchasing power parity between countries may create a concrete, albeit intangible, barrier for leisure travel and shopping tourism for residents of a poorer country to a more expensive destination country (Boonchai & Freathy, 2020). Similarly, Boehmer and Peña (2012, p. 279) note that economic differences between neighboring states influence the level of border openness: "The larger the income gap between neighboring states, the less open the wealthier states will be to the people of the poorer neighbor, but the more open the poorer state will be to people from the richer nation". As noted previously, this is the case on the Mexico–USA frontier. Strict currency requirements and fluctuations of currency exchange rates influence cross-border travel, sometimes very abruptly (Prokkola, 2019; Timothy, 2001).

Wars, tense geopolitical relationships between countries, and border disputes (see Timothy 2001, pp. 24–25) often constitute concrete institutional barriers, as well as collective and personal mental obstacles. Examples of bilateral travel restrictions between neighboring countries due to political conflicts include Armenia and Azerbaijan, Somalia and most of its neighbors, and South and North Korea (Prideaux & Kim, 2018). American travel to Cuba has been heavily restricted due to the US government's ideological opposition to the island's communist regime. The US government has also sometimes advised against travel to the Philippines because that country failed to renew the US Bases Treaty (Bianchi, 2006).

Borders as manifestations of interstate political relations affect mobility and travel in more complex directions than only bilaterally. For example, most Middle Eastern countries prohibit Israelis from entering, but even more, many Middle Eastern countries prohibit entry to travelers whose passports bear evidence of a visit to Israel (Whyte, 2008, p. 137), which led Israel to cease stamping foreign passports on arrival. Likewise, citizens of Iran, Iraq, Libya, Somalia, Sudan, Syria, and Yemen face many restrictions on travel to the United States (Seyfi & Hall, 2020), and international travelers to the USA are required to undergo additional scrutiny and visa procedures after visiting these countries and the Democratic People's Republic of Korea (State Department, 2020). Moreover, tourists are particularly susceptible to perceived security threats related to political instability and health risks (Bringas & Verduzco, 2008). Examples of countries where terrorist attacks have been directed towards tourists and tourism interests have been common in the past few decades and where political violence has affected tourist flows and travel behavior, including Egypt, Israel, Northern Ireland, Syria, Pakistan, and Peru (Sönmez, Apostolopoulos & Tarlow, 1999).

Despite their preponderance to keeping people out, there are numerous examples of how border walls and monuments act as tourist attractions. The Norwegian–Russian border, which was largely closed for crossings during the Cold War period, became a thrilling object of tourist attention, as one could experience a physically closed border and gaze upon the forbidden otherness on the opposite side. In the 1980s, a Norwegian air company offered so-called "border flights" along the Norwegian–Soviet border for adventurous tourists (Fors, 2018, p. 167). The closed Finnish–Russian border had a similar allure during the Cold War, when "many Finns used to visit the Finnish–Soviet frontier … to feel the mystique of the place … seeking to experience a geopolitical thrill" (Medvedev, 1999, p. 43). The Finnish–Russian (Soviet) border provides a fitting example of how border transitions influence tourism. Many scholars have documented the transformation of the border from the strictly guarded and almost entirely closed border of the Soviet era to a tourist destination (Izotov & Laine, 2013; Laine, 2017; Paasi & Raivo, 1998).

## Visa Politics, Sanctions, and Case-specific Regulations

Border regulations, visa politics, sanction regimes, and case-specific regulations impact international travel mobility. The barriers that border and visa regulations create for travel are unstable and interlinked with the development of the system of modern states and their attempt to regulate movement (Franklin, 2003, pp. 38–45). State border regulation and visa systems evolved to meet the need for states to control their territory and international travel mobility that was gradually becoming more common among the "masses" instead of being merely an elitist endeavor (Towner, 1996).

Visa and border regulations create multiple barriers to international travel. Mobility restrictions may be introduced by both home and host countries (Timothy, 2001, p. 16). When tourists apply for visas, the time, distance, and expenses associated with travel increase. Moreover, many countries require an official letter of invitation from an organization or a relative for people arriving from specific countries. Recently, tourism and border scholars have turned their attention to the fact that borders do not create similar physical and institutional barriers to all people and nationalities. Rather, they afford varying degrees of access to different groups of people (Bianchi, 2006; Wang, 2004). Passports issued by different states are valued differently.

For instance, Taiwan's passport is not recognized by PR Chinese authorities (Wang, 2004), and at the time of writing in 2021, the United States still does not offer citizens of Romania, Bulgaria, Cyprus, and Croatia visa-free access, even though they are EU citizens, whereas the other 23 EU states are able to enter the USA without a visa.

Regulations and barriers to international travel are established by foreign countries but also sometimes by one's own government. Some countries do not allow all their citizens or groups of citizens to undertake international travel; heavy regulation of women's travel mobilities is common in some Muslim countries. Likewise, some professional groups in some countries have restricted access to foreign travel. Chinese military personnel and government officials must leave their passports with their employers, and they are usually granted permission to travel only under special circumstances (Zhang, 2013, p. 98).

Political borders pose constraints and obstacles to travel mobilities in a highly unequal way. States often welcome, and compete for, travelers from wealthy countries, while simultaneously strongly regulating travel mobilities by residents of poor countries (Cohen, 2021). The 9/11 events and the "war on terror" have added to the restrictions faced by many travelers and especially by non-white travelers of "Middle Eastern" origin. Many governments have introduced new biometric surveillance methods that enable officials to profile, identify, and pre-empt the entry of "risky" travelers (Amoore, 2006). The racial profiling of passengers at points of entry and the denying of access to visas and other travel documents (thus foreign entry) are acts of bordering and differentiative barriers to international mobilities (Adey, 2009; Bianchi, 2006). The deep inequality towards and diverse causes of the right to international mobility become highly visible in the process of acquiring tourist visas and entering ports of entry. Thus, "a seamless cross-border travel has only materialized for a privileged minority of the world's citizens", in which citizens of more affluent states have more visa-free travel options (Bianchi, Stephenson & Hannam, 2020, p. 297).

Van Houtum and Lacy (2020, p. 706) conceptualize the documents that regulate the mobility of people from visa-obliged countries as a form of "pre-border". These "paper borders", or e-borders, pre-screen eligible border crossers before they actually arrive at a physical border. In such a manner border control is outsourced to government offices far from the actual borderline (van Houtum & Lacy, 2020). Similarly, Salter (2012, p. 736) points out that "traditional models of the territorial state borders are confounded by the presence of border functions that are not at the edges of the state". In addition to visa procedures, these include traveler pre-screening "by airline agents and border officials prior to departure on international flights" (Salter, 2012, p. 736). Because of the COVID-19 pandemic, additional entry requirements have been imposed on international arrivals, including a negative COVID-19 test, strict quarantines, and in some cases proof of vaccination. Thus, a physical border has a widespread network of infrastructure and agents that perform the filtering functions of the border away from the actual boundary.

Notably, "possession of a visa or eligibility for a visa-free privilege does not constitute a right to enter a foreign country. Additional requirements may need to be met at the border" (Whyte, 2008, p. 136). Travel bans, blacklisting, and sanctions are forms of travel barriers that can be multilaterally, regionally, or unilaterally applied by governments. Sanctions have become "an increasingly popular tool for exercising foreign policy and politico-economic pressure on targeted actors" (Seyfi & Hall, 2020, p. 761). They range in scope from economic, financial, and diplomatic sanctions to restrictions on travel and cross-border mobility (Seyfi & Hall, 2020). In addition to restricting entry of certain nationals or groups of individuals, sanctions also create a negative image of a destination and construct psychological barriers, increase perceived risk, and "thus contribute to lower tourist arrivals" (Seyfi & Hall, 2020, p. 758).

The outbreak of COVID-19 has reinforced the physical presence of borders through international travel-related non-pharmaceutical interventions (NPIs). NPIs aim to slow the spread of infectious diseases and delay epidemic peaking (Ryu et al., 2020), and they have major impacts on tourism. NPIs vary from traveler screenings and testing at borders for symptoms of illness, travel restrictions between particular states or groups of states, quarantine requirements, and border closures. For many years, China has quietly gauged arriving passengers' temperatures with thermal imaging to detect any sign of illness.

The current pandemic has changed both the functional characteristics of borders and their meanings. For example, in the case of Russian second-home tourism in Finland, the Finnish–Russian border is a real physical barrier with a strict visa regime. However, in addition to being an actual obstacle, the border has played the role of perceived barrier that protects safe and desirable second-home locations in Finland and delineates sociocultural and linguistic barriers (Hannonen, 2016; Hannonen, Tuulentie & Pitkänen, 2015). During the 2020–2021 pandemic outbreak, the border became a stumbling block and reinforced its role as an actual barrier that restricts access to recreational properties (Pitkänen et al., 2020).

## Mental and Symbolic Barriers

Political borders are tangibly manifested in physical landscapes with tangible barriers, demarcation signs, administrative infrastructures, and institutional practices. This has contributed to a strong symbolic psychological significance in the human psyche. While a distinction is often made between mental boundaries and material boundaries, the two are, in fact, inseparable. The material border defines the legal jurisdiction and territorial limits of states, nationality, and citizenship. The physical border also provokes mental images of a particular country and its residents, and reinforces certain stereotypes and associations that are used, among other practices, in tourism promotions (Sofield, 2006) (see Table 9.1). In such a manner, "the border will thus combine both the material and the conceptual/mental, and tourism is interrelated intimately to both elements" (Sofield, 2006, p. 103).

Physical expressions of borders, and border symbols such as walls, watchtowers, fences, and fortresses, also play a performative role in tourism, attracting visitors to observe and photograph the borderscape (Fors, 2018; Timothy, 2001). The Berlin Wall is one of the most illustrative examples of a former physical and mental barrier that was, and continues to be, a significant tourist attraction. Borders as mental barriers refer to how the boundary is perceived and imagined by potential tourists on both sides. In this regard, perceived borders are social constructions that are constantly (re)produced. Borders as attractions and barriers are not just located in their physical geographical context but also in wider societal practices and in imagined cultural landscapes and metaphors that are reinforced through novels, movies, and folklore (Paasi & Raivo, 1998; Prokkola, 2010). Symbolic barriers are constructed and maintained by various tourist attractions such as war museums, heritage sites, and exhibitions (Mansfeld & Korman, 2015; Prokkola & Lois, 2016).

According to Paasi (1996), mental borders—borders in the mind—can be conceptualized as subjective representations or interpretations of demarcations between people and their territories. Mental barriers mean that even if the "other side" is physically proximate, it can be mentally distant. Thus, borders as mental and symbolic barriers can be viewed from the perspective of meanings that are attached to the border. For instance, the Berlin Wall was a symbol of the contrast between the capitalist West and the communist East—a miniature laboratory of the entire Iron Curtain that divided Europe socially, economically, politically, and ideologically. The West Bank barrier between Israel and Palestine is a physical barrier that has become "the ultimate activity holiday destination for graffiti writers" (Banksy, 2005, n.p.), who aim to modify people's representations of the wall, questioning its role and meaning (Fors, 2018, p. 40).

Politically motivated violence towards travelers presents a real risk, and perceived insecurities and fear can restrict travel even in destinations that are considered safe. People's insecurities and fear are often derived from a lack of knowledge, as well as psychocentric distances they create for themselves by fearing other languages and cultures, both of which can create a sense of insecurity and vulnerability. This kind of experience with insecurity often means different things to different individuals depending on nationality, age, education, gender, and previous travel experience (Lepp & Gibson, 2003). Likewise, travelers with different national or cultural backgrounds may perceived risks in different ways (Kozak, Crotts & Law, 2007).

Mental barriers do not only exist at geopolitically sensitive borderlands (Spierings & van der Velde, 2013; Timothy, 2019). Timothy and Tosun (2003) examine tourist perceptions of the Canada–USA border with a particular focus on experience barriers. They find that, for most people, that particular border does not create a considerable barrier. The countries are considered secure destinations that share good bilateral relations, and their citizenry shares the same language and similar cultures. Research shows that when tourists have a greater degree of knowledge about the border tourism, they often value border destinations more than tourists who know little (Del Río et al., 2017). For some people, however, borders seem to create a "subjective hindrance" that restricts their travel mobility. The perceived barrier effects of the border usually derive from previous experiences, hearsay from others, the necessary inconveniences related to crossing, and necessary encounters with intimidating frontier officials, in addition to general ignorance. Mental barriers are often so robust that they keep many people from crossing altogether and enjoying the pleasures that often exist abroad. Even open frontiers, such as those between EU and Schengen states, persist in the minds of latent travelers, even after years of border formalities having been eliminated in most cases (Paasi & Prokkola, 2008; Paasi et al., 2019; Spierings & van der Velde, 2013; Więckowski & Saarinen, 2019).

Clearly the removal of elements of the physical border and many administrative functions does not eliminate all perceived differences, for borders "carry a heavy weight of symbolism" (O'Dowd, 2002, p. 27). Even many ancient or more recent relict borders, which no longer function as lines of sovereignty, continue to sway the minds, cultures, and daily practices of borderlanders (Schmidtke, 2008), especially in former conflict or war zones (Lagiewski & Revelas, 2004). Thus, in addition to the physical boundaries themselves, the bordering process, the way borders are constructed and imagined, and the way people perceive and act on them are also impactful (Newman, 2006; Timothy, 2001). Even when physical demarcations are removed and political agendas change, borders "persist in peoples' minds" (Schack, 2000, p. 203). Strong mental and physical attachment to one's home in relation to the border mentally upholds the idea of the border and maintains the sociocultural condition of the borderlands (Gielis & van Houtum, 2012).

Political troubles between states can create mental divisions and hindrances to cross-border relations and tourism, but mental barriers can also be a product of the symbolic borders of tourism development. An example is the enclavic tourism growth in Los Cabos, Mexico, which fosters an increasing concentration of investment, income inequality, and social exclusion. This leads to spatial and social segregation and the marginalization of the local population and the erection of internal borders (Gamez & Angeles, 2010; Saarinen, 2017; Saarinen & Wall-Reinius, 2021).

While the physical border represents the top-down separation of the "self" from the "other" initiated by government, the perception of differences, individual border narratives, and experiences represent the bottom-up or the bordering process. Bordering entails "distinguishing between those who belong and those who do not" (Newman, 2006, p. 147), differentiating between "us" and "them", "insiders" and "outsiders". Thus, to define bottom-up bordering it is important to "listen to their personal and group narratives" (Newman, 2006, p. 154). The group narratives can refer to stereotypes and attitudes, political and social discourses, in relation to a particular group and/or citizen of a particular state, such as Finnish societal discourse on Russian second-home tourists in Finland (Hannonen, 2019).

In relation to crossing borders, how people perceive formalities and restrictions, administrative differences, costs, and opposing ideologies is significant (Van Houtum, 2010). Travel may be avoided entirely by many people if services are not available on the other side in the tourists' own language, for example. Scholars have discussed how border crossings may involve unpleasant and even humiliating bodily experiences and encounters that can reinforce mental barriers and hinder future travel (Wang, 2004; Zhang, 2013). In the case of the Croatia–Montenegro border, Lagiewski and Revelas (2004) examined the physical inconvenience of crossing, as well as the poor treatment by frontier staff, which are considered significant barriers for greater cross-border tourism development. Different languages and cultures on opposing sides of the border create an added barrier (see Table 9.1). Newman (2006, pp. 147–148) considers language the biggest chasm that "remains difficult to cross". Studies show that mental borders appear as significant barriers to tourism development and can repel first-time visitors and hinder people's intentions to revisit.

## Borders as Barriers to Tourism Development

Borders are traditionally perceived as obstacles to tourism industry development, functioning as barriers to human interactions, goods, and services (Bianchi, Stephenson & Hannam, 2020; Weidenfeld, 2013). From a physical perspective, security mechanisms (e.g., walls, fences, guard towers, and minefields) associated with borders are inconducive to the friendly, collaborative, and safe conditions that need to exist in successful tourism development. Even though research has shown that these often serve as tourist attractions in their own right, they more likely repel potential tourism investments, as well as individual tourist arrivals, and the tangible scars in the border landscape may damage natural ecosystems or cultural areas that lie adjacent to, or across, national frontiers. On the USA–Mexico border, where the recent Trump administration constructed approximately 740 km of a new border wall in 2019–2020, natural wildlife habitats and animal migration routes were truncated, pristine natural landscapes were divided, and ecosystems were disturbed (Best, 2021), making it difficult to protect certain natural and cultural assets and develop wilderness tourism along the border.

Perceptual boundaries, however, are more impactful than physical ones when it comes to tourism growth and development. Border regulations, political environments, and a lack of sociocultural cohesion affect border permeability and the potential for transfrontier tourism development. Despite the boundary and all that it entails, holistic and sustainable tourism planning should consider what is happening on the other side of the border and how it affects the developing destination. Planning and collaboration across an international divide is important, but binational or multinational cooperation is difficult at best, especially if legal regulations differ considerably and different levels of government are responsible for tourism development and policy-making (Timothy, 2001, pp. 162–163). Moreover, mismatched levels of socioeconomic development, cultural and institutional differences, and national traditions create hurdles that complicate communication and trust-building, which are essential ingredients in sustainable tourism management and development (Timothy, 2001, pp. 162–165). Even between countries in the EU, which share many multilateral policies and regulations, borders remain a salient obstacle to tourism planning and development (Mayer et al., 2019).

Border areas embody specific tourism landscapes where transnational social relations merge and where geopolitical assemblages are re-articulated (Mostafanezhad & Norum, 2016; Prokkola, 2007; Rowen, 2016). Tourism development simultaneously constitutes and reflects political discourses and "spatializes international politics as they are linked to global and local tourism industries" (Mostafanezhad & Norum, 2016). Thus, bilateral travel restrictions, sanctions, and differentiated visa policies are a few examples geopolitical restrictions on travel.

The impacts of tourism on borders and borders on tourism growth and development are widely studied. In the case of Croatia and Montenegro, visa requirements are considered a major hindrance to greater tourism flows and regional tourism development (Lagiewski & Revelas, 2004). Since Lagiewski and Revelas's work in 2004, this particular border has opened up somewhat with both countries now having some similar visa policies, though Croatia has since joined the European Union, while Montenegro remains outside it as of mid-2022. Thus, their common border on the Prevlaka Peninsula is an EU external border, which has major implications not only for cross-border mobility but also for transboundary tourism development in a region that shares a history and many cultural and natural assets. There are many examples of border constraints to regional tourism development (Poulaki et al., 2022; Saarinen 2017), partitioned states (e.g., northern and southern Cyprus, see Webster & Timothy, 2006), and conflicted and contested borders (e.g., Israel–Palestine, see Gelbman, 2008; and Peru-Ecuador, see Saba, 1999).

The level of border permeability influences tourism development on both sides, including infrastructure, transportation, services and facilities, as well as marketing activities and attraction development. Border locations are often remote and peripheral. Thus, travel is frequently more expensive and burdensome. The development of tourism in peripheral areas is not always supported by national decision-makers. Even in Europe where cross-border mobilities and economic zones of activity have been supported with EU structural funds, tourism development in border regions faces many challenges (Prokkola, 2007; Stoffelen et al., 2017).

In the German–Czech borderlands, Stoffelen et al. (2017) identified obstacles to cross-border tourism governance, including institutional incompatibility between the tourism governance systems in neighboring states, destination management complexities on two sides of the border, weak structural alignment and an over-reliance on short-term European funding to support tourism projects, and sociocultural differences that hinder operational collaboration (Stoffelen et al., 2017, p. 136). Moreover, in cross-border destinations that have similar tourist attractions and services, open borders may not only suffer from a lack of collaboration but may also experience increased competition between neighboring borderland destinations and tourism enterprises. Ioannides, Nielsen, and Billing (2006) examine cross-border cooperation from the perspective of tourism at the Finnish–Swedish border. Their research concluded that competition for visitors and customers, combined with national cultural differences, are apt to maintain and even strengthen the mental barriers between Finnish and Swedish stakeholders. Other research similarly concludes that national interests are usually prioritized over tokenistic transfrontier outreach in the development of tourism destinations, and the costs and benefits of border tourism continue to be measured separately (Fors, 2018; Prokkola, 2009).

A lack of knowledge and even mistrust towards stakeholders on the other side of the border often restricts local and regional cooperation. In many border areas, cultural, linguistic, and organizational differences form institutional and mental barriers that are difficult to bypass. Local and regional conflicts of interest are common within state territories; however, in cross-border tourism development, national institutions and cultural differences create additional barriers to collaborative tourism development (Blasco et al., 2014; Quack, 2006). Although administrative and organizational hindrances and competition are common in state-centric destination development, these are often easier to manage and overcome.

Tourism development in border areas is often rather vulnerable to external shocks and high-level political tensions. The opening of a closed state border or the sudden closure of a previously open border can have sudden and dramatic impacts on tourism and enterprises in border areas. This has been illustrated by the COVID-19 pandemic but also by various geopolitical and economic events that have stagnated travel mobilities. In borderlands, where the customer base is largely homogeneous (e.g., focusing on cross-border shopping tourism), changes to transfrontier mobility can essentially freeze all tourism growth and development (Prokkola, 2019). Moreover, since geopolitical troubles between states often strengthen transborder divisions, both perceptual and physical, new hurdles to cross-border tourism and tourism development are created.

## Discussion and Conclusion

Borders have featured prominently in discussions of international mobility during 2020–2021 (e.g., Häkli, 2021; Więckowski & Timothy, 2021). Borders as physical barriers have been re-established even within the promised "borderless" Europe. For many travelers, tightened border and visa regulations are not new, however. International travel mobility has been "subject to intense political scrutiny" in recent years, and many countries have strengthened their control over mobilities within and across their sovereign boundaries (Bianchi, Stephenson & Hannam, 2020, p. 290). The COVID-19 pandemic that started in 2020 has showed that travel restrictions and border closures are a powerful means of restricting travel mobilities in the name of domestic security. COVID-19 travel restrictions created barriers to almost all worldwide travel at some point in 2020–2021. If previous popular and academic discourse has focused on debordering processes, easy travel access with lists of the best passports for travel being written, and rankings of the most open destinations being compared, the barrier function of border has re-entered the discourse. This emphasizes that, regardless of the utopian vision of a "borderless world", the functions of international frontiers as barriers to human mobility have never been fully quelled.

The COVID-19 pandemic offers a unique moment to study the relationships between tourism and borders, and it may influence both physical and mental barriers regarding international travel in the long term. In some countries like Sweden, in recent years, new mental barriers to international travel mobility started to emerge even before the pandemic. Research suggests that in some countries people are taking more responsibility for their own greenhouse gas emissions and adaptations to climate change. A major societal change like COVID-19 can entail major behavioral changes and lower people's interest in air travel, for example (Becken, 2007), and open a more hopeful and sustainable path for international tourism (Crossley, 2020). The physical and mental barriers that borders create for international air travel and slow rail travel during the pandemic and in a post-COVID-19 world may have many similarities and differences, and will require additional scholarly attention.

The outbreak of COVID-19 and examples of previous regional health risks (e.g., Ebola and SARS) have resulted in the erection of administrative barriers in terms of travel restrictions and constructed a perception of destinations as risky and unsafe. This emphasizes the fluid nature of borders and their multilayered structures and functions. Depending on the situation, different border layers are either lifted or constructed as constraints to travel. Geopolitical tensions often uphold physical and mental borders. However, physical borders become barriers in increasingly diverse ways. Recent border control practices show that borders are used by governments as tools for actions against individual persons, groups of people, states, or groups of states in the form of "pre-borders", "paper borders", "e-borders, and sanctions. In this way, particular borders become uneven barriers for citizens of one state and open doors for others.

Drawing on the most recent studies on barriers in tourism and empirical cases of rebordering, we conclude that borders as barriers to tourism development and travel mobilities will persist, while modes of bordering will be diverse in their forms and targets.

## References

Adey, P. (2009). Facing airport security: Affect, biopolitics, and the preemptive securitisation of the mobile body. *Environment and Planning D: Society and Space*, 27(2), 274–295.

Amoore, L. (2006). Biometric borders: Governing mobilities in the war on terror. *Political Geography*, 25(3), 336–351.

Banksy, R. (2005). *Wall and piece*. London: Century.

Bätzner, A.N., & Stephenson, M.L. (2017). Towards an integrated transport network in the GCC region: Fostering tourism and regional cooperation. In M.L. Stephenson, & A. Al-Hamarneh (eds), *International tourism development and the Gulf Cooperation Council states: Challenges and opportunities*, pp. 76–91. London: Routledge.

Becken, S. (2007). Tourists' perception of international air travel's impact on the global climate and potential climate change policies. *Journal of Sustainable Tourism*, 15(4), 351–368.

Best, S. (2021). The costs of a wall: The impact of pseudo-security policies on communities, wildlife, and ecosystems on the US-Mexico border. In N. Khazaal, & N. Almiron (eds), *Like an animal: Critical animal studies approaches to borders, displacement, and othering*, pp. 255–280. Leiden: Brill.

Bianchi, R. (2006). Tourism and the globalisation of fear: Analysing the politics of risk and (in)security in global travel. *Tourism and Hospitality Research*, 7(1), 64–74.

Bianchi, R.V., Stephenson, M.L., & Hannam, K. (2020). The contradictory politics of the right to travel: Mobilities, borders & tourism, *Mobilities*, 15(2), 290–306.

Blasco, D., Guia, J., & Prats, L. (2014). Emergence of governance in cross-border destinations. *Annals of Tourism Research*, 49, 159–173.

Boehmer, C.R., & Peña, S. (2012). The determinants of open and closed borders. *Journal of Borderlands Studies*, 27(3), 273–285.

Boonchai, P., & Freathy, P. (2020). Cross-border tourism and the regional economy: A typology of the ignored shopper. *Current Issues in Tourism*, 23(5), 626–640.

Bringas, N., & Verduzco, P. (2008). The construction of the northern border as a tourist destination in a context of security alerts. *Region and Society*, 20(42), 3–36.

Brown, W. (2010). *Walled states, waning sovereignty*. New York: Zone Books.

Cohen, E. (2021). Mobility regimes, subversive mobilities, and tourism. *Tourism Analysis*, 26(1), 91–103.

Crossley, É. (2020). Ecological grief generates desire for environmental healing in tourism after COVID-19. *Tourism Geographies*, 22(3), 536–546.

Del Río, J., Agüera, F., Cuadra, S., & Morales, P. (2017). Satisfaction in border tourism: An analysis with structural equations. *European Research on Management and Business Economics*, 23(2), 103–112.

Fors, B.S. (2018). *Border performances: Politics, art and tourism where Norway meets Russia*. Doctoral Dissertation. Tromsø: University of Tromsø, Norway.

Franklin, A. (2003). *Tourism: An introduction*. London: SAGE.

Gamez, A., & Angeles, M. (2010). Borders within: Tourism growth, migration and regional polarization in Baja California Sur (Mexico). *Journal of Borderlands Studies*, 25(1), 1–18.

Gelbman, A. (2008). Border tourism in Israel: Conflict, peace, fear and hope. *Tourism Geographies*, 10(2), 193–213.

Gelbman, A., & Timothy, D.J. (2011). Border complexity, tourism and international exclaves: A case study. *Annals of Tourism Research*, 38(1), 110–131.

Gielis, R., & van Houtum, H. (2012). Sloterdijk in the house! Dwelling in the borderscape of Germany and the Netherlands. *Geopolitics*, 17(4), 797–817.

Häkli, J. (2021). COVID-19 certificates as a new form of mobility control. *European Journal of Risk Regulation*, 12(2), 362–369.

Hannonen, O. (2016). *Peace and quiet beyond the border: The trans-border mobility of Russian second home owners in Finland*. Tampere: Juvenes Press.

Hannonen, O. (2019). Bordering mobilities: The case of Russian trans-border second-home ownership in Finland. *Journal of Finnish Studies*, 22(1&2), 241–264.

Hannonen, O., Tuulentie, S., & Pitkänen, K. (2015). Borders and second home tourism: Norwegian and Russian second home owners in Finnish border areas. *Journal of Borderlands Studies*, 30(1), 53–67.

Hartman, K. (2006). Destination management in cross-border regions. In H. Wachowiak (ed), *Tourism and borders. Contemporary issues, policies and international research*, pp. 89–109. Aldershot: Ashgate.

Ioannides, D., Nielsen, P., & Billing, P. (2006). Trans-boundary collaboration in tourism: The case of the Bothian Arc. *Tourism Geographies*, 8(2), 122–142.

Izotov, A., & Laine, J. (2013). Constructing (Un)familiarity: Role of tourism in identity and region building at the Finnish–Russian border. *European Planning Studies*, 21(1), 93–111.

Jones, R. (2012). *Border walls: Security and the war on terror in the United States, India, and Israel*. London: Zed Books.

Kozak, M., Crotts, J.C., & Law, R. (2007). The impact of the perception of risk on international travellers. *International Journal of Tourism Research*, 9, 233–242.

Lagiewski, R.M. & Revelas, D.A. (2004). *Challenges in cross-border tourism regions*. Rochester, NY: Rochester Institute of Technology.

Laine, J. (2017). Finnish-Russian border mobility and tourism: Localism overruled by geopolitics. In D. Hall (ed), *Tourism and geopolitics: Issues and concepts from central and Eastern Europe*, pp. 178–190. Boston: CABI.

Leimgruber, W. (1998). Defying political boundaries: Transborder tourism in a regional context. *Visions in Leisure and Business*, 17(3), 8–29.

Lepp, A. & Gibson, H. (2003). Tourist roles, perceived risk and international tourism. *Annals of Tourism Research*, 30(3), 606–624.

Mansfeld, Y. & Korman, T. (2015). Between war and peace: Conflict heritage tourism along three Israeli border areas. *Tourism Geographies*, 17(3), 437–460.

Matznetter, J. (1978). Border and tourism: Fundamental relations. In G. Gruber, H. Lamping, W. Lutz, J. Matznetter, & K. Vorlaufer (eds), *Tourism and borders: Proceedings of the meeting of the IGU working group – geography of tourism and recreation*, pp. 61–73. Frankfurt: Institut für Wirtschafts – und Sozialgeographie der Johann Wolfgang Goethe Universitat.

Mayer, M., Zbaraszewski, W., Pieńkowski, D., Gach, G., & Gernert, J. (2019). Cross-border politics and development in the European Union with a focus on tourism. In M. Mayer, W. Zbaraszewski, D. Pieńkowski, G. Gach, & J. Gernert (eds) *Cross-border tourism in protected areas: Potentials, pitfalls and perspectives*, pp. 65–84. Cham, Switzerland: Springer.

Medvedev, S. (1999). Across the line: Borders in post-Westphalian landscapes. In H. Eskelinen, I. Liikanen, & J. Oksa (eds), *Curtains of iron and gold: Reconstructing borders and scales of interaction*, pp. 43–56. Aldershot: Ashgate.

Mostafanezhad, M. & Norum, R. (2016). Towards a geopolitics of tourism. *Annals of Tourism Research*, 61, 226–228.

Newman, D. (2006). The lines that continue to separate us: Borders in our 'borderless' world. *Progress in Human Geography*, 30(2), 143–161.

Nijkamp, P. Rietveld, P. & Salomon, I. (1990). Barriers in spatial interactions and communications. A conceptual exploration. *The Annals of Regional Science*, 24, 237–252.

O'Dowd, L. (2002). The changing significance of European borders. *Regional & Federal Studies*, 12(4), 13–36.

Paasi, A. (1996). *Territories, boundaries and consciousness*. New York: Wiley.

Paasi, A. & Prokkola, E-K. (2008). Territorial dynamics, cross-border work and everyday life in the Finnish–Swedish border area. *Space and Polity*, 12(1), 13–29.

Paasi, A., Prokkola, E.K., Saarinen, J., & Zimmerbauer, K. (eds) (2019). *Borderless worlds for whom? Ethics, moralities and mobilities*. New York: Routledge.

Paasi, A. & Raivo, P. (1998). Boundaries as barriers and promoters: Constructing the tourist landscapes of Finnish Karelia. *Visions in Leisure and Business*, 17(3), Article 4.

Pitkänen, K., Hannonen, O., Toso, S., Gallent, N., Hamiduddin, I., Halseth, G., Hall, C.M., Müller, D.K., Treivish, A., & Nefedova, T. (2020). Second homes during corona – safe or unsafe haven and for whom? Reflections from researchers around the world. *Finnish Journal of Tourism Studies*, 16(2), 20–39.

Poulaki, I., Papatheodorou, A., Panagiotopoulos, A., & Liasidou, S. (2022). Exclave accessibility and cross-border travel: The pene-exclave of Ceuta, Spain. *Tourism Geographies*, 24(1), 152–176.

Prideaux, B. & Kim, S. (2018). Protocols as a strategy to reduce travel barriers between countries experiencing or have recently experienced serious political difficulties. *Tourism Recreation Research*, 43(2), 197–208.

Prokkola, E.K. (2007). Cross-border regionalization and tourism development at the Swedish-Finnish border: Destination Arctic circle. *Scandinavian Journal of Hospitality and Tourism*, 7(2), 120–138.

Prokkola, E.K. (2009). Resources and barriers in tourism development: Cross-border cooperation, regionalization and destination building at the Finnish-Swedish border. *Fennia*, 186, 31–46.

Prokkola, E.K. (2010). Borders in tourism: Transformation of the Swedish-Finnish border landscape. *Current Issues in Tourism*, 13, 223–238.

Prokkola, E.K. (2019). Border-regional resilience in EU internal and external border areas in Finland. *European Planning Studies*, 37(8), 1587–1606.

Prokkola, E.K. & Lois, M. (2016). Scalar politics of border heritage: An examination of the EU's northern and southern border areas. *Scandinavian Journal of Hospitality and Tourism*, 16(1), 14–35.

Quack, H.D. (2006). Organizing destination management: France and Germany compared. In H. Wachowiak (ed), *Tourism and borders. Contemporary issues, policies and international research*, pp.77–87. Aldershot: Ashgate.

Rowen, I. (2016). The geopolitics of tourism: mobilities, territory, and protest in China, Taiwan, and Hong Kong. *Annals of the American Association of Geographers*, 106(2), 385–393.

Ryu, S., Gao, H., Wong, J.Y., Shiu, E.Y.C., Xiao, J., Fong, M.W., & Cowling, B.J. (2020). Nonpharmaceutical measures for pandemic influenza in nonhealthcare settings – international travel-related measures. *Emerging Infectious Diseases*, 26(5), 961–966.

Saarinen, J. (2017). Enclavic tourism spaces: Territorialization and bordering in tourism destination development and planning. *Tourism Geographies*, 19(3), 425–437.

Saarinen, J., & Wall-Reinius, S. (Eds.) (2021). *Tourism enclaves: Geographies of exclusive spaces in tourism.* London: Routledge.

Saba, R. (1999). From peace to partnership: Challenges of integration and development along the Peru-Ecuador Border. *Journal of Borderlands Studies*, 14(2), 1–22.

Salter, M.B. (2012). Theory of the / : The Suture and Critical Border Studies. *Geopolitics*, 17, 734–755.

Schack, M. (2000). On the Multicontextual character of border regions. In M. van der Velde & H. van Houtum (eds), *Borders, regions, and people*, pp. 202–219. London: Pion Limited.

Schack, M. (2001). Regional identity in border regions: The difference borders make. *Journal of Borderlands Studies*, 16(2), 99–114.

Schmidtke, O. (2008). Borders in public perception. In O. Schmidtke, & S. Ozcurumez (eds) *Of states, rights, and social closure: Governing migration and citizenship*, pp. 91–110. New York: Palgrave Macmillan.

Seyfi, S. & Hall, C.M. (2020). Sanctions and tourism: Effects, complexities and research. *Tourism Geographies*, 22(4–5), 749–767.

Sofield, T.H.B. (2006). Border tourism and border communities: An overview. *Tourism Geographies*, 8(2), 102–121.

Sönmez, S.F., Apostolopoulos, Y., & Tarlow, P. (1999). Tourism in crisis: Managing the effects of terrorism. *Journal of Travel Research*, 38(1), 13–18.

Spierings, B. & van der Velde, M. (2013). Cross-border differences and unfamiliarity: Shopping mobility in the Dutch-German Rhine-Waal Euroregion. *European Planning Studies*, 21(1), 5–23.

State Department (2020). U.S. Department of State – bureau of consular affairs: Visa waiver program. https://travel.state.gov/content/travel/en/us-visas/tourism-visit/visa-waiver-program.html

Stoffelen, A., Ioannides, D. & Vanneste, D. (2017). Obstacles to achieving cross-border tourism governance: A multi-scalar approach focusing on the German-Czech borderlands. *Annals of Tourism Research*, 64, 126–138.

Timothy, D.J. (1995). Political boundaries and tourism: Borders as tourist attractions. *Tourism Management*, 16(7), 525–532.

Timothy, D.J. (2001). *Tourism and political boundaries.* Routledge: London.

Timothy, D.J. (2019). Tourism, border disputes and claims to territorial sovereignty. In R.K. Isaac, E. Çakmak, & R. Butler (eds) *Tourism and hospitality in conflict-ridden destinations*, pp. 25–38. London: Routledge.

Timothy, D.J., Saarinen, J. & Viken, A. (2016). Editorial: Tourism issues and international borders in the Nordic region. *Scandinavian Journal of Hospitality and Tourism*, 16(1), 1–13.

Timothy, D.J., & Teye, V. (2004). Political boundaries and regional cooperation in tourism. In A. Lew, C.M. Hall, & A. Williams (eds), *A companion to tourism*, pp. 584–585. Malden, MA: Blackwell.

Timothy, D.J., & Tosun, C. (2003). Tourists' perceptions of the Canada–USA border as a barrier to tourism at the International Peace Garden. *Tourism Management*, 24(4), 411–421.

Towner, J. (1996). *A historical geography of recreation and tourism in the Western World 1540–1940*. New York: Wiley.

Vallet, É. & Charles-Philippe, D. (2012). Introduction: The (re)building of the wall in international relations. *Journal of Borderlands Studies*, 27(2), 111–119.

Van der Velde, M. & Spierings, B. (2010). Consumer mobility and the Communication of Difference: Reflecting on cross-Border shopping practices and experiences in the Dutch-German borderland. *Journal of Borderlands Studies*, 25(3&4), 191–205.

Van Houtum, H. (2010). Waiting before the Law: Kafka on the border. *Social and Legal Studies*, 19(3), 285–297.

Van Houtum, H. & Lacy, R.B. (2020). The autoimmunity of the EU's deadly b/ordering regime; Overcoming its paradoxical paper, iron and camp borders. *Geopolitics*, 25(3), 706–733.

Wang, H. (2004). Regulating transnational flows of people: An institutional analysis of passports and visas as a regime of mobility. *Identities*, 11(3), 351–376.

Webster, C. & Timothy, D.J. (2006). Travelling to the 'other side': The occupied zone and Greek Cypriot views of crossing the Green Line. *Tourism Geographies*, 8(2), 162–181.

Weidenfeld, A. (2013). Tourism and cross border regional innovation system. *Annals of Tourism Research*, 42, 191–213.

Whyte, B. (2008). Visa-free travel privileges: An exploratory geographical analysis. *Tourism Geographies*, 10(2), 127–149.

Więckowski, M., & Saarinen, J. (2019). Tourism transitions, changes, and the creation of new spaces and places in Central-Eastern Europe. *Geographia Polonica*, 92(4), 369–377.

Więckowski, M., & Timothy, D.J. (2021). Tourism and an evolving international boundary: Bordering, debordering and rebordering on Usedom Island, Poland-Germany. *Journal of Destination Marketing & Management*, 22, 100647.

Zhang, J.J. (2013). Borders on the move: Cross-strait tourists' material moments on 'the other side' in the midst of rapprochement between China and Taiwan. *Geoforum*, 48, 94–101.

# 10
# ENCLAVE TOURISM
## Bounded Spaces and Social Exclusion

*Adam Weaver*

## Introduction

In 2020, as a result of the COVID-19 pandemic, the word "bubble" became synonymous with the management of a highly contagious disease. Bubbles are a "protected" space and can exist at different scales. Bubbles may include a group of individuals, perhaps members of one household or more than one household, who restrict their social interactions to those within a collectively agreed-upon cluster. As well as bubbles operating at the scale of individuals and households, others may include two or more countries. Transnational bubbles could conceivably encompass two or more countries that have successfully tamed COVID-19 (Fusté-Forné & Michael, in press; Sharun et al., 2020). Travel between or among these countries, while closely monitored, was sanctioned during the pandemic, as in the case of the Australia–New Zealand travel bubble, which was established, disestablished, and re-established in 2021 (Baratti, 2021), and the Baltic Bubble, which was effective for a short time in 2020, enabling barrier-free travel between Estonia, Latvia, and Lithuania (Mzezewa, 2020).

With respect to tourism, the word "bubble" has a meaning that predates COVID-19. In this context, bubbles refer to enclaved environments (Cohen, 1972; Jaakson, 2004; Jacobsen, 2003), or touristic spaces that are set apart from the normative spaces of the destination where residents live and work. They typically manifest in a built form, separate—or separable—from other places. People or activities deemed to be troubling, controversial, or unwelcome can be removed and prohibited entry. Tourist bubbles, or enclaves, include urban entertainment districts, resort complexes, casino hotels, theme parks, cruise ships, and backpacker zones (Saarinen & Wall-Reinius, 2019). A commercial logic usually underpins their creation and functioning (Saarinen, 2017), wherein their spatial configuration is designed to profit directly from tourism. Enclosing tourist spaces is deployed in ways that are most conducive to generating revenue. Even tourist spaces that evolve organically (e.g., backpacker enclaves), rather than being planned purposively, become centres of profit-making.

Tourism occurs in many different types of places, some of which could be described as enclavic spaces—not to be confused with the geopolitical and legal state territories known as enclaves or exclaves. The premise of this chapter is that tourism enclaves, when considered in broad terms, possess a complexity that runs counter to their seemingly straightforward physical attributes, namely their bounded or bordered character. Clearly and distinctly demarcated leisure spaces for tourism have prompted a wide range of scholarly studies that have examined their composition and structure (e.g., Freitag, 1994; Howard, 2007; Jacobsen, 2003; Saarinen & Wall-Reinius, 2019).

This chapter reviews four prominent themes relevant to the study of enclaved tourism spaces. Each theme explores different dimensions of tourism enclaves that relate to their borders and bounded spaces. First, tourism enclaves encompass a variety of types, for enclaves assume many different forms. Enclosuring manifests itself in a variety of ways and across an array of contexts. The second theme addresses the benefits and drawbacks of enclaved environments. These benefits and drawbacks have been debated extensively and are related to the circumscribed nature of enclaves. Third, bounded enclavic places are connected to the wider world. They are both separate from, and integrated with, broader socioeconomic systems and processes. The fourth theme is related to the physical features of tourist enclaves—their material attributes and borders, as well as their symbolic or image-oriented qualities. These four themes encompass ideas and arguments that have defined the study of tourism enclaves to date. Research into these exclusive tourist spaces, furthermore, reveals divisions and separation that are not dissimilar to normative social stratification.

## Enclaved Tourism Spaces: A Diversity of Types

Words such as "enclave" and "bubble" are applied to different spatial forms and physical environments in the tourism industry. They are usually physically removed from their broader environmental contexts and encompass spaces as diverse as entertainment districts in cities, beach resorts, casino resorts, theme parks, urban backpacker zones, wildlife game parks in Africa, and cruise ships (Carlisle & Jones, 2012; Mbaiwa, 2005; Mbaiwa & Hambira, 2020; Saarinen & Wall-Reinius, 2019; Timothy & Zhu, 2022). The means of separation offered by the tourist bubble, the boundary between the contained holiday environment and its surroundings, vary. A cruise ship at sea is bounded by water; gated beach resorts or tourist-only game preserves may have security checkpoints, border fencing, and security walls, much like the securityscapes of many international borders. Urban tourism enclaves represent neighbourhoods or zones within a city where opportunities to shop, meet, and mingle with fellow travellers, gamble, and attend concerts or professional sporting events are concentrated (Krakover & Wang, 2008; Simpson, 2016). The boundaries separating tourist spaces and residents may not be physically comprised of walls, barricades, or gates, as in the case of many city-based tourist bubbles, but these methods of demarcation and fortification are common surrounding many high-end beach resorts and golf clubs where local residents without financial means or social capital are generally unwelcome. Exclusion is sometimes far subtler than fences and walls. It may be in the form of high admission fees or retail prices that keep many people out or make them feel out of place. These exclusionary zones are also often used to create staged environments that erase visible evidence of poverty or squalor from the frame of the tourist gaze.

Tourist bubbles sometimes represent points of intersection between wealthier and poorer countries. For example, many resort enclaves are nodes of Western amenities, which may not be widely available outside of the tourist bubble (Saarinen, 2017; Timothy & Zhu, 2022; Torres & Momsen, 2005). Cruise ship passengers, for example, can visit ports of call in impoverished countries and then retreat to the confines, comforts, and first-world environments of their vessels whenever they wish to do so. Resorts, theme parks, and cruise ships are free of permanent inhabitants other than the employees who support the visitor experience. In these enclavic spaces, tourists are insulated from the nuisances, or even repulsions, that may be created by the presence of local inhabitants.

Urban tourist bubbles have resident neighbours, many of whom may live in squalid conditions, but most urban tourism enclaves are typically safe, prettified (perhaps even idealized) versions of a town for those who wish to avoid the gritty, raw environment of an underdeveloped city (Che, 2008; Silk, 2007). Some scholarly research is critical of elements of the present-day city: the way it emphasizes spectacle, its fixation with economic growth, the obsession with image and civic boosterism (often gratuitous promoting), and the increasing privatization of public spaces (Harvey, 1989; Simpson, 2016). Sharp distinctions between environments devoted to consumption and play (i.e., manicured tourist zones) and those plagued by physical decay, dereliction, and deteriorating of infrastructure—the province of the locals—often alienate residents.

Tourism enclaves are commodified domains designed to please consumers. They signal the existence of markets that desire to spend increasingly available discretionary income in predictable, non-threatening spaces. These tourist bubbles appeal to different market segments, from budget backpackers (Howard, 2007; Timothy & Zhu, 2022; Wilson & Richards, 2008) to affluent tourists seeking premium services (Atkinson & Blandy, 2009; Brenner & Aguilar, 2002). This diversity of markets, as well as the wide range of existing enclave environments, are accompanied by, from the perspective of some commentators, a perceived sense of sameness, or the McDonaldization of the tourist bubble (Ritzer & Liska, 1997), which provides the same comforts and conveniences of home.

Some enclaves or parts of them are enclosed, indoor environments that are climate controlled; air conditioning is a standard feature within warm-climate tourist bubbles. Other enclaves, however, are open-air spaces. There are mobile enclaves (e.g., cruise ships) and those that are territorially fixed. Most bubbles, despite their differences, share a common set of attributes. They are insular spaces geared to commerce; retail is interwoven with other activities and events. They host a variety of amenities, and underpinning the boundaries and barriers that define the enclave, from the perspective of the destination and investors, is a desire for territorial control, exclusion, and profit-making.

## The Benefits and Drawbacks of Enclosure

The wide array of bubbles in existence makes it particularly difficult to arrive at definitive conclusions related to their benefits and drawbacks. For some observers, the source of their popularity is puzzling. For example, this form of tourism, especially resorts, is out of favour with those who wish to have an immersive cultural experience rather than a getaway oriented towards a pleasurable escape (Cohen, 1972). To consumers who find tourism enclaves appealing, they promise security and even prestige, as well as a clean, calm environment: the perceived opposite of nearby busy streets teeming with vendors, hawkers, and poor people. Tourism enclaves ensure safer and more predictable consumption spaces and create an appealing stage that idealizes the destination for visitors.

Shopping and relaxation are combined according to a carefully determined formula. The obsessive management that underpins the operation of Disney-owned theme parks is, in part, responsible for the global reverence they have cultivated amongst consumers (Wasko, 2001; Zukin, 1991). Nonetheless, enclaved tourism is the subject of sharp social and academic criticism, but it is undeniably regarded with great favour and approval by many consumers (Wall-Reinius et al., 2019).

Most of the benefits of enclave tourism are retained by the organizations that own the bubble environments (Mbaiwa, 2005). Most resorts are self-contained, offering multiple food services, shopping opportunities, recreational activities, and even tours outside the walls of the resort property. Cruise ship companies have developed mobile enclaves that are particularly effective at capturing a growing proportion of passenger-spending both onboard and in port (Weaver, 2005). Even in backpacker enclaves, certain businesses cluster to form critical masses of services (e.g., food, lodging, internet service, and tours), ensuring that backpacker tourists do not have to go beyond the borders of their bubbles to purchase services and activities.

Tourism is typically presented as a vehicle for urban, regional, and national development. Residents may benefit but not necessarily benefit handsomely, especially in countries of the Global South. The bounded nature of tourist enclaves often has negative implications for local entrepreneurs, who are often unable to compete with the resorts and cruise ships (Freitag, 1994). Many globally branded enclaves are owned and operated by outside investors, causing severe economic leakages of income from tourism, with relatively few of the profits remaining in the destination. Despite these challenges, many destinations choose enclaved tourism as an economic alternative, because they feel that, in light of a lack of options, some tourism-derived income is better than none at all. Despite its pitfalls, for cities and countries with few options for economic growth, enclave tourism can provide much needed hard currency for the state and create jobs for some local residents (Naidoo & Pearce, 2018; Nunkoo & Ramkissoon, 2016).

This form of tourism creates a spatially polarized domain—an "inside" and an "outside", an "us" versus "them" relationship that segregates visitors from residents for the most part but can, as already noted, create some connectivity through the creation of employment, even though these jobs are typically low-wage service sector positions. Although enclaved spaces do not necessarily create a considerable stock of wealth for a destination community, there are some socioeconomic benefits. For instance, enclaves can assist in managing the impacts of concentrated visitor numbers and simultaneously act as a social, cultural, and environmental showcase for the destination (Saarinen & Wall-Reinius, 2019). Their insularity and defined boundaries, while controversial in many respects with regard to social exclusion, may be a means of controlling some of the visitor-related impacts of tourism.

The insularity of tourist bubbles and the increased safety they provide, for instance a secure distillation of downtowns and holiday destinations for those who wish to avoid potentially unsavoury environments, simultaneously poses a threat in the era of COVID-19. Close quarters provide ideal environments for the transmission of contagious viruses. Travel news headlines throughout 2020 and 2021 were plastered with cruise cancellations and resort shutdowns. Buffets, concerts, children's play areas, casinos, and other spaces and occasions on board a cruise ship or in a casino resort present serious hazards. The cruise industry and many vacation destinations have a long and difficult path to recovery after the current global pandemic becomes manageable (Assaf & Scuderi, 2020; Papathanassis & Klein, 2020). Consideration must be given to what can easily circulate within the confines of a tourist bubble, as well as what it seeks to exclude.

## Tourism Enclaves and the Wider World

Tourism enclaves have developed in response to the rise of tourism globally. In terms of amenities for tourists, enclaves are often islands of Western comfort within a sea of unfamiliarity (Saarinen, 2017; Torres & Momsen, 2005). Enclaved spaces usually feature pristine and modern facilities. They often appear to be separate from the wider world and shielded from the possibility of intrusion. However, studying tourism enclaves is a valuable entrée to understanding wider social and economic configurations.

Tourism enclaves are spaces that are simultaneously bounded and connected. The construction of physical boundaries and barriers is as old as human settlement itself (Newman, 1973).

Separation and detachment are part of the appeal of enclaves. From the perspective of many tourists, the world outside an enclave features potential threats. Ensuring that certain people remain outside is as important as ensuring that a measurable volume of people enter and spend their money inside.

As contained spaces, it is tempting to try to understand tourism enclaves in isolation. Bubbles and their immediate surroundings may reflect processes within the wider world. Many attributes of cruise ships, for example the international division of labour on board, flags of convenience, and deterritorialization, are emblematic of globalization (Timothy, 2006; Wood, 2000). Brands of various types dominate the world inside and outside of tourist bubbles. For example, Coca Cola or Pepsi products are widely available within theme parks, specifically from on-site concessions, as well as outlets and popular chain restaurants around the world.

Commerce defines the world within circumscribed tourism spaces, even beyond their established boundaries. The presence and popularity of tourist bubbles are arguably a response to, and reflection of, growing inequalities in the world. Tourists seek to protect themselves from the intrusion of danger, crime, or visual unpleasantries assumed to threaten them from the outside. The same motives and desire for enclosure can be seen in the residential domain, namely in gated communities (Bartling, 2006; Saarinen & Wall-Reinius, 2019). Many people travel to, and play within, enclaves, as well as reside within fortified communities. The desire for safety and seclusion is present at home and away. This phenomenon, if taken to the extreme, becomes a manifestation of the "succession of the successful" described by Reich (1991).

Two other factors—constant virtual connectivity and political ideology—reinforce a comfort with and demand for separation. First, the increasing connectedness of the world at large via the internet and social media potentially intensifies the longing for greater privacy. Tourism enclaves provide opportunities for people to retreat into more cloistered domains, even if they decide to continue to read and answer work-related emails and engage their broader world through social media. Second, bubbles extend to the realm of ideology. The United States, in political terms, can be characterized as two polarized bubbles, for example red and blue states (Gelman, 2010). These country-wide divisions may normalize other types of segregation or division, including tourism-based ones.

## Tourism Enclaves: Material and Symbol-rich Spaces

Aside from some backpacker areas that develop organically, most tourism enclaves are not only planned environments but also engineered ones. The barriers that define such enclaves are physical and include boundary fences and security checkpoints in response to perceived threats. Those who are not sufficiently affluent to be part of the enclaved market are excluded, and a fortress mentality often leads enclaves' development and management, as they become pseudo-fortresses. Even backpacker enclaves, however, evolve into protected areas meant for a foreign market, which might not be affluent, but does desire a respite from the difficult world to which backpacker tourists are constantly exposed.

There are symbolic and physical dimensions to tourism enclaves (Kothari, 2015). Boosterism and marketing help propel their commercial success. The construction of tourism-oriented amenities in urban areas is a way for a city to secure status and prominence (Simpson, 2016). Promotional efforts, as one would anticipate, circulate favourable images of enclaves. Producers of widely disseminated representations and images—travel writers and bloggers, website content creators, social media influencers, and television travel program producers—have generated images of tourism enclaves for a mass audience. These producers have imagined bubbles embodying positive traits such as hospitality, relaxation, and a carefree holiday experience.

They may also reflect or embody the personal aspiration of travellers to access a standard of comfort and service at a level unavailable at home.

The closed, self-contained nature of tourism enclaves provides a visible and powerful imagery of exclusion (Schmid, 2008), and many holidaymakers pay handsomely for exclusivity. Bounded tourism spaces are visual reminders of social distinctions that make tourists feel special, pampered, and extraordinary in a life that is otherwise rather ordinary. For some consumers, the distinction is important. The reinforcement of social stratification and exclusivity necessarily requires the isolation of the affluent away from the poor.

Themed environments are found within many different types of enclaves. If physical spaces require sophisticated engineering, they may be characterized by an element of "Disneyfied imagineering". Theming features design motifs and follows a standard formula, even a branded one. The inspiration for themes often derives from sports, fantasy, history, travel, and the entertainment industry. Business competition has shaped the demand for symbol-rich spaces, to differentiate products and experiences from their competition and to satisfy a desire for entertaining and meaningful spaces (Erb & Ong, 2017; Gottdiener, 2001). The pursuit of profit, meaning, and branding through competitive marketing has prompted the spread and acceptance of themed commercial spaces. Theme parks, in particular, contain domains conjured up by image makers who design spaces that recreate other places, "real" or otherwise. Resorts may also contain themed environments, such as safaris or space travel, in an effort to provide a unique selling point and develop a certain brand. The process of enclosing buttresses the fantasy of theming by shutting out the wider world and immersing guests in a fantastical landscape that takes them from the ordinary to the extraordinary.

## Conclusion

In the same way that the study of mobility exposes complex flows, there is also complexity with respect to spaces characterized as enclaves. This enclavic complexity manifests itself in terms of the types of enclaves that exist, their benefits and drawbacks, their relationship with the wider world, and their symbolic qualities. There are potentially other complexities that apply to enclaved tourism and even tourism more generally, for example, a longing amongst tourists to be both surprised and reassured at the same time. Enclaves provide opportunities for tourists to escape their normative environments temporarily, and yet these spaces reflect the harsh social realities of the parallel dualisms of a world divided between production and consumption, work and play, and wealth and poverty.

A profound social distance characterizes many tourism encounters, vis-à-vis the visitors and the visited, and the way in which the relative impermeability of tourist bubbles works to maintain this distance. Through enclavic spaces, tourists are shielded from preconception-challenging interactions with residents—a form of separation that most high-end tourist experiences encourage. Holidaymakers without care or concern happily inhabit "filter bubbles" (Pariser, 2011): information-based enclaves wherein people close themselves off from points of view that might contradict their own assumptions, prejudices, and suppositions. In these virtual bubbles, customized information is provided through various algorithms based upon internet users' website browsing history. Users are caught up in a self-reinforcing cycle of isolation from articles, videos, and other content that might run counter to their worldviews and, in turn, receive more material that suits their personal interests.

Tourism enclaves are simultaneously complex and simple, but for enclave tourists, the complexities are minimized by managers and service providers *in situ*, and travel agents and tour operators at home. Tourist bubbles prevent the unexpected and the undesirable. In them, travel consumers are cocooned, removed from experiences that might disrupt their view of the world or the holiday experience of a lifetime—a non-normative world that is antiseptically comfortable for the guests but whose boundaries symbolize and reinforce the "exotic other", social exclusion, and a sense of disempowerment within the destination community.

## References

Assaf, A., & Scuderi, R. (2020). COVID-19 and the recovery of the tourism industry. *Tourism Economics*, 26(5), 731–733.

Atkinson, R., & Blandy, S. (2009). A picture of the floating world: Grounding the secessionary affluence of the residential cruise liner. *Antipode*, 41(1), 92–110.

Baratti, L. (2021, November 01). Australia-New Zealand travel bubble resumes in run-up to reopening. *Travel Pulse*. https://www.travelpulse.com/news/destinations/australia-new-zealand-travel-bubble-resumes-in-run-up-to-reopening.html

Bartling, H. (2006). Tourism as everyday life: An enquiry into the Villages, Florida. *Tourism Geographies*, 8(4), 380–402.

Brenner, L., & Aguilar, A.G. (2002). Luxury tourism and regional economic development in Mexico. *The Professional Geographer*, 54(4), 500–520.

Carlisle, S., & Jones, E. (2012). The beach enclave: A landscape of power. *Tourism Management Perspectives*, 1, 9–16.

Che, D. (2008). Sports, music, entertainment and the destination branding of post-Fordist Detroit. *Tourism Recreation Research*, 33(2), 195–206.

Cohen, E. (1972). Toward a sociology of international tourism. *Social Research*, 39(1), 164–182.

Erb, M., & Ong, C-E. (2017). Theming Asia: Culture, nature and heritage in a transforming Environment. *Tourism Geographies*, 19(2), 143–167.

Freitag, T. (1994). Enclave tourism development: For whom the benefits roll? *Annals of Tourism Research*, 21(3), 538–554.

Fusté-Forné, F., & Michael, N. (in press). Limited tourism: Travel bubbles for a sustainable future. *Journal of Sustainable Tourism*, https://doi.org/10.1080/09669582.2021.1954654

Gelman, A. (2010). *Red state, blue state, rich state, poor state: Why Americans vote the way they do*. Princeton: Princeton University Press.

Gottdiener, M. (2001). *The theming of America: Dreams, media fantasies, and themed environments*, 2nd edn. London: Routledge.

Harvey, D. (1989). *The condition of postmodernity: An enquiry into the origins of cultural change*. Oxford: Blackwell.

Howard, R.W. (2007). Five backpacker tourist enclaves. *International Journal of Tourism Research*, 9(2), 73–86.

Jaakson, R. (2004). Beyond the tourist bubble? Cruise ship passengers in port. *Annals of Tourism Research*, 31(1), 44–60.

Jacobsen, J.K.S. (2003). The tourist bubble and the Europeanisation of holiday travel. *Journal of Tourism & Cultural Change*, 1(1), 71–88.

Kothari, U. (2015). Reworking colonial imaginaries in post-colonial tourist enclaves. *Tourist Studies*, 15(3), 248–266.

Krakover, S., & Wang, Y.C. (2008). Spatial dimensions of the Orlando destination region *Tourism Analysis*, 13(3), 245–258.

Mbaiwa, J.E. (2005). Enclave tourism and its socio-economic impacts in the Okavango Delta, Botswana. *Tourism Management*, 26(2), 157–172.

Mbaiwa, J.E., & Hambira, W.L. (2020). Enclaves and shadow state tourism in the Okavango Delta, Botswana. *South African Geographical Journal*, 102(1), 1–21.

Mzezewa, T. (2020, April 29). 3 Baltic states announced a 'travel bubble'. What is it and could it work in the US? *New York Times*. https://www.nytimes.com/2020/04/29/travel/coronavirus-travel-bubble.html

Naidoo, P., & Pearce, P. (2018). Enclave tourism versus agritourism: The economic debate. *Current Issues in Tourism*, 21(17), 1946–1965.

Newman, O. (1973). *Defensible space: Crime prevention through urban design*. New York: Collier Books.

Nunkoo, R., & Ramkissoon, H. (2016). Stakeholders' view of enclave tourism: A grounded theory Approach. *Journal of Hospitality & Tourism Research*, 40(5), 557–588.

Papathanassis, A., & Klein, R. (2020). Editorial: The "liquid-modern" cruise sector: Growth, responsibility, and the failure of moral relativism. *Tourism in Marine Environments*, 15(2), 59–63.

Pariser, E. (2011). *The filter bubble: How the new personalized web is changing what we read and how we think.* London: Penguin Books.

Reich, R.B. (1991, January 20). Secession of the successful. *The New York Times Magazine*, 16.

Ritzer, G., & Liska, A. (1997). "McDisneyization" and "post-tourism": Complementary perspectives on contemporary tourism. In C. Rojek, & J. Urry (eds) *Touring cultures: Transformations of travel and theory*, pp. 96–109. London: Routledge.

Saarinen, J. (2017). Enclavic tourism spaces: Territorialization and bordering in tourism destination development and planning. *Tourism Geographies*, 19(3), 425–437.

Saarinen, J., & Wall-Reinius, S. (2019). Enclaves in tourism: Producing and governing exclusive spaces for tourism. *Tourism Geographies*, 21(5), 739–748.

Schmid, K.A. (2008). Doing ethnography of tourist enclaves: Boundaries, ironies, and insights. *Tourist Studies*, 8(1), 105–121.

Sharun, K., Tiwari, R., Natesan, S., Yatoo, M.I., Malik, Y.S., & Dhama, K. (2020). International travel during the COVID-19 pandemic: Implications and risks associated with "travel bubbles". *Journal of Travel Medicine*, 27(8), 1–3.

Silk, M.L. (2007). Come downtown & play. *Leisure Studies*, 26(3), 253–277.

Simpson, T. (2016). Tourist utopias: Biopolitics and the genealogy of the post-world tourist city. *Current Issues in Tourism*, 19(1), 27–59.

Timothy, D.J. (2006). Cruises, supranationalism and border complexities. In R.K. Dowling (ed) *Cruise ship tourism*, pp. 407–413. Wallingford: CABI.

Timothy, D.J., & Zhu, X. (2022). Backpacker tourist experiences: Temporal, spatial and cultural perspectives. In R. Sharpley (ed) *Routledge handbook of the tourist experience*, pp. 249–261. London: Routledge.

Torres, R.M., & Momsen, J.D. (2005). Gringolandia: The construction of a new tourist space in Mexico. *Annals of the Association of American Geographers*, 95(2), 314–335.

Wall-Reinius, S., Ioannnides, D., & Zampoukos, K. (2019). Does geography matter in all-inclusive resort tourism? Marketing approaches of Scandinavian tour operators. *Tourism Geographies*, 21(5), 766–784.

Wasko, J. (2001). *Understanding Disney: The manufacture of fantasy*. Cambridge: Polity Press.

Weaver, A. (2005). Spaces of containment and revenue capture: "Super-sized" cruise ships as mobile tourism enclaves. *Tourism Geographies*, 7(2), 165–184.

Wilson, J., & Richards, G. (2008). Suspending reality: An exploration of enclaves and the backpacker experience. *Current Issues in Tourism*, 11(2), 187–202.

Wood, R.E. (2000). Caribbean cruise tourism: Globalization at sea. *Annals of Tourism Research*, 27(2), 345–370.

Zukin, S. (1991). *Landscapes of power: From Detroit to Disney World*. Berkeley: University of California Press.

# 11
# GLOBALIZATION, MOBILITY, AND BORDER RESTRICTIONS
## Tourism Perspectives

*Aharon Kellerman*

## Introduction

This chapter was written during the global COVID-19 pandemic—a time when international travel mobility had almost entirely ceased but with expectations for its gradual renewal, assuming there would be an eventual decline in the spread of the virus. Following the introduction and adoption of effective vaccines, global tourism has begun its return to pre-coronavirus levels, though probably involving increased health measures to be taken as a precaution against any possible future outbreaks of old or new viruses (Gössling et al., 2021; Kellerman, 2020b).

International tourism involves voluntary and temporary global movements of people for leisure, business, work, and many other purposes, excluding migration and refugee movements. International travel accounts for half of all global tourism receipts with the rest deriving from domestic travel, although many estimates suggest that domestic trips outnumber international by several times (UNWTO, 2020). Domestic and international tourism varies significantly among countries, with domestic tourism being extremely popular in geographically large countries such as the USA, Russia, and China, whereas international tourism (outbound and inbound) is greater on a per capita basis in the smaller and more affluent countries of Europe and the Middle East (Lew, 2011).

International tourism requires motives and purposes for travel and is based upon people's mobility rights and their ability to travel, but travel patterns differ between countries of origin, by the means of global mobility, and by the choices of destinations. Following a short introduction to globalization and tourism, I discuss global tourism from two perspectives: personal globalization (or the motives, rights, and capabilities to travel) and the governance and transportation perspectives on global mobility, including how home states control outgoing travel and destination states control incoming travel, as well as changes in the airline sector, which is the preferred means of international travel worldwide.

## International Tourism and Globalization

International tourism has emerged within the wider context of globalization, which is the "increasing integration of economies, societies, and civilizations" (Hjalager, 2007, p. 437, see also Aramberri, 2009 and Timothy, 2019a). Perhaps more modestly, globalization may be viewed as bringing about a "widening, deepening and speeding up of worldwide interconnectedness in all aspects of contemporary life" (Held et al., 1999, p. 2). Thus, tourism is both a result of globalization and a driver of globalization (Timothy, 2019a). The relationships between tourism and globalization manifest in many different ways, including economic development, technology, commerce and trade, the international corporatization of businesses, education, governance and supranationalism, transportation, and even diseases, as the COVID-19 pandemic clearly demonstrates. Although there are many types of globalization, this chapter touches only on a few of these, including technology, transportation, and governance.

From the perspective of spatial mobility, contemporary globalization is characterized by increasingly easier movements of people, objects, and information across international borders, thus bringing about a sharp decline in the differences between domestic and international mobilities. Today, information moves freely across national borders, except in a few cases of censorship (Fu & Timothy, 2021; Warf, 2013), whereas people and objects typically require permits (i.e., passports and visas) to move internationally. The relationship between domestic and international mobilities may also change. For example, security requirements, which were originally imposed only on international passengers, have now been imposed on domestic travelers as well, particularly with airport security (Kellerman, 2008).

People's global mobility has expanded vastly in recent decades, now involving primarily two-way short trips for pleasure and business, undertaken mainly by means of large and efficient airplanes, guided by technology heretofore unseen. International tourism is a striking manifestation of contemporary globalization and spurred by constant exposure to information through the internet and other technologies, and eventually resulting in people reserving their own tourism services through online providers (Kellerman, 2014). Thus, contemporary globalization does not occur only through government and large-scale commercial activities but also by individuals located elsewhere in the world through user-generated geographic information provided by their social media presence and use of travel ratings.

Growing international tourism is an expression of globalization, side by side with increased flows of information through social media and travel websites generated by individuals and marketing organizations. The growth in international tourism has been aided by the introduction of low-cost airlines and secondary airports in more locations, increased global affluence, social media, and various other information and communication technologies, as well as many other modern forces. Even overtourism, or excessive mass tourism, is a manifestation of globalization. Rapid tourism growth has brought about objections by residents of highly visited cities where overtourism has become an important point in public debate, such as in Barcelona, Venice, and Amsterdam (Pechlaner et al., 2020; Vargas-Sánchez et al., 2014). Although growing local objections to incoming tourism may not reduce global tourism, it may be effective in channeling some of it to other destinations.

Besides general globalization, we might also speak of "personal globalization" when referring to conditions that affect individuals and translates into them becoming global travelers. Three personal conditions must exist on the demand side of tourism for it to flourish and for people to be empowered to travel. First, there must be a desire to travel. Push factors entail the forces in a person's home environment that cause one to want to get away. Boredom, stress, exhaustion, curiosity, a desire to learn, and the need for social interaction are common motivations for taking a journey. Pull factors are the characteristics of a potential destination that draws people to it, including warm weather, beautiful natural and cultural landscapes, famous iconic attractions, and attractive beaches. The pull factors are the things in the destination that will satisfy the push factors. The second element of personal globalization is the right to travel; and the third is the financial means to travel, which entails not only personal finances but also macroeconomic forces that determine one's ability to travel. The two latter points—travel as a human right and the means to travel—are examined briefly below within the broader context of globalization and mobility.

## *International Tourism and the Right to Travel*

Since the end of World War II, the basic human right to travel has been reaffirmed several times, including first in the 1948 UN Universal Declaration of Human Rights, in 1980 with the Manila Declaration, in 1999 with the Global Code of Ethics for Tourism, and with the 2017 Framework Convention on Tourism Ethics, all of which reflect the widespread growth of international tourism (Bianchi et al., 2020; Bianchi & Stephenson, 2013). This global recognition of people's right to travel has served as a basis for some government policies regarding human mobility and tourism. Modern global tourism had its roots earlier than World War II, but was generally a right reserved, at the time, for specific social classes only. Although many observers have suggested that the modern-day notion of tourism derived historically through medieval pilgrimages, the modern notion of leisure-oriented international tourism can be traced back to seventeenth and eighteenth-century Europe (Veblen, 1912; Williams, 2009). Europe was, therefore, the laboratory for introducing the contemporary and globally oriented phenomenon of international tourism.

The first phase of international tourism consisted of the Grand Tour, which prevailed in the seventeenth century, peaking in the second half of the eighteenth century, and ending in the early nineteenth century. The Grand Tour entailed youth of aristocratic families traveling to familiarize themselves with centers of classical art and culture, through prolonged tours of Europe, focusing primarily on Renaissance Italian cities (e.g., Rome, Venice, Padua, and Florence), as well as several sophisticated and artistic locales in Austria, Germany, and France.

Following the end of the Napoleonic Wars in 1815 there was a second wave of European international tourism, this time of a more bourgeoisie nature, focusing on much shorter sightseeing tours of the Alps in Switzerland, Italy, France, and Austria. In the mid-1800s, Thomas Cook began organizing tours in various parts of Europe and the Holy Land.

The third phase of European international tourism focused on exclusive, albeit non-aristocratic, tourism centered on the Mediterranean French Riviera, attracting northern Europeans in the winter months beginning in the late nineteenth century. Following World War I, this trend became popular throughout Europe, aided in large part by the region's burgeoning railway transportation network. Current global tourism is the fourth development phase, following World War II, with the technological growth of international aviation, coupled with the rise in incomes of the middle classes, first in North America, then in Western Europe, and eventually reaching East Asia and Eastern Europe (Williams, 2009).

The general international consensus that humans have a right to travel globally for tourism purposes, coupled with the continued growth in international tourism, has led to the conceptualization of an increasingly borderless world (Ohmae, 1990; Paasi et al., 2019), coupled with proposed "global" (Butcher, 2019; Heater, 2002), "world" (Isin & Turner, 2007), or "flexible" (Ong, 1999) citizenships. However, although debordering processes continue to make the world a smaller place and bring people together in tourism settings (Więckowski & Cerić, 2016; Więckowski & Timothy, 2021), a truly borderless world is still a faraway reality.

## *Economic Ability to Travel*

Although the right to travel internationally has been globally recognized, its acceptance is not universal. Not all governments have honored this claim, and even in conditions where people are permitted to travel, many still cannot afford such a luxury. Thus, people's economic constraints may be a bigger obstacle to international mobility than a lack of desire or political obstacles to travel.

An increasing number of countries have experienced phenomenal economic growth in recent decades, which normally results in a growing middle class and translates into more people traveling abroad. China and Russia are two prominent examples of countries that have undergone not only major political reorientations but also economic revolutions that percolate down to the ordinary population, providing them with more opportunities for global mobility.

Outbound tourism is currently led by wealthy and highly populated countries, especially China, Germany, Hong Kong (counted statistically as separate from China), and the United States, rather than poorer large countries, or the countries that serve as the main destinations of these wealthier tourists. In 2017, these four countries together produced over a quarter (26.4 percent) of all international tourist trips. Other leading source countries the same year included large and wealthy countries, as well as emerging Eastern European states that now enjoy the ease of travel within Europe since they joined the European Union and the Schengen Accord (Kellerman, 2020a; Timothy, 2019b). The majority of outbound international travel derives overwhelmingly from the three wealthy global cores of North America, Europe, and Asia Pacific, which means that international tourism cannot be considered truly globally integrated (Aramberri, 2009). The "tourism gap" in access to international travel is not only between rich and poor countries but is also intra-national, since lower-income populations within wealthier states, including the top tourist-generating countries, cannot themselves afford overseas visits.

## Governance and Transportation Perspectives

The discussion so far has focused on individuals' rights and the financial ability to travel. Three additional parameters, pertaining specifically to individual tourists but operationalized at a normative rather than personal globalization level, are examined in the sections that follow. These are namely the policies of tourists' countries of origins, their modes of travel, and the policies of the destination countries. Although there are several transportation options for international travel, the airline section below focuses specifically on air transport as the preferred means of global travel and the best manifestation of transportation globalization.

### *Home State: Controlling Outbound Tourism*

As noted above, national and personal economic dimensions are a key factor in the volume of outgoing global travel. The assumptions noted earlier are that people want to participate in foreign travel and overseas vacations, they are permitted to do so given the global recognition of travel as a human right, and they can afford to take holiday trips. Unfortunately, however, state borders may be closed, partially or fully, not only for incoming tourists (discussed later), but also for outgoing residents.

Since the beginning of the nineteenth century, nearly all international travelers have required valid passports or equivalent travel documents. The EU and its associated Schengen Agreement have enabled free and open travel between signatory states, which has resulted in increased levels of intra-European tourism, although some restrictions have been imposed recently by some EU countries in an attempt to stave off illegal immigration (Bianchi et al., 2020; Ramji-Nogales & Goldner Lang, 2020) and in 2020–2021 to slow the spread of COVID-19. Some countries require exit visas/permits of their own citizens. For example, in the 1930s and 1940s, Germans were required to obtain exit visas to leave Germany. Today, China requires an "Exit–Entry

Permit" of its citizens who desire to visit Macau or Hong Kong, and the Chinese government indirectly controls where its citizens can spend their vacations abroad. Most Chinese tourists travel overseas on pre-arranged package tours. The People's Republic of China allows these tour groups only to visit countries that the government has pre-approved through its so-called "Approved Destination Status" list (Smed & Bislev, 2022). Likewise, until just a few years ago, Cuba required a lengthy and arduous exit visa process for its citizens wishing to travel abroad.

Similarly, if the destination country requires an entry visa, departing passengers may be required to show it to border officials or airline employees at the point of departure. In some countries, citizens may be prohibited from leaving if they have a criminal record or if there are any ongoing legal proceedings against them.

In recent history, many totalitarian regimes prohibited their citizens from leaving the country, including for tourism. For example, the Soviet Union heavily restricted its citizens' foreign travel, prohibiting most journeys abroad except for pre-approved holidays in other communist states. Today, few countries prohibit their citizens from going abroad, but the most notable one is North Korea, which heavily restricts foreign and domestic travel by its citizens. Some countries require exit visas for resident foreigners, as is the case in Saudi Arabia, Kuwait, and the United Arab Emirates, where foreign workers must present departure permits from their employers.

The COVID-19 pandemic has made it difficult for people to leave their home countries, not necessarily due to exit restrictions, but rather because of reduced international transportation and lockdowns for incoming travelers imposed by many destinations. Although these are not home-country-imposed restrictions, they function de facto as such in that they restrict people's ability to leave their countries of origin and limit their destination choices.

## *Means of International Transportation*

Once people are able to leave their countries, flights are the preferred travel mode. Air travel has become the leading means of international mobility, implying that "flights are central to performing the global order" (Urry, 2009, p. 30). Some 57 percent of international tourists in 2017 arrived by air, and the International Air Transport Association (IATA, 2018) reported some 4.1 billion domestic and international air passengers in 2017. Simultaneously, the World Tourism Organization (UNWTO, 2018a) reported some 1.323 billion international tourist arrivals by air the same year which, including the return flights, amounted to approximately 2.646 billion international tourist person-trips by air, or 65 percent of the total for air passengers in 2017. Only one-third of the total flight volume in 2017 was domestic, which means that international air travel has become extremely voluminous in recent years. In 2004, demand for domestic and international air travel was almost completely opposite, with the percentage of international flights that year standing at 35 percent (Kellerman, 2008). Thus, in only 13 years, this share had almost doubled. The tremendous growth in international flights reflects the liberalization and globalization of the airline sector, expressed through internet-based self-booking systems, volumes of online information, more destinations being served through systems restructuring, and the flourishing of low-cost carriers, which has brought about a general decline of air fares in a more competitive global environment (Duval & McIlree, 2019; Spasojevic & Lohmann, 2019).

In overseas tourism, flights have become almost the sole mode of transportation, with only a few exceptions, such as international ferry services (e.g., between Tallinn, Estonia, and Helsinki, Finland), international underwater tunnels (e.g., under the La Manche/English Channel between France and the UK), or ships. Air travel began to take precedent over maritime travel shortly after World War II and has since then grown exponentially to all but almost entirely replacing trans-Atlantic and trans-Pacific ship-based transportation.

The airline industry is extremely dispersed. IATA (2018) reported for 2018 a membership of 270 airlines providing some 82 percent of global air traffic. Although some countries' air transportation is monopolized by a single service provider (often a flag carrier or government-owned national airline) or a small group of providers, on a global scale the airline industry is not dominated by a single airline or handful of carriers that monopolize a significantly large share of global air traffic, as is the case with marine shipping (Kellerman, 2020a). In 2010, the global international air traffic measure of "revenue ton kilometers" (RTK), showed that Lufthansa (Germany) was the world's leading airline, with some 4.86 percent of the global RTK, followed by Emirates (UAE) with 4.81 percent. Air France (France), the third-ranked provider, stood at 3.7 percent (Scheelhaase et al., 2012). Today, Turkish Airlines, Air France, British Airways, and Ethiopian Airlines serve the largest number of countries worldwide. The airlines serving the highest number of passengers prior to the COVID pandemic were American Airlines, Delta Airlines, Southwest Airlines, United Airlines, and Ryanair.

This dispersed structure of the airline industry reflects the prominent use of airplanes for international travel, which implies several features of the industry. First, people require a wider range of options for their international mobility, compared to commodities shipping. The airline system provides a great deal of flexibility and travel options, particularly since the 1980s with major changes in routing and flight networks throughout the world. Second, the speed of international travel by airplane is usually cited as the most obvious advantage over other modes of transportation. This allows people to spend more time in the destination than in transit, extending the holiday time and opportunities abroad. Third, air travel tends to be much more comfortable than ocean-based or even train travel. Fourth, the number and locations of airports are far greater than sea ports. Geographically, airports can be built inland, whereas ports are obviously confined to coastal areas. Thus, airports provide more locational advantages within the geography of tourism. Finally, many countries maintain a special relationship with a particular airline, which may, as noted above, be considered the national carrier. This often appeals to citizens who prefer to support their national airline out of pride, solidarity, and trust.

The international air transport system has undergone numerous transitions since the 1970s, which have facilitated the liberalization, restructuring, and profitability of the airline industry. These changes have come about through the growing demand for international tourism. Simultaneously, however, the reduced cost of airfares, the larger number of served destinations, and increased access to travel with a growing middle class in most parts of the world are major catalysts for the continued growth of international tourism, and its spread to a wider range of destinations.

Mergers, takeovers, deregulation, privatization, and open-sky agreements have affected numerous airlines worldwide and effected new flight routes, competitive pricing, and better-quality service (Duval, 2007; Duval & McIlree, 2019). The airline industry has become more flexible through the emergence of low-cost carriers (LCCs) since the 1970s and their rapid growth in the 2000s, reaching some 28 percent of the world's air traffic in 2016 (Allianz Partners, 2017). In 2020, LCCs accounted for 35 percent of total global seat capacity (Mazareanu, 2021). With the growth of LCCs and the benefits they were offering tourists and destinations, veteran airlines began to cooperate with one another in the 1990s in large airline alliances, with Oneworld, SkyTeam, and Star Alliance being the largest. These three global alliances enabled integrated schedules for their airline members through code sharing and a common passenger rewards system, creating global networks that were more efficient and profitable (Douglas & Tan, 2017). In 2012, these three alliances accounted for some 60 percent of all global air transportation (Lordan et al., 2014).

The airline industry, particularly the LCCs, have suffered enormously from the coronavirus pandemic. Billions of dollars have been lost, and many estimates suggest that it may take at least a decade for some airlines to recover. At the beginning of 2022, it is still too early to assess how the industry will survive the crisis, and which transitions it may have to undergo to remain viable.

## *Controlling Inbound Tourism*

Government permissions to enter a country or restrictions from entering constitute a significant additional dimension of patterns of international tourism. All states control human mobilities across their national frontiers, either strictly or minimally. This usually depends on bilateral relationships. This is the nature of sovereignty and reflects one of the primary purposes of political borders: filtering, monitoring, and regulating cross-border flows of people (Timothy, 2001). The main exceptions are the member states of the European Union and the Schengen Agreement, which have deputed their border controls and some sovereign rights to the supranational alliance to which they belong (Timothy, 2019b).

The most common regulatory tool for a country's entrance policies is the visa, which is normally issued to foreign citizens in their home countries by representatives of the destination country. For some nationalities, the visa regulations of other countries may be strict and onerous, while for some citizens, they may be relatively easy and straightforward (Whyte, 2008). To increase greater global mobility and to encourage the growth of tourism, during the past two decades, more countries have begun easing and streamlining visa requirements, including implementing visa waiver programs. The economic interests involved in these processes sometimes conflict with national security interests, notably during times of growing illegal immigration and threats of terrorist attacks (Czaika & Neumayer, 2017; Webster & Ivanov, 2016). The policies of countries in light of these contradictory interests have been mixed. Recently, the USA ceased issuing visas to citizens of countries it regards as sponsors of terrorism. Likewise, the EU has tightened control of its land and maritime borders (Bianchi et al., 2020; Diener & Hagen, 2009).

Mau and his colleagues (2015) conducted a comparative study of 155 countries, evaluating the number of visa waivers for their passport holders in 1969 and 2010. They found that the average number of visa waivers per national passport increased from 24 in 1969 to 32 in 2010, or by some 33 percent. This change seems to represent a geographical expansion of destinations and an easing of travel for international tourists worldwide. However, the trend has also been coupled with a growing polarization of visa waivers when the continents or regions of tourists' origins are compared. Whereas travelers from most regions of the world have seen an increase in visa-free travel during the past several decades, tourists from Africa are the exception; for most Africans, visa regulations have not eased. Europeans, who enjoyed the most widespread visa-free travel regimes in the 1960s, continue in this position today (Whyte, 2008). Specific country comparisons revealed that Latin American and Eastern European countries have enjoyed the greatest expansion of visa waivers in recent decades. This pattern of differential visa-waiver rights across the globe reflects "a new system of stratification built on an unequal access to mobility rights" (Mau et al., 2015, p. 1194). Another study shows that citizens of Global North countries receive more visa-waiver preferences than citizens of the Global South, making people from more affluent countries feel more globalized, while simultaneously the affluent countries continue to impose stricter visa requirements on citizens from the Global South (Webster & Ivanov, 2016).

In recent years, a class of "global nomads" has emerged (Bianchi & Stephenson, 2013), consisting of certain businesspeople, field experts, and backpackers or "wanderers", who are constantly on the move and do not necessarily feel attached to any specific country. In 2017, some 13 percent of international tourists were classified as business travelers (UNWTO, 2018b). However, the so-called global nomads constitute a small share of business tourists and today include a wider range of people who feel disconnected to territory and national citizenship. This rather small group of travelers may truly enjoy a sense of borderlessness and mobility freedom, though they too must undergo entry and exit procedures at airports and border crossings. Today's global nomads are a modern version of "domestic nomads" (Castells, 1989), identified by their placelessness and rootlessness (Relph, 1976).

Certain classes of international travelers fit the definition of "traveling workers", or employees whose very work includes travel, such as pilots, flight attendants, cruise ship employees, and train engineers. These classes of travelers often fall under special visa regimes and immigration statuses that enable them certain entry and exit privileges not available to regular tourists (Cohen, 1974; Uriely, 2001).

Urry (1990) and Mau (2010) used the term "mobility citizenship" to distinguish between the right to cross-boundary mobility, which is granted through temporary visitor visas or visa waivers on the one hand, and the right of abode, which relates primarily to permanent immigrants. A group of travelers lies between these two ends of the travel mobility spectrum and consists of temporary expatriate professionals and workers. Many international trade agreements have provided for special multiannual visas for such individuals, including, for instance, professionals in finance, business, medical care, telecommunications, construction, agriculture, domestic help, child care, and tourism (Sassen, 2007). The workforce of many countries in the Middle East, such as Qatar, Saudi Arabia, Kuwait, Bahrain, and the UAE, is comprised largely of expatriate workers who fall into this category (Hannam & Paris, 2019). Likewise, students who study abroad are also a type of temporary migrant, and tourist, in some cases. The common thread among these classes of transnational workers is their longer stay in the host country, which may last months or even years, compared to leisure and business tourists whose stays normally last only days or weeks. For EU citizens, relocating or moving within the EU can be done without work, student, or residence visas, given that the EU functions as a single labor market and because citizens of all EU member states are also citizens of the EU, which gives them complete freedom of movement, work, and residence within the bloc.

Security concerns vis-à-vis tourists and tourism, as manifested through visa policies, have been intensified with the growing number of terrorist attacks in recent years. This fear has led to enhanced security and surveillance measures applied in airports and at border crossings (Andersen & Prokkola, 2022; Bianchi et al., 2020). Furthermore, a "border-like" atmosphere has emerged with resort and beach-based tourism, where armored police and military personnel have been deployed to protect so-called "enclaved tourism spaces" (e.g., beach resorts that exclude local people) (Saarinen, 2017) and other tourism installations in host countries where there are significant security concerns or where the contrast between wealthy foreign tourists and poor locals is distinct and clear (Bianchi et al., 2020).

## Conclusion

In this chapter I have interpreted several elements of international tourism from the perspective of globalization and human mobility. In terms of "personal globalization", I have described the global recognition of humankind's desire and right to international travel, and followed this with a discussion of the economic capabilities of individuals to pay for such travels. Restrictions imposed by travelers' home countries, changes in the airline industry that have affected global mobility, and how countries control inbound tourism through visas and waiver programs have all been highlighted within the purview of globalization.

The right of international travel has been agreed upon through various international treaties, but it is not a guarantee in all countries. Scholars recognize that the right to travel is not based only on home government policies but also on socioeconomic status. Level of affluence (wealth) and social standing may in fact be more influential variables to people's ability to travel than home-state-imposed restrictions. Thus, the "right" to travel is perhaps a greater de facto right in the Global North than it is in the Global South, and even within individual countries, one's socioeconomic status may determine the level of "right" one has to travel.

Certain countries restrict almost all international travel by their citizens. Others restrict or regulate the destinations their citizens can visit. Some countries require an exit visa or other arduous process to get permission to travel abroad. These sorts of home-state controls over their own citizens usually reflect totalitarian approaches to population control and the desire to restrict contact between peoples, or they reflect poor bilateral relations between home and host state. Controls established by host countries are usually in the form of visas, although some citizens are entirely precluded from visiting certain countries.

Air transportation has become the preferred mode of international travel worldwide, and technology and the globalization of transportation have enabled much more efficient, less-expensive, and more comfortable journeys that encourage people to utilize flights more than any other means of overseas travel. Airline deregulation and other elements of globalization have resulted in the emergence of low-cost carriers that provide a less expensive air service to secondary airports in more locations.

Globalization is manifested in many different ways, from the foods we eat and the clothes we wear, to modern technology and supranational governance. Tourism is both a stimulator of globalization and a product of globalization in every sense of the word. From the perspective of global tourism mobility, borders, and border policies, tourism is especially sensitive to restrictions enacted by home and host country and by advances in travel technology, especially that related to air travel. As globalization processes continue to unfold and as we learn to live with the effects of COVID-19, international tourism will continue to exert change on the global stage and will continue to be affected by every globalization process and mobility control.

# References

Allianz Partners (2017). Low-cost airlines increased air traffic in 2016, accessed 28 January 2019 at https://allianzpartners-bi.com/banque-en/trading-en/video-low-cost-airlines-increased-air-traffic-in-2016-a9bc-333d4.html

Andersen, D.J., & Prokkola, E-K. (eds) (2022). *Borderlands resilience: Transactions, adaptation and resistance at borders*. London: Routledge.

Aramberri, J. (2009). The future of tourism and globalization: Some critical remarks. *Futures*, 41, 367–376.

Bianchi, R.V., & Stephenson, M.L. (2013). Deciphering tourism and citizenship in a globalized world. *Tourism Management*, 39, 10–20.

Bianchi, R.V., Stephenson, M.L., & Hannam, K. (2020). The contradictory politics of the right to travel: Mobilities, borders and tourism. *Mobilities*, 15, 290–306.

Butcher, J. (Ed.) (2019). *Tourism, cosmopolitanism and global citizenship*. London: Routledge.

Castells, M. (1989). *The informational city: Information, technology, economic restructuring and the urban-regional process*. Oxford: Blackwell.

Cohen, E. (1974). Who is a tourist? A conceptual clarification. *Sociology*, 22, 527–555.

Czaika, M., & Neumayer, E. (2017). Visa restrictions and economic globalization. *Applied Geography*, 84, 75–82.

Diener, A.C., & Hagen, J. (2009). Theorizing borders in a 'borderless world': Globalization, territory and identity. *Geography Compass*, 3, 1196–1216.

Douglas, I., & Tan, D. (2017). Global airline alliances and profitability: A difference-in-difference analysis. *Transportation Research Part A*, 103, 432–443.

Duval, D. T. (2007). *Tourism and transport: Modes, networks and flows*. Bristol: Channel View Publications.

Duval, D.T., & McIlree, J. (2019). Globalisation and transportation innovation. In D.J. Timothy (ed.) *Handbook of globalization and tourism*, pp. 225–234. Cheltenham: Edward Elgar.

Fu, Y., & Timothy, D.J. (2021). Social media constraints and destination images: The potential of barrier-free internet access for foreign tourists in an internet-restricted destination. *Tourism Management Perspectives*, 37, 100771.

Gössling, S., Scott, D., & Hall, C.M. (2021). Pandemics, tourism and global change: A rapid assessment of COVID-19. *Current Issues in Tourism*, 29(1), 1–20.

Hannam, K., & Paris, C.M. (2019). Tourism, migration and an expatriate workforce in the Middle East. In D.J. Timothy (ed.) *Routledge handbook on tourism in the Middle East and North Africa*, pp. 330–339. London: Routledge.

Heater, D. (2002). *World citizenship: Cosmopolitan thinking and its opponents*. London: Continuum.

Held, D., McGrew, A., Goldblatt, D., & Perraton, J. (1999). *Global transformation: Politics, economics and culture*. Cambridge: Polity.

Hjalager, A-M. (2007). Stages in the economic globalization of tourism. *Annals of Tourism Research*, 34, 437–457.

IATA (International Air Transport Association) (2018). Traveler number reach new heights, accessed 25 January 2019, at https://www.iata.org/pressroom/pr/Pages/2018-09-06-01.aspx

Isin, E.F., & Turner, B.S. (2007). Investigating citizenship: An agenda for citizenship studies. *Citizenship Studies*, 11, 5–17.

Kellerman, A. (2008). International airports: Passengers in an environment of 'authorities'. *Mobilities*, 3, 161–178.

Kellerman, A. (2014). *The internet as second action space*. London: Routledge.

Kellerman, A. (2020a). *Globalization and spatial mobilities: Commodities and people, capital, information and technology*. Cheltenham: Edward Elgar.

Kellerman, A. (2020b). The post-corona city: Virus imprints and precautions. *Environment and Planning B: Urban Analytics and City Science* 47 (forthcoming).

Lew, A.A. (2011). Tourism's role in the global economy. *Tourism Geographies*, 13, 148–151.

Lordan, O., Sallan, J.M., & Simo, P. (2014). Study of the topology and robustness of airline route networks from the complex network approach: A survey and research agenda. *Journal of Transport Geography*, 37, 112–120.

Mau, S. (2010). Mobility citizenship, inequality and the liberal state: The case of visa policies. *International Political Sociology*, 4, 339–361.

Mau, S., Gülzau, F., Laube, L., & Zaun, N. (2015). The global mobility divide: How visa policies have eroded over time. *Journal of Ethnic and Migration Studies*, 41, 1192–1213.

Mazareanu, E. (2021). Low cost carriers' worldwide market share from 2007 to 2020. *Statista*, 14 April, 2021. Online: https://www.statista.com/statistics/586677/global-low-cost-carrier-market-capacity-share/

Ohmae, K. (1990). *The borderless world: Power and strategy in the interlinked economy*. New York: Harper Business.

Ong, A. (1999). *Flexible citizenship: The cultural logics of transnationality*. Durham, NC: Duke University Press.

Paasi, A., Prokkola, E-K., Saarinen, J., & Zimmerbauer, K. (eds) (2019). *Borderless worlds for whom? Ethics, moralities and mobilities*. London: Routledge.

Pechlaner, H., Innerhofer, E., & Erschbamer, G. (eds) (2020). *Overtourism: Tourism management and solutions*. London: Routledge.

Ramji-Nogales, J., & Goldner Lang, I. (2020). Freedom of movement, migration, and borders. *Journal of Human Rights*, 19(5), 593–602.

Relph, E. (1976). *Place and Placelessness*. London: Pion.

Saarinen, J. (2017). Enclave tourism spaces: Territorialization and bordering in tourism destination development and planning. *Tourism Geographies*, 19, 425–437.

Sassen, S. (2007). *A sociology of globalization*. New York: W.W. Norton.

Scheelhaase, J., Schaefer, M., Grimme, W., & Maertens, S. (2012). Cost impacts of the inclusion of air transport into the European Emissions Trading Scheme in the time period 2012-2020. *European Journal of Transport and Infrastructure Research*, 12, 332–348.

Smed, K.M., & Bislev, A. (2022). Framing Chinese tourism in Europe: Golden geese or gaggles? In L. Xing (ed.) *China-EU relations in a new era of global transformation*, pp. 273–290. London: Routledge.

Spasojevic, B., & Lohmann, G. (2019). Air route development and transit tourism in the Middle East. In D.J. Timothy (ed.) *Routledge handbook on tourism in the Middle East and North Africa*, pp. 290–306. London: Routledge.

Timothy, D.J. (2001). *Tourism and political boundaries*. London: Routledge.

Timothy, D.J. (2019a). Globalisation: The shrinking world of tourism. In D.J. Timothy (ed.) *Handbook of globalisation and tourism*, pp. 323–332. Cheltenham: Edward Elgar.

Timothy, D.J. (2019b). Supranationalism and tourism: Free trade, customs unions, and single markets in an era of geopolitical change. In D.J. Timothy (ed.) *Handbook of globalisation and tourism*, pp. 100–113. Cheltenham: Edward Elgar.

UNWTO (2018a). *2017 annual report*, accessed 25 January 2019 at https://www.e-unwto.org/doi/pdf/10.18111/9789284419807

UNWTO (2018b). *Tourism highlights 2018 edition*, accessed 2 February 2019 at https://www.e-unwto.org/doi/pdf/10.18111/9789284419876

UNWTO (2020). UNWTO highlights potential of domestic tourism to help drive economic recovery in destinations worldwide. Online at: https://www.unwto.org/news/unwto-highlights-potential-of-domestic-tourism-to-help-drive-economic-recovery-in-destinations-worldwide

Uriely, N. (2001). 'Travelling workers' and 'working tourists': Variations across the interaction between work and tourism', *International Journal of Tourism Research*, 3, 1–8.

Urry, J. (1990). *The Tourist Gaze*. Thousand Oaks, CA: Sage.

Urry, J. (2009). Aeromobilities and the global. In S.C. Werner, S. Kesselring, & J. Urry (eds) *Aeromobilities*, pp. 25–38. London: Routledge.

Vargas-Sánchez, A., Porras-Bueno, N., & Plaza-Mejía, M.d.L.Á. (2014). Residents' attitude to tourism and seasonality. *Journal of Travel Research*, 53, 581–596.

Veblen, T. (1912). *The theory of the leisure class*. New York: Macmillan.

Warf, B. (2013). *Global geographies of the internet*. Dordrecht: Springer.

Webster, C., & Ivanov, S. (2016). The ideologies of national security and tourist visa restrictions. *International Journal of Tourism Policy*, 6, 171–190.

Whyte, B. (2008). Visa-free travel privileges: An exploratory geographical analysis. *Tourism Geographies*, 10(2), 127–149.

Więckowski, M., & Cerić, D. (2016). Evolving tourism on the Baltic Sea coast: Perspectives on change in the Polish maritime borderland. *Scandinavian Journal of Hospitality and Tourism*, 16(1), 98–111.

Więckowski, M., & Timothy, D.J. (2021). Tourism and an evolving international boundary: Bordering, debordering and rebordering on Usedom Island, Poland-Germany. *Journal of Destination Marketing & Management*, 22, 100647.

Williams, S. (2009). *Tourism geography: A new synthesis*, 2nd edition. London: Routledge.

# 12
# MILITARY OCCUPATIONS AND TOURISM

*Jack Shepherd and Daniel Laven*

## Introduction

"While inspecting this gate and hearing accounts of the battle from his soldier guide, Noyori noticed an unpleasant odour. His hosts informed him that it likely came from the corpses of Chinese soldiers buried haphazardly in the area" (Ruoff, 2014, p. 183). Kenneth Ruoff's account of Japanese tourism in Occupied China is deeply disturbing. His description of Noyori Hideichi's visit to Nanjing in April 1938, in which Noyori sought out Nanjing's most famous attractions along with postcards to send home, came only five months after the infamous "Rape of Nanjing" where thousands of Chinese civilians were murdered by the invading Japanese army. As the quote above demonstrates, the recent conflict was all too evident. Yet it was not long before Imperial Japan established a tourist office in the city that offered Japanese citizens patriotic tours of Nanjing, assisted by direct flights from Tokyo (ibid.). Surprisingly, 1940, in the midst of World War II, was the year that Imperial Japanese tourism reached its zenith (ibid., p. 171). Although we might struggle to fathom tourism at such a time and place, tourism and conflict are often deeply entwined (Isaac et al., 2019). This chapter focuses on one important dimension of the tourism–conflict nexus, that of military occupations.

Our intention here is to provide an holistic overview of the various relationships tourism has to military occupations, which are an historically important manifestation of bordering, shifting sovereignty, and geopolitical change. Such an overview is so far missing from the tourism literature. In exploring these various avenues of inquiry, we rely on a wealth of literature that has looked at the tourism–occupation nexus in different historical and contemporary contexts, stretching from the early nineteenth century to the present day. For the most part, we present a descriptive review of the literature on military occupations and tourism, yet we supplement the knowledge found in this literature with insights from our research in the occupied Palestinian Territories.

## Military Occupations

In this chapter we carefully consider what could be described as a "military occupation". Although the application of the term "military occupation" can be uncontroversial, such as during the fascist occupations of World War II, the label of occupation is often highly contested. For example, although the United Nations (UN) and the European Union (EU) consider Crimea, Northern Cyprus, Palestine, and Western Sahara to be occupied territories, this labelling would likely be contested by many (if not most) Russians, Turks, Israelis, and Moroccans respectively. Moreover, many parts of the world are home to inhabitants that may consider themselves as living under occupation, even if the major global players do not share this position. For example, Tibetans living in China, Irish living in Northern Ireland, and Palestinians living in Israel may all consider themselves under occupation. Some observers, like Noam Chomsky and Pappé (2015, p. 67), have even gone as far as saying that the US state of Arizona should be considered Occupied Mexico! Despite UN opinion statements on occupied territories, there exists no official body for deciding when or where international law on military occupations should apply (Roberts, 1984), rendering the term "military occupation" decidedly contestable. Therefore, when looking at military occupations, it is important to understand both the ambiguity of the term and its emotional baggage.

Despite this messiness, the term "military occupation" is not inoperable. For example, the UN General Assembly and Security Council regularly express views regarding when military occupations are underway. In addition, there are a series of internationally accepted treaties that define the circumstances under which a military occupation is in effect. The 1907 Hague Regulations, the 1949 Geneva Conventions, and the 1977 Geneva Protocol lay out the basis for such circumstances and the associated obligations of occupying powers to the people and the territories they occupy (Roberts, 1984). Taken together, these treaties suggest a military occupation is in existence when "the armed forces of a State [are] exercising some kind of coercive control or authority over inhabited territory outside the accepted international frontiers of their state" (ibid., p. 255). Naturally, this definition leaves much open to interpretation, and thus it is not surprising that Roberts (1984) lists 17 different types of military occupation.

Within this context, this review focuses on the literature on military occupations that have been internationally recognised by major international bodies such as the UN or EU, or which fit well with one of Roberts's (1984) examples. In doing so, we do not deny the experiences of those who feel they live under an unrecognised military occupation, nor do we intend to offend the sensibilities of those who feel the use of such terminology is inappropriate. This *is* a sensitive topic. Rather than shy away from it, we feel the subject demands thorough investigation.

## Military Occupation as an Exercise in Tourism

The French-language newspaper, *Le Courrier de l'Air*, frames the arrival of German troops in Morocco in 1941 within the lexicon of tourism (Figure 12.1). The soldiers are described as "tourists" and "technicians", who take up residence in the hotels of Casablanca, and whose visas are all "perfectly in order". Yet these "tourists" are also securing petrol supplies, patrolling airfields, and engaging in "the most suspicious activities along the coast".

This is the first relationship we wish to highlight between military occupations and tourism, namely that military occupation can serve as a mass exercise in tourism, as it often necessitates the movement of thousands of people into new and foreign landscapes (Stein, 2008; Torrie, 2011). Although the primary role of soldiers is to serve the military aims of the state, seeing soldiers as mere military functionaries ignores the human curiosity occupying soldiers have for the lands and peoples they occupy, as well as the non-combatant roles that soldiers can play in assisting a military occupation. Importantly, although military occupation may serve as a mass exercise in tourism, it does so within a context rife with ideological intentions as well as severe power imbalances between "host and guest", occupied and occupier.

*Figure 12.1* "Les touristes allemands au Maroc" ("The German tourists in Morocco"). Front cover of Free French Newspaper, *Le Courrier de l'Air*, March 10, 1941.

Photo: Jack Shepherd at the Musée de la Libération in Paris, August 2020

The occupying armies of World War II (1939–1945) provide perhaps the best examples of military occupation as tourism. Nowhere was this more evident than in German-occupied Paris (1940–1944). One of the most iconic images from World War II is of Adolf Hitler, flanked by architect Albert Speer and sculptor Arno Beker, striding forward with the Eiffel Tower as their backdrop.[1] The image is interesting as it intentionally positions Hitler's visit to Paris as an exercise in tourism. It also stresses the dual role of the occupying German army in Paris: to both occupy the city militarily and enjoy it sensuously. As Torrie (2011, p. 310) explains, German soldiers "alternated between the role of occupiers and tourists, sometimes taking on both roles simultaneously". Given the touristic appeal of the City of Light, it is not surprising that German soldiers were commonly seen wandering the streets of Paris with a German *Baedeker* guide in their hands. Nor was it surprising that the city's brothels did a roaring trade, or that Paris's finest restaurants found themselves exempt from the strict rationing imposed on the city (Gordon, 2017, 2018; Torrie, 2011). Recognising the importance of satisfying this touristic demand, the German authorities established organised tours of Paris that took almost 1 million German soldier-tourists around the city during the war (Torrie, 2011). This effort was supported by the publication of guides such as the *Deutsches Gesehen*, which served as both a tourist guide and a rationale for the occupation (Torrie, 2018), as well as newspapers such as *Pariser Nächte* that listed the various attractions and vices of the city (Gordon, 2017). The hope was that tourism would satisfy the desires of the troops, serve as recuperation from and a reward for the horrific toils of the Eastern Front, and instill in the men a craving to continue possessing this desirable city (Torrie, 2011). In essence, their hope was that tourism would render "the occupation palatable" (Torrie, 2018, p. 127).

Equally, for the Allies who occupied Italy from 1943 onwards, military occupation was seen as a rare opportunity for international tourism. Buchannan (2016, p. 594) explains how American soldiers wrote home describing how they felt more like tourists than soldiers when stationed in Italy. In fact, the US Army newspaper, *Stars and Stripes*, reported that the American occupation was run by a "tourist army" (ibid., p. 597). American soldiers stationed in Italy were issued guidebooks such as *The Pocket Guide to Italian Cities*, offered tours to Capri and surrounding Mediterranean countries, and advised about the best cultural events in cities like Rome and Venice (ibid., pp. 594–595). Moreover, during the invasion of Italy, the Allied armies ensured that they occupied the finest hotels in the country's beautiful cities (Freyberg, 2013)—cities that may have been spared the most brutal bombing because of their touristic appeal (Buchannan, 2016; Freyberg, 2013).

Yet soldier tourism during a military occupation is far from benign. The gaze of both tourist and soldier cannot be disentangled. Therefore, the rampant sex tourism that occurred in both Nazi-occupied Paris and Allied-occupied Italy is much more than simply sex tourism; it as an occupying of occupied bodies within a new imbalanced power structure. For example, Buchannan (2016, p. 601) reports that between 70 and 76% of American GIs paid for sex during their occupation of Italy, often in the form of army food rations. Given the privations that affected the Italian people at that time, such transactions must be seen within a power structure juxtaposing occupying soldiers and occupied women. Similarly, in Corsica, when American troops arrived in 1944, troops wanting to escape the heat started damming the Alto River to create their own swimming pools. Naturally, local farmers complained but to no avail (Buchannan, 2016). Therefore, far from existing in a vacuum, the tourist gaze of occupying soldiers is also an occupying gaze, informed by a perceived entitlement to occupied bodies and lands, and assisted by the perception that the occupied lie "prostrate and apparently accommodating" (Miles & Gerster, 2018, p. 120).

## The Changing Shape of Tourism under Military Occupation

Tourism from the occupying power's military personnel represents one new form of tourism under occupation, and one that can prove particularly lucrative for those in the right line of business. Paris's night scene catered willingly to German soldiers on break from patrol or from the Russian winter (Gordon, 2018), Beirut's restaurants did a roaring trade amongst Israeli soldiers during their occupation of South Lebanon in the 1980s (Stein, 2008), and in the early 1950s, Japanese hotels hosted thousands of occupying US soldiers, as well as those on leave from the Korean War (Endo, 2018).

For occupied peoples, however, restrictions on movement, economic hardships, and oppression make participating in tourism challenging, yet equally, even more important. The stress of living under occupation only hastens the perceived need for leisure and escape. In such circumstances, tourism can be a cathartic outlet from the drudgery of life under occupation. Gordon (2018) describes how during World War II French people living in the Nazi-occupied north would try to spend their holidays in the unoccupied south of the country in order to reconnect with loved ones and experience landscapes free from the sight of Nazi tyranny. In Palestine, we have heard in our own research how tourism abroad can act as a reminder of what a "normal" life should be, as this quote from a hostel worker in Ramallah attests:

> The moment you realize that it [the situation] is not normal is the moment you leave Palestine, you go somewhere else … Really simple things outside Palestine can tell you how much we are oppressed here. I spent 16 hours on a bus in the US, and that was horrible for an American, they don't want this, but it was fascinating for me because I did not get stopped at any checkpoint … here in the West Bank, a trip [of] five hours, you get stopped every half an hour or so.[2]

Just as the frustrating and humiliating experiences of living under occupation may force people to seek tourism opportunities elsewhere, similar emotions can rob an occupied territory of previously stable tourism markets. A military occupation often leads to a mass movement of people, as inhabitants flee or are forcibly removed from the occupied territory. Following such traumatic experiences, these people are likely to share a lifelong disdain for the new occupying authority. It might also turn once cherished homelands into landscapes of fear and humiliation. Consequently, previously popular tourism destinations might become stigmatised in the national tourism imaginary.

Cyprus offers an instructive example. Before the Turkish invasion in 1974, some of the most popular tourism resorts in Cyprus, such as Famagusta and Kyrenia, were in the north of the island. Cypriots would make little distinction between holidaying in the south or the north of the island (Ioannides, 2020, personal communication). This changed when Cyprus was sliced in two following the Turkish invasion, which was in response to a Greek-backed coup of the island's government. As a result, the island was divided, with the north falling under a Turkish military occupation. For the next 30 years, travel across the "Green Line" separating north and south was not possible for Cypriots. Although this "border" opened in 2003, Webster and Timothy (2006) suggest that Greek Cypriots remain uncomfortable about holidaying on the Turkish side. In their survey conducted a year after the opening, Greek Cypriots felt that even if it was perhaps acceptable to visit places related to their family's past, contributing in any way to the North's tourism economy was considered highly inappropriate. Many Greek Cypriots also objected to having to show their passport to visit what they see as a part of their own country.

Conversely, for the occupier, newly acquired territories may represent fertile ground for revelling in opposite emotions: pride and patriotism. Whereas for Greek Cypriots, *avoiding* the occupied North is a question of patriotic duty, for Russians, *visiting* the occupied territory of Crimea is a patriotic duty (MacFarquhar, 2015). The Russian government has actively encouraged its citizens to travel to Crimea, including subsidising travel to the peninsula and boosting connections between Moscow and Sevastopol (MacFarquhar, 2015). The authorities in Crimea are all too happy to draw a link between tourism in Crimea and patriotism. Under the title "Keep abreast of patriotism", the official tourism website of the "Republic of Crimea" encourages Russian tourists to visit sites associated with Russia's military. The website claims "patriotic memorial places are especially popular today" (Republic of Crimea, 2020, n.p.). This new form of patriotic tourism helps explain why, within one year of annexation, Russian tourism to Crimea increased by 340% (Berryman, 2017, p. 66). This kind of tourism in occupied territory is nothing new. Reynolds (2020) reminds us that British tourists visiting Occupied France[3] (1815–1818) in the wake of the Battle of Waterloo routinely commented on feelings of pride and patriotism. Similarly, a century later, when Italy occupied Libya, tourists were encouraged to visit the newly acquired African territory to demonstrate their patriotism. The national tourism board of Italy, the Touring Club Italiano, described visiting Libya in 1931 as a "national duty" (Hom, 2012, p. 290). It seems likely that patriotic tourism in occupied territories will continue in the coming years, especially among the BRIC countries who have demonstrated their willingness to use tourism as a geopolitical weapon in contested spaces (Timothy, 2019).

Military occupations, themselves, can also be a tourism pull factor. Those tourists who came to revel in the hedonic atmosphere following the 1815 defeat of Napoleon also came to witness the extraordinary "grand reviews" of the occupying Allied army. Parades of up to 55,000 troops from all over Europe were a sight to behold and drew crowds from across Western Europe for whom the occupation was a spectacle not to be missed (Reynolds, 2020). Today, tourists are even offered the opportunity to partake in such military fetishism. In the Occupied Palestinian Territories, companies such as Caliber 3 (www.caliber3range.com) offer tourists the chance to mimic the military operations of the occupying Israeli army in, for example, training for a terror attack, learning how to respond to a Molotov cocktail attack, or partaking in an "IDF shooting adventure".

On the other hand, occupations can draw tourist interest of a very different kind, where rather than gaining access to the experience of the occupier, tourists wish to show solidarity with the occupied. Accordingly, scholars have forwarded the idea of "solidarity tourism" (Guia, 2021; Kassis et al., 2016) and have largely focused on the Occupied Palestinian Territories where solidarity tourists prioritise learning about life under the Israeli occupation and try to engage with the daily struggle of Palestinians. Sometimes this can mean putting their bodies on the front line of the conflict by, for example, joining weekly Palestinian protests against the Israeli army (Belhassen et al., 2013), or assisting Palestinians in picking their olive crops near Israeli settlements—a task that is increasingly dangerous for Palestinian farmers (Kassis et al., 2016).

For many tourists, however, there is no desire to roll up one's sleeves in fighting an occupation or in promoting it. For these tourists, an occupation represents an interesting and complex political situation of which they want a greater understanding. Innovative tourism products cater for these tourists such as the "dual narrative tours" that exist in Israel and Palestine, where tourists visit contested cities with two guides, one representing the occupier's (Israel) narrative, and one representing the occupied (Palestinians) (Schneider, 2019).

## Profiteering from Military Occupation through Tourism

Based on the Fourth Geneva Convention, an EU report states that "an occupying power may not dispose of the resources of occupied territory for her own good" (Wrange, 2015, p. 8). The understanding in the report appears to be that these resources are most likely to be extractable, physical resources. For example, the authors describe how phosphates and oil are being illegally extracted in Western Sahara with Morocco's acquiescence (ibid., p. 41). Yet tourism resources are also potentially lucrative to an occupying power and provide the possibility for a military power to profit from its occupation.

One striking example is the Yemeni island of Socotra. The island is famous for its stunning landscapes, and is described as the "Galapagos of Arabia", as it hosts many unique and endemic species of flora and fauna (Towers, 2018). Its tourism potential, largely untapped, has recently drawn the attention of some of the industry's big names, such as *Bradt Guides* and *Wanderlust* founder Hilary Bradt (Hardingham-Gill, 2020). This potential has not been lost on its new occupier, the United Arab Emirates (UAE), which has exerted increasing control over the island since Yemen descended into civil war in 2014. Initially welcomed on the island to improve Socotra's poor infrastructure, the UAE has now firmly taken control of the island, with troops in the streets and the UAE's flag adorning public buildings (Al Jazeera, 2018). Now in control, the UAE is reportedly developing mass tourism on the island. Locals report that Emirati businessmen have been buying up land and destroying swathes of the island's natural environment to construct hotels and pools, in what has been seen as a planned Dubai-ification of the island (Kedam, 2018; Towers, 2018). Validating these claims is the emergence of a direct charter flight between the island and Abu Dhabi, operated by Emirati airline Rotana Jet (Towers, 2018). These reports suggest that the UAE intends to profit from its occupation through the development of tourism and control of tourism flows. Such development appears to ignore the wishes of the occupied people of Socotra, thereby contravening occupation law, which states that the use of occupied resources should be for the benefit of the occupied peoples (Wrange, 2015).

The Socotra example mirrors a long history of occupying powers seeking profit through tourism. Even during World War II, occupying powers were busy envisioning tourism development in their newly acquired territories. For example, only one month after the Italian invasion of Albania in 1939, Italy's Director of Tourism, Probo Magrini, was dispatched to the country to inventory Albanian tourism resources and develop a tourism master plan (Hom, 2012).

Two decades later, when Israel occupied the Egyptian Sinai after the 1967 war, it also rapidly set about developing tourism along the peninsula's pristine coastline (Glassner, 1974). Within a few years, Israel constructed several basic tourist resorts along the Sinai coast and built roads to previously inaccessible places such as St. Catherine's monastery, which quickly became a popular tourism site (Glassner, 1974). A *New York Times* article written only three years after the Sinai was occupied recalls that, "in Israel, where tourism is only one step behind occupation, the holiday potential of the Southern Sinai is being developed almost as quickly as its military defences" (Feron, 1970, n.p.). Naturally, all this development contributed to sustaining the Israeli settlements that had popped up in the Sinai, and profited Israeli companies such as Egged, Israel's largest bus company, which had a monopoly on tours to the Sinai (Glassner, 1974).

Incidentally, that same bus company was listed in 2020 by the United Nations as profiteering from another occupation: Israel's ongoing occupation of the West Bank (Office of the United Nations High Commissioner for Human Rights, 2020). Egged runs bus services and tours to and from Israel's civilian infrastructure in the West Bank. Its services do not serve any Palestinian centres in the territory and therefore cannot be considered as services provided by the occupier for the occupied people. Ensuring tourist mobility to and from the illegal settlements in the West Bank not only profits Egged but also contributes to the longevity of the settlement project. Egged is not alone in this regard, and according to Amnesty International's (2019) recent report on tourism and the occupation of Palestine, giant multinational tourism companies such as Airbnb, TripAdvisor, and Booking.com have also profited from tourism in Israel's West Bank settlements. These cases demonstrate that it is not just an occupying power that can profit from military occupation, but also international companies. Yet Israel also profits from its occupation by forcibly taking control of tourism sites from occupied Palestinians.

Through its architecture of occupation, which includes a convoluted system of checkpoints and walls, Israel has managed to syphon off a number of important archaeological and heritage sites throughout the occupied territories (Isaac & Platenkamp, 2016). This ensures that important tourism and pilgrimage sites, such as Rachel's Tomb in Bethlehem, are only accessible by employing an Israeli tour guide, or buying a bus ticket from an Israeli bus company, such as the aforementioned Egged! This is despite the fact that the tomb lies well within the internationally recognised boundaries of Palestine.

## Tourism as Normalising Military Occupation

Along with generating revenue, tourism also plays a role in normalising military occupations. Through tourism, ordinary citizens help in obfuscating the violence of military occupations and propagating the occupier's narrative. Together, these can foster an attachment between the occupier and the occupied territory that makes letting go of that territory much harder.

As already noted, occupation does not mean the cessation of tourism. In fact, the opposite often happens. One example is the aftermath of the Israeli victory in the 1967 Six Day War. Having fought off Egypt, Syria, and Jordan, Israel occupied territories in the West Bank, Gaza, Golan Heights, and the Sinai Peninsula. Formerly inaccessible to Israelis, these territories were suddenly transformed into spaces of leisure (Stein, 2008). Within a matter of days after hostilities ended, Israeli tourists were flooding occupied East Jerusalem, which was previously forbidden territory for them. These Israelis were particularly set on visiting the holy Western Wall. On the first day the wall was opened to the public (June 14, 1967), some 200,000 Israelis visited (ibid., p. 650). What these tourists may not have known was that their visit was only made possible by the rapid destruction of the Palestinian Maghariba quarter that had previously existed in the space now forming the Western Wall Plaza (Weizman, 2017, p. 38). The tourism rush continued unabated and before long Israelis were indulging in tourism throughout the occupied territories, in what Stein (2008) portrays as a frenzy of consumption, with Israelis gleefully enjoying the restaurants and souks of newly captured Palestinian cities. Here, tourism played a perceived role in reassuring the newly occupied Palestinians that Israeli control could be mutually beneficial and non-violent. To summarise, Stein (2016, p. 551) states, "the occupation was recast as mere consumptive opportunity, generative of new cartographies of leisure rather than violence, thereby fictively denuding the occupation of its violence". Tourism made tangible the benefits of the occupation to the Israeli public (Stein, 2008) and thus gave Israelis a personal stake in the continuation of the occupation.

For the Axis powers in World War II, the use of tourism to sanitise military occupation was far more explicit. Imperial Japan saw tourism as a form of "patriotic citizenship training" (Ruoff, 2014, p. 194), and Japanese citizens were encouraged to travel to the newly occupied territories in China. The hope was that as tourists visited sites of former Chinese cultural and political agencies, such as the home of Confucius in Qufu, which had rapidly become mummified into a heritage site, Japanese tourists would come away with a reaffirmed belief in not only Japanese superiority, but also in Japan's self-proclaimed role as the guardian of Asian civilization (Ruoff, 2014).

During its occupation of Libya (1911–1943), Italy also saw tourism as way of communicating the value of occupation. Tourism was encouraged as a means of connecting the Italian people to the increasingly concrete existence of a "new Roman Empire". Italians were encouraged to "re-possess" Roman territories like Libya, the Greek Islands, and Albania (Hom, 2012, p. 286). Indeed, the Touring Club Italiano said in 1912 that tourism was "a means to restore that dominion of ours that the Romans had … and that we should force ourselves to resurrect for the benefits of those countries, Italy and civilization" (ibid., p. 287). Visiting Occupied Libya was therefore a way of making communion with Italy's *mission civilisatrice* and normalising its associated violence.

Yet it is not just domestic audiences whose tourist gaze is instrumentalised to normalise occupation. Given the exponential growth of international tourism and communication networks, it has become increasingly important that occupations are also validated by international observers—tourists not from the countries in conflict. International tourists represent important potential agents in the wider field of international geopolitics. Thus, giving tourists the "right narrative" about the occupation is important to an occupying power. Yang (2020) argues that Israel, for example, has deftly used tourism as a tool for normalising its occupation of Palestinian areas. Her work has looked at West Bank tours run by Israeli companies and argues that such tours support the Israeli occupation by propagating a vision of the West Bank where Israeli military violence is occluded. The focus of such tours on religious heritage, depoliticised aspects of life in Palestine, and a self-gratifying encounter with the architecture of the Israeli occupation, such as the Separation Wall, leads tourists to become, in Yang's (2020, p. 1086) words, "complicit in sustaining Israeli state violence".

## Challenges for Tourism Development under Military Occupation

So far, our focus has been largely on the occupying powers. Now our attention turns to the consequences of military occupation on those who are occupied, and in particular, on their ability to continue to develop tourism. These challenges can come as a direct result of the actions of the occupying power, but also as a result of the actions of the international community, whose attempts to punish a state for invading and occupying a territory can have unwelcome consequences on tourism actors under occupation.

Regarding the challenges created by an occupying power, firstly, an occupying power can be downright destructive. The devastation wrought by the Islamic State (ISIS) during its occupation of vast swathes of Iraq and Syria testifies to the destructive potential of an occupying power. In destroying large parts of the Roman ruins in Palmyra or the Assyrian remains in Nimrud (Al-Kanany, 2020; Curry, 2015), ISIS not only annihilated priceless global cultural heritage, but also damaged the future tourism potential of both countries. ISIS may seem unparalleled in its thirst for wanton destruction, but military occupations have an established record of looting and vandalism. A quick stroll around some of Europe's finest museums, like the British Museum in London, reveals just how kleptomaniac a foreign occupation can be.

Tourism infrastructure can also be the target of an occupier's wrath. This was the case in 2001 when Israel purposefully destroyed Palestine's only airport in the Gaza Strip (Weizman, 2017). Alternatively, tourism infrastructure might suffer due to the crossfire between contesting armies of occupied territories. For example, popular tourism sites in Armenian-occupied Nagorno-Karabakh, such as Ghazanchetsots Cathedral in Shushi, have faced significant damage in the tug of war between Azeri and Armenian forces (Mirovalev, 2020).

An occupying power may also deliberately frustrate the tourism development of an occupied territory so that the occupied people remain economically weak and dependent, thereby retaining the upper hand in the regional tourism market. It is no secret that the Israeli occupation of the West Bank has created such conditions (Isaac et al., 2016). These include control over Palestine's external borders, restricting Palestinian tour guide access to Israel, imposing curfews on Palestinian cities, and frustrating Palestinian mobility through the use of checkpoints, the Separation Wall, and apartheid roads (Çakmak & Isaac, 2012; Isaac, 2019; Isaac et al., 2016).

On a less sinister note, the change in administration that accompanies an occupation may lead to new legislative rules, currencies, and taxation that would present challenges for any tourism business. Ivanov et al. (2016) describe how businesses in Crimea faced such challenges after the Russian takeover. Even though the companies they surveyed in Crimea found the legal transition smooth, they did say that other changes, such as the introduction of the Russian rouble, which suffered a severe devaluation because of the occupation, as well as higher taxes, made the day-to-day operation of their businesses increasingly difficult.

These conditions can be aggravated when an occupied territory is subject to international sanctions due to the occupation. Following the 2014 Russian invasion of Crimea, for example, the majority of the world did not consider Russia's actions and the subsequent referendum of the Crimean people as legitimate. Accordingly, the European Union, the United States, Canada, Australia, Japan, and others imposed sanctions on Russia. The consequence of non-recognition and associated sanctions proved devastating to the Crimean tourism industry (Ivanov et al., 2016; MacFarquhar, 2015). Direct flights and cruise ships from Europe, which used to be a regular feature in cities such as Sevastopol and Yalta, ground to a complete halt (MacFarquhar, 2015). As a result, tourism from outside Russia sank drastically, and by 2019, 85% of all Crimean tourism was coming from Russia (Ayres, 2019). In fact, one tour guide in Yalta told a *Los Angeles Times* journalist that he had not seen a foreign tourist in three years (Ayres, 2019). The sanctions also meant foreign investment in Crimean tourism became illegal, forcing the region's tourism actors to become completely dependent on financing from the occupying power (Ayres, 2019). Furthermore, with sanctions clamping the economy, inflation in Crimea rose to 42% within one year of occupation (Berryman, 2017). Accordingly, the running costs for hotels rose markedly and business owners felt compelled to raise their prices (Ivanov et al., 2016).

Tourism developers in Northern Cyprus face similar issues. Given the lack of international recognition for the Turkish Republic of Northern Cyprus (TNRC), it is not possible for tourists to fly from major tourism supply markets, like the European Union, directly to North Cyprus. Because of ongoing sanctions, the largest airport on the island only receives direct flights from Turkey (Alipour & Kilic, 2005). This represents a growing problem for North Cyprus given it has seen rapid growth in demand from tourism markets outside of Turkey in recent decades (Yasarata et al., 2010). However, like Crimea, the TNRC remains heavily reliant on tourism from the occupying power, with Turkish arrivals making up the overwhelming majority of tourism arrivals (Alipour & Kilic, 2005).

## Mobility Regimes under Military Occupation

The last relationship between tourism and military occupation highlighted here relates to the new and uneven mobility regimes that emerge from military occupations, which result in differing levels of what Kaufmann et al. (2004, p. 750) refer to as "motility", meaning "the capacity of entities to be mobile" between tourists, locals, and occupiers.

For the citizens of an occupying power, military occupation might mean new access to previously inaccessible territories. As mentioned above, the tourism rush that occurred into East Jerusalem in 1967 should not be seen as a sudden outburst of curiosity amongst Israelis, but rather the result of a whole nation of Jews having been excluded from their holiest site for decades. During the Jordanian occupation of parts of the city (1948–1967), Jews were forbidden from entering East Jerusalem, whilst other tourists had to provide a baptismal certificate proving their non-Jewish status to gain entry (Idinopoulos, 1994). Jordan also forbade tourists from re-entering Israel once they had passed into the West Bank, making Christian pilgrimage itineraries challenging. The advent of the Israeli occupation of the West Bank, therefore, expedited both Israeli and international tourist mobility (Feron, 1970). Although the Oslo Agreements have created a convoluted system of "areas" with differing access rights for Israelis and Palestinians, thus reducing somewhat Israeli mobility in the West Bank, there remain few impediments in place for tourists who wish to travel between Israel and the Palestinian territories.

As in Israel–Palestine, in Moldova, tourists are not impeded if they wish to travel from the Moldovan capital Chişinău to the occupied city of Tiraspol in Transnistria. Interestingly, there are also cases where the view is taken by governments that areas under a military occupation are considered safer than non-occupied areas. For example, the British Foreign and Commonwealth Office's (FCO) travel guidelines for Moroccan-occupied Western Sahara show as "safe" all the areas under Moroccan occupation and as "advising against all travel" to those parts under the control of the native Sahrawi people's representative authority, the Polisario Front (FCO, 2020). This is despite the fact that the United Kingdom does not officially recognise Morocco's stewardship of Western Sahara.

Some occupied areas are, to all intents and purposes, off-bounds to international tourists. It is unlikely that many tourists would find their movements into Turkish-occupied Northern Syria assisted by powers on either side of the divide. Other occupied areas, however, simply become far more challenging for a tourist to access once a homogeneous territory is fragmented into occupied and unoccupied zones. Formerly, for example, a tourist could enter Crimea from mainland Ukraine in less than half an hour. Later, the same journey took up to half a day (Ayres, 2019). It is not just time that such mobility regimes can cost the tourist. The experience of crossing these "borders", of facing armed soldiers at checkpoints, or being interrogated by suspicious guards can leave tourists feeling a mixture of fear, shock, and anger—emotions that can define the travel experience in occupied territories (Buda et al., 2014; Shepherd et al., 2020).

For those living under occupation, an entirely different type of mobility regime may be in place. As a statement of power and to facilitate control, an occupying power tends to restrict the freedom of movement of the people it occupies. This has consequences for tourism. A West Bank Palestinian, for example, seeking to take a holiday outside of Palestine faces the difficult process of obtaining a permit to leave the West Bank or Gaza, followed by unpredictable Israeli border guards, and the prospect of having to travel to Amman, Jordan, three days in advance of their flight in order to insure against any border-related hassles. As a general rule, West Bank Palestinians are forbidden from flying out of the far more convenient airport in Tel Aviv. Similarly, residents of Crimea, who before were served by multiple direct flights to Europe, may now only leave via Russia (Ayres, 2019). This makes formerly short international trips to places like Istanbul more time consuming as flights are routed back via Moscow. Moreover, whereas Ukrainians can travel visa-free to the European Union, Crimean residents with Russian passports now have to obtain visas in Moscow if they want to travel to Europe.

As these examples illustrate, military occupation installs a new "government of mobilities" that dictates which bodies can move freely and which ones cannot (Sheller, 2016, p. 16), where tourists may have freedom of movement, but locals do not. This has been described by Sheller (2016) as "uneven mobility". To demonstrate these uneven mobilities in an occupied tourism setting, the first author, Jack Shepherd, recalls his experience on a group tour in Hebron, in the Occupied Palestinian Territories:

*Figure 12.2* Entrance to Shuhada Street, Hebron.

Photo: Jack Shepherd, September 2018

After lunch, our guide wanted us to witness the impact of Israeli occupation on the Old City of Hebron. Sadly, our guide was forbidden from entering some parts of the city because he is Palestinian. In contrast, our (mostly European) passports allowed us the privilege of accessing these areas. Despite feeling uneasy about leaving our guide behind, we went through the Israeli checkpoint (Figure 12.2) with instructions from him of how to navigate the interior. Meanwhile, our guide started his run to "the other side". A 15-minute jog to make sure our 15-minute walk would coincide with his arrival. In fact, on several occasions throughout that tour, the Israeli occupation provided "divergent pathways [and] differential access" (Sheller, 2016, p.16) to us tourists and to our Palestinian guide. Although our position as non-Palestinians gave us a freedom of movement, it certainly made us uncomfortable, embarrassed even. I must admit, in the end, I preferred treading the Palestinian pathways (Figure 12.3). I did not want the occupation to use my passport against (indeed, for) me.[4]

This example speaks both to the existence of uneven mobility regimes under occupation and to the affective ramifications of such systems. Visweswaran (2012, p. 441) also reflected on these imbalances when travelling to Occupied Kashmir as an Indian citizen, stating "I was 'free' to see the Pari Mahal or Shankaracharya temple under armed guard and behind barbed wire, but the Kashmiris I saw were not free … not in the least". Such situations bring up a whole host of questions that relate to justice in tourism during occupation and the degree to

*Figure 12.3* Divergent pathways—an example of apartheid infrastructure in Hebron. While Israelis and tourists can walk on the left side of the barrier, Palestinians must walk on the right.

Photo: Jack Shepherd, September 2018

which we can consider tourists as complicit with the (re)production of these uneven mobility regimes (Yang, 2020).

## Conclusion

This chapter began with the assumption that military occupations represent barriers and challenges to tourism. Along with demonstrating how and why this happens, our analysis has revealed the far more nuanced and complex relationships shared between tourism and military occupations. Although an occupation can frustrate tourism development, it can also usher in new, innovative, and at times controversial forms of tourism. Similarly, although occupations can reduce the tourism mobility of occupied peoples, other tourists might find their mobility increased as part of a new, uneven mobility regime.

What speaks through all the relationships that were highlighted between tourism and military occupation is the way in which tourism reflects, projects, and often amplifies power. Who has the right to move? Who has the right to build? Who has the right to a narrative platform? These questions are all embedded in the production and performance of tourism. In light of this, as tourism scholars, we should continually ask ourselves: whom does tourism serve? Perhaps as Yang (2020) encourages, we should also reflect on our own complicity as tourists within an ever more complex and interconnected geopolitical order.

Despite our critical approach, we would like to conclude this chapter by offering an alternative view, that occupations also offer opportunities for peacebuilding through tourism.

Reynolds (2020) unabashedly forwards the thesis that tourism assisted a process of growing cultural exchange and understanding between Britain and France during the Allied occupation of France (1815–1818). Endo (2018) also suggests that the American occupation of Japan (1945–1952) was a crucial moment in the formation of a co-constructed peace narrative, one made tangible through tourism. Our own research in Israel and Palestine gives us hope that tourism is well-placed for promoting transformational dialogue between occupier and occupied (Shepherd & Laven, 2021; Shepherd et al., 2020). Therefore, going forward, we hope that tourism studies continues to probe tourism's ability to be both the cancer and the cure in areas under occupation.

## Notes

1 This image can be found in the German National Archives: www.bild.bundesarchiv.de/dba/en/search/?query=Bild%20183-H28708
2 Data are excerpted from previously unpublished interviews conducted at Area D Hostel, Ramallah, by Jack Shepherd in September 2018.
3 The Allied Occupation of France is considered the world's first modern military occupation (Reynolds, 2020).
4 Data are excerpted from previously unpublished field notes written by Jack Shepherd in September 2018.

## References

Al Jazeera (2018, May 3). Anger erupts on Yemen's Socotra as UAE deploys over 100 troops. https://www.aljazeera.com/news/2018/05/03/anger-erupts-on-yemens-socotra-as-uae-deploys-over-100-troops/
Alipour, H., & Kilic, H. (2005). An institutional appraisal of tourism development and planning: The case of the Turkish Republic of North Cyprus (TRNC). *Tourism Management, 26*, 79–94.
Al-Kanany, M.M.R. (2020). Extremist iconoclasm versus real Islamic values: Implications for heritage-based tourism development in Iraq. *Journal of Heritage Tourism, 15*(4), 472–478.
Amnesty International (2019). *Destination occupation: Digital tourism and Israel's illegal settlements in the Occupied Palestinian Territories.* London: Amnesty International.
Ayres, S. (2019, January 28). Four years after Russia annexed Crimea, the peninsula remains in limbo. *Los Angeles Times.* https://www.latimes.com/world/la-fg-crimea-20190128-story.html
Belhassen, Y., Uriely, N., & Assor, O. (2013). The touristification of a conflict zone: The case of Bil'in. *Annals of Tourism Research, 49*, 174–189.
Berryman, J. (2017). Crimea: Geopolitics and tourism. In D. Hall (ed.) *Tourism and geopolitics: Issues and concepts from Central and Eastern Europe*, pp. 57–70. Wallingford: CABI.
Buchannan, A. (2016). "I Felt like a Tourist instead of a Soldier": The occupying gaze – war and tourism in Italy, 1943-1945. *American Quarterly, 68*(3), 593–615.
Buda, D.M., d'Hauterre, A-M., & Johnston, L. (2014). Feeling and tourism studies. *Annals of Tourism Research, 46*, 102–114.
Çakmak, E., & Isaac, R. (2012). What destination marketers can learn from their visitors' blogs: An image analysis of Bethlehem, Palestine. *Journal of Destination Marketing and Management, 1*, 124–133.
Chomsky, N., & Pappé, I. (2015). *On Palestine.* London: Penguin Books.
Curry, A. (2015, September 1). Here Are the ancient sites ISIS has damaged and destroyed. *National Geographic.* https://www.nationalgeographic.com/news/2015/09/150901-isis-destruction-looting-ancient-sites-iraq-syria-archaeology/
Endo, R. (2018). Reforming heritage and tourism in occupied Kyoto (1945-1952). How to create peace when surrounded by the atmosphere of war. *Asian Journal of Tourism Research, 3*(2), 95–120.
Feron, J. (1970, February 22). Israelis build up on heels of occupation. *The New York Times.* https://www.nytimes.com/1970/02/22/archives/israelis-build-up-on-heels-of-occupation.html
The Foreign & Commonwealth Office (2020). *Foreign travel advice: Western Sahara.* https://www.gov.uk/foreign-travel-advice/western-sahara

Freyberg, A. (2013, May 17). *The Telegraph*. Venice: Wartime haven on the Grand Canal. https://www.telegraph.co.uk/travel/destinations/europe/italy/veneto/venice/articles/Venice-wartime-haven-on-the-Grand-Canal/

Glassner, M.I. (1974). The Bedouin of southern Sinai under Israeli administration. *Geographical Review*, 64(1), 31–60.

Gordon, B. (2017). Tourism and erotic imaginaries in wartime Paris: French and Germans during the occupation, 1940-1944. *Via Tourism Review*, 11–12, 1–15.

Gordon, B. (2018). *War tourism: Second World War France from defeat and occupation to the creation of heritage*. Ithaca, NY: Cornell University Press.

Guia, J. (2021). Conceptualizing justice tourism and the promise of posthumanism. *Journal of Sustainable Tourism*, 29(2–3), 503–520.

Hardingham-Gill, T. (2020, September 7). How a crowdfunded travel guidebook could help protect Socotra island. *CNN Travel*. https://edition.cnn.com/travel/article/socotra-travel-guide/index.html

Hom, S.M. (2012). Empires of tourism: Travel and rhetoric in Italian colonial Libya and Albania, 1911-1943. *Journal of Tourism History*, 4(3), 291–300.

Idinopoulos, T.A. (1994). *Jerusalem: A history of the holiest city as seen through the struggles of Jews, Christians, and Muslims*. Chicago: Ivan R. Dee Publishing.

Isaac, R.K. (2019). Tourism as a tool for colonization, segregation, displacement and dispossession: The case of East Jerusalem, Palestine. In D.J. Timothy (ed.) *Routledge handbook on tourism in the Middle East and North Africa*, pp. 213–230. London: Routledge.

Isaac, R.K., & Platenkamp, V. (2016). Concrete U(dys)topia in Bethlehem: A city of two tales. *Journal of Tourism and Cultural Change*, 14(2), 150–166.

Isaac, R.K., Çakmak, E., & Butler, R. (Eds.) (2019). *Tourism and hospitality in conflict-ridden destinations*. London: Routledge.

Ivanov, S., Idzhylova, K., & Webster, C. (2016). Impacts of the entry of the Autonomous Republic of Crimea into the Russian Federation on its tourism industry: An exploratory study. *Tourism Management*, 54, 162–169.

Kassis, R., Solomon, R., & Higgins-Desbiolles, F. (2016). Solidarity tourism in Palestine: The alternative tourism group of Palestine as a catalyzing instrument of resistance. In R.K. Isaac, C.M. Hall, & F. Higgins-Desbiolles (eds), *The politics and power of tourism in Palestine*, pp. 37–52. London: Routledge.

Kaufmann, V., Bergman, M.M., & Joye, D. (2004). Motility: Mobility as capital. *International Journal of Urban and Regional Research*, 28(4), 745–756.

Kedam, S. (2018, May 10). The UAE appears to be building a Dubai-style resort on Yemen's island of Socotra. *Verdict*. https://www.verdict.co.uk/uae-building-dubai-style-resort-on-yemens-otherworldly-island-of-socotra-officials-and-islanders-say/

MacFarquhar, N. (2015, August 19). Russia's pitch to vacationers: Crimea is for patriots. *The New York Times*. https://www.nytimes.com/2015/08/20/world/europe/russias-pitch-to-vacationers-crimea-is-for-patriots.html

Miles, M., & Gerster, R. (2018). Japan for the taking: Images of the occupation. In M. Miles & R. Gerster (eds), *Pacific exposures*, pp.113–151. Canberra: Australian National University Press.

Mirovalev, M. (2020, October 15). Armenia, Azerbaijan battle an online war over Nagorno-Karabakh. *Al Jazeera*. https://www.aljazeera.com/features/2020/10/15/karabakh-info-war

The Office of the United Nations High Commissioner for Human Rights (2020). *Annual report of the United Nations High Commissioner for Human Rights and reports of the Office of the High Commissioner and the Secretary-General Human rights situation in Palestine and other occupied Arab territories*. (Report No. A/HRC/43/71).

Republic of Crimea (2020). *Excursions to Crimea in autumn: Patriotism, intellectual tourism and a new trend*. https://en.travelcrimea.com/news/20200917/1466226.html

Reynolds, L. (2020). There John Bull might be seen in all his glory: Cross-Channel tourism and the British army of occupation in France, 1815-1818. *Journal of Tourism History*, 12(2), 139–155.

Roberts, A. (1984). What is a military occupation? *The British Year Book of International Law*, 55(1), 249–305.

Ruoff, K. (2014). Japanese tourism to Mukden, Nanjing, and Qufu, 1938-1943. *Japan Review*, 27, 171–200.

Schneider, E.M. (2019). Touring for peace: The role of dual-narrative tours in creating transnational activists. *International Journal of Tourism Cities*, 5(2), 200–218.

Sheller, M. (2016). Uneven mobility futures: A Foucauldian approach. *Mobilities*, *11*(1), 15–31.

Shepherd, J., Laven, D., & Shamma, L. (2020). Autoethnographic journeys through contested space. *Annals of Tourism Research*, *84*: 103004.

Shepherd, J., & Laven, D. (2021). Hostels in hostile territory: The role of tourism spaces in transformative dialogue. In J.T. Da Silva, Z. Breda, & F. Carbone (eds), *Role and impact of tourism in peacebuilding and conflict transformation*, pp. 195–217. Hershey, PA: IGI Global.

Stein, R. (2008). Souvenirs of conquest: Israeli occupations as tourist events. *International Journal of Middle East Studies*, *40*, 647–669.

Stein, R. (2016). #StolenHomes: Israeli tourism and/as military occupation in historical perspective. *American Quarterly*, *68*(3), 545–555.

Timothy, D.J. (2019). Tourism, border disputes and claims to territorial sovereignty. In R. Isaac, E. Çakmak, & R. Butler (eds) *Tourism and hospitality in conflict-ridden destinations*, pp. 25–38. London: Routledge.

Torrie, J. (2011). 'Our rear area probably lived too well': Tourism and the German occupation of France, 1940-1944. *Journal of Tourism History*, *3*(3), 309–330.

Torrie, J. (2018). *German soldiers and the occupation of France, 1940-1944*. Cambridge: Cambridge University Press.

Towers, L. (2018, May 3). Socotra island: The UNESCO-protected 'Jewel of Arabia' vanishing amid Yemen's civil war. *The Independent*. https://www.independent.co.uk/news/world/middle-east/socotra-island-yemen-civil-war-uae-military-base-unesco-protected-indian-ocean-a8331946.html

Visweswaran, K. (2012). Occupier/Occupied. *Identities*, *19*(4), 440–451.

Webster, C., & Timothy, D.J. (2006). Travelling to the 'Other Side': The occupied zone and Greek Cypriot views of crossing the Green Line. *Tourism Geographies*, *8*(2), 162–181.

Weizman, E. (2017). *Hollow land: Israel's architecture of occupation*. London: Verso.

Wrange, P. (2015). *Occupation/annexation of a territory: Respect for international humanitarian law and human rights and consistent EU policy*. Brussels: European Parliament.

Yang, C. (2020). Staging Israel/Palestine: The geopolitical imaginaries of international tourism. *Politics and Space*, *38*(6), 1075–1090.

Yasarata, L., Altinay, M., Burns, P., & Okumus, F. (2010). Politics and sustainable tourism development – Can they co-exist? Voices from North Cyprus. *Tourism Management*, *31*, 345–356.

# 13
# CULTURAL BOUNDARIES AND ETHNIC REPRESENTATION IN CROSS-BORDER TOURISM DESTINATIONS

*Min (Lucy) Zhang and Jaume Guia*

## Introduction

Here–there, us–them, inside–outside, include–exclude, self–other: such linguistic dichotomies reflect the idea that borders exist almost everywhere and divide society into groups who belong and those who do not (Newman, 2006b). "Borders determine the nature of group belonging, affiliation, and membership, and the way in which the processes of inclusion and exclusion are institutionalized" (Newman, 2006a, p. 33). Sofield (2006) likewise claims that borders today are boundaries of inclusion as much as they are lines of exclusion.

In addition to being physical borders, "boundaries constitute a mental device for distinguishing between 'Them' and 'Us'. They draw the lines of 'difference' and are thus a crucial ingredient in any imagined community and its collective identity" (Hageman et al., 2004, cited in Sofield, 2006). Although international borders may divide nations, borderland communities may remain unified by culture, ethnicity, language, and/or religion (Underiner, 2011). Such ethnic and cultural boundaries bridge bordered territories, and there are many examples worldwide, including the Flemish, the Basques, and the Catalans in Europe; the Akha in Asia; and the Maya in Mesoamerica—to name but a few. These borderland and trans-frontier communities demonstrate a continued process of de-bordering and re-bordering over the past several decades (Newman, 2006a; Paasi & Prokkola, 2008).

Academics have paid considerable attention to borderlands from multidisciplinary backgrounds, adopting diverse approaches to the study of borders. To bring together the hierarchical nature of borders and their multidisciplinary character (Newman, 2004), scholars like Paasi (2011) interrogate whether a border theory is an unattainable dream or a realistic aim. Any theory evolves with challenges in practice, like the Regional Comprehensive Economic Partnership (RCEP) which integrates 15 Asia-Pacific countries, including the ASEAN states (China, Japan, South Korea, Australia, and New Zealand) in November 2020, which resulted in the largest free trade zone in the world. Another example of regional integration is the African Continental Free Trade Area (AfCFTA) launched in January 2021. In contrast, Brexit, which came into effect at the beginning of 2021, perforated European integration which had been the world's exemplary laboratory of regional collaboration and integration for decades. Such rapidly transforming contexts might turn current border studies in a different direction, aside from the traditional laboratories like the USA–Mexico border and the EU's internal and external borders.

The aim of this chapter is to review current issues and reflect on some key challenges at borders from a performative and dynamic perspective on the relationship between cultural boundaries and ethnic representation. Yet, our brief discussion of the topic is not a comprehensive examination; instead, it is an introduction and invitation to further explore border complexities in different geographical and sociocultural contexts. We conceptualize borders and boundaries, and ethnic communities at borderlands. We then explore significant issues in border regions concerning mobility and ethnic heritage, and their cultural representation. Instead of confining the debate within the traditional discourse of authenticity, we attempt to explain the dynamic nature of cultural boundaries and ethnic representation with the concept of performativity and the process of authentication. Finally, the key challenging relations in borderlands are discussed before the conclusion.

## Conceptualization

### *Borders and Boundaries*

Borders, boundaries, frontiers, and borderlands are human creations that are grounded in various ethical and political traditions (Brunet-Jailly, 2010). "Border", originally, was used to delimit the territorial possessions of sovereign states; borders were central to the nationalist agenda and the development of nation states. In line with Paasi (1999), who identifies boundaries as institutional constructs from a political perspective, Donnan and Wilson (1998) argue that borders are concerned with the study of power in and between nations and states at the local level of borders. While taking the perspective of social anthropology, the breakthrough work by Fredrik Barth (1969) on "Ethnic Groups and Boundaries" considers boundary formation to be a dynamic process of social interaction. In fact, there is a wide consensus among many scholars engaged in border studies that although a distinction is often drawn between physical and cultural (or material and mental) boundaries (Newman, 2006b; Sofield, 2006; Timothy, 2001), the two are integrated as two sides of one coin. Kearney (2004, p.132) confirms this point:

> a border is a vaguely defined area that exists on both sides of a boundary. Cultural borders demarcate identities such as nationality, citizenship, ethnicity, and so forth. A border defined in both senses is a composite geographic, legal, institutional, and sociocultural structure and process.

A "new generation" of border studies emerged in the 1990s with the geopolitical changes that took place in Europe, the Soviet Union and the USA–Mexico borderlands (Newman & Paasi, 1998; Newman, 2006b). Borders became a widespread research theme, not only in geography but also in other social sciences and cultural studies. Moreover, border studies as a multidisciplinary field has attracted much academic attention. Researchers in different academic fields have studied borders largely from their own disciplinary perspectives, and as a result, social, economic, political, and cultural "layers" within borders have been widely examined (e.g., Horstmann, 2014; Kearney, 2004; Qian, 2017).

Rather than focusing strictly on physical borders, the bordering perspective also entails the everyday construction of borders among communities and groups (Scott, 2015). Therefore, borders are not given, but are highly penumbral; as Paasi and Zimmerbauer (2016) observe, borders can be insignificant or "soft" in many practices and instances, yet at other times and in some practices, they can be meaningful and "hard", depending on certain conditions. In this sense, the traditions and values that create a sense of community are what define the cultural layer of borders (Paasi, 2019). As such, ethnic minority communities often bear on the realm of sociocultural boundaries whereby limits and boundaries are an essential part of life (Hageman et al., 2004; Holt, 2018; Leimgruber, 1999).

Scholars have proposed studying borders and boundaries at various scales. It is argued that existing boundaries are relatively inconstant. There are three types of boundaries according to Paasi (2011) from a rather macro-perspective: some are open, for instance the boundaries inside the EU; some are strictly guarded, like the border between North and South Korea; and some others are in-between, so as to be selectively open, so that flows between states are somehow flexible depending on bilateral agreements, such as the external borders of the EU, the USA–Mexico border, and the borders of China and its ASEAN neighbors. In particular, Newman (2006a, p.143) takes a micro-scalar view, suggesting that:

> borders should be studied not only from a top-down perspective but also from the bottom-up, with a focus on the individual border narratives and experiences, reflecting the ways in which borders impact upon the daily life practices of people living in and around the borderland and trans-boundary transition zones.

This perspective has guided studies towards the bordering processes of ethnic communities.

## *Ethnic Communities at Borders*

Borders are not only associated with territory and political demarcations; more importantly, the social, cultural, and ethnic meanings of a border are influenced by local communities who live in their presence. Communities are socially constructed by the people who identify themselves as part of a group and associated with certain beliefs, perceptions, images, and discourses (Anderson, 1997). Ethnic minorities that are split between different states by international borders often find themselves in a complex reality of living "in the middle", between two societies and cultures, between two economic systems, in the shadow of changing international relations (Gelbman & Timothy, 2011). Although there is no consensus, the crucial role of borderland communities with regard to cultural boundary formation and maintenance has been identified (Zhang, 2019a), and thus the importance of their local culture is underscored.

The practice of crossing international borders in a routine fashion has important implications for our understanding of the spatial and social organization of society and culture. In marginal spaces, where one state ends and another begins, ethnic communities play with their identities or make use of the border for their advantage (Horstmann, 2014). Thus, border communities play a significant role in making and transforming identity by negotiating the highly ambiguous spaces of the borderlands. Why this point is significant in the border context will be further elaborated in a later section on performativity.

The cultural border is never definitive, and cultural boundaries between communities may reach much further beyond the territorial limits of the sovereign state. Ethnic boundaries are an outcome of the classificatory struggles and negotiations between actors situated in a social field (Barth, 1969; Gao et al., 2019). Wimmer (2008) articulates that the conditions under which these negotiations will lead to a shared understanding of the meaning of boundaries vary from case to case. The institutional order, distribution of power, and political networks determine which actors will adopt which strategy of ethnic boundary making. A recent case study conducted by Zhang (2019a) reveals the strategy-making process of an ethnic group, the Jing people on the China–Vietnam border, which demonstrates how the sociocultural boundaries of ethnic communities are established and maintained through tourism activities. Hence, the ethnic community is a salient force in producing and negotiating the cultural boundaries of borderlands.

We now turn our discussion to several current issues based upon our own observations and evaluation of what constitutes important topics for problem-oriented work in border contexts.

## Issues

### *Mobilities*

From "spaces of places" to "spaces of flows" (Castells, 2000), globalized mobility makes borderlands a more complex type of space (Timothy & Michalkó, 2016). The concept of mobility is an interpretation of the formation process of geographical forms, as well as an important theoretical tool to connect social and spatial theories, which facilitates the understanding of the significance of human beings in the process of spatial movement through specific social and cultural representations (Tang et al., 2016). The freedom of mobility not only reflects actors' initiatives, but also means the ability to obtain resources and opportunities to a large extent. Thus, (cross-)border mobility has become an important factor in the continuous reconstruction of multiple social relations (Gao et al., 2019).

Urry (2000, p.186) argues that "diverse mobilities of peoples, objects, images, information, and wastes are materially transforming the 'social as society' into 'social as mobility', including imaginative travel, movements of images and information, virtual travel, object travel and corporeal travel". Indeed, mobility puts borderlands in a new spotlight in two ways. First, ethnic minorities in border areas use marginal spaces where their everyday life takes place to reconstruct transnational communities due to the flow of people, commodities, and ideas based on historical ethnic and religious ties in local spaces, as Horstmann (2014) demonstrates with several examples in Southeast Asia. Second, international borders as tourist attractions and cross-border tourism cooperation are both salient components of tourism motilities (Gelbman & Timothy, 2011; Sofield, 2006). As many cases demonstrate (Esman, 1984; Zhang, 2019a; Zhu, 2012), tourism facilitates the expression of ethnic culture and it can revive "pride of belonging" (Cohen, 1988). Moreover, these two aspects are sometimes intertwined. For instance, the debate about whether mobility blurs cultural boundaries has inspired academic research, such as that by Sun and Zhang (2015), who examine how boundaries in the context of mobility have been maintained in a heterogeneous host community. These authors argue that the boundary between different ethnic groups is constructed and maintained in two ways: internally, the core cultural values of ethnic groups, and externally, by the ecology of the tourism industry based on inter-group interactions.

Such flows of people and goods create marketplaces across borders where local commerce and petty trade take place (Borzooie et al., 2021; Tömöri, 2010). These frequently involve local ethnic communities sharing and working together in border areas (Schoenberger & Turner, 2008). As recent research illustrates, border markets, especially as venues of petty trade, develop as an important part of community livelihoods (Zhang, 2019b). In the example of the border of China and its ASEAN neighbors, small-scale petty border trade between communities remains the major economic contribution to local development, despite the fact that local governments seek a larger-scale, more market-oriented and rapid pro-growth track. Thus, border regions must confront the dilemma between the marketized economy, which by nature prioritizes profits in the short term, and community-based local entrepreneurship embedded in the trans-frontier social networks that are oriented toward collaboration and cooperation in the longer term. Aside from the economic implications, Tang et al. (2016) observe that cross-border flows and frequent commercial interactions have become an important means of establishing social relations and maintaining cross-border ethnic identities. Through the exchange of folk activities, the sharing of ordinary livelihood elements, and communication through similar languages (including local dialects), the ethnic cultural genes of the border are inherited, and the ethnic cultural identity is thus maintained, often even developed further (Konrad et al., 2019).

Although mobility is related to grassroots freedom of community exchange, it is also associated with power and governance. If borders and territories are both subject to state power, mobility is what the daily management at borders deals with. Therefore, border areas are constantly negotiated and shaped not only by limiting flows, but also by making use of them to operate and strengthen state power (Stefanova, 2013). At the supranational level, as in the case of the General Agreement on Tariffs and Trade (GATT) and the International Monetary Fund (IMF) in the late twentieth century, multinational agreements effectively fomented economic collaboration in Europe and North America (Blatter & Clement, 2000), with such trade agreements between governments acting as a mobility management tool impacting border negotiations. For instance, managers of the China–Vietnam border reached a "tacit understanding" of mobilities based on a long bordering experience (Tang et al., 2014). As previously mentioned, the RCEP agreement not only helps reduce the threshold of tariff preferences, but also greatly promotes intra-regional trade cooperation, and stabilizes and strengthens the regional industrial supply chain. Against this backdrop, some scholars (e.g., Laine, 2016, p. 470) have noted that increasing mobility and migration might cultivate xenophobia rather than create tolerance, as mixed and newly hybrid cultures have increasingly prompted people to turn towards their own culture in search of their identities (Keating, 2001). In short, "the mobilities paradigm … argues against the ontology of distinct places or people" (Hannam et al., 2006, p.13) and creates a new dimension of borders and boundaries.

## *Ethnic Heritage and Cultural Representation*

The *Oxford English Dictionary* defines heritage as "property that may be passed from one generation to the next, something that can be conserved or inherited, and something that has historic or cultural value" (Oxford English Dictionary, 2021). In fact, heritage is a fundamental element in the construction of community identity, as well as a central focus of tourism (Ballesteros & Ramírez, 2007; Timothy, 2021). In this sense, heritage has a dual role to play due to its convergence of ethnic communities and visitors.

Dela and Anril (2019) conceptualized heritage broadly as the natural and cultural environment and resources of a community. They further claim that the value of heritage is commonly determined by the values of the community. Their community-based understanding of heritage opposes the "ideological apparatus of the dominant authority, typically the state, which has a tendency to impose its perspective instead of engaging community members in conversations" (Dela & Anril, 2019, p. 301). This perspective is consistent with UNESCO's (2003) definition of intangible heritage: "the practices, representations, expressions, knowledge, skills—as well as the instruments, objects, artifacts and cultural spaces associated therewith—that communities, groups and, in some cases, individuals recognize as part of their cultural heritage". Moreover, heritage is not merely an object to be preserved and protected but a process that involves constant re-creation "by communities and groups in response to their environment, their interaction with nature and their history, and provides a sense of identity and continuity" (Harrison, 2013, p.134). Heritage is often used in making cultural references, "in the definition of the values, signs, supports and markers of identity" (Lanfant, 1995, p. 8). Although a large body of scholarship investigates representation of others, few regard how the "Other" represents itself (Yang et al., 2016). Muzaini (2017), for example, discusses how a theme park is utilized by Malaysian authorities to embody Malaysian statehood and nationality. Yet, Malays adjust the official narrative conveyed by cultural artifacts and stories by drawing from their own personal experiences at the park. Other examples showcase how the tensions of cultural representation are often complicated between different ethnic groups in border regions. Yang et al. (2016) explore the operational mechanism of impersonation in multi-ethnic communities, showing how indigenous culture is (mis)represented by other ethnic groups in Xinjiang. Similarly, the study by Zhang (2019b) reveals how a Ha festival, an intangible living heritage manifestation of the Jing people (originally from Vietnam and currently located in Dongxing, Guangxi Autonomous Region, China), is commodified by Han tourism enterprises. These examples demonstrate the contested cultural representations of ethnic heritage both for communities and tourists and exemplify the vagarious boundaries between cultures and ethnicities. Timothy (2021) highlights similar examples in other parts of the world, where "cultural imposters" can, in some people's eyes, deteriorate a sense of cultural and ethnic authenticity. In borderlands, the subjective notion of cultural "authenticity" may be blurred even further than in non-border regions.

The representation of minority cultures is central to ethnic and indigenous tourism development (Ruhanen & Whitford, 2019; Yang, 2013). Especially in remote areas like border regions, tourism is often associated with ethnicity (historical and cultural), which involves the representation of the Other and the heritage of native peoples (Wang, 1999). In practice, many cases demonstrate that tourism is embraced as an instrument for economic growth based on the value(s) of culture and ethnicity. For example, the reinvention of Lijiang Dongba cultural products not only attracts millions of tourists, but also presents an opportunity for the representation of Naxi ethnic culture (Zhu, 2012), which reveals how tourism can develop "new meanings" to support local identities (Cohen, 1988). On the one hand, tourism assists ethnic minorities in showcasing their traditions and their cultural reviving (Buzinde et al., 2006; Zhu, 2012), while simultaneously bringing economic growth and social benefits to the community. However, it can also adversely impact the sociocultural structure, ethnic groups' identity, and their sense of belonging (Li & Hunter, 2015; Oakes, 1998). In terms of the role tourism plays in the cultural representation of ethnic heritage, some scholars (e.g., Timothy, 2021; Yang, 2011) underline the importance of tourism as a creator of heritage, or a catalyst of change in the way people see themselves in relation to cultural artifacts or traditions. As such, at the physical level, tourism has led to the reconstruction and restoration of many heritage sites (Gravari-Barbas, 2018). In the process of heritage-making at the symbolic level, it has been argued that the "tourist gaze" (Urry, 1990) transforms heritage sites, and not always in positive ways. Studies have pointed to the significance of tourism in transferring the cultural representations of ethnic heritage through the processes of cultural globalization and homogenization (Logan, 2001), and as icons of cultural identity (Breathnach, 2006; Edson, 2004). Nevertheless, as previously noted, authenticity from the perspectives of the ethnic community and tourists is another strand to deepen the discussion of cultural representation at political borders and within the context of social borders between cultural groups.

## *Authenticity and Performativity*

The concept of authenticity entails being in a "natural state" for local communities (Taylor, 2001), or so-called "host authenticity", which means that local communities have the right to interpret for themselves what is authentic or not (Zhou et al., 2015). In tourism studies, situated in the center of academic debates, "authenticity" has experienced several phases from objectivism to constructivism and finally to postmodernism as the tourism industry evolves. Early objectivists assert that "true" (authentic) culture is a vital component in the production of touristic values; as Benjamin (1968, p.220) suggests, "the presence of the original is the prerequisite to the concept of authenticity". As such, the criteria to judge whether cultural tourist products, such as ethnic festivals, religious rituals, even cuisine or dress, are authentic or not rely on whether they are enacted by locals according to tradition. MacCannell (1973, 1976) introduced the concept of "staged authenticity" to explain tourists' experiences and travel motivations, suggesting that people do travel to seek authentic places and experiences but are fooled into believing that "staged" places are authentic, genuine, or real.

The constructivist perspective renders tourism an embodying communicative event, a dialectic between object and subject (Taylor, 2001). Thus, according to this school of thought, authenticity is negotiated and contextually determined (Cohen, 1988; Salamone, 1997). However, "both objective and constructive authenticity, as object-related notions, can only explain a limited range of tourist experiences" (Wang, 1999, p. 350). Because of this, Wang (1999) further raises the notion of "existential authenticity" with activity-orientation, as conducive to explaining a greater variety of "personal or inter-subjective feelings activated in tourism activities". Furthermore, the notion of performative authenticity is illustrated with the dynamic interaction between memory, habitus, and embodied practice (Zhu, 2012). Knudsen and Waade (2010, p.1) agree that it is "an instrumental embodiment aroused through the dynamic interaction between individual agency and the external world. In this sense, authenticity is neither objective nor subjective, but rather performative". "Hot" authentication produced by the performative conduct of the attending public is proposed by Cohen and Cohen (2012), who conceptualize processes of authentication as "cool" and "hot" by investigating the nature of power instead of focusing on the discourse of authenticity per se. They argue that the authoritative, declarative cool authentication of an object, site, or event is conducive to its isolation from the "flow of everyday life", and might eventuate its stagnation or fossilization (Cohen & Cohen, 2012, p. 1303). In contrast, hot authentication with performative acts from both locals and tourists might create opportunities to co-produce borders and tourist attractions. This is supported by Edensor (2001, p.71): "tourist space is also (re)produced by tourists, who perform diverse meanings about symbolic places". Thus, ethnic communities in border areas and tourists are implicated in the process of hot authentication, thereby constituting, or transforming, the forces of borders.

There is a "complex relationality between places and persons connected through both performances and performativity" (Hannam et al., 2006, p. 13). In this vein, Lugosi (2014) further clarified "performative practices" as embodied acts, including physical actions like gestures, and verbal and non-verbal communication, which are actively involved in the social construction of identity. In addition, it is necessary to distinguish two terms: performance and performative, although they are not mutually exclusive. According to Erving Goffman (1959), performances are behavioral acts as strategic means of self-representation and impression management in everyday life. In this sense, performances are what one actively plays, whilst performativity on the other hand is more effect-producing oriented, as opposed to merely reproducing. Performativity theory posits the inherent instability of identity. Hence, a fixed or stable identity does not exist.

Drawing from the cool and hot authentication modes and performativity, we now attempt to identify several challenges as important areas at the intersections of globalization, modernity, and tourism development in borderlands, namely, the relation between ethnic and state identity at borders, and the relation between trust-based networks and marketized logic.

## Challenges

### *Ethnic versus State Identity*

Identity is a complex and often contested concept that concerns how we understand who we are (Katz, 2009). Borderlands are localities where political, cultural, and social identities converge, coexist, and sometimes even conflict, because many ethnic communities are arbitrarily divided by international boundaries which ignore Indigenous cultural groups and socio-ethnic boundaries (Flynn & William, 1997). However, "the constructions of identities are implicitly linked to the production of social space" (Lugosi, 2014, p. 167). Thus, border identity has been identified as playing a critical role in nation-building and cultural revival, which leads to a challenge confronted widely in border regions on how to construct an identity through common border experiences (Martinez, 1994)—an identity that allows the (re)negotiation of cultural boundaries on a local, national, or international level in ongoing processes of identity formation at borders since "places are not only contexts or backdrops, but also an integral part of identity" (Hauge, 2007, p. 50).

Tourism can play a dual role in reinforcing or crippling both ethnic identity and state identity in borderlands. For instance, some scholars observe that preserving traditional ethnic culture has become important for China's nationalism and modernization (Oakes, 1998; Yang et al., 2008). An example at the China–Vietnam border showcases that the ethnic culture of the borderland Jing people, through the designation process of national heritage, became much more visible and appreciated not only by Jing groups, but also by other local ethnic groups. Furthermore, Jing culture has gained significant market success as an ethnic cultural tourist attraction, which reinforces both the Jing ethnic identity and the state identity simultaneously (Zhang, 2019a). As such, "tourism promotes the restoration, preservation, and fictional recreation of ethnic attributes" (MacCannell, 1984, p. 377) and thus ethnic identity is reconstructed in response to tourism development.

However, the dynamic interplay between tourism and identity in (cross)border contexts is more complex due to the fact that performativity has a significant impact in understanding (geo)political processes and enacting cultural boundaries. A case study demonstrates that the Catalans of French Catalonia have experienced some revival of their identity as France–Spain cross-border tourism flows increase based on proximity, cultural similarity, and more importantly trust (Blasco et al., 2014). Drawing upon this line, the ethnic and state identities are not always consistent. On the one hand, cross-border ethnic groups share a common sense of ethnic identity; on the other hand, they hold a different sense of belonging because their life is closely linked to the states they live in. Thus, when ethnic policies are preferential on one side of the border, social stability and economic prosperity in the host country may be an impetus to unify the ethnic identity and national belonging of cross-border ethnic groups. On the contrary, if a country fails to treat cross-border ethnic groups fairly, it might lead to greater inconsistencies and chasms between ethnic and national interests; in this case, the ethnic identity is more likely to conflict with the state identity (e.g., He, 2012).

### *Trust-based Networks versus Marketized Logic*

With the deepening of globalization and modernization, the cultures of nations and ethnic groups have been increasingly exposed to the world and brought into the context of modernity, more specifically, the dynamics of market relations. However, aside from economic connections, and more importantly, border communities are culturally and ethnically connected, which creates a different logic of border economy as Emerson observed (1976, p. 354):

> each transaction is one of a series between members of a trade friendship or partnership. Under such conditions, each transaction must preserve the trust and solidarity built by previous transactions and prepare the ground for future transactions. There emerges in longitudinal relations—if the parties enjoy a balance of power—equity and even a touch of altruism as exchange rules.

This means that trust-based economic practices and related cultural and ethnic networks at borderlands are not within the reference of pure capitalism or a marketized logic.

Furthermore, trust plays the role of a transformer from negotiated to reciprocal relations. Lewicki et al. (1995, 1996, 2006) specify three forms of trust, indicating the contingency of transformation from negotiated to reciprocal relations: (1) calculus-based trust involves economic calculation; (2) knowledge-based trust refers to the understanding between partners about the other, which helps predict their behavior, thus reducing uncertainty; and (3) identity-based trust is grounded on shared visions and strategies among members. The first is similar to negotiated relations, and the last is closer to "productive exchange", which is group-oriented, a coordinated task whereby actors seek to produce a valued result through their joint collaboration (Lawler, 2001). Productive exchange with identity-based trust allows stakeholders to co-create value that benefits all within a coherent social exchange network. Thus, border micro-economies between cross-border ethnic communities are different from rational individual decision making in a competitive market (Emerson, 1976). As Sahlins (1972) argued, apart from self-interest, mutual concern and more generalized concern also could be important motives in exchange relations. Therefore, the motivations and drivers of value creation usually follow different principles and logic at borders. Mukherjee and Dutta (2018) further conclude that the market, as social globalization, depends on community everyday bordering processes, which improve border regions and countries to better enjoy the benefits from economic globalization.

## Conclusion

This chapter has attempted to contextualize borderlands with analytical lenses in line with Brunet-Jailly's (2005) border theory. We have identified three current hot research issues, which are significant for understanding the relationships between cultural boundaries and ethnic representation in border settings: mobility, ethnic heritage and cultural representation, as well as authenticity and performativity. Clearly, these issues are far too expansive to provide an exhaustive assessment in a book chapter. There are further important issues which deserve deeper exploration and discussion, such as border governance at various levels, the impact of pandemics on border policies, different responses in border communities in safe-guarding and using their cultural heritage, gambling, smuggling, and prostitution, to name only a few. Moreover, the chapter has identified two important challenges in the duality of ethnic and state identities at borders, and that between trust-based networks and marketized logic.

There are two wider implications of this analysis for border and tourism studies. The first is that scholars should give more attention to the cultural complexity of borderland communities and to their transnational networks based on trust. In addition to the emphasis on interactions in ethnic minorities embedded in ethnic cultural networks, the second implication concerns local identity (re)construction in the processes of border-crossing activities against the rapidly changing backdrop of borderlands. In addition, future research both in border studies and in tourism should widen their focus on border regions in understudied areas such as South America, Africa, and Asia (Brunet-Jailly, 2010).

## References

Anderson, M. (1997). *Frontiers: Territory and state formation in the modern world*. Cambridge: Polity Press.
Ballesteros, E.R., & Ramírez, M.H. (2007). Identity and community-reflections on the development of mining heritage tourism in southern Spain. *Tourism Management*, 28(3), 677–687.
Barth, F. (1969). Ethnic groups and boundaries: Introduction. In F. Barth (ed.) *Ethnic groups and boundaries: The social organization of culture difference*, pp. 9–38. Boston: Little Brown.
Benjamin, W. (1968). The work of art in the age of machanical reproduction. In H. Arendt (ed.) *Illuminations*, pp. 217–252. New York: Shocken Books.
Blasco, D., Guia, J., & Prats, L. (2014). Emergence of governance in cross-border destinations. *Annals of Tourism Research*, 49, 159–173.
Blatter, J., & Clement, N. (2000). Cross-border cooperation in Europe: Historical development, institutionalization, and contrasts with North America. *Journal of Borderlands Studies*, 15(1), 15–53.
Borzooie, P., Lak, A., & Timothy, D.J. (2021). Designing urban customs and border marketplaces: A model and case study from Lotfabad, Iran. *Journal of Borderlands Studies*, 36(3), 469–486.
Breathnach, T. (2006). Looking for the real me: Locating the self in heritage tourism. *Journal of Heritage Tourism*, 1(2), 100–120.
Brunet-Jailly, E. (2005). Theorizing borders: An interdisciplinary perspective. *Geopolitics*, 10, 633–649.
Brunet-Jailly, E. (2010). The state of borders and borderlands studies 2009: A historical view and a view from the Journal of Borderlands Studies. *Eurasia Border Review*, 1(1), 1–15.
Buzinde, C.N., Santos, C.A., & Smith, S.L.J. (2006). Ethnic representations: Destination imagery. *Annals of Tourism Research*, 33(3), 707–728.
Castells, M. (2000). *The rise of the network society*. Oxford: Blackwell.
Cohen, E. (1988). Authenticity and commoditization in tourism. *Annals of Tourism Research*, 15, 371–386.
Cohen, E., & Cohen, S.A. (2012). Authentication: Hot and cool. *Annals of Tourism Research*, 39(3), 1295–1314.
Dela, S.E., & Anril, T. (2019). Tourism, heritage and cultural performance: Developing a modality of heritage tourism. *Tourism Management Perspectives*, 31, 301–309.
Donnan, H., & Wilson, T.M. (ed.) (1998). *Border identities: Nation and state at international frontiers*. Cambridge: Cambridge University Press.
Edensor, T. (2001). Performing tourism, staging tourism: (Re)producing tourist space and practice. *Tourist Studies*, 1(1), 59–81.
Edson, G. (2004). Heritage: Pride or passion, product or service? *International Journal of Heritage Studies*, 10(4), 333–348.
Emerson, R.M. (1976). Social exchange theory. *Annual Review of Sociology*, 2, 335–362.
Esman, M.R. (1984). Tourism as ethnic preservation: The Cajuns of Louisiana. *Annals of Tourism Research*, 11, 451–467.
Flynn, D.K., & William, D.K.F. (1997). "We are the border": Identity, exchange, and the state along the Bénin-Nigeria border. *American Ethnologist*, 24(2), 311–330.
Gao, J., Ryan, C., Cave, J., & Zhang, C. (2019). Tourism border-making: A political economy of China's border tourism. *Annals of Tourism Research*, 76, 1–13.
Gelbman, A., & Timothy, D.J. (2011). Border complexity, tourism and international exclaves: A case study. *Annals of Tourism Research*, 38(1), 110–131.
Goffman, E. (1959). *The presentation of self in everyday life*. New York, Doubleday.
Gravari-Barbas, M. (2018). Tourism as a heritage producing machine. *Tourism Management Perspectives*, 25, 173–176.
Hageman, K., Berger, S., Gemie, S., & Williams, C. (2004). *Creating and crossing borders: The state, future and quality of border studies*. Glamorgan: University of Glamorgan.
Hannam, K., Sheller, M., & Urry, J. (2006). Editorial: Mobilities, immobililties, moorings. *Mobilities*, 1(1), 1–22.
Harrison, R. (2013). *Heritage: Critical approaches*. London: Routledge.

He, Q. (2012). Research on the identity of cross-border ethnic groups in Yunnan. *Journal of Yunnan Agricultural University*, 6(2), 37–40.

Holt, Y. (2018). Performing the Anglo-Scottish border: Cultural landscapes, heritage and borderland identities. *Journal of Borderlands Studies*, 33(1), 53–68.

Horstmann, A. (2014). Incorporation and resistance: Border-crossings and social transformation in Southeast Asia. *Antropologi Indonesia*, 26, 12–19.

Katz, C. (2009). Social systems: Thinking about society, identity, power and resistance. In N. Clifford, S. Holloway, S. Rice, & G. Valentine (eds) *Key concepts in geography*, pp. 236–250. London: Sage.

Kearney, M. (2004). The classifying and value-filtering missions of borders. *Anthropological Theory*, 4(2), 131–156.

Keating, M. (2001). *Plurinational democracy: Stateless nations in a post-sovereignty era*. Oxford: Oxford University Press.

Knudsen, B.T., & Waade, A.M. (2010). Performative authenticity in tourism and spatial experience: Rethinking the relation between travel, place and emotion. In B. Knudsen, & A.M. Waade (eds) *Re-investing authenticity: Tourism, place and emotions*, pp. 1–19. Bristol: Channel View Publications.

Konrad, V., Laine, J.P., Liikanen, I., Scott, J.W., & Widdis, R. (2019). The language of borders. In S. Brunn, & R. Kehrein (eds) *Handbook of the changing world language map*, pp. 2175–2191. Cham, Switzerland: Springer.

Laine, J.P. (2016). The multiscalar production of borders. *Geopolitics*, 21(3), 465–482.

Lanfant, M-F. (1995). International tourism, internationalization and the challenge to identity. In M-F. Lanfant, J. Allcock, & E.M. Bruner (eds) *International tourism: Identity and change*, pp. 24–43. London: Sage.

Lawler, E.J. (2001). An affect theory of social exchange. *American Journal of Sociology*, 107(2), 321–352.

Leimgruber, W. (1999). Border effects and the cultural landscape: The changing impact of boundaries on regional development in Switzerland. In H. Knippenberg, & J. Markusse (eds) *Nationalising and denationalising European border regions, 1800-2000: Views from geography and history*, pp. 199–221. Dordrecht: Kluwer.

Lewicki, R.J., & Bunker, B.B. (1995). Trust in relationships: A model of development and decline. In B.B. Bunker, & J.Z. Rubin (eds) *Conflict, cooperation and justice: Essays inspired by the work of Morton Deutsch*, pp. 133–173. San Francisco: Jossey-Bass.

Lewicki, R.J., & Bunker, B.B. (1996). Developing and maintaining trust in work relationships. In R. Kramer, & T.R. Tyler (eds) *Trust in organizations: Frontiers of theory and research*, pp. 114–139. Thousand Oaks: Sage.

Lewicki, R.J., Tomlinson, E.C., & Gillespie, N. (2006). Models of interpersonal trust development: Theoretical approaches, empirical evidence, and future directions. *Journal of Management*, 32, 991–1022.

Li, Y., & Hunter, C. (2015). Community involvement for sustainable heritage tourism: A conceptual model. *Journal of Cultural Heritage Management and Sustainable Development*, 5(3), 248–262.

Logan, W.S. (2001). Globalizing heritage: World heritage as a manifestation of modernism and challenges from the periphery. In *Proceedings of the Australia ICOMOS National Conference 2001*, pp. 51–57.

Lugosi, P. (2014). Mobilising identity and culture in experience co-creation and venue operation. *Tourism Management*, 40, 165–179.

MacCannell, D. (1973). Staged authenticity: Arrangements of social space in tourist settings. *American Journal of Sociology*, 79(3), 589–603.

MacCannell, D. (1976). *The tourist: A new theory of the leisure class*. New York: Schocken.

MacCannell, D. (1984). Reconstructed ethnicity tourism and cultural identity in third world communities. *Annals of Tourism Research*, 11(3), 375–391.

Martinez, O.J. (1994). *Border people: Life and society in the US-Mexico borderlands*. Tucson: University of Arizona Press.

Mukherjee, D., & Dutta, N. (2018). What determines governance across nations: Do economic and social globalization play a role? *Economic Modelling*, 69, 103–113.

Muzaini, H. (2017). Informal heritage-making at the Sarawak Cultural Village, East Malaysia. *Tourism Geographies*, 19(2), 244–264.

Newman, D. (2004). Conflict at the interface: The impact of boundaries and borders on contemporary ethno-national conflict. In C. Flint (ed.) *Geographies of war and peace*, pp. 192–214. Oxford: Oxford University Press.

Newman, D. (2006a). Borders and bordering: Towards an interdisciplinary dialogue. *Journal of Asian and African Studies*, 41(3), 171–186.

Newman, D. (2006b). The lines that continue to separate us: Borders in our 'borderless' world. *Progress in Human Geography*, 30(2), 143–161.

Newman, D., & Paasi, A. (1998). Fences and neighbours in the postmodern world: Boundary narratives in political geography. *Progress in Human Geography*, 22(2), 186–207.

Oakes, T. (1998). *Tourism and modernity in China*. London: Routledge.

Oxford English Dictionary (2021). Online: www.oed.com.

Paasi, A. (1999). The political geography of boundaries at the end of the millennium: Challenges of the de-territorializing world. In H. Eskelinen, I. Liikanen, & J. Oksa (eds) *Curtains of iron and gold: Reconstructing borders and scales of interaction*, pp. 9–24. Aldershot: Ashgate.

Paasi, A. (2011). A border theory: An unattainable dream or a realistic aim for border scholars? In D. Wastl-Walter (ed.) *The Ashgate research companion to border studies*, pp. 1–40. Farnham: Ashgate.

Paasi, A. (2019). Borderless worlds and beyond: Challenging the state-centric cartographies. In A. Paasi, E-K. Prokkola, J. Saarinen, & K. Zimmerbauer (eds) *Borderless worlds for whom? Ethics, moralities and mobilities*, pp. 21–36. London: Routledge.

Paasi, A., & Prokkola, E-K. (2008). Territorial dynamics, cross-border work and everyday life in the Finnish–Swedish border area. *Space and Polity*, 12(1), 13–29.

Paasi, A. & Zimmerbauer, K. (2016). Penumbral borders and planning paradoxes: Relational thinking and the question of borders in spatial planning. *Environment and Planning A*, 48(1), 75–93.

Qian, X. (2017). Research on the cooperative of cross border ethnic cultural tourism between China and Vietnam under the background of "the Belt and Road Initiatives". *Guizhou Ethnic Studies*, 3(38), 173–177.

Ruhanen, L., & Whitford, M. (2019). Cultural heritage and Indigenous tourism. *Journal of Heritage Tourism*, 14(3), 179–191.

Sahlins, M. (1972). *Stone age economics*. New York: Aldine de Gruyter.

Salamone, F. (1997). Authenticity in tourism: The San Angel Inns. *Annals of Tourism Research*, 24(2), 305–321.

Schoenberger, L., & Turner, S. (2008). Negotiating remote borderland access: Small-scale trade on the Vietnam–China border. *Development and Change*, 39(4), 667–696.

Scott, J.W. (2015). Bordering, border politics and cross-border cooperation in Europe. In R.C.F. Celata (ed.) *Neighbourhood policy and the construction of the European external borders*, pp. 27–37. New York: Springer.

Sofield, T.H.B. (2006). Border tourism and border communities: An overview. *Tourism Geographies*, 8(2), 102–121.

Stefanova, B. (2013). Crossborder dynamics at the southeastern periphery of the European Union: The unusual case of Bulgaria's ethnic Turkish minority. *European and Regional Studies*, 3, 65–91.

Sun, J., & Zhang, A. (2015). Host of destination from the perspective of ethnic boundary theory: The case of Yangshuo. *Tourism Tribune*, 30(6), 102–110.

Tang, X., Yang. X., & Qian. J. (2014). Conceptualizing border from a social constructionist perspective: Current progress and implications for future research. *Progress in Geography*, 33(7), 969–978.

Tang, X., Yang, X., & Qian, J. (2016). Meanings and practices of borders from the perspective of cross-border mobility: A case study of village X, Hekou, Yunnan at the Sino-Vietnamese borderlands. *Geographical Research*, 35(8), 1535–1546.

Taylor, J.P. (2001). Authenticity and sincerity in tourism. *Annals of Tourism Research*, 28(1), 7–26.

Timothy, D.J. (2001). *Tourism and political boundaries*. London: Routledge.

Timothy, D.J. (2021). *Cultural heritage and tourism: An introduction*, 2nd edn. Bristol: Channel View Publications.

Timothy, D.J., & Michalkó, G. (2016). European trends in spatial mobility. *Hungarian Geographical Bulletin*, 65(4), 317–320.

Tömöri, M. (2010). Investigating shopping tourism along the borders of Hungary—A theoretical perspective. *GeoJournal of Tourism and Geosites*, 6(2), 202–210.

Underiner, T.L. (2011). Playing at border crossing in a Mexican indigenous community…seriously. *TDR:Drama Review*, 55(2), 11–32.

UNESCO. (2003). Text of the Convention for the Safeguarding of the Intangible Cultural Heritage. Online: https://ich.unesco.org/en/convention#art2

Urry, J. (1990). *The tourist gaze: Leisure and travel in contemporary societies*. London: Sage.

Urry, J. (2000). Mobile sociology. *British Journal of Sociology*, 51(1), 185–203.

Wang, N. (1999). Rethinking authenticity in tourism experience. *Annals of Tourism Research*, 26(2), 349–370.

Wimmer, A. (2008). The making and unmaking of ethnic boundaries: A multilevel process theory. *American Journal of Sociology*, 113(4), 970–1022.

Yang, J., Ryan, C., & Zhang, L. (2016). Impersonation in ethnic tourism: The presentation of culture by other ethnic groups. *Annals of Tourism Research*, 56, 16–31.

Yang, L. (2011). Ethnic tourism and cultural representation. *Annals of Tourism Research*, 38(2), 561–585.

Yang, L. (2013). Ethnic tourism and minority identity: Lugu Lake, Yunnan, China. *Asia Pacific Journal of Tourism Research*, 18(7), 712–730.

Yang, L., Wall, G., & Smith, S.L.J. (2008). Ethnic tourism development: Chinese government perspectives. *Annals of Tourism Research*, 35(3), 751–771.

Zhang, M. (2019a). Boundaries versus borders: Transforming ethnic cultural representation into place identity through tourism. *Tourism, Culture and Communication*, 19(4), 243–251.

Zhang, M. (2019b). *Community participation in the tourism governance at the Chinese border: Power, boundaries and values*. Tarragona: University of Rovira i Virgili.

Zhou, Q.B., Zhang, J., Zhang, H., & Ma, J. (2015). A structural model of host authenticity. *Annals of Tourism Research*, 55, 28–45.

Zhu, Y. (2012). Performing heritage: Rethinking authenticity in tourism. *Annals of Tourism Research*, 39(3), 1495–1513.

# PART III

# The Anomalous Border Landscape: Tourism Values and Assets

# 14
# BORDERLINES
## Linear Tourist Attractions in Liminal Space

*Marek Więckowski*

## Introduction

The most attractive borders, including ancient walls, frontier fortifications, and boundary curiosities, play a significant role in tourism. Borders simultaneously construct their own liminal spaces, economies, heritages, identities, and sociocultural norms that are often much different from the conditions at the national core (Martinez, 1994). These differences, as well as those clearly demarcated by the border, create circumstances that are often conducive to tourism (Gelbman & Timothy, 2019; Timothy et al., 2016). Some ancient boundaries and lines of defence are key tourist attractions, such as China's Great Wall, old Roman limes such as Hadrian's Wall and the Antonine Walls, as well as dividing lines with major symbolic significance, including the former border between West and East Germany and other fragments of the former Iron Curtain in Europe. China's most recognizable monument—the Great Wall—is an intrinsic element of the country's heritage brand and attracts approximately 20 million tourists a year. Likewise, the border between the two Koreas, the DMZ, also attracts tens of thousands of visitors every year and is an important tourism asset in both North and South Korea (Hunter, 2015; Shin, 2007; Timothy et al., 2004). The Berlin Wall remains one of the main symbols of the Cold War, and its remnants, the famed Checkpoint Charlie, and various border monuments, museums, and parks are the main tourist attractions of the German capital.

Borderlines have long served as barriers to human mobility and as determiners of the spatial development of places. Sometimes they have been closed, and even subject to such a level of enforcement that any activity or movement into border zones was itself restricted or forbidden, with borderlands thus representing areas of isolation, forbidden zones, or "no-man's-lands". Paradoxically, even under such conditions, political boundaries proved to be curiosities and attractions for many people who, for reasons best known to themselves, were keen to see the border, how it was marked or fortified, and to gaze on what lay on the other side. Such was the appeal of most visits to the border between the two Germanies in the 1960s, 1970s, and 1980s (Eckert, 2019). In the modern world where tourism plays such an important role in society, borders have come to represent important tourist attractions and elements of heritage, including a sense of place and social identity (Timothy, 2001). The debordering processes of today facilitate frontier crossings and the further development of borderline tourism. This chapter examines boundary lines as tourist attractions and shows how borders, their environs, and their associated landscapes are of interest to curiosity-seekers and the tourist gaze.

## Interest in Borders and Borderlands

The most familiar borders are those that separate independent states (i.e., sovereign territories established under international law) from one another, while at the same time constituting interfaces between them, regardless of whether the borders are sharp lines, areas, or zones. In legal terms, a border is an invisible vertical plane without width or depth that separates (or adjoins) two or more territories. Thus, it establishes a meeting place of neighbouring sovereign entities (Kristoff, 1959; Pounds, 1963) and marks the maximum extent to which a state may exercise its legal and sovereign authority (Prescott, 1987).

On maps and satellite images a border is usually represented by a simple line, while on the ground it typically features boundary markers of many different types, as well as signs, fences, or walls. Even on the ground, international boundaries are sometimes demarcated with lines drawn on the earth, which effectively differentiates sociocultural, economic, political, and historical regimes on opposite sides. Regardless of how boundaries manifest on the ground or on maps, they are socially constructed human institutions based upon legal definitions, treaties, and ancient or modern practices (Jones, 2009). The state and its associated boundaries are a tool for spatially organizing territory. A border's main purposes are to mark the limits of state territory, to filter undesirable forces, and to protect the state and its population and resources, often as a defensive mechanism (Madsen, in press).

Borders are thus an integral part of the state and have become increasingly acknowledged as such throughout history (Elden, 2010). Most scholars until now have emphasized borders as barriers to human interaction and travel (Canally & Timothy, 2007; Gelbman & Timothy, 2010, 2019; Timothy, 2001; Timothy & Gelbman, 2015) with a heavy emphasis on Western concepts of sovereignty and division in the evolution of borders and the construction of their associated functions. Far less attention has been paid to ways in which tourism can help improve transfrontier relations and capitalize on the intrinsic socioeconomic value of borders, especially how borders may stimulate regional and local development through tourism, trade, and transit. Nevertheless, growing academic interest has shown that borders in many cases can be tourism assets, not only barriers. The borderlines themselves may exude a unique tourism appeal, and many borders educe conditions favourable to the development of tourism, such as lower taxes and product prices, more permissive activities, different laws and policies, and cultural differences (Galluser, 1994; Matznetter, 1979; Timothy, 1995, 2001; Wachowiak, 2006, Więckowski, 2010, in press; Zhang et al., 2019). Borders become tourist attractions and borderlands become tourist destinations not only because of these variables that stimulate shopping, gaming, medical mobility, prostitution, and recreational opportunities, but also as a result of certain curiosities in border landscapes, borders' peripheral locations on the margins of the state, and the sociocultural and sociopolitical differences they separate (Timothy, 2001; Więckowski, in press).

In all of these cases, access to borders is obviously required for them to become attractions or destinations. However, many borders, especially those in Central and Eastern Europe, were for many decades scarcely accessible to the average person, and were thus largely neglected as attractions. The exceptions were transit localities, such as official border-crossing points, although even in that case, physical access to the borderline was heavily restricted or entirely prohibited, such as the case of the Finland–USSR and the Czechoslovak–West German frontiers. In remote environments hiking trails often parallel borders or extend to a borderline but are truncated by the line. Tourist activity in these cases is therefore almost always limited to one side of the border only (Eckert, 2019; Timothy, 2001, Więckowski, 2010), resulting in two parallel sets of developments or one-sided development only.

Various debordering processes (e.g., supranationalism and transfrontier cooperation) in recent years have highlighted more examples of borders serving as nodes of tourism development. Through these processes, new tourist spaces are created and more open borders are becoming tourism growth poles with transboundary planning, strategy formulation, governance, and marketing becoming easier and more balanced. Tourism as a geopolitical force has even been known to effect changes in borders and national sovereignty, such as the exchange of territory and the redrawing of borders between France and Andorra to enable the construction of an Andorran access tunnel, and between France and Switzerland to enable the international airport in Geneva to remain entirely within the borders of Switzerland (Timothy et al., 2014).

Many borderlands are attractive destinations because they are located in peripheral regions where, in most cases, they lie at a distance from the national core. Thus, they are often located in natural areas with scenic landscapes and a living cultural heritage. The Himba tribe of Namibia and Angola has been able to preserve most of its unique living culture in large part because of its borderland location on the edge of the state, away from the two countries' core areas. Besides natural and cultural heritage, contrasting political and economic systems on either side of a border and the resulting social, economic, and political differences (Raffestin, 1986; van Houtum & van Naerssen, 2002) also account for the appeal of borders as tourist attractions. Although most of these contrasts manifest in shopping, gaming, and other such activities as noted earlier, borders themselves may also then be valued because of their geopolitical, historical, and symbolic values and meanings. Thus, the very act of crossing a border may be a motivation for travel, especially when it entails straddling or crossing a line that marks the interface between socially, culturally, and economically different political regimes (Ioannides et al., 2006; Timothy, 1995, 2001).

Borders interest tourists as curiosities, symbolic referents, items of heritage interest, and sources of education and learning. In some cases, they also symbolize cooperation and peaceful neighbourly relations. The public fascination with place uniqueness has been acknowledged by the tourism industry, and for the most part tourists seek a sense of "otherness" in travelling specifically to see something beyond their normative and ordinary lives (Picard & Di Giovine, 2014). Borderlines may satisfy that very desire for some place or something unique. In the contexts of international borders, "when lines are marked on the ground by tangible objects, and when they mark socio-economic differences, they have the potential to attract tourists and shape socio-economic trends and patterns" (Gelbman & Timothy, 2010, p. 240).

According to Timothy (1995, 2001) and Timothy et al. (2016), borders exert most of their appeal as and when:

- They are represented by interesting anomalies in the landscape, such as walls, fences, guard towers, gateways, and unique demarcation methods;
- They separate opposing ideological systems or adversarial neighbours, which causes many people to want to observe life "over there" in the forbidden or highly restricted "other side";
- Attractions or sites are partitioned by a border (e.g., golf courses or buildings), which have a unique appeal for visitors wishing "to be in two places at once";
- Natural or cultural areas are divided, including beaches, waterfalls, archaeological sites, and historic bridges;

- Border-themed attractions are developed to commercialize the political divide (e.g., in peace parks, customs museums, or border theme parks);
- Borders are commemorated and consumed as heritage sites and attractions.

In addition to political borders, certain "symbolic borders" are regarded as important attractions in certain localities, such as highest or lowest points, unique geometric lines (e.g., the Equator or the Arctic Circle), or territorial extremes (e.g., northernmost or easternmost) (Löytynoja, 2008; Timothy, 1998; Varnajot, 2019, 2020). These appeal to humankind's basic interests in extremes, edges, and superlatives, as well as our desire to have "been there and done that" (Timothy, 1998).

A border that can offer excitement, entertainment, cultural diversity, and sometimes even a certain dose of danger has a competitive advantage and has the potential to attract tourists' attention. "Border tourism" may be both a serious pursuit among a small niche market that shares interests in political history, war, peace, and cultural differences, and a casual attraction that people decide on the spot might be of interest or enough of a curiosity to pose for pictures. However, even closed or dangerous borders attract tourists, examples being the borders between the two parts of Germany during the Cold War (Eckert, 2019), currently between the Korean states at the DMZ (Hunter, 2015; Shin, 2007), and the present militarized border between India and Pakistan (Chhabra, 2018; Timothy, 2019).

## Boundaries Attracting Tourists

As already noted, many aspects of geopolitical borders, including the elements of their physicality and the narratives associated with them, prove attractive to certain tourists. Based on the work of Timothy (1995, 2001), Timothy et al. (2016), and Więckowski (2010), the following sections outline several aspects and characteristics (but not all) of borders that create a touristic appeal: border markings; border crossings; defensive fortifications; divided objects and attractions; border stories, narratives, events, and semantics; border trails and pathways; and special geographical points associated with non-political borders.

### *Borderlines and Boundary Markers*

Almost all international borders on the earth today are entirely defined and delimited, and most are marked physically on the ground, although some have yet to be demarcated because of difficult topography, a lack of political will between states, or because the precise location of a particular boundary line is disputed between neighbours (Glassner & de Blij, 1989). The demarcation of borderlines is part of the responsibility of adjacent countries to show precisely where one state's authority ends and another begins; in most cases every metre (or centimetre) of territory is covetously possessed and controlled (Timothy, 2001).

Boundary markers are usually the most permanent features of borders, and many still remain in the landscape even in some locations where a border has ceased to exist. Border markers are the physical representation of legal limits and require accurate surveying, erection, and maintenance to ensure the physical integrity of the state (Prescott, 1987). As such, they divide places into "here" and "there", "us" and "them" (Newman, 2006), creating distinctions in culture, governance, economic development, and history. Most international borders today are marked with concrete or stone pillars or obelisks, carved markings on natural stone surfaces, metal or cement plates in pavements, wood logs, plastic or fibreglass signs, or lines painted or paved in stone across roads, pavements, and car parks. These markers are legally surveyed indicators of where one country's sovereign authority ends and that of another begins. Some tourists show an interest in seeing and photographing a border, touching it, taking classic selfies with border markers, welcome signs, or displays of flags and coats of arms, and straddling the line (Timothy, 2001; Więckowski, in press) in a style that Ryden (1993) argues reflects people's desire to be in more than one place at a time.

In addition to boundary markers, other physical features are used to monumentalize the border, especially in locations where borders are either contested and embroiled in conflict, or commemorated as meeting points between friends and peaceful transfrontier neighbours. Prominent examples include the Peace Arch on the USA–Canada border, the ornate gateways prominent on many international borders in Asia and Latin America, and in the case of conflict, the Wagah border gate between Pakistan and India.

At many borderlines, including tripoints, where three countries meet, tourism and leisure facilities have been developed to encourage curiosity-seekers to stay longer and enjoy the border environment. These include such features as picnic areas and firepits, children's playgrounds, interpretive panels, walking trails, opposing national flags, historic markers, cafes and souvenir shops, and car parks, creating unique border tourismscapes (Więckowski, in press).

Borders that no longer function as geopolitical boundaries but are still noticeable in the landscape are known as "relict" borders. While no longer officially marking national borders, some continue to play a significant economic and sociocultural role (e.g., the former East–West German divide). This is common in many places in Europe and Asia from ancient and medieval days. In some of these cases, former border markers have become historic monuments worthy of protection and interpretation as heritage memorials. Some ancient or medieval boundary stones continue to function as current markers, such as Prussian border stones that still mark the current frontier of Germany and Belgium and Germany and the Netherlands. Likewise, an old 1841 United States–Republic of Texas border marker, which at the time demarcated an international boundary, now indicates the location of the subnational border between Louisiana and Texas and is an important historic site in both states.

Others are no longer located on any border but remain part of relict historical border landscapes. Prime examples exist in Finland, where several of the 1595 carved boulders that marked the former Swedish–Russian border, and in Russia, where some of the pre-World War II boundary stones marked the former Finland–USSR border have become important heritage attractions and historic sites (Aleksandrova & Stupina, 2014; Kolosov, 2020). The same heritage values are attached to several 1919 Treaty of Versailles markers in Poland, which demarcated the German–Polish frontier until 1939.

A particularly unique type of borderline is the tripoint, where three countries meet at a single point. In Europe, most of these are accessible to the public and tourism/recreation infrastructure has been developed to commemorate the location and satisfy curiosity-seekers' interests. Many tripoints are ensconced in symbolic meaning and are special places decorated with border markers, national flags, and commemorative monuments. On a regional scale, tripoints provide an impetus for more than bilateral cooperation; they provide legal and socioeconomic reasons for transboundary cooperation between three or more countries (Kałuski, 2006; Sohn et al., 2009, Więckowski, in press). In recent decades, several such locations have transformed into international tourist attractions. A few examples include the point where Germany, the Netherlands, and Belgium meet near Vaals (Timothy et al., 2014); where Germany, France, and Switzerland meet at Basel (Leimgruber, 2005; Reitel, 2013); at Schengen where Germany, France, and Luxemburg come together (Sohn et al., 2009), and at the meeting point of Belgium, Germany, and Luxemburg, which is commemorated with a European Union Park, recreational infrastructure, and historic border markers. Photo platforms, museums, and riverside reference indicators mark the tripoint of Myanmar, Thailand, and Laos in the Mekong River at the so-called "Golden Triangle".

Historically, one of the first documented tourism focus on a tripoint in Europe occurred at the meeting point of the Austro-Hungarian, Russian, and Prussian Empires in the mid-nineteenth century (Kałuski, 2006, Więckowski, in press). There, even more than a century ago, souvenir stands, observation platforms, and picnic areas were built as part of the touristic appeal of this historic tripoint. One of the oldest relict tripoints in Europe is currently situated in Poland, with an historic border marker in Bogusze-Prostki, which marks the spot where the Kingdoms of Poland, Prussia, and Lithuania converged almost 500 years ago.

## *Border Crossings*

Border crossings, or ports of entry, represent important thresholds of a travel experience and can make significant first impressions, since a border is often the first area of a foreign country a traveller encounters (Kwanisai et al., 2014; Mayer et al., 2019; Timothy, 2001). These are the places where states identify and inspect the people and products entering or departing. Here, a unique infrastructure is built to facilitate human movement or to hinder it. The entire symbolism of the border entry point, particularly at contentious borders, is interesting and may exude a sense of danger or personal risk, allowing a tourist to cross an imaginary line from freedom to oppression, from one sociopolitical system to another. In some cases, the differences are remarkable, such as formerly between the communist states of Central and Eastern Europe and their Western European neighbours.

The infrastructure associated with border crossings can also provide a certain level of appeal, even intimidation, which, while seemingly contradictory sensations, are part of the experience of border crossing (Medvedev, 1999; Timothy, 2001). Customs and immigration buildings dominate the structures at ports of entry. Their architectural styles may be modern, historical, or otherwise unique. Physical barriers, guardhouses, observation towers, frontier officials, guard dogs, and surveillance equipment are important components of border landscapes, which satisfy official purposes and help create a sense of intimidation and proper behaviour. In addition to official administrative features, related border infrastructure, such as transportation, customs and immigration offices, duty-free shops, petrol stations, and highways and bridges, all combine to create unique border-crossing landscapes not found in other locations. Kałuski (2017, pp. 108–109) argues that scholars spend little time on the attractiveness of border crossings. They can be very different and can be an unforgettable experience: the Eurotunnel crossing from France to the UK, the cross-border bridge over the Øresund, the Mont Blanc tunnel, the Col de Clapier Pass, where Hannibal carried his elephants are all salient components of border infrastructure that have a certain charm.

In this instance, too, the notion of relict versus active border crossings is relevant. There are many examples of famous former border checkpoints having been transformed into tourist attractions. Checkpoint Charlie is one of Berlin's most visited tourist attractions (Eckert, 2019) (Figure 14.1) and the old Ledra border checkpoint is one of the most visited spots in Nicosia, Cyprus (Díaz-Sauceda et al., 2015). A nearby skyscraper is home to the Ledra Observatory Museum, which interprets the history of the island's division, and enables visitors to view the entire divided city. From 1977 until 2007, this checkpoint was one of the most visited places in the UN buffer zone between North Cyprus and South Cyprus (Gelbman, 2010; Scott, 2012; Timothy, 2001; Webster & Timothy, 2006). While Cyprus remains divided, the border has opened a great deal since 2004, and the Ledra crossing has become a busy commercial shopping area with less emphasis being placed on the divide. The observation platform that

*Figure 14.1* Checkpoint Charlie, one of Berlin's top tourist attractions.
(Photo: M. Więckowski)

once stood nearby to enable visitors and locals to gaze into the occupied other side has now been dismantled and a new crossing thoroughfare created.

The border between India and Pakistan exemplifies a difficult binational history, mainly a result of the unfinished Kashmir conflict, creating one of the most dangerous geographies on the planet. There are only a couple of crossing points along this conflicted border, but at the most important of these, at Wagah, between Amritsar, India, and Lahore, Pakistan, the border crossing has become a very popular tourist attraction (Timothy, 2019). Each evening when it is time to lower national flags and close the border gate, soldiers from the opposing sides line up side by side on their respective sides of the line and in a competitive, albeit theatrical, show of strength they demonstrate their military might. The show attracts thousands of spectators to both sides each year and is one of the most celebrated touristic and geopolitical events in the region (Chhabra, 2018).

## *Defensive Lines*

There are many elements in this category that may prove interesting to tourists, not least are closed and guarded borders, fences, minefields, ploughed greenbelts or sand pits, walls, control towers, bunkers, and trenches. Defensive lines and their constituent elements such as walls and guard towers can remain attractions in the landscape for many years, even decades or centuries, after the relevant border has altogether disappeared. For centuries, the easiest territories to defend and protect were borders featuring strong natural barriers (e.g., mountains, swamps, rivers, and deserts). However, in the process of striving to form linear boundaries and adhering to modern international law with precision boundary-making, the defensive significance of nature zones decreased. In addition, technological advancements made crossing traditionally formidable natural barriers much easier, which meant that states or proto-states were required then to create their own foreboding barriers. Thus, on land, defensive walls began to be built to separate emerging polities from barbarians, or people who plundered, especially border areas. The best examples of this that have become major tourist attractions are the Great Wall of China and the Roman limes in Great Britain (e.g., Hadrian's Wall and the Antonine Wall) and the Upper German–Raetian Limes in Germany, all of which have been inscribed on UNESCO's World Heritage List. Following the seventeenth-century Peace of Westphalia, borderlines and sovereignty became codified in European national and international law, with states marking their borders precisely and building border fortifications not only to indicate the locations of their borders but also to defend against would-be invaders. Today, the states of Europe continue to build border fortifications, particularly since the immigration crisis of 2015–2022. The same is true on many borders in North America, Asia, and southern Africa.

The remnants of the Berlin Wall remain one of the German capital's main tourist attractions (Light, 2000), and the entire East–West Germany former divide has become a significant heritage attraction throughout Germany where the former Iron Curtain once ran (Havlick, 2014; Zmelik et al., 2011). At least 22 border museums have been established, dedicated to protecting the dark heritage of the East–West divide (Grinko, 2016; Kolosov, 2020). In Berlin, wall remnants, the Berlin Wall Trail, and several museums and parks form an indelible part of the heritage fabric of the city.

Not all border fortifications are located precisely at international boundaries and may be established some distance from them. Nonetheless, they may be part of the broader border fortification network. The famous Maginot Line in France, a series of obstacles, artillery installations, and fortifications, was erected in the 1930s near the French–German border to prevent the Germans from invading France (Smart, 1996). Although it did not prevent the invasion, it deterred it and forced the Germans to enter through Belgium. The Maginot Line fortifications still stand and are an important heritage attraction near the French–German border.

One of the main attractions in Israel is the country's extremely well-fortified borders with Lebanon and Syria. At Mount Bental in the Golan Heights, visitors can gaze into the UN buffer zone and Syrian territory from observation posts (Gelbman, 2008, 2010). This has become an especially important tourist attraction for domestic Israeli tourists but also for foreigners. Likewise, gazing beyond the heavily fortified Lebanese border is a favoured pastime among many visitors to northern Israel. As noted earlier, the same phenomenon is true at the borders of North and South Korea, Pakistan and India, and North and South Cyprus. At all of these locations, the border and its fortifications, as well as the perceived security threat, create an allure unmatched in other borderland locations (Timothy, 2019).

## *Attractions Bisected by a Border and Border-themed Attractions*

As a result of often complex historical and geopolitical processes, boundaries come into contact with numerous objects and even divide them in one of two ways. The first is when a border is drawn through a previously settled and developed area (superimposed boundary): villages and towns, buildings, streets, farmers' fields, and even individual businesses and homes are sometimes split, creating unique situations with their own stories, histories, and touristic interests. There are also buildings which, as a result of legal regulations, remain straddling the border, most often as a means of taking advantage of special legal regulations or property issues. The second way is when buildings or other attractions are built intentionally and directly on borderlines, where legal, to create a unique appeal or to take advantage of property law differences.

Attractions can be natural or human-created, and there are many examples of both types being divided by an international border. Ancient heritage sites may be divided by more recent boundaries, such as the French–Spanish border established in 1659, which divides the small classical-era ruins of Panissars, requiring close collaboration between municipalities in both

*Figure 14.2* The Haskell Free Library and Opera House is divided by the US-Canada border. (Photo: M. Więckowski)

countries for the site's protection and promotion. Many cultural sites and historic buildings are divided by the USA–Canada border east of the Great Lakes, including the Haskell Library and Opera House (Quebec-Vermont), and several homes, shops, and bars (Figure 14.2). Likewise, the famous hotel and restaurant Arbez is divided by the Swiss–French border, and the mountain hut Purtschellerhaus used by hikers lies precisely on the border of Austria and Germany. In the perplexing boundary labyrinth of Baarle-Nassau, Netherlands, and Baarle-Hertog, Belgium, many homes, shops, and public buildings are divided by the international boundary, providing a unique border landscape that is demarcated inside and outside of some of the villages' buildings providing the community's main tourist attraction, together with the retail advantages stimulated by the unique frontier situation (Gelbman & Timothy 2011; Timothy, 2021).

Several types of border-themed attractions have also been developed intentionally at borderlines and crossings as tourist attractions, including but not limited to international parks/gardens, golf courses, amusement parks, museums, and recreation areas. Many international "peace parks" have been established across or adjacent to borders with the aim of commemorating peaceful and friendly relations between neighbours (Timothy, 2001, Timothy et al., 2016). Two such places on the USA–Canada border are Peace Arch Park (Washington-British Columbia) and the International Peace Garden (North Dakota-Manitoba) (Gelbman & Timothy, 2019). Similar parks are found in parts of Asia and Europe.

The Tornio golf course was built to bestride the Swedish–Finnish border, with greens and holes in both countries and in two different time zones. The business's unique selling point is its border-straddling position. The International Golf Maastricht course is similarly divided by the Belgian–Dutch border with holes, greens, and fairways in both countries. Similarly, the Aroostook Valley Country Club and golf course straddles the Canada–USA border. The clubhouse and most of the golf course is in Canada, but the car park and some of the greens are in the USA. There are several ski resorts that overlap European borders (Mayer et al., 2019), including a lodge that lies astride the Switzerland–Italy border.

Border museums are particularly common in Europe and are often manifested as part of the relict border landscapes described earlier. Although most of the former customs and passport control buildings at EU and Schengen borders have been removed or abandoned, some of

*Figure 14.3* The tripoint where Belgium, Germany, and the Netherlands meet has been developed into a tourist attraction and amusement park.

(Photo: M. Więckowski)

them have been repurposed into tourism information offices, shops, or museums that interpret the history of the border and the former activities of national border patrols. At the point where Belgium, the Netherlands, and Germany come together at a tripoint, a border-themed amusement park and recreational area has been developed in the Dutch portion of the site, including coffee shops, children's rides and games, an observation tower to oversee three countries, and shops (Figure 14.3).

Similarly, simulated borders have been purposefully built to satiate visitors' desires to see, straddle, and cross boundary lines that might otherwise not be permitted (Löytynoja, 2007; Timothy, 2001). These mock boundaries enable visitors to feel the sensation of crossing borders without actually having to do so. In central Mexico, tourists can purchase fake illegal border-crossing experiences. These simulate the experiences of illegal border crossers on the USA–Mexico border 1,300 km south of the actual frontier. At Parque EcoAlberto, tourists (especially middle-class Mexicans) can experience the "thrills and chills of an illegal border crossing" at a staged USA–Mexico border. The three-hour encounter involves being handled by human traffickers, sneaking through fences, and enduring "sirens, dogs, chases and the fake border patrol yelling threats" (Fronteras, 2013, n.p.). In eastern Finland, fake Finland–Russia borders and checkpoints have been erected near the actual border that enable people to pretend to straddle and cross it. Replica boundary markers, staged passport controls, and Russian-speaking actors dressed in uniform and acting out stereotypical elements of Russian culture (e.g., drinking vodka) are part of the staged border experience (Löytynoja, 2007).

Many natural features are bisected by national borders, including mountain summits and passes, lakes, rivers, waterfalls, forests, caves, islands, and beaches. All of these are popular natural attractions that should be managed collaboratively by cross-border jurisdictions, although in many cases, some sides are managed better than others. The existence of a border can both enhance and detract from the natural heritage value of a locality. Many protected natural areas have been founded along or across national frontiers to created transfrontier nature protection areas. These are plentiful in Africa and Europe and are often labelled international parks, transnational biosphere reserves, or transfrontier protected areas (Ramutsindela, 2014; Timothy, 2001; Więckowski, 2013).

Many national borders terminate on coastlines, dividing beaches and other such natural tourism assets. On Usedom Island, Poland–Germany, the borderline was demarcated, fenced off, and patrolled by border police from 1945 until 2007, when Poland fully implemented the Schengen Agreement. Examples abound where borders are truncated on beaches, providing limits to tourists' sunbathing and swimming activities but adding a degree of appeal to the beach-going experience (Estrada Milán & Escala Rabadan, 2021; Więckowski & Timothy, 2021).

## *Border Stories, Narratives, Events, and Semantics*

In many areas, contrasting development can be seen taking place on either side of a border. This may reflect different histories, settlement patterns, urban morphologies, and socioeconomic conditions. With the physical and symbolic opening of the EU's internal frontiers, cross-border regions there have become spaces of communication, interaction and development, of which tourism plays an important part in regional identity formation and image-building (Prokkola, 2008), and are being transformed into a salient element of cross-border heritage (Prokkola & Lois, 2016).

Borders may long remain tangible in practice and in people's spatial behaviours, even as they also go on serving tourism, heritage, and remembrance functions. There are different processes by which these kinds of oddities can be created, with classical solutions involving transformations of past border-control points (Cantine di Gandria, Switzerland–Italy, home to the Swiss Customs Museum), while contemporary ones create symbolic places of European integration (in the Schengen Zone) or else an open-air museum linking exhibitions and internet resources supported by European funds. A good case of the latter is the Cieszyn/Český Těšín, cross-border open-air museum in Poland and Czechia, which aims to commemorate the commonalities of a once united town that has been divided since 1920.

One of the most common borderland folklore traditions are stories of smuggling and other clandestine undertakings and the actors, events, and activities associated with them. In the multi-enclaved village of Baarle-Hertog/Baarle-Nassau, tales of smuggling and the evasion of authorities play an important role in local folklore and community identity, especially during the German occupations of World Wars I and II. These smuggling narratives also permeate USA–Canada and USA–Mexico border communities (Gelbman & Timothy, 2019). Clandestine meetings between opposition forces during the communist period of Europe are also commemorated on border trails in the Polish–Czech Karkonosze/Krkonoše Mountains. Other storied themes involve animosities toward, stereotypical perceptions of, and jokes about the neighbours that continue to impact on community activities and transfrontier relations in the present day. Many of these tales are part of local oral tradition, and some are etched in stone, literally, on monuments and interpretive boards along trails or in village squares.

Likewise, battlefields, war memorials, and sites of conflict are of interest to tourists and are frequently located in border areas (Prokkola & Lois, 2016), since territorial disputes and borders have formed the basis of much conflict throughout history. Thus, these narratives, too, create underlying border-specific senses of place and community identity, pride, and solidarity. Very often, trails, interpretive centres, information boards, and monuments are created to commemorate these sorts of historical conflicts or to demarcate the location where a famous person might have crossed the border at some point in history.

Similarly, the semantic use of the words "border", "tripoint", and "frontier" is frequent in branding, marketing, and promoting activities for tourism, including in the names of hotels, restaurants, and attractions (Timothy & Gelbman, 2015). This is often a result of the border heritage of places in the borderlands that wish to capitalize on their frontier-located markers of identity, senses of place, and borderland heritage narratives. Smuggler's Inn, which abuts the USA–Canada border but is located on the US side is an example of a tourism enterprise capitalizing on its border lore, as is the Hotel Frontera on the Mexican side of the USA–Mexico border, and the Grenzbäckerei (Border Bakery) adjacent to the Austrian border in the German village of Oberstaufen.

## *Border Trails and Pathways*

Throughout the world, many hiking trails or other natural and cultural routes have developed organically or intentionally along, or adjacent to, international borders, with some of them even crossing the respective frontiers more than once (Timothy & Boyd, 2015). For example, the 800-km Haute Route Pyrénées for the most part follows along, and weaves back and forth across, the Spanish–French border in the Pyrenees Mountains, and there are many hiking trails in the Carpathian Mountains along and across the Polish–Slovakian border, in the Karkonosze/Krkonoše Mountains on the Czech–Polish border (Więckowski, 2013, 2018), and in most other mountain systems where borders are less fortified and non-militarized (Hisakawa et al., 2013).

Tourist routes allow borders and their vicinities to be explored in natural or cultural surroundings. They "bind" places, stories, and traditions together, making them easier to share, interpret, and narrate. There are many spatial types of border paths and routes, which depend on the role of a particular border (Więckowski, 2010). In areas of difficult topography and when borders are physically or administratively closed, trails frequently run alongside the boundary but do not provide a means of crossing. However, relatively good relations between neighbours, even in politically contentious times, sometimes enable hiking trails to connect contiguous national parks and protected areas, and also can result in "friendship trails". During the communist era in Europe, locals could cross the Polish–Czechoslovak border informally on what was then known as "friendship trails", which provided local access to eateries, shops, and bars on the other side of the border. In this specific context, Poles crossing over for Czech beer was especially popular. Many cross-border paths have been created or expanded in open border areas of Europe (e.g., the Alps and Tatra Mountains) after the implementation of the Common Market and the Schengen Treaty (Timothy, 2021).

Many themed routes and trails have been created along former (and current) borders, with a prime example being EuroVelo, which runs along the route of the former Iron Curtain. The Iron Curtain Trail (ICT), also known as EuroVelo 13 (EV13), is a partially completed long-distance cycling route, which traces the full length of the former Iron Curtain (Timothy & Boyd, 2015) (Figure 14.4). The trail runs along local roads and paths that are situated as close to the former border as possible, and in fact crosses it often in many areas (Zmelik et al., 2011). The trail features many historical sites and natural areas along the way. Under a resolution of the European Parliament dated September 9, 2005, the ICT is categorized as an example of soft transfrontier mobility and a symbol of European unity.

The number of new thematic trails is growing. A recent example is the "Smugglers' Route" on the border of Belgium and Luxembourg. Trails along border walls, such as the Antonine Wall and the Berlin Wall, are very popular tourist attractions (Timothy & Boyd, 2015). In the United States, disused and derelict railways have a long history of being repurposed into recreational trails. The same is happening in Europe and elsewhere. In many localities, these previously made linear routes are being transformed into cycling and walking routes that zigzag

*Figure 14.4* The Iron Curtain Trail (*EuroVelo* 13) near the Czech-Austria border.

(Photo: M. Więckowski)

across international borders (e.g., the Vennbahn between Belgium and Germany; Stoffelen, 2018) or cross them at a single point.

## *Special "Borders" and Geographical Extremities*

There are other types of borders that are not legal political boundaries but function much like borders in terms of being thresholds, geodetic lines, or geographical extremities. These geodetic lines and places, or superlative locations, may also function as border-like tourist attractions (Timothy, 1998). These include such places as the Arctic Circle, the Equator, the Prime Meridian, the Tropic of Capricorn, and various superlative localities, including the easternmost, northernmost, precise centre, highest point, lowest elevation, and furthest spot—examples that have received considerable travel media attention and are heavily promoted in their respective regions (Jacobsen, 1997; Löytynoja, 2008; Timothy, 1995, 1998, 2001; Varnajot, 2019, 2020; Więckowski, in press). These are largely symbolic and have little effect in real terms in the way that political borders do. Nonetheless, many such points have symbolic significance and have been transformed into tourist attractions. The Arctic Circle near Rovaniemi, Finland, is perhaps the best example of this, where a Santa Claus village was established decades ago and is one of Finland's main tourist attractions. Much of the appeal of that geometric line is the psychological affirmation that crossing it means one is officially entering "the Arctic" and a space of otherness (Varnajot, 2019).

These locations tend to provide geographical anomalies and therefore prove interesting to curiosity-seekers, just as political borders do. Extreme points, or extreme geographies, are often located on sea coasts and are frequently manifested with commemorative markers, interpretive signs, and trails to enhance the extremity itself and its uniqueness and touristic value (Löytynoja, 2008; Timothy, 1998). Such markings are not the same as actual borders, but they may appeal to visitors in much the same way, because "they express the limits of territories or of natural phenomena" (Löytynoja, 2008, p. 16). The southernmost point of the United States at Key West, Florida, is hyped by the fact that it lies only 90 miles from Cuba; Smygehuk is the southernmost point of Sweden and the Scandinavian Peninsula; the southernmost shoreline of the Baltic Sea (and northernmost part of Poland) in Jastrzębia Góra is an important attraction; and the southernmost point of continental Asia on Singapore's Palawan Island are all monumentalized for tourism purposes. In Nuorgam, Finland, a stone monument marks the northernmost point of the European Union, while a nice tourism setup was established on Tripiti Beach, Crete, to denote the southernmost point of Europe. Near the village of L'Agulhas, South Africa, the southernmost tip of Africa is celebrated with a monument, which also indicates where the Atlantic and Indian Oceans collide. The highest or lowest points of a country, region, or mountain range are part of the same extreme geography phenomenon.

## Discussion and Conclusion

Regarding tourism, international borders have traditionally been represented as barriers, destinations, transit spaces, and creators or modifiers of tourism landscapes (Timothy, 1995, 2001; Timothy & Gelbman, 2015). The purpose of this chapter was to illustrate many of the ways in which international boundaries and their associated landscapes and functions can be seen as tourist attractions at peaceful and open borders, as well as in closed border areas that are heavily fortified and more contentious. Many tourist attractions related to borderlines have been well documented in various locations (see Gelbman, 2008; Timothy, 2001; Więckowski, in press), and especially in relation to the extreme cases of the East–West German divide and other parts of the former Iron Curtain (Eckert, 2019), the buffer zone between North Cyprus and South Cyprus (Díaz-Sauceda et al., 2015; Gelbman, 2010; Scott, 2012), the current DMZ between North and South Korea (Hunter, 2015; Shin, 2007), and even in more tranquil settings such as USA–Canada, India–Nepal, Spain–France, Spain–Portugal, and Finland–Sweden (Blasco et al., 2014; Gelbman & Timothy, 2019; Prokkola, 2008; Prokkola & Lois, 2016).

Borders separate different "worlds", even between similar states (e.g., USA–Canada and Poland–Czech Republic), and in the very act of crossing them people can see perceptible changes in the environment—laws, cultures, languages, behaviours, currencies, road signs, religious practices, driving standards, architectural styles, and land-use patterns. Over a distance of only a few metres, these differences and this otherness may be vividly evident and tangible, proving fascinating, even mystical, for some (Medvedev, 1999; Ryden, 1993; Timothy, 2001). Even being near a border or seeing what lies beyond adds appeal to a touristic encounter, which was the rationale for observation platforms in West Berlin and in Nicosia, Cyprus.

People are curious. Heavily fortified borders simultaneously repel many people and attract many others, but certain borderlands are not conducive to the development of tourism if the border is unapproachable. Nonetheless, a sense of foreboding or even a tinge of danger can motivate some curiosity-seekers to visit an armoured borderline. Although two (or three in the case of tripoints) states share a common border, it may be attractive only on one side, but in many cases there is mutual interest, and cross-boundary attractions develop on both sides. Unique anomalies in the landscape with regard to markers, cleared boundary vistas, walls, and memorials attract tourists because of the otherness associated with borders and the desire to straddle, look across, or photograph what legally and politically is a distinctly different place. Likewise, disused or relict borders have considerable heritage value, and in many cases this translates to tourist visits. In these ways, borders influence the physical and socioeconomic development of tourism and the creation of a brand image in many borderland areas that is used as a foundational marketing tool (Timothy & Gelbman, 2015; Więckowski, 2010).

Political boundaries are frequently defined by, and located in, elements of nature. Although the primary touristic appeal of these borderlands is their natural beauty, the borderlines often add a degree of intrigue and may become a secondary attraction that benefits peripheral regions. Seeing or crossing a border in a remarkable natural landscape can further augment the attractiveness of the locality. The same is true of cultural landscapes, some of which differ significantly because of the historical development of human activity that was largely determined by the border.

During the past few decades, global debordering processes have ushered in many changes and enhanced the potential for border resources and environments to be used for tourism. Given the unique peripheral, political, and controversial positions and roles of state boundaries, tourism near, on, and across national frontiers requires good management, government tolerance, and in many cases sound transfrontier networks and cooperation frameworks (Blasco et al., 2014; Guo, 2015; Stoffelen, 2018; Stoffelen & Vanneste, 2017; Timothy & Saarinen, 2013). The degree of a border's openness and permeability determines the level of transfrontier tourism development on both sides and offers an opportunity for cross-border attractions to be established, marketed, and managed for tourism.

## Acknowledgement

This chapter was prepared as part of project 2018/29/B/HS4/02417, financed by the National Science Centre, Warsaw, Poland.

## References

Aleksandrova, A., & Stupina, O.G. (2014). *Turistskoe regionovedenie: Vliyanie regionalnoi integratsii na mirovoi turistskii rynok* (Tourism regional studies: The impact of regional integration on the world tourist market). Moscow: Knorus.
Blasco, D., Guia, J., & Prats, L. (2014). Emergence of governance in cross-border destinations. *Annals of Tourism Research*, 49, 159–173.
Canally, C., & Timothy, D.J. (2007). Perceived constraints to travel across the US-Mexico border among American university students. *International Journal of Tourism Research*, 9(6), 423–437.
Chhabra, D. (2018). Soft power analysis in alienated borderline tourism. *Journal of Heritage Tourism*, 13(4), 289–304.
Díaz-Sauceda, J., Palau-Saumell, R., Forgas-Coll, S., & Sánchez-García, J. (2015). Cross-border tourists' behavioral intentions: The Green Line of Nicosia, Cyprus. *Tourism Geographies*, 17(5), 758–779.
Eckert, A. (2019). *West Germany and the Iron Curtain: Environment, economy, and culture in the borderlands*. Oxford: Oxford University Press.
Elden, S. (2010). Land, terrain, territory. *Progress in Human Geography*, 34(6), 799–817.
Estrada Milán, J., & Escala Rabadan, L. (2021). Riding waves on the Mexico–United States border: Beaches, local surfers and cross-border processes. *Journal of Sport and Social Issues*, 45(2), 217–232.
Fronteras (2013, January 24). Mexican amusement park offers fake border crossing attraction. *PBS News Hour*. Online: https://www.pbs.org/newshour/world/fake-border-crossing-is-amusement-park-attraction
Galluser, W.A. (ed) (1994). *Political boundaries and coexistence*. Bern: Peter Lang.
Gelbman, A. (2008). Border tourism in Israel: Conflict, peace, fear and hope. *Tourism Geographies*, 10(2), 193–213.
Gelbman, A. (2010). Border tourism attractions as a space for presenting and symbolizing peace. In O. Moufakkir, & I. Kelly (eds) *Tourism, progress and peace*, pp. 83–98. Wallingford: CABI.
Gelbman, A., & Timothy, D.J. (2010). From hostile boundaries to tourist attractions. *Current Issues in Tourism*, 13(3), 239–259.

Gelbman, A., & Timothy, D.J. (2011). Border complexity, tourism and international exclaves: A case study. *Annals of Tourism Research*, 38(1), 110–131.

Gelbman, A., & Timothy, D.J. (2019). Differential tourism zones on the western Canada-US border. *Current Issues in Tourism*, 22(6), 682–704.

Glassner, M., & de Blij, H. (1989). *Systemic political geography*. New York: Wiley.

Grinko, I.A. (2016). Muzeinye' granitsy i formirovanie novykh identichnostei (Border museums and formation of new identities). *Samarskii nauchnyi vestnik* (Samara Scientific Bulletin), 4(17), 149–152.

Guo, R. (2015). *Cross-border management: Theory, method and application*. Berlin: Springer.

Havlick, D.G. (2014). The Iron Curtain Trail's landscapes of memory, meaning, and recovery. *Focus on Geography*, 57(3), 126–133.

Hisakawa, N., Jankowski, P., & Paulus, G. (2013). Mapping the porosity of international border to pedestrian traffic: A comparative data classification approach to a study of the border region in Austria, Italy, and Slovenia. *Cartography and Geographic Information Science*, 40(1), 18–27.

van Houtum H., & van Naerssen T. (2002). Bordering, ordering and othering. *Tijdschrift voor Economische en Sociale Geografie*, 93(2), 125–136.

Hunter, W.C. (2015). The visual representation of border tourism: Demilitarized zone (DMZ) and Dokdo in South Korea. *International Journal of Tourism Research*, 17(2), 151–160.

Ioannides, D., Nielsen, P., & Billing, P. (2006). Transboundary collaboration in tourism: The case of the Bothian Arc. *Tourism Geographies*, 8(2), 122–142.

Jacobsen, J.K.S. (1997). The making of an attraction: The case of North Cape. *Annals of Tourism Research*, 24(2), 341–356.

Jones, R. (2009). Sovereignty and statelessness in the border enclaves of India and Bangladesh. *Political Geography*, 28(6), 373–381.

Kałuski, S. (2006). Border tripoints as transborder cooperation regions in Central and Eastern Europe. In J. Kitowski (ed.) *Regional trans-border co-operation in countries of Central and Eastern Europe: A balance of achievements*, pp. 27–36. Warsaw: Geopolitical Studies.

Kałuski, S. (2017). *Blizny historii: Geografia granic politycznych współczesnego świata*. Warsaw: Wydawnictwo Akademickie Dialog.

Kolosov, V. (2020). Phantom borders: The role in territorial identity and the impact on society. *Belgeo: Revue belge de géographie*, 2, 1–19.

Kristoff, L. (1959). The nature of frontiers and boundaries. *Annals of the Association of American Geographers*, 49, 269–282.

Kwanisai, G., Mpofu, T., Vengesayi, S., Mutanga, C.N., Hurombo, B., & Mirimi, K. (2014). Borders as barriers to tourism: Tourists experiences at the Beitbridge Border Post (Zimbabwean side). *African Journal of Hospitality, Tourism and Leisure*, 3(1), 1–13.

Leimgruber, W. (2005). Boundaries and transborder relations, or the hole in the prison wall: On the necessity of superfluous limits and boundaries. *GeoJournal*, 64, 239–248.

Light, D. (2000). Gazing on communism: heritage tourism and post-communist identities in Germany, Hungary and Romania. *Tourism Geographies*, 2(2), 157–176.

Löytynoja, T. (2007). National boundaries and place-making in tourism: Staging the Finnish-Russian border. *Nordia Geographical Publications*, 36(4), 35–45.

Löytynoja, T. (2008). The development of specific locations into tourist attractions: Cases from northern Europe. *Fennia*, 186(1), 15–29.

Madsen, K.D. (in press). Terminus unleashed: Divine antecedents of contemporary borders. *Journal of Borderlands Studies*. DOI: 10.1080/08865655.2020.1865185.

Martinez, O.J. (1994). The dynamics of border interaction – New approaches to border analysis. In C.H. Schofield (ed.) *World boundaries, global boundaries*, pp. 1–15. London: Routledge.

Matznetter, J. (1979). Border and tourism: Fundamental relations, In G. Gruber, & H. Lamping (eds) *Tourism and borders: Proceedings of the Meeting of the IGU Working Group - Geography of Tourism and Recreation*, pp. 61–73. Frankfurt: Institut fur Wirtschafts und Sozialgeographie der Johann Wolfgang Goethe Universität.

Mayer, M., Zbaraszewski, W., Pieńkowski, D., Gach, G., & Gernert, J. (2019). *Cross-border tourism in protected areas: Potentials, pitfalls and perspectives*. Cham, Switzerland: Springer.

Medvedev, S. (1999). Across the line: Borders in post-Westphalian landscapes. In H. Eskelinen, I. Liikanen, & J. Oksa (eds) *Curtains of iron and gold: Reconstructing borders and scales of interaction*, pp. 43–56. Aldershot: Ashgate.

Newman, D. (2006). Borders and bordering: Towards an interdisciplinary dialogue. *European Journal of Social Theory*, 9(2), 171–186.

Picard, D., & Di Giovine, M.A. (Eds) (2014). *Tourism and the power of otherness: Seductions of difference*. Bristol: Channel View Publiations.

Pounds, N. (1963). *Political geography*. New York: McGraw Hill.

Prescott, J.R.V. (1987). *Political frontiers and boundaries*. London: Allen & Unwin.

Prokkola, E.-K. (2008). Resources and barriers in tourism development: Cross-border cooperation, regionalization and destination building at the Finnish-Swedish border. *Fennia*, 186(1), 31–46.

Prokkola, E.-K., & Lois, M. (2016). Scalar politics of border heritage: An examination of the EU's northern and southern border areas. *Scandinavian Journal of Hospitality and Tourism*, 16(1), 14–35.

Raffestin, C. (1986). Eléments pour une théorie de la frontière. *Diogène*, 134, 3–21.

Ramutsindela, M. (ed.) (2014). *Cartographies of nature: How nature conservation animates borders*. Newcastle upon Tyne: Cambridge Scholars.

Reitel, B. (2013). Border temporality and space integration in the European transborder agglomeration of Basel. *Journal of Borderlands Studies*, 28(2), 239–256.

Ryden, K.C. (1993). *Mapping the invisible landscape: Folklore, writing and the sense of place*. Iowa City: University of Iowa Press.

Scott, J. (2012). Tourism, civil society and peace in Cyprus. *Annals of Tourism Research*, 39(4), 2114–2132.

Shin, Y.S. (2007). Perception differences between domestic and international visitors in the tourist destination: The case of the borderline, the DMZ area. *Journal of Travel & Tourism Marketing*, 21(2–3), 77–88.

Smart, N. (1996). The Maginot Line: An indestructible inheritance. *International Journal of Heritage Studies*, 2(4), 222–233.

Sohn, C., Reitel, B., & Walther, O. (2009). Cross-border metropolitan integration in Europe: The case of Luxembourg, Basel, and Geneva. *Environment and Planning C: Government and Policy*, 27(5), 922–939.

Stoffelen, A. (2018). Tourism trails as tools for cross-border integration: A best practice case study of the Vennbahn Cycle Route. *Annals of Tourism Research*, 73, 91–102.

Stoffelen, A., & Vanneste, D. (2017). Tourism and cross-border regional development: Insights in European contexts. *European Planning Studies*, 25(6), 1013–1033.

Timothy, D.J., (1995). Political boundaries and tourism: Borders as tourist attractions. *Tourism Management*, 16(7), 525–532.

Timothy, D.J. (1998). Collecting places: Geodetic lines in tourist space. *Journal of Travel and Tourism Marketing*, 7(4), 123–129.

Timothy, D.J. (2001). *Tourism and political boundaries*. London: Routledge.

Timothy, D.J. (2019). Tourism, border disputes and claims to territorial sovereignty. In R.K. Isaac, E. Çakmak, & R. Butler (eds) *Tourism and hospitality in conflict-ridden destinations*, pp. 25–38. London: Routledge.

Timothy, D.J. (2021). *Tourism in European microstates and dependencies: Geopolitics, scale and resource limitations*. Wallingford: CABI.

Timothy, D.J., & Boyd, S.W. (2015). *Tourism and trails: Cultural, ecological and management issues*. Bristol: Channel View Publications.

Timothy D.J., & Gelbman A. (2015). Tourist lodging, spatial relations, and the cultural heritage of borderlands. *Journal of Heritage Tourism*, 10(2), 1–11.

Timothy, D.J., Guia, J., & Berthet, N. (2014). Tourism as a catalyst for changing boundaries and territorial sovereignty at an international border. *Current Issues in Tourism*, 17(1), 21–27.

Timothy, D.J., Prideaux, B., & Kim, S.S. (2004). Tourism at borders of conflict and (de)militarized zones. In T.V. Singh (ed.) *New horizons in tourism: Strange experiences and stranger practices*, pp. 83–94. Wallingford: CABI.

Timothy, D.J., & Saarinen, J. (2013). Cross-border cooperation and tourism in Europe. In C. Costa, E. Panyik, & D. Buhalis D. (eds) *Trends in European tourism planning and organisation*, pp. 64–74. Bristol: Channel View Publications.

Timothy, D.J., Saarinen, J., & Viken, A. (2016). Tourism issues and international borders in the Nordic region. *Scandinavian Journal of Hospitality and Tourism*, 16(1), 1–13.

Varnajot, A. (2019). "Walk the line": An ethnographic study of the ritual of crossing the Arctic Circle—Case Rovaniemi. *Tourist Studies*, 19(4), 434–452.

Varnajot, A. (2020). Digital Rovaniemi: Contemporary and future arctic tourist experiences. *Journal of Tourism Futures*, 6(1), 6–23.

Wachowiak, H. (ed.) (2006). *Tourism and borders: Contemporary issues, policies, and international research*. Farnham: Ashgate.

Webster, C., & Timothy, D.J. (2006). Traveling to the 'Other Side': The occupied zone and Greek Cypriot views of crossing the Green Line. *Tourism Geographies*, 8(2), 162–181.

Więckowski, M. (2010). Tourism development in the borderlands of Poland. *Geographia Polonica*, 83(2), 67–81.

Więckowski, M. (2013). Eco-frontier in the mountainous borderlands of Central Europe: The case of Polish border parks. *Journal of Alpine Research/Revue de géographie alpine*, 101(2), 1–13.

Więckowski, M. (2018). From periphery and the doubled national trails to the cross-border thematic trails: New cross-border tourism in Poland. In D. Müller, & M. Więckowski (eds) *Tourism in transitions: Recovering decline, managing change*, pp. 173–186. Cham, Switzerland: Springer.

Więckowski M. (in press). How border tripoints offer opportunities for transboundary tourism development. *Tourism Geographies*. DOI: 10.1080/14616688.2021.1878268.

Więckowski, M., & Timothy, D.J. (2021). Tourism and an evolving international boundary: Bordering, debordering and rebordering on Usedom Island, Poland-Germany. *Journal of Destination Marketing & Management*, 22, 100647.

Zhang, S., Zhong, L., Ju, H., & Wang, Y. (2019). Land border tourism resources in China: Spatial patterns and tourism management. *Sustainability*, 11, 236.

Zmelik, K., Schindler, S., & Wrbka, T. (2011). The European Green Belt: International collaboration in biodiversity research and nature conservation along the former Iron Curtain. *Innovation*, 24(3), 273–294.

# 15
# BORDERS OF CONFLICT AS TOURIST ATTRACTIONS

*Alon Gelbman*

## Introduction

Border regions are often broadly connected with geopolitical disputes. While the potential for actual danger in frontier regions has little allure for most tourists, the excitement of visiting a politically controversial area appeals to many others (Butler, 1996; Chhabra, 2018; Timothy, 2019). Many borders are integral parts of geopolitical tensions, conflict, and war, while most wars in recent years have had borders and contested national territory at the heart of the dispute (Timothy, 2013; Timothy, Prideaux & Kim, 2004). Several present borders came into being as wartime ceasefire lines or armistice lines, creating what in the realm of geopolitics is described as partitioned states (Butler & Mao, 1996; Waterman, 1987). Timothy (2001) emphasized "contrast" as a major element drawing tourists to a potential border attraction, encompassing the desire to experience past or present differences of conflicts and fortified boundaries.

Typical examples of such border areas are the former Berlin Wall separating east from west, and the lines that divide Cyprus or the Korean Peninsula. These borders serve to partition incompatible ideological systems, societies, and economies, and ironically they have become significant tourist attractions despite their original function, which was to hinder the flow of travel (Shin, 2004; Timothy, 1995, 2000). They are tourist attractions because people have always been interested in "otherness", and in this case, in the "forbidden" or "inaccessible". "Nostalgia for" and "curiosity about" also attract tourists, as can be seen at the former east–west divide in Germany. Checkpoint Charlie and the Berlin Wall as global symbols of the collapse of the Iron Curtain have spurred the establishment of some 30 border museums along the corridor that once formed this infamous boundary (Blacksell, 1998; Borneman, 1998; Frank & Spengler, 2016; Light, 2000).

Borders have significant historical, structural, and etymological connections with present or past violence and conflicts. Borders have long been a tool for establishing, asserting, maintaining, and spreading political power. From the expansion of Imperial Rome to contemporary state sovereignty, the setting of borders and the foundation of political order in modern Western societies have been indissolubly linked (Brambilla & Jones, 2020). Border-making as a violent founding act of separation also gave rise to the idea of civil society based on private property and enclosures, which are the keystone to the uneven development of capitalistic landscapes (Mezzadra & Neilson, 2013). Borderlines and border regions often constitute a focal point for hostilities and disputes between the countries lying beyond these borders. Such tensions are a drawing card for certain types of visitors and tourists, as can be seen in tourism visits to hostile border areas (Timothy, 2019; Timothy et al., 2004).

The topic of this chapter, borders of conflict as tourist attractions, is connected to several familiar phenomena in tourism development, which will also be mentioned later on, including dark tourism, war and battlefield tourism, danger zone tourism, heritage tourism, and political tourism. In this chapter I describe and analyze the salient characteristics linking conflict areas and tourism attractions, as well as providing some insights and theories about the subject from the literature. The chapter includes references to the characteristics of tourism attractions in conflict areas and their classification according to their timeframe—present vs. past—in other words, border tourism attractions of present conflicts (such as the borders of North and South Korea, or Israel and Syria) versus conflict heritage sites of a past dispute that has become a heritage tourist attraction (e.g., the Iron Curtain borders in Europe).

## Conflicted Borders as Tourist Attractions

Tourists' interest in so-called "dark tourism"—visiting sites of death, disaster, and atrocity—has been growing since the 1990s. Expansion of global communication networks, anxiety over changes caused by modernity, and the commodification of death and disaster all play a role in producing and reproducing dark tourism (Lennon & Foley, 1999). War often stimulates a curiosity factor among some groups of tourists "whereby tourists are interested in seeing a place they may have seen or read about during a period of political instability, and which is now safe to visit" (Hall & O'Sullivan, 1996, p. 118). This may manifest either in visits to active war zones or regions where the war no longer exists or poses an existential threat.

Geopolitical post-conflict border tourism attractions may create or exacerbate tensions connected to the disparity between commodification and authenticity. This occurs when local communities at a particular locale view their commemorations and memorials as sacred places and daily reminders of past violence and injustices suffered. The tourists, on the other hand, are usually motivated by a search for authenticity and "otherness". Local communities may be in danger of being marginalized or becoming mere objects of the voyeuristic tourist gaze if they are not empowered to tell their own version of the past (Wiedenhoft Murphy, 2010).

"Danger zone tourism" is related, and entails people traveling to places of active conflict because they are curious, they want to test their endurance or personal abilities, or they have a desire to "conquer" a unique destination that others do not visit (Lisle, 2016; Mahrouse, 2016). Tours to Taliban strongholds or al-Qaida training camps in Afghanistan prior to the US military's August 2021 pull-out, or visits to the highly contentious Line of Control between Indian and Pakistani controlled areas of Jammu and Kashmir, are examples of this unusual type of dark or danger zone tourism.

Timothy (2001) emphasizes the contrast factor of border areas as an important element that creates tourist interest and curiosity to visit a place and perhaps illuminate the substantial differences between countries. He notes that physical elements that illustrate this contrast may become tourist attractions (e.g., fences, flags, signs, or border markings) (see also Więckowski & Timothy, 2021), and the more significant the geopolitical contrast between the countries in the past or present, the more fascinating and intense the visit experience may be. This is especially salient in conflicted border areas. Thus, for example, a visit to the DMZ border separating North and South Korea has become one of the most important attractions for tourists to South Korea (also available from the North), and in this area border tourism sites have been commercially developed to relate and illustrate the reality of this conflict area (Hunter, 2015; Shin, 2007; Timothy et al., 2004).

Gelbman (2008), studying the development of border tourism along the fortified and conflicted frontier of Israel and its neighbors, identified a typology with four main categories of supply, which constitute a draw for visits and tourism activity linked to an unmediated first-hand experience of the conflicted border area: (1) old remains of buildings or infrastructure (e.g., an old customs station, remains of former cross-border train lines and stations, old cross-border bridges); (2) remains of military activities and memorials (e.g., bunkers, watch towers, tanks, and remains of weaponry); (3) boundary markers and icons (e.g., border gates, signs, fences and markers, and national flags); and (4) border observatories from which the neighboring country can be viewed, as well as museums. In the Israeli case, and in the cases of many other ongoing border conflicts (e.g., Pakistan–India, North–South Korea, Armenia–Azerbaijan), these types of attractions are considered "one-sided" border attractions, because visitors cannot cross freely to visit the other side. Border tourism sites in Israel are affected by conditions often dictated by geopolitical relations with its neighboring states. Throughout the world, some border sites are located near hostile and closed frontiers, whereas others are in close proximity to highly permeable borders (Timothy, 2001).

Visiting Israel's border-tourism sites is an exercise in observation which offers tourists a special experience. They can feel the danger and fear connected to battles that took place near the border, as well as the ongoing tensions (e.g., between Israel and Lebanon, and Israel and Syria), and they also have a close and clear look at the land on the other side of the border. These sites may also simultaneously be places of hope for a better future of peace and cooperation with the neighbors on the other side. In many cases, the observation points can grow to signify both the core of the conflict and a prayer for peace, a special mixture of fear and hope (Gelbman, 2008). For example, the summit of Mount Bental, located in the northern part of the Golan Heights, offers a spectacular panoramic view of Syria, Lebanon, and Israel. The extensive Israel Defense Forces bunker system located there has been turned into a tourist attraction. The wars of 1967 and 1973 have made the Golan Heights a highly strategic and conflicted border area. Between 1948 and 1967, when Syria controlled the Golan Heights, the area was used by Syria as a military stronghold. On the site are remains of tanks and weapons and the highest coffee shop in the country, at 1,165 meters above sea level. Visitors to Mount Bental and those walking through the bunkers can look out at the landscape beyond the borders with Syria and Lebanon, touch the remains of tanks and weapons, which have been recycled in part as works of art, and hear or read the Israeli version of the history of the borders and battles in the Golan Heights (Gelbman, 2008) (Figure 15.1).

South Korea's border with North Korea divides the Korean peninsula at the 38th parallel. This land border, negotiated at the end of Korean War hostilities in 1953 as part of an armistice agreement, was brokered between UN forces and North Korea and is commonly known as the demilitarized zone (DMZ). This border is considered temporary because technically the two Koreas are still at war, and sporadic hostilities keep tensions high in the borderlands (Hunter, 2015). This heavily fortified boundary is 4 km wide and runs 248 km coast to coast from the Incheon Northern Limit Line in the west, through Gyeonggi and Gangwon provinces to the east.

The DMZ is a symbolic artifact of the Cold War and features various war heritage or dark tourism attractions including the Joint Security Area (JSA), Imjingak and Tongil Observatory, the Punch Bowl Battlefield, and Dorasan Station (the last stop on the Gyeonggi railway before North Korea) (Bigley et al., 2010; Shin, 2007). Attempts are ongoing at additional sites, including Seorak Mountain and Baekdan Temple, to use tourism to transform the DMZ into that

*Figure 15.1* Bental Mountain Observatory view of Syria, Lebanon, and Israel.
(Photo: A. Gelbman)

of an ecological recreation zone (Hunter, 2015; Lee et al., 2007) or a peace park (Kim et al., 2019). In South Korea, the DMZ is an alienated borderland, and prohibitions against crossing it similarly emphasize the border area, the borderline itself, and the mysteries about what lies on the other side. Beyond its physical barriers, the DMZ is a socially constructed borderland, whose identity was formed in part by political and economic elites, by war and diplomatic effects, and also by the activities of those who visit this periphery of the Koreas (Hunter, 2015; Shin, 2004).

The Dorasan train station is an example of a related tourist attraction (Figure 15.2). Opened in 2002, it is located near the edge of the DMZ (Kim et al., 2007) and, depending on how one looks at it, is either the last train stop in South Korea or the first stop in North Korea from the south. Although the tracks are connected, the communist regime to the north does not allow trains to pass through, so the $40 million station sits unused (Burke, 2012). Under the watchful eye of the local hosts, South Korean soldiers and travelers wander around the train station taking in the impressive artwork and advertisements that adorn the walls. The chairs in the lobby look new, the floor is shiny, and a screen provides information to visitors. Travelers see their reflections in the bulletproof glass on the facade. A man behind the ticket counter is ready to sell boarding passes to anyone passing through the turnstiles before heading outside to its platforms. This situation coincides with the tourist experience of visiting one side of a closed and fortified border (Matznetter, 1979; Timothy, 2001), and with Gelbman's (2008) duality model: fear of the present threatening reality but also hope for a better future. But a question that arises is: What do tourists see when they look at the immaculately maintained station? Do they perceive it as a waste of money or a beacon of hope for reunification on the Korean Peninsula (Gelbman, 2017)?

*Figure 15.2* The Dorasan train station is located just inside South Korea near the border of the contentious Demilitarized Zone between the North and the South.

(Photo: A. Gelbman)

## From Conflicted Border to Heritage Attraction

The connection between conflicts, wars, and tourism can be complicated from two perspectives: how conflicts are remembered and how they are symbolically perpetuated. This provides a new dimension to the reproduction of the collective memory of war through tour operators and tourists (Arthur, 1997; Prokkola & Lois, 2016; Wiedenhoft Murphy, 2010). Tourism has the potential to keep past conflicts in the present and may constrain efforts at peace-making. Tourism in post-conflict societies has the potential to create new conflicts, particularly if tour operators compete for tourists in order to sell their version of history (Wiedenhoft Murphy, 2010). Researchers have emphasized the need to be especially aware of the narratives presented at war sites and localities of conflict, including those in border areas, and to allow different points of view to be expressed at the site, in order to avoid one version arousing emotional opposition in any particular community (Arthur, 1997). Tour operators in post-conflict areas should ask themselves whether they hope to arouse passion or create an environment of forgiveness through their tours (Tarlow, 2005). These senses have long been closely connected to heritage tourism. The central issues surrounding tourism in most heritage contexts are identity, contestation, and representation (Hall & Tucker, 2004; Timothy, 2021).

In border regions that have been closed and hostile due to geopolitical tensions and ideological differences, the end of the crisis usually leads to the removal of geopolitical and physical obstacles and the opening of the borders for people to pass (Gelbman, 2010; Więckowski &

Timothy, 2021). Despite the removal of many physical barriers, the historical border continues to exist as a memory of significance for local residents and tourists, as many border (or former border) communities commemorate their unique geopolitical heritage with border monuments and heritage narratives (Andersen & Prokkola, 2021; Więckowski & Timothy, 2021). This process can be seen in different border areas around the world, such as in Ireland, at the Golden Triangle in Southeast Asia, and along the former Berlin Wall and the entire inner-German border that divided Germany until 1990, all of which underwent this transformation (Borovik, 2019; Boyd, 1999; McClelland, 2016). The result of the change was that the borders became commemorative spaces of past events, keeping alive an awareness and understanding of former disagreements, with an emphasis on the positive elements of transformation and its symbolic power for the present and future.

The result of this process is often tourism development, which can draw large numbers of tourists. Tourism development is often based on concrete elements of the physical landscape of the border area, which may become quasi-monuments commemorating the heritage of the past and relating the story of the place (Chhabra, 2018; Gelbman, 2019). The development also creates a feeling among visitors that they are following in the footsteps of important historical processes—local and global—that transpired in the not-so-distant past. At times, even if the physical border was a sealed barrier over many years but has opened completely today, it may continue to exist as a symbol of a dark heritage that should be remembered but not repeated. This is often the central message of border museums and parks, preserved segments of contentious borders, observation points, and explanatory materials available to visitors (Gelbman, 2010).

The Berlin Wall was a formidable partition that split the German capital into the communist East German sector and the capitalist-dominated West German sector. East Berlin served as the capital of East Germany, but West Berlin was merely an enclave within East Germany, so West Germany's capital was transferred to Bonn. Berlin was divided in 1945, but the split became much more significant with the erection of the wall in 1961 and the deepening of the Cold War and inter-bloc hostilities, which had begun after World War II. Political control of the city was unevenly divided between the USSR on the one hand and France, Britain, and the USA on the other, with the Soviet sector constituting a much larger portion than the combined area of the other three sectors. As early as the late 1940s a serious conflict about the city erupted between the East and West blocs, leading to a blockade of West Berlin. On August 13, 1961, the Soviets began to construct a fence, which was later fortified several times, eventually becoming the infamous wall (Koenig, 1981).

The wall extended more than 155 km around West Berlin and included many guard towers, anti-vehicle trenches, bunkers, minefields, and barbed wire. For 28 years, the residents of Berlin were divided and could not pass from East to West, although some West Berliners were permitted to visit the East. Of the many people who tried to escape westward, a few succeeded, while many others failed, sometimes paying with their lives because of the "shoot-to-kill" orders the East German border guards were working under.

On the night of November 9, 1989, the wall was breached by throngs of Germans from both East and West Berlin, opening the barrier to a free flow of human mobility. Less than one year later, on October 3, 1990, Germany was reunited. Today, only a few segments of the wall remain standing as commemorative monuments throughout the city. Most of the wall was destroyed quickly by the masses, who hurriedly took pieces of the original concrete from the wall as souvenirs. Other parts of the barrier were dismantled by the newly unified German government in various stages after 1990. The remaining sections of the wall do not look today as they did during the period of 1961 to 1989. Still standing is the 1300-meter-long "East Side

Gallery", near the Ostbahnhof train station. The eastern side of the wall today is covered by graffiti, most of it on subjects of peace and the solidarity of nations. Such a phenomenon would not have been possible under East German rule. At that time, only the western side of the wall was covered by graffiti (Borneman, 1998; Kinzer, 1994). A few remains of the wall still stand in various parts of the city, some of it interpreted for visitors, and some left nearly abandoned.

To commemorate the dark heritage of the urban scar, a Berlin Wall Trail (Berliner Mauerweg) was established shortly after the reunification of Germany and developed in sections between 1991 and 2006. Today, the 160-km walking and cycling trail generally follows the course of the Berlin Wall and is a popular tourist attraction in the city. It passes by wall remains, pieces of the East German security landscape, and includes displays, commemorative markers, and interpretive placards for trail users to better understand the history of one of Europe's most memorable and momentous borders (Gelbman, 2019; Timothy, 2021).

The process the Berlin Wall underwent is both interesting and unique, especially because it became a global tourist attraction and an object lesson for future international geopolitical relationships. When most cross-border travel was barred, the wall served as a magnet for Westerners wishing to observe the other side (Koenig, 1981; Timothy, 2001). After the demise of the East–West divide in 1989–1990, the same wall became a unique tourist attraction symbolizing the Cold War (Light, 2000). Some remains of the wall became an exhibit at Checkpoint Charley Museum, the place from which visitors could observe a different "world" during the years the wall stood (Frank & Spengler, 2016; Wachowiak & Engels, 2006) and one of the city's main crossing points. Several other border museums have been established since 1990 along the former East Germany–West Germany frontier where guard towers, fences, walls, and patrol tracks are preserved and interpreted as memorials to the East–West Cold War conflict (Eckert, 2019; Kolosov & Więckowski, 2018; Timothy & Boyd, 2015; Timothy et al., 2004).

This collective memory is directly connected to a border's symbolic, natural, and built landscapes, serving as a source of interest and curiosity for tourists who wish to experience history and visit the places where famous events occurred. This process leads to the development of tourist attractions. A border fence or wall, guard tower, national flag, border markers, bunkers, and military posts are examples of elements from a built political landscape that may take on exceptional symbolic meaning when a borderline undergoes the transformation from being closed and hostile to one that is open and peaceful (Więckowski, in press). Thus, heritage is an important part of the transformation of the border from closed and hostile to open and peaceful. In this conceptualization, the contentious past of the place is commemorated, highlighting its present status and offering the positive transformation as a symbol of belief for a better future (Gelbman & Timothy, 2010).

## Conclusion

Political borderlines and boundaries constitute a significant element in the political landscape that can develop into unique regional and international tourist attractions. Borderline areas on the peripheries of countries engaged in disputes and wars are places fraught with incipient danger and intrigue (Timothy, 2019). As such, they fascinate a certain type of tourist interested in visiting authentic places where dangerous events occurred in the recent or distant past, or where conflict is ongoing. These types of border tourism attractions belong simultaneously to the market niches of dark tourism, battlefield and war tourism, heritage tourism, danger zone tourism, and political tourism. Indeed, the growing demand to visit conflict-related border sites, such as the Korean DMZ or the Berlin Wall, is part of the growing travel segment who desire to visit dark sites of death, disaster, and atrocities. This reflects the desire among more tourists to visit sites with added value and deeper meaning. This meaning may include learning about history or past events through a process of identifying with, or connecting to, conflicted events and the lessons to be learned from them.

The cross-border contrast factor as described by Timothy (2001) takes on special meaning for border tourism in conflict zones. The physical elements that symbolize or define boundaries and/or events that occurred in the borderlands (e.g., border fences, signs, boundary markers, flags and military infrastructure, remains of old buildings, relict remains of military activities and memorials, boundary symbolisms, and border observatories) draw tourists' interest and help connect them to the concrete and abstract elements of the borderlands (Gelbman, 2008; Więckowski, in press). Tourism visits to most heavily fortified and conflicted border areas, such as the border between Israel and Syria or the DMZ separating the two Koreas, allow people to visit only one side of the border at a given time. There they can experience a true sense of place authenticity, because of the restrictions placed upon them and their activities, as well as the ever-presence of military personnel and heavy security landscapes. Thus, they can see up close the source and manifestation of international hostilities and get a feel for certain dangers. At the same time, however, it might be possible to sense a glimmer of hope for a better future if only hostilities would end and peaceful relations prevail (Gelbman, 2008). Such visits might even encourage participants to take action to help effect change between hostile neighbors.

In border areas that were once sites of disputes and war but have since become peaceful frontiers or ceased to be international boundaries entirely, such as the former Berlin Wall and the entire East–West Germany border, conflict-related heritage attractions frequently develop into national and international symbols of transformation from conflict to benevolence, embodying the lessons learned from the dark history of the place (Gelbman & Timothy, 2010). Many of these attractions perpetuate stories of the past and protect physical remnants of the past, such as parts of the original Berlin Wall or museums that recount the story of the years during which the border was closed or during which a war was waged. The case of the Berlin Wall emphasizes the intensity of the site's touristic importance. Even though most of the original wall and its associated security landscape are gone, its tangible and intangible legacy remains and continues to serve as a unique and important border tourist site that attracts thousands of tourists from around the world each year. Thus, border-related heritage sites serve as tourist attractions, but conversely, tourism helps to revive and preserve the heritage of past conflicts and recount the unique stories of the borders that were once the core of the conflict.

## References

Andersen, D.J., & Prokkola, E-K. (2021). Heritage as bordering: Heritage making, ontological struggles and the politics of memory in the Croatian and Finnish borderlands. *Journal of Borderlands Studies, 36*(3), 405–424.

Arthur, P. (1997). "Reading" violence: Ireland. In D. Apter (ed.) *The legitimization of violence*, pp. 234–291. London: Palgrave Macmillan.

Bigley, J.D., Lee, C.K., Chon, J., & Yoon, Y. (2010). Motivations for war-related tourism: A case of DMZ visitors in Korea. *Tourism Geographies, 12*(3), 371–394.

Blacksell, M. (1998). Redrawing the political map. In D. Pinder (ed.) *The new Europe: Economy, society and environment*, pp. 23–42. Chichester: Wiley.

Borneman, J. (1998). Grenzregime (border regime): The wall and its aftermath. In T.M. Wilson, & H. Donnan (eds) *Border identities: Nation and state at international frontiers*, pp. 162–190. Cambridge: Cambridge University Press.

Borovik, S. (2019). The wall's legacy still lingers three decades after the dawn of a 'new Europe'. *New Europe*, 01 November. Online at: https://www.neweurope.eu/article/the-walls-legacy-still-lingers-three-decades-after-the-dawn-of-a-new-europe/

Boyd, S.W. (1999). North-south divide: The role of the border in tourism to Northern Ireland. *Visions in Leisure and Business*, 17(4), 50–71.

Brambilla, C., & Jones, R. (2020). Rethinking borders, violence, and conflict: From sovereign power to borderscapes as sites of struggles. *Environment and Planning D: Society and Space*, 38(2), 287–305.

Burke, M.M. (2012). South Korea: Dorasan train station in DMZ still waiting for a connection, stars and stripes, January 11 [online], available from http://www.stripes.com/lifestyle/south-korea-dorasan-train-station-in-dmz-still-waiting-for-a-connection-1.165731 [6 December 2016].

Butler, R.W. (1996). The development of tourism in frontier regions: Issues and approaches. In Y. Gradus, & H. Lithwick (eds.) *Frontiers in regional development*, pp. 213–229. Lanham, MD: Rowman & Littlefield.

Butler, R.W., & Mao, B. (1996). Conceptual and theoretical implications of tourism between partitioned states. *Asia Pacific Journal of Tourism Research*, 1(1), 25–34.

Chhabra, D. (2018). Soft power analysis in alienated borderline tourism. *Journal of Heritage Tourism*, 13(4), 289–304.

Eckert, A. (2019). *West Germany and the Iron Curtain: Environment, economy, and culture in the borderlands*. Oxford: Oxford University Press.

Frank, S., & Spengler, J. (2016). *Wall memorials and heritage: The heritage industry of Berlin's Checkpoint Charlie*. London: Routledge.

Gelbman, A. (2008). Border tourism in Israel: Conflict, fear, peace and hope. *Tourism Geographies*, 10(2), 193–213.

Gelbman, A. (2010). Border tourism as a space of presenting and symbolizing peace. In O. Moufakkir, & I. Kelly (eds) *Tourism progress and peace*, pp. 83–89. Wallingford: CABI.

Gelbman, A. (2017). The heritage of geopolitical borders as peace tourism attractions. In D. Walter, P. Davis, & D. Laven (eds) *Heritage and peacebuilding*, pp. 191–204. Suffolk: Boydell & Brewer Ltd.

Gelbman, A. (2019). Tourism, peace, and global stability. In D.J. Timothy (ed.) *Handbook of globalisation and tourism*, pp. 149–160. Cheltenham: Edward Elgar.

Gelbman, A., & Timothy, D.J. (2010). From hostile boundaries to tourist attractions. *Current Issues in Tourism*, 13(3), 239–259.

Hall, C.M., & O'Sullivan, V. (1996). Tourism, political stability and violence. In A. Pizam, & Y. Mansfeld (eds), *Tourism, crime and international security issues*, pp. 105–121. Chichester: Wiley.

Hall, C.M., & Tucker, H. (Eds.). (2004). *Tourism and postcolonialism: Contested discourses, identities and representations*. London: Routledge.

Hunter, W.C. (2015). The visual representation of border tourism: Demilitarized zone (DMZ) and Dokdo in South Korea. *International Journal of Tourism Research*, 17(2), 151–160.

Kim, H., Choe, Y., & Lee, C.K. (2019). Differential effects of patriotism and support on post-development visit intention: The Korean DMZ Peace Park. *Journal of Travel & Tourism Marketing*, 36(3), 384–401.

Kim, S. Prideaux, B., & Prideaux, J. (2007). Using tourism to promote peace on the Korean Peninsula. *Annals of Tourism Research*, 34, 291–309.

Kinzer, S. (1994, December 18). At checkpoint Charlie, a museum remembers. *New York Times*, p. 3.

Koenig, H. (1981). The two Berlins. *Travel Holiday*, 156(4), 58–63.

Kolosov, V., & Więckowski, M. (2018). Border changes in Central and Eastern Europe: An introduction. *Geographia Polonica*, 91(1), 5–16.

Lee, C.K., Yoon, Y.S., & Lee, S.K. (2007). Investigating the relationships among perceived value, satisfaction, and recommendations: The case of the Korean DMZ. *Tourism Management*, 28(1), 204–214.

Light, D. (2000). Gazing on communism: Heritage tourism and post-communist identities in Germany, Hungary and Romania. *Tourism Geographies*, 2(2), 157–176.

Lisle, D. (2016). *Holidays in the danger zone: Entanglements of war and tourism*. Minneapolis: University of Minnesota Press.

Lennon, J.J., & Foley, M. (1999). Interpretation of the unimaginable: The US Holocaust Memorial Museum, Washington, DC, and "dark tourism". *Journal of Travel Research*, 38(1), 46–50.

Mahrouse, G. (2016). War-zone tourism: Thinking beyond voyeurism and danger. *ACME: An International Journal for Critical Geographies*, 15(2), 330–345.

Matznetter, J. (1979). Border and tourism: Fundamental relations. In G. Gruber, H. Lamping, W. Lutz, J. Matznetter, & K. Vorlaufer (eds) *Tourism and borders: Proceedings of the meeting of the IGU working group – Geography of tourism and recreation*, pp. 61–73. Frankfurt: Institut fur Wirtschafts und Sozialgeographic der Johann Wolfgang Goethe Universität.

McClelland, A. (2016). The management of heritage in contested cross-border contexts: Emerging research on the island of Ireland. *Journal of Cross Border Studies in Ireland*, 11, 91–104.

Mezzadra, S., & Neilson, B. (2013). *Border as method, or, the multiplication of labor.* Durham, NC: Duke University Press.

Prokkola, E-K., & Lois, M. (2016). Scalar politics of border heritage: An examination of the EU's northern and southern border areas. *Scandinavian Journal of Hospitality and Tourism, 16*(1), 14–35.

Shin, Y.S. (2004). Tourists' perceptions and attitudes towards political boundaries and tourism. *International Journal of Tourism Sciences, 4*(1), 17–37.

Shin, Y.S. (2007). Perception differences between domestic and international visitors in the tourist destination: The case of the borderline, the DMZ area. *Journal of Travel & Tourism Marketing, 21*(2–3), 77–88.

Tarlow, P.E. (2005). Dark tourism: The appealing 'dark' side of tourism and more. In M. Novelli (ed) *Niche tourism – contemporary issues, trends and cases*, pp. 47–58. Oxford: Elsevier.

Timothy, D.J. (1995). Political boundaries and tourism: Borders as tourist attractions. *Tourism Management, 16*(7), 525–532.

Timothy, D.J. (2000). Borderlands: An unlikely tourist destination. *IBRU Boundary and Security Bulletin, 8*(1), 57–65.

Timothy, D.J. (2001). *Tourism and political boundaries.* London: Routledge.

Timothy, D.J. (2013). Tourism, war and political instability: Territorial and religious perspectives. In R. Butler, & W. Suntikul (eds) *Tourism and war*, pp. 12–25. London: Routledge.

Timothy, D.J. (2019). Tourism, border disputes and claims to territorial sovereignty. In R.K. Isaac, E. Çakmak, & R. Butler (eds) *Tourism and hospitality in conflict-ridden destinations*, pp. 25–38. London: Routledge.

Timothy, D.J. (2021). *Cultural heritage and tourism: An introduction*, 2nd Edn. Bristol: Channel View Publications.

Timothy, D.J., & Boyd, S.W. (2015). *Tourism and trails: Cultural, ecological and management issues.* Bristol: Channel View Publications.

Timothy, D.J., Prideaux, B. & Kim, S.S. (2004). Tourism at borders of conflict and (de)militarized zones. In T.V. Singh (Ed.) *New horizons in tourism: Strange experiences and stranger practices*, pp. 83–94. Wallingford: CABI.

Wachowiak, H., & Engels, D. (2006). Academics on cross-border issues in tourism around the world: A commentary international literature bibliography. In H. Wachowiak (ed.) *Tourism and borders: Contemporary issues, politics and international research*, pp. 149–266. Aldershot: Ashgate.

Waterman, S. (1987). Partitioned states. *Political Geography Quarterly, 6*(2), 151–170.

Więckowski, M. (in press). How border tripoints offer opportunities for transboundary tourism development. *Tourism Geographies.*

Więckowski, M., & Timothy, D.J. (2021). Tourism and an evolving international boundary: Bordering, debordering and rebordering on Usedom Island, Poland-Germany. *Journal of Destination Marketing & Management, 22*, 100647.

Wiedenhoft Murphy, W.A. (2010). Touring the troubles in West Belfast: Building peace or reproducing conflict? *Peace & Change, 35*(4), 537–560.

# 16
# BORDERS AS DARK TOURISM SPACES

*Richard Sharpley*

## Introduction

In her novel *The Sunrise*, Victoria Hislop (2014) weaves fact and fiction into a story set in Cyprus in the early 1970s. At that time, the island was becoming an increasingly popular tourist destination—more than a quarter of a million international arrivals were recorded in 1973 (Ayers, 2000)—and the tourism sector was developing rapidly, particularly in the resort areas of Kyrenia and Famagusta. In her book, Hislop tells the story of the opening of a new (fictitious) hotel, The Sunrise, by the beach at Famagusta and how it quickly becomes one of the most successful and exclusive resort hotels on the island. That success is, however, short-lived. In reality, the development of Famagusta as a tourist destination was brought to an abrupt halt by Turkey's invasion and subsequent annexation of the northern part of Cyprus in 1974 (Sharpley, 2003), and it is in the context of that event that Hislop's story unfolds. As Famagusta falls under Turkish control, she relates the destruction brought upon the city and its inhabitants through the experiences of two families, one Greek Cypriot and the other Turkish Cypriot, who are connected through sons who both work at the Sunrise hotel. Finding themselves isolated in a part of the city which was cleared of residents and cut off from the rest of the island, the families manage to take refuge in the empty hotel for a number of months, finally being obliged to escape. Eventually, they meet up again in north London to where, in actuality, many Cypriots emigrated following the Turkish invasion.

Cyprus today remains, of course, a divided island, with the (Greek) Republic of Cyprus to the south and the self-declared Turkish Republic of Northern Cyprus (TRNC) separated by a border, the UN Buffer Zone. At the eastern end of that buffer zone, but controversially remaining under Turkish rather than UN control, the former beach resort of Famagusta (or Varosha as it is now known to distinguish it from the contemporary city of Famagusta of which it was once a part) has, since 1974, been an inaccessible ghost town, a "no-man's-land". It was the distant sight of Varosha that first inspired Hislop's novel but the ironic point here is that, whereas once tourists were attracted to the resort to enjoy its beach, hotels and local culture, nowadays they go there to gaze upon it from the outside. Not only is it possible to look down along the beach from the northern, Turkish side but also there are more distant viewing platforms in the Greek sector from which the city can be seen (Figure 16.1). In other words, Varosha, as an inaccessible border space, has become a tourist attraction.

*Figure 16.1* View towards Varosha.

Photo: R. Sharpley

As discussed later in this chapter, other sections of the border that divides Cyprus are also tourist attractions, particularly within the capital city of Nicosia. As such, the Cypriot Buffer Zone, together with Varosha, is but one of innumerable examples of border spaces, whether actual (physical or perceived) borders or border regions, to which tourists are for one reason or another attracted; indeed, in this context, reference is frequently made to Cyprus in the literature. For example, Timothy (2006) describes how transformations in the nature of cross-border tourism on the island have reflected the dynamic and, arguably, improving wider political context, whilst Díaz-Sauceda et al. (2015) explore cross-border tourists' behavioural intentions at the "Green Line" border crossing in Nicosia (see also Webster & Timothy, 2006). It is, therefore, not surprising that the relationship between tourism and borders, from borders as barriers to tourism to borders as attractors of tourism, has been the focus of increasing academic attention (e.g., Blasco, Guia & Prats, 2014; Sofield, 2006; Stoffelen & Vanneste, 2017; Timothy, 1995, 2001; Wachowiack, 2006).

A review of this literature is beyond the scope of this chapter, not least because many key themes and issues are considered elsewhere in this volume. However, what is perhaps surprising is that, given the very nature of borders as "demarcations of 'us' and 'them'" (Sofield, 2006: 102), of nations, societies, cultures and political systems and, hence, of borders as spaces that are potentially difficult or problematic, no attempt has been made to conceptualize particular manifestations of border tourism as such. More specifically, not only may borders and border regions be sites of conflict, whether in the literal sense of physical, armed conflict between groups or nations or where competing political, social, economic, legal or cultural systems meet and conflict, but also their attraction to tourists might lie in the evidence or outcome of that conflict. That is, as spaces of human tragedy or suffering, of deprivation or crime, or even as spaces that separate the known from the unknown or the secure from the threatening, borders can possess or convey a "darkness" that is in some way appealing or intriguing to tourists.

This is not to say that what might be referred to as dark border tourism has been overlooked in the literature. For instance, a number of studies focus on tourism to the demilitarized zone (DMZ) between North and South Korea (e.g., Bigley et al., 2010; Koh, 2019; Lee, Yoon & Lee, 2007; Shin, 2007). Tourism to borders that Israel shares with various neighbouring countries has also attracted academic attention (e.g., Gelbman, 2008; Mansfeld & Korman, 2015) whilst, unsurprisingly, the Mexico–USA border has been the focus of much research both as a border space in general and from a tourism perspective in particular (e.g., Arts, 2019; Berdell & Ghoshal, 2015; Payan, 2014; Shirk, 2014; Staudt, 2014). Nevertheless, the extent to which the concept of dark tourism, as an increasingly popular topic within tourism studies, can be applied and potentially contribute to understanding the phenomenon of border tourism has yet to be considered.

The purpose of this chapter, therefore, is to address this gap in the literature. Specifically, I seek to explore the relevance of dark tourism to the study of borders as tourist attractions and, in so doing, to propose a taxonomy of borders as dark tourism spaces. As such, I do not attempt to theorize borders or border regions as dark tourism spaces, not least because, as discussed shortly, the concept of dark tourism itself remains widely contested and, as argued elsewhere, "theoretically fragile" (Sharpley, 2009: 6). Rather, I seek to identify the diversity of characteristics of borders that might contribute to them being understood as dark spaces and, consequently, the significance of their attraction to tourists. Evidently, then, the first task is to review briefly the concept of dark tourism as a framework for the subsequent discussions in this chapter.

## Towards an Understanding of Dark Tourism

The term "dark tourism" was first coined more than two decades ago (Foley & Lennon, 1996), though the touristic phenomenon it refers to significantly predates this; as Seaton (1999) and others observe, a relationship between death, suffering and tourism has been in evidence for centuries, indeed for as long as people have been able to travel (Sharpley, 2009). Nevertheless, it is only more recently, even within the history of tourism studies, that dark tourism has emerged as an identifiable focus of academic attention, the catalyst undeniably being the publication of Lennon and Foley's (2000) text *Dark Tourism: The Attraction of Death and Disaster*. Since then, and perhaps reflecting what some consider to be wider societal interest or fascination in death (Howarth, 2007; Walter, 2009), not only has it evolved into one of the more popular areas in the study of tourism but also, in practice, recent years have witnessed an apparent increase in both the provision and consumption of dark tourism experiences. As Stone (2013: 307) observes, "the commodification of death for popular touristic consumption, whether in the guise of memorials and museums, visitor attractions, special events and exhibitions or specific tours, has become a focus for mainstream tourism providers".

However, despite the burgeoning research into dark tourism within both the tourism literature and related fields of study, it remains, as noted above, a controversial and contested concept; what appear to be straightforward definitions tend to disguise its complexity and inherently subjective and pejorative nature, particularly when considered in terms of the (dark) tourist experience. Broadly speaking, dark tourism can be thought of as "tourism associated with sites of death, disaster and depravity" (Lennon & Foley, 1999: 46) or, as Light (2017: 277) suggests, "an umbrella term for any form of tourism that is somehow related to death, suffering, atrocity, tragedy or crime". From this perspective, it is apparent that the concept of dark tourism embraces an enormous diversity of sites and attractions from, at one extreme, sites of or related to genocide to, at the other extreme, what Stone (2006: 152) refers to as "dark fun factories", such as houses or horror. Hence, not only is a precise understanding and analysis of the concept challenged by its increasingly broad application—as Sharpley and Stone (2009: 250) conclude, "the blanket categorisation of ... places or events of, or associated with, death as 'dark tourism' simplifies and hides a multitude of meanings and purposes with respect to both their production and consumption", but also the distinction between dark tourism and other labels/categorizations attached to such sites and events, whether sub-categories of dark tourism (e.g., disaster tourism, battlefield tourism) or alternative conceptualizations (e.g., heritage tourism, genealogy tourism), becomes increasingly fuzzy. For this reason, it is not surprising that some suggest the term "dark tourism" should be abandoned (Bowman & Pezzullo, 2009).

In addition, a tension continues to exist in the literature between the production and consumption of dark tourism or, in other words, between viewing it from the perspective of supply (as a "product"—a place or an event) or demand (motivation, experience). Much of the initial work on the topic was concerned with the former and was devoted to identifying and justifying the categorization of different tourist sites and attractions as "dark", as well as to their management and interpretation. Indeed, the complexities of interpreting dark or difficult heritage can be traced back to Uzell's (1989) work on the "hot" interpretation of conflict sites whilst, contemporaneously with Foley and Lennon's (1996) ground-breaking writing on dark tourism, Tunbridge and Ashworth (1996) introduced the notion of dissonant heritage as a framework for exploring the challenges facing the management and interpretation of dark sites (see also Ashworth & Hartmann, 2005). In these earlier works, the role of the tourist—their motivations and experiences—was largely overlooked or, more precisely, the potentially thorny issue that tourists might positively seek out "dark" experiences was neatly sidestepped. Lennon and Foley (2000: 23), for example, suggested that visits to dark sites simply occur serendipitously or out of curiosity amongst those "who happen to be in the area".

Nevertheless, the great majority of definitions of dark tourism, or alternatively "thanatourism" (Seaton, 1996), the distinction between the two being considered in detail by Light (2017), establish dark tourism as a form of consumption, with numerous commentators referring to it as travel to or visiting sites of death and suffering (e.g., Johnston & Mandelartz, 2016; Preece & Price, 2005; Stone, 2006; Tanaś, 2014; Tarlow, 2005), although Best (2007: 38) suggests more explicitly that visitors to dark sites are individuals who are "motivated primarily to experience the death and suffering of others for the purpose of enjoyment, pleasure and satisfaction". In so doing, she alludes to the problem (and prejudicial assumptions) that emerge from aligning "tourism" with "dark". Though an intriguing juxtaposition, the word "dark" is considered, at least in Western cultures, to connote "something disturbing, troubling, suspicious, weird, morbid or perverse" (Bowman & Pezzullo, 2009: 190). Hence, the suggestion might be that not only are dark sites distasteful, unethical or exploitative in the way they interpret or commemorate tragic events but also that those who visit them (that is, "dark" tourists) possess a morbid fascination or curiosity with death, or engage in voyeurism or *Schadenfreude*.

To some, this is undoubtedly the case. Schaller (2007), for example, argues that tourism to genocide sites such as those in Rwanda can only be described as voyeuristic, while Cole (1999: 115) admits that "there can be little doubt that an element of voyeurism is central to Holocaust tourism". However, the increasingly extensive research into the consumption and experience of dark tourism reveals that numerous other factors may stimulate visits to dark sites. Indeed, as Light (2017: 285) notes in his review, "there is little evidence that an interest in death (including morbid curiosity) is an important motive for visiting places and attractions that are labelled dark". This is supported by Raine (2013) who found that there exists amongst visitors to burial sites a continuum of purposes, from "devotion" (mourning/pilgrims), through "experience" (morbid curiosity) and "discovery" (information seekers/hobbyists) to "incidental" (sightseers/recreationists). In other words, although dark sites and attractions can be categorized by their varying association with death and suffering, the same cannot be said for visitors to them; their motives are as diverse as for engaging in any other form of tourism. Hence, it is argued that the experience of dark sites might be best understood in terms of tourists' emotional responses to visiting such sites (Ashworth & Isaac, 2015).

This, in turn, suggests that dark tourism should be thought of as neither a category of site or attraction—such is the diversity of places or events that fall under the increasingly expansive umbrella of dark tourism that the term is becoming meaningless—nor as a specific form of tourism consumption. Indeed, only in highly specific circumstances is the term "dark tourist" applicable (Sharpley, 2005). Rather, acknowledging that its significance lies primarily in the role which dark sites and attractions play in mediating between the event(s) they represent and visitors to them, dark tourism should perhaps be seen as a *context* for exploring this relationship and, hence, the ways in which tourists understand or confront the death and suffering that the site signifies, represents or memorializes (Stone & Sharpley, 2008). And it is from this perspective on the concept of dark tourism that I now consider the ways in which borders and border regions might be considered dark spaces or, more precisely, the manner in which different types or categories of borders offer tourists the opportunity to confront death, suffering and the "darker side".

## Towards a Taxonomy of Dark Tourism Border Spaces

As widely acknowledged, borders are fundamental to tourism (Prokkola, 2010). International tourism involves, by definition, the crossing of tangible national (political) borders (Timothy, 1995) or, more precisely, the physical movement of tourists from one country or jurisdiction to another. At the same time, all tourism, including domestic tourism, is in a sense defined by the crossing of a perceived or imagined (or liminal) border from one condition to another, such as from being at work to being on holiday or perhaps from the familiar to the unfamiliar (Sharpley, 2022). And as has also long been argued, borders (tangible or imagined) may, on the one hand, act as barriers to tourism but, on the other hand, as tourist attractions (Timothy, 1998). Reflecting a variety of factors including improvements in international political and trade relations and regional development programmes, recent decades have witnessed a decline in the former, although many international borders were closed in 2020–2021 in response to the COVID-19 pandemic. Equally, the latter has also increasingly become the case; rather than simply being crossed, a greater number of borders and border regions have become tourist attractions in their own right, often, and ironically, for the very same reasons that they previously acted as barriers, such as political instability, criminal activities and armed conflicts (Mansfeld & Korman, 2015).

In other words, the "darkness" of borders and border regions that, in some cases, once discouraged tourism now stimulates it. Moreover, it is possible to categorize such borders as dark tourism spaces according to the nature of their dark character (but not to the "shade" or intensity of darkness that has underpinned other such taxonomies) (see Sharpley, 2005 and Stone, 2006) and the manner in which that darkness is significant to the tourist experience. Hence I now propose a number of distinctive manifestations of dark border spaces that may attract tourists. However, it is important to commence this discussion by first acknowledging that, in contrast, there remain dark border spaces which may not be entered or crossed by tourists owing to the darkness that lies (or is perceived to exist) beyond. These are referred to here as impenetrable dark borders.

## *Impenetrable Dark Borders: A Barrier to the Darker Side*

There are two principal reasons why borders cannot be crossed by, or are impenetrable to, tourists. On the one hand, and quite evidently, nations might wish to deny entry to international visitors and hence close their borders or, at least, permit entry for only specific reasons. Traditionally, this would usually have been for political or ideological reasons, although this has become increasingly rare in recent decades. However, national responses to the COVID-19 crisis are a contemporary manifestation of border closures. On the other hand, tourists themselves may choose not to cross particular national borders, often as an outcome of risk aversion (Yang & Nair, 2014) but also because they may simply not be interested in visiting certain countries.

In the context of this chapter, however, particular borders might be considered impenetrable by some tourists because of the perceived darkness that lies beyond. That is, given the significance of dark tourism destinations as places which tourists choose (for whatever reason) to visit in order to confront the death and/or suffering with which they are associated, it is perhaps inevitable that a desire to avoid such confrontation will result in avoidance behaviour. Putting it another way, it is claimed that participation in dark tourism may enhance an individual's sense of ontological security (Stone & Sharpley, 2008). In contemporary societies in which death and dying are increasingly bracketed out (Giddens, 1991), dark tourism offers tourists a legitimized space to contemplate their and others' suffering and mortality. Equally, however, it may have the opposite effect. When confronted by the death or suffering of others, tourists may feel uncomfortable, the parameters of their life-world might be challenged and the fragility of their existence might be emphasized. Hence, rather than transforming "the seemingly meaningless into the meaningful" (Stone & Sharpley, 2008: 588), dark tourism may in fact enhance an individual's ontological insecurity. For instance, anecdotal evidence suggests that some people are unwilling to visit India because, despite the country's innumerable cultural attractions, they are unwilling, unlike so-called slum tourists (Dyson, 2012; Slikker & Koens, 2015), to confront its endemic poverty. Similarly, although research has demonstrated that visiting Rwanda's genocide sites can, for some tourists, be a cathartic experience (Sharpley & Friedrich, 2016), it is likely that the country is rejected by many others as a potential destination owing to widespread evidence of the events of 1994. In both cases, the counties' borders are, therefore, an impenetrable (dark) barrier.

## *"Dicing with Death" Border Regions*

In his playful alliterative categorization of dark tourism, Graham Dann (1998) identifies "dicing with death" as a potential motive for participation in dark tourism. The thrill of travelling to dangerous places (and surviving them) has long been encouraged by publications such as P. J. O'Rourke's (1988) *Holidays in Hell* and Robert Pelton's (2003) *The World's Most Dangerous Places*, whilst a variety of websites offer contemporary lists of, for example, the ten most dangerous cities worth visiting (World Travel Guide, 2018) and variations on the theme of the world's ten most dangerous places to travel to or in (e.g., Ball, n.d.; Maheshwari, n.d.). Amongst these, an interesting inclusion is the resort of Acapulco in Mexico which, in the mid-twentieth century, was one of the world's most famous beach tourism destinations. Travelling to such "perilous places" (Dann, 1998) might be undertaken simply for the challenge. Equally, it may be seen as a means of enhancing self-identity; "I survived El Salvador" T-shirts were popular in the 1980s amongst backpackers traversing Central America—or heightening one's sense of mortality.

Though not usually appearing in popular lists of dangerous places to visit (or avoid), the appeal of some border regions to tourists might lie in their potential threat to personal safety and security. That is, tourists may purposefully decide to travel to or across particular border spaces in the full knowledge that they may be endangered in one way or another, whether through being caught up in cross-border conflict or becoming the target of criminal activities, from robbery to kidnapping. Equally, some may visit dangerous border spaces either unaware of the potential risk or in the belief that "it won't happen to them". In 2011, for example, tourists were advised to avoid travelling to the northern Kenyan coastal area bordering Somalia following a small number of cross-border kidnappings of tourists staying at resorts in that area (*Telegraph*, 2011). However, those who do choose to travel to dangerous border regions, such as along the (in)famous Khyber Pass on the Pakistan–Afghanistan border or across the Turkish–Syrian border, are knowingly or, perhaps more precisely, perceiving themselves to be "dicing with death", for it might be logically assumed that such tourists expect to survive and, hence, to be able to relate their adventures on social media; as Calamur (2017) observes, travel in war zones accords tourists with "ultimate bragging rights". Nevertheless, the extent to which tourists are indeed dicing with death in such dark borders regions is debatable. Some organizers of such travel experiences, such as Untamed Borders (see untamedborders.com), claim that their purpose is to bring prosperity to conflict areas through tourism and to educate tourists, while in a powerful critique, Mahrouse (2016) suggests that war zone tourism is little more than a form of controlled adventure tourism. That is, with tourists often being guided (or protected) by ex-military security professionals, they are consuming not danger but safety marketed as risk. Conversely, independent travel through dark border regions is undoubtedly more risky but, irrespective of whether it is actual or perceived, it is the inherent danger of travelling in dark border regions that, for whatever reason, is the allure for tourists.

## *Dark Borders of (Past) Conflict*

In contrast to dark border spaces defined by ongoing conflict and other immediate threats to the safety and security of tourists, there exist many border spaces where conflict occurred in the past. Indeed, it is likely that, collectively, such borders comprise the greatest number of dark border tourism spaces. This is not perhaps surprising. It has long been claimed that warfare-related sites, including battlefields, museums, memorials and graveyards, "probably constitute the largest single category of tourist attraction in the world" (Smith, 1996: 248; see also Butler & Suntikul, 2013), and inevitably, border regions are often sites of warfare. At same time, however, and for the purposes of this chapter, other forms of conflict resulting in human death and suffering, such as between competing political systems (e.g., the Berlin Wall) or between social groups based upon religious or ethnic differences, the sectarian violence in Northern Ireland being a notable example, can be included in this category (Wiedenhoft Murphy, 2010).

Given the enormous diversity of dark border spaces that might be defined as sites of past conflict, within the context of this chapter it is a difficult, if not impossible, task to explore comprehensively and completely the nature and the attraction to tourists of such dark sites. Nevertheless, on the one hand, dark border spaces of past (though not necessarily resolved) conflict can be conceptualized simply as places which offer evidence of that conflict through physical structures and/or physical evidence of conflict (e.g., damaged buildings), museums, memorials to the victims and other forms of interpretation, the significance of which is likely to be enhanced by their border location. On the other hand, the motives for tourist visits are likely to be complex and diverse, varying from education or historical interest to personal commemoration, from simple curiosity to positive support for peace and reconciliation. Again, the border location may well be a significant factor in both the desire to visit and in the experience of such places, not least because the border itself represents tangible, physical evidence of the divide between the competing sides in the conflict. One notable example of this are the so-called "peace walls" in Belfast, Northern Ireland. These are not only popular attractions in their own right (many boast political and philosophical murals) but, standing as they do between (or more precisely, segregating) the city's two communities, they serve as both a stark reminder of the sectarian divide (a cultural and political divide within the city) and "the Troubles" but also compete with the contemporary political peace narrative (Byrne & Gormley-Heenan, 2014).

It should also be noted that examples of past (or post-) conflict border sites can be found around the world and, given both the diversity of both sites that may be labelled as "dark" and wider understandings of borders (e.g., an island nation's coastline can be considered to be its border), the category of "dark borders of past conflict" is potentially both broad and imprecise. For example, many well-known (and much visited) coastal battlefield sites, such as Gallipoli (Çakar, 2020), are technically located in border spaces but, arguably, would not be considered conceptually as border tourism destinations. Hence, for definitional purposes, it is only land borders (between or within nations) as sites of past conflict that we are concerned with here, some of which, such as Israel's borders with its neighbouring countries and the Korean DMZ have, as previously noted, benefited from academic attention. Returning to the case of Cyprus, the border between north and south can also be considered a powerful example. Although it is the contemporary crossing between the Greek and Turkish sectors of Nicosia (a dark site that can equally be thought of as a dark "us and them" border—see next section) that is most widely considered in the literature, it is the border buffer zone across the city displaying material evidence of the conflict (see Figure 16.2) as well as abandoned villages and military

*Figure 16.2* UN Buffer zone in Nicosia, Cyprus.

Photo: R. Sharpley

look-out towers alongside the road leading east towards Famagusta that offer tourists a more tangible sense of the darkness of the yet-unresolved "Cyprus Problem".

## Dark "Us and Them" Borders

A recognized sub-category of dark tourism is what some refer to broadly as "poverty tourism" (Rolfes, 2010), embracing more specific touristic experiences such as slum tourism (Dyson, 2012; Steinbrink, 2012), favela tourism (Frisch 2012) or township tourism (Booyens, 2010). Irrespective of terminology, however, a common factor is tourists visiting and gazing upon people living in less fortunate circumstances than their own or, from a "dark" perspective, witnessing the (typically poverty related) suffering of others. As with other forms of dark tourism, it is likely that a variety of motives are at play amongst those participating in poverty tourism, although the limited research in this regard is inconclusive. Chhabra and Chowdhury (2012), for example, identified a significant degree of voyeurism amongst slum tourists in India, suggesting that visits may be motivated by a degree of *Schadenfreude*. More positively, Rolfes's (2010) research revealed an interest in local culture and the desire to learn more about life in townships as dominant motives to join a township tour, whilst Ma (2010) concludes, somewhat ambiguously, that slum tourists are primarily driven by curiosity. Interestingly, although poverty tourism is often organized by and contributes to the well-being of the local poor community, the extant research does not point to social responsibility motives on the part of tourists, implying that the principal attraction of poverty tourism is to witness the contrast between "us" and "them".

Most, if not all, research into poverty tourism focuses on communities within countries. However, the concept can be translated into the context of border tourism where, in a sense, different worlds collide or, more precisely, where borders demarcate richer and poorer societies and/or states with opposing political systems, resulting in citizens enjoying what are perceived to be (by "us") greater or (in the case of "them") lesser degrees of well-being. This, in turn, suggests that the attraction of such dark border regions to tourists is to witness what they consider to be the suffering (or at least, the disadvantaged) lifestyles of others.

There are numerous examples of what might be described as cross-border inequality, where a relatively wealthy and politically stable country borders one which is more impoverished and unstable. An extreme example is the border between Saudi Arabia and Yemen, in which approximate per capita GDP is, respectively, USD47,000 and USD2,300 (Trading Economics, 2020). Clearly, this border region is not visited by tourists; indeed, the same could be said for many such borders around the world. Nevertheless, as noted in the previous section, one manifestation of this can arguably be found in Nicosia, Cyprus, where tourists from the south can cross into the culturally and economically distinctive northern Turkish sector of the city; however, although per capita income in the TRNC is roughly half of that in the Greek Republic of Cyprus, it is more likely the political context that adds a dark dimension to a visit.

In contrast, the more than 3,000-kilometre-long border between Mexico and the USA not only divides two countries but separates the "global north" and the "global south" (Shirk, 2014). It also offers significant opportunities for tourists from the USA to engage in a form of poverty tourism. Not only is the Mexico–USA border one of the world's most popular (in terms of daily numbers) but also "tourism has been particularly important in Mexico's border states" (Berdell & Ghoshal, 2015: 15). The great majority of tourists are *excursionistas*, or day visitors, crossing the border for work, family visits or shopping but, according to Arts (2019), border-crossing tours have become increasingly popular with a number of companies based in both countries offering tours of various kinds. For most companies, the stated objective is to inform or educate tourists on the challenges of living in Mexico's border regions. As such, they can be considered a form of dark border tourism. Interestingly, however, Arts's (2019: 56) research reveals that the tours are typically promoted as "entertainment, sensation, experiencing the out of the ordinary and fun", highlighting the difference between the two countries but not necessarily the problematic or even dangerous nature of life in the border regions. Hence, the potential mediating or educative role of (dark) tourism along the Mexico–USA border appears to be diluted and, arguably, more akin to the voyeuristic experiences identified in other research into poverty tourism. Whether this is the case in other potential "us and them" tourism border regions, such as that between South Africa and Mozambique, would however require further research.

## Dark Crossing Borders

The final category of dark tourism space to be proposed in this chapter is "dark crossing borders". Borders are the site of both the legitimate and illegitimate physical movement of people and goods. Legitimate movement includes recognized, authorized trade and, of course, tourism, whilst illegitimate movements include smuggling, the trafficking of illegal substances and illegal immigration which can collectively be thought of as the darker side of cross-border activity. Such illegitimate or criminal activities are, according to Moré (2011), most prevalent across borders of high inequality, although they undoubtedly occur across most, if not all, borders. Less certain, however, is the extent to which a relationship exists between border tourism and the illegitimate movement of goods and people. On the one hand, tourists may, for example, travel to border regions to see refugee camps and, perhaps, to volunteer to help the participants in (or victims of) illegal immigration, whilst they might also witness it unintentionally. It is not unusual for tourists at the Calais ferry terminal in northern France to see groups of refugees seeking to travel (illegally) across to the UK. In the extreme, they might even seek the experience, popularized by David Farrier in the Netflix series *The Dark Tourist* and discussed by Arts (2019), of participating in a tour which simulates the challenges faced by immigrants attempting to cross illegally from Mexico into the USA, although this should perhaps be more accurately defined as a lighter, themed form of dark tourism (Stone, 2006). Equally, just as tourists now travel to the city of Medellín, Colombia, attracted by its association with Pablo Escobar and his Medellín drug cartel (Van Broek, 2018), Gelbman and Timothy (2010) discuss the manner in which the history of drug smuggling is part of the attraction for tourists visiting the Golden Triangle region where the borders of northern Thailand, eastern Myanmar and western Laos converge.

On the other hand, tourists may travel to border regions with the explicit intention of purchasing illicit substances or participating in other activities, such as gambling or sex tourism, which may be legally permitted or perhaps tolerated by the authorities in liminal border spaces. In other words, border tourism becomes a form of dark tourism when tourists cross borders with the intention of engaging in illicit (dark) activities, with the added dimension of not "dicing with death" but "avoiding the authorities" should they attempt to carry drugs or other illicit goods back across the border.

## Conclusion

Over the last 25 years, dark tourism has attracted increasing academic attention; however, to date it has not been applied conceptually to the specific context of border tourism. This is, perhaps, a surprising omission given that many border regions may possess an intrinsic darkness reflecting competing or conflicting peoples, cultures and ideologies. In other words, borders may be sites of human suffering, of deprivation or crime or, as suggested in the introduction, simply spaces that separate the known from the unknown. In this chapter, then, in seeking to address this gap in the literature, I have offered an exploratory and, perhaps, speculative perspective on border tourism through the lens of dark tourism, a concept which itself remains contested in academic circles. In so doing, I have proposed a taxonomy of "dark border spaces" based upon the way in which they mediate between dark events/activities and tourists who are attracted to them. In addition to impenetrable dark borders, four other categories have been suggested: "dicing with death" border regions; dark borders of (past) conflict; dark "us and them" borders; and dark crossing borders. Inevitably, these are not necessarily mutually exclusive; some borders (or, rather, their attraction to tourists) might be identifiable with more than one, if not all, of these categories. At the same time, borders which are the site of dark tourism may equally be defined according to other parameters, reflecting the fuzziness of the concept of dark tourism more generally. Nevertheless, it is hoped that the chapter adds an additional dimension to the study of border tourism whilst providing a conceptual foundation for empirical research into the darker side of tourism in border regions.

# References

Arts, A. (2019). *Now Let Us Show It You: A Multimodal Discourse Analysis of Websites Offering United States-Mexico Border Crossing Tours*. Unpublished master's thesis, Radboud University Nijmegen.

Ashworth, G., & Hartmann, R. (2005). *Horror and Human Tragedy Revisited: The Management of Sites of Atrocities for Tourism*. New York: Cognizant.

Ashworth, G., & Isaac, R. (2015). Have we illuminated the dark? Shifting perspectives on 'dark' tourism. *Tourism Recreation Research*, 40(3), 316–325.

Ayers, R. (2000). Tourism as a passport to development in small states: The case of Cyprus. *International Journal of Social Economics*, 27(2), 114–133.

Ball, R. (n.d.). *The 10 Most Dangerous Places to Travel to Around the Globe*. Available at: https://www.mapquest.com/travel/most-dangerous-places-to-travel/ (Accessed 28 July 2020).

Berdell, J., & Ghoshal, A. (2015). US–Mexico border tourism and day trips: An aberration in globalization? *Latin American Economic Review*, 24(15), 1–18.

Best, M. (2007). Norfolk Island: Thanatourism, history and visitors' emotions. *Shima: The International Journal of Research into Island Cultures*, 1(2), 30–48.

Bigley, J.D., Lee, C.K., Chon, J., & Yoon, Y. (2010). Motivations for war-related tourism: A case of DMZ visitors in Korea. *Tourism Geographies*, 12(3), 371–394.

Blasco, D., Guia, J., & Prats, L. (2014). Emergence of governance in cross-border destinations. *Annals of Tourism Research*, 49, 159–173.

Booyens, I. (2010). Rethinking township tourism: Towards responsible tourism development in South African townships. *Development Southern Africa*, 27(2), 273–287.

Bowman, M., & Pezzullo, P. (2009). What's so 'dark' about 'dark tourism'? Death, tours, and performance. *Tourist Studies*, 9(3), 187–202.

Butler, R., & Suntikul, W. (Eds) (2013). *Tourism and War*. Abingdon: Routledge.

Byrne, J., & Gormley-Heenan, C. (2014). Beyond the walls: Dismantling Belfast's conflict architecture. *City*, 18(4-5), 447–454.

Çakar, K. (2020). Investigation of the motivations and experiences of tourists visiting the Gallipoli Peninsula as a dark tourism destination. *European Journal of Tourism Research*, 24, 1–30.

Calamur, K. (2017). Why vacation in war zones? *The Atlantic*, 13 October. Available at: https://www.theatlantic.com/international/archive/2017/10/war-zone-tourism/542814/ (Accessed 25 August 2020).

Chhabra, D., & Chowdhury, A. (2012). Slum tourism: Ethical or voyeuristic. *Tourism Review International*, 16(1), 69–73.

Cole, T. (1999). *Selling the Holocaust. From Auschwitz to Schindler: How history Is Bought, Packaged and Sold*. New York: Routledge.

Dann, G. (1998). *The Dark Side of Tourism*. Aix-en-Provence: Centre International de Recherches et d'Études Touristiques.

Díaz-Sauceda, J., Palau-Saumell, R., Forgas-Coll, S., & Sánchez-García, J. (2015). Cross-border tourists' behavioral intentions: The Green Line of Nicosia, Cyprus. *Tourism Geographies*, 17(5), 758–779.

Dyson, P. (2012). Slum tourism: Representing and interpreting 'reality' in Dharavi, Mumbai. *Tourism Geographies*, 14(2), 254–274.

Foley, M., & Lennon, J. (1996). JFK and dark tourism: A fascination with assassination. *International Journal of Heritage Studies*, 2(4), 198–211.

Frisch, T. (2012). Glimpses of another world: The favela as a tourist attraction. *Tourism Geographies*, 14(2), 320–338.

Gelbman, A. (2008). Border tourism in Israel: Conflict, peace, fear and hope. *Tourism Geographies*, 10(2), 193–213.

Gelbman, A., & Timothy, D.J. (2010). From hostile boundaries to tourist attractions. *Current Issues in Tourism*, 13(3), 239–259.

Giddens, A. (1991). *Modernity and Self Identity*. Cambridge: Polity Press.

Hislop, V. (2014). *The Sunrise*. London: Headline Publishing Group.

Howarth, G. (2007). *Death and Dying: A Sociological Introduction*. Cambridge: Polity Press.

Johnston, T., & Mandelartz, P. (2016). Introduction. In T. Johnston & P. Mandelartz (Eds), *Thanatourism: Case Studies in Travel to the Dark Side*. Oxford: Goodfellow.

Koh, D.Y. (2019). The Placeness of the DMZ: The rise of DMZ tourism and the real DMZ project. *Positions Asia Critique*, 27(4), 653–685.

Lee, C.K., Yoon, Y.S., & Lee, S.K. (2007). Investigating the relationships among perceived value, satisfaction, and recommendations: The case of the Korean DMZ. *Tourism Management*, 28(1), 204–214.

Lennon, J.J., & Foley, M. (1999). Interpretation of the unimaginable: The US Holocaust Memorial Museum, Washington, DC, and 'dark tourism'. *Journal of Travel Research*, 38(1), 46–50.

Lennon, J.J., & Foley, M. (2000). *Dark Tourism: The Attraction of Death and Disaster*. London: Continuum.

Light, D. (2017). Progress in dark tourism and thanatourism research: An uneasy relationship with heritage tourism. *Tourism Management*, 61, 275–301.

Ma, B. (2010). A trip into the controversy: A study of slum tourism travel motivations. *2009-2010 Penn Humanities Forum on Connections*, 12, 1–50.

Maheshwari, E. (n.d.). 10 Most Dangerous Places in The World. Available at: https://traveltriangle.com/blog/most-dangerous-places-in-the-world/ (Accessed 28 July 2020).

Mahrouse, G. (2016). War-zone tourism: Thinking beyond voyeurism and danger. *ACME: An International Journal for Critical Geographers*, 15(2), 330–345.

Mansfeld, Y., & Korman, T. (2015). Between war and peace: Conflict heritage tourism along three Israeli border areas. *Tourism Geographies*, 17(3), 437–460.

Moré, I. (2011). *The Borders of Inequality: Where Wealth and Poverty Collide*. Tucson: University of Arizona Press.

O'Rourke, P.J. (1988). *Holidays in Hell*. London: Picador.

Payan, T. (2014). Ciudad Juárez: A perfect storm on the US–Mexico Border. *Journal of Borderlands Studies*, 29(4), 435–447.

Pelton, R. (2003). *The World's Most Dangerous Places*, 5th Edn. London: Harper.

Preece, T., & Price, G. (2005). Motivations and participants in dark tourism: A case study of Port Arthur, Tasmania, Australia, in C. Ryan, S. Page, & M. Aicken (Eds), *Taking Tourism to the Limits: Issues, Concepts and Managerial Perspectives*, pp. 191–198. Oxford: Elsevier.

Prokkola, E-K. (2010). Borders in tourism: The transformation of the Swedish–Finnish border landscape. *Current Issues in Tourism*, 13(3), 223–238.

Raine, R. (2013). A dark tourist spectrum. *International Journal of Culture, Tourism and Hospitality Research*, 7(3), 242–256.

Rolfes, M. (2010). Poverty tourism: Theoretical reflections and empirical findings regarding an extraordinary form of tourism. *GeoJournal*, 75(5), 421–442.

Schaller, D. (2007). Genocide tourism: Educational value or voyeurism? *Journal of Genocide Research*, 9(4), 513–515.

Seaton, A. (1996). Guided by the dark: From thanatopsis to thanatourism. *International Journal of Heritage Studies*, 2(4), 234–244.

Seaton, A. (1999). War and thanatourism: Waterloo 1815-1914. *Annals of Tourism Research*, 26(1), 130–158.

Sharpley, R. (2003). Tourism, modernisation and development on the island of Cyprus: Challenges and policy responses *Journal of Sustainable Tourism*, 11(2/3), 246–265.

Sharpley, R. (2005). Travels to the edge of darkness: Towards a typology of dark tourism. in C. Ryan, S. Page, & M. Aicken (Eds), *Taking Tourism to the Limits: Issues, Concepts and Managerial Perspectives*, pp. 217–228. Oxford: Elsevier.

Sharpley, R. (2009). Shedding light on dark tourism: An introduction. in R. Sharpley, & P. Stone (Eds), *The Darker Side of Travel: The Theory and Practice of Dark Tourism*, pp. 3–22. Bristol: Channel View Publications.

Sharpley, R. (2022). Tourist experiences: Liminal, liminoid or just doing something different? in R. Sharpley (Ed.), *The Routledge Handbook of the Tourist Experience*, pp. 89–110. London: Routledge.

Sharpley, R., & Friedrich, M. (2016). Genocide tourism in Rwanda: Contesting the concept of the 'dark tourist'. in G. Hooper, & J. Lennon (Eds), *Dark Tourism: Practice and Interpretation*, pp. 134–146. London: Routledge.

Sharpley, R., & Stone, P. (2009). Life, death and dark tourism: Future research directions and concluding comments. in R. Sharpley, & P. Stone (Eds), *Travels on the Darker Side: The Theory and Practice of Dark Tourism*, pp. 247–251. Bristol: Channel View Publications.

Shin, Y.S. (2007). Perception differences between domestic and international visitors in the tourist destination: The case of the borderline, the DMZ area. *Journal of Travel & Tourism Marketing*, 21(2-3), 77–88.

Shirk, D.A. (2014). A tale of two Mexican border cities: The rise and decline of drug violence in Juárez and Tijuana. *Journal of Borderlands Studies*, 29(4), 481–502.

Slikker, N., & Koens, K. (2015). 'Breaking the silence': Local perceptions of slum tourism in Dharavi. *Tourism Review International*, 19(1–2), 75–86.

Smith, V. (1996). War and its attractions. in A. Pizam, & Y. Mansfeld (Eds), *Tourism, Crime and International Security Issues*, pp. 247–264. Chichester: Wiley.

Sofield, T. (2006). Border tourism and border communities: An overview. *Tourism Geographies*, 8(2), 102–121.

Staudt, K. (2014). The border, performed in films: Produced in both Mexico and the US to 'Bring out the worst in a country'. *Journal of Borderlands Studies*, 29(4), 465–479.

Steinbrink, M. (2012). 'We did the Slum!' Urban poverty tourism in historical perspective. *Tourism Geographies*, 14(2), 213–234.

Stoffelen, A., & Vanneste, D. (2017). Tourism and cross-border regional development: Insights in European contexts. *European Planning Studies*, 25(6), 1013–1033.

Stone, P. (2006). A dark tourism spectrum: Towards a typology of death and macabre related tourist sites, attractions and exhibitions. *Tourism*, 54(2), 145–160.

Stone, P. (2013). Dark tourism scholarship: A critical review. *International Journal of Culture, Tourism and Hospitality Research*, 7(3), 307–318.

Stone, P., & Sharpley, R. (2008). Consuming dark tourism: A thanatological perspective. *Annals of Tourism Research*, 35(2), 574–595.

Tanaś, S. (2014). Tourism, 'death space' and thanatourism in Poland. *Current Issues of Tourism Research*, 3(1), 22–27.

Tarlow, P. (2005). Dark tourism: The appealing 'dark' side of tourism and more. in M. Novelli (Ed.), *Niche Tourism: Contemporary Issues, Trends and Cases*, pp. 47–57. Oxford: Elsevier.

*Telegraph* (2011). Tourists warned away from 100 miles of Kenyan coast after second kidnap by Somalians. *The Telegraph*, 2 October. Available at: https://www.telegraph.co.uk/news/worldnews/africaandindianocean/kenya/8802013/Tourists-warned-away-from-100-miles-of-Kenyan-coast-after-second-kidnap-by-Somalians.html (Accessed 25 August 2020).

Timothy, D.J. (1995). Political boundaries and tourism: Borders as tourist attractions. *Tourism Management*, 16(7), 525–532.

Timothy, D.J. (1998). Tourism and international borders: Themes and issues. *Visions in Leisure and Business*, 17(3), 3–7.

Timothy, D.J. (2001). *Tourism and Political Boundaries*. London: Routledge.

Timothy, D.J. (2006). Relationships between tourism and international boundaries. in H. Wachowiack (Ed.) *Tourism and Borders: Contemporary Issues, Policies and International Research*, pp. 9–19. Aldershot: Ashgate.

Trading Economics (2020). Indicators: Countries. Available online: tradingeconomics.com Accessed July 5, 2020.

Tunbridge, J., & Ashworth, G. (1996). *Dissonant Heritage: The Management of the Past as a Resource in Conflict*. Chichester: Wiley.

Uzell, D. (1989). The hot interpretation of war and conflict. in D. Uzell (Ed.), *Heritage Interpretation, Volume I: The Natural and Built Environment*, pp. 33–47. London: Belhaven Press.

Van Broek, A-M. (2018). 'Pablo Escobar tourism' – unwanted tourism: Attitudes of tourism stakeholders in Medellín, Colombia. in P. Stone et al. (Eds), *The Palgrave Handbook of Dark Tourism Studies*, pp. 291–318. London: Palgrave Macmillan.

Wachowiack, H. (Ed.) (2006). *Tourism and Borders: Contemporary Issues, Policies and International Research*. Aldershot: Ashgate.

Walter, T. (2009). Dark tourism: Mediating between the dead and the living. in R. Sharpley, & P. Stone (Eds), *The Darker Side of Travel: The Theory and Practice of Dark Tourism*, pp. 39–55. Bristol: Channel View Publications.

Webster, C., & Timothy, D.J. (2006). Travelling to the 'other side': The occupied zone and Greek Cypriot views of crossing the Green Line. *Tourism Geographies*, 8(2), 162–181.

Wiedenhoft Murphy, W.A. (2010). Touring the Troubles in West Belfast: Building peace or reproducing conflict? *Peace & Change*, 35(4), 537–560.

World Travel Guide (2018). The ten most dangerous cities worth visiting. Available at: https://www.worldtravelguide.net/features/feature/the-10-most-dangerous-cities-worth-visiting/ (Accessed 28 July 2020).

Yang, E., & Nair, V. (2014). Tourism at risk: A review of risk and perceived risk in tourism. *Asia-Pacific Journal of Innovation in Hospitality and Tourism*, 3(2), 1–21.

# 17
# BORDERS, HERITAGE, AND MEMORY

*Dallen J. Timothy and Marek Więckowski*

## Introduction

Heritage is what humankind inherits from the past, values and uses today, and hopes to pass on to future generations (Eskilsson & Högdahl, 2009; Graham et al., 2000; Timothy, 2021a). It is broad in scope and includes both natural and cultural, as well as tangible and intangible, inheritances. Cultural heritage assets are among the most utilized tourism resources in the world, and many destinations' tourism sectors rely almost entirely on heritage tourism of various sorts. In many places, built heritage is the sole tourist referent, the iconic image of place and something that is used to brand destinations for tourist consumption and global visibility. Tourism largely focuses on the grandest scale of heritage with the most opulent remnants of the past being the sole focus of development, sometimes at the expense of small-scale and local elements of the human past.

Although tangential in many respects, as vestiges of state power, social organization, and history, political boundaries have become significant heritage attractions in many locales and may demonstration local, national, and international heritage. Among Berlin's most popular tourist attractions are the Berlin Wall remnants, the Checkpoint Charlie Museum, and various other border-related heritage sites (Gelbman & Timothy, 2010; Light, 2000; Stoffelen & Vanneste, 2019; Yan et al., 2019). The same is true of the entire former East–West Germany frontier, where dozens of border museums have been established (Eckert, 2011, 2019; Pelkmans, 2012). Likewise, the Great Wall of China, an ancient boundary, is one of that country's leading heritage attractions, not only for its grandiose structure and imprint on the cultural landscape, but also because of the historical sense of Chinese identity it evokes. Although borders, famous and grand, as well as those of lesser renown, are an important part of the world's heritage, they have not been well examined from the perspective of heritage and heritage tourism. This chapter examines several of the ways in which political borders may be viewed as cultural heritage and its tourism implications.

## Heritage Tourism

Every place has heritage. It may be personal, local, regional, national, or international in its reach, touristic appeal, and commemorative value (Timothy, 1997). Cultural heritage manifests

DOI: 10.4324/9781003038993-20

in tangible artifacts, such as archaeological remains, buildings and structures, cemeteries, battlefields, war memorials, sites of dark events and human suffering, museums, galleries, and agricultural landscapes, or intangible features inherited from previous generations, including music, dance, art forms and handicrafts, folklore, poetry, cuisine and culinary traditions, beliefs, rituals and celebrations, knowledge, and family traditions, to name but a few (Timothy, 2021a). These assets combined create most of the world's tourism resources, and there are multitudes of motivations for visiting heritage places and consuming cultural products, including curiosity, seeking knowledge, personal or family ties, a desire to connect with the past, satisfying hobby and leisure pursuits, or using up free time. Together the heritage supply and the demand for it create the phenomenon of heritage tourism (Timothy, 2021a).

Heritage is ensconced with certain values, and indeed for something to be heritage, it typically needs to be esteemed as heritage by an individual or group of people. Heritage is cherished by society for its aesthetics, economic worth, scientific and educational value, scarcity value, and its ability to tell stories and protect the most important elements of the past. Heritage is a crucible of knowledge and a protector of the human story. It imbues individuals and societies with national pride and solidarity, and often provides a foundation for ethnic and religious identity. These values are what makes heritage assets important tourism resources.

## Heritage and Political Borders

Political borders have several functions, including lines of military and security defense, filters against undesirable elements (e.g., narcotics and diseases), barriers to the flow of people, goods, and ideas, and perhaps most importantly, they demarcate the limits of a state's sovereign authority. The functions of borders are not static but are in a constant state of change, with many disappearing as polities unite or their locations change, or appearing as regimes change and territories become divided. Geopolitical relations between neighbors also reflect cycles of forming, opening and closing, or bordering, debordering, and rebordering (Newman, 2006; Stetter, 2005).

Despite their dynamic nature, international borders have traditionally functioned primarily as barriers to human mobility and trade in goods and services, although they have throughout history also attracted the attention of curious onlookers, including tourists, who are intrigued by the differences they indicate and the recreational and commercial opportunities they foster. Thus, in addition to their role as barriers, lines of exclusion, and differentness, state borders are also simultaneously symbolic social and cultural lines of inclusion, material and imagined, physical and intangible (Nash et al., 2013; Zhang, 2019).

Since World War II, the various processes and forces associated with globalization and supranationalization have reduced the barrier effects of borders, enabling increased trade, travel, cooperation, and exchange of ideas (Timothy, 2019a, 2021b). This debordering process recently is best illustrated in Europe with the collapse of state communism in the early 1990s and the emergence and expansion of the European Union as a single, cohesive common market and travel area (Coles & Hall, 2005). However, with the increasing global migration crisis, security threats, human trafficking, trade in illicit drugs, and more recently the COVID-19 pandemic, the world has seen a course of rebordering unlike any in recent history. Higher and more technologically advanced walls and fences have recently been built or are currently being built on the borders of the United States and Mexico, Spain and Morocco (at Melilla and Ceuta), Botswana and Zimbabwe, Oman and the United Arab Emirates, and Brunei and Malaysia, and elsewhere. Even in largely debordered Europe, temporary barriers have been erected between EU and Schengen co-member states to stem illegal immigration and the spread of the coronavirus. Some intra-EU countries have even erected more permanent barriers (e.g., Austria and

Slovenia, and Slovenia at its border with Croatia), and permanent blockades have recently been built between some of the EU's outermost states and their non-EU neighbors (e.g. Hungary–Serbia and Bulgaria–Turkey since 2015, and Poland–Belarus since 2021).

Globalization and debordering have diminished the constraints educed by national frontiers and helped to create new identities (Kolosov & O'Loughlin, 1998). Within the European Union, for instance, macro-regional identities are beginning to develop (Timothy, 2001, 2021b), including pan-European heritage through the efforts of the European Commission and the Council of Europe. Indeed, European integration has brought about a new kind of border heritage, wherein old divisions and old wars have been superseded by new symbols of cooperation, integration, neighborliness, and a newfound sense of European solidarity.

Källén (2019, p. 7) rightfully notes that borders enclose and define stable national identities. Even in the shadows of massive geopolitical change, debordering, and supranationalism, borders continue to reinforce a sense of national identity and belonging (Andersen & Prokkola, 2022). As such, borders continue to narrate important histories about faith, family, culture, and nationality. They are crucibles of history, both conflicted and peaceful.

Heritage-making, or heritagization, is the process of commoditizing the past as a resource for consumption today. Owing to its economic rationale, tourism is one of the most prevalent uses of the past, in company with scientific research, education, government propaganda, and conservation. As already noted, heritagization denotes political processes, power relations, economic rationales, decision-making, and memorialization, valorization, and veneration. Although not a common approach to understanding geopolitics and political boundaries, heritage is a suitable framework for understanding some of the relationships between borders and tourism (Lähdesmäki & Mäkinen, 2019; Lois, 2019; Lois & Cairo, 2015; Więckowski & Timothy, 2021). Borders have significant potential as heritage tourist attractions, as they wield an appeal for curiosity-seekers in many ways for their geopolitical, historical, and modern symbolic values (Prokkola & Lois, 2016; Timothy, 2001; Timothy et al., 2016).

Although national borders have been a relatively neglected part of most states in socioeconomic and political terms, borders are imbued with many heritage values, histories, senses of place, place-making, mobilities, and immobilities. The geopolitical changes of the past three decades in Europe and elsewhere have highlighted the important role of borders and have set in motion the broader heritagization of borders and borderlands. In this very real sense, border landscapes become heritage landscapes as they represent a present linked to an important past.

When heritage becomes the institutionalized memory of a nation, it may be understood as acts of bordering and rebordering, inclusion and exclusion, where some heritages are inherited while others are disinherited and left out of the official state narrative. In relation to geopolitical borders, border heritagization refers to an understanding of borders as enacted, located, and bearing significance in more locations than in their physical manifestation as border control posts. Borders are thus understood as manifested and reproduced in various social and cultural practices and narratives of inclusion and exclusion, as has been suggested by several border scholars (e.g., Andersen & Prokkola, 2021; Newman & Paasi, 1998; Rumford, 2006; van Houtum & van Naerssen, 2002).

Even if heritage is understood to be an important foundation of national identity, the memorialization and commemoration of border heritage (including war) may simultaneously strengthen the experienced boundaries within and between communities, sometimes resulting in new conflicts between groups (Andersen & Prokkola, 2021). The 1648 Peace of Westphalia, which partially established the current legal and political understandings of sovereign states and their boundaries in Europe, in effect, ushered in the role of national boundaries as part of the national identity and national story (Kolosov, 2020).

From a heritage perspective, borders may be viewed from many different viewpoints. First, current borders exhibit heritage value, depending on the history of the border and how long it has existed in its present form. Second, former borders between current states may be situated in a different locale away from the present border. For example, part of the former German–Polish border is now located inside Poland and is interpreted for heritage consumption. Likewise, the former Polish–Russian border can be found inside the territory of Russia. Third, there are examples of disbanded former borders between polities that no longer exist, such as the boundary between Poland and the Free City of Danzig, between Belgium and Neutral Moresnet, and between the Republic of Texas and the United States of America. Finally, relict boundaries of former polities, such as the Limes of the Roman Empire, comprise an important heritage in various parts of the world.

Borders can also undergo change at certain points in time, when for instance the fading of established meanings goes hand in hand with a "remembrance" of spatial experiences or configurations that were relevant in the distant past (von Hirschausen et al., 2019). Thus, former or phantom borders and their adjacent landscapes acquire the status of cultural heritage. Commemoration and heritagization strongly depend on local, regional, and national authorities. When heritage becomes the institutionalized memory of a nation, it may be understood as acts of bordering and rebordering. When historic borders are enacted by multiple actors, research shows that it is their practices that come to shape borders even more than state intervention (Andersen & Sandberg, 2012). The high symbolic significance of relict borders is due to the fact that the events associated with them serve as a lesson for the future, reminding societies about the controversies of the past and the importance of historical reconciliation between neighboring countries (Kolosov, 2020).

Bordering and rebordering processes are inherent in the very notion of heritage-making, not least because of the close connections between heritage-making and nation-building (Andersen & Prokkola, 2021). Through time and with the struggles of nation-building and national heritage-making, borders may become symbolic representations of nationhood and educe a strong sense of cultural solidarity (van Houtum, 2005).

As this discussion indicates, the role of borders in the context of heritage can be examined from several different perspectives. These include, but are not limited to, sites of power and nationalism, borders and a heritage of darkness, borders as meeting grounds, border stories and heritage narratives, border landscapes as heritagescapes, and border-spanning cultural resources.

## *Symbolic Sites of Power and Nationalism*

Heritage as commemoration of the past is often said to be the result of power. Traditionally, most heritage has reflected the ideologies, wishes, and desires of people or organizations with the most power and influence. The old adage, "history is written by the winners of war", is a truism in many aspects of heritage commemoration. This is, in part, why so much of what societies value as heritage symbolizes power and represents powerful elites, including palaces, castles, cathedrals and temples, government buildings, fortresses, and other historical remains that exemplify vestiges of power and prestige, as opposed to the heritage of ordinary people (Timothy, 2014).

Many border-related tourist attractions are physical demonstrations of power and assertions of control. Given the main purposes of borders, such assertions of power may be necessary to repel unwanted forces or to keep people from leaving. Even in ancient days, before the Westphalian notion of precise borders and full sovereignty had gained widespread currency, frontier ramparts were erected as defensive fortifications against the unknown other or to protect crown territory from invading marauders. One of the best examples in the context of heritage tourism is the Great Wall of China, a UNESCO World Heritage Site and one of China's most popular tourist attractions (Su & Wall, 2012).

Rather than being a single linear defense, the Great Wall of China is actually a series of walls built over vast areas, east to west and north to south at different times, beginning in the seventh century BC. The most popular among tourists, easiest to access, and best-preserved portions of the wall were built in the Ming Dynasty between the fourteenth and seventeenth centuries AD. Most of the earliest walls have deteriorated significantly and lie in ruins, but those from the Ming Dynasty are popular tourist attractions. Although the main purpose of the Great Wall was defense against raiders from the north, it also served as a way station along the Silk Road where taxes could be levied and the movement of people controlled (Shelach-Lavi et al., 2020). The successive walls built in what is today northern China essentially demarcated the limits of various ancient Chinese states and later a unified China in about 220 BC.

Shortly after the 1949 division of Germany into East and West, the inner-German border was demarcated and border fortifications erected. In 1961 in Berlin, the border between the eastern sector (occupied by the Soviet Union) and the western sector (occupied by France, the United Kingdom, and the United States) was erected and through various iterations became the infamous Berlin Wall. The wall was erected to keep East Berliners from defecting to the West and is one of the most powerful modern manifestations of power effected at a state boundary.

Another interesting facet of border heritage landscapes of power is the competitive nature of each side outfoxing the other that has prevailed at some boundary locations. In a cunning show of regional dominance, South Korea erected a 98-meter flagpole used to fly a 130-kilogram South Korean flag within its Daeseong-dong village inside the DMZ. In response, and in a concerted show of one-upmanship, the North right away constructed an even higher flagpole (160 meters) with a larger flag in its "propaganda village" Kijŏng-dong (Atanasova, 2019). This nicknamed "flagpole war" is an important part of the tourism narrative of the region, and both flags continue to fly against each other across the line of demarcation. A similar situation exists in Cyprus near the buffer zone dividing the north from the south. In the Turkish-occupied north, only ten kilometers from the Green Line, one of the world's largest flags is painted on a mountainside in full view of Nicosia, the divided capital, and other parts of the Republic of Cyprus (Kliot & Mansfield, 1997). The Turkish Republic of Northern Cyprus flag was painted on the hillside in the 1980s in a taunting show of independence, Turkish ethnic pride, and a constant reminder to the Greek South of the Turkish domination over the North (Figure 17.1). A similar prominent example of this one-upmanship can be seen at the main border crossing between India and Pakistan, where each evening the border gate is closed in an elaborate ceremony in which the Pakistani and Indian border officers compete theatrically to show which side is more fearsome (Chhabra, 2018; Timothy, 2001). Every year, thousands of Indian, Pakistani, and foreign tourists gather at this border town to witness the theater at Wagah.

## Borders and a Heritage of Darkness

Despite the relative neglect by many central governments, borders are an important part of a state's history, particularly with regard to territorial losses and gains, the formation of states, and how wars, invasions, or even natural accretion have altered the shapes of countries and their territorial extent. Dark tourism, a form of heritage tourism, has gained prominence in the tourism industry and in academic research. This form of tourism entails people traveling to localities associated with suffering, death, and the macabre to satisfy a wide variety of motives and experiences (Stone et al., 2018). The idea that borders are spaces of darkness is not new.

*Figure 17.1* The extraordinarily large Turkish Republic of Northern Cyprus flag visible from the Republic of Cyprus.

(Photo: D.J. Timothy)

Because borders and frontiers have often been theaters of war, borderlands throughout the world are riddled with military cemeteries and war memorials (Janicki, 2009; Kolosov, 2020; Timothy, 2013), some of which perpetuate the memory of battles, vilifying invaders and glorifying national heroes (Balibar, 2004; Le & Pearce, 2011).

In a few momentous cases, a country's heritage may also be a stimulus for cross-border conflicts, which tend to create a stronger sense of nationalism in each respective country. The example of Preah Vihear in Cambodia, which has long been a point of contention and even armed conflict between Thailand and Cambodia because of the archaeological site's extreme value for national and regional heritage identity, is a significant case in point (Williams, 2011). The contested David Gareja monastery complex on the border of Azerbaijan and Georgia is another prominent example that has created additional layers of conflict between neighboring states and affirmed each country's resolve that the site is representative of its own past and not that of the other.

The intimate connections between borders and conflict are some of the strongest foundations of border heritage. The Berlin Wall and the entire Iron Curtain were clear examples of darkness (Lennon & Foley, 2001). The boundaries between the communist east and the capitalist west denoted the differences between democracies and autocracies. The heavy border fortifications associated with the Iron Curtain were synonymous with fear, intimidation, and human rights abuses. Border soldiers in the East were ordered to shoot to kill anyone who dared cross the border, and even in some recorded cases, to approach the border closely. In the West, the Iron Curtain became a symbol of oppression and human rights violations. May people died or were imprisoned in an attempt to escape to the West, and the borderline separated two opposing socioeconomic and political systems that contrasted significantly with each side promoting its own form of propaganda to make the other side seem worse than it probably was. Today, remnants of the Iron Curtain can be seen throughout Central and Eastern Europe and are frequently interpreted from the lens of oppression, autocracy, and places of death (e.g., numerous monuments at places where people were executed trying to escape communist dictatorships, with common examples being in Berlin and in Devín, Slovakia).

Israel's borders with Palestine, Lebanon, Syria, Jordan, and Egypt have long been flashpoints of violence. The violence associated with these borders and the constant threat of violence continue to maintain these borders as important dark attractions in Israel. Conflict, nowadays particularly that between Israel and Syria, Israel and Lebanon, and Israel and Palestine, plays an important role in the region's heritage milieu, and is the very essence of heritage along Israel's frontiers (Gelbman, 2008; Gelbman & Timothy, 2010). Conflict underscores a significant portion of the heritage of Israel and its borders' defensive purpose is a major part of Israeli national identity and fuels its sense of solidarity.

The USA–Mexico border has gone through several lifecycles of darkness, beginning with Prohibition (1920–1933) in the United States, which outlawed the production, selling, or consumption of alcoholic beverages. During this time, the Mexican border towns thrived as popular destinations for Americans who crossed to consume alcohol and participate in prostitution, illicit gambling, and rowdy behaviors. This deviant tourism environment earned the Mexican borderlands a negative reputation as centers of mischief, hedonism, and danger. Later, the Mexican government enacted policies to improve the border communities' reputation and socioeconomic status, which also had the effect of growing tourism. However, as recent as the early 2000s, drug cartels had taken over much of the commercial environment of Mexican border areas and had dominated the security climate with kidnappings, executions, wanton acts of larceny, and general lawlessness. Added to that was the growing crisis of illegal immigration and human trafficking. All of these problems have plagued the USA–Mexico border for years but have become especially prominent since around 2005. The US government's responses have been varied, including additional security personnel and border patrol agents at the border, increased surveillance, and the construction of fences and walls to keep drug and human trafficking at bay. All of these conditions combine to create an overall sense of darkness at the Mexico–USA border that both repels and attracts tourist interests. In this sense, then, the heritage of this particular frontier is one of darkness—crime, drug and human smuggling, sex trafficking, and a general atmosphere of danger and violence.

National boundaries are often associated with painful memoryscapes, especially in cases of partition by foreign powers when societies and ethnic groups were divided (e.g., the multiple partitions of Poland between 1772 and 1918). These superimposed partitions that sever cohesive cultural groups are particularly painful for a nation, because not only do they divide loved ones and co-nationalists, they are also reminders and testaments of complete or partial failure. The partition of a state, the secession of part of it, or the forced transfer of territory are especially painful turning points in history, which can leave deep emotional scars on a people's psyche and national identity that can live on for many generations (Kolosov, 2020).

## *Borders as Meeting Grounds*

Modern thinking about borders suggests that they are not only lines of exclusion but also lines of inclusion. Sanguin (1983) distinguished between borders that divide and those that connect, mirroring relations between neighbors through conflict, competition, subordination, and eventually cooperation (Kolosov et al., 2018). As other chapters in this book have rightly noted, tourism in borderlands demonstrates unique characteristics that do not exist elsewhere. Among these, shopping, prostitution, gambling, alcohol use, protected natural areas, and even medical care have become a salient part of the heritage narrative of borderlands as they represent these activities in ways unlike in other regions of the state (Arreola & Curtis, 1993; Więckowski, 2010).

A prominent theme of research in the social sciences has been the melding of cultures at borders to create unique borderland heritages (Brown, 1997; Husmann, 2013; Marsico, 2016). Perhaps the most researched borderland in this regard has been the Mexico–USA frontier, although work has been done along similar lines in other border regions (Husmann, 2013). The USA–Mexico borderlands have distinct elements of culture that distinguish them from other regions of Mexico and the USA (Arreola, 2002; Cuevas Contreras & Zizaldra Hernández, 2015; Martínez, 1994; Stavans, 2010) in areas of cross-border family and personal linkages, economic interdependence, commerce and shopping, language ("Spanglish"), religious traditions, smuggling, migration, education, holiday celebrations, food traditions, and architecture, to name only a few (Cuevas Contreras & Zizaldra Hernández, 2015; Martínez, 1994; Walker, 2013). Other borderland cultures in Europe and Asia integrate some of these issues, as well as collaboration in law enforcement, joint tourism marketing, and planning major events (Stoffelen et al., 2017). For people who grow up in the shadows of national borders, their daily lives are affected directly by the boundary, and they tend to develop a unique perspective of their own identities as borderlanders. For them, border life is a personal heritage.

Borders as meeting grounds may also be thought of as places of remembrance and symbolic commemorations of peace. Borders commonly play host to major events, cultural exchanges, and even high-level political encounters. In 1659, the Treaty of the Pyrenees was signed between France and Spain on tiny Pheasant Island in the Bidasoa River on the two countries' border. The treaty effected peace between France and Spain, settled several boundary contests, and established the French–Spanish border that remains to this day. Today, Pheasant Island is an international condominium, where both countries share sovereignty over it, and a historical marker commemorates the major geopolitical event that took place there nearly 400 years ago (Timothy, 2021b).

Another prominent example of remembrance and symbolic representations of border heritage are the growing number of border parks in Europe, North America, and elsewhere. These include the Europe Monument at the tripoint of Belgium, Luxembourg, and Germany; the Peace Arch Park on the USA–Canada border; the International Peace Garden on the USA–Canada border; and the Dreiländereck park at the tripoint where Czechia, Germany, and Poland meet (Więckowski, in press). At these parks, peaceful relations are celebrated through monuments, border markers, interpretive signs, pathways, picnic areas, and in some cases shops and vendors (Figure 17.2). Many such parks have been developed at international borders in Europe, and perhaps one of the most important to commemorate the border as meeting place is the Pan-European Picnic Memorial Park at the border of Hungary and Austria.

On August 19, 1989, a peace demonstration was held at the Hungarian–Austrian border near Sopron, attended largely by East Germans who were vacationing in Hungary and who had heard about the relaxed Austro-Hungarian border and the dismantling of the barbed-wire boundary fences earlier that year. During the event, the border gate was opened, and with the Hungarian guards not intervening, several hundred East Germans rushed unfettered into Austria. From that time forward, Hungary kept open its border with Austria. This "picnic" is seen by many observers as the first major event in the fall of the Berlin Wall only a couple of months later, and the collapse of the Iron Curtain and communism in 1990–1991 (Gioielli, 2020). Today, a commemorative park has been built in the location of the Pan-European Picnic and stands for a unified Europe (Barcza & Szabolcs, 2017). Sculptures, monuments, interpretive plaques, remnants of the boundary fence, pieces of the Berlin Wall, and other

*Figure 17.2* The authors working on this chapter astride an historic border marker in the Krkonise-Karkonisze Transfrontier Biosphere Reserve. Marek is in Poland. Dallen is in the Czech Republic.

(Photo: D.J. Timothy)

symbols commemorate the events of that day in 1989. In 2014, the park was added to the European Union's list of European Heritage Label sites, which symbolize the creation of modern-day Europe and European ideals, values, history, and integration (Balogh, 2019; European Commission, 2022; Harlov-Csortán, 2017).

## Border Stories and Heritage Narratives

The heritagization process includes written stories, oral traditions, and legends associated with places, people, and events, and the values and meanings ascribed to them. Such traditions underscore borderland lore and cross-border relations (Andersen & Prokkola, 2021). For example, stories of smuggling or transborder raids are endemic to borderlands throughout the world and have become a salient part of local identities and folklore, even to the extent of heroifying famous local outlaws and valorizing a general sense of lawlessness.

Through this process, border heritages are created and through tourism they are maintained. The lore of smuggling continues to captivate the attention of visitors in various places along the USA–Canada border, the Thailand–Malaysia border, the Andorran–French and Andorran–Spanish borders (Augustin, 2009; Gelbman & Timothy, 2019). Likewise in the enclaved patchwork of Baarle Nassau and Baarle Hertog (Netherlands-Belgium), where the puzzle of enclaves in the small village provided tiny bits of Belgian refuges vis-à-vis the German occupation of Belgium proper during World War I and afterwards protection for smugglers when customs formalities existed between the two countries, the heritage of smuggling is a critical part of local lore and borderland identity (Farran, 1955; Gelbman & Timothy, 2011; Robinson, 1959). The checkered history of the Baarles plays an important part of the identity of the village and border region, and has translated into the area's heritage tourism narrative in public memory, as well as in stories, books, articles, brochures, and interpretive media at the local visitor center. Similarly, on the USA–Mexico border, the stories associated with the Mexican outlaw Poncho Villa and his raids on America during the Mexican Revolution (1919–1920) pervade much of the local storied narrative in New Mexico and Chihuahua (Cuevas et al., 2016; Pick, 2010).

This manifestation of intangible heritage exists in almost all borderlands and most commonly takes place at a very local level. Local frontier-related legends create a particular distinctiveness that sets borderlands apart from other areas. In protecting local border heritage, people find an important way to signify their distinctiveness in an ever increasingly homogeneous world. Such local lore can help build a sense of cultural solidarity, particularly in the face of the difficulties of borderland living, and has proved to be a salient part of the heritage narrative packaged, marketed, and sold to tourists.

## *Border Infrastructure as Heritage Landscape*

As noted earlier, the physical manifestations of power and state responsibilities (e.g., customs, immigration, security apparatuses, and health inspections) are a salient part of the border landscape. The tangible manifestations of borders, as well as their intangible (symbolic) representations, help to create unique border heritagescapes comprised of boundary markers and related administrative infrastructure. Crossing boundaries, straddling their markers, and photographing guard towers are a few ways in which people consume the border landscape.

From a spatio-temporal and heritage perspective, border landscapes and infrastructure can be seen as relict borders (also referred to as phantom borders) which no longer function as political boundaries, but once did, and whose remnants and impacts are still visible in the landscape (Hartshorne, 1936). Some defensive lines and state borders can be seen from three perspectives: relict borders, currently functioning borders, or a combination of the two. Disused boundaries discussed earlier, including the Berlin Wall, are examples of relict borders, and parts of many of the pre-World War II frontiers of Europe in places such as Poland, Germany, France, and Belgium continue to be maintained as historic monuments, including several border markers of the Treaty of Versailles, the Maginot Line in France near the German frontier, remains of the original border fences built during World War I along the Belgian–Dutch border, and the reconstruction of some for today's tourism purposes (Figure 17.3).

Whereas relict border landscapes may be appealing heritage assets for what they used to represent or symbolically continue to represent today (Löytynoja, 2008), current border landscapes are attractions for what they presently represent. Most international borders today are demarcated (Biger, 1995). Demarcation is an important part of the boundary creation and maintenance process (Jones, 1945) and takes on many forms, including concrete or steel pillars and obelisks, wood or plastic poles, metal plates embedded in bedrock or pavement, fences, survey markers, wood or fiberglass signs, blazes carved or painted on trees or stones, or other means of precisely marking the vertical planes where one sovereign state meets another. Although seemingly simple means of marking human-created imaginary lines, these signs and symbols not only demarcate sovereign space, they also serve as symbolic representations of nationhood, social solidarity, or cultural identity (Więckowski & Timothy, 2021). As indicators

*Figure 17.3* Reconstructed Dodendraad (Wire of Death) on the Dutch-Belgian border from WWI with interpretive signs.

(Photo: D.J. Timothy)

of place, space, and identity, these demarcation tools also represent divisions of differentness, or life as lived in one place and life as lived in another (Timothy, 2001). For many people, then, these markers are meant to be straddled, leaned against, photographed, or climbed upon.

Besides markers, border administration requires other infrastructure, such as passport inspection and immigration offices, and customs and agricultural inspection stations. These still play a crucial part of the intrigue of borders, but in Europe, with increasing debordering, many of these former administrative buildings have become derelict, sitting empty like sores that represent past times and places. Most intra-EU and intra-Schengen inspection stations have been demolished, although many have been repurposed into local heritage museums, coffee shops, bars, souvenir stores, or tourism information offices (Timothy, 2001; Więckowski & Saarinen, 2019). Keeping their customs signs and state insignias intact, however, is an effort to maintain the heritage values of these historic structures.

Combined derelict and current border functions are common in areas where borders continue to function as lines of state sovereignty, but they (or elements of them) no longer serve as checkpoints. The disused inspection stations noted earlier are examples of this in the EU. Thus, the borderline duality of relictness and functioning presentness remains, but the border services and administrative functions no longer do.

A country's flag, landmarks, emblems and symbols, and welcome signs are all heritage elements that are widely used at border crossings and are recognized as symbols of national identity (Więckowski, in press). Just north of the DMZ, when entering North Korea from the

South, travelers are greeted with an entire political landscape devoted to the Kim dynasty and Juche, North Korea's unique brand of communist ideology. Signs, statues, and placards clarify in no uncertain terms that one has entered the sphere of Kim Il-sung's juche system, which dictates every aspect of life for North Koreans.

Border landscapes, thus, become heritage monuments (Prokkola, 2010). They provide a unique regional heritage narrative that is often associated with barbed wire, depictions of power, and strong nationalist symbolisms (Gelbman & Timothy, 2010; Timothy et al., 2016; Więckowski, in press).

Border-hunting has been an interesting, albeit esoteric, activity for a long time among a small population of curiosity-seekers. Nineteenth and early twentieth-century accounts of ordinary people exploring historic borders and hunting old border markers are common in some early literature because of what the border markers represent and because of the historic stories they tell (e.g., Griswold, 1939; Woodward, 1907). Today, elements of the border, including markers, infrastructure, and related icons, continue to draw tourists' attention.

Where borders separate hostile or malevolent neighbors, they are usually more clearly marked and often heavily fortified with ancillary devices. Walls, fences, minefields, patrol roads, guard towers, warning signs, bunkers, anti-vehicular trenches or barricades, and other dissuasive material elements form an endemic part of the heritage securityscapes of many belligerent borders and simultaneously function as tourist attractions, even where there is an element of danger (Timothy, 2019b). Even between friendly neighbors, fences, walls, and patrol paths may become part of the border landscape where illegal activities prevail, such as the USA–Canada and USA–Mexico borders.

Many border landscapes also have a commercial element including clusters of duty-free shops, currency exchange booths, supermarkets and petrol stations, insurance dealers, and other service clusters that cater to the needs of border crossers. These too demonstrate elements of border heritage, particularly when they are part of the lore associated with the borderlands. For example, in the Swedish–Finnish borderlands, it was common practice in the 1980s and at other times for Finns to patronize thriving Swedish supermarkets near the border to buy Finnish butter, which was cheaper than in Finland due to government policies there. The activity of a day in Sweden shopping for butter and participating in other activities became part of familial heritage, memories of times spent together. The supermarkets were an indelible part of the border servicescape on the Swedish side and tales of illicit butter smuggling abounded. The clustering of shops and services in Andorra very near the French and Spanish borders, because of Andorra's much lower VAT, is part of the past and present border landscapes of this microstate. Both examples from Sweden and Andorra play a crucial role in the local lore of bootlegged merchandise and the commercial competitive advantage of the border.

## Cross-border Cultural Resources

Another perspective is the situation where heritage is bisected by national frontiers. Research on transfrontier nature preserves has a long history. Many studies have covered global (e.g., Andersson et al., 2017) and regional contexts, in Southern Africa (Duffy, 2006), Central Europe (Więckowski, 2013), and the Balkan states (Markov, 2015; Noe, 2010). Likewise, multitudes of living cultures and their intangible heritages divided by national borders have been well researched (e.g., Aykan, 2016; Blasco et al., 2014; Dorvlo, 2017; Horjan, 2011; Leza, 2018), including among thousands of others, the lifestyles and celebrations of the Yaqui Native Americans on both sides of the USA–Mexico border, the Ewe culture that straddles the Ghana–Togo boundary, the Maya culture across the Mexico–Guatemala frontier, and the Bengali traditions of Bangladesh and India. However, with only a few exceptions (e.g., Metreveli, 2019; Sternberg, 2017; Timothy, 2021a; Timothy & Gelbman, 2015), divided tangible heritage and historic sites are not well examined in the literature.

In terms of geography and scale, divided cultural heritage may be seen as transboundary or transnational. Transboundary heritage refers to a single heritage area that is divided by a political border, such as the Stone Circles of Senegambia. Transnational heritage typically occurs at a larger scale and may not have spatial continuity across a national frontier. Instead, it refers to many different sites situated in more than two countries but which are united in their historical connections and common themes. An example of the latter is the UNESCO-listed Architectural Work of Le Corbusier, which can be found in far-flung localities in Asia, Latin America, and Europe. Table 17.1 illustrates the 43 World Heritage Sites (as of 2022) designated as "transboundary" by UNESCO because they share common elements in more than one state. Although UNESCO only utilizes the term "transboundary", we have differentiated the properties based on their relationship with the border.

Clearly the transboundary condition of much of the world's heritage has major implications for planning and policy-making, funding, resource management, protection, interpretation, and tourist use. Most transnational heritage is recognized and delineated at a supranational level, such as in the context of UNESCO World Heritage or the Council of Europe's Cultural Routes program. Thus, these international organizations facilitate and coordinate the "branding" and promotion of, as well as structural support for, transnational heritage. Transboundary (or cross-border) heritage typically occurs on a smaller scale (although UNESCO sees it differently) and requires major coordination efforts between neighboring states to ensure access, promote common use (e.g., tourism), and enact parallel or compatible protective legislation. Funding is rarely available in cross-border settings for heritage protection, except in the European Union where structural funds in recent decades (i.e., Interreg) have enabled transfrontier euroregions to work together to protect their common heritage and promote its use through tourism (Dołzbłasz, 2018; Prokkola, 2011; Shepherd & Ioannides, 2020; Studzieniecki, 2005). Challenges to the cross-border management of heritage also include contestations about whose heritage and which heritage, as well as a frequent lack of political will to collaborate equitably across political lines (McClelland, 2016).

Transboundary heritage, or heritage divided physically by a boundary, requires more significant cooperation than transnational heritage, because the sites are either directly divided or are part of a larger cultural ecosystem that is divided between sovereign states. Scale is important with regard to cross-border heritage and bordering (Laine, 2016). For example, when individual historic buildings or archaeological sites are partitioned by a boundary, effective hands-on management must take place on a local level, with legislative support from higher-order agencies (Timothy & Gelbman, 2015). For example, the Haskell Free Library and Opera House in Derby Line, Vermont (USA), and Stanstead, Quebec (Canada), is shared by both communities as a common library and heritage site. Both communities participate in managing and maintaining the historic building, but their activities must be aligned within the legal frameworks and border restrictions established by the US and Canadian governments and the International Boundary Commission. Likewise, the Roman archaeological site of Panissars is a small area of ancient ruins straddling the modern border of France and Spain. Although each country has its own heritage protective legislation, the day-to-day management of Panissars is done at a very local level by local heritage organizations (Timothy, 2021a) (Figure 17.4).

In some instances, divided heritage can be a center of geopolitical contestation. One of the best examples today is the David Gareja Monastery complex on the border of Georgia and Azerbaijan. The border divides this religious heritage area, which is considered by Georgians to

Table 17.1 UNESCO World Heritage List, transboundary properties

| Name | countries | Date of Inscription | Extension | Type | |
|---|---|---|---|---|---|
| Natural and Cultural Heritage of the Ohrid region | Albania, North Macedonia | 1979 | 1980, 2019 | mixed | transboundary |
| Ancient and Primeval Beech Forests of the Carpathians and Other Regions of Europe | Albania, Austria, Belgium, Bosnia and Herzegovina, Bulgaria, Croatia, Czechia, France, Germany, Italy, North Macedonia, Poland, Romania, Slovakia, Slovenia, Spain, Switzerland, Ukraine | 2007 | 2011, 2017, 2021 | natural | transnational |
| Jesuit Missions of the Guaranis: San Ignacio Mini, Santa Ana, Nuestra Señora de Loreto and Santa Maria Mayor (Argentina), Ruins of Sao Miguel das Missoes (Brazil) | Argentina, Brasil | 1983 | 1984 | cultural | transnational |
| Qhapaq Ñan, Andean Road System | Argentina, Bolivia, Chile, Colombia, Ecuador, Peru | 2014 | – | cultural | transnational |
| The Architectural Work of Le Corbusier, an Outstanding Contribution to the Modern Movement | Argentina, Belgium, France, Germany, India, Japan, Switzerland | 2016 | – | cultural | transnational |
| Fertö/Neusiedlersee Cultural Landscape | Austria, Hungary | 2001 | – | cultural | transboundary |
| Prehistoric Pile Dwellings around the Alps | Austria, France, Germany, Italy, Slovenia, Switzerland | 2011 | – | cultural | transnational |
| Frontiers of the Roman Empire – The Danube Limes (Western Segment) | Austria, Germany, Slovakia | 2021 | – | cultural | transnational |
| The Great Spa Towns of Europe | Austria, Belgium, Czechia, France, Germany, Italy, United Kingdom | 2021 | – | cultural | transnational |
| Białowieża Forest | Belarus, Poland | 1979 | 1992, 2014 | natural | transboundary |
| Struve Geodetic Arc | Belarus, Estonia Finland, Latvia, Lithuania, Norway, Moldova, Russia, Sweden, Ukraine | 2005 | – | cultural | transnational |
| Belfries of Belgium and France | Belgium, France | 1999 | 2005 | cultural | transboundary |

*Borders, Heritage, and Memory*

| Name | Countries | Year | Year2 | Type | Scope |
|---|---|---|---|---|---|
| Colonies of Benevolence | Belgium, Netherlands | 2021 | – | cultural | transboundary |
| W-Arly-Pendjari Complex | Benin, Burkina Faso, Niger | 1996 | 2017 | natural | transboundary |
| Stećci Medieval Tombstone Graveyards | Bosnia and Herzegovina, Croatia, Montenegro, Serbia | 2016 | – | cultural | transboundary |
| Sangha Trinational | Cameroon, Central African Republic, Congo | 2012 | – | natural | transboundary |
| Kluane/Wrangell-St. Elias/Glacier Bay/Tatshenshini-Alsek | Canada, United States of America | 1979 | 1992, 1994 | natural | transboundary |
| Waterton Glacier International Peace Park | Canada, United States of America | 1995 | – | natural | transnational |
| Silk Roads: the Routes Network of Chang'an-Tianshan Corridor | China, Kazakhstan, Kyrgystan | 2014 | – | cultural | transnational |
| Talamanca Range-La Amistad Reserves/La Amistad National Park | Costa Rica, Panama | 1983 | 1990 | natural | transboundary |
| Mount Nimba Strict Nature Reserve | Côte d'Ivoire, Guinea | 1992 | – | natural | transboundary |
| Venetian Works of Defence between the 16th and 17th Centuries: Stato da Terra – Western Stato da Mar | Croatia, Italy, Montenegro | 2017 | – | cultural | transnational |
| Erzgebirge/Krušnohoří Mining Region | Czechia, Germany | 2019 | – | cultural | transboundary |
| Wadden Sea | Denmark, Germany, Netherlands | 2009 | 2014 | natural | transboundary |
| High Coast/Kvarken Archipelago | Finland, Sweden | 2000 | 2006 | natural | transboundary |
| Pyrénées - Mont Perdu | France, Spain | 1997 | 1999 | mixed | transboundary |
| Stone Circles of Senegambia | Gambia, Senegal | 2006 | – | cultural | transboundary |
| Frontiers of the Roman Empire | Germany, United Kingdom | 1987 | 2005, 2008 | cultural | transnational |
| Muskauer Park/Park Mużakowski | Germany, Poland | 2004 | – | cultural | transboundary |
| Frontiers of the Roman Empire – The Lower German Limes | | 2021 | – | cultural | transboundary |
| Historic Centre of Rome, the Properties of the Holy See in that City Enjoying Extraterritorial Rights and San Paolo Fuori le Mura | Holy See, Italy | 1980 | 1990 | cultural | transboundary |
| Caves of Aggtelek Karst and Slovak Karst | Hungary, Slovakia | 1995 | 2000 | natural | transboundary |

(*Continued*)

233

Table 17.1 (Continued)

| Name | countries | Date of Inscription | Extension | Type | |
|---|---|---|---|---|---|
| Monte San Giorgio | Italy, Switzerland | 2003 | 2010 | natural | transboundary |
| Rhaetian Railway in the Albula/Bernina Landscapes | Italy, Switzerland | 2008 | – | cultural | transboundary |
| Western Tien-Shan | Kazakhstan, Kyrgystan, Uzbekistan | 2016 | – | natural | transboundary |
| Maloti-Drakensberg Park | Lesotho, South Africa | 2000 | 2013 | mixed | transboundary |
| Curonian Spit | Lithuania, Russian Federation | 2000 | – | cultural | transboundary |
| Uvs Nuur Basin | Mongolia, Russian Federation | 2003 | – | natural | transboundary |
| Landscapes of Dauria | Mongolia, Russian Federation | 2017 | – | natural | transboundary |
| Wooden Tserkvas of the Carpathian Region in Poland and Ukraine | Poland, Ukraine | 2013 | – | cultural | transboundary |
| Prehistoric Rock Art Sites in the Côa Valley and Siega Verde | Portugal, Spain | 1998 | 2010 | cultural | transboundary |
| Heritage of Mercury. Almadén and Idrija | Slovenia, Spain | 2012 | – | cultural | transnational |
| Mosi-oa-Tunya/Victoria Falls | Zambia, Zimbabwe | 1989 | – | natural | transboundary |

Source: UNESCO (2022)

*Figure 17.4* This boundary obelisk inside the Roman ruins of Panissars demarcates the French-Spanish border.

(Photo: D.J. Timothy)

have extremely important religious heritage value and in fact constitutes part of the Georgian national identity. Because of the border's location through this heritage compound, its definition and delineation have not been fully accepted by either country. Both claim the border extends further into the neighboring state, creating significant contestation and questions about sovereignty over the site (Metreveli, 2019). Obviously, this has important management implications, as neither Georgia or Azerbaijan is able to fully exercise its will over the complex and develop it fully for tourism. The contest over this heritage space has created a stronger sense of nationalism among Georgians and enflamed a deeper sense of solidarity in a region where Georgia feels encroached upon by other neighbors, namely Russia.

Historic villages and towns divided by international borders are important tourist attractions. There are essentially two types of divided border communities: those that were bisected by a border through border changes after the communities had already been established, and twin towns that organically (or intentionally) developed opposite one another on either side of a frontier (Jańczak, 2009). Hundreds of such villages, towns, and cities exist in all parts of the world, but Table 17.2 lists a handful of both types that are important heritage communities and regional tourism destinations.

In addition to their interesting histories and built heritage, divided villages often take on a strong retail orientation and become shopping destinations whose tourism product is more geared toward differential taxes and merchandising than they are about built heritage. In many cases, however, the commercial and retail traditions then become part of the heritage nuances

*Table 17.2* Examples of divided or twin heritage towns and cities

| Twin Towns | Locations | Estimated Population |
|---|---|---|
| Chuí – Chuy | Brazil and Uruguay | 6,770 (Chuí) |
| | | 9,700 (Chuy) |
| Konstanz – Kreuzlingen | Germany and Switzerland | 84,500 (Konstanz) |
| | | 22,000 (Kreuzlingen) |
| Gorizia – Nova Gorica | Italy and Slovenia | 34,400 (Gorizia) |
| | | 13,030 (Nova Gorica) |
| Herzogenrath – Kerkrade | Germany and Netherlands | 46,225 (Herzogenrath) |
| | | 45,700 (Kerkrade) |
| Komárom – Komárno | Hungary and Slovakia | 18,800 (Komárom) |
| | | 33,500 (Komárno) |
| Derby Line – Stanstead | United States and Canada | 687 (Derby Line) |
| | | 2,850 (Stanstead) |
| Sátoraliaújhely – Slovenské Nové Mesto | Hungary and Slovakia | 16,300 (Sátoraliaújhely) |
| | | 1,100 (Slovenské Nové Mesto) |
| Rivera – Santana do Livramento | Uruguay and Brazil | 64,500 (Rivera) |
| | | 76,300 (Santana do Livramento) |
| Laufenburg – Laufenburg | Germany and Switzerland | 9,020 (German side) |
| | | 3,650 (Swiss side) |
| Valka – Valga | Latvia and Estonia | 4,510 (Valka) |
| | | 11,800 (Valga) |
| Baarle Hertog – Baarle Nassau | Netherlands and Belgium | 2,700 (Baarle Hertog) |
| | | 6,850 (Baarle Nassau) |
| Rheinfelden – Rheinfelden | Switzerland and Germany | 13,550 (Swiss side) |
| | | 33,000 (Germany side) |
| Niagara Falls – Niagara Falls | Canada and United States | 88,200 (Canadian side) |
| | | 48,700 (US side) |
| Zgorzelec – Görlitz | Poland and Germany | 30,040 (Zgorzelec) |
| | | 56,000 (Görlitz) |

*Source:* compiled from multiple sources

of the place (e.g., Baarle-Hertog/Baarle-Nassau), illustrated by colorful historical narratives and public memory (Timothy, 2021b).

## Conclusion

Boundaries are human creations that represent the outermost membrane of a state's sovereign control, and they separate places, peoples, histories, and times. Thus, they educe different experiences and are replete with meaning and influence (Prescott, 1987; Timothy, 2001). International borders are full of heritage narratives and historic sites that are in many cases quite unique from heritage sites and narratives in other regions. Because they are indicators of statehood, nationhood, struggles with conflict, and other such important elements of nationhood and heritage, borderlands are fascinating laboratories for understanding heritage-making, national ideals, and what it means to belong or to be excluded.

Borderlines and their hinterlands educe senses of awe, fear, identity, solidarity, and value. They are often revered and valorized as crucial heritage areas, or vilified as places to fear and avoid. Tourism capitalizes on these emotions and on the histories of borderlands in a way that heritagizes once-neglected or forgotten landscapes on the margins of the state. Borders affect the everyday life of everyone on the planet in one way or another. Most directly impacted are borderland residents, for the border is their own heritage, as well as the heritage of the nation. Tourism is frequently used by borderland communities at current or former borders to protect, commemorate, and even fund the protection of this past, which may be rather ordinary or in some cases extraordinary. In either case, border heritage is worthy of protection and commemoration to sustain memory, build solidarity, and to archive the past so that it is not forgotten in a rapidly debordering world.

## Acknowledgment

This chapter was prepared as part of project 2018/29/B/HS4/02417, financed by the National Science Centre, Warsaw, Poland.

## References

Andersen, D.J., & Prokkola E-K. (2021). Heritage as bordering: Heritage making, ontological struggles and the politics of memory in the Croatian and Finnish borderlands. *Journal of Borderlands Studies*, 36(3), 405–424.

Andersen, D.J., & Prokkola, E-K. (Eds.) (2022). *Borderlands resilience: Transitions, adaptation and resistance at borders*. London: Routledge.

Andersen, D.J., & Sandberg, M. (2012). Introduction. In D.J. Andersen, M. Klatt, & M. Sandberg (Eds.), *The border multiple: The practicing of borders between public policy and everyday life in a re-scaling Europe*, pp. 1–21. Aldershot: Ashgate.

Andersson, J., de Garine-Wichatitsky, M., Cumming, D., Dzingirai, V., & Giller, K. (Eds.). (2017). *Transfrontier conservation areas: People living on the edge*. London: Taylor & Francis.

Arreola, D.D. (2002). *Tejano south Texas*. Austin: University of Texas Press.

Arreola, D.D., & Curtis, J.R. (1993). *The Mexican border cities: Landscape anatomy and place personality*. Tucson: University of Arizona Press.

Atanasova, L. (2019). The Korean Demilitarized Zone (DMZ) as liminal space and heterotopia. *Sociological Problems*, 51, 410–424.

Augustin, B. (2009). *Cultures of the world: Andorra*. Tarrytown, NY: Marshall Cavendish International.

Aykan, B. (2016). The politics of intangible heritage and food fights in Western Asia. *International Journal of Heritage Studies*, 22(10), 799–810.

Balibar, É. (2004). *We, the people of Europe? Reflections on transnational citizenship*. Princeton, NJ: Princeton University Press.

Balogh, P. (2019). The revival of cultural heritage and borders. In A. Källén (ed.) *Heritage and borders*, pp. 13–35. Stockholm: The Royal Swedish Academy of Letters, History and Antiquities.

Barcza, A., & Szabolcs, L. (2017). Destination: Europe 2020 transforming parks to promote cities as valuable tourist destinations. *World Leisure Journal*, 59(1), 61–68.

Biger, G. (1995). *The encyclopedia of international boundaries*. Durham: University of Durham, International Boundaries Unit.

Blasco, D., Guia, J., & Prats, L. (2014). Heritage tourism clusters along the borders of Mexico. *Journal of Heritage Tourism*, 9(1), 51–67.

Brown, T.C. (1997). The fourth member of NAFTA: The US-Mexico border. *Annals of the American Academy of Political and Social Science*, 550(1), 105–121.

Chhabra, D. (2018). Soft power analysis in alienated borderline tourism. *Journal of Heritage Tourism*, 13(4), 289–304.

Coles, T., & Hall, D. (2005). Tourism and European Union enlargement: Plus ça change? *International Journal of Tourism Research*, 7(2), 51–61.

Cuevas Contreras, T.J., & Zizaldra Hernández, I. (2015). A holiday celebration in a binational context: Easter experiences at the US–Mexico border. *Journal of Heritage Tourism*, 10(3), 296–301.

Cuevas, T., Blasco, D., & Timothy, D.J. (2016). The Pink Store: A unique tourism enterprise at the US-Mexico border. *European Journal of Tourism Research*, 13, 122–131.

Dołzbłasz, S. (2018). A network approach to transborder cooperation studies as exemplified by Poland's eastern border. *Geographia Polonica, 91*(1), 63–76.

Dorvlo, K. (2017). From restitution to redistribution of Ewe heritage: Challenges and prospects. In D. Merolla, & M. Turin (Eds.) *Searching for sharing: Heritage and multimedia in Africa*, pp. 61–80. Cambridge: Open Book Publishers.

Duffy, R. (2006). The potential and pitfalls of global environmental governance: The politics of transfrontier conservation areas in Southern Africa. *Political Geography, 25*(1), 89–112.

Eckert, A.M. (2011). 'Greetings from the zonal border': Tourism to the Iron Curtain in West Germany. *Studies in Contemporary History, 8*, 9–36.

Eckert, A.M. (2019). *West Germany and the Iron Curtain: Environment, economy, and culture in the borderlands*. Oxford: Oxford University Press.

Eskilsson, L., & Högdahl, E. (2009). Cultural heritage across borders? Framing and challenging the Snapphane story in southern Sweden. *Scandinavian Journal of Hospitality and Tourism, 9*(1), 65–80.

European Commission (2022). European Heritage Label sites. Accessed from https://culture.ec.europa.eu/cultural-heritage/initiatives-and-success-stories/european-heritage-label-sites

Farran, C.O. (1955). International enclaves and the question of state servitudes. *International & Comparative Law Quarterly, 4*(2), 294–307.

Gelbman, A. (2008). Border tourism in Israel: Conflict, peace, fear and hope. *Tourism Geographies, 10*(2), 193–213.

Gelbman, A., & Timothy, D.J. (2010). From hostile boundaries to tourist attractions. *Current Issues in Tourism, 13*(3), 239–259.

Gelbman, A., & Timothy, D.J. (2011). Border complexity, tourism and international exclaves: A case study. *Annals of Tourism Research, 38*(1), 110–131.

Gelbman, A., & Timothy, D.J. (2019). Differential tourism zones on the western Canada–US border. *Current Issues in Tourism, 22*(6), 682–704.

Gioielli, E. (2020). From crumbling walls to the fortress of Europe: Changing commemoration of the 'Pan-European Picnic'. In J. von Puttkamer, M. Kopeček, & W. Borodziej (Eds.), *Cultures of history forum*, pp. 1–14. Jena, Germany: Herder-Institut für Historische Ostmitteleuropaforschung.

Graham, B.J., Ashworth, G.J., & Tunbridge, J.E. (2000). *A geography of heritage: Power, culture and economy*. London: Edward Arnold.

Griswold, E.N. (1939). Hunting boundaries with car and camera in the northeastern United States. *Geographical Review, 29*(3), 353–382.

Harlov-Csortán, M. (2017). From the borderland of the Iron Curtain to European and world cultural heritage. *Folklore: Electronic Journal of Folklore, 70*, 193–224.

Hartshorne, R. (1936). Suggestions on the terminology of political boundaries. *Annals of the Association of American Geographers, 26*, 56–57.

von Hirschhausen, B., Grandits, H., Kraft, C., Müller, D., & Serrier, T. (2019). Phantom borders in Eastern Europe: A new concept for regional research. *Slavic Review, 78*(2), 368–389.

Horjan, G. (2011). Traditional crafts as a new attraction for cultural tourism. *International Journal of Intangible Heritage, 6*(7), 46–56.

van Houtum, H. (2005). The geopolitics of borders and boundaries. *Geopolitics, 10*(4), 672–679.

van Houtum, H., & van Naerssen, T. (2002). Bordering, ordering and othering. *Tijdschrift voor Economische en Sociale Geografie, 93*(2), 125–136.

Husmann, C. (2013). *Curling alone: Transnational social capital on the Canada-United States border*. Unpublished doctoral dissertation, Idaho State University, Pocatello.

Jańczak, J. (Ed.) (2009). *Conflict and cooperation in divided cities*. Berlin: Verlag.

Janicki, W. (2009). Possibilities of tourism development on Polish eastern borderland: Expectations versus potential. *GeoJournal of Tourism and Geosites, 4*(2), 133–144.

Jones, S.B. (1945). *Boundary making*. Washington, DC: Carnegie Endowment.

Källén, A. (2019). Heritage and borders. In A. Källén (ed.) *Heritage and borders*, pp. 7–12. Stockholm: The Royal Swedish Academy of Letters, History and Antiquities.

Kliot, N., & Mansfield, Y. (1997). The political landscape of partition: The case of Cyprus. *Political Geography, 16*(3), 495–521.

Kolosov, V. (2020). Phantom borders: The role in territorial identity and the impact on society. *Belgeo: Revue Belge de Géographie, 2*, 1–19.

Kolosov, V., Medvedev, A., & Zotova, M. (2018). Comparing the development of border regions with the use of GIS (the case of Russia). *Geographia Polonica, 91*(1), 47–61.

Kolosov, V., & O'Loughlin, J. (1998). New borders for new world orders: Territorialities at the fin-desiecle. *GeoJournal, 44*(3), 259–273.

Lähdesmäki, T., & Mäkinen, K. (2019). The 'European significance' of heritage. In T. Lähdesmäki, S. Tomas, & Y. Zhu (Eds.) *Politics of scale: New directions in critical heritage studies*, pp. 36–49. New York: Berghahn Books.

Laine, J.P. (2016). The multiscalar production of borders. *Geopolitics, 21*(3), 465–482.

Le, D.T.T., & Pearce, D.G. (2011). Segmenting visitors to battlefield sites: International visitors to the former demilitarized zone in Vietnam. *Journal of Travel & Tourism Marketing, 28*(4), 451–463.

Lennon, J.J., & Foley, M. (2001). *Dark tourism: The attraction of death and disaster*. London: Cengage.

Leza, C. (2018). Indigenous identities on the US-Mexico border. *Journal of the Southwest, 60*(4), 914–936.

Light, D. (2000). Gazing on communism: Heritage tourism and post-communist identities in Germany, Hungary and Romania. *Tourism Geographies, 2*(2), 157–176.

Lois, M. (2019). The politics of border heritage: EU's cross-border cooperation as scalar politics in the Spanish-Portuguese border. In T. Lähdesmäki, S. Tomas, & Y. Zhu (Eds.) *Politics of scale: New directions in critical heritage studies*, pp. 81–94. New York: Berghahn Books.

Lois, M., & Cairo, H. (2015). Heritage-ized places and spatial stories: B/Ordering practices at the Spanish-Portuguese *Raya/Raia*. *Territory, Politics, Governance, 3*(3), 321–343.

Löytynoja, T. (2008). The development of specific locations into tourist attractions: Cases from Northern Europe. *Fennia: International Journal of Geography, 186*(1), 15–29.

Markov, I. (2015). Cross-border landscape: Construction of natural heritage and local development at Bulgarian-Serbian borderlands. *Venets: The Belogradchik Journal for Local History, Cultural Heritage and Folk Studies, 6*(2), 159–184.

Marsico, G. (2016). The borderland. *Culture & Psychology, 22*(2), 206–215.

Martínez, O.J. (1994). *Border people: Life and society in the U.S.-Mexico borderlands*. Tucson: University of Arizona Press.

McClelland, A. (2016). The management of heritage in contested cross-border contexts: Emerging research on the island of Ireland. *Journal of Cross Border Studies in Ireland, 11*, 91–104.

Metreveli, R. (2019). David Gareji Monastery complex–an integral part of ancient cultural heritage of Georgia. *Bulletin of the Georgian National Academy of Sciences, 13*(2), 161–167.

Nash, C., Reid, B., & Graham, B. (2013). *Partitioned lives: The Irish borderlands*. London: Routledge.

Newman, D. (2006). The lines that continue to separate us: borders in our 'borderless' world. *Progress in Human geography, 30*(2), 143–161.

Newman, D., & Paasi, A. (1998). Fences and neighbours in the postmodern world: Boundary narratives in political geography. *Progress in Human Geography, 22*(2), 186–207.

Noe, C. (2010). Spatiality and 'borderlessness' in transfrontier conservation areas. *South African Geographical Journal, 92*(2), 144–159.

Pelkmans, M. (2012). Chaos and order along the (former) Iron Curtain. In T.M. Wilson, & H. Donnan (Eds.) *A companion to border studies*, pp. 269–282. Oxford: Blackwell.

Pick, Z.M. (2010). *Constructing the image of the Mexican Revolution*. Austin: University of Texas Press.

Prescott, J.V.R. (1987). *Political frontiers and boundaries*. London: Unwin Hyman.

Prokkola, E-K. (2010). Borders in tourism: The transformation of the Swedish–Finnish border landscape. *Current Issues in Tourism, 13*(3), 223–238.

Prokkola, E-K. (2011). Regionalization, tourism development and partnership: The European Union's North Calotte sub-programme of INTERREG IIIA North. *Tourism Geographies, 13*(4), 507–530.

Prokkola, E-K., & Lois, M. (2016). Scalar politics of border heritage: An examination of the EU's northern and southern border areas. *Scandinavian Journal of Hospitality and Tourism, 16*(1), 14–35.

Robinson, G.W.S. (1959). Exclaves. *Annals of the Association of American Geographers, 49*, 283–295.

Rumford, C. (2006). Theorizing borders. *European Journal of Social Theory, 9*(2), 155–169.

Sanguin A.L. (1983). L'architecture spatiale des frontières politiques: Quelques réflexions théoriques à propos de l'exemple Suisse. *Regio Basiliensis, 24*, 1–10.

Shelach-Lavi, G., Wachtel, I., Golan, D., Batzorig, O., Amartuyshin, C., Ellenblum, R., & Honeychurch, W. (2020). Medieval long-wall construction on the Mongolian steppe during the eleventh to thirteenth centuries AD. *Antiquity, 94*, 724–741.

Shepherd, J., & Ioannides, D. (2020). Useful funds, disappointing framework: Tourism stakeholder experiences of INTERREG. *Scandinavian Journal of Hospitality and Tourism, 20*(5), 485–502.

Stavans, I. (Ed.) (2010). *Border culture*. Santa Barbara, CA: Greenwood.

Sternberg, M. (2017). Transnational urban heritage? Constructing shared places in Polish–German border towns. *City*, *21*(3–4), 271–292.

Stetter, S. (2005). *Theorising the European neighbourhood policy: Debordering and rebordering in the Mediterranean*. Florence: European University Institute.

Stoffelen, A., Ioannides, D., & Vanneste, D. (2017). Obstacles to achieving cross-border tourism governance: A multi-scalar approach focusing on the German-Czech borderlands. *Annals of Tourism Research*, *64*, 126–138.

Stoffelen, A., & Vanneste, D. (2019). Commodification of contested borderscapes for tourism development: Viability, community representation, and equity of relic Iron Curtain and Sudetenland heritage tourism landscapes. In A. Paasi, E-K. Prokkola, J. Saarinen, & K Zimmerbauer (Eds.), *Borderless worlds for whom? Ethics, moralities and mobilities*, pp. 139–153. London: Routledge.

Stone, P., Hartmann, R., Seaton, A., Sharpley, R., & White, L. (Eds.) (2018). *The Palgrave handbook of dark tourism studies*. Basingstoke: Palgrave Macmillan.

Studzieniecki, T. (2005). Euroregions—new potential destinations. *Tourism Review*, *60*(4), 26–32.

Su, M.M., & Wall, G. (2012). Global–local relationships and governance issues at the Great Wall World Heritage Site, China. *Journal of Sustainable Tourism*, *20*(8), 1067–1086.

Timothy, D.J. (1997). Tourism and the personal heritage experience. *Annals of Tourism Research*, *34*(3), 751–754.

Timothy, D.J. (2001). *Tourism and political boundaries*. London: Routledge.

Timothy, D.J. (2013). Tourism, war, and political instability: Territorial and religious perspectives. In R. Butler, & W. Suntikul (Eds.) *Tourism and war*, pp. 12–25. London: Routledge.

Timothy, D.J. (2014). Contemporary cultural heritage and tourism: Development issues and emerging trends. *Public Archaeology*, *13*(3), 30–47.

Timothy, D.J. (2019a). Globalisation: The shrinking world of tourism. In D.J. Timothy (Ed.), *Handbook of globalisation and tourism* (pp. 323–332). Cheltenham: Edward Elgar.

Timothy, D.J. (2019b). Tourism, border disputes and claims to territorial sovereignty. In R.K. Isaac, E. Çakmak, & R. Butler (Eds.) *Tourism and hospitality in conflict-ridden destinations*, pp. 25–38. London: Routledge.

Timothy, D.J. (2021a). *Cultural heritage and tourism: An introduction*, 2nd Edn. Bristol: Channel View Publications.

Timothy, D.J. (2021b). *Tourism in European microstates and dependencies: Geopolitics, scale and resource limitations*. Wallingford: CABI.

Timothy, D. J., & Gelbman, A. (2015). Tourist lodging, spatial relations, and the cultural heritage of borderlands. *Journal of Heritage Tourism*, *10*(2), 202–212.

Timothy, D. J., Saarinen, J., & Viken, A. (2016). Tourism issues and international borders in the Nordic Region. *Scandinavian Journal of Hospitality and Tourism*, *16*(1), 1–13.

UNESCO (2022). World Heritage List. Online at https://whc.unesco.org/en/list/

Walker, M.A. (2013). Border food and food on the border: Meaning and practice in Mexican haute cuisine. *Social & Cultural Geography*, *14*(6), 649–667.

Więckowski, M. (2010). Tourism development in the borderlands of Poland. *Geographia Polonica*, *83*(2), 67–81.

Więckowski, M. (2013). Eco-frontier in the mountainous borderlands of Central Europe: The case of Polish border parks. *Journal of Alpine Research/Revue de Geographie Alpine*, *101*(2), 1–13.

Więckowski, M. (in press) How border tripoints offer opportunities for transboundary tourism development. *Tourism Geographies*. https://doi.org/10.1080/14616688.2021.1878268

Więckowski, M., & Saarinen, J. (2019). Tourism transitions, changes, and the creation of new spaces and places in Central-Eastern Europe. *Geographia Polonica*, *92*(4), 369–377.

Więckowski, M., & Timothy, D.J. (2021). Tourism and an evolving international boundary: Bordering, debordering and rebordering on Usedom Island, Poland-Germany. *Journal of Destination Marketing & Management*, *22*, 100647.

Williams, T. (2011). The curious tale of Preah Vihear: The process and value of World Heritage nomination. *Conservation and Management of Archaeological Sites*, *13*(1), 1–7.

Woodward, F.E. (1907). A ramble along the boundary stones of the District of Columbia with a camera. *Records of the Columbia Historical Society, Washington, DC*, *10*, 63–87.

Yan, L., Xu, J. B., Sun, Z., & Xu, Y. (2019). Street art as alternative attractions: A case of the East Side Gallery. *Tourism Management Perspectives*, *29*, 76–85.

Zhang, M.L. (2019). Boundaries versus borders: Transforming ethnic cultural representation into place identity through tourism. *Tourism Culture & Communication*, *19*(4), 243–251.

# 18
# TOUR GUIDING IN CONTESTED GEOPOLITICAL BORDERLANDS: NARRATIVES AND APPROACHES

*Alon Gelbman and Rachel Schweitzer*

## Introduction

Tour guides serve as important intermediaries in conveying messages that help shape visitors' experiences in tourism destinations. This role takes on more significance at border areas, which once were, or still are, centres of controversy and conflict, where tourists are exposed to subjective interpretations of facts. Many researchers have emphasized the great potential appeal of border and post-conflict heritage sites among tourists wishing to experience a current troubled environment or explore the authentic places where political events occurred, and the mediating role of tour guides at such sites (Bowman, 1992; Brin, 2006; Brin & Noy, 2010; Dahles, 2002; Gelbman, 2008; Gelbman & Maoz, 2012; Gelbman & Timothy, 2010; Ngo & Bui, 2019; Quinn & Ryan, 2016; Schlegel & Pfoser, 2021; Skinner, 2016; Wiedenhoft Murphy, 2010; Zhao & Timothy, 2017a). The World Federation of Tourist Guide Associations (2021, n.p.) defines a tour guide as "a person who guides visitors in the language of their choice and interprets the cultural and natural heritage of an area". This definition takes on special meaning in contested heritage sites, such as many border areas, where the message tourists hear depends on the interpretation provided by their tour guide.

This chapter presents and analyses approaches and methods used by tour guides in areas of ongoing conflict and at tourist attractions near former and present hostile borders. It reviews the roles of tour guides as mediators and narrators, and of contested heritage borders as tourism attractions. It focuses on several tour guiding approaches and narrative strategies at borderland attractions based on concepts of tour guides as mediators and narrators.

Tour guide narratives at borders and contested heritage sites, especially geopolitical messages and narratives, can be divided into four selected guiding approaches and strategies: the official narrative (Brin, 2006; Dahles, 2002; Ngo & Bui, 2019; Zhao & Timothy, 2017a); the personal beliefs approach (Gelbman & Maoz, 2012; Quinn & Ryan, 2016; Skinner, 2016; Wiedenhoft Murphy, 2010); the adapted narrative approach (Bowman, 1992; Brin & Noy, 2010); and the dialogue-promoting approach (Gelbman & Maoz, 2012; Gelbman & Timothy, 2010; Wiedenhoft Murphy, 2010).

## Tour Guides as Mediators and Narrators

Tour guides do more than welcome and inform. They convey the essence of a place and open windows into a site, region, or country (Dahles, 2002; Pond, 1993; Weiler & Black, 2015). The functions of tour guides are diverse and include information-givers, founts of knowledge, teachers or instructors, and even entertainers (Cohen, 1985; Holloway, 1981; Timothy, 2021). They are also leaders, educators, ambassadors, hosts, and facilitators (Pond, 1993, cited in Ap & Wong, 2001). They may also be interpreters of language and information, social catalysers, site navigators, tour managers, and of course representatives of the company that employs them (Leshem, 2018).

The job of the modern tour guide combines elements of two types of roles. First, the "pathfinder" geographical guide leads tourists through an environment with which they are unfamiliar, or which is an inaccessible socially defined territory. Second, the "mentor"/guru guides seekers (tourists) toward insight, enlightenment, or some other desired outcome (Cohen, 1985). Pathfinders facilitate access, whereas mentors/gurus build on the access tourists already have, integrating what they see into a coherent and meaningful story and image of place (Bowman, 1992). The role of the mentor guide resembles that of a teacher or advisor by pointing out objects of interest, explaining them, and telling tourists where and when to look. Narratives may include historic facts, comments on architecture, or cultural information (Dahles, 2002). Guides must display a high level of professional skills and an intimate knowledge of local culture (Cohen, Ifergan & Cohen, 2002), and they should create the desired touristic image of the host setting (Cohen, 1985; Weiler & Black, 2015). For mentor guides, information is essential as they help their clients understand the attractions, the character, and the uniqueness of the destination (Reisinger & Steiner, 2006).

Cohen (1985) identifies four general types of tour guides: originals, who are pathfinders, instrumental leaders, responsible for navigating a safe and secure route; animators, who focus on social interaction with the tourists; tour-leaders, who facilitate tourist–host interactions; and professionals, who perform communicative functions. Professionals, like the mentors mentioned above, make local sites and cultures accessible to the tourists by selecting objects of interest—what to see, as well as what not to see; disseminating correct and precise information; interpreting the experience; and fabricating information. Cohen (1985, p. 21) argues that the role of guides is transitioning from leadership towards mediating, from logistical aspects to facilitating experiences, from pathfinding to mentoring, with the communicative component becoming the centre of the professional role.

The most defining communicative function of tour guides is interpretation (Cohen, 1985), which means telling the story and revealing the meaning of a place, event, person, or combination of these (Timothy, 2021). Whether they serve as mediators or cultural brokers, their interpretation often plays a vital role in enhancing the visitor experience and visitors' understanding of a destination (Ap & Wong, 2001). Culture brokering entails bridging, linking, or mediating between groups or persons of different cultural backgrounds to reduce conflict or produce change (Jezewski & Sotnik, 2001, cited in Reisinger & Steiner, 2006). As culture brokers, guides select, gloss, and interpret attractions (Bowman, 1992; Cohen, 1985; Holloway, 1981; Salazar, 2005; Schmidt, 1979; Weiler & Black, 2015). This means that the image of the place as seen by the tourist is not necessarily verification of their expectations, but rather a more nuanced understanding that emerges from the dialogue between the guide and the tourists, which mediates between the tourist gaze and the object of their gaze (Bowman, 1992). According to Urry (1990), guides direct the tourists' gaze, instructing visitors what to observe and what to ignore, and especially how to interpret what they see (Gelbman & Maoz, 2012).

Guides interpose themselves between tourists and the environment, serving both to integrate and to insulate tourists into and from the locality, thus making it less threatening and more inviting. In this way, guides can potentially help bridge conflicted relations and build understandings across communities (Feldman & Skinner, 2018).

Different approaches to guiding emphasize the mediation role of guides (Dahles, 2002). Tour guides may build bridges between people as they deal with money, services, activities, and information (Gurung, Simmons & Devlin, 1996, cited in Ngo & Bui, 2019). They also mediate the cultural gaps between visitors and locals by means of transcultural interpretation that "takes the form of translation of the strangeness of a foreign culture into a cultural idiom familiar to the visitors" (Cohen, 1985, p.15). As interpreters, tour guides not only present facts but also show the importance and meaning of the facts (Leshem, 2018). Yet guides are not merely "translators" of other cultures in the limited sense of the word. In effect, they are mediators who enable tourists to experience other cultures and spaces of otherness (Dahles, 2002). Using communication skills, knowledge, and interpretive abilities, guides can transform an itinerary into an experience (Ap & Wong, 2001). By referencing tourists' cultural knowledge, guides can translate incomprehensible elements of the landscape into familiar ones (Bowman, 1992). As gatekeepers, guides decide which previous knowledge and associations to relate. To gain the attention of as wide a range of tourists as possible, stories are often built on well-known historic events and persons, or on internationally known fictional figures (Nilsson & Zillinger, 2020). In summary, the process of mediation is more than telling tourists how and what to think and feel about their experiences. It is about leading them to their own conclusions and facilitating their learning (Reisinger & Steiner, 2006).

Despite the common denominators shared by many different guiding approaches (e.g., the strong emphasis on the guides' mediation role), guiding cannot be operationalized solely as a harmonious model of mediation intended to satisfy all parties (Dahles, 2002). Personal viewpoints and outside factors also impact guiding. For example, Cohen (1985) observes that guides select objects of interest based on their own personal preferences, professional training, directions from employers or tourism authorities, or the assumed interests of the tour group. Tour guides may have their own agendas based on their country's sociocultural, historical, political, and economic regulations (Ap & Wong, 2001; Zhao & Timothy, 2017a). Through their interpretations or stories, tour guides plant ideas in their guests' minds, with either positive or adverse effects (Leshem, 2018). Quinn and Ryan (2016) found that tour guides face more serious challenges when the difficult heritage and contested past of a site are not immediately apparent to visitors, and interpretation of their meaning is open to negotiation and disagreement. Tour guides articulate difficult memories of past events through their narratives, which are selective and subjective, and in effect they act as gatekeepers of memory (Quinn & Ryan, 2016). Brin and Noy (2010) report that guides interpret scenes and their meanings based on their own beliefs, which can potentially reshape the identities, places, and histories covered in and by the tour. Other studies concur, noting that tour guides tend not to filter out their own philosophical worldviews, so that their gaze may actually distort reality, either to make it more positive or more negative (Gelbman & Collins-Kreiner, 2018). One study of guided tours concluded that because guides have the power to choose which attractions, movements, and stories to highlight, they actually contribute to the reconstruction of history and place image, so that it may not correspond to the identity familiar to the locals (Nilsson & Zillinger, 2020).

Thus, the tourist experience can be moulded as the guide represents heritage and constructs the experiences (Dahles, 2002), based on information designed to influence clients' impressions and attitudes (Cohen, 1985). Often, the message is political and ideological (Ngo & Bui, 2019; Zhao & Timothy, 2017a). Governments may use tourism and tour guides strategically to address issues of national significance and to promote a country's image (Dahles, 2002; Gelbman & Maoz, 2012), as well as to garner sympathy for a cause on the global stage of tourism. Some countries and sites strictly control the guides' narratives and explanations (Feldman & Skinner, 2018; Zhao & Timothy, 2017b). In these cases, guided tours may "whitewash" history by providing a glimpse of what the authorities want tourists to see and know without revealing undesirable elements of the past. This has proven to be an effective instrument for controlling tourists and their contact with the host society, as well as the images and narratives the host society wants to present to outsiders (Dahles, 2002).

Nowhere are the roles of tour guides as gatekeepers, political propagandizers, mediators, and information brokers as apparent as in areas of geopolitical sensitivity and in conflicted border zones (Evangelou, 2019; Leonard, 2007; Timothy, Prideaux & Kim, 2004). Here, guides tend to be highly partisan in their attempts to garner sympathy for a cause or a specific side of a conflict. The narratives on opposites sides may even diverge so much that they might share little in common and could be seen as representing entirely different events and places (Kuntz, 2019; Yang, 2020).

## Borders and Contested Heritage as Tourist Attractions

The relationship between tourism and borders is fundamental. Travel usually involves crossing a border, whether political or otherwise, domestic or international, and borderlands are often the first or last areas of a state that travellers encounter (Prokkola, 2010). Tourism is influenced by political boundaries, by border-related government policies and administrative management on both sides, and by the actual physical barriers they create. Borders also have a dynamic influence on tourism by creating barriers, tourist attractions, and modifications of the tourism landscape (Timothy, 2001). Borderlines reflect socio-political values and attract visitors who have a fascination with them. Lines marked on the ground by tangible objects have the potential to attract tourists and shape socio-economic trends and patterns (Gelbman and Timothy, 2010; Timothy, 2001). The same border that deters some travellers may attract others who take an interest in comparing differences in languages, cultures, and politics (Gelbman, 2008; Gelbman & Timothy, 2010).

When a crisis ends and a border opens, that border frequently becomes a commemorative space for a region's political heritage (Więckowski, 2010). It can be used to teach awareness and understanding of the nature of disagreements, with an emphasis on the positive elements of transformation and its symbolic power for the present and the future (Gelbman, 2010; Gelbman & Timothy, 2010). Still, post-conflict sites associated with difficult memories offer serious challenges as to which aspects of history should be selected and represented and which should be ignored (Quinn & Ryan, 2016). Achieving a balance between ownership, power, and interpretation can also be problematic (Causevic & Lynch, 2011). Sometimes a previously closed border can serve as a symbol of a darker heritage to be remembered but not repeated (Gelbman & Timothy, 2010). Alternatively, tourism in post-conflict areas has the bivalent potential to both build peace and keep past conflict in the present (Wiedenhoft Murphy, 2010). Visitors are drawn to formerly closed and hostile borderlines mainly because of the historic events enacted there and the heritage, historic remains, and local myths that developed around the events (Gelbman & Timothy, 2010). At such localities, tour guides take on the additional roles of storytellers and meaning-makers for the tourists. By sharing viewpoints and stories, reflection and understanding can emerge (Ngo & Bui, 2019).

Tourists may be attracted to destinations suffering from ongoing hostility and violence, specifically because they seek a unique and exciting experience. Brin (2006) introduced the concept of politically oriented tourism, in which tourists visit a place marked by political instability to demonstrate their solidarity with one or the other conflicting party residing there or, if they are more politically neutral, simply to learn more about the conflict.

## Tour Guiding Approaches at Geopolitical Borderlands

As noted previously, the literature examines a variety of roles for tour guides, the most significant of which are mediator and interpreter between the tourist and the destination. This aspect becomes more complex at border sites enmeshed in a past of historic conflict or a troubled conflicted present where both sides vie to transmit their political agenda to the tourists. At contested borderland attractions, four main guiding approaches are discernable, which differ in terms of the tour guides' motives and the content of their narrative (Figure 18.1). The following four guiding approaches are illustrated in border and conflict situations and are discussed below: the official narrative approach, the personal belief approach, the adapted narrative approach, and the dialogue promoting approach.

### *Official Narrative Guiding Approach*

The first and most top-down regulated guiding approach is the official narrative. In this scenario tour guides' agendas are determined in advance by the government or another body promoting a particular political message. Tour guides serving such political objectives follow an officially authorized narrative and convey "facts" approved by the government in an attempt to distance tourists from undesirable aspects of the host society, as well as to control the images and narratives through which the host society is presented. Government-approved guides are instructed on what to tell, where and when, and how to represent the country or locality correctly, thus minimizing the guides' subjective interpretive role (Dahles, 2002; Zhao & Timothy, 2017a). By exposing tourists to certain messages and sites, it is hoped that they will propagate the authority's desired political messages when they return to their communities of origin (Brin, 2006).

The official guiding approach is employed in guided tours of the historical sites of Quang Tri Province in Vietnam. From 1954 to 1976, the Geneva Accords established the 17th parallel as the military demarcation line and the de facto political boundary between North and South Vietnam. Quang Tri Province, located in the centre of Vietnam, was the backdrop for the

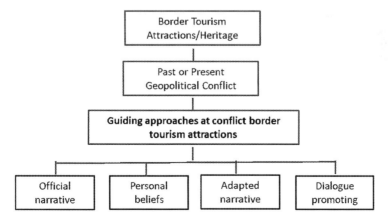

*Figure 18.1* Selected tour guiding approaches at contested border tourism destinations.

fiercest battles of the Vietnam War and enormous loss of lives, which earned the area a sacred place in the national memory. The region encompasses many war-related historic sites of the former demilitarized zone where tour guides are tasked with conveying an official political message to visitors and educating younger generations. Only professional, trained guides are permitted to deliver the highly regulated and politically charged official narratives of national history and symbolic interpretation associated with the sites (Ngo & Bui, 2019).

The Korean demilitarized zone (DMZ) is becoming an increasingly popular tourist attraction, which can be visited on day-trip package tours from both sides of the border (Hunter, 2015; Kim, Choe & Lee, 2019; Kim & Thapa, 2018; Timothy, 2001). Unique to this locality, on the South Korean side, the tours are led by US and Korean military personnel. Besides protecting the border, one of the troops' main duties is to protect and guide visitors at the Panmunjom truce village and other areas of the DMZ. After arriving at the destination, tourists are funnelled from private buses into military vehicles, which take them to the appointed locations in the zone and where tour-guide-trained soldiers depict a narrative that reflects the view of the South (and conversely the view of the North on the northern side) regarding who won the (ongoing) war and the potential reunification of the Koreas (Grinker, 1995; Shin, 2007; Timothy et al., 2004).

Another case that illustrates the official narrative approach is the city of Jerusalem, which lies at the core of the Israeli-Palestinian conflict. Jerusalem is the capital of Israel and the holiest city in the world for Jews and Christians, and the third holiest city for Muslims. As such, the city has always been a focus of pilgrimages among the three Abrahamic faiths and the main destination in the Holy Land (Shoval & Cohen-Hattab, 2001). During the 1948 War of Independence, Jerusalem was divided between Israel and Jordan but was unified following the 1967 war. Since then, Jews and Palestinians have coexisted in the contested city with fluctuating political violence, tension, and instability. In this situation the official and unofficial representatives of the conflicting parties promote their political agendas, in order to defend their international image or garner sympathy by selecting the messages delivered to visitors throughout the city (Brin, 2006).

More than providing tourists with carefully selected historic and cultural information about contested heritage sites and restricting the tour guides' interpretive role, the official narrative approach is used to create a positive image of contested places in the international community, which tourists represent.

## *Personal Beliefs Guiding Approach*

Tour guides employing the second approach at borderland sites transmit a message based on their own personal beliefs and points of view, as opposed to a top-down regulated political message. Guides' personal interests and experiences can substantially influence their narratives and their representation of difficult events of the past (Quinn & Ryan, 2016). The spiritual belief of some tour guides may cause them to view guiding as a mission to spread goodwill or a specific message. If they do not filter out their own point of view, they may present reality as more positive or more negative than it really is (Gelbman & Collins-Kreiner, 2018).

Tour operators in conflict or post-conflict societies attempt to sell their version of history to win tourists' support (Wiedenhoft Murphy, 2010). Tour guides' sense of affiliation with a national reference group shapes the type of words they use, especially regarding sites and events that hold a special place in the reference group's collective memory (Brin & Noy, 2010).

Evidence of this approach is found in Belfast, Northern Ireland, where the peace lines are a salient part of local tours. The walls that separate Catholic and Protestant areas of the city were

*Tour Guiding in Contested Borderlands*

first built in 1969 during the early years of "the Troubles" as a way to keep Irish Republicans and British Loyalists apart. Today the walls have gates to allow passage from one area to another during the day and are closed at night. Local tour guides in Belfast capitalize on the conflict to express their own historic narratives and identities. They function as "gatekeepers" of the collective memory and representation of the historic conflict (Wiedenhoft Murphy, 2010). This phenomenon is intensified several fold when the tour guide is, for example, an Irish Republican ex-prisoner whose mission is to educate and promote the Republican ideology through his or her historical narrative and not to interpret both sides of the Troubles (Skinner, 2016). Moreover, when asked about narrating the Troubles, such individuals claim that only local guides can "tell the truth" and that tour operators from outside the local communities distort the history of the past conflict (Wiedenhoft Murphy, 2010).

At another conflicted border attraction, the Israeli-Jordanian Island of Peace border site (Figure 18.2), tour guides tend to express their personal attitudes when referring to the war heritage and geopolitical conflict narratives of the past, with little reference to today's peace between Israel and Jordan (Gelbman & Maoz, 2012).

The drawback of this approach is that it can help to keep the former conflict alive. At the Island of Peace, for example, the guiding narrative can plant seeds of fear instead of sending messages of hope and peace. Therefore, tour guides must be careful not to express their personal viewpoints but instead adjust the discourse to strengthen the positive narratives and transmit the message of peace the border site is supposed to convey, as demonstrated by its name (Gelbman & Maoz, 2012).

*Figure 18.2* Tour guiding at the 'Island of Peace' on the Israeli-Jordanian border.

## Adapted Narrative Guiding Approach

Tour guides who use the third guiding approach are essentially formulating and adapting their narrative to fit what the audience expects or would like to hear. Tour guides may use drama to heighten tourists' interest and create a dark tourism atmosphere at sites commemorating a heavy tragedy that is imprinted in the collective memory of visitors (Gelbman & Maoz, 2012). On the other hand, guides may also avoid controversial topics, thus side-stepping conflict and creating a pleasurable experience by regulating the information they convey and selectively silencing contested aspects of the past (Schlegel & Pfoser, 2021).

Investigating Israeli and Palestinian tour guides leading non-Jewish tourists in Israel and the Occupied Territories, Bowman (1992) found that guides tended to modify their nationalist visions to accommodate what tourists wanted to see and hear, so as not to alienate them. However, while the only option for Palestinian guides was to avoid any mention of their national vision, Israeli guides could establish bridges through guide–tourist cultural discourses. Bowman noted that Israeli guides claimed they told tourists what they wanted to hear and not what a government ministry instructed them to say. Furthermore, guides used tourists' responses to shape their presentations. Satisfied tour groups benefit not only the tour guides themselves financially but also their nation, by sending home tourists who are convinced that the rewarding visit helped them gain new insights into old beliefs (Bowman, 1992). Ron and Timothy (2019) discuss similar conditions where Israeli tour guides adapt their narratives to accommodate the wishes, desires, and viewpoints of different Christian denominations regarding the ongoing political conflict in the Holy Land.

Similarly, tour guides are careful not to anger or alienate their listeners, and therefore avoid topics that might cause uneasiness. For the same reason, certain terminology may be used to create empathy with the narrative. For example, during a tour of a Jerusalem neighbourhood, a Jewish-Israeli tour guide leading a Jewish-Israeli group mentioned public army and political figures by their popular nicknames, thus making it easier for the listeners to identify with them, endearing the leaders to them, and imbuing the entire narration with a sense of shared intimacy, as well as to satisfy high public demand for a feeling of belonging (Brin & Noy, 2010).

Even where the official narrative approach is used, the narrative is at times adapted to suit different visitors. Such is the case with the on-site guides in Quang Tri, Vietnam, where the stories told to younger audiences emphasize survival in the face of hardships and the darkness of war. For Vietnamese tourists, the guides are mediating agents connecting present and past, while for international tourists, their interpretation promotes mutual understanding and brings a new perspective of the war to foreigners (Ngo & Bui, 2019). With this approach, tour guides aim to create a pleasant experience and avoid confrontation with tourists. By adapting their narrative to the type of audience, guides present visitors at borderland sites with the image they expect to encounter, or with a message that resounds positively with them, and thereby strengthen their existing beliefs in the dynamics of the conflict. This is in contrast to the first two approaches, which introduce visitors to new information, whether dictated from above or by the guides' beliefs.

## Dialogue-promoting Guiding Approach

The fourth guiding approach presented in this chapter refers to tour guide narratives that offer an opportunity for tourists at contested border areas to observe and learn about the existing reality and to engage in dialogue and discourse about it. Guides may function as more neutral facilitators or information brokers to help guide interactive learning and provide historical knowledge from a more balanced perspective.

Tourism has the potential to promote cross-border and cross-community cooperation, particularly if tour guides can provide a neutral narrative of the other side, be it ethnic or religious groups, and to highlight shared history and heritages (Wiedenhoft Murphy, 2010). Likewise, tour operators at sites where past tragedies have occurred must determine whether "to arouse passions or to create a sense of forgiveness" (Tarlow, 2005, p. 56). For example, in the case of three former borders of conflict—the Island of Peace on the Israeli-Jordanian border, the Golden Triangle of Southeast Asia, and the Berlin Wall—the opening of borders resulted in the emergence of commemorative spaces of the past at those sites, promoting understanding of former disagreements and emphasizing a more peaceful present and future (Gelbman, 2019; Gelbman & Timothy, 2010; Litvin, 2020).

Israel's border tourism sites can be viewed as places of hope for a better future of peace and cooperation with neighbours on the other side. In many cases, the observation point can grow to signify both the core of the conflict and a prayer for peace (Gelbman, 2008). A border tourism attraction like the Island of Peace on the Israeli and Jordanian border has the potential to function as an important place for discussing and even promoting coexistence and cooperation between the countries. Tour guides who encourage bridging discourse for understanding may contribute to an atmosphere of peace and understanding (Gelbman & Maoz, 2012).

A study of tour guiding conducted at post-conflict tourism sites in Bosnia and Herzegovina found that guides typically avoided aspects of nationalism and politics and instead emphasized the meaningful experiences of ordinary people, to inspire reflection and to present a message of peace (Causevic & Lynch, 2011). It is interesting to observe that along with their political and educational role, tour guides in the Quang Tri province of Vietnam also perform a symbolic role of bridging between past and present, reconciling conflicts between opposing sides and promoting common understanding and empathy (Ngo & Bui, 2019).

## Conclusions

One of the significant roles of tour guides is to serve as a mediator and interpreter between visitors and the tourist attraction and to communicate the meaning of the place. This role becomes even more challenging at borderland sites and locations suffused with suffering from ongoing troubles or difficult memories, where interpreted meaning is open to negotiation and contestation (Quinn & Ryan, 2016). This chapter has focused on four selected approaches and narrative strategies adopted by tour guides for guiding tourists through border and contested heritage sites. The first approach, the official narrative approach, is the most top-down regulated of them, and is mainly used by hosts wishing to control the particular political message they wish to convey and to create a positive image of the place. In this strategy, carefully selected facts are presented to control the narratives and distance visitors from undesirable aspects of the host society (Brin, 2006; Dahles, 2002).

The second style, the personal belief guiding approach, is similar to the first in the sense that the guides transmit a predetermined message to tourists visiting the border site. The difference is that in this approach, the tour guide promotes a personal rather than an official, politically imposed agenda. Therefore, the narrative and representation of difficult memories can vary from guide to guide according to each one's personal interests, viewpoints, and experiences (Quinn & Ryan, 2016), and can potentially bias reality so that it appears more positive or negative than it is (Gelbman & Collins-Kreiner, 2018). Guides can also plant seeds of fear instead of sending messages of hope and peace (Gelbman & Maoz, 2012).

The third guiding approach entails an adaptation of the character of the presented narrative to the identity of the tourists themselves. Tour guide strategies may include the use of drama

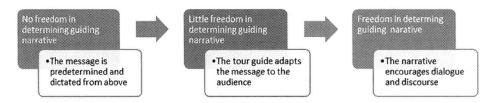

*Figure 18.3* Tour guiding narrative and freedom at conflict and contested border tourism attractions.

to heighten interest and create a specific atmosphere in places suffused with difficult memories (Gelbman & Maoz, 2012). They may also dwell on positive aspects and avoid controversial issues of the past, to create a positive experience for visitors (Schlegel & Pfoser, 2021).

Unlike the previous three approaches, in the fourth one, the tour guide has complete freedom regarding the nature of the narrative and strives to use words that encourage open dialogue with their clients. The importance of the dialogue-promoting method is its ability to promote an atmosphere of peace and understanding (Causevic & Lynch, 2011; Gelbman & Maoz, 2012), foster respect for cross-community history and heritage (Wiedenhoft Murphy, 2010), and encourage coexistence and cooperation between countries (Gelbman & Maoz, 2012).

Despite the different approaches, a particular narrative may at times fall into more than one scheme. For example, a guide may convey a predetermined message that is tailored to a specific target audience, such as children, locals, or tourists (Ngo & Bui, 2019). Similarly, tour guides who deliver a message based on personal beliefs can also encourage bridge-building discourse and understanding (Gelbman & Maoz, 2012). This review of four tour guiding approaches in contested border areas and other regions of geopolitical conflict reveals a process of movement from the micro, with little or no freedom in determining the guiding narrative, to the macro, with significant freedom in determining what guides say and how they say it (Figure 18.3).

In this sense, at the lower level, the messages conveyed are predetermined and dictated from above and tourists are perceived as a target for promoting the host's political agenda. At the intermediate level, guides adapt themselves to the audience and therefore the narrative presented may at times be detached from a specific script. Finally, at the high level of freedom, tour guides encourage dialogue and discourse between themselves and tourists, and perhaps even between tourists and hosts. On the one hand, this approach may provoke discomfort and even disagreements. On the other hand, such openness can stimulate interesting discourse and new insights, especially at borderland destinations with present and/or past histories of geopolitical conflicts and disagreements.

The discussion in this chapter has demonstrated the potential inherent in the narrative of tour guides at contested border attractions and other areas of geopolitical dissonance, which on the one hand can serve as a political tool by the host, and on the other hand has the ability to encourage bridge-building processes and understanding between communities.

# References

Ap, J. & Wong, K. K. (2001). Case study on tour guiding: Professionalism, issues and problems. *Tourism Management*, 22(5), 551–563.

Bowman, G. (1992). The politics of tour guiding: Israeli and Palestinian guides in Israel and the Occupied Territories. In D. Harrison (ed) *Tourism and the less-developed countries*, pp. 121–134. London: Belhaven Press.

Brin, E. (2006). Politically-oriented tourism in Jerusalem. *Tourist Studies*, 6(3), 215–243.

Brin, E., & Noy, C. (2010). The said and the unsaid: Performative guiding in a Jerusalem neighbourhood. *Tourist Studies*, 10(1), 19–33.

Causevic, S., & Lynch, P. (2011). Phoenix tourism: Post-conflict tourism role. *Annals of Tourism Research*, 38(3), 780–800.

Cohen, E. (1985). The tourist guide: The origins, structure and dynamics of a role. *Annals of Tourism Research*, 12(1), 5–29.

Cohen, E. H., Ifergan, M., & Cohen, E. (2002). A new paradigm in guiding: The Madrich as a role model. *Annals of Tourism Research*, 29(4), 919–932.

Dahles, H. (2002). The politics of tour guiding: Image management in Indonesia. *Annals of Tourism Research*, 29(3), 783–800.

Evangelou, E. (2019). Theatre beyond nationalism: Participatory art in the Cyprus buffer zone. *The Cyprus Review*, 31(1), 193–207.

Feldman, J., & Skinner, J. (2018). Tour guides as cultural mediators. *Ethnologia Europaea*, 48(2), 5–13.

Gelbman, A. (2008). Border tourism in Israel: Conflict, peace, fear and hope. *Tourism Geographies*, 10(2), 193–213.

Gelbman, A. (2010). Border tourism attractions as a space for presenting and symbolizing peace. In O. Mouffakkir & I. Kelly (eds) *Tourism, progress and peace*, pp. 83–98. Wallingford: CABI.

Gelbman, A. (2019). Tourism, peace, and global stability. In D.J. Timothy (ed) *Handbook of globalisation and tourism*, pp. 149–160. London: Edward Elgar.

Gelbman, A., & Collins-Kreiner, N. (2018). Cultural and behavioral differences: Tour guides gazing at tourists. *Journal of Tourism and Cultural Change*, 16(2), 155–172.

Gelbman, A., & Maoz, D. (2012). Island of peace or island of war: Tourist guiding. *Annals of Tourism Research*, 39(1), 108–133.

Gelbman, A., & Timothy, D. J. (2010). From hostile boundaries to tourist attractions. *Current Issues in Tourism*, 13(3), 239–259.

Grinker, R. R. (1995). The "Real Enemy" of the nation: Exhibiting North Korea at the demilitarized zone. *Museum Anthropology*, 19(2), 31–40.

Gurung, G., Simmons, D., & Devlin, P. (1996). The evolving role of tourist guides: The Nepali experience. In R.W. Butler, & T. Hinch (eds) *Tourism and indigenous peoples*, pp. 107–128. London: Thomson.

Holloway, J. C. (1981). The guided tour a sociological approach. *Annals of Tourism Research*, 8(3), 377–402.

Hunter, W. C. (2015). The visual representation of border tourism: Demilitarized zone (DMZ) and Dokdo in South Korea. *International Journal of Tourism Research*, 17(2), 151–160.

Jezewski, M. A., & Sotnik, P. (2001). *The rehabilitation service provider as culture broker: Providing culturally competent services to foreign born persons.* Buffalo, NY: Center for International Rehabilitation Research Information and Exchange.

Kim, H., Choe, Y., & Lee, C. K. (2019). Differential effects of patriotism and support on post-development visit intention: the Korean DMZ Peace Park. *Journal of Travel & Tourism Marketing*, 36(3), 384–401.

Kim, M., & Thapa, B. (2018). The influence of self-congruity, perceived value, and satisfaction on destination loyalty: A case study of the Korean DMZ. *Journal of Heritage Tourism*, 13(3), 224–236.

Kuntz, A. F. (2019). Battir: Creative resistance in a front line—Opportunities and dilemmas of tourism development in a conflict zone. *Tourism Culture & Communication*, 19(4), 265–276.

Leonard, M. (2007). A little bit of history and a lot of opinion: Biased authenticity in Belfast and Nicosia. *Kıbrıs Araştırmaları Dergisi*, 13(33), 53–77.

Leshem, A. (2018). Guiding the dark and secondary trauma syndrome: Tour guides' coping mechanisms for guiding in dark tourism sites. *Journal of Tourismology*, 4(2), 107–127.

Litvin, S. W. (2020). Tourism and peace: A review and commentary. *Tourism Review International*, 23(3–4), 173–181.

Ngo, P. M., & Bui, H. T. (2019). Contested interpretation of Vietnam war heritage: Tour guides' mediating roles. *Journal of Tourism & Adventure*, 2(1), 61–84.

Nilsson, J. H., & Zillinger, M. (2020). Free guided tours: Storytelling as a means of glocalizing urban places. *Scandinavian Journal of Hospitality and Tourism*, 20(3), 286–301.

Pond, K. L. (1993). *The professional guide: Dynamics of tour guiding.* New York: Van Nostrand Reinhold.

Prokkola, E-K. (2010). Borders in tourism: The transformation of the Swedish–Finnish border landscape. *Current Issues in Tourism*, 13(3), 223–238.

Quinn, B., & Ryan, T. (2016). Tour guides and the mediation of difficult memories: The case of Dublin Castle, Ireland. *Current Issues in Tourism*, 19(4), 322–337.

Reisinger, Y., & Steiner, C. (2006). Reconceptualising interpretation: The role of tour guides in authentic tourism. *Current Issues in Tourism*, 9(6), 481–498.

Ron, A.S., & Timothy, D.J. (2019). *Contemporary Christian Travel: Pilgrimage, Practice and Place*. Bristol: Channel View Publications.

Salazar, N. B. (2005). Tourism and glocalization "local" tour guiding. *Annals of Tourism Research*, 32(3), 628–646.

Schlegel, S., & Pfoser, A. (2021). Navigating contested memories in a commercialised setting: Conflict avoidance strategies in Kyiv city tour guiding. *International Journal of Heritage Studies*, 27(5), 487–499.

Schmidt, C. J. (1979). The guided tour: Insulated adventure. *Urban life*, 7(4), 441–467.

Shin, Y-S. (2007). Perception differences between domestic and international visitors in the tourist destination: The case of the borderline, the DMZ area. *Journal of Travel and Tourism Marketing*, 21(2/3), 77–88.

Shoval, N., & Cohen-Hattab, K. (2001). Urban hotel development patterns in the face of political shifts. *Annals of Tourism Research*, 28(4), 908–925.

Skinner, J. (2016). Walking the Falls: Dark tourism and the significance of movement on the political tour of West Belfast. *Tourist Studies*, 16(1), 23–39.

Tarlow, P. E. (2005). Dark tourism – The appealing 'dark' side of tourism and more. In M. Novelli (ed) *Niche tourism*, pp. 47–58. London: Routledge.

Timothy, D. J. (2001). *Tourism and political boundaries*. London: Routledge.

Timothy, D.J. (2021). *Cultural heritage and tourism: An introduction*, 2nd edn. Bristol: Channel View Publications.

Timothy, D. J., Prideaux, B., & Kim, S. S. (2004). Tourism at borders of conflict and (de)militarized zones. In T.V. Singh (ed) *New horizons in tourism: Strange experiences and stranger practices*, pp. 83–94. Wallingford: CABI.

Urry, J. (1990). *The tourist gaze*. London: Sage.

Weiler, B., & Black, R. (2015). *Tour guiding research: Insights, issues and implications*. Bristol: Channel View Publications.

Więckowski, M. (2010). Tourism development in the borderlands of Poland. *Geographia Polonica*, 83(2), 67–81.

Wiedenhoft Murphy, W. A. (2010). Touring the troubles in West Belfast: Building peace or reproducing conflict? *Peace & Change*, 35(4), 537–560.

World Federation of Tourist Guide Associations (2021). What is a tourist guide? Online: https://wftga.org/about-us/what-is-a-tourist-guide/

Yang, C. (2020). Staging Israel/Palestine: The geopolitical imaginaries of international tourism. *Environment and Planning C: Politics and Space*, 38(6), 1075–1090.

Zhao, S., & Timothy, D.J. (2017a). The dynamics of guiding and interpreting in red tourism. *International Journal of Tourism Cities*, 3(3), 243–259.

Zhao, S., & Timothy, D.J. (2017b). Tourists' consumption and perceptions of red heritage. *Annals of Tourism Research*, 63, 97–111.

# 19
# TOURISTS' PERFORMANCES AT BORDER LANDMARKS IN THE ERA OF SOCIAL MEDIA

*Alix Varnajot*

## Introduction

This chapter explores tourists' border-crossing performances around border markers and landmarks. Borders have traditionally been understood as barriers for tourism by hindering and filtering the mobility of people (Gao et al., 2019; Webster & Timothy, 2006). However, it is now well understood that borders are also geographic spaces with great potential for the development of tourism (Orgaz-Agüera & Moral-Cuadra, 2022; Sofield, 2006; Timothy, 1995). Indeed, on the one hand, borders can be understood as tourist destinations, where tourists will take advantage of different political and economic policies and regulations available on "the other side" for activities including cross-border shopping, prostitution and gambling (Timothy, Saarinen & Viken, 2016) or even for medical reasons (Cuevas Contreras, 2016). The Pyrenean region, for instance, provides a great example of such cross-border tourism. In villages located at the Spanish (e.g., Arnegi, Ibardin and Dantxaria) or Andorran (e.g., El Pas de la Casa) borders, one can observe the ritualized practices of people walking from stores back to their cars, loaded with alcohol and tobacco goods, taking advantage of tax differences between France and Spain or Andorra.

On the other hand, borders have also become tourist attractions, visited by millions of people and generating as many border-crossings and ritualized performances. For example, Grenier (2007) noted that crossing the borderline of the Arctic Circle is an inescapable ritual for tourists visiting Rovaniemi, Finland, for the first time. Here, these rituals are defined as "stereotyped [sequences] of activities involving gestures, words and objects" (Turner, 1973, p. 1100) invariably performed and reproduced by tourists (see Varnajot, 2019a). In this chapter, borders refer to all forms of borderlines that separate different territories (not just states or countries) and that are celebrated by visible markers in the landscape. They might be national or subnational boundaries, as well as geodetic lines, also called "ghostly lines" by Tim Ingold (2007, p. 47), including the Equator, the Tropics of Cancer and Capricorn, the Polar Circles or meridian lines (Timothy, 1998). These markers—or landmarks—can be as various as a simple sign by the side of the road, or lines painted on the ground or on globes, cairns, poles, monuments, interpretative boards or tourist centres organized around tourism clusters including museums, catering services and souvenir shops, such as La Ciudad Mitad del Mundo and the Santa Claus Village, respectively celebrating the Equator in Ecuador and the Arctic Circle in Finland.

People's performances and mobilities around borders have gained significant interest in the context of state border securitization through studies on the surveillance of individual bodies at border-crossing checkpoints, on discrimination against migrant women and vulnerable borderland populations, or on border guard services (see Prokkola & Ridanpää, 2015). However, little interest has been given to the practices and rituals performed around touristic border landmarks. Therefore, by examining tourists' border-crossing practices and bodily performances, I aim to further conceptualize developments in the study of borders in tourism, and particularly on borders as being tourist attractions. First, I concentrate on the narratives of otherness induced by borders, briefly discussing how the essence of borderlines generates specific expectations and performances. Focus then shifts to descriptions of these border-crossing performances and to an examination of both "border-crossing postures" and "line-crossing ceremonies". In recent years, the rise of social media, assisted by new technological tools (e.g., smartphones, Wi-Fi services and mobile apps), has significantly influenced tourists' experiences, performances and practices (Du et al., in press; Gretzel, 2017; Kokkinou et al., 2022; Munar & Jacobsen, 2014), and therefore the last section of the chapter explores the role of social media in the reproduction of these border-crossing rituals.

## Crossing Borders and the Narrative of Otherness

As recalled by Newman (2003, p. 15), "all borders share a common function to the extent that they include some and exclude many others". Thus, by separating, delimiting and defining territories, borders create differences and otherness, and by extension, they also define the identity of these separated territories (Balibar, 2002; Newman & Paasi, 1998; Timothy, 1995; Varnajot, 2019a). As a result, borders serve as demarcation lines between the "familiar" and the "unusual", the "us" and the "them" or the "here" and the "there" (Newman, 2003, 2006). These differences, shaped by borderlines, are seductive (Picard & Di Giovine, 2014) and the "otherness" they create raises curiosity, mystery and fascination (Gelbman & Timothy, 2010; Newman, 2006; Ryden, 1993; Timothy, 2003a; Varnajot, 2020).

The otherness induced by borderlines triggers feelings of curiosity and fascination almost in spite of what type of boundary is present, as long as one is aware that one is about to cross a border, which is not always the case, particularly in the case of ghostly lines, as showed by Varnajot (2019a) with the Arctic Circle. For example, Medvedev (1999, p. 43) shared his experience of crossing the border of Finland and Russia. Being moved by the love of geography and plain curiosity, he wrote:

> Borders have fascinated me since childhood. [...] Approaching the Finnish–Russian boundary, I was feeling this boyish excitement, an anticipation of mystery. [...] Likewise, many Finns used to visit the Finnish–Soviet frontier, especially in the olden days of a sealed border, to feel the mystique of the place, take photos of the prohibited sign, or even to step in the restricted border zone seeking to experience a geopolitical thrill – taking a small step towards the Other, into the realm of shadows.

The Finnish–Russian border is a highly symbolic line (Laurén, 2012; Paasi, 1999). Indeed, more than delimiting two countries, it also delimits the European Union from Russia and was even considered the border between the communist East and capitalist West for most of the twentieth century. This led to an intense culturally and socially construed border with semiotically encoded sides that are still well exploited in media discourses (Koch & Vainikka, 2019; Vainikka & Vainikka, 2018). Although today "the Finnish–Russian border is utilitarian and

*Figure 19.1* Approaching the restricted area of the Finnish-Russian border, in Näränkä, south of Kuusamo, Finland.

Photo: A. Varnajot, June 2019

there is more interaction and transnational movement than in the period of the Iron Curtain" (Laurén, 2012, p. 40), these passionate narratives on restrictions and otherness, associated with the physical items such as fences and prohibited entry signs (Figure 19.1), have triggered desires and feelings of curiosity to go see the mysterious "Other" side, as Medvedev (1999) relates.

Nevertheless, borders do not have to be as symbolic as the Finnish–Russian frontier in order to fascinate. The geographer Kent Ryden (1993, pp. 1–2), for example, recounts his experience of walking along the subnational border between Rhode Island and Connecticut in the United States:

> In the space of a few feet, we pass from a geographical entity to another which looks exactly the same but is unique, has a different name, is in many ways a completely separate world from the one we just left. […] Now, on a brilliant blue May morning, I stand […] on the border between Connecticut and Rhode Island, looking one way and then the other, letting each place tell me what it means. The signs on each side do their best to let me know that their state is distinctive and significant, that I would be glad should I decide to cross the line in that direction. They invite me with strenuous bonhomie.

The signs embodying the border emphasize the narrative of otherness and its associated curiosity factor. Albeit the border between Rhode Island and Connecticut is free to cross and

*Figure 19.2* The state of Alaska welcoming us on the Klondike Highway, on our way to Skagway.

Photo: A. Varnajot, June 2018

is not as symbolic as the Finnish–Russian borderline, the signs serving as border landmarks incite feelings about the crossing. Indeed, on both sides, the signs are welcoming; they invite people to discover the distinctive qualities that make their respective state unique and above average (see Zelinsky, 1988). Therefore, the persuasiveness and geographical messages painted on welcome signs aim to shape and manipulate tourists' feelings by creating both narratives of otherness and intangible distinctions between Rhode Island and Connecticut (Ryden, 1993; Varnajot, 2019a). In other words, welcoming signs epitomize the transition between two realms of experience that borders in tourism are all about: they offer opportunities for photos and for visitors to perform border-crossing postures (Więckowski, in press), such as at the Alaska welcome sign near the Canadian border (see Figure 19.2).

Although the markers might not be located at the exact borderline (see Löytynoja, 2007; Timothy, 2001), their presence in the landscape is imperative for effecting a feeling of excitement or geographical thrill of crossing a border to be complete. Indeed, if one is aware of entering or leaving another territory or region and there is no visible marker, the crossing might lead to completely opposite feelings, such as frustration or disappointment, such as the experience of the British traveller Cutcliffe Hyne (1898, p. 271) when crossing the Arctic Circle, during a trip to northern Europe:

> On this stage, we were due to recross that imaginary boundary, the Arctic Circle, and come once more in that Temperate Zone which was our more native atmosphere, and we were on the keen lookout for some official recognition of its whereabouts. I do

not quite know what we expected to see – a cairn or a wooden notice would have satisfied us – but the absence of any mark whatever jarred upon us. That a country which could mark off the kilometres on its roads with fine red posts, should ignore a geographical acquisition like the Arctic Circle, seemed a piece of unappreciative barbarism.

Ghostly lines such as the Arctic Circle and other geodetic positions are usually abstract and invisible in the landscape, unlike most political boundaries. They need to be marked on the ground to exist in the minds of tourists (Löytynoja, 2008; Timothy, 1998). Gunn (1988, p. 48) goes even further and argues that in modern tourism, sites cannot "become true attractions until they are provided with access, lookout points, parking areas, interpretation programs, and linkages with service centers". As a consequence, the lack of border markers is also a lack of notification of otherness. It erases the induced differences as well as the mystery; there is no "here" and "there" anymore. In addition, it hinders the potential interest and sense of excitement usually raised by borders, as shown by Hyne's account. The author of this chapter (Varnajot, 2020) felt a similar irritation when crossing the Arctic Circle for the first time onboard a Norwegian train. Without any crossing notification, the supposedly different side of the arctic line felt boringly similar. The narrative of otherness was eliminated, as was the opportunity to take photographs.

The narrative of otherness is tightly connected to the presence of border landmarks visible in the landscape (Więckowski, in press; Więckowski & Timothy, 2021). Although the fascination and mystery of otherness is infused in border imaginaries and is intangible, it is only when approaching a border marker or other boundary landmark that the narrative of otherness is felt and becomes concrete.

## Border-crossing Performances

Border-crossing rituals include specific postures performed by tourists, as well as more or less organized and authentic ceremonies. The former refers to what Varnajot (2019a, p. 446) terms "border-crossing postures", which he defined as "recognizable postures, practices or actions that are performed individually or in groups around borders' landmarks, typically a line, that clearly suggest the crossing of a borderline or the fact of being in two different places at once". The latter, however, refers to what has been called "crossing-line ceremonies", which often take place onboard cruise ships, when crossing symbolic lines like the Equator (Cashman, 2019) or when entering micro-nations (see Timothy, 2003b, 2021) and remote territories, for example.

### *Border-crossing Postures*

In his essay "Borders", the American writer Barry Lopez (1989, p. 97) recounts his experience of approaching the border between Alaska and Canada, on the shore of the Beaufort Sea, and how he performed a simple border-crossing posture:

> Far ahead, through a pair of ten-power binoculars, I finally see what appears to be a rampart of logs, weathered gray-white and standing on a bluff where the tundra falls of fifteen or twenty feet to the beach. Is this the border? […] We examine the upright, weathered logs and decide on the basis of these and several pieces of carved wood that this is, indeed, the border. No one, we reason, would erect something like this on a coast so unfrequented by humans if it were not. […] Yet we are not sure. The bluff has

a certain natural prominence, though the marker's placement seems arbitrary. But the romance of it – this foot in Canada, that one in Alaska – is fetching.

Although these border-crossing postures differ from one person to another, the baseline performance rarely changes: one foot here, one foot there, as described by Lopez. As Varnajot (2019a) observed at Arctic Circle landmarks, by moving their bodies in similar ways around border landmarks, all tourists engage with the narrative of otherness through these specific performances (e.g., jumping over the line, standing over the line with a foot on each side, or staying immobile while faking a crossing). Indeed, the essence of these actions is to involve otherness by either saying "Look! I'm in two places at once" (Figure 19.3) or "Hey! I'm entering another region" (Figure 19.4). In other words, tourists invariably reproduce analogous border-crossing postures around border markers or landmarks, and as such, these specific practices have become recycled performances (Larsen, 2005). Therefore, border-crossing postures are not personal, lone and isolated performances. Rather, they belong to a collective sense that certain practices must be performed at certain sights (MacCannell, 1976; Varnajot, 2020). In line with this, border-crossing postures can be seen as a "forced repetition of norms" (Larsen, 2005, p. 419) when wandering around border landmarks.

At the origin of these border-crossing postures are three factors that can influence tourists' performances. First, the way border landmarks usually look—some kind of linear marking—naturally incites tourists to perform these specific practices. Indeed, according to Edensor (2001, p. 63), "the organization, materiality and aesthetic and sensual qualities of the tourist space influence – but do not determine – the kinds of performances that tourists undertake". Second, tourists reproduce what they might have seen while preparing for their trip by reading travel magazines, websites or looking for photos on social media posted by people who visited

*Figure 19.3* One foot here, one foot there at the Arctic Circle in Rovaniemi, Finland.

Photo: A. Varnajot, December 2017

*Tourists' Performances at Border Landmarks*

*Figure 19.4* Leaving the mundane world for the unfamiliar Arctic.

Photo: A. Varnajot, December 2017

the place before. As recalled by Adler (1989, p. 1367), "travel literatures have served as a means of preparation, aid, documentation, and vicarious participation", which constitutes the anticipatory phase of the tourist experience (Buhalis, 2000; Cox et al., 2009; Narangajavana et al., 2017; Xiang & Gretzel, 2010). For example, the Ecuador Hop (2021) website, an Ecuadorian travel agency offering bus trips across the country, provides information about La Ciudad Mitad del Mundo, a major Ecuadorian tourism cluster that commemorates the equatorial line, with a couple of photos of people performing border-crossing postures. A similar webpage can be found on the Visit Rovaniemi (2021) website explicitly telling and showing how to cross the Arctic Circle. Third, similarly to guidebooks (see Bhattacharyya, 1997), these websites regulate and direct on-site tourist performances. Edensor (2001) even goes further and argues that if tourists do not follow the recommendations provided in guidebooks or on websites, they will most likely not appreciate the experience at its fullest and their performances will be considered deficient and incomplete.

## *Line-crossing Ceremonies*

The second type of border-crossing performances refers to line-crossing ceremonies and are often associated with the crossing of geodetic and symbolic lines. Although these ceremonies have deep roots in nautical folklore (Cashman, 2019; Eyers, 2011), they can also take place on land, as shown by Saarinen and Varnajot (2019) with Arctic Circle crossing ceremonies organized in Rovaniemi. Tourists will gather under a supposedly traditional Sami tent wherein a host will tell stories about the Arctic and perform shamanistic practices, as if crossing the Arctic Circle was an esoteric experience associated with Sami folklore (which it is not), leading to an unethical commoditization of the Sami culture (see Cohen, 1988; Greenwood, 1977; Saarinen, 1999). At the end of the ceremony, as proof of having crossed the Arctic Circle, participants will all receive an "original" certificate.

Although in the maritime tradition these ceremonies were rites, marking the transition from inexperienced to accomplished sailor, today they usually take place onboard cruises, celebrating a tourist's first crossing of a symbolic line, a first encounter with the Other (Bronner, 2006). A popular example is one's first crossing of the Equator onboard a cruise vessel: crew members dressed as King Neptune and Mermaids will, after some incantation, make volunteers undertake strange practices such as kissing a fish or jumping in a pool, so they can transform from "pollywogs" to "shellbacks" and receive a certificate (Cashman, 2019). In these ceremonies, the mythical and nautical figures of Neptune and the Mermaids serve to mark the crossing but also represent the boundary between the human, mundane, above-the-sea world and the enchanted undersea realm, filled with unknown aquatic marvels and monsters (Robertson, 2013). Similar ceremonies are performed onboard Hurtigruten cruise vessels for example, when passengers cross the Arctic Circle for the first time, with whistle signals and symbolic on-deck baptisms (Hurtigruten, 2021). By using the mystic and fascinating narratives of otherness associated with borderlines, these line-crossing ceremonies transport the observer towards the Other, "into a fantastic and actual aquatic realm" (Porter, 2019, p. 251; see also Porter & Lück, 2018).

The mystification of both the Sami culture and of the appearance of nautical figures taking place in these line-crossing ceremonies are designed to manipulate appearances and create what might be termed "staged authenticity" performances (MacCannell, 1973; Wang, 1999). Indeed, geodetic lines remain invisible in the landscape until they are marked or celebrated. Their crossing cannot be celebrated without ceremonies or at least without being able to spot a landmark (Hyne, 1898). However, they still might be experienced as authentic from the participant's point of view (Saarinen & Varnajot, 2019), as Löytynoja (2007) showed in her study on the role of staged Finnish–Russian border markers in tourism.

Nevertheless, line-crossing ceremonies can be more minimalistic, and among the most common ones is getting a stamp in a passport, whether from an official and recognized country or from a quirky, often fictitious, territory, micro-nation (as opposed to a micro-state) or self-proclaimed entity. These passport stamps will serve as souvenirs or symbolic tokens used to celebrate entry into a noteworthy and unique destination, and which can be proudly exhibited afterward. Among "cool" officially recognized stamps are those acquired after reaching remote territories (e.g., Tristan da Cunha or the Pitcairn Islands), destinations with opposing socio-political systems (e.g., North Korea) or countries perceived as troubled by terrorism or political instability (e.g., Afghanistan and Syria) (Korstanje & Clayton, 2012; Timothy, 1998). However, grounded in a romanticized and entertaining approach to borders and bordering practices (i.e., getting a visa stamped in one's passport), some other passport stamps are completely fictitious from a diplomatic perspective. They might be offered when one crosses a symbolic geodetic line like the Arctic Circle (Figure 19.5) or the Equator. They can also be acquired at any destination with a distinctive feature such as Port Lockroy, Antarctica (after reaching Earth's last frontier), at micro-nations such as Whangamōmona in New Zealand or at a place like Llanfairpwllgwyngyllgogerychwyrndrobwllllantysiliogogogoch, Wales, for its distinctive long name.

Getting these passport stamps, however, is only perceived as a line-crossing ceremony or act from the tourist's point of view because they represent a unique experience and marker of place. From the perspective of border officials or local tourist office employees, they are contrarily simple routinized actions—part of their daily duties. From the tourist's perspective, crossing unique borders can also be motivated by "collecting places" purposes, which can then be used

*Figure 19.5* A passport stamp from the Arctic Circle in Rovaniemi, Finland.

Photo: A. Varnajot, April 2021

as proof one has reached or been to a noteworthy location and provides a sense of belonging to an exclusive club (Timothy, 1998). Timothy (1998, p. 126) defined the purpose of collecting places as "a process whereby locations visited are enumerated, and wherein there is a desire to visit additional places for competitive reasons". Nevertheless, although these passport stamps are often simple tourism souvenirs or sometimes considered as propaganda stratagems (in the case of micro-nations (not micro-states) for example) (Timothy, 2021), acquiring one tends to shift the meaning of these border-crossing performances to "Look where I've been!" rather than conveying images of being at two places at once. As a result, border-crossing postures and line-crossing ceremonies can engage with the narrative of otherness in different ways.

## The Influence of Social Media

Social media has been defined as "internet-based applications that build on the ideological and technological foundations of Web 2.0, and that allow the creation and exchange of user-generated content" (Kaplan & Haenlein, 2010, p. 61). Although social media emerged with text-based tools, "they quickly evolved to include audio, visual and animated content" (Gretzel, 2019, p. 62). As a result, they include blogs (e.g., Tumblr), photo- and video-sharing applications or platforms (e.g., Instagram, Snapchat or TikTok) and social networks (e.g., Facebook), which are among the most common ones (Aichner & Jacob, 2015; Varnajot, 2019b). Depending on their respective functions, social media also incorporate various features such as messaging, following other users, sharing contents in various formats (permanent or only available for 24-hour "stories", photos and videos) and live broadcasting (Gretzel, 2019). The rapid growth of social media use has had various significant implications for tourism (Sigala, 2019). Indeed, it has had increasing influence in the anticipatory phase of the tourist experience (Cox et al., 2009; Narangajavana et al., 2017; Varnajot, 2019b; Xiang & Gretzel, 2010), the experiential phase during a journey (Kokkinou et al., 2022; Samala et al., 2022; Varnajot, 2019a) and the reflective phase after a trip (Gretzel, 2017; Kim & Fesenmaier, 2017; Lo et al., 2011; Munar

& Jacobsen, 2014). Social media also has roots in photography. Indeed, according to Urry and Larsen (2011, p. 147), the development of social media belongs to the last stage of the history of tourist photography, which they termed "digitization and internetization".

The growing influence of social media in tourist experiences has affected how tourists cross borders, particularly when borders are considered attractions. For example, Varnajot (2019a) shows that tourists only performed border-crossing postures at the Arctic Circle when they were photographed. Otherwise, they remained indifferent to Arctic demarcation lines on the ground. Nevertheless, although Varnajot's observation connects only indirectly with social media and more directly with photography (people were performing border-crossing postures long before the invention of social media), there are other ways social media can influence border-crossing performances, as explored in the following.

Online publications have started listing must-get passport stamps, and therefore have encouraged travellers to cross unique, iconic and the most sought-after borders. A brief search on Google using the keywords "unique", "passport" and "stamps" shows a list of blogs such as "cool and rare passport stamps from around the world", "most coveted passport stamps in the world" or "11 rare passport stamps you may never get", which keep records of the most incongruous borders to cross and symbolic passport stamps to acquire. Although collecting places is not a new phenomenon (Timothy, 2001), these blogs establish checklists of borders to cross and passport stamps to get, giving more visibility to these off-the-beaten-track locations, and by extension, exacerbate the feeling of competition with other travellers. Indeed, as recalled by Gretzel (2019, p. 62), "[social] media allow users to affiliate with other users, with contents and with events, which explains why they are referred to as 'social'". In other words, by easing communication between travellers, social media also intensifies the desire for collecting unique places. In addition, given the visual nature of many popular social media, such as Instagram, it becomes easier to share visual proof that one has been to a unique destination in order to impress friends and relatives (Timothy, 1998), but also hundreds and sometimes thousands of followers.

This resonates with what Canavan (2020, p. 9) calls the "tourist celebrity gaze", referring to tourists travelling to be gazed upon while performing places. Contrary to the traditional tourist gaze developed by John Urry (1990, 1992) where tourists are gazing at places and people, the tourist celebrity gaze is an inverted gaze, whereby the traveller seeks to be observed by others (Canavan, 2020; Woods & Shee, 2021). This inverted gaze has been made possible by the growing use of social media allowing travellers to become the centre of attention, a celebrity, an "influencer". By sharing on social media their peregrinations to the most symbolic borders and remote locations, "[anyone] now has the potential to leverage and expand their position within their networks of followers, and thus establish themselves as an 'influencer'" (Woods & Shee, 2021, p. 7). The more remote, incongruous or dangerous the border crossing is, the more observers will ascribe glamourous, notorious or adventurous values to a traveller posting visual contents on social media (see Rojek's (2001) definition of a celebrity).

Nevertheless, the growing use of social media in the tourist experience also raises a contradictory perspective. Indeed, social media have had implications for the meanings of borders in a tourism context, and somehow have "depreciated" or demystified the meanings and narratives of otherness conveyed by border-crossing performances by popularizing what was once unique and exclusive. Borders have traditionally been depicted as delineations between the familiar and the unfamiliar (Newman, 2003, 2006). In other words, they are the symbolic lines between mundane life and an extraordinary, mystic, unknown world (Herva, Varnajot & Pashkevich, 2020; Medvedev, 1999).

Authors like Carr (2002), Cohen (2010), Larsen (2008) and Uriely (2005) show how the boundaries between tourism experiences and everyday life are becoming increasingly blurred and intricate. In addition, more recently, some studies have demonstrated the increasing role of social media and new technologies in blurring the distinctions between tourism and mundane, daily lived experiences (Dinhobl and Gretzel, 2015; Du et al., in press, Jansson, 2018). This is illustrated by Du et al. (in press, p. 1), where everyday use of social media "has extended to the tourism context, resulting in the eroding boundaries between tourism experiences and everyday life". As a result, although border-crossing performances delineate, simultaneously straddling the familiar and the unfamiliar, the mystic and the usual, the extensive use of social media has obliterated some of the symbolic actions that characterized specific border-straddling practices. Social media, therefore, can help develop the "fame" of a border place and its symbolic crossing through the tourist celebrity gaze (Canavan, 2020), while at the same time it also turns border performances into everyday practice, thereby de-emphasizing the narrative of otherness so that border crossing becomes less significant and symbolic.

## Conclusion

This chapter has explored tourists' practices and performances around border markers and other landmarks at geopolitical frontiers or more abstract geodetic lines. Border-crossing performances refer to both border-crossing postures and line-crossing ceremonies. Both originate from the narrative of otherness that is infused in border imaginaries, although line-crossing ceremonies are collectively organized practices and border-crossing postures are simple practices performed independently by tourists. This chapter has revealed that what is important from the tourist perspective is to be able to perform at some kind of border landmark but not necessarily at the actual borderline, which might be invisible in the landscape. This is important to know for destinations that are home to borders or which have a significant geodetic line within their territory. This can better help them arrange tourist sites and border symbols by enabling access to certain landmarks through road networks for example, rather than erecting markers in locations that might be geographically accurate but difficult to reach.

The growing use of social media has had major implications for tourist experiences and tourism in general. This includes tourism at borders and geodetic landmarks and experiences of crossing borderlines. In addition to documenting tourists' border-crossing performances and actions, this chapter has briefly detailed how social media has affected the meanings of border-crossing performances and borders as tourist attractions. Border-crossing ceremonies highlight the symbolic straddling of boundary lines or bodily frontier crossings towards Otherness. However, with the rise of social media, these border-crossing ceremonies and postures have become a new means of reaching the "other" in a virtual world that everyone can share.

## References

Adler, J. (1989). Travel as performed art. *American Journal of Sociology*, 94(6), 1366–1391.
Aichner, T., & Jacob, F. (2015). Measuring the degree of corporate social media use. *International Journal of Market Research*, 57(2), 257–276.
Balibar, E. (2002). *Politics and the other scene*. London: Verso.
Bhattacharyya, D.P. (1997). Mediating India: An analysis of a guidebook. *Annals of Tourism Research*, 24(2), 371–389.
Bronner, S.J. (2006). *Crossing the line: Violence, play, and drama in naval Equator traditions*. Amsterdam: Amsterdam University Press.

Buhalis, D. (2000). Marketing the competitive destination of the future. *Tourism Management, 21*(1), 97–116.

Canavan, B. (2020). Let's get this show on the road! Introducing the tourist celebrity gaze. *Annals of Tourism Research, 82*, 102898.

Carr, N. (2002). The tourism–leisure behavioural continuum. *Annals of Tourism Research, 29*(4), 972–986.

Cashman, D. (2019). King Neptune, the mermaids, and the cruise tourists: The line-crossing ceremony in modern passenger shipping. *Coolabah, 27*, 90–105.

Cohen, E. (1988). Authenticity and commoditization in tourism. *Annals of Tourism Research, 15*(3), 371–386.

Cohen, E. (2010). Tourism, leisure and authenticity. *Tourism Recreation Research, 35*(1), 67–73.

Cox, C., Burgess, S., Sellitto, C., & Buultjens, J. (2009). The role of user-generated content in tourists' travel planning behavior. *Journal of Hospitality Marketing & Management, 18*(8), 743–764.

Cuevas Contreras, T. (2016). An approach to medical tourism on Mexico's northern border. *Eurasia Border Review, 6*(1), 45–62.

Dinhobl, A., & Gretzel, U. (2015). Changing practices/new technologies: Photos and videos on vacation. In I. Tussyadiah, & I. Alessandro (eds) *Information and communication technologies in tourism*, pp. 777–788. Cham: Springer.

Du, X., Liechty, T., Santos, C.A., & Park, J. (in press). 'I want to record and share my wonderful journey': Chinese millennials' production and sharing of short-form travel videos on TikTok or Douyin. *Current Issues in Tourism*. https://doi.org/10.1080/13683500.2020.1810212

Ecuador Hop (2021). *Mitad del Mundo: Visiting the middle of the world*. https://www.ecuadorhop.com/mitad-del-mundo-ecuador/

Edensor, T. (2001). Performing tourism, staging tourism: (Re) producing tourist space and practice. *Tourist Studies, 1*(1), 59–81.

Eyers, J. (2011). *Don't shoot the albatross! Nautical myths and superstitions*. London: A&C Black.

Gao, J., Ryan, C., Cave, J., & Zhang, C. (2019). Tourism border-making: A political economy of China's border tourism. *Annals of Tourism Research, 76*, 1–13.

Gelbman, A., & Timothy, D.J. (2010). From hostile boundaries to tourist attractions. *Current Issues in Tourism, 13*(3), 239–259.

Greenwood, D.J. (1977). Culture by the pound: An anthropological perspective on tourism as cultural commoditization. In V.L. Smith (ed) *Hosts and guests*, pp. 129–139. Philadelphia: University of Pennsylvania Press.

Grenier, A.A. (2007). The diversity of polar tourism: Some challenges facing the industry in Rovaniemi, Finland. *Polar Geography, 30*(1–2), 55–72.

Gretzel, U. (2017). #travelselfie: A netnographic study of travel identity communicated via Instagram. In M. Levina, & G. Kien (eds) *Post-global network and everyday life*, pp. 41–58. New York: Peter Lang.

Gretzel, U. (2019). The role of social media in creating and addressing overtourism. In R. Dodds, & R. Butler (eds) *Overtourism: Issues, realities and solutions*, pp. 62–75. Berlin: De Gruyter.

Gunn, C.A. (1988). *Vacationscape: Designing tourist regions*, 2nd Edn. New York: Van Nostrand Reinhold.

Herva, V.P., Varnajot, A., & Pashkevich, A. (2020). Bad Santa: Cultural heritage, mystification of the Arctic, and tourism as an extractive industry. *The Polar Journal, 10*(2), 375–396.

Hurtigruten. (2021). The Arctic Circle. *Hurtigruten Norwegian Coastal Express*. https://global.hurtigruten.com/destinations/norway/inspiration/attractions/the-arctic-circle-monument-on-vikingen/?_hrgb=2&_ga=2.34100833.1135656677.1619524506-1564440832.1618211814

Hyne, C. (1898). *Through arctic Lapland*. London: Adam and Charles Black.

Ingold, T. (2007). *Lines: A brief history*. London: Routledge.

Jansson, A. (2018). Rethinking post-tourism in the age of social media. *Annals of Tourism Research, 69*, 101–110.

Kaplan, A.M., & Haenlein, M. (2010). Users of the world, unite! The challenges and opportunities of Social Media. *Business Horizons, 53*(1), 59–68.

Kim, J., & Fesenmaier, D.R. (2017). Sharing tourism experiences: The posttrip experience. *Journal of Travel Research, 56*(1), 28–40.

Koch, K., & Vainikka, V. (2019). The geopolitical production of trust discourses in Finland: Perspectives from the Finnish-Russian border. *Journal of Borderlands Studies, 34*(5), 807–827.

Kokkinou, A., Tremiliti, E., van Iwaarden, M., Mitas, O., & Straatman, S. (2022). Are you traveling alone or with your device? The impact of connected mobile device usage on the travel experience. *Journal of Hospitality and Tourism Insights, 5*(1), 45–61.

Korstanje, M.E., & Clayton, A. (2012). Tourism and terrorism: Conflicts and commonalities. *Worldwide Hospitality and Tourism Themes, 4*(1), 8–25.

Larsen, J. (2005). Families seen sightseeing: Performativity of tourist photography. *Space and Culture, 8*(4), 416–434.

Larsen, J. (2008). De-exoticizing tourist travel: Everyday life and sociality on the move. *Leisure Studies, 27*(1), 21–34.

Laurén, K. (2012). Fear in border narratives: Perspectives of the Finnish-Russian border. *Folklore, (52)*, 39–62.

Lo, I.S., McKercher, B., Lo, A., Cheung, C., & Law, R. (2011). Tourism and online photography. *Tourism Management, 32*(4), 725–731.

Lopez, B. (1989). *Crossing open ground*. New York: Vintage.

Löytynoja, T. (2007). National boundaries and place-making in tourism: Staging the Finnish-Russian border. *Nordia Geographical Publications, 36*(4), 35–45.

Löytynoja, T. (2008). The development of specific locations into tourist attractions: Cases from Northern Europe. *Fennia, 186*(1), 15–29.

MacCannell, D. (1973). Staged authenticity: Arrangements of social space in tourist settings. *American Journal of Sociology, 79*(3), 589–603.

MacCannell, D. (1976). *The tourist*. New York: Schocken Books.

Medvedev, S. (1999). Across the line: Borders in post-Westphalian landscapes. In H. Eskelinen, I. Liikanen, & J. Oksa (Eds.) *Curtains of iron and gold: Reconstructing borders and scales of interaction*, pp. 43–56. Aldershot: Ashgate.

Munar, A.M., & Jacobsen, J.K.S. (2014). Motivations for sharing tourism experiences through social media. *Tourism Management, 43*, 46–54.

Narangajavana, Y., Callarisa Fiol, L.J., Moliner Tena, M.Á., Rodríguez Artola, R.M., & Sánchez García, J. (2017). The influence of social media in creating expectations: An empirical study for a tourist destination. *Annals of Tourism Research, 65*, 60–70.

Newman, D. (2003). On borders and power: A theoretical framework. *Journal of Borderlands Studies, 18*(1), 13–25.

Newman, D. (2006). The lines that continue to separate us: Borders in our 'borderless' world. *Progress in Human Geography, 30*(2), 143–161.

Newman, D., & Paasi, A. (1998). Fences and neighbours in the postmodern world: Boundary narratives in political geography. *Progress in Human Geography, 22*(2), 186–207.

Orgaz-Agüera, F., & Moral-Cuadra, S. (2022). The relevance of the souvenirs, food, experiences and facilities of a bordered destination on the key relationship of perceived value, attitudes and satisfaction. *Journal of Borderlands Studies, 37*(3), 513–532.

Paasi, A. (1999). Boundaries as social practice and discourse: The Finnish-Russian border. *Regional Studies, 33*(7), 669–680.

Picard, D. & Di Giovine, M.A. (2014). *Tourism and the power of Otherness: Seductions of difference*. Bristol: Channel View Publications.

Porter, B.A. (2019). A multimethods exploration of knowledge sharing platforms in "enchanted" mermaiding events. *Event Management, 23*(2), 239–253.

Porter, B.A., & Lück, M. (2018). Mermaiding as a form of marine devotion: A case study of a mermaid school in Borocay, Philippines. *Shima: The International Journal of Research into Island Cultures, 18*(2), 231–249.

Prokkola, E.K., & Ridanpää, J. (2015). Border guarding and the politics of the body: An examination of the Finnish Border Guard service. *Gender, Place & Culture, 22*(10), 1374–1390.

Robertson, V.L.D. (2013). Where skin meets fin: The mermaid as myth, monster and other-than-human identity. *Journal for the Academic Study of Religion, 26*(3), 303–323.

Rojek, C. (2001). *Celebrity*. London: Reaktion Books.

Ryden, K.C. (1993). *Mapping the invisible landscape: Folklore, writing, and the sense of place*. Iowa City: University of Iowa Press.

Saarinen, J. (1999). Representations of indigeneity: Sami culture in the discourses of tourism. In P.M. Sant, & J.N. Brown (eds), *Indigeneity: Constructions and re/presentations*, pp. 231–249. New York: Nova Science.

Saarinen, J., & Varnajot, A. (2019). The Arctic in tourism: Complementing and contesting perspectives on tourism in the Arctic. *Polar Geography, 42*(2), 109–124.

Samala, N., Katkam, B.S., Bellamkonda, R.S., & Rodriguez, R.V. (2022). Impact of AI and robotics in the tourism sector: A critical insight. *Journal of Tourism Futures*, *8*(1), 73–87.

Sigala, M. (2019). The bright and the dark sides of social media in tourism experiences, tourists' behaviors and well-being. In D.J. Timothy (ed) *Handbook of globalisation and tourism*, pp. 247–259. London: Edward Elgar.

Sofield, T.H. (2006). Border tourism and border communities: An overview. *Tourism Geographies*, *8*(2), 102–121.

Timothy, D.J. (1995). Political boundaries and tourism: Borders as tourist attractions. *Tourism Management*, *16*(7), 525–532.

Timothy, D.J. (1998). Collecting places: Geodetic lines in tourist space. *Journal of Travel & Tourism Marketing*, *7*(4), 123–129.

Timothy, D.J. (2001). *Tourism and political boundaries*. London: Routledge.

Timothy, D.J. (2003a). Border regions as tourist destinations. In G. Wall (ed) *Tourism: People, places and products*, pp. 81–100. Waterloo: University of Waterloo, Department of Geography.

Timothy, D.J. (2003b). Where on Earth is this place? The potential of non-nations as tourist destinations. *Tourism Recreation Research*, *28*(1), 93–96.

Timothy, D.J. (2021). *Tourism in European microstates and dependencies: Geopolitics, scale and resource limitations*. Wallingford: CABI.

Timothy, D.J., Saarinen, J., & Viken, A. (2016). Tourism issues and international borders in the Nordic region. *Scandinavian Journal of Hospitality and Tourism*, *16*(1), 1–13.

Turner, V.W. (1973). Symbols in African ritual. *Science*, *179*, 1100–1105.

Uriely, N. (2005). The tourist experience: Conceptual developments. *Annals of Tourism Research*, *32*(1), 199–216.

Urry, J. (1990). *The tourist gaze*. London: Sage.

Urry, J. (1992). The tourist gaze "revisited". *American Behavioral Scientist*, *36*(2), 172–186.

Urry, J., & Larsen, J. (2011). *The tourist gaze 3.0*. London: Sage.

Vainikka, V., & Vainikka, J. (2018). Welcoming the masses, entitling the stranger–commentary to Gill. *Fennia*, *196*(1), 124–130.

Varnajot, A. (2019a). "Walk the line": An ethnographic study of the ritual of crossing the Arctic Circle—Case Rovaniemi. *Tourist Studies*, *19*(4), 434–452.

Varnajot, A. (2019b). Digital Rovaniemi: Contemporary and future Arctic tourist experiences. *Journal of Tourism Futures*, *6*(1), 6–23.

Varnajot, A. (2020). Rethinking Arctic tourism: Tourists' practices and perceptions of the Arctic in Rovaniemi. *Nordia Geographical Publications*, *49*(4), 1–108.

Visit Rovaniemi (2021). Cross the Arctic Circle. *Rovaniemi*. https://www.visitrovaniemi.fi/love/arctic-circle/

Wang, N. (1999). Rethinking authenticity in tourism experience. *Annals of Tourism Research*, *26*(2), 349–370.

Webster, C., & Timothy, D.J. (2006). Travelling to the 'other side': The occupied zone and Greek Cypriot views of crossing the Green Line. *Tourism Geographies*, *8*(2), 162–181.

Więckowski, M. (in press). How border tripoints offer opportunities for transboundary tourism development. *Tourism Geographies*. https://doi.org/10.1080/14616688.2021.1878268

Więckowski, M., & Timothy, D.J. (2021). Tourism and an evolving international boundary: Bordering, debordering and rebordering on Usedom Island, Poland-Germany. *Journal of Destination Marketing & Management*, *22*, 100647.

Woods, O., & Shee, S.Y. (2021). "Doing it for the 'gram"? The representational politics of popular humanitarianism. *Annals of Tourism Research*, *87*, 103107.

Xiang, Z., & Gretzel, U. (2010). Role of social media in online travel information search. *Tourism Management*, *31*(2), 179–188.

Zelinsky, W. (1988). Where every town is above average: Welcoming signs along America's highways. *Landscape*, *30*(1), 1–10.

# PART IV

# The Competitive Advantage of the Border

# 20
# OUTSHOPPING ABROAD
## Cross-border Shopping Tourism and the Competitive Advantage of Borders

*Teemu Makkonen*

### Introduction

Borders are commonly regarded as barriers to tourism (Timothy, 1995), but at the same time they create many advantages in areas such as marketing and branding for tourism in borderlands (Sohn & Licheron, 2018). One specific tourism pull factor that borders invite is the potential for cross-border shopping. Tourism and shopping are inextricably intertwined. Shopping is a fundamental part of the overall appeal of tourism destinations and nearly all travel experiences. Thus, it is a significant factor shaping the destination decisions of tourists and an important feature in determining the overall economic impact of tourism (Makkonen, 2016).

Although shopping is a very common tourist activity, most tourists make decisions about where to buy souvenirs, gifts and food items only after they reach the destination. However, in border regions, shopping is an important motivation for transboundary journeys. For some consumers, the opportunity to shop abroad is the primary reason for their trip (Timothy & Butler, 1995). For example, before the contemporary crises (COVID-19 and the Russian invasion of Ukraine), retail was the main motive for travelling for millions of tourists who cross the Finnish–Russian border every year (Laine, 2017). Thus, the local service sector and even individual stores can play a significant role in attracting tourist-consumers (Wong & Lam, 2016). An example of this is the IKEA store situated in the town of Haparanda on the Swedish side of the Finnish–Swedish Tornio River Valley cross-border region. The store is among the main tourist attractions in the entire region (Nilsson, Eskilsson & Ek, 2010).

Cross-border shopping trips rarely entail only shopping but more often also include leisure elements and combinations of other motives and attractions that affect travel decisions (Bygvrå, 2019; Tömöri, 2010). As such, cross-border shopping tourism comprises a multi-layered destination experience that includes not only retail opportunities but also leisure activities, services, a different atmosphere and cultural experiences (Ramsey, Thimm & Hehn, 2019; Timothy & Butler, 1995). Cross-border shopping can act as a catalyst for the development of a more diversified tourism sector with a variety of tourist attractions and services organised around it (Leick, Schewe & Kivedal, 2021).

The remainder of this chapter proceeds as follows. First, a definition of cross-border shopping tourism is provided. Second, in line with Yeung and Yee's (2012) typology, the preconditions and rationale for crossing borders to shop are discussed in two thematic areas:

(i) product attributes and (ii) shopping experiences. Third, the negative and positive impacts of cross-border shopping tourism are examined against the reactions of the local population and policymakers towards hindering or promoting it. The chapter combines the above issues (preconditions, rationales, impacts and reactions) into an overarching framework and discusses the policy implications of cross-border shopping tourism. Finally, a discussion of the benefits of borders and the opportunity of utilising cross-border shopping opportunities as a regional competitive tourism advantage concludes the chapter.

## Understanding Cross-border Shopping Tourism

Cross-border shopping is a subcategory of outshopping (Wong & Lam, 2016)—a phenomenon frequently studied by consumer and retail specialists. Outshopping entails people shopping outside their local communities. By extension, international outshopping occurs when consumers travel outside their local area and cross a national boundary primarily for retail purposes (Sullivan, Bonn, Bhardwaj & DuPont, 2012). In addition to local inhabitants taking advantage of retail opportunities across a nearby boundary, often on a daily or weekly basis, cross-border shopping also attracts visitors from areas farther away from the border (Szytniewski & Spierings, 2018). Timothy and Butler (1995) refer to the first instance as "proximal shopping", which is common in many borderlands throughout the world where frontiers are relatively open and local residents shop frequently in neighbouring countries for everyday practical items, such as groceries, housewares, petrol or clothing. People who live away from the border but travel to shop on the other side comprise what Timothy and Butler (1995) call "medial shopping" or "distal shopping". For these non-local consumers, international outshopping tends to be far less frequent, less utilitarian, often entails purchases of big-ticket items and more frivolous merchandise, and is inclined to include a more recreational element.

Shopping, whether for souvenirs or groceries, is among the most popular activities undertaken by tourists and often ends up being an unplanned ancillary activity rather than an intended primary reason for travel (Lehto, Chen & Silkes, 2014). Therefore, a distinction can be made between "tourist shopping" and "shopping tourism". Tourist shopping connotes shopping as a secondary travel activity that is often decided on or discovered after being in a destination for other primary reasons, whereas shopping tourism implies retail as the main reason for travel and choice of destination (Jin, Moscardo & Murphy, 2017; Saayman & Saayman, 2012; Timothy, 2005). Finally, as reasoned by van der Velde and Spierings (2010, see also Spierings & van der Velde, 2013), cross-border shopping tourism can be both goal-oriented "daily shopping", "run shopping" or "purposeful shopping" (i.e., utilitarian shopping for ordinary consumer goods), and experience-oriented "fun shopping" or "recreational shopping" (i.e., leisure shopping for specialised products, services and experiences).

These concepts lead to a key distinction between same-day visitors, cross-border tourists and cross-border shopping tourists based on their motivation for the trip and their length of stay in the destination (Di Matteo & Di Matteo, 1996; Makkonen, 2016; Studzińska, Sivkoz & Domaniewski, 2018; Timothy, 2005). In the retail context, same-day visitors are motivated almost entirely by economic reasons. They cross the border back and forth the same day without overnighting abroad. Thus, although they do not conform to the official World Tourism Organization definition of a tourist (i.e., someone who stays overnight away from home) and are therefore usually not counted as tourists in national tabulations, they nonetheless participate in tourism by crossing state frontiers, spending money abroad, utilising services and undertaking leisure activities (Timothy, 2005, see also Gelbman & Timothy, 2019). Cross-border tourists are people who cross an international border for personal or business purposes, not necessarily directly related to shopping. Finally, cross-border shopping tourists are consumers who primarily cross the border for shopping purposes and spend at least one night abroad. Thus, the push (motives of tourists for visiting a certain location) and pull (characteristics of destinations that attract visitors) factors of tourism apply also in the case of cross-border shopping.

Although the definitions of cross-border shopping and cross-border shopping tourism are conceptually clear, their empirical treatment is problematic for a number of reasons (Studzińska et al., 2018). First, since cross-border trips usually combine multiple purposes (e.g., business, leisure and shopping), determining the primary reason for the trip is not straightforward. Second, the primary motivations (as different from purposes) for crossing the border for shopping is hard to define, because it too is commonly a combination of different motivating factors. Third, there is no consensus on whether to consider same-day retail visitors as "tourists", even when day-trips also clearly entail leisure and recreational components, such as sightseeing or outdoor recreation. However, for the purposes of this chapter, all manifestations of cross-border shopping will be discussed within the framework of tourism.

## Rationales for Cross-border Shopping

### *Preconditions: Border Permeability, Regulations and Knowledge*

As noted at the outset, state frontiers sometimes hinder international tourist mobility, but in the case of cross-border shopping, borders and the economic and social differences they create form the appeal of borderland retail and are needed to sustain and promote cross-border mobility in this arena (Spierings & van der Velde, 2013; van der Velde & Spierings, 2010). For cross-border shopping tourism to grow and succeed, a border needs to be permeable enough, physically and psychologically, to allow consumers to cross (Timothy, 2001). Second, convenient, effective and efficient regulations (policies and border procedures—customs and passport and visa requirements) and sufficient infrastructure affect the time required and money needed to cross the border, facilitate border crossings and enable cross-border shopping. Unrestricted frontier permeability, such as that between Schengen countries in Europe (except during the COVID-19 pandemic), facilitates higher levels of cross-border mobility, whereas restricted border permeability limits the growth of cross-border shopping tourism. Shocks to border permeability (e.g., the September 11 terror attacks, Brexit, the re-establishment of border controls in Europe due to the asylum seeker situation from 2015 until now, and the closing of many international boundaries due to the pandemic) constrain and complicate frontier crossings, often disturbing or collapsing border permeability, exacting severe negative impacts on cross-border shopping (Prokkola, 2019). Additionally, customs regulations can either allow (e.g., due to the realisation of the single European market), prohibit or limit the amount or volume of certain products that can be imported, such as alcohol (Hellman & Ramstedt, 2009). The latter is the case, for example, at the Finnish–Russian border, where the volume of alcohol has been strictly regulated in connection with day-trips by Finns to the Russian side of the border (Smętkowski, Németh & Eskelinen, 2017). These types of regulations can have dual effects. One the one hand, they can discourage same-day outshopping trips abroad. On the other hand, they can encourage longer stays on the other side, which increases people's duty-free and import allowances. Finally, improvements in cross-border infrastructure, such as roads, railways and border crossing points (the textbook example being the opening of the Oresund bridge between Sweden and Denmark), increase the volume of cross-border traffic and the number of cross-border shopping trips (Bygvrå & Westlund, 2004).

As already stated, the time and money it takes to cross the border are important factors in the travel decisions of would-be cross-border shoppers. Therefore, distance to the border also matters. As a general rule, an inverted relationship exists between geographical distance to the border and the likelihood of crossing; the greater the distance an individual has to travel to the border, the more expensive it is and the less frequently she or he will engage in cross-border shopping (Timothy & Butler, 1995). However, consumers coming from more distant locations commonly spend more money during their infrequent visits than shoppers who live close to the border and may shop abroad more often (Asplund, Friberg & Wilander, 2007; Bygvrå, 2009; Segerer, Hommerová & Šrédl, 2020; Timothy & Butler, 1995).

Finally, in addition to border permeability, regulations and infrastructure as major preconditions for cross-border shopping, prospective tourists must be aware of the shopping opportunities on the other side of the border and perceive the potential benefits of shopping abroad. That is, they need to have knowledge (awareness) of cross-frontier retail opportunities. This awareness can be raised, for example, via official communication or word of mouth, and intentional promotional efforts and marketing (Bygvrå, 2019).

## *Product Attributes (Economic Rationale)*

One of the most often noted rationales for cross-border shopping is the price differences across the border. Retail tourists usually act rationally and cross borders for economic reasons to buy products priced lower than in their home countries. Most consumers purchase ordinary, utilitarian goods such as alcoholic drinks, tobacco and fuel on the condition that the savings compensate for the real and perceived costs (Leal, Lopez-Laborda & Rodrigo, 2010). Cross-border price differentials are usually caused by one or more of the following conditions:

- Labour costs: higher or lower labour costs affect the cost of supply, which is reflected in the prices of the final product;
- Taxation: lower value added taxes create lower product prices abroad;
- Currency exchange rates: fluctuations in currency exchange rates create situations where shopping abroad is (temporarily) more lucrative;
- Structure of retailing and economy of scale: consumer prices are generally lower in large countries (with large markets) and countries with large numbers of hypermarkets and discount stores;
- Consumption patterns: since high demand for a product typically increases its price, varying consumer patterns can affect the consumer prices of products across the border.

*(Aalto-Setälä, Nikkilä & Pagoulatos, 2004)*

Perceived quality differences also draw shoppers abroad or keep them at home. Perceived poor quality and perceived risk of purchasing fake or unsafe products abroad naturally deters cross-border shopping (Sharma, Chen & Luk, 2018). Likewise, perceived risk, fake or unsafe products at home can stimulate increased cross-border retail activity. For example, in China in 2008, nearly 300,000 children were severely sickened and several babies died from contaminated milk and formula to which melamine had been intentionally added to increase the products' nitrogen content in an effort to dilute the product to increase profits (Branigan, 2008). This led to massive waves of Mainland Chinese travelling to Hong Kong and Macau to purchase caseloads of baby formula, both for their own consumption or for resale at home. There are many instances of foreign products being deemed higher quality and safer, driving a substantial amount of international outshopping in border areas.

Likewise, larger assortments of products and services abroad are also major pull factors for cross-border shopping. For example, a study on the outshopping preferences of Croatian, Serbian and Montenegrin consumers concluded that "shopping trips to the 'old' EU countries (Austria, Italy and Greece) are motivated mostly by a larger selection and a better quality of consumer goods, whereas out-shopping in 'new' EU countries (Slovenia and Hungary) is motivated primarily by low prices" (Dmitrovic & Vida, 2007, p. 388). This finding illustrates how economic gaps between countries can create a two-way flow of cross-border shopping, where consumers from the more affluent country cross the border because of lower prices (due to, for example, lower labour costs), whereas consumers from the less-advantaged country cross the border to shop for (perceived) higher quality products and services.

Bar-Kołelis and Wendt (2018) note that economic differences can converge over time, and they describe this convergence as an evolutionary process that starts from petty cross-border trading (see also Michalkó & Timothy, 2001; Szytniewski, Spierings & van der Velde, 2020) and economically driven and goal-oriented cross-border shopping between countries of different levels of economic development towards a more experiential and leisure-oriented shopping tourism between equally developed countries (see also Stryjakiewicz, 1998). In other words, if cross-border regions experience increased integration, for example due to accession to the EU, these types of price–quality differences may decrease over time (Baláž & Williams, 2005), although in many cases, even in the EU, price differentials continue to drive cross-border shopping, such as Germans to Poland, the French to Spain and Belgians to Luxembourg. Therefore, differences in product attributes alone are not enough to explain the rationale for cross-border shopping. Rather, experience-related factors also influence the travel decisions of potential cross-border shopping tourists.

## *Shopping Experiences*

Cross-border shopping tourists not only try to satisfy their consumer needs (i.e., lower prices and product availability) but also seek shopping experiences that are connected to elements of authenticity, relaxation, pleasure and learning (Moscardo, 2004; Tosun, Temizkan, Timothy & Fyall, 2007). Therefore, other factors beyond strict economics can affect people's decision to cross a border to do their shopping. According to research, these factors include pleasant and enjoyable, or unique, shopping facilities and atmospheres, as well as good customer service (Guo & Wang, 2009; Lau, Sin & Chan, 2005). Additionally, opportunities to experience local heritage, customs and cultures may be added benefits to a transfrontier shopping excursion (Spierings & van der Velde, 2013). Cross-boundary differences may create a sense of exoticism (i.e., something different from one's everyday surroundings), contributing to the attractiveness of cross-border shopping tourism (Szytniewski, Spierings & van der Velde, 2017). In fact, an opportune mix of exotic "attractive unfamiliarity" (relating to unfamiliar physical surroundings or new sociocultural encounters) and mundane "comfortable familiarity" (relating to the avoidance of uncertainty, unexpected and annoying experiences and a feeling of displacement), that is "familiar unfamiliarity", has been noted as a contributor to cross-border shopping decisions (Spierings & van der Velde, 2008; van der Velde & Spierings, 2010). On the one hand, visiting shopping centres across the border should be a reasonably familiar experience, as too much difference may lead to some sort of culture shock and thereby deter shopper tourists from crossing. On the other hand, if shopping centres on two sides of a border are too similar, cross-border shopping will have less appeal for visitors who want a "foreign" experience. Naturally, what is considered attractive or comfortable and familiar or unfamiliar differs between people and may change over time.

## Economic Impact of, and Reactions to, Cross-border Shopping

Cross-border shopping-based tourism induces both negative and positive economic impacts. First, many border regions are concerned about the "substitution effect" of cross-border commerce in which residents do much of their shopping on the other side of the border, rather than in their home region, thereby hurting the domestic service sector and thus inducing negative economic impacts, or a leakage effect (Makkonen, 2016). This was especially problematic in Canada in the early and mid-1990s, when Canadians shopping in the United States en masse was a major phenomenon owing largely to favourable Canadian dollar exchange rates. In this situation, the national and provincial governments appealed to the patriotism and common sense of Canadian consumers, and even "guilted" them to a degree, by enacting counter-marketing measures to encourage Canadian borderlanders to stay home to shop rather than spend their money in neighbouring US regions (Timothy & Butler, 1995).

Increases in the volume of cross-border shopping can lead to subsequent inflated retail property prices in the receiving region, which is often a concern for the local inhabitants, as commercial properties become unaffordable for new entrepreneurs. This has been a significant concern in Hong Kong and Macau as a result of the massive growth in cross-border shopping from PR China (Li, Cheung & Han, 2018). Local entrepreneurs on the less retailed side of the boundary commonly feel that the benefits of cross-border shopping are unidirectional and disproportionately distributed (or exclusively so) only on one side of the border (Prokkola, 2008), leaving them few opportunities to develop entrepreneurial endeavours. This often feeds into nationalistic sentiments and discontent, and fuels discourses and demands for legislation and policies that will protect the local retail sector. Ultimately, if these concerns are shared by policymakers, they can lead to actions to protect domestic services against the competition from retailers across the border, for example by restricting certain products (Hampton, 2010) or limiting people's cross-border mobility.

The main positive impact of cross-border shopping is the source of income it provides for local entrepreneurs in many receiving border regions (Rogerson, 2011). The amount of money that cross-border shoppers spend during their visits depends on a number of variables, including their length of stay (day-trippers or overnight tourists), frequency of crossing the border, income level, psychological traits, and various other socioeconomic and demographic characteristics of the travellers (Asgary, De Los Santos, Vincent & Davila, 1997). Predictably, in general, shopping tourists tend to spend more money per capita than leisure-activity-oriented tourists during their stays (Choi, Heo & Law, 2016) and are thus seen as a lucrative market segment for borderland destinations. Cross-border shoppers' expenditures provide economic benefits to the regional economy by generating income and creating jobs, both directly and indirectly through the so-called multiplier effect (Archer, 1976; Khan, Phang & Toh, 1995; Makkonen & Hokkanen, 2013; Sullivan et al., 2012). Direct multiplier effects are the initial injection of tourist expenditures that provide direct revenue, for example to hotels, restaurants and shops. Indirect multipliers occur as tourism facilities and services require contributions from other providers (e.g., food producers, construction companies and fishing enterprises), spreading the benefits of tourism to other industries. Induced effects come when the beneficiaries of direct and indirect earnings spend their income on non-tourism-related products and services.

The scale of the multiplier effect varies between regions depending on their size and the structure of the local economy (Wall, 1997), but the main rationale, that, besides profiting the regional tourism industry, cross-border shopping tourism indirectly benefits a wide range of related and unrelated sectors, is valid for all regions. Taken together, the tourist expenditures ($TE$), coupled with the multiplier effect ($ME$), minus the substitution effect ($SE$) (including negative indirect and induced costs) to local demand make up the total regional economic impact (*REI*) of cross-border shopping:

$$REI = TE * ME - SE.$$

The above equation is naturally a simplification, since not all the impacts of cross-border shopping can be easily measured. However, it does provide an indication of whether the total regional economic impacts of cross-border shopping are positive or negative for a particular frontier region. If the impact is perceived to be positive, the region will (or at least should) promote cross-border shopping tourism. That international outshopping is important for many regional economies has led to regional marketing strategies to raise the visibility of retail opportunities and to lobby for improving cross-border infrastructure and abolishing regulatory barriers that might hinder cross-border retail (Henderson, Chee, Mun & Lee, 2011; Rogerson, 2011). As such, borderland destination authorities actively promote their attractiveness by providing appealing shopping environments and by improving border-crossing facilities to soften the process of cross-frontier consumer mobility. For example, many Finnish regions adjacent to the Russian border adopted Russian retail travel into their development strategies to tap into the opportunities it offered for regional economic growth (Smętkowski et al., 2017) before the COVID-19 crisis and the Russian invasion of Ukraine. As a result, cross-border shopping has also been a catalyst for developing higher-quality physical infrastructure (e.g., roads and electricity) through investments by national and regional authorities (Boonchai & Freathy, 2020). The local population also benefits from improved public transportation developed to cater to the needs of shopping tourists from abroad (Dascher & Haupt, 2011). However, as noted above, if the total economic impact of cross-border shopping is perceived to be negative, regional authorities will frequently try to restrict it. Thus, the "direction" of shopping flows and the total economic impact of cross-border shopping affects whether regions aim to decrease or increase border permeability and whether or not they actively raise awareness about shopping opportunities on the other side of the border.

Additionally, cross-boundary differences act as drivers of knowledge transfer and innovation in borderlands (Makkonen, Williams, Weidenfeld & Kaisto, 2018). Since human interaction is an important source of learning in the service industries, customers are a potential source of new ideas. Managers of retail services can benefit from potentially different and foreign customer feedback and innovative ideas stemming from cross-border shoppers (Weidenfeld, Björk & Williams, 2016, 2021). Thus, the shoppers are also a medium of knowledge transfer and a potential source of innovation in terms of novel products and services. While innovation is important for the total regional economic development of border regions, these types of additional advantages of the border are rarely considered, at least partly due to the difficulties of assessing and measuring their monetary value (Makkonen et al., 2018). In summary, the main impacts of cross-border shopping of interest to borderland regions are economic in nature.

## Synthesis and Policy Implications

As noted previously, the basic preconditions of cross-border shopping are that: (1) the border is permeable enough to allow crossings with relative ease; (2) there are no (or only a few) regulations relating to customs and visa requirements that prohibit cross-border shopping tourism; (3) the local infrastructure facilitates cross-border consumer spending; and (4) people have knowledge or awareness of the retail opportunities across the border. If these preconditions are conducive to cross-border shopping, consumers will be motivated either solely based on economic expediency or more likely a combination of factors related to product attributes, including lower prices, better merchandise quality or larger assortments of goods and services, and/or as a means of seeking leisure experiences. Cross-boundary retail activity needs to offer something exotic, unique or unfamiliar, while at the same time remaining convenient and familiar enough to alleviate stress and reduce any potential culture shock. This balance between the familiar and unfamiliar is termed here "familiar unfamiliarity".

Retail opportunities abroad attract tourists' expenditures which, when coupled with indirect and induced multipliers, can lead to significant economic gains for borderland shopping destinations, which are otherwise often economically disadvantaged peripheral regions of the state. However, from the perspective of the homeland of the travelling consumers, shopping on the other side of a frontier often pilfers domestic demand and thus leads to a negative substitution effect. Depending on the total regional economic impact of cross-border shopping, or the general perception of it, the regions where shoppers live will normally try to protect domestic retail against transboundary competition via restrictions when the substitution effect is dominant. Conversely, under the same conditions, the side of the frontier with the best retail opportunities will promote outshopping tourism by lobbying for increased border permeability and by intensifying marketing campaigns to raise awareness among their foreign neighbours about shopping opportunities. Figure 20.1 summarises the main antecedents and impact of motivations for, and reactions to, cross-border shopping into an overarching framework.

As previously stated, increased border permeability is an important factor in cross-border shopping decision-making. However, at the same time, the home and destination differences (or unfamiliarity) that borders create are also needed; too much similarity will reduce the attractiveness of shopping abroad. Thus, borders create competitive advantages for tourism, and policies aiming to abolish borders in an effort to increase boundary permeability and mobility while strengthening transfrontier cohesion (e.g., supranationalism, such as the EU) can result in the disappearance of price–quality–merchandise disparities that fuel cross-border

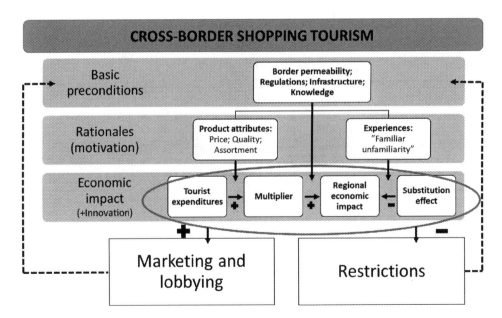

*Figure 20.1* Cross-border shopping tourism: Preconditions, rationales, impact, and reactions.

outshopping. Such debordering efforts can also result in too much product and environmental standardization or familiarity, so that the attractiveness of the other side decreases for visitors wanting to experience something distinctive (Baláž & Williams, 2005; Spierings & van der Velde, 2008; Szytniewski et al., 2017). Policymakers thus need to strike a balance between supporting cross-border mobility for retail consumption and maintaining the advantages that the border creates for the region.

Although there has been research on the market segmentation of cross-border shoppers as a means of benefitting target marketing and promotion campaigns (e.g., Yeung & Yee, 2012, 2015), much less effort has been made to determine all of the beneficiaries of cross-border shopping. What we do know is that the economic benefits of borderland shopping are unlikely to be felt by all residents in exactly the same way. Developing cross-border shopping tourism yields better results for entrepreneurs and workers who are capable and enjoy working with foreigners. However, higher incomes usually drive up rents, and as a result, some persons, for example those lacking language skills, might be crowded out of tourist areas (Dascher & Haupt, 2011).

These issues create difficult policy conundrums related to increasing cross-border permeability without completely abolishing state frontiers and designing policies that do not disproportionately favour certain groups of people to the detriment of others.

## Concluding Remarks: Cross-border Shopping as a Competitive Advantage

While this chapter has mainly elaborated on the potential positive and negative impacts of cross-border shopping from the perspective of the phenomenon benefitting one side of the border over the other, international outshopping should ideally benefit communities on both sides—if not equally, then at least in some symbiotic way. Although one side of a state boundary cashes in on its ability to sell local (or imported) products to cross-border consumers, the opposite side of the border can simultaneously benefit from transboundary collaborative marketing. Combining domestic travel with cross-border shopping can be an advantage in terms of attracting visitors to the region, hosting them, and serving as their anchor point, even if their main goal is to cross over the border to shop in a neighbouring country. Many visitors who come from further away, from the medial or distal zones of the home country, to shop abroad will frequently also visit domestic attractions and use local services on their own side of the border. Thus, their retail travel decisions can lead to both international and domestic expenditures (Stoffelen & Vanneste, 2017).

Makkonen (2016) surmises that cross-border shopping can make a significant contribution to the overall attractiveness of borderlands; it can be a pull factor to draw large numbers of domestic tourists into the region, so that both sides benefit. Therefore, in situations where cross-border shopping is mostly unidirectional, its economic impacts can still benefit both halves of the borderlands. Many of the products purchased abroad are goods that shoppers would not have bought from retailers in their home regions anyway. This realization might help appease naysayers or those who try to quell the outshopping phenomenon in border regions. Notwithstanding this, over-dependence on cross-border-shopping tourism can potentially lead to substantial fluctuations in the economy, because transboundary shopping tourism is vulnerable to changes in entry requirements (Li et al. 2018), bilateral state relations and other socio-political or health conditions as exemplified by many border closures in reaction to the COVID-19 outbreak in 2020–2021.

## References

Aalto-Setälä, V., Nikkilä, M., & Pagoulatos, E. (2004). *Elintarvikkeiden hintaerojen syyt Euroopan maiden välillä [Price Differences in a European Single Market]*. Helsinki: Kuluttajatutkimuskeskus.

Archer, B.H. (1976). The anatomy of a multiplier. *Regional Studies*, *10*(1), 71–77.

Asgary, N., De Los Santos, G., Vincent, V., & Davila, V. (1997). The determinants of expenditures by Mexican visitors to the border cities of Texas. *Tourism Economics*, *3*(4), 319–328.

Asplund, M., Friberg, R., & Wilander, F. (2007). Demand and distance: Evidence on cross-border shopping. *Journal of Public Economics*, *91*(1–2), 141–157.

Baláž, V., & Williams, A.M. (2005). International tourism as bricolage: An analysis of Central Europe on the brink of European Union membership. *International Journal of Tourism Research*, *7*(2), 79–93.

Bar-Kołelis, D., & Wendt, J.A. (2018). Comparison of cross-border shopping tourism activities at the Polish and Romanian external borders of European Union'. *Geographia Polonica*, *91*(1), 113–125.

Boonchai, P., & Freathy, P. (2020). Cross-border tourism and the regional economy: A typology of the ignored shopper. *Current Issues in Tourism*, *23*(5), 626–640.

Branigan, T. (2008, December 2). Chinese figures show fivefold rise in babies sick from contaminated milk. *The Guardian*. Online at: https://www.theguardian.com/world/2008/dec/02/china

Bygvrå, S. (2009). Distance and cross-border shopping for alcohol: Evidence from Danes' cross-border shopping 1986–2003. *Nordic Studies on Alcohol and Drugs*, *26*(2), 141–163.

Bygvrå, S. (2019). Cross-border shopping: Just like domestic shopping? A comparative study. *GeoJournal*, *84*(2), 497–518.

Bygvrå, S., & Westlund, H. (2004). Shopping behaviour in the Øresund region before and after the establishment of the fixed link between Denmark and Sweden. *GeoJournal*, *61*(1), 41–52.

Choi, M.J., Heo, C.Y., & Law, R. (2016). Progress in shopping tourism. *Journal of Travel & Tourism Marketing*, *33*, 1–24.

Dascher, K., & Haupt, A. (2011). The political economy of regional integration projects at borders where poor and rich meet: The role of cross-border shopping and community sorting. *Journal of Urban Economics*, *69*(1), 148–164.

Di Matteo, L., & Di Matteo, R. (1996). An analysis of Canadian cross-border travel. *Annals of Tourism Research*, *23*(1), 103–122.

Dmitrovic, T., & Vida, I. (2007). An examination of cross-border shopping behaviour in South-East Europe. *European Journal of Marketing*, *41*(3–4), 382–395.

Gelbman, A., & Timothy, D.J. (2019). Differential tourism zones on the western Canada-US border. *Current Issues in Tourism*, *22*(6), 682–704.

Guo, C., & Wang, Y.J. (2009). A study of cross-border outshopping determinants: Mediating effect of outshopping enjoyment. *International Journal of Consumer Studies*, *33*(6), 644–651.

Hampton, M.P. (2010). Enclaves and ethnic ties: The local impacts of Singaporean cross-border tourism in Malaysia and Indonesia. *Singapore Journal of Tropical Geography*, *31*(2), 239–253.

Hellman, M., & Ramstedt, M. (2009). Cross-border purchase of alcohol in the Nordic countries. *Nordic Studies on Alcohol and Drugs*, *26*(2), 111–115.

Henderson, J.C., Chee, L., Mun, C.N., & Lee, C. (2011). Shopping, tourism and retailing in Singapore. *Managing Leisure*, *16*(1), 36–48.

Jin, H., Moscardo, G., & Murphy, L. (2017). Making sense of tourist shopping research: A critical review. *Tourism Management*, *62*, 120–134.

Khan, H., Phang, S.Y., & Toh, R.S. (1995). The multiplier effect: Singapore's hospitality industry. *Cornell Hotel and Restaurant Administration Quarterly*, *36*(1), 64–69.

Laine, J. (2017). Finnish–Russian border mobility. In D. Hall (ed) *Tourism and geopolitics: Issues and concepts from Central and Eastern Europe*, pp. 178–190. Wallingford: CABI.

Lau, H.F., Sin, L.Y.M., & Chan, K.K.C. (2005). Chinese cross-border shopping: An empirical study. *Journal of Hospitality & Tourism Research*, *29*(1), 110–133.

Leal, A., Lopez-Laborda, J., & Rodrigo, F. (2010). Cross-border shopping: A survey. *International Advances in Economic Research*, *16*(2), 135–148.

Lehto, X.Y., Chen, S.Y., & Silkes, C. (2014). Tourist shopping style preferences. *Journal of Vacation Marketing*, *20*(1), 3–15.

Leick, B., Schewe, T., & Kivedal, B.K. (2021). Tourism development and border asymmetries: An exploratory analysis of market-driven cross-border shopping tourism. *Tourism Planning & Development*, 18(6), 673-698.

Li, L.H., Cheung, K.S., & Han, S.Y. (2018). The impacts of cross-border tourists on local retail property market: An empirical analysis of Hong Kong. *Journal of Property Research*, 35(3), 252–270.

Makkonen, T. (2016). Cross-border shopping and tourism destination marketing: The case of southern Jutland, Denmark. *Scandinavian Journal of Hospitality and Tourism*, 16(1), 36–50.

Makkonen, T., & Hokkanen, T.J. (2013). ICT innovation and local economy: Mobile game as a tourist attraction. *Scandinavian Journal of Hospitality and Tourism*, 13(3), 257–268.

Makkonen, T., Williams, A.M., Weidenfeld, A., & Kaisto, V. (2018). Cross-border knowledge transfer and innovation in the European neighbourhood: Tourism cooperation at the Finnish-Russian border. *Tourism Management*, 68, 140–151.

Michalkó, G., & Timothy, D.J. (2001). Cross-border shopping in Hungary: Causes and effects. *Visions in Leisure and Business*, 20(1), 4–22.

Moscardo, G. (2004). Shopping as a destination attraction: An empirical examination of the role of shopping in tourists' destination choice and experience. *Journal of Vacation Marketing*, 10(4), 294–307.

Nilsson, J.H., Eskilsson, L., & Ek, R. (2010). Creating cross-border destinations: INTERREG programmes and regionalisation in the Baltic Sea area. *Scandinavian Journal of Hospitality and Tourism*, 10(2), 153–172.

Prokkola, E-K. (2008). Resources and barriers in tourism development: Cross-border cooperation, regionalization and destination building at the Finnish-Swedish border. *Fennia-International Journal of Geography*, 186(1), 31–46.

Prokkola, E-K. (2019). Border-regional resilience in EU internal and external border areas in Finland. *European Planning Studies*, 27(8), 1587–1606.

Ramsey, D., Thimm, T., & Hehn, L. (2019). Cross-border shopping tourism: A Switzerland-Germany case study. *European Journal of Tourism, Hospitality and Recreation*, 9(1), 3–17.

Rogerson, C.M. (2011). Urban tourism and regional tourists: Shopping in Johannesburg, South Africa. *Tijdschrift voor Economische en Sociale Geografie*, 102(3), 316–330.

Saayman, M., & Saayman, A. (2012). Shopping tourism or tourists shopping? A case study of South Africa's African tourism market. *Tourism Economics*, 18(6), 1313–1329.

Segerer, M., Hommerová, D., & Šrédl, K. (2020). Why do Czech customers come to Upper Palatinate? Motives, sales volume, and the importance of distance: A case study of shopping in Bavaria. *Sustainability*, 12(9), 3836.

Sharma, P., Chen, I.S., & Luk, S.T. (2018). Tourist shoppers' evaluation of retail service: A study of cross-border versus international outshoppers. *Journal of Hospitality & Tourism Research*, 42(3), 392–419.

Smętkowski, M., Németh, S., & Eskelinen, H. (2017). Cross-border shopping at the EU's Eastern edge: The cases of Finnish-Russian and Polish-Ukrainian border regions. *Europa Regional*, 24(1/2), 50–64.

Sohn, C., & Licheron, J. (2018). The multiple effects of borders on metropolitan functions in Europe. *Regional Studies*, 52(11), 1512–1524.

Spierings, B., & Van Der Velde, M. (2008). Shopping, borders and unfamiliarity: Consumer mobility in Europe. *Tijdschrift voor Economische en Sociale Geografie*, 99(4), 497–505.

Spierings, B., & Van der Velde, M. (2013). Cross-border differences and unfamiliarity: Shopping mobility in the Dutch-German Rhine-Waal Euroregion. *European Planning Studies*, 21(1), 5–23.

Stoffelen, A., & Vanneste, D. (2017). Tourism and cross-border regional development: Insights in European contexts. *European Planning Studies*, 25(6), 1013–1033.

Stryjakiewicz, T. (1998). The changing role of border zones in the transforming economies of East-Central Europe: The case of Poland. *GeoJournal*, 44(3), 203–213.

Studzińska, D., Sivkoz, A., & Domaniewski, S. (2018). Russian cross-border shopping tourists in the Finnish and Polish borderlands. *Norsk Geografisk Tidsskrift-Norwegian Journal of Geography*, 72(2), 115–126.

Sullivan, P., Bonn, M.A., Bhardwaj, V., & DuPont, A. (2012). Mexican national cross-border shopping: Exploration of retail tourism. *Journal of Retailing and Consumer Services*, 19(6), 596–604.

Szytniewski, B.B., & Spierings, B. (2018). Place image formation and cross-border shopping: German shoppers in the Polish bazaar in Słubice. *Tijdschrift voor Economische en Sociale Geografie*, 109(2), 295–308.

Szytniewski, B.B., Spierings, B., & Van der Velde, M. (2017). Socio-cultural proximity, daily life and shopping tourism in the Dutch–German border region. *Tourism Geographies*, 19(1), 63–77.

Szytniewski, B.B., Spierings, B., & Van Der Velde, M. (2020). Stretching the border: Shopping, petty trade and everyday life experiences in the Polish–Ukrainian borderland. *International Journal of Urban and Regional Research*, 44(3), 469–483.

Timothy, D.J. (1995). Political boundaries and tourism: Borders as tourist attractions. *Tourism Management*, 16(7), 525–532.

Timothy, D.J. (2001). *Tourism and political boundaries*. London: Routledge.
Timothy, D.J. (2005). *Shopping tourism, retailing and leisure*. Bristol: Channel View Publications.
Timothy, D.J., & Butler, R.W. (1995). Cross-border shopping: A North American perspective. *Annals of Tourism Research, 22*(1), 16–34.
Tömöri, M. (2010). Investigating shopping tourism along the borders of Hungary—A theoretical perspective. *GeoJournal of Tourism and Geosites, 6*(2), 202–210.
Tosun, C., Temizkan, S.P., Timothy, D.J., & Fyall, A. (2007). Tourist shopping experiences and satisfaction. *International Journal of Tourism Research, 9*(2), 87–102.
Van der Velde, M., & Spierings, B. (2010). Consumer mobility and the communication of difference: Reflecting on cross-border shopping practices and experiences in the Dutch-German borderland. *Journal of Borderlands Studies, 25*(3–4), 191–205.
Wall, G. (1997). Scale effects on tourism multipliers. *Annals of Tourism Research, 24*(2), 446–450.
Weidenfeld, A., Björk, P., & Williams, A.M. (2016). Cognitive and cultural proximity between service managers and customers in cross-border regions: Knowledge transfer implications. *Scandinavian Journal of Hospitality and Tourism, 16*(1), 66–86.
Weidenfeld, A., Björk, P., & Williams, A.M. (2021). Identifying cultural and cognitive proximity between managers and customers in Tornio and Haparanda cross-border region. *Journal of Borderlands Studies, 36*(1), 99–118.
Wong, I.A., & Lam, I.K.V. (2016). A multilevel investigation of the role of retail stores in cross-border shopping. *Journal of Travel & Tourism Marketing, 33*(6), 837–853.
Yeung, R.M., & Yee, W.M. (2012). A profile of the mainland Chinese cross-border shoppers: Cluster and discriminant analysis. *Tourism Management Perspectives, 4*, 106–112.
Yeung, R., & Yee, W. (2015). Application of cluster analysis and discriminant analysis in market segmentation and prediction. *Leading Issues in Business Research Methods, 2*, 63–79.

# 21
# BORDERS AND HEALTHCARE
## Medical Mobility, Globalization and Borderland Tourism

*Tomás Cuevas Contreras and Isabel Zizaldra Hernández*

### Introduction

At first glance, the crossover between tourism and the practice of medicine seems to be an incongruous fit, perhaps even contradictory or oxymoronic. This is largely owing to the common misunderstanding that "tourism is a frivolous pursuit: fun, sometimes educational in the lightest sense, often romantic, even exotic" (Becker, 2013, p. 8), whereas in fact this describes only a part of the global tourism phenomenon, which entails traveling away from home for any reason, and a tourist is essentially anyone who travels away from home for at least one night regardless of motivations and activities undertaken in the destination. Likewise, same-day return trips (excursions) and the activities undertaken are part of the tourism system (World Tourism Organization, 2021). Healthcare, thus, may be as strong a motivation for travel (and tourism) as lounging on a beach, touring an historic city or visiting friends and family.

Healthcare is a high priority for the general population and for most governments and has received considerable policy attention in recent years. For millennia, the need for medical treatments has led many of the world's affluent citizenry to seek healthcare beyond the borders of their home regions or countries. The ancient Greeks, Romans and Sumerians notoriously traveled for spiritual healing, thermal spa treatments and medical care to areas inside and outside their respective empires. Likewise, Indigenous people throughout history have long embarked on quests to heal or strengthen themselves. These are two manifestations of the antecedents to modern medical tourism, also variously known as health tourism, surgery tourism, healthcare tourism, reproductive tourism, dental tourism, pharmaceutical tourism, medical mobility and other related terminologies (Bolton & Skountridaki, 2017; Connell, 2006, 2011; Eissler, 2010; Foley et al., 2019; Gómez et al., 2012; Hall, 2013; Wong & Hazley, 2021; Yang, 2020; Zermeño Flores et al., 2020). During the past two decades, medical tourism (MT) has gained momentum throughout the world, due in large part to dissimilar healthcare systems prevailing in different countries, including the costs of medical care, the quality of service and the types of treatments available. The growth of medical tourism has expanded geometrically to the point where in many cases it may be considered a form of mass tourism, despite its being a niche form of specialized travel. In many border regions, cross-frontier medical care is one of the most vital forms of tourism, and through the process of globalization, healthcare seekers now commonly travel much further, unfettered by national frontiers or the policies and

DOI: 10.4324/9781003038993-25

laws of home. This chapter first looks at general and global perspectives on MT beyond the confines of state borders. It then hones in on MT in borderland contexts.

## Medical Tourism

As noted in the introduction, medical mobility took place in ancient times and has become an ever-present part of healthcare in the modern day. Thermalism, or the therapeutic use of hot springs, arose in ancient days among the Arabs, Greeks, Turks and Romans for relaxation and healing, and thermal baths developed throughout the Roman Empire as "holiday" destinations for military officers, political leaders and social elites (Jackson, 1990). Simultaneously, spas developed in East Asia and people also sought treatments there by practitioners of traditional medicine, who were also often spiritual leaders. For many people, healthcare travel in ancient times throughout the world was somewhat like a pilgrimage, and the aristocracy commonly traveled great distances not only for spa treatments but also for medical care at the hands of known faraway specialists at the time.

Research on medical mobility has gained prominence in the fields of economics, geography, politics, healthcare and tourism, owing to increasing numbers of people traveling to receive planned medical treatments (Hall, 2013; Koehn, 2018), which sometimes also includes a leisure or pleasure element (Alegría Carrasco et al., 2014). MT entails people traveling away from their home environments, in most cases to a foreign country, for the purpose of seeking healthcare services and medical treatments. It is a rapidly growing niche or subsector of tourism worldwide, benefiting the healthcare industry, local economies in the destination and tourism services (e.g., accommodation, food services, tour companies, transportation providers, museums and attractions), which not only serve traditional tourists but also satisfy the needs of visiting patients.

In Asia and Latin America, the economic crisis of the late 1990s reduced the size of the middle-class population and collapsed regional markets for privately funded healthcare (BioSocieties, 2007, p. 312). At the same time, healthcare is increasingly being seen as a basic human right, which has expanded to see governments and employers having to do more to care for their citizens and employees (Plotnikova, 2012). As part of these trends, people are increasingly traveling abroad for medical care and other health services. MT has increased substantially through globalization, due to expanded opportunities for people to obtain health services at lower prices than those in their place of origin, often shorter wait times, better quality of care abroad, geographical proximity, cultural affinity on opposite sides of a border, certain procedures not being available in a patient's home country, and even the tourist attractions of the destination providing part of the motivation (Alegría Carrasco et al., 2014; Connell, 2019; Zermeño Flores et al., 2018). MT has emerged as a multi-billion-dollar industry, and many countries, especially developing countries, actively promote it as a means of stimulating their economies. In response to this trend, MT's costs and benefits to the host country have been discussed extensively in the tourism, healthcare and medical literature (e.g., Beladi et al., 2019; Hadian et al., 2021). However, the recent COVID-19 pandemic, which nearly halted global travel, is an excellent example of why health tourism's future will probably evolve through technological advancements. Healthcare is no longer only about local access but about crossing national borders, whether physically or virtually (Wong & Hazley, 2021). The rapid innovation of IR 4.0 technology has enabled virtual MT, which has opened doors for people to consult, and even undertake certain procedures remotely, with medical experts in faraway countries. Like other forms of tourism, technology has both facilitated travel and replaced some of it with virtual experiences.

Traditionally, wealthy people from the less-developed world traveled to the Global North to seek medical services. Today, however, the tide has turned, and countries of the Global North are the main sources of medical tourists who seek healthcare services in the less expensive but high-quality medical destinations of the Global South.

> In the past, people from developing countries traveled to developed countries in search of medical care. Today the panorama is different, given that patient flows are in the opposite direction and developing countries are benefiting the most from the growing influx of cross-border patients.
>
> *(Arias Aragones et al., 2012, pp. 94–95)*

Patients from developed countries have the financial capacity to pay for procedures that might not be covered by their insurance at home or which might not be available. Many destinations specialize in certain medical procedures, and consumers frequently choose their destination based on their specific medical needs (De la Hoz-Correa et al., 2018), together with other vacation opportunities available in the same locale. People frequently seek physical, mental and spiritual treatment for reasonable prices, taking advantage of the opportunity to leave their home countries to visit different and sometimes exotic places (Zermeño Flores et al., 2018).

The most requested treatments are shown in Figure 21.1 and include cosmetic surgery; dentistry; cardiology and heart surgery; orthopedic surgery; bariatric surgery; fertility treatments and gender reassignment; organ, cell and tissue transplants; eye surgery; and diagnostics and check-ups. Several of these services involve treatments and procedures that are especially conducive to international travel, such as cases of gender reassignment surgeries, experimental cancer treatments, stem cell research-based treatments and alternative medicines, any of which may be illegal or stigmatized in the patient-traveler's home country.

Although MT is now a megatrend, it remains too complex to quantify at a global scale, although individual countries and researchers continue to try to understand its parameters, impacts and motives. What many destination countries do realize is the phenomenon's extremely lucrative potential as a tourism income source, causing them to train and hire medical

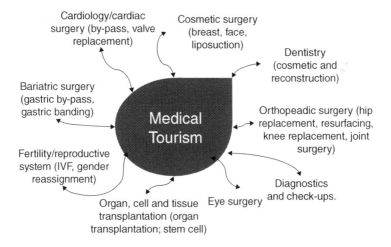

*Figure 21.1* Most requested treatments in medical tourism.

Source: compiled by the authors from various sources

*Table 21.1* Top ten medical tourism destinations, 2021

| Ranking | Destination |
|---|---|
| 1 | Canada |
| 2 | Singapore |
| 3 | Japan |
| 4 | Spain |
| 5 | United Kingdom |
| 6 | Dubai |
| 7 | Costa Rica |
| 8 | Israel |
| 9 | Abu Dhabi |
| 10 | India |

*Source:* Stephano (2021).

specialists (or provide more liberal work visas for healthcare workers) and build world-class hospitals and care facilities to brand themselves as prime medical destinations. According to the Medical Tourism Association (Stephano, 2021), the most popular medical destination countries overall include several in the Global North (see Table 21.1). However, the majority of other healthcare destinations are in the Global South and include Malaysia, Mexico, Thailand, Brazil, Cuba, China, Pakistan, and several others in the Caribbean, Asia and Latin America (Connell, 2011, 2019; De la Hoz-Correa et al., 2018).

## Medical Tourism and Travel Decisions

Branding themselves as MT destinations is an increasingly common tourism development strategy and has supplanted other forms of tourism in certain destinations. MT, thus, is seen to offer a competitive advantage over other destinations when a place becomes specialized in this tourism sector and when it receives support and buy-in from the community, the private sector and government agencies (Cuevas Contreras et al., 2019; Gómez et al., 2012). This multi-sectoral buy-in is important, because MT is a unique form of tourism, which has its own unique policies and practices, client needs and service requirements from the community.

In common with many forms of tourism, information and shared experiences are an important part of the decision-making process for medical tourists. Shared experiences on social media, for example, are especially important in the context of MT, as recommendations and shared experiences might be a matter of one's health, or life and death. Thus, travel and treatment decisions with regard to social media and ratings websites may be taken more seriously than in leisure tourism situations. Loyalty is an important factor in people's decisions in MT, as well as variables such as self-confidence, familiarity with the destination, destination image and trust (Stylidis et al., 2020). A patient's social networks (actual and virtual) are very influential in decision-making. A great deal of research shows the importance of people's online networks in travel decision-making (e.g., Bae et al., 2017; Sederaa et al., 2017), which is no less important in the context of MT. Positive recommendations through social media, e-WOM (word of mouth) or person-to-person WOM will help provide the information and recommendations needed to choose a medical destination and healthcare provider. By the same token, one's social networks may also indicate which places and service providers to avoid.

As noted above, trustworthiness is a major factor in the success of MT in many localities and something healthcare consumers value a great deal. For instance, Singapore, Canada and Japan are all prosperous MT destinations, owing largely to their reputations as having high-quality medicine and healthcare with exceptional hygiene standards. Likewise, we are seeing a major trend in Muslim patients traveling to Muslim-majority countries, or countries with large Muslim populations, such as Egyptians seeking healthcare in Malaysia and India, where they can be treated by Muslim physicians and nurses, and where women patients can be cared for by female Muslim doctors and nurses. In this latter instance, the interconnected globalization of medicine, religion and travel combine to provide a treatment and recovery environment that appeals to certain lucrative markets (Kamassi et al., 2021; Rahman et al., 2017). For this same reason and to cater to this high-value market, several Muslim-majority countries have begun devoting much energy and investment in this form of tourism (Moghimehfar & Nasr-Esfahani, 2011; Rahman et al., 2021).

Familiarity and geographic proximity are important variables in relation to national borders and transfrontier healthcare. For example, research evidence suggests that in many, if not most, situations, cross-border patients originate from neighboring countries (Adams et al., 2018; Bochaton, 2015; De Arellano, 2007; Lautier, 2008; Ormond & Sulianti, 2017), which reflects patients' desire for foreign but geographically proximal and culturally and linguistically similar destinations (John & Larke, 2016; Zarei et al., 2020); this demonstrates the principles of trust and familiarity. In Lautier's (2008) study, for example, most of Tunisia's foreign medical tourists came from neighboring Arab states. Likewise, in Thailand, 89% of foreign patients treated in 2002 were mostly regional expatriates or Asian neighbors. In Singapore, 84% of foreign patients came from nearby Indonesia and Malaysia (Lautier, 2008)—a pattern which remains true today (Rashid et al., 2020).

Quality of life is garnering considerable attention from tourism scholars, suggesting that travel should enhance one's quality of life and living standards (Moscardo, 2009). MT is closely aligned with this powerful concept and has the potential to enhance people's quality of life through various treatments and therapies. As previously noted, in their search for quality medical services (Figure 21.2), patient-travelers seek high-quality care, affordable prices, high health and hygiene standards, and experienced physicians, nurses and other medical personnel. Part of this decision, however, also includes location features (tourism features, recreational facilities and opportunities to relax), facility standards, and particular treatments and services on offer (Cuevas Contreras et al., 2019; Holliday et al., 2015; Lunt et al., 2015), which all contribute to a higher quality of life.

Kumar, Breuing and Chahal (2012) outline the variables that are most important in medical tourists' decisions to travel to the United States, India and Thailand. These include clinical safety, cost of the experience, the destination region and its characteristics, and patient safety (Table 21.2).

The total tourist experience generally takes place in three major phases: pre-travel preparation and anticipation, the journey itself, and a post-trip reflective period. In the first phase, people begin to recall former experiences and plan their upcoming journey. The second phase involves leaving home, spending time in the destination and undertaking activities there, and returning home. The post-trip phase occurs after the journey and includes memories, enjoying souvenirs, gift-giving, storytelling, posting experiences on social media and looking at photographs (Bae et al., 2017). Such a process also takes place in the context of MT.

In the pre-travel phase, mobile patients may regard the healthcare limitations in their home countries as a major push factor. For example, Cameron and her colleagues (2014) describe how many older Canadians are dissatisfied with the healthcare system in Canada. Many are unable to receive adequate care, particularly with regard to limited availability and long wait times for knee and hip replacements/resurfacing, sometimes in the range of two to four years. This drives many middle-aged and older Canadians to seek these surgeries abroad, providing motivation, justification and the normalization of such practices. This anticipatory and preparation

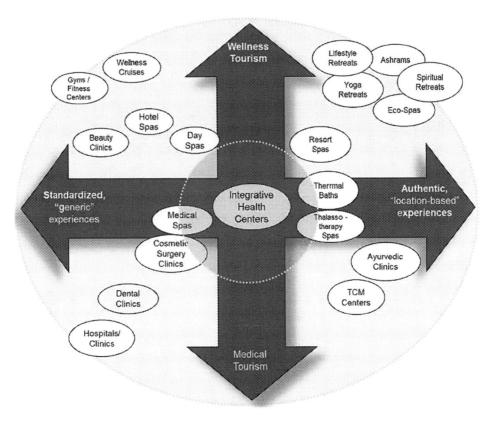

*Figure 21.2* Medical tourism, health, and wellness market.

Source: redrawn from Cuevas Contreras et al. (2019) and Global Spa Summit (2011)

*Table 21.2* Important variables that promote medical tourism mobility

| Clinical Safety | Cost | Region | Patient safety |
| --- | --- | --- | --- |
| Increasing level of surgeons professionals | Surgery cost difference | Visa requirements to any | Category of travelers |
| Prevention of bacteria that is resistant to antibiotics | Community of care domestically | Exchange rate | Eligible for long distance travel |
| Processor standards of sanitization | Traveling expense | Political risk | Sufficient savings in cash |
| Lack of proper diagnostic technology at home | Hidden billing cost | Forging versus domestic | Insurance companies abilities to cover expenses |
|  | Exchange rate | Prompt and consistent palsied treatment | Willingness to travel |
|  | Cost of failure, reward cost Medical Tourism | Legal systematical practice Language Barriers | Needed surgery performed overseas |

Source: based on information in Kumar et al. (2012)

phase requires a great deal of background research, examining insurance and payment options, reading reviews, deciding which caregivers to work with and which medical destination to choose. Once again, the last point usually includes considerations of leisure activities, sightseeing opportunities, a place's image and reputation, and the local cultural scene as determining the choice as well, especially during the recovery period.

During the journey, the main objective is to receive medical therapy. However, before the scheduled treatment, patients often sightsee and take a tour, enjoy a region's culinary traditions, stay in hotels, shop or other normative tourist activities. Likewise, following the procedure, many patients participate in the same sorts of activities, but many post-treatment times are characterized by a recovery period, which is often spent in a hospital or other recovery center, which may resemble a resort or spa with physical therapy, massages, swimming, exercise and healthy eating. Many destination hospitals and recovery centers have become hybridized spaces that double as hospitals and hotels/resorts, attracting a significant international clientele to a safe, caring, clean, culturally immersed and comfortable environment (Whittaker & Leng, 2015).

Once the healthcare trip is over, many patient-tourists have long recoveries, while others may recover fully in the destination. Depending on the specific treatment, in the post-travel phase, patients are often instructed on how best to care for themselves and are given restrictions on activities, foods and other behaviors that will lessen stress on their bodies. Some patients require additional hospitalization and aftercare once they arrive in their home countries (Lautier, 2008). Follow-up appointments with their own family physicians are common, and many must continue taking medications prescribed abroad. They share their experiences with friends and family and post stories, photographs and ratings on social media (John et al., 2018; Medhekar, 2018).

MT worldwide is a vast and growing phenomenon as described so far in this chapter. In all of its forms, it has received critical examination and a considerable share of criticism, particularly with regard to issues of socioeconomic inequity—where the rich can receive quality care abroad but the poor remain outside the reach of medical care—medical ethics, patients' rights and safety (Cohen, 2014; Hodges et al., 2012). Medical certifications vary between countries and regions, and patients are often discouraged by their own caregivers from traveling abroad for treatment. Ethical issues derive largely from the use of unapproved alternative or experimental treatments, stem-cell-based therapies and the health implications of inaccessibility for the poor. Regardless of these challenges, MT continues to thrive and grow in both the Global North and the Global South.

## Medical Tourism in the Borderlands

From the discussion so far in this chapter, it is clear that healthcare is a major push factor for people traveling abroad, and the globalization of medicine, including technology and new treatments, has accelerated cross-border medical mobility throughout the world. The destinations which patient-tourists choose to visit also exude pull factors, which might include prices, available medical specialties, fewer treatment restrictions, the availability of experimental treatments and technology innovations that might not be available at home. In border regions, all of these factors come into play. As previously noted, border areas are common destinations for medical tourists. For the most part, border health services attract patients due to lower costs, different treatments available, higher quality care and shorter wait times (Martínez Almanza et al., 2019). However, in most cases, geographic proximity and lower cost are the main catalysts for medical treatments in border areas.

Research on healthcare tourism in this specific geographic context shows that border MT is far less about "vacation" opportunities than it is about purely utilitarian needs. In fact, most borderland health tourism is far less about appreciating the destination than the procedures sought, and much MT in border areas is comprised of day-trips abroad. Thus, economic necessity and proximity are the two main variables that stimulate the growth of borderland MT. In the context of the USA–Mexico border, Horton and Cole (2011) consider convenience and proximal opportunity as important influential variables in border clinics on the Mexican side, and according to one industry source:

> The main driving force [of Mexican border MT] is cost, however other factors include speed of service, the ability to "vacation" while recovering and access to procedures not available in one's home country. Savings can amount to 90% of medical costs in the US or Canada.
>
> *(McDade, 2021, n.p.)*

MT in border regions frequently relies on cross-border linkages and networks (Bochaton, 2015; Hanefeld et al., 2015), including insurance coverage, transfrontier medical associations, inter-governmental collaboration, supplier–consumer relations, and social and personal connections. One of the best recent examples of transborder health networks is the case of Hospital de Cerdanya, which is located in the Catalonian (Spain) city of Puigcerdà in the Cerdanya Valley near the French border. Hospital de Cerdanya/Hôpital de Cerdagne was completed in 2014 and is a unique model in the world. With the realization that the isolated Cerdanya Valley needed a hospital to care for the needs of the area's 33,000 residents (on both sides of the French–Spanish border), the idea was conceived to build a facility that would not physically straddle the border but would be located close enough to serve the needs of the valley's French and Catalan/Spanish residents (Ferrer-Roca et al., 2022). In 2007, an agreement was signed between the French government and the regional government of Catalonia to ensure that both Catalan and French healthcare systems would work side by side in the facility and that the care standards of both countries would be upheld. The building was constructed with European Union regional funds, Catalan regional funds and French government funds on land donated by the city of Puigcerdà. Operational capital derives from both sides of the border. Today, the hospital cares for the needs of patients from both countries, and services are offered in Catalan, French and Spanish. This development has enabled French patients from La Cerdanya to receive high-quality healthcare near their homes without having to travel to distant hospitals in other parts of France (Berzi, 2017).

Along the USA–Mexico border, MT has replaced most traditional manifestations of border tourism there (e.g., gambling, shopping, cultural tourism) to become one of the most salient economic sectors on the Mexican side (Cuevas Contreras, 2015; Cuevas Contreras et al., 2016; Timothy, 2020a, 2020b; Timothy & Canally, 2008). Health tourism developed so rapidly in the 2000s, that it has changed the physical layout of the Mexican border cities (Boda & Harris, 2013; Cuevas Contreras, 2015; Martínez Almanza et al., 2016), much the same way prostitution, gambling, alcohol consumption and shopping determined their urban morphology in the early and mid-twentieth century (Arreola & Curtis, 1993). Many former souvenir shops and restaurants have been repurposed into dental clinics and pharmacies. New hospitals and rehab centers are being built in Mexican border cities such as Ciudad Juárez, Tijuana, Nuevo Laredo and Matamoros. Older hospitals are being renovated and updated to cater to American and Canadian patient-tourists (Timothy, 2019). The physical development of the border cities through MT enables Mexico's neighbors to the north easy access and proximity to their home country while receiving less-expensive services available abroad.

People who live near the border in major metropolitan areas (e.g., San Diego, Tucson, Las Cruces, El Paso and Laredo) and even further inland (e.g., Los Angeles, Phoenix, San Antonio and Corpus Christi) routinely cross into Mexico for healthcare. However, people from other parts of the United States and Canada, far from the border itself, are also known to fly (or drive) to a border city and cross over to take advantage of Mexico's lower prices and quality care. Canada's public healthcare system does not generally cover dental work or most routine vision care. Thus, Canadians are especially avid "dental tourists" in Mexico, especially those who spend their winters in the US Southwest (Adams et al., 2018; Coates et al., 2002).

Two main geographical patterns characterize Mexico's border MT. The first is how it has caused a physical evolution of the urban landscape, as noted above (Boda & Harris, 2013; Martínez Almanza et al., 2019). While hospitals that cater to the needs of foreign patients (but also to Mexicans) are located throughout larger towns and cities, there is a distinct clustering of dentists, optometrists and pharmacies, most of which are located very near border ports of entry (Figure 21.3). This allows American and Canadian patients to park in the United States and walk across the border without having to venture too far into Mexico. In this sense, they can comfortably remain near the United States but reap the monetary benefits of seeking healthcare in Mexico.

The second geographical perspective is that certain cities specialize in particular healthcare services. In the larger Mexican border cities, nearly all medical services are available, and even the

*Figure 21.3*  Part of the medical tourism landscape of Mexicali, a 'medical tourism lane' enables American medical tourists a quicker return to the US border crossing. Note the US border fence on the right.

(Photo: D.J. Timothy)

*Figure 21.4* The medical landscape of Los Aldgodones is dominated by dental services but is also comprised of many other healthcare services.

(Photo: D.J. Timothy)

smallest border communities (e.g., Naco, Sasabe and Puerto Palomas) are home to at least a small number of pharmacies, dentists and optometrists who cater to the needs of nearby Americans or "snowbirding" Canadians (Cuevas Contreras et al., 2016). Mexicali and Nogales are best known as dental and pharmacy destinations. The small town of Los Algodones (population *c.*5,400) is particularly famous for its dental services (Adams et al., 2019; Oberle & Arreola, 2004) and is sometimes referred to as the "dental tourism" capital of Mexico, although it is also a sought-out destination for eye care, chiropractic, gynecology and pharmacies (Figure 21.4). The large city of Tijuana is particularly known for bariatric surgery, cosmetic/plastic surgery and orthopedics. Likewise, Ciudad Juárez is famous for dental services and surgeries that require hospitalization.

The COVID-19 pandemic has severely affected the tourism industry, which many observers argue will require at least a decade to recover. MT is perhaps one of the most affected forms of tourism, as even day-trips by Americans were curtailed severely in 2020 and 2021, with upwards of an 80% decline in patient and pharmaceutical visits in Mexico's border communities. The pandemic's effect on MT can be seen in all of the main destinations, but perhaps the borderlands once again provide a vivid perspective on this crisis (Cuevas Contreras, 2021; Timothy, 2020b). In November 2021, the border was reopened in both directions, which has seen significant growth in medical arrivals. Although Americans were permitted to cross into Mexico for healthcare purposes during the pandemic, many stayed home because of US government travel warnings and perceptions of an easily contagious virus.

## Conclusions

Health-related tourism has ancient origins, and it is becoming an increasingly popular form of human medical mobility today. In many ways, through globalization processes, MT has become a borderless phenomenon that is occurring in many corners of the globe, with a mix of developed and developing countries being among the top healthcare destinations in North America, Latin America, Asia, the Caribbean and Europe. Although the draw of international MT is primarily healthcare, destination exoticness, opportunities to visit famous localities and the chance to recover in a scenic location with many cultural and natural amenities are other important variables that affect patient-tourists' destination decisions, as well as their pre-trip travel and post-travel experience. This pattern resembles other forms of tourism in this regard, despite MT's core motive being almost purely utilitarian.

MT continues to undergo an evolutionary process as technology changes and advances, alternative treatments are devised, medical destinations brand and market themselves as "the best" healthcare destinations, especially for certain treatments, and as e-WOM continues to influence people's decision-making through social media and other internet-based platforms. With new technologies, virtual borders have opened opportunities that physical borders have long prevented, including remote doctor appointments and remote treatments.

As healthcare and medical procedures continue to advance and as more countries jump on the MT wagon, the future will likely see new subtypes of MT developing to serve the needs of specific markets. For instance, the industry has heretofore focused only on patient travel, with little regard for the tourism implications of medical professionals' travel patterns and experiences. Medical volunteer tourism is widespread and has a long history in many parts of the Global South. This traditionally has been viewed as volunteer tourism only, but it is in fact a major crossover between voluntourism and medical tourism (Abbott et al., 2017; Citrin, 2010). More research needs to be done on the globalization of, and sectoral crossover between, volunteer tourism and MT, for is not caregiver travel also a form of medical tourism? Likewise, we have seen new forms of MT appear in recent years, such as so-called "vaccine tourism", where people have traveled to other countries to receive vaccinations when these are in short supply in their homelands. This has been an especially noticeable trend in 2020–2021 with regard to COVID-19 injections (Espindola & Vaca, 2022). Another recent trend that has major globalization, border and citizenship implications is known as "birth tourism" or "citizenship tourism", which has become a critical talking point in the United States as pregnant women from other countries arrive in the USA to give birth, thereby granting the child automatic *jus soli* US citizenship (Jaramillo et al., 2019). These and other unique medical travel trends need further examination.

During the past three decades and through the accelerated pace of globalization, international borders have become less meaningful in the Westphalian sense, and internationalized healthcare for those who can afford it goes far beyond national borders and the boundaries of insurance or state healthcare. Millions of people travel on their own expense each year to undergo a wide range of medical treatments. As a result, many borderlands throughout the world have become popular MT destinations. In the European Union, all EU citizens get free healthcare, but proximity to hospitals and doctors on one side of the border can be a determining factor for someone to travel abroad for healthcare services (Verra et al., 2016). On the USA–Mexico border and at other international frontiers in Asia and Latin America, lower costs, geographic proximity and convenience continue to dominate the pull factors that stimulate medical tourism. International borders continue to facilitate the growth of MT as they mark differences in administration, laws, policies and healthcare standards, and often demarcate different cultural and leisure environments that are frequently part of the MT experience.

## References

Abbott, K.L., Woods, C.A., Halim, D.A., & Qureshi, H.A. (2017). Pediatric care during a short-term medical mission to a Syrian refugee camp in northern Jordan. *Avicenna Journal of Medicine*, 7(4), 176–181.

Adams, K., Snyder, J., & Crooks, V.A. (2019). Narratives of a "dental oasis": Examining media portrayals of dental tourism in the border town of Los Algodones, Mexico. *Journal of Borderlands Studies*, 34(3), 325–341.

Adams, K., Snyder, J., Crooks, V.A., & Berry, N.S. (2018). A critical examination of empowerment discourse in medical tourism: The case of the dental tourism industry in Los Algodones, Mexico. *Globalization and Health*, 14(1), 1–10.

Alegría Carrasco, D., Berríos Lara, J., & Díaz Tobar, C. (2014). *Hedonismo en el turismo médico*. Santiago: Facultad de Economía y Negocios, Universidad de Chile.

Arias Aragones, F.J., Caraballo Payares, A.M., & Matos Navas, R.E. (2012). El turismo de salud: Conceptualización, historia, desarrollo y estado actual del mercado global. *Clío América*, 6(11), 72–98.

Arreola, D.D., & Curtis, J.R. (1993). *The Mexican border cities: Landscape anatomy and place personality*. Tucson: University of Arizona Press.

Bae, S.J., Lee, H., Suh, E.K., & Suh, K.S. (2017). Shared experience in pretrip and experience sharing in posttrip: A survey of Airbnb users. *Information and Management*, 54(6), 714–727.

Becker, E. (2013). *Overbooked: The exploding business of travel and tourism*. New York: Simon & Schuster.

Beladi, H., Chao, C-C., Ee, M.S., & Hollas, D. (2019). Does medical tourism promote economic growth? A cross-country analysis. *Journal of Travel Research*, 58(1) 121–135.

Berzi, M. (2017). The cross-border reterritorialization concept revisited: The territorialist approach applied to the case of Cerdanya on the French-Spanish border. *European Planning Studies*, 25(9), 1575–1596.

BioSocieties (2007). *First world health care at third world prices: Globalization, bioethics, and medical tourism*. London: London School of Economics and Political Science.

Bochaton, A. (2015). Cross-border mobility and social networks: Laotians seeking medical treatment along the Thai border. *Social Science & Medicine*, 124, 364–373.

Boda, P.J., & Harris, J. (2013). Root canals and crowns: An analysis of the spatial distribution of dental offices in Ciudad Juárez, Chihuahua, Mexico, 1996-2011. *International Journal of Geosciences*, 4(6), 38–43.

Bolton, S., & Skountridaki, L. (2017). The medical tourist and a political economy of care. *Antipode*, 49(2), 449–516.

Cameron, K., Crooks, V., Chouinard, V., Snyder, J., Johnston, R., & Casey, V. (2014). Motivation, justification, normalization: Talk strategies used by Canadian medical tourists regarding their choices to go abroad for hip and knee surgeries. *Social Science & Medicine*, 106, 93–100.

Citrin, D. (2010). The anatomy of ephemeral healthcare: "Health Camps" and short-term medical voluntourism in remote Nepal. *Studies in Nepali History and Society*, 15(1), 27–72.

Coates, K.S., Healy, R., & Morrison, W.R. (2002). Tracking the snowbirds: Seasonal migration from Canada to the USA and Mexico. *American Review of Canadian Studies*, 32(3), 433–450.

Cohen, I.G. (2014). *Patients with passports: Medical tourism, law, and ethics*. Oxford: Oxford University Press.

Connell, J. (2006). Medical tourism: Sea, sun, sand and … surgery. *Tourism Management*, 27(6), 1093–1100.

Connell, J. (2011). *Medical tourism*. Wallingford: CABI.

Connell, J. (2019). Medical mobility and tourism. In D.J. Timothy (ed.) *Handbook of globalisation and tourism*, pp. 305–315. Cheltenham: Edward Elgar.

Cuevas Contreras, T.J. (2015). An approach to medical tourism on Mexico's northern border. *Eurasia Border Review*, 6(1), 45–62.

Cuevas Contreras, T., Blasco, D., & Timothy, D.J. (2016). The Pink Store: A unique tourism enterprise at the US-Mexico border. *European Journal of Tourism Research*, 13, 122–131.

Cuevas Contreras, T.J., Delgado Guzmán, A., & Gómez Hinojosa, C. (2019). Turismo médico, salud y bienestar como una vocación del destino de Ciudad Juárez, Chihuahua. In R. Covarrubias Ramírez, C. Gómez Hinojosa, T. Cuevas Contreras, & G. Gómez Ceballos (Eds) *Turismo y vocación, una aproximación interpretativa teórico-metodológica*, pp. 97–128. Mexico City: Universidad de Colima.

Cuevas Contreras, T.J., Zermeño Flores, S.G., Zizaldra Hernández, I., & Villa Zamorano, Z.M. (2021). Challenges of tourism in northwestern Mexico between Ciudad Juárez, Chihuahua and San Luis Rio Colorado in the face of COVID 19 uncertainty. In A. Abreu, D. Liberato, González, E.A., & J.C. Garcia Ojeda (eds) *Advances in tourism, technology and systems: Selected papers from International Conference on Tourism, Technology and Systems*, pp. 509–520. Singapore: Springer.

De Arellano, A.B.R. (2007). Patients without borders: The emergence of medical tourism. *International Journal of Health Services*, 37(1), 193–198.

De la Hoz-Correa, A., Muñoz-Leiva, F., & Bakucz, M. (2018). Past themes and future trends in medical tourism research: A co-word analysis. *Tourism Management*, 65, 200–211.

Eissler, L. A. (2010). *The lived experience of seeking healthcare through international medical tourism: An interpretative phenomenological study of Alaskan patients travelling internationally for medical and dental care*. Unpublished PhD thesis, University of Hawaii at Manoa.

Espindola, J., & Vaca, M. (2022). On the morality of vaccination tourism. *Bioethics*. 36(1), 93–99.

Ferrer-Roca, N., Guia, J., & Blasco, D. (2022) Partnerships and the SDGs in a cross-border destination: The case of the Cerdanya Valley. *Journal of Sustainable Tourism*. 30(10), 2410–2427.

Foley, B.M., Haglin, J.M., Tanzer, J.R., & Eltorai, A.E. (2019). Patient care without borders: A systematic review of medical and surgical tourism. *Journal of Travel Medicine*, 26(6), taz049.

Global Spa Summit (2011). Research report: Wellness tourism and medical tourism: Where do spas fit? Key findings & analysis. Online: www.globalspasummit.org

Gómez, D., Morales, A., Pérez, A., & Woolfolk, L. (2012). Turismo de salud, ventaja competitiva para el estado de Sonora: Caso específico-reactivación de la Asociación de turismo médico del estado de Sonora. *Global Conference on Business and Finance Proceedings*, 7(2), 803–807.

Hadian, M., Jabbari, A., Mousavi, S.H., & Sheikhbardsiri, H. (2021). Medical tourism development: A systematic review of economic aspects. *International Journal of Healthcare Management*, 14(2), 576–582.

Hall, C.M. (2013). Medical and health tourism: The development and implications of medical mobility. In C.M. Hall (ed.) *Medical tourism: The ethics, regulation, and marketing of health mobility*, pp. 3–27. London: Routledge.

Hanefeld, J., Lunt, N., Smith, R., & Horsfall, D. (2015). Why do medical tourists travel to where they do? The role of networks in determining medical travel. *Social Science & Medicine*, 124, 356–363.

Hodges, J.R., Turner, L., & Kimball, A.M. (2012). *Risks and challenges in medical tourism: Understanding the global market for health services*. Santa Barbara, CA: ABC-CLIO.

Holliday, R., Bell, D., Cheung, O., Jones, M., & Probyn, E. (2015). Brief encounters: Assembling cosmetic surgery tourism. *Social Science & Medicine*, 124, 298–304.

Horton, S., & Cole, S. (2011). Medical returns: Seeking health care in Mexico. *Social Science & Medicine*, 72(1), 1846–1852.

Jackson, R. (1990). Waters and spas in the classical world. *Medical History*, 34(10), 1–13.

Jaramillo, J., Goyal, D., & Lung, C. (2019). Birth tourism among Chinese women. *MCN: The American Journal of Maternal/Child Nursing*, 44(2), 94–99.

John, S.P., & Larke, R. (2016). An analysis of push and pull motivators investigated in medical tourism research published from 2000 to 2016. *Tourism Review International*, 20(2–3), 73–90.

John, S.P., Larke, R., & Kilgour, M. (2018). Applications of social media for medical tourism marketing: An empirical analysis. *Anatolia*, 29(4), 553–565.

Kamassi, A., Manaf, N.H.A., & Omar, A. (2021). The need of international Islamic standards for medical tourism providers: A Malaysian experience. *Journal of Islamic Marketing*, 12(1), 113–123.

Koehn, P.H. (2018). *Transnational mobility and global health: Traversing borders and boundaries*. London: Routledge.

Kumar, S., Breuing, R., & Chahal, R. (2012). Globalization of health care delivery in the United States through medical tourism. *Journal of Health Communication*, 17(2), 177–198.

Lautier, M. (2008). Export of health services from developing countries: The case of Tunisia. *Social Science & Medicine*, 67(1), 101–110.

Lunt, N., Exworthy, M., Hanefeld, J., & Smith, R. (2015). International patients within the NHS: A case of public sector entrepreneurialism. *Social Science & Medicine*, 124, 338–345.

Martínez Almanza, M.T., Guía Julve, J., Morales Muñoz, S.A., & Esparza Santillana, M.A. (2019). Border medical tourism: The Ciudad Juárez medical product. *Anatolia*, 30(2), 258–266.

Martínez Almanza, M.T., Morales Muñoz, S.A., & Zizaldra Hernández, I. (2016). El turismo médico: Tendencia de transformación para Ciudad Juárez, México. *TURyDES: Revista Turismo y Desarrollo Local*, 9(21), n.p.

McDade, R.B. (2021). Have you considered medical tourism in Juarez, Mexico? Mexpro.com. Online: https://www.mexpro.com/blog/medical-tourism-juarez-mexico/

Medhekar, A. (2018). The role of social media for knowledge dissemination in medical tourism: A case of India. In K-P. Mehdi (ed.) *Medical tourism: Breakthroughs in research and practice*, pp. 132–161. Hershey, PA: IGI Global.

Moghimehfar, F., & Nasr-Esfahani, M.H. (2011). Decisive factors in medical tourism destination choice: A case study of Isfahan, Iran and fertility treatments. *Tourism Management*, 32(6), 1431–1434.

Moscardo, G. (2009). Tourism and quality of life: Towards a more critical approach. *Tourism and Hospitality Research*, 9(2), 159–170.

Oberle, A.P., & Arreola, D.D. (2004). Mexican medical border towns: A case study of Algodones, Baja California. *Journal of Borderlands Studies*, 19(2), 27–44.

Ormond, M., & Sulianti, D. (2017). More than medical tourism: Lessons from Indonesia and Malaysia on South–South intra-regional medical travel. *Current Issues in Tourism*, 20(1), 94–110.

Plotnikova, E.V. (2012). Cross-border mobility of health professionals: Contesting patients' right to health. *Social Science & Medicine*, 74(1), 20–27.

Rahman, M.K., Sarker, M., & Hassan, A. (2021). Medical tourism: The Islamic perspective. In A. Hassan (ed.) *Tourism products and services in Bangladesh: Concept analysis and development suggestions*, pp. 87–99. Singapore: Springer.

Rahman, M.K., Zailani, S., & Musa, G. (2017). Tapping into the emerging Muslim-friendly medical tourism market: Evidence from Malaysia. *Journal of Islamic Marketing*, 8(4), 514–532.

Rashid, I.M.A., Ibrahim, S., & Yusoff, S. (2020). Recent performance in Singapore's tourism industry using normality test correlation and regression analysis: The effect of medical tourism, service sector and exchange rate. *European Journal of Molecular and Clinical Medicine*, 7(8), 1354–1362.

Sederaa, D., Lokugea, S., Atapattua, M., & Gretzel, U. (2017). Likes—the key to my happiness: The moderating effect of social influence on travel experience. *Information & Management*, 54, 825–836.

Stephano, R-M. (2021). Top ten medical tourism destinations in the world. Medical Tourism Association. Online at: https://www.magazine.medicaltourism.com/article/top-10-medical-tourism-destinations-world

Stylidis, D., Woosnam, K.M., Ivkov, M., & Kim, S.S. (2020). Destination loyalty explained through place attachment, destination familiarity and destination image. *International Journal of Tourism Research*, 22(5), 604–616.

Timothy, D.J. (2019). Cooperation, border tourism, and policy implications. In K. Andriotis, D. Stylidis, & A. Weidenfeld (eds) *Tourism policy and planning implementation: Issues and challenges*, pp. 155–171. London: Routledge.

Timothy, D.J. (2020a). Borderscapes and tourismscapes: The place of postcards in Mexican border town tourism. *Geographia Polonica*, 93(4), 553–568.

Timothy, D.J. (2020b). La pandemia ha devastado al turismo médico, necesitamos soluciones creativas. *El Universal*, October 23, 2020. https://www.eluniversal.com.mx/opinion/dallen-j-timothy/la-pandemia-ha-devastado-al-turismo-medico-necesitamos-soluciones-creativa

Timothy, D.J., & Canally, C. (2008). The role of the US-Mexico border as a destination: Student traveler perceptions. *Tourism Analysis*, 13(3), 259–269.

Verra, S.E., Kroeze, R., & Ruggeri, K. (2016). Facilitating safe and successful cross-border healthcare in the European Union. *Health Policy*, 120(6), 718–727.

Whittaker, A., & Leng, H. (2015). Perceptions of "an international hospital" in Thailand by medical travel patients: Cross-cultural tensions in a transnational space. *Social Science & Medicine*, 124, 290–297.

Wong, B.K.M., & Hazley, S.A.S. (2021). The future of health tourism in the industrial revolution 4.0 era. *Journal of Tourism Futures*, 7(2), 267–272.

World Tourism Organization (2021). Glossary of tourism terms. Online: https://www.unwto.org/glossary-tourism-terms Accessed November 3, 2021.

Yang, I.C.M. (2020). A journey of hope: An institutional perspective of Japanese outbound reproductive tourism. *Current Issues in Tourism*, 23(1), 52–67.

Zarei, A., Feiz, D., Maleki Minbashrazgah, M., & Maleki, F. (2020). Factors influencing selection of medical tourism destinations: A special niche market. *International Journal of Healthcare Management*, 13(1), 192–198.

Zermeño Flores, S.G., Cuevas Contreras, T.J., & Timothy, D.J. (2018). Turismo médico y de salud: Una oportunidad para México. In S.A. Gómez, M.R. Llamas Paz, & R.M. Jiménez (eds) *Turismo médico en el Norte de México: Oportunidades, retos, dilemas y políticas públicas*, pp. 99–118. San Luis Río Colorado: Universidad Estatal de Sonora.

Zermeño Flores, S.G., Amaya Molinar, C.M., & Cuevas Contreras, T.J. (2020). Turismo de salud y redes colaborativas en innovación: Caso Los Algodones, Baja California. *Turismo y Sociedad*, 26, 67–88.

# 22
# CROSSING BORDERS AND BORDER CROSSINGS
## Sex, Tourism, and Travelling in the Sensual Spaces of Borderlands

*C. Michael Hall and Kimberley J. Wood*

### Introduction

Borders and borderlands are innately linked to boundaries and the promises of the "Other". Because of the legal and social differences between jurisdictions, what is not acceptable or legal in one polity, may be acceptable in another. Border zones are therefore frequently marked by a variety of illicit activities, such as smuggling and trafficking and, depending on the laws and mores of juxtaposed jurisdictions, drugs, gambling, and prostitution, some of which, especially the latter, have long been recognised as significant attractions for cross-border tourism (Askew & Cohen, 2004; Chan, 2008; Curtis & Arreola, 1991; Luna, 2018; Timothy, 2001).

However, sex is tied into borders and borderlands in far more subtle and complex ways than the often-noted connection with prostitution. Legal and cultural differences facilitate spaces in which sexual and sensual demands and needs that cannot be enjoyed in one jurisdiction without risk of condemnation or prosecution may be satisfied in another. Depending on the context, such demands may include same-gender sex, sex between people from different ethnic backgrounds or religious affiliations, premarital sex, extramarital affairs (or even to get married), or the opportunity to enjoy certain sexual practices, such as oral sex, masturbation, bestiality, kink, and anal sex, without it being illegal or declared a pathology (Kwon, 2021). Even the opportunity to bare more flesh, or do something potentially as seemingly innocuous as holding hands or kissing in public (Karibo, 2015) may be more tolerated in other jurisdictions. Given this context, it should therefore not be surprising that borderlands can be framed as spaces of creative and destructive processes resulting from confrontations of different culturally, economically, legally, and politically specific constructions of the body, sensuality, and sexuality where "the basic stuff of sexuality—intimacy, marriage, courtship, love—are all in flux" (Kennedy & Ullman, 2003, p. xiii).

Tourism is intimately tied up in such matters as not only does difference serve as an attraction for people from outside of the immediate location but the mere act of crossing a border statistically, if not liminally and economically, creates the category of being a tourist. Such identity and meaning-making rests not only on crossing political borders but also the various identities attached to border crossings, including cultural, economic, and sexual boundaries (Kennedy & Ullman, 2003). Because of the appeal of border regions, border tourism also generates employment (both legal and illegal) and livelihoods, as well as a wider infrastructure to support visitors and their needs. Borderlands can therefore serve as liminal and often marginal spaces of attraction that appeal to people on the premise that they can do things that they would otherwise likely not be able to do at home without cultural, legal, or moral sanction.

However, to categorise such tourism as "just being" sex tourism would constitute not only lazy labelling and thinking, it would also be wrong. Instead, frameworks broader than the one's primarily used to examine sex tourism are needed, which can account for the provisional practices and identities that constitute sensual and sexual travel markets and that can envelop notions of attraction, infrastructure, labour, the body, and sex as more fluid categories that shift in space and time. To echo the reasoning of Cabezas (2004, p. 1010), we need more sophisticated approaches that enhance our understanding of sensual pleasure as part of the tourism experience and which place sexual citizenship at the core of the analysis of labour, tourism, and the promotion and development of border spaces.

The relationship between tourism and sex has arguably become more important in the age of mass tourism. While travel, border crossings, and the sexual and sensual imaginary of the other side of the border have long been a part of tourism and are inseparable from mercantilism and colonialism, globalisation and modernity have hastened attention to the sex and tourism relationship. From the demand side, the global expansion of tourism has led to travellers seeking sexual relationships in other places, often within the liminal space of the tourist-local encounter. The extent to which these are commercialised transnational sexual relationships will vary given different notions of what constitutes sex work in different cultures and societies. Nevertheless, the sensualisation, if not sexualisation, of the local is intrinsic to much tourism advertising and the tourist imaginary in which promises of satisfying fantasy, social needs, and personal wellbeing are often mixed with the exotic. Nearly everyone in advertising images is smiling. Couples hold hands, the locals are beautiful, the sky and sea are always clear and blue, the people are welcoming, and the body is presented in sensual ways (Berno & Jones, 2001; Cohen, 2001; Hall, 1998; Jeffreys, 2008). Situation normal for tourism advertising!

In terms of supply, commercial sex work and transnational sexual contacts have increased in the wake of post-Cold War neoliberal globalisation and transition which embody "ambiguous conceptions of gift and commodity, work and pleasure, and coercion and empowerment", what can otherwise be framed as the "industrialised vagina" and penis (Jeffreys, 2008), as well as less nuanced discourses of victimisation (Campbell, 2007, p. 263). The latter issue highlights the significance of gaining a better understanding of forms of agency, such as obtaining greater consumer purchasing power, as well as the escape from restrictive gender relationships (Campbell, 2007, p. 263). However, as well as issues of individual agency, there is the development of the infrastructure and locations that make transnational sexual opportunities and spaces available for tourism, which may or may not occupy the same space as other forms of tourism. While overlaying such spaces of interaction, the legal and governance frameworks of jurisdictions may also include health concerns (Sönmez, Wiitala & Apostolopoulos, 2019).

The border spaces of sex, perhaps like sex itself, are sticky and messy. Sticky in that they serve to attract and retain people and messy in that they are complex and often contested environments. In this chapter we aim to provide an account of some of the main themes and issues in discussing sex and tourism in borderlands. We first provide a framework for discussing some of the main themes before looking at several issues in more depth, including liminality, sexual mores, workers, legality, and, of course, the tourists themselves. The chapter concludes with some comments on the importance of normalising sex and border-crossing rather than academically or economically fetishising it, perhaps for the purpose of ignoring much more serious problems.

## Framing and Blurring the Border

Borders are more than a line between nations or, sometimes, even within nations. They constitute a legal boundary that can also serve to reinforce cultural, political, and economic difference. From a tourism perspective such difference can prove extremely attractive. However, it is important to recognise that while the legal differences at the border may prove abrupt, their interpretation and implementation, together with other aspects of society, may prove less so as different national spaces can overlap, even if only informally (Hu-DeHart, 2012; Ford & Lyons, 2020). Borderlands, the political and cultural spaces either side of a border, are therefore spaces in which "overlapping and contradictory legal systems operate; local residents and foreigners meet and interact". By their very nature, therefore, "borderlands are disputed and pulled in multiple directions" (Hooks, 2020, p. 2). Chávez-García and Castillo-Muñoz (2020, p. 5), for example, define the USA–Mexico borderlands as a "region of diverse social, political, economic, and cultural interactions, contradictions, and conflicts. Bisected by an international boundary, it encompasses and brings together diverse peoples of different genders, races, ethnicities, classes, and sexualities".

Reyes (2015, 2019) takes a broader approach and proposes the concept of "global borderlands"—those semi-autonomous, often foreign-controlled geographic locations geared toward international socioeconomic exchange which, she argues, includes overseas military bases, special economic zones, tourist resorts, embassies, cruise ships, port cities, and colonial trading forts. Reyes's concept clearly takes the notion of borders and borderlands away from the traditional use of national borders to highlight the embeddedness of national and transnational space with processes of contemporary globalisation and the particular hybrid nature of such spaces which makes their difference often inherently attractive to tourists and, in political terms, messy. As Hooks (2020, p. 2) observed, the notion of global borderlands highlights the complex and contradictory forces operating "at different levels—state to state, employer employee, buyers and sellers, individuals and justice systems, lovers, and family members".

The nature of borderlands means that differences and categories that may otherwise be clear further away from the border become blurred either at or in crossing borders. For example, many societies assume that someone who is romantically involved with a foreign tourist or soldier is a sex worker. Yet some relationships blur "the boundary between romance and transaction" (Hooks, 2020, p. 2) and the intersections between romance, sex work, marriage, friendship, leisure, money, supervision, and consumption in a sexual tourist setting (Spanger, 2013). Stout (2015, p. 668) suggests that because some foreign tourists "never pay directly for sexual services and spend extended lengths of time with sex workers, sex tourist encounters tend to blur the lines between transactional sex and less overtly commodified forms of intimacy". Similarly, Cabezas (2004, p. 1000) argues:

> With gifts seen as expressions of love and not as payment for services rendered, men and women hope to obscure the dichotomy between love and money. Emotional labor is used to break down the boundaries of commercial exchanges or at least to blur the lines between intimacy and labor and to preserve the dignity of the local participant. This liminal space is marked by fluidity, ambiguity, and heterogeneity and provides opportunities that direct commercial transactions cannot.

However, labour is still work, even though the relative ambiguity of such encounters may serve to lessen the notion that services are being provided to a tourist as a straight economic transaction to communities, self, and perhaps even for the tourist.

Prostitution, for example, arguably becomes harder to define at the border and possibly even in wider society as a result of the global borderland of the Internet. Prostitution has usually been defined in terms of largely indiscriminate sexual relationships, "without affection, and frequently anonymous", which represents "a severe deviation from the explicit or stated sexual mores" of a society (Karibo, 2015, pp. 60–61). Yet, in the age of hook-up culture, Grindr, and Tinder, it is difficult to see how such "traditional" notions of sexual relations still apply (Choi & DeLong, 2019; Horley & Clarke, 2016), even as many moral crusaders try to influence policy to make it so. Definitions of prostitution that imply multiple sexual partners and a "high rate of acquisition of new partners" and which imply no commitments to future relationships or subsequent exchanges (Wardlow, 2004, p. 1025) are not too different from contemporary hook-up culture. Brennan (2017, p. 1), for example, notes the emergence of mobile pornographers, men seeking payment for sex via Grindr, "a concept that embodies their willingness to exploit the affordances of mobile technology and the profits to be gained from youth and sex, without the digital traces of more traditional pornographic forms". Instead, a definition of prostitution perhaps can best be created around the exchange of sex for money, or perhaps other items of value, and discrete pay per sexual transaction, which may involve a broker. However, this can also be enacted online and does not necessarily require an identified physical space, although such designated and often promoted spaces are of course significant for tourism promotion.

In seeking to connect prostitution and sexual relations in borderlands to tourism it is also important to recognise that implicit in many studies of prostitution, "and probably in Western folk notions of (hetero)sexuality more generally, is a pseudobiologistic assumption that men are the sexual desirers and women the desirables" (Wardlow, 2004, p. 1027). Yet such assumptions may start to break down when examining the behaviours of female tourists and resident male sexual interrelationships with female tourists. For example, males are usually portrayed in the tourism literature as "sex tourists" while women who engage in exactly the same behaviours are framed as "romance tourists" (Pruitt & LaFont, 1995; Ryan & Hall, 2001). This (artificial) division may possibly make female tourists' sexual behaviour more acceptable to some researchers, readers, and perhaps journal reviewers and editors, but it is also empirically untrue and represents a completely false divide (Bauer, 2014; Taylor, 2006). This division is actually a mechanism to deny, or impose particular fictions on, female sexuality and a failure to acknowledge that both women and men may actually like and want to have consensual sex with someone of their own choosing.

> A number of critics of this assumption have asserted that prostitution has little to do with biologically based desire and everything to do with power, the implication being that if women were the ones with economic and political power, then they just might find themselves paying men for sex—and perhaps more to the point, women might be constructed as the "natural" desirers and buyers of male sexuality. Nevertheless, the ideology that women are the "natural" objects of desire is quite powerful.
> 
> *(Wardlow, 2004, p. 1027)*

This is not to deny that women can be forced into prostitution or harassed or sexually assaulted when travelling or in other environments. However, it is to argue that sexual roles and relations should not be examined by simplistic binary notions of sexuality and the acceptability, or not, of sexual practices and relationships (Locke, Lawthom, & Lyons, 2018). Indeed, feminist perspectives on prostitution are extremely useful here because of the way in which transactional sexual relations can be simultaneously conceptualised as both "indicating and reinforcing female subordination" and "as a potentially emancipatory practice that exposes, transgresses, and thereby undermines dominant discourses about gender" (Wardlow, 2004, p. 1023).

The inappropriateness of binary conceptualisations is arguably inherent in the way that sex tourism has often been approached, especially given that as a result of increased mobility and globalisation, the sex industry has been increasingly subject to "touristification" (Sacramento, 2011, p. 377), which also represents the internationalisation of the sex industry's consumer base. In Western countries, Wardlow (2004) argues that, for a number of elements in society, prostitution and monetary-based sex tourism embodies and epitomises the anxieties of some about the commoditisation of human relationships. According to Wardlow (2004, p. 1029), "in the Western popular imaginary, love is only love if it is 'freely given,' thus, a monetized transaction is, by definition, devoid of the emotional attachments that define genuine, heartfelt relationality". Prostitution and some forms of sex tourism that are "presumably not motivated by love violates this gendered moral imperative. By commoditizing that which ideally signifies the transcendence of commoditization, prostitutes represent the possibility of a world in which all relationships are instrumental and mediated by cash" (Wardlow, 2004, p. 1030). Yet it is that same commercial dimension that intrinsically distinguishes tourism from recreation and leisure. Given that tourism is an explicitly commercial transaction of engaging in commoditised leisure, including sex, it therefore often becomes a focus of moral opposition because it is almost inherently sexualised and often charged with the sexualities of the other, particularly in borderlands (Gabbert, 2003), even though members of the local community may similarly engage in paid and transactional sexual relations.

Karibo (2015, p. 60) suggests that at the centre of the appeal of border sex tourism destinations is "the commodification of illicit sexual pleasure, which allow[s] participants to cross sexual, spatial, and racial boundaries simultaneously". Such crossings may come from individual consumption or, and what is just as important but is not so well recognised in the literature, for couples and other sexual groupings to cross borders and be able to engage in practices without necessarily having sexual relations with those who live in the border space but with themselves, because it becomes permissible or maybe even just possible (Dion, 2021). From this perspective, crossing borders allows for participation in acts such as anal and oral sex, as well as consensual sex outside of marriage, adultery, open relationships, or access to sex aids or even online sexual material that would otherwise be unavailable. Crossing borders and entering borderlands is therefore a way of avoiding or escaping some of the constraints of state policing of sexuality and imposed notions of sexual citizenship (Cossman, 2007). As Lee (2011, p. 2) comments, much state regulation of sexuality,

> imposes constraints and punishment on those who seek to engage in consensual behaviour, between adults and usually in private. But in a world which displays great diversity – religiously, economically, geographically, and politically – States commonly seek to prevent certain forms of sexuality from being expressed, even when, as is often the case, the country concerned has a rich history of diverse and socially legitimate sexual conduct.

Given such diversity and the fluidity of the relationships between sex, sexuality, tourism, and place, we therefore embrace the borderlands of sex and tourism "as a landscape for a multiplicity and range of gradations of erotic, affectional, and even spiritual practices and as a landscape with some institutions and practices that mark sexual activities as work or labor" (Cabezas, 2004, p. 1003).

## The Temptation of the Border

Border regions are tempting spaces for tourists with respect to sex for a multiplicity of reasons. Because of their nature, plural/multiple legal frameworks simultaneously operate and coexist, providing relatively safer spaces for sexual practices (Dell-Era, 2020). These are also overlain with different cultural and ethical layers. As Askew and Cohen (2004, p. 93) comment, "differences in legal-political and social conditions prevailing in Thailand, compared to those in Malaysia and Singapore, are critical factors underlying the continued flow of tourism into Thailand and help to explain the predominant forms it takes, namely sex-oriented tourism". The rigorous enforcement of legal sanctions against the sex industry in Malaysia and the application of the strict shariah law in some states "contrasts strikingly with the openness and ease of access to sex workers in Thailand across the border" (Askew & Cohen, 2004, p. 93).

Nevertheless, the temptations to cross borders may be substantially different for tourists and workers. For example, persons entering the United States and suspected as "likely to become a public charge" or "arrested for any other immoral purpose", including prostitution, face being denied admittance (Chávez-García & Castillo-Muñoz, 2020, p. 8). Furthermore, it is still common for trafficked victims in general, and especially for women in prostitution cases, to be treated as criminals (Chong, 2014). With respect to crossing the Mexico–USA border, Chávez-García and Castillo-Muñoz (2020, p. 7) report on a case where

> suspecting the single women had intentions to cross the border to work in brothels located in El Paso and beyond or to in other ways engage in non-normative gender roles, the border inspectors pried [into] women's private lives, probing their personal motivations and intimate relationships as well as their sexuality to determine if they subscribed to what state officials believed to be immoral lives.

Border towns have become destinations and centres of sex tourism and commercial sex work because they are crossroads that connect different cultures (with different sexual values) and provide anonymity for sexual activity which may be clandestine (Kennedy & Ullman, 2003; Martinez, 1994). In some cases, it has also been suggested that the attractiveness of such destinations is related to their geographically peripheral location on the border leading to lesser visibility and institutional control from central governments (Sacramento, 2011). Nevertheless, peripheral or not, it is clear that political and legal differences are integral to borderlands' relative attraction to some tourists for whom sexual opportunities serve as an element of their motivation to visit a destination because they are perceived as being relatively safe. Cultural and religious difference and tolerance also play a substantial part in the meaning-making of visitors associated with such sites (Dell-Era, 2020). Yet, most border tourism appears driven by a mix of both familiarity and difference, including legal, political, and economic difference (Askew & Cohen, 2004; Lei & Hanh, 2011).

Significantly, an important part of the attractiveness of such areas is the way in which sex has been commoditised as part of the commercial practice of tourism and its role in economic development (Lei & Hanh, 2011), which reflects the transactional view of sex noted above and is in keeping with broader neoliberal practices and the marketisation of the body. In the case of the latter, it has long been recognised that tourism promotion is clearly connected with sexualisation and the promotion of fantasy, whether real or imagined, to consumers as part of the process by which a destination or a product becomes differentiated and othered. As Campbell (2007, p. 276) recognises, "clearly, the play of fantasy and imagery, the manipulation of cultural representations, the erotic construction of the other and the performance of stereotypes – as well as power imbalances – are all critical to cross-border sexual exchanges".

Nevertheless, not all cross-border sexual exchanges are the same and, in order to gain a better understanding of the sexual identities of borderlands, there is potentially a need to disaggregate between the different exchanges that exist: from the purely commercial through to the romantic. Both may be forbidden or frowned upon in the tourist's home country, yet they are occurring in different spaces. In many countries, areas that explicitly exist to provide a location where visitors can be sexually entertained may be explicitly zoned under planning regulations or may be confined and restricted by a combination of formal and informal sanction and surveillance. In Batam, the largest city in the Riau Islands of Indonesia and only a short ferry ride from Singapore, the Singaporean government attempted to control the sexual transgressions of its citizens "by enforcing new techniques of surveillance at its borders" (Lindquist, 2010, p. 286). In Vietnam, control has been attempted by such measures as the registration of sex workers at police stations and the imposition of taxes on individual "entertainment" businesses (Lei & Hanh, 2011). As a result, such spaces may therefore become separated from other notions of the everyday and often come to be regarded as deviant or "immoral" landscapes (Symanski, 1981), within the broader tourism borderscape. Symanski (1981, p. xii) observes that "much of the social problem of prostitution and its solution are eminently geographic" with a need to keep deviant and immoral space socially invisible from an otherwise hypocritical host community that enjoys the economic benefits (Lei & Hanh, 2011). For example, countries such as South Korea and Thailand have historically enjoyed the economic benefits of sex tourism. In the case of Thailand,

> although the sale of sexual services is currently illegal ..., the Thai government does little to curb the existence of businesses that cater to sex tourists. In fact, the government has historically supported sex tourism due to its military and economic positioning in the area.
> 
> *(Bernstein & Shih, 2014, p. 436)*

Perhaps ironically, the othering of such spaces actually enables them to be more effectively commoditised and controlled, providing a clear location for the satisfaction of different sexual and other practices, although this may create policy issues. For example, in the case of the Texas borderlands with Mexico, "for El Paso's civic leaders, what was 'morally correct' was not always economically sound; they had to choose whether to represent El Paso as a 'Sin City' or a 'Sun City'" (Gabbert, 2003, p. 576). The overlap of spatial and sexual identity therefore enables both promotion and access by providing the experience of another crossing of a border, one that is sexual rather than just a political crossing, although the two can often not be separated. As well as offering commercialised sexual performance, such spaces therefore also provide opportunities for tourists to look in and experience the frisson of deviance even if they do not directly partake.

A number of authors argue that the identified deviant border spaces can serve as physical liminal spaces that can impact individuals, given that daily social norms are suspended in such spaces and transgressions and "Dionysian indulgence" are encouraged (Sacramento, 2011). However, while such spaces are temporarily occupied by tourists, their actual liminal nature becomes somewhat problematic given that they are also highly commoditised and provide an already anticipated known encounter, even if it is different from that experienced in the home environment. Furthermore, tourism—even of a deviant kind—has also become greatly routinised. A truer sexualised liminal space is provided when tourists experience the unexpected and unscripted desire or encounter with local people, other tourists, and/or even those they are travelling with. These will, almost certainly, not be commoditised encounters although they may occur in commercialised tourist spaces, most obviously in hotels, restaurants, and bars, which may loosen personal restraint. Indeed, we would argue that it is the very unexpectedness of the sexual experience that is the essence of liminal notions of being out of time and space. Therefore, the sensualscapes of the borderlands and their different sights, smells, and feel provide the possibilities of crossing sexual borders simply by not being in the home environment.

The crossing of sexual borders to experience the erotic other, even if not fully commoditised, may, in some situations, still be socially and economically constructed. For example, ethnosexuality in which sex and sexuality are bound up with the social and cultural implications of race, racism, and nationalism (Chong, 2014) can be a motivation for sexual exploration across borders. Such racialized constructions of desire (Wardlow, 2004) can take several forms. In terms of prostitution, it may mean paying for women or men from different races and nationalities to provide the illusion of experiencing the "exotic" (Chong, 2014). Another form is the desire of tourists to experience sex with someone from a different ethnicity out of interest and curiosity which is played out by the deliberate search for such opportunities. Such motivations have been recognised in the literature from both male and female tourists with it often being connected to supposed Western desires for a "black experience" (Aston, 2008; Garland, 2015). According to Pruitt and LaFont (1995, p. 423), with their new economic power,

> many Euro-American women are seeking an identity beyond the confines of the traditional gender scripts offered in their cultures … With the ease and popularity offered by mass tourism, part of this negotiation is being conducted around the world as women travel independently of men. Free from their own society's constraints, female tourists have the opportunity to explore new gender behaviour.

However, such ethnosexual motivations still remain bound up with economic inequalities. A third racialized construction is ethnosexual encounters themselves become "borderlands on either side of ethnic divides" which, as Chong (2014, p. 199) observes, "skirt the edges of ethnic communities; they constitute symbolic and physical sensual spaces where sexual imaginings and sexual contact occur between members of different racial, ethnic and national groups". Finally, the constructed racialized stereotypes of "the sexual anxieties of white men, the sexual submissiveness of Asian woman, the sexual looseness of white woman, [and] the sexual potency of black men" are found to be similar in the sexual imaginings of both heterosexuals and homosexuals (Chong, 2014, p. 200). The continuation of such stereotypes is perhaps all the more remarkable given that the consumers of such imaginaries are themselves coming from increasingly multicultural spaces, thereby raising the possibility that it is the border crossings of tourists that serve to promote stereotypes of stereotypes.

Nevertheless, the economic disparities between the consumer and the ethnic other raises broader questions with respect to involvement in the supply of monetized sexual exchange and the economic position of the provider of such services (Campbell, 2007). In considering such issues, Wardlow (2004, p. 1018) argues that consideration must be given to, "first, local constructions of gender and sexuality, particularly the role female gender plays in social reproduction, and second, the ways in which economic structures are mediated by gendered meanings and processes to shape women's motivations and agency". Much of the research on sex work, for example, whether in Western or non-Western contexts, stresses either economic desperation or, although largely voluntary, the awareness that sex work potentially pays better than other work (Wardlow, 2004), an observation borne out in a number of studies (Askew & Cohen, 2004; Lindquist, 2004). Askew and Cohen (2004, p. 100), for example, argue that

> Thai women, through their work with their bodies, have sexualized the Thai-Malaysian border, serving to act collectively as a major source of attraction, using the border in their own way towards strategies of economic recovery and improvement, often through relationships of varying intensity and duration with the cross-border visitors.

Similarly, Lei and Hanh (2011, p. 84) observe that the China–Vietnam borderlands "have become a place where sexual dreams of Chinese men and economic dreams of Vietnamese women meet and materialize, for better or for worse". This quote also highlights, as noted above, that considerable debate exists in feminist and other scholarship with respect to the exploitative nature of such economic relations. For example, in the case of the Huli women of Papua New Guinea (Wardlow, 2004), females began their journey into sex work for emotional reasons and the feeling of control of their body before asking for money for sex.

## Conclusion: Crossing Borders?

As discussed at the beginning of the chapter, sex is inherently a messy subject. The relationship between sex and tourism is also an essentially contested subject that is fraught with the key issue of how it should be defined and framed as a research or policy problem. Much of the research on sex and tourism is also tied up with different philosophies, ideologies, and moralities that affect not only the framing of research but also how the results are interpreted. As noted in this chapter, one substantial issue is how different sex and tourism relationships are represented. In this we have argued that there is now substantially no difference between male and female tourists—if there ever was—although we readily acknowledge the highly gendered nature of many tourism spaces and practices and that there has been much more writing of males taking advantage of female tourists than females taking sexual advantage of other tourists.

Historically, female tourists' relations with men at destinations or even with fellow travellers have been portrayed as being more romantic and emotional rather than overtly sexual and, therefore, much more "acceptable". The physical contact that followed was therefore only a natural step in the development of a romantic relationship between host and guest. The distinction between the "abominable sex tourism of men and the kind, loving relationship of women" (Bauer, 2014, p. 22) led Pruitt and LaFont (1995, p. 423) to invent the term "romance tourism", which encompassed positive features such as the possibility "to explore new avenues for negotiating femaleness and maleness" by allowing women to explore their gender identity and the men to benefit economically, with neither partner supposedly regarding this activity as paid prostitution. Yet, other researchers have shown that whatever women were doing still fits the criteria for sex tourism (Bauer, 2014; Taylor, 2006). "The fact that parallels between male and female sex tourism are [deliberately?] widely overlooked reflects and reproduces weaknesses in existing theoretical and commonsense understandings of gendered power, sexual exploitation, prostitution and sex tourism" (Taylor, 2006, p. 43). In a review of the empirical research on transactional sex where women form the demand (buyer) and men the supply (seller), Berg, Molin, and Nanavati (2020, p. 104) concluded:

> While the women appear to be mature and financially independent, the men are young and socioeconomically vulnerable. Men's main motivation for the sexual-economic

exchanges with women is financial, whereas women's motivations are largely satisfaction of sexual needs and a stereotyped erotic fantasy of black male hypersexuality. Condoms are often not used. Our review shows that there is a – possibly growing and diversifying – female consumer demand for male sexual services, and transactional sex where women trade sex from men is a complex social phenomenon firmly grounded in social, economic, political, and sexual relations.

As such, Jeffreys's (2003, p. 223) argument, that "careful attention to the power relations, context, meanings and effects of the behaviours of male and female tourists who engage in sexual relations with local people, makes it clear that the differences are profound", really no longer holds, if it ever did. Indeed, by idealising sex tourists as romanticists who travel in pursuit of emotional relationships, and by failing to account for the wider set of socio-economic and sexual relations involved, "one may easily overlook the fact that these romanticists use and reproduce sex tourism as a social institution" (Taylor, 2006, p. 55). Increasingly, social media and the neoliberalisation and marketisation of sex have led to a growth in transactional sexual relations in which tourism is inexorably bound, given its own commoditisation of pleasure and the body. In many ways such a shift in the nature of sexual relations and the desire for people to do as they wish with their own bodies represents a continuation in the ongoing change of sexual mores, behaviours, and rights (Todd, 2020).

The borders that the tourists cross here, therefore, represent a shift to a space where such behaviours may be allowed or at least less frowned upon than in the home environment. Ford and Lyons (2020) suggest that studies should identify the origins of regulatory authority over sexual practices and distinguish between political authority (is it legal?) and social authority (is it licit?) if they are to understand the nuances of cross-border activities. It has also long been recognised that notions of escape on the part of tourists are also potentially shared by some of the local sexual partners that tourists may have (Bowman, 1989; Cohen, 1971). Although, as Bowman (1989, p. 78) rightly acknowledged, unless appropriately framed and contextualised, the "metaphorics of sexuality functions to displace, and in its failure to do so reasserts, the structure of relations between the socially and economically empowered and those without power".

Our argument with respect to sex tourism is not to deny the existence of socio-economic, gendered, and political inequalities that are open to exploitation which is, at its worst, to be identified as trafficking and child rape tourism (Tepelus, 2008) (we use this last phrase advisedly, but we believe that it is more appropriate than child sex tourism given that, almost by definition, children are not able to give informed consent to sexual acts). At its worst, tourism only serves to reinforce and exploit inequalities which, in many contexts, severely affect the most vulnerable. Nevertheless, essentialist models of gender and sexuality, and dominant understandings of the term "sexual exploitation", often preclude the possibility that a woman can sexually exploit a man (Taylor, 2001), and it is that need to develop a broader understanding of contemporary exchange values that are attached to sex that we would support and encourage (Taylor, 2006).

Three other areas also provide rich ground for future research and intervention. First, while borderlands and the destination are the focus for much of the research on sex and tourism, particularly because of local economic and sexual exchange, there is insufficient attention given to what it is that tourists are escaping from in their home environment to want to engage in sexual practices elsewhere. Because of the lack of lifecourse and longitudinal studies we do not know how practices change (or not) over time or how the experiences as a tourist are transferred back to the home environment and the mundane sexuality of the everyday. Second, accounts of sexuality on and in the borderlands are often framed as heteronormative

(Pérez, 2003). As a result, it often appears that civil society is conceptualised "as a heterosexual (as well as patriarchal and racist) construction that serves to make entry into the public realm very difficult for [the lesbians, bisexuals, gays, queers, transgendered, and others] whose sexual lives are judged 'immoral'" (Hubbard, 2001, p. 55). Taylor (2006) argued that a greater level of equality is assumed to be present in homosexual sex work between male clients and sellers. Research suggests that, in some contexts, "queer tourists similarly establish long-term relationships with male sex workers, many of whom perform heterosexual identities in their everyday lives, and send remittances for extended periods of time" (Stout, 2015, p. 667). However, the field remains relatively unexplored as only a limited number of researchers have examined the relationships between gay pleasure tourism, global border spaces, and late-capitalist affective economies (Ram et al., 2019; Stout, 2015).

Finally, we come to the role of researchers and the study of sex and tourism relationships. Arguably, some of the arguments presented by researchers on sex tourism may represent more about the researchers' own sexualities, moralities, vulnerabilities, and biases than the phenomena they are studying. They certainly do not seem to have sex, and they almost never "fuck" (De Graeve & De Craene, 2019). One reason for this is undoubtedly connected to the veneer of scientific objectivity and concern over the perceived loss of scientific credibility. As De Craene (2017, p. 449) observed, "despite earlier calls to acknowledge and include the eroticisms of the researcher, accounts where the desiring researcher's body is a central focus remain exceptions to the rule" and instead "sustain the cover of the asexual, disembodied researcher".

Cupples (2002) identified three reasons for the inclusion of researchers' sexuality/ies. First, researchers cannot escape their sexuality in the field; therefore, it should be acknowledged and addressed. Second, the subject and field itself can have "a seductive quality" (p. 383) for the researcher. Third, we are sexually positioned by those we research. Nevertheless, while there are calls for greater reflexivity and self-disclosure in tourism research and its importance for positionality, it invariably rarely includes details of our own preferred sexual positions. Similarly, as Vause (2004, p. 58) observed with respect to auto-eroticism, "no matter how pragmatic and innocuous masturbation is from a rational perspective, it nonetheless remains a topic shrouded in shame and secrecy—and a topic that can still turn heads, especially as it pertains to women"—a comment that can be extended to many of the sexual practices and expressions of sexuality noted in this chapter.

Indeed, the creation of distance "between the 'asexual' researcher and the sexual, desiring, perverted researched and research, might be perceived as embodied survival strategies" (De Craene, 2017, p. 456). A key issue, therefore, in the majority of research on tourist sexual behaviour and sex tourism, whether in the borderlands or elsewhere, is that

> there seems to be a remarkable dichotomy between the desiring informant versus the non-desiring researcher. This dichotomy is not only problematic from a methodological point of view – why would the desires of a researcher not influence our interpretations and understandings of the desires of the informant? – it also confronts us with the epistemological question of how a non-desiring body can investigate desire in its very existence … [Academic] disclaimers on non-normative practices such as paedophilia or sex work, but also on pornography, cheating or BDSM … serves as a tool to create a distance between academic interests and personal desires, and is therefore a strategy of doing sex (research) without incorporating the stigma and having all the "dirt" on the body of the researcher.
>
> *(De Craene, 2017, p. 455)*

Firsthand, detailed, fieldwork and ethnographic research is also greatly limited given the issues involved (Briggs et al., 2011; De Graeve, 2021). Nevertheless, valuable data can be gained via the co-construction of intimacy in sex and tourism studies (Miles, 2020), which can also highlight the intersubjective vulnerability of such research which De Graeve (2021, p. 1) also argues can help produce a "multidimensional and embodied understanding of power relations".

In concluding this border-crossing, we therefore concur with the importance of acknowledging the emotional labours and vulnerabilities of those engaged in sex work, transactions, and tourism, including those of the researchers, and the need for greater transparency in the sexualities or positionality of sex tourism research. Such sensitivities may potentially improve the quality of the research undertaken, as well as empower those at the sexual margins, on which much attention is given. However, that noted, we also acknowledge our own privilege within academia and society, of being white, heterosexual, relatively well off, and abled, and that, for many, such avowed positionality at the borders may be easier said than done.

## References

Askew, M., & Cohen, E. (2004). Pilgrimage and prostitution: Contrasting modes of border tourism in lower south Thailand. *Tourism Recreation Research*, 29(2), 89–104.

Aston, E. (2008). A fair trade? Staging female sex tourism in sugar mummies and trade. *Contemporary Theatre Review*, 18(2), 180–192.

Bauer, I.L. (2014). Romance tourism or female sex tourism? *Travel Medicine and Infectious Disease*, 12(1), 20–28.

Berg, R.C., Molin, S-B., & Nanavati, J. (2020). Women who trade sexual services from men: A systematic mapping review. *The Journal of Sex Research*, 57(1), 104–118.

Berno, T., & Jones, T. (2001). Power, women, and tourism development in the South Pacific. In A. Apostolopoulos, S. Sönmez, & D.J. Timothy (eds) *Women as producers and consumers of tourism in developing regions*, pp. 93–109. Westport, CT: Praeger.

Bernstein, E., & Shih, E. (2014). The erotics of authenticity: Sex trafficking and "reality tourism" in Thailand. *Social Politics*, 21(3), 430–460.

Bowman, G. (1989). Fucking tourists: Sexual relations and tourism in Jerusalem's old city. *Critique of Anthropology*, 9(2), 77–93.

Brennan, J. (2017). Cruising for cash: Prostitution on Grindr. *Discourse, Context & Media*, 17, 1–8.

Briggs, D., Tutenges, S., Armitage, R., & Panchev, D. (2011). Sexy substances and the substance of sex: Findings from an ethnographic study in Ibiza Spain. *Drugs and Alcohol Today*, 11(4), 173–187.

Cabezas, A., (2004). Between love and money: Sex, tourism, and citizenship in Cuba and the Dominican Republic. *Signs: Journal of Women in Culture and Society*, 29(4), 987–1015.

Campbell, H. (2007). Cultural seduction: American men, Mexican women, cross-border attraction. *Critique of Anthropology*, 27(3), 261–283.

Chan, Y.W. (2008). Cultural and gender politics in China-Vietnam border tourism. In M. Hitchcock, V.T. King, & M. Parnwell (eds), *Tourism in Southeast Asia: Challenges and new directions*, pp. 206–221. Copenhagen: Nordic Institute of Asian Studies.

Chávez-García, M., & Castillo-Muñoz, V. (2020). Gender and intimacy across the US-Mexico borderlands. *Pacific Historical Review*, 9(1), 4–15.

Choi, D., & DeLong, M. (2019). Defining female self sexualization for the twenty-first century. *Sexuality & Culture*, 23(4), 1350–1371.

Chong, N.G. (2014). Human trafficking and sex industry: Does ethnicity and race matter? *Journal of Intercultural Studies*, 35(2), 196–213.

Cohen, C.B. (2001). Island is a woman: Women as producers and products in British Virgin Islands tourism. In A. Apostolopoulos, S. Sönmez, & D.J. Timothy (eds) *Women as producers and consumers of tourism in developing regions*, pp. 47–72. Westport, CT: Praeger.

Cohen, E. (1971). Arab boys and tourist girls in a mixed Jewish Arab community. *International Journal of Comparative Sociology*, 12(1), pp. 217–233.

Cossman, B. (2007). *Sexual citizens: The legal and cultural regulation of sex and belonging*. Stanford, CA: Stanford University Press.

Cupples, J. (2002). The field as a landscape of desire: Sex and sexuality in geographical fieldwork. *Area*, 34(4), pp. 382–390.

Curtis, J., & Arreola, D. (1991). Zonas de tolerancia on the northern Mexican border. *Geographical Review*, 81(3), 333–346.

De Craene, V. (2017). Fucking geographers! Or the epistemological consequences of neglecting the lusty researcher's body. *Gender, Place & Culture*, 24(3), 449–464.

De Graeve, K. (2021). Beyond the crazy ex-girlfriend: Drawing the contours of a radical vulnerability. *Sexualities*, 1–16, 1363460719876817.

De Graeve, K., & De Craene, V. (2019). The researcher's erotic subjectivities: Epistemological and ethical challenges. *Documents d'anàlisi geogràfica*, 65(3), 587–601.

Dell-Era, A. (2020). Global borderlands: Fantasy, violence, and empire in Subic Bay, Philippines. *New Global Studies*, 14(2), 213–216.

Dion, M.L. (2021). Regulation of sexuality in the Global South. In: *Oxford research encyclopedia of politics*. Oxford University Press, Oxford. https://doi.org/10.1093/acrefore/9780190228637.013.1183

Ford, M. & Lyons, L. (2020). The illegal as mundane: Researching border-crossing practices in Indonesia's Riau Islands. *Indonesia and the Malay World*, 48(140), 24–39.

Gabbert, A. (2003). Prostitution and moral reform in the borderlands: El Paso 1890-1920. *Journal of the History of Sexuality*, 12(4), 575–604.

Garland, C. (2015). The visual rhetoric of 'voluntourists' and aid workers in post-earthquake Haiti. *Social and Economic Studies*, 64(3/4), 79–102.

Hall, C.M. (1998). The legal and political dimensions of sex tourism: The case of Australia's child sex tourism legislation. In M. Oppermann (Ed.), *Sex tourism and prostitution*, pp. 87–96. New York: Cognisant.

Hooks, G. (2020). Global borderlands: Fantasy, violence, and empire in Subic Bay, Philippines by Victoria Reyes (review). *Social Forces*, 99(1), 14.

Horley, J., & Clarke, J. (2016). *Experience, meaning, and identity in sexuality*. London: Palgrave Macmillan.

Hubbard, P. (2001). Sex Zones: Intimacy, citizenship and public space. *Sexualities*, 4(1), 51–71.

Hu-DeHart, E. (2012). Chinatowns and borderlands: Inter-Asian encounters in the diaspora. *Modern Asian Studies*, 46(2), 425–451.

Jeffreys, S. (2003). Sex tourism: Do women do it too? *Leisure Studies*, 22(3), 223–238.

Jeffreys, S. (2008). *The industrial vagina: The political economy of the global sex trade*. London: Routledge.

Karibo, H.M. (2015). *Sin city north: Sex, drugs, and citizenship in the Detroit-Windsor Borderland*. North Carolina: UNC Press Books.

Kennedy, K., & Ullman, S.R. (eds) (2003). *Sexual borderlands: Constructing an American sexual past*, Ohio: Ohio State University Press.

Kwon, R.O. (2021). It's time to talk more about kink – and take the shame away from it. *The Guardian*. 9 February, https://www.theguardian.com/lifeandstyle/2021/feb/09/kink-anthology-book-fear-shame

Lee, J.C. (2011). *Policing Sexuality: Sex, society, and the state*. London: Zed Books.

Lei, Z., & Hanh, D.B. (2011). Sex work in the Sino-Vietnamese borderlands. *Asian Anthropology*, 10(1), 81–100.

Lindquist, J. (2004). Veils and ecstasy: Negotiating shame in the Indonesian borderlands. *Ethnos*, 69(4), 487–508.

Lindquist, J. (2010). Putting ecstasy to work: Pleasure, prostitution, and inequality in the Indonesian borderlands. *Identities: Global Studies in Culture and Power*, 17(2–3), 280–303.

Locke, A., Lawthom, R., & Lyons, A. (2018). Social media platforms as complex and contradictory spaces for feminisms: Visibility, opportunity, power, resistance and activism. *Feminism & Psychology*, 28(1), 3–10.

Luna, S. (2018). Affective atmospheres of terror on the Mexico–US border: Rumors of violence in Reynosa's prostitution zone. *Cultural Anthropology*, 33(1), 58–84.

Martinez, O.J. (1994). *Border people: Life and society in the US-Mexico borderlands*. Tucson: University of Arizona Press.

Miles, S. (2020). "I've never told anyone this before": Co-constructing intimacy in sex and sexualities research. *Area*, 52(1), 73–80.

Pérez, E. (2003). Queering the borderlands: The challenges of excavating the invisible and unheard. *Frontiers: A Journal of Women Studies*, 24(2/3), 122–131.

Pruitt, D., & LaFont, S. (1995). For love and money: Romance tourism in Jamaica. *Annals of Tourism Research*, 22, 422–40.

Ram, Y., Kama, A., Mizrachi, I., & Hall, C.M. (2019). The benefits of an LGBT-inclusive tourist destination. *Journal of Destination Marketing & Management*, 14, 100374.

Reyes, V. (2015). Global borderlands: A case study of the Subic Bay freeport zone, Philippines. *Theory and Society*, 44(4), 355–384.

Reyes, V. (2019). *Global borderlands: Fantasy, violence, and empire in Subic Bay, Philippines*. Stanford, CA: Stanford University Press.

Ryan, C., & Hall, C.M. (2001). *Sex tourism: Marginal people and liminalities*. London: Routledge.

Sacramento, O. (2011). Liminal spaces: Reflections on the proxemia of cross-border demand for prostitution. *Space and Culture*, 14(4) 367–383.

Sönmez, S., Wiitala, J., & Apostolopoulos, Y. (2019). How complex travel, tourism, and transportation networks influence infectious disease movement in a borderless world. In D.J. Timothy (ed.) *Handbook of globalisation and tourism*, pp. 76–88. Cheltenham: Edward Elgar.

Spanger, M. (2013). Doing Love in the borderland of transnational sex work: Female Thai migrants in Denmark. *NORA: Nordic Journal of Women's Studies*, 21(2), 92–107.

Stout, N. (2015). When a yuma meets mama: Commodified kin and the affective economies of queer tourism in Cuba. *Anthropological Quarterly*, 88(3), 665–691.

Symanski, R. (1981). *The immoral landscape: Female prostitution in Western societies*. Toronto: Butterworth-Heinemann.

Taylor, J.S. (2001). Dollars are a girl's best friend? Female tourists' sexual behaviour in the Caribbean. *Sociology*, 35(3), 749–764.

Taylor, J.S. (2006). Female sex tourism: A contradiction in terms? *Feminist Review*, 83(83), 42–59.

Tepelus, C.M. (2008). Social responsibility and innovation on trafficking and child sex tourism: Morphing of practice into sustainable tourism policies? *Tourism and Hospitality Research*, 8(2), 98–115.

Timothy, D.J. (2001). *Tourism and political boundaries*. London: Routledge.

Todd, M. (2020). *Sexualities and society: An introduction*. Sage: London.

Vause, M. (2004). Doing it ourselves: Female masturbation past and present. *Iris: A Journal About Women*, 48, 58–64.

Wardlow, H. (2004). Anger, economy, and female agency: Problematizing "prostitution" and "sex work" among the Huli of Papua New Guinea. *Signs: Journal of Women in Culture and Society*, 29(4), 1017–1040.

# 23
# TRANSBOUNDARY SECOND-HOME TOURISM

*Olga Hannonen*

## Introduction

Borders are considered barriers to tourism development, human interaction, and movement of goods and services (Gelbman, 2008; Weidenfeld, 2013). However, borders are not only physical or mental barriers. They produce various forms of interactions, relations, and activities across them, which would not exist without the presence of the border (Newman, 2006; Schack, 2001; Timothy, 2000; Van der Velde & Spierings, 2010). The border itself or what lies across it can also become an attraction as a curiosity in the cultural landscape and a symbol of differences and national identities (Gelbman & Timothy 2010; Hannonen, Tuulentie & Pitkänen, 2015; Prokkola 2010; Timothy 2001). This is particularly the case in transboundary second-home tourism, in which the benefits of foreign property ownership often outweigh domestic locations. Patterns and trajectories of transboundary second-home tourism are dependent on types of borders and interstate relations that these borders represent.

Depending on the character and intensity of cross-border interactions, borderlands can be characterised as alienated, co-existent, interdependent, and integrated (Martinez, 1994). Alienated borderlands are the least integrated, as the cross-border interaction and interchange is "practically non-existent" (Martinez, 1994, p. 2). The border remains slightly open, allowing for the development of limited bilateral interaction in the case of coexistent borderlands. Interdependent borderlands are characterised by friendly and cooperative relationships between the borderlanders, while integrated borderlands allow unrestricted movement of people and goods across the boundary (Martinez, 1994). Consequently, types of interaction and touristic activity are predetermined by interstate relations and the type and form of the borderland. It has been argued that the level of interaction between people across the border depends on the border and its functions. Interactions tend to be high across soft borders and low when the border is strong (Schack, 2001). However, in the tourism context, borders act in a more complex way. In relation to tourism, borders as political boundaries can be destinations or modifiers of tourism landscapes (Timothy, 2001). Real and perceived borders can also be barriers to tourism. Borders act as tourist attractions when they offer unique cultural landscapes or attractive economic, legal, and cultural differences. The nature of borders and human factors influence the spatial development of border regions, turning borders into modifiers of tourism landscapes (Timothy, 2001).

It is important to note that the components of Martinez's and Timothy's typologies are not mutually exclusive. In tourism, alienated borderlands are not always barriers, while integrated borders are not necessarily destinations. Studies and empirical examples around the world show that alienated borderlands can be barriers to tourism but also destinations or attractions (Gelbman, 2008). In a similar vein, open integrated borderlands can have limitations or restrictions on certain touristic activities, such as second-home tourism (Müller, 2011b; Tress, 2002).

One may distinguish between three types of border tourism depending on how tourism relates to the boundary (Fors, 2018). First, border is a context, a locale, or a setting for tourism: "It has no real effect on tourism, nor is it of particular interest for the tourists" (Fors, 2018, p. 42). Second, the border can serve as a locale but also as a generator of tourism. The most common example of this type of border-tourism entanglement are cross-border retail tourism and gambling, which are encouraged by economic and legal dissimilarities across frontiers. The third type is when tourism focuses on the border itself both as a destination and an attraction (Fors, 2018; Timothy, 2001).

Border regions can become tourist attractions due to the differences in how the societies on both sides function. Various laws and policies applied to frontier regions may give rise to many tourist-oriented activities that are restricted in other areas or in the home country (Fors, 2018; Gelbman & Timothy, 2010). The activities that are allowed or available on the other side of the border include cross-border shopping, gambling, and snowmobiling, among many others (Hannonen, Tuulentie & Pitkänen, 2015; Timothy, 2000).

Studying border regions is important, as the presence of the border changes daily life practices in the borderland (Gielis & Van Houtum, 2012; Newman, 2006), often resulting in unique socioeconomic and cultural practices and identities not found elsewhere within the state. Furthermore "cross-border regions may offer relatively large differences in a relatively small area and therefore at a relatively close distance – that is, in the physical sense because the mental distance towards the other side may be much larger" (Spierings & Van der Velde, 2013, p. 8), which provide borderlanders with rich opportunities for various recreational activities, shopping, or even dwelling (Hannonen, 2016). Thus, borders often offer opportunities, not only challenges.

There are a number of studies on the relationships between tourism and borders (e.g., Gelbman & Timothy, 2010, 2011; Prokkola, 2010; Timothy, 2001; Van der Velde & Spierings, 2010). However, despite the growing transborder second-home tourism phenomenon in different parts of the world, it has been largely overlooked in both border studies and in cross-border tourism research. Among the few exceptions are Russian and Norwegian second-home owners in Finland (Hannonen, 2016; Hannonen, Tuulentie & Pitkänen, 2015) and Hong Kong residents in Mainland China (Hui & Yu, 2009). Most of the studies in transboundary second-home tourism define the border as a context for an empirical case, identifying sociocultural and legislative differences and barriers. Despite the limited number of discussions on borders in studies of transboundary second-home tourism, they collectively highlight valuable empirical insight to support conceptual elaboration on borders in second-home tourism. Moreover, studies on motivation, destination choice, and mobility patterns in transboundary second-home tourism also bring valuable facets of advantages and opportunities of locations beyond borders. Thus, in this chapter I draw upon studies of transboundary second-home tourism that both directly and indirectly refer to the border.

In relation to the competitive advantage of the border, the literature on lifestyle and retirement migration provides important insights. Lifestyle mobility researchers unite to explain all types of lifestyle movements and migrations through the prism of the pursuit of the "good life" (O'Reilly & Benson, 2009). Lifestyle mobilities are primarily driven by aspirations to increase quality of life (Åkerlund, 2013). From the perspective of lifestyle mobility research, a foreign location of (semi-)permanent residence, seasonal or second home, serves the purpose of a positive change and a better life.

This chapter illustrates the competitive advantage(s) of borders in the context of transboundary second-home tourism. Perspectives on the competitive advantage of the border have (at least) two sides: the second home owners' standpoint and the destination perspective. I start with a definition of "transboundary second-home tourism" and define its main trajectories that are formed in part at least due to the competitive advantage of a foreign locality. The discussion continues with the border as a source of benefits and opportunities for recreational property ownership, which attracts significant numbers of owners across the border. Then, the perspective of foreign governments to increase the attractiveness of second-home locations is presented. The chapter ends with a discussion.

## Transboundary Second Homes and Recreational Properties

International second-home ownership and residential mobility have grown rapidly since the 1980s. Simultaneously both domestic and international second-home tourism has witnessed an increase in research attention (Hall & Müller, 2004; Mottiar & Quinn, 2003; Müller, 2011a). The rapid growth of second homes abroad is the result of socio-political factors like globalisation, de-bordering processes, increased international experience and mobility, increased affordability of foreign property markets through the loosening of restrictions on foreign ownership and transport accessibility, the digitalisation of real estate, the flexibility of working lives, and increases in global relative wealth (Gustafson, 2009; Hannonen, 2018a; Mottiar & Quinn, 2003; Müller, 1999; O'Reilly & Benson, 2009; Paris, 2011). Research on international second homes is rather modest in comparison to studies on other types of tourism. It originates from studies of "snowbirds"—people who migrate seasonally to sunnier and warmer locations (O'Sullivan & Stevens, 1982). While being an impulse for studies on second homes on the international scale, seasonal migration currently represents a separate branch of scholarly inquiry. Different disciplinary perspectives and empirical contexts have resulted in a terminological abundance of like phenomena that often leads to confusion. Thus, it is important to define what is regarded as a second home.

A second home is defined as a property owned as the occasional residence of a household that usually lives elsewhere, and which is primarily used for recreational purposes (Coppock, 1977; Paris, 2011). In the case of transboundary second homes, this also means that such properties are owned by someone whose permanent place of residence is in another country and who may also have citizenship of a country other than that where the second home is located. Other phenomena that intersect and overlap with second-home ownership are residential tourism, permanent tourists, lifestyle mobility, lifestyle migration, heterolocal lifestyles, multi-local living, and multiple dwellings. Müller and Hall (2018, p. 4) suggest that second-home tourism is an umbrella concept, as other terms refer to "roughly the same phenomenon". For example, the term "residential tourism" refers not least to the seasonal second-home practices of northern retirees in the south (Müller & Hall 2018). Thus, I use "second home" as an overarching concept but also include other types of transboundary phenomena in the discussion to emphasise different facets of borders as opportunities and their competitive advantages.

The term "transboundary second-home tourism" concerns both international and domestic forms of ownership. In the international context it presumes transborder ownership, while domestic second-home tourism occurs across internal jurisdictions or municipal borders within the same state. The latter, however, rarely provides unique opportunities or competitive advantages. On the contrary, examples and discussions of second-home ownership in different municipalities concern restrictions or specific regulations. Among these are the autonomous Åland Islands in Finland, in which non-Ålander Finnish citizens are required to have the right of domicile in order to own property. Likewise, even within the European Union's (EU) legislation on free mutual property purchases, Denmark and the Czech Republic have maintained restrictive legislation on land ownership by foreigners (Haldrup, 2009; Hannonen, 2016; Müller, 2011b; Tress, 2002).

It is important to note that the term "second home" has also been used to define a permanent move to a foreign country, predominantly for retirement. One of the best-known examples of a promotional campaign in this arena is the "Malaysia My Second Home" programme, which targets foreign retirees and encourages them to relocate to Malaysia on a long-term or permanent basis. Similarly, a number of studies that examine retirement migration to Malaysia refer to second-home ownership, which contrasts with the definition of the term (e.g., see the case of the Japanese in Malaysia described in Aminudin, Rahman, and Othman, 2014). In second-home scholarship and in this chapter, the second home is regarded as the residence that is occupied on a non-permanent basis and which is primarily used for leisure and recreation.

## Trajectories of Transboundary Second-home Tourism

With international mobility, people tend to move to places that require a minimal investment of time and money. Another important factor in lifestyle-related mobility is the amenity of the destination and its attractive differences (Hall & Müller, 2004; Van der Velde & van Naerssen, 2011). Utilising attractive climatic, economic, and sociocultural differences, physical proximity to primary residence, and the amenities of a destination, certain individual trajectories of transboundary lifestyle and second-home mobility have been established.

The first trajectory is the "snowbird" phenomenon, or seasonal and retirement migration from north to south. This type of migration is popular among retirees both in Europe and North America and is dominated by examples of permanent or semi-permanent movement to the southern parts of Europe and Latin America, or in North America from Canada to the southern United States (Åkerlund, 2013; Haldrup, 2009; Mottiar & Quinn, 2003). Examples of second-home ownership along the north–south axis are geographically dominated by cases from the West. They include but are not limited to Northern European and Benelux nationals in France (Buller & Hoggart, 1994; Calzada & Le Blanc, 2006; Chaplin 1999; Fareniaux & Verlhac, 2008; Goujard, 2002; Paris, 2011), German-speaking nationals in Spain (Breuer, 2005; Hannonen, 2018a) (see Figure 23.1), and US nationals in Mexico (Janoschka, 2009). Another pattern of tourism mobility in Europe is from "old" European Union states to "new" member countries, from Western Europe to Eastern Europe—a pattern that is largely driven by economic advantages and debordering processes. Prominent examples are Germans and Austrians in Hungary (Csordás, 1999; Illés & Michalkó, 2008), and Austrians and Italians in Slovenia (Lampič & Mrak, 2012). A similar trend of economically driven second-home ownership, in which foreign owners take advantage of more affordable properties and cheaper costs of living in the destination country, can be observed in the case of Singaporeans in Malaysia (Paris, 2011) and Hong Kong residents in Mainland China (Hui & Yu, 2009).

Economic differences, housing demands, differing tax schemes, and recreational opportunities are both push and pull factors for citizens of adjacent states to move across internal EU and European Economic Area (EEA) borders, forming the third trajectory: second-home ownership between neighbouring states within a single market alliance. It has become increasingly common to work and reside on different sides of a border, to shop across a border, or to spend

*Figure 23.1* German and other foreign-owned second homes on the island of Gran Canaria, Spain.
(*Source:* O. Hannonen)

free time in a second home in a neighbouring country. The majority of studies on transborder and transnational mobility within Europe are undertaken with the conceptual guidance of "debordering" and "intensifying mobility". Examples of this third phenomenon include German and Spanish second-home owners in France, Norwegian second-home owners in Sweden and Finland, and German recreational home owners in Sweden (Buller & Hoggart, 1994; Fareniaux & Verlhac, 2008; Hannonen, Tuulentie & Pitkänen, 2015; Müller, 1999, 2011b). The key factor in this mobility is nationality and shared membership in supranational institutions, such as the EU, EEA, and Schengen zone, all of which provide degrees of open cross-border mobilities. In a study of German second-home owners in the Swedish countryside, Müller (1999, p. 39) states that given the EU's de-emphasis on internal borders, "the location abroad should not play any significant role". The process of European integration has indeed had an impact on the proliferation of second-home tourism (Hannonen, 2016), wherein "the establishment of the European Union can be read as an institutional symbol for the ongoing internationalization" (Müller, 1999, p. 40). A common political and legal framework within the EU creates trust in property investments abroad (Müller, 1999, 2011b). Open and integrated European borders provide an increasingly unified space for mobilities (Timothy & Michalkó, 2016). These advantages have been recently reinforced by Brexit, as British nationals have been caught in the situation of limited rights and potentially limited stays at their foreign properties in EU countries, unless they are registered as legal residents. Moreover, the question of continued British freedom of movement within the EU (and vice versa) remained unresolved by the Withdrawal Agreement (Hall, 2020; O'Reilly, 2020).

In relation to second-home mobility, Müller and Hoogendoorn (2013, p. 362) note that the internationalisation of second-home ownership might change its vector as new flows "could come from economies and regions that traditionally have fallen outside the gaze of second-home research". This statement is supported by the examples of pre-2022 growing Russian transboundary second-home tourism. The case of Russian second-home tourism in Finland centres on the heavily guarded physical border that demarcates not only two sovereign states, as well as the EU and the non-EU "other", but also one of the highest transfrontier economic disparities in the world and which does not fit easily into any of the major patterns of second-home tourism flows described earlier (Hannonen, 2016). This underscores the importance of studying multiple facets of international borders in second-home tourism for the advantages and the opportunities they unveil.

Studies on transborder second homes have shown that buying a property abroad involves a different type of reasoning and integration strategy than buying a second home in one's own country (Åkerlund, 2013; Buller & Hoggart, 1994; Lipkina, 2013; Müller, 2011b). Citizens of different countries have very different mobility capacities, both in terms of the financial costs of, and rights to, mobility (Paris, 2006, p. 14). Purchasing real estate abroad is often associated with risk and uncertainty (Müller, 1999). Crossing national borders can also entail crossing substantial cultural, social, economic, and language borders as well. It is easier to cross borders if no language barrier exists or if crossing formalities are rather relaxed (Schack, 2001). However, Müller (2006) states that an important factor in explaining the reasons for transnational property ownership is the cultural background of second-home owners, which can help explain the reasons behind people's choice of a foreign location.

## The Competitive Advantage of the Border

Gelbman and Timothy (2011, p. 112) define the importance of borders in tourism and their attractiveness for visitors in the following way: "The populations on the two sides of a border are usually different, as they belong to different regimes and have developed different lifestyles and cultures, separate economies and different cultural landscapes". While differences are considered a major part of the appeal of transborder tourism, including second-home ownership, the disparities across borders should be attractive but not too unfamiliar. Thus, to stimulate mobility across borders, the balance between unfamiliar (but not too exotic) and somewhat familiar (but not too commonplace) is ideal. The so-called "bandwidth of unfamiliarity", an interplay between rational and emotional differences, forms case-specific and subjective perspectives on acceptable and unacceptable differences across borders (Van der Velde & Spierings, 2010). The bandwidth of unfamiliarity is a useful analytical tool to understand which functional, physical, and sociocultural differences can explain certain cross-border activities, including transboundary second-home tourism (Hannonen, Tuulentie & Pitkänen, 2015).

In second-home mobility, people cross borders for cheaper properties, fewer restrictions in planning, warmer climates, and better investments (Müller, 2011b; Paris, 2006). In addition to economic factors, the border can also provide access to a society and environment that are perceived to be more picturesque or harmonious for a recreational property location (Buller & Hoggart, 1994; Lipkina, 2013). In such a manner, the border may be(come) an opportunity. The crossing of national borders provides an opportunity to experience and perform another space. Trajectories of transboundary second-home tourism already reveal a number of advantages offered by a foreign location. Following empirical examples, this section discusses opportunities and advantages of transboundary second-home tourism in more detail.

## Climate and Amenities

Climate is one of the desired differences that has produced the snowbird phenomenon, the first version of transboundary second-home ownership. A favourable climate is one of the benefits that has established the strong transboundary second-home trajectory. Academics have written extensively on this type of residential mobility from northern European countries to the Mediterranean and Atlantic islands and coastal regions (see, among others, Åkerlund, 2013; Breuer, 2005; Casado-Diaz, Kaiser & Warnes, 2004; Gustafson, 2009; O'Reilly & Benson, 2009). Thus, international second-home ownership in Europe intersects with the North American snowbird phenomenon referring to the consumption of seasonal amenities (Müller, 2011b, p. 435). Among others, German second-home owners in Spain use their properties to escape the unpleasant winter climate of Central Europe (Breuer, 2005; Hannonen, 2018a; Müller, 2011b). In some cases, even an adjacent state can provide diverse climatic conditions, such as in case of US–Mexican transboundary ownership.

Climate as a competitive advantage does not always presume sharp contrasts between climatic conditions. Many second-home owners long for places with similar climates and environments. Examples include the British in rural France (Buller & Hoggart, 1994), Germans in Sweden (Müller, 1999), Singaporeans in Malaysia (Paris, 2011), and Russians in Finland (Lipkina, 2013). Müller (2011, p. 435) argues that "assets other than the usual sun, sea and sand lure people abroad". The possibility of purchasing a cottage in an amenity-rich area in another country might be more significant than its foreign location. In some cases, it is not possible to afford purchasing a second home domestically. An absence of plots with a desirable location (such as a lakeshore or a mountain area) in the home country and significant differences in housing prices can push cottage buyers to a neighbouring state or other foreign destination (Müller, 2006). Aesthetic criteria, such as scenery and place amenities, are considered significant directing forces in longer distance home acquisitions (Buller & Hoggart, 1994). Studies show that British second-home owners are looking for a perceived lost British countryside that they ostensibly rediscover in rural France (Buller & Hoggart, 1994); German second-home owners in Sweden are attracted by an imagined rural idyll and Swedish culture that was created by Swedish children's books and movies (Müller, 1999). Likewise, Russians in Finland seek lakeside locations, which are unavailable in Russia due to legislative restrictions there (Lipkina, 2013).

Opportunities to own a second home abroad in a desired location are enabled not least by economic incentives and favourable property prices. As Lipkina (2013, p. 313) concludes, "with the lower price for leisure, Russian cottagers get such conditions for a holiday they yearn for in the homeland: rich amenities and lower prices have made the Finnish second home property market more attractive to Russians" (Figure 23.2). Thus, economic differences and price rates are another competitive advantage of transboundary second-home tourism.

## Economic Disparities

Economic disparities between states produce labour and tourism mobility across borders in different parts of the world. This is what Urry (2007) calls "economic distance", as it contrasts the geographical proximity of regions and countries. Economic disparities have played a significant role in forming north-to-south and west-to-east transboundary mobilities. In Asia the overarching mobility vector is directed from the "Asian Tiger" states—Hong Kong, Singapore, and Taiwan—to neighbouring China and Malaysia (Hui & Yu, 2009; Paris, 2011; Wang, 2008). Economic differences enable desirable living and recreational conditions that are financially unattainable back home. This is a common incentive in lifestyle and retirement migration

*Figure 23.2* A Russian-owned second home in the Finnish countryside.
(*Source:* O. Hannonen)

because "money can go further" and allow "access to opportunities for the good life, such as early retirement or a larger consumption space" (Åkerlund, 2013, p. 35).

It should, however, be noted that "while competitive advantages in price levels are another attraction adding to the scenic beauty of the area", these can be subject to quick macroeconomic changes (Müller, 2011b, p. 444). Thus, certain trajectories are more persistent than others. Volatility of exchange and interest rates can result in a sharp decline in second home purchases (e.g., Russian second-home tourism in Finland; see Hannonen, 2016) and even cause owners to return to their home countries (e.g., British property owners in Turkey; see Waller, 2017).

Many studies that describe the economic advantages of the border originate from regions that have high economic disparities, such as the US–Mexican border (Janoschka, 2009). However, diverging economic development in other less fiscally contrasting regions, such as the Nordic realm, has also caused second-home flows across intraregional borders (e.g., Norwegians in Sweden) (Müller, 2011b). The most common assumption, however, is that mobility vectors that take advantage of economic disparities are always formed in a direction from more affluent to less affluent states. A contrasting situation can be seen on the Finnish–Russian border, which accentuates very different standards of living between neighbouring states. A justifiable assumption would be that the more affluent Finns shop for cheaper properties and take advantage of lower living costs on the Russian side of the border. Finns, however, own very few plots of land in Russia, whereas Russians are now the largest group of foreign second-home owners in Finland (Hannonen, 2016). Thus, economic disparities are an advantage in one context but a barrier in another. The latter emphasises the importance of looking into multifaceted advantages of borders that outweigh real barriers, such as economic boundaries.

## *Sociocultural Characteristics*

The structural framework of "home" and "away" enhances the understanding of the competitive advantages of transboundary second-home tourism. Borders nearly always raise the question of cultural differences and similarities that make certain destinations more attractive and appealing than others. Depending on second-home owners' cultural backgrounds, they search either for similar or contrasting sociocultural characteristics in the destination. Empirical evidence shows that the sociocultural characteristics of a second-home destination can include a desire for the same legal space and shared culture, safer environment, and attractive natural and built environments (Buller & Hoggart, 1994; Hannonen, 2016, 2018a; Krasteva-Blagoeva, 2020; Lipkina, 2013; Müller, 2011a). Moreover, the culture of the second-home locality may have experienced different historical and cultural development even between adjacent neighbours. Thus, transboundary second homes exude a feeling of cultural difference at least in part owing to the physical characteristics of the dwelling and the spatial organisation of second-home settlements. The overcrowded urban infrastructure of Hong Kong serves as an illustrative example here. Many Hong Kong residents try to escape the busy everyday life of the city by looking for more spacious recreational and residential environments in Mainland China (Hui & Yu, 2009).

Socio-political situations are another factor that facilitates or restrains transboundary second-home mobility. Differing levels of political and economic stability, as well as public order between the home and host country, are some of the biggest factors in producing amenity mobility across the border (Hannonen, 2016). Foreign real estate is often perceived as a safe investment when insecure and unstable political and economic situations dominate in the homeland. The case of Russian second homes in Finland traditionally demonstrates that many Russians are in search of a safe haven abroad, a "socially just place to live". Instability is thus the main reason behind the asymmetry of the phenomenon; Russians are active second-home buyers abroad, yet reciprocal second-home purchases in Russia are uncommon (Åkerlund, Lipkina & Hall, 2015). Russian second-home ownership in Finland illustrates how the border is an opportunity for certain leisure conditions that are linked to socio-political and economic order and safety in Finland.

In addition to contrasting social and political environments, familiarity is an important factor in transboundary second-home tourism. In the case of Russian second homes in Bulgaria, familiarity with the destination has become one of the leading factors driving Russian transboundary second-home tourism. Krasteva-Blagoeva (2020) argues that cultural proximity between Bulgarians and Russians is a crucial determinant in second-home purchases and use. Unofficially regarded as the "16th republic of the USSR", the most loyal country to Russia among all former socialist states, Bulgaria is an old friend that creates a "sense of being at home" (Krasteva-Blagoeva, 2020, p. 102). The attitude of Russians towards Bulgaria can be summarised in a popular Russian expression: "The hen is not a bird, Bulgaria is not abroad" (Russian: *Курица не птица, Болгария – не заграница*). Similar findings have been reported in Norwegian cross-border tourism in Sweden. There, Norwegians "enter the area with very different economic preconditions, but similar cultural values and traditions" (Müller, 2011b, p. 442). With Russian holiday homes in Bulgaria, the familiarity factor is enhanced by the attractive fact that the latter is an EU member state, which comes with certain advantages (Krasteva-Blagoeva, 2020).

EU membership has been an important factor also in internal EU second-home purchases. Among other nationalities, Germans in Spain made their choice of second-home location largely based on the institutional advantage and similar legal spaces between the two EU states, which reinforces a sense of security in transboundary property ownership (Hannonen, 2018a) and social services, such as health care. Despite shared supranational membership, state borders also mark the borders of national regulations that may signify desirable differences. The case of Norwegian recreational homes in Finland serves as an example here: "The main positive difference, and for many Norwegians one of the main reasons, to spend time on the Finnish side is related to snowmobiling regulations", which are less restrictive on the Finnish side (Hannonen, Tuulentie & Pitkänen, 2015, p. 61).

Second homes often symbolise family attachments and connections to childhood in a domestic context, although a few rare examples of these filial ties also exist in some cases of transboundary second-home ownership. Hong Kong second-home owners have social, historical, and cultural attachments to the Chinese mainland either through pre-existing connections or previous experiences (Hui & Yu, 2009). Also, some Taiwanese second-home owners in Mainland China are looking for an "attachment to their roots" (Hui & Yu 2009, p. 110). The example of British owners in France demonstrates that, for many Britons, a search for a French home is "spurred by nostalgic visions of rural Britain" (Buller & Hoggart, 1994, p. 201). Thus, they seek a familiar rural landscape, something which "actually appears to them as genuine British" (Müller, 1999, p. 42). Thus, the French countryside provides a desired degree of familiarity that is unattainable in Britain. In contrast to Britons in France, Russians in Finland achieve a desirable difference, rather than familiarity, in second-home culture. Burdened by the Soviet heritage of the ideology of "productive leisure" and "rational recreation" at Russian dachas (second homes) (Hannonen, 2018b), in Finland, Russians do not need to engage in certain activities at their leisure homes, such as growing fruits and vegetables (Lipkina, 2013).

As noted previously, transboundary second-home tourism is characterised by several trends and trajectories predominantly based on the major advantages of climate and economic differences. Property location abroad in a different climatic and/or socioeconomic and cultural context provides access to a different set of touristic activities. At seaside or lakeside locations, second-home owners engage in water-related activities. In northern and mountainous locations seasonal activities may include skiing and snowmobiling. Locationally determined activities form other border-induced opportunities.

## *State-induced Advantages*

Foreign second-home tourists' economic, social, and environmental contributions to the host country have been recognised by governments, fostering the development of favourable policies to attract foreign interest (Åkerlund, Lipkina & Hall, 2015). The role of governments and state institutions at various scales to attract international lifestyle mobility, including second homes, are normally geared toward economic interests but are often tempered by political concerns. Governments usually wish to encourage second-home development on the basis of increasing tax revenue but also generating economic and employment benefits through the purchasing power of second-home owners and their visitors. Measures to encourage such transboundary second-home ownership can include not only place promotion but also changes to migration and property laws, including the creation of special visas and residency schemes (Åkerlund, 2013; Åkerlund, Lipkina & Hall, 2015; Aminudin, Rahman & Othman, 2014).

Property agents are considered key players as intermediaries in influencing the purchaser's decisions. "Because of their superior expertise on property transaction procedures and regulations, area characteristics and contact networks, agents may influence buyers' decisions" (Åkerlund, 2013, p. 43). Foreign interest also stimulates the development of specific real estate and property management services that are crafted for foreign second-home segments (Åkerlund, Lipkina & Hall, 2015; Hiltunen, Pitkänen, Vepsäläinen & Hall, 2013; Müller, 2011). Åkerlund (2013, p. 43) states that

> many property agents act as "lifestyle brokers", promoting the acquisition of a new lifestyle rather than just the purchase of a property, and present and promote the destination in a way similar to the performance of tourist guides, for example emphasizing opportunities for leisure activities and experiences.

In such a manner, property agents become intercultural communicators, who skilfully communicate the advantages and opportunities of foreign locations. Among growing incentives attached to foreign property ownership are residence permits and a guaranteed rent for return investment.[1]

It is common knowledge that some countries (e.g., Malta and Malaysia) enact effective policies to attract second-home owners, while others (e.g., Australia) tend to restrict and control the phenomenon instead (Åkerlund, Lipkina & Hall, 2015; Aminudin, Rahman & Othman, 2014). Meeting foreign demand for properties, Malta has introduced specially designated areas that are designed to meet the needs of foreign owners, such as seafront locations and proximal central areas with intensive tourism infrastructure (Åkerlund, Lipkina & Hall, 2015). Empirical studies show that governments of home countries in some cases also promote foreign second-home ownership due to domestic planning problems that raise barriers to recreational second home ownership at home (for the Netherlands example, see Priemus, 2005).

## Conclusion

The presence of a border and the differences that it demarcates may become a resource for intensive transboundary activities, which is especially the case in transborder second-home tourism. In addition to acting as a barrier, in tourism mobility, borders also act as attractions, opportunities, and modifiers of tourism landscapes (Gelbman & Timothy, 2010; Van der Velde & Spierings, 2010). Both physical lines and the differences across them attract visitors (Timothy, 2001). The border as an attraction and opportunity maintains the destination's attractiveness and produces mobilities that otherwise would not take place. On the other hand, the border as a barrier makes the destination either attractively or unattractively unfamiliar (Spierings & Van der Velde, 2013). To maintain tourism mobility across borders, a complex interplay and set of negotiations between the familiar and the unfamiliar, attractive and unattractive, advantageous and disadvantageous, is required. Despite a wide range of studies on tourism and borders, transborder second-home tourism and its influences have not been addressed from the border perspective. The relationship between second-home tourism and borders differs from other types of transborder tourism. While ordinary tourists pass through a destination, second-home owners make a permanent connection with the destination through property ownership. Thus, while second-home owners are permanent visitors, the border sustains the advantages and opportunities of a destination and maintains its attractiveness.

Established trajectories of second-home flows reflect the persistent and prevailing advantages of transboundary tourism. Other border-induced opportunities are contextual and often depend on the cultural characteristics of the destination, as well as the type of border involved, such as an internal or external border of a supranational alliance (e.g., the EU), or an open or closed border. I have argued that in the case of transboundary second-home tourism, the border appears to be an opportunity for better leisure conditions, such as increased possibilities for recreation, amenities, safe environments, or a favourable climate. While borders are usually considered an obstacle to tourism development (Timothy, 2001; Weidenfeld, 2013), transboundary second-home tourism in many cases is the result of the very presence of the border, because the opportunities that are provided and safeguarded by the national frontier outweigh its barrier functions. Thus, in transboundary second-home tourism, the areas and their benefits beyond the border are more important than the mere presence of the border.

## Note

1  Author's observation at the real estate fair in Saint Peterburg, Russia, Spring 2017.

## References

Åkerlund, U. (2013). *The best of both worlds – Aspirations, drivers and practices of Swedish lifestyle movers in Malta*. Umeå: Umeå University.

Åkerlund, U., Lipkina, O., & Hall, C.M. (2015). Second home governance in the EU: In and out of Finland and Malta. *Journal of Policy Research in Tourism, Leisure and Events*, 7(1), 77–97.

Aminudin, N., Rahman, A.S., & Othman, N.H. (2014). Country attractiveness among cross-border second-homers. *Tourism, Leisure and Global Change*, 1(1), 106–122.

Breuer, T. (2005). Retirement migration or rather second-home tourism? German senior citizens on the Canary Islands. *Die Erde*, 136(3), 313–333.

Buller, H., & Hoggart, K. (1994). The social integration of British home owners into French rural communities. *Journal of Rural Studies*, 10(2), 197–210.

Calzada, C., & Le Blanc, F. (2006). Attractivité résidentielle: les résidences secondaires allemandes en Lorraine. *INSEE Lorraine*, 49, 1–8.

Casado-Diaz, M., Kaiser, C., & Warnes, A. (2004). Northern European retired residents in nine Southern European areas: Characteristics motivations and adjustment. *Ageing and Society*, 24(3), 353–381.

Chaplin, D. (1999). Consuming work/productive leisure: the consumption patterns of second home environments. *Leisure Studies*, 18(1), 41–55.

Coppock, J.T. (1977). Second homes in perspective. In J.T. Coppock (ed) *Second homes: Curse or blessing?*, pp. 1–16. Oxford: Pergamon Press.

Csordás, L. (1999). Second homes in Hungary. In A. Duró (ed) *Spatial research in support of the European integration*, pp. 145–160. Pécs: Centre for Regional Studies.

Fareniaux, B., & Verlhac, E. (2008). Le dysfonctionnement des marchés du logement en zone touristique. Paris: Ministère de l'écologie, du développement et de l'aménagement durables.

Fors, B.S. (2018). *Border performances: Politics, art and tourism where Norway meets Russia*. Unpublished doctoral dissertation. University of Tromsø, Norway.

Gelbman, A. (2008). Border tourism in Israel: Conflict, peace, fear and hope. *Tourism Geographies*, 10(2), 193–213.

Gelbman, A., & Timothy, D.J. (2010). From hostile boundaries to tourism attractions. *Current Issues in Tourism*, 13(3), 239–259.

Gelbman, A., & Timothy, D.J. (2011). Border complexity, tourism and international exclaves: A case study. *Annals of Tourism Research*, 38(1), 110–131.

Gielis, R., & Van Houtum, H. (2012). Sloterdijk in the house! Dwelling in the borderscape of Germany and the Netherlands'. *Geopolitics*, 17(4), 797–817.

Goujard, A. (2002). *Résidences secondaires des etrangers et territoire Français: Localisation et retombées économique locales, la valorisation d'un capital Symbolique*, Paris: Université de Paris –Val-de-Marne.

Gustafson, P. (2009). Your home in Spain: Residential strategies in international retirement migration. In M. Benson, & K. O'Reilly (eds) *Lifestyle migrations: Expectations, aspirations and experiences*, pp. 69–86. Aldershot: Ashgate.

Haldrup, M. (2009). Second homes. In R. Kitchin, & N. Thrift (eds) *International encyclopedia of human geography*, pp. 50–55. Oxford: Elsevier.

Hall, C.M., & Müller, D.K. (2004). Introduction: Second homes, curse or blessing? Revisited. In C.M. Hall & D.K. Müller (eds) *Tourism, mobility and second homes: Between elite landscape and common ground*, pp. 3–14. Clevedon: Channel View Publications.

Hall, D. (2020). *Brexit and tourism: Process, impacts and non-policy.* Bristol: Channel View Publications.

Hannonen, O. (2016). *Peace and quiet beyond the border: The trans-border mobility of Russian second home owners in Finland.* Tampere: Juvenes Press.

Hannonen, O. (2018a). Second home owners as tourism trend-setters: A case of residential tourism in Gran Canaria. *Journal of Spatial and Organizational Dynamics*, 6(4), 345–359.

Hannonen, O. (2018b). Stretching the boundaries: building the Russian dacha dream. In C.M. Hall & D.K. Müller (eds) *The Routledge handbook of second home tourism and mobilities*, pp. 179–190. London: Routledge.

Hannonen, O., Tuulentie, S., & Pitkänen, K. (2015). Borders and second home tourism: Norwegian and Russian second home owners in Finnish border areas. *Journal of Borderlands Studies*, 30(1), 53–67.

Hiltunen, M.J., Pitkänen, K., Vepsäläinen, M., & Hall, C. M. (2013). Second home tourism in Finland: Current trends and eco-social impacts. In Z. Roca (ed), *Second homes in Europe: From lifestyle to policy issues*, pp. 165–198. Aldershot: Ashgate.

Hui, E.C.M., & Yu, K.H. (2009). Second homes in the Chinese Mainland under "one country, two systems": A cross-border perspective. *Habitat International*, 33, 106–113.

Illés, S., & Michalkó, G. (2008). Relationships between international tourism and migration in Hungary: Tourism flows and foreign property ownership'. *Tourism Geographies*, 10(1), 98–118.

Janoschka, M. (2009). The contested spaces of lifestyle mobilities: Regime analysis as a tool to study political claims in Latin American retirement destinations. *Die Erde*, 140(3), 1–20.

Krasteva-Blagoeva, E. (2020). Russian real estate owners on Bulgarian Black Sea coast: Culture and ethnic relations (the case of Tsarevo). *Zeszyty Łużyckie*, 54, 97–114.

Lampič, B., & Mrak, I. (2012). Globalization and foreign amenity migrants: The case of foreign home owners in the Pomurska region of Slovenia. *European Countryside*, 4(1), 45–56.

Lipkina, O. (2013). Motives for Russian second home ownership in Finland. *Scandinavian Journal of Hospitality and Tourism*, 13(4), 299–316.

Martinez, O.J. (1994). The dynamics of border interaction: New approaches to border analysis. In C.H. Schofield (ed) *World boundaries - Vol. 1: Global boundaries*, pp. 1–15. London: Routledge.

Mottiar, Z., & Quinn, B. (2003). Shaping leisure/tourism places – the role of holiday home owners: a case study of Courtown, Co. Wexford, Ireland. *Leisure Studies*, 22(2), 109–127.

Müller, D.K. (1999). *German second home owners in the Swedish countryside: On the Internationalization of the leisure space.* Umeå: Department of Social and Economic Geography.

Müller, D.K. (2006). The attractiveness of second home areas in Sweden: A quantitative analysis. *Current Issues in Tourism*, 9(4–5), 335–350.

Müller, D.K. (2011a). Second homes in rural areas: Reflections on a troubled history. *Norsk Geografisk Tidsskrift – Norwegian Journal of Geography*, 65(3), 137–143.

Müller, D.K. (2011b). The internationalization of rural municipalities: Norwegian second home owners in Northern Bohuslän, Sweden. *Tourism Planning & Development*, 8(4), 433–445.

Müller, D.K., & Hall, C.M. (2018). Second home tourism: An introduction. In C.M. Hall & D.K. Müller (eds) *The Routledge handbook of second home tourism and mobilities*, pp. 3–14. London: Routledge.

Müller, D.K., & Hoogendoorn, G. (2013). Second homes: Curse or blessing? A review 36 years later. *Scandinavian Journal of Hospitality and Tourism*, 13(4), 353–369.

Newman, D. (2006). The lines that continue to separate us: Borders in our 'borderless' world. *Progress in Human Geography*, 30(2), 143–161.

O'Reilly, K. (2020, March 6). *Brexit and the British in Spain. Reports.* https://brexitbritsabroad.org/about-the-project/reports.html

O'Reilly, K., & Benson, M. (2009). Lifestyle migration: escaping to the good life? In M. Benson, & K. O'Reilly (eds) *Lifestyle migrations: Expectations, aspirations and experiences*, pp. 1–13. Aldershot: Ashgate.

O'Sullivan, D.A., & Stevens, S.A. (1982). Snowbirds: seasonal migrants to the Sunbelt. *Research on Ageing*, 4(2), 159–177.

Paris, C.M. (2006). Multiple homes, dwelling, hyper-mobility & emergent transnational second home ownership. *The ENHR conference 'Housing in an expanding Europe: theory, policy, participation and implementation'*, July 2006. Ljubljana, Slovenia.

Paris, C.M. (2011). *Affluence, mobility and second home ownership.* London: Routledge.

Priemus, H. (2005). Importing and exporting spatial needs: A Dutch approach. *European Planning Studies*, 13(3), 371–386.

Prokkola, E.K. (2010). Borders in tourism: Transformation of the Swedish-Finnish border landscape. *Current Issues in Tourism*; 13, 223–238.

Schack, M. (2001). Regional identity in border regions: The difference borders make. *Journal of Borderlands Studies*, 16(2), 99–114.

Spierings, B., & van der Velde, M. (2013). Cross-border differences and unfamiliarity: Shopping mobility in the Dutch-German Rhine-Waal Euroregion', *European Planning Studies*, 21(1), 5–23.

Timothy, D.J. (2000). Borderlands: An unlikely tourist destination? *IBRU Boundary and Security Bulletin*, 8(1), 57–65.

Timothy, D.J. (2001). *Tourism and political boundaries*. Routledge: London.

Timothy, D.J., & Michalkó, G. (2016). European trends in spatial mobility. *Hungarian Geographical Bulletin*, 65(4), 317–320.

Tress, G. (2002). Development of second-home tourism in Denmark. *Scandinavian Journal of Hospitality and Tourism*, 2(2), 109–122.

Urry, J. (2007). *Mobilities*. London: SAGE.

Van der Velde, M., & Spierings, B. (2010). Consumer mobility and the communication of difference: Reflecting on cross-border shopping practices and experiences in the Dutch-German borderland. *Journal of Borderlands Studies*, 25(3&4), 191–205.

Van der Velde, M., & Van Naerssen, T. (2011). People, borders, trajectories: An approach to cross-border mobility and immobility in the European Union. *Area*, 43(2), 218–224.

Waller, I. (2017). A case study of the perceptions, experiences and relations of British permanent tourists with the host community in Didim, Turkey. *e-Review of Tourism Research*, 14(3.4), 102–116.

Wang, R. (2008, February 25). Red hot real estate. *China Daily*. http://www.chinadaily.com.cn/cndy/2008-02/25/content_6480512.htm

Weidenfeld, A. (2013). Tourism and cross border regional innovation systems. *Annals of Tourism Research*, 42, 191–213.

# 24
# MERCHANTS, SMUGGLERS, AND WANGLERS:

## Non-conventional Tourism and Trade across Political Borders

*Gábor Michalkó, Mihály Tömöri, and Noémi Ilyés*

### Introduction

The history of humanity is the history of the demarcation, protection, and adjusting of borders (Guo, 2018; Parker, 2006). The peace treaties closing World War II and the establishment of the United Nations have also sought to create stability with regard to the dividing lines between states (Weiss, 2015). Although the historical paradigm of thousands of years cannot be changed overnight, recent decades have demonstrated that it is possible to reinterpret the functions of state borders. In this process, economic interests often override political interests, and there is a growing awareness that tourism, the so-called "peace industry", has considerable potential for economic recovery in border regions (D'Amore, 1988; Franch et al., 2017; Litvin, 1998).

The dichotomy in understanding borders is rooted in the bordering of a "world without borders", or the extent to which policies and laws allow the traditional barrier functions of state boundaries to be diminished (Diener & Hagen, 2009). While the economic and socio-political processes of the second half of the twentieth century (e.g., supranationalism) led to a reduction in the restrictive role of national frontiers, or debordering, we are witnessing an opposite process (i.e., rebordering) in the first half of the twenty-first century (Paasi, 2019). The world's largest multi-state integration process, the creation and growth of the European Union, is founded on the idea of creating a frontier-free Europe by lifting border restrictions on trade and human mobility (Dedman, 1996; Schimmelfennig, 2021). The most important directive of the European Union, the free movement of goods, services, capital, and people, is antithetical to the essential character of borders as set out in the 1648 Peace of Westphalia and subsequent treatments of state frontiers: to maintain distinctiveness and sovereign control over territory. The almost limitless freedom of mobility within the EU and its associated Schengen Area has shown that tourism plays a key role in maintaining and exploiting the economic, social, and cultural differences along state borders (Timothy & Saarinen, 2013; Więckowski, in press). Border regions in Europe, and increasingly elsewhere, are now unoccupied by the military might of adjacent countries. This has given way to an occupation by tourists and the landscapes that follow their consumption behaviours. European borders in most cases no longer constitute a threat but rather a tangible benefit for the regions concerned (Irimiás, 2014).

The geopolitical events of the first decades of the twenty-first century have highlighted the difficulties rooted in the dual interpretation of borders. Overtourism and some anti-tourist movements have also raised the possibility of reintroducing or tightening border controls as a means of slowing the flow of tourists (Butler, 2019; Higgins-Desbiolles et al., 2019). Likewise, the trans-Mediterranean migration/refugee crisis of 2015 hit Europe particularly hard and forced decision makers to enact policies and practices to prevent large numbers of refugees from passing through their countries or entering the EU using technical barriers established temporarily at their borders and with the help of their armed forces (Kocsis et al., 2017). The current COVID-19 pandemic has severely curtailed tourists' mobilities by closing borders and creating strict conditions for crossing (Gössling et al., 2021).

Research on the role of borders in tourism has revealed many elements of the specific symbiosis of tourism mobility and security (Gelbman, 2008; Gelbman & Timothy, 2019; Timothy & Tosun, 2003). This work defines the nature of border areas, which manifest an order (as well as the backstage dichotomy of disarray) that offers social and economic stability. In border regions the state guarantees a high level of security, which is in the interest of borderlanders. By the same token, legal commercial and tourism services in the borderlands, which are created to exploit business opportunities that arise from cross-border differences, also have the potential to create informal and illegal economic activities (Gao et al., 2019; Gelbman & Timothy, 2011; Timothy & Teye, 2005; Yalçın-Heckmann & Aivazishvili, 2012). The purpose of this chapter is to provide an overview of the unusual trade activities, smuggling, and commerce-related endeavours as a form of cross-border "tourism". This will help scholars and community leaders understand better the social, economic, and environmental phenomena and processes taking place on the peripheries of states throughout the world, which can, ultimately, be classified as a unique form of tourism.

## Non-conventional "Tourism" Mobilities in Border Regions

Border regions are notoriously venues of "non-conventional tourism". Non-conventional tourism here refers to travel activities that are not recorded (or not fully recorded) and where travel behaviour and motivations fall outside the traditional scope of leisure-oriented tourism or business travel most commonly recognized by the public and many industry organizations (De Cantis et al., 2015; Heung-Ryel et al., 2019; Klemm, 2002; Novelli, 2005; Rátz et al., 2015).

Non-conventional tourism mobility has existed for a long time in areas where borders could be crossed with relative ease by borderland residents. It has grown in recent years, however, because of the rapid growth of tourism in the twenty-first century, changing transportation business models (Dobruszkes, 2006), the emergence of collaborative economies (Heo, 2016), the blurring boundaries between work and leisure (Pécsek, 2018), the decline of the barrier effects of international boundaries (i.e., access, passports, visas) (Bigo & Guild, 2005), increasing levels of migration (including student migration) and human mobility in general (Raghuram, 2013), the popularity of second homes abroad (Hall, 2014; Hannonen et al., 2015), and technological advancements (Jansson, 2020)—all of which, among other variables, have changed the nature of all types of tourism.

Community planners and destination management organizations must now consider broader human mobilities, including short-haul, same-day visitors, who might not be considered "tourists" in the strictest statistical sense (they do not stay overnight in the destination), or who may not even be motivated by leisure or pleasure, but who do indeed participate in the broad phenomenon of tourism and contribute to the local economy (Tomonori et al., 1994). These may be visitors who return home the same day or utilize non-registered accommodation (e.g., second homes, free accommodation, or home exchanges) (Gallent et al., 2016). They may be visiting friends and relatives (VFR) tourists, who often stay in the homes of their acquaintances

(Zátori et al., 2019); people working or studying temporarily in a tourist destination (Lundberg et al., 2009); people in transit (Tóth et al., 2017); and those who disguise their actual travel motivations and activities for various legal reasons, such as petty traders (Ryan & Kinder, 1996). "Quasi-tourists" are the main players in non-conventional tourism, partly overlapping with new tourists whose consumer behaviour is closer to the traditional understanding of tourism (Back & Marjavaara, 2017). Border regions are premier laboratories for understanding quasi-tourists because borders are transit points, spaces for shopping and commerce, places to tap into health care and education services, and locations for traditional vices such as prostitution, gaming, drug use, and smuggling.

Non-conventional tourism and economic activities in border regions and the merchants and suppliers serving them are located at different points along a scale of legality, with legal activities at one end of the spectrum, informal and semi-legal somewhere in the middle, and illegal and illicit at the other end of the spectrum. The main characteristic of this dubious market is that, on the one hand, it seeks to exploit the potential synergies between services, while on the other hand, through overlaps it is possible to place visitors on different points of the legal–informal–illegal scale of travel. We often think of this issue being relegated to land borders (contact zones), but maritime and fluvial border areas are also spaces of "unofficial tourism" and tourisms of dubious legality (Bowers & Koh, 2019). Thus, these same issues and concerns pertain to islands, coastal microstates, port areas, border control points, and customs areas connected with shipping routes.

## The (Border) Economics of Tourism

Border regions are essentially reflections of the state. Even in countries with diverse natural and socioeconomic conditions, borders reflect a unique blend of culture, economy, politics, society, and history. Frontier regions are areas where travellers' first impressions are made and they are often the scenes of "culture shock", which is reinforced by the physical security structures of the boundary and the border control procedures (Byrne, 2001; Furnham, 1984; Gelbman & Timothy, 2019).

The main driver of the economies of most border regions is trade and commerce, enhanced by the distinctness that borders create, which can be exploited by commerce and tourism separately or symbiotically. This distinctness can be traced back to border-associated natural, political, and social variables and their interactions (Rumley & Minghi, 2014). Cross-border distinctions and their appeal are most noticeable in populated border regions that have undergone centuries of socioeconomic development. The contrasts between two national spaces can trigger a sense of otherness or exoticness often associated with travelling abroad (Cohen & Avieli, 2004; Seddighi & Theocharous, 2002), or they can create contrasting socioeconomic conditions that are conducive to both formal and informal trade.

### *Informal Trade*

Trade is one outcome of these cross-border differences. The infrastructure of formal commercial trade consists of warehouses, container sites, and customs zones, including duty-free zones, duty-free warehouses, and transit areas. Cross-border trade to a large extent serves the demand of freight traffic by road, rail, and waterway. In these circumstances, there is a need for a particularly extensive infrastructure to facilitate shipping and transhipment along trade routes. Cross-border trade zones also have high labour needs in the areas of storage, customs, product processing, packaging, infrastructure management, security, and other needs. The infrastructure needed to transport the workforce, cater to their needs (food services and retail), supply them with consumer goods (shops, pharmacies, fuel stations), and accommodate them (hotels, apartments, and motels) also serves the needs of tourism (Chen et al., 2016) (Figure 24.1).

Another manifestation of formal trade is cross-border shopping. The retail sector in border areas supplies residents and non-resident workers in the region, but in its development the needs of freight transport, transit passengers, and tourists play a determining role. Within conventional and non-conventional tourism at the border, shopping tourism has played a special role, based on lower prices and taxes, different product offerings, and a perceived higher quality of goods sold in retail shops (Timothy, 2005). Cross-border shopping-based tourism is characterized by relatively short shopping trips (i.e., same-day returns or brief overnight stays), is done mostly by car or on foot, and usually takes place at hypermarkets and supermarkets, outlets, or marketplaces with easy access and parking. Cross-border shopping is motivated primarily by price differences, and its processes can be described as a see-saw mechanism based on the balance of benefits and cost (Michalkó et al., 2014). One of the essential features of borderland shopping tourism is that retail is often combined with other leisure motivations.

Informal and unofficial trade is also a by-product of the unique conditions of transfrontier areas. Petty trade is an informal economic activity, sometimes referred to as the "shadow economy", that takes place at many international borders. The informal economy is comprised of income-generating activities that are not controlled or officially enumerated by the state because they function outside the purview of state agents (Castells & Portes, 1989; Portes & Haller, 2005; Timothy & Wall, 1997). The informal economy runs parallel to the formal economy and can only be understood with respect to its relationship to the formal economy (Sassen, 1994).

*Figure 24.1*  The Corozal Free Trade Zone lies just inside Belize before Belizean customs. Here, Mexican consumers shop at much lower prices for merchandise for their own use, as well as to re-sell at home. This commercial zone provides retail opportunities for legal and illegal trade.

(Photo: D.J. Timothy)

The informal economy involves all kinds of unregistered activities that are functionally "invisible" to the state and its taxing and regulatory agencies. In many cases, it is a concerted effort at tax evasion and profiteering that would otherwise be legal (Xheneti, Smallbone & Welter, 2013). In many cases there is no sharp distinction between the formal and the informal, since they often overlap, thus it is better to view them on a continuum from formal and legal to informal and illicit, with a sort of "shadow economy" in between.

Informal cross-border petty trading is a form of arbitrage, wherein participants try to make profits by exploiting price differentials between states by purchasing products in low-price regions and selling them across the border where higher prices dominate (Michalkó & Timothy, 2001; Tömöri, 2010; Williams & Baláž, 2002). Cross-border petty trading occurs in three stages (Egbert, 2006). During the first stage traders raise capital, which enables them to travel abroad and buy products for resale. The second stage involves transporting the purchased merchandise through the border. The third stage is the process of selling the imported items. Cross-border retailing and consumption is a legal activity as long as the items purchased are licit according to the legal systems of the states concerned and as long as the products are purchased, transported, imported, and sold through formal channels. However, experience from borderlands throughout the world shows that a substantial part of small-scale transfrontier trade does not meet these criteria and is therefore an informal or illegal activity (Szytniewski et al., 2020).

In most cases, the formal, informal, and illegal elements of cross-border petty trade cannot be separated clearly from one another. For instance, a common characteristic of informal cross-border trade is that participants skirt paying tariffs, duties, and other taxes (Afrika & Ajumbo, 2012; Lesser & Moisé-Leeman, 2009). However, many traders only partially avoid paying taxes (Cantens, Ireland & Raballand, 2015), since they might pay certain taxes (e.g., local sales taxes, VAT), while avoiding others, such as social security contributions. It is also common for licensed merchants that are thought to be part of the formal sector to purchase items through informal or illegal channels (i.e., smuggling) to achieve greater profit margins (Cantens, Ireland & Raballand, 2015).

The phenomenon of small-scale cross-border trade exists along nearly all international borders (Chikanda & Raimundo, 2017; Karrar, 2019; Peberdy, 2000; Soto Bermant, 2015). However, the social, economic, and political circumstances at the borders of the developing and former socialist countries of Central and Eastern Europe provide particularly favourable conditions for this activity in and around those countries (Hall, 2017; Williams & Baláž, 2002) (Figure 24.2). In these countries the shadow or illicit economy in cross-border trade is an important source of (supplemental) income, since employment opportunities and wages on the formal labour market are rather limited. Generally, people looking for extra income (opportunity seekers), as well as those fighting for everyday survival, are involved in cross-border petty trade; nevertheless, motivations show great variability in time and space. Small-scale cross-border trade can be interpreted as a temporary survival strategy, but also as an alternative space for economic activities (Michalkó & Timothy, 2001; Smith, 2000). Research illustrates that it is usually not the poorest who are most actively involved in cross-border trade, but rather those who have better financial backgrounds and wider social networks that help them exploit the benefits of this activity (Nagy, 2017; Xheneti, Smallbone & Welter, 2013).

Small-scale cross-border trade is a risky activity, since traders operate fully or partly illegally, and institutions and laws across the border are often unfamiliar to them (Smallbone & Welter, 2012). In addition, minor traders also have to face risks related to untrustworthy business partners, organized crime syndicates, a constantly changing regulatory framework, as well as police and customs officials. Entrepreneurial risk-taking is also present in the decision-making process, as traders have to consider carefully what goods to carry across which borders in what quantity and at what time (Ngo & Hung, 2019). Therefore, social capital accumulated in the form of trust, familial relationships, ethnic ties, friendships, and other types of social linkages play a vital role in the success of small-scale cross-border trade, since this web of social relations may contribute to the reduction of risks. Cross-border traders' special relationships with border guards and customs officials, which sometimes includes a system of bribery, is also an example of risk management (Williams & Baláž, 2005).

Informal cross-border trade and political power relations are inseparable, since the traders aim to circumvent laws and regulations created and enforced by the state (Sik, 2012). Before the political transition (1990–1991) of the former socialist countries of Eastern Europe it was evident that the special informal international trade system among these states could survive not because of the creativity of petty traders, but because of the tolerant attitude of the state, which turned a blind eye to this phenomenon (Wessely, 2002). From the perspective of the communist state, it was a rational decision to sustain international cross-border petty trade, since the activity contributed to social stability by orienting people's attention to satisfying their material needs instead of political reforms (Holešovský, 1965). Thus, the benefit (i.e., preserving political power) that came from the maintenance of the status quo kept states and political leaders from acting against informal and illicit economic activities.

## *Smuggling and Illicit Trade*

Today borders between nations represent "opportune" spaces; the differences along the two sides of the border (i.e., asymmetry of markets, laws, and enforcement) create the opportunity to profit through criminal and informal cross-border exchange. The dual nature of borders, that is their barrier and bridge function, enhances the profitability of criminal and trading activities. Moving drugs, guns, and humans (e.g., for the purpose of illegal forms of labour, such as sex work or slavery) across the border enhances, rather than creates, their market value (McCrossen, 2009).

Smuggling and illicit trade should be interpreted in the context of the evolution of nation-states and the creation of political boundaries. By creating borders and (customs) laws, states attempt to establish order and restrict mobility; they try to monitor and control (sometimes also prevent) cross-border flows of goods, services, people, ideas, and technologies, and they also try to extract revenue from the movement of goods (Pearson, 2016). Ultimately, it is the state that defines the border between the legal and the illegal and therefore sets up the legal framework by which all actors, including cross-border traders and entrepreneurs, should abide (Bruns et al., 2011). However, some traders do not comply with border laws and thus become smugglers. From a legal perspective, both smuggling and informal cross-border trade are illicit activities, but smuggling is relatively intentional and based on the wish to pay no taxes or fewer taxes, or to profit from trade in prohibited goods, while in informal trade, non-compliance with border regulations may be less intentional (Cantens et al., 2015).

Although globalization is sometimes interpreted as a homogenization process that reduces geographical, economic, and cultural differences, experience shows that globalization rather reorders differences and inequalities without eliminating them. Therefore, it is not surprising that trade blocs (such as the former North American Free Trade Agreement—NAFTA) or the economic and/or political integration of states (such as the European Union), which are one manifestation of globalization, undoubtedly foster cross-border activities, including informal trade and smuggling. For instance, McCrossen (2009) states that the USA–Mexico borderland has always provided opportunities for criminal economic activity, but as NAFTA removed many trade barriers, the region saw increased criminal activity, much of which was related to trade.

*Figure 24.2* Hegyeshalom—former border checkpoint between Austria and Hungary, where smuggling was common. Nowadays, as both countries are EU and Schengen states, it is no longer used and sits deserted.

(Photo: G. Michalkó, 2006)

However, the example of Central and Eastern Europe shows that globalization may also have a negative impact on small-scale cross-border trade and smuggling. Although the regime changed, the transition from planned economies to market economies, and the opening of borders at the beginning of the 1990s, created extremely favourable conditions for petty traders and smugglers in Central and Eastern Europe (Williams & Baláž, 2002); from the second half of the 1990s conditions altered significantly. Due to increasing income levels, the growth of international trade, which increased the availability of a wider range of higher-quality goods, and the emergence and spread of transnational retail corporations (e.g., Tesco and Auchan), prices in formal retail markets dropped markedly, making smuggling less profitable (Nagy, 2001; Williams & Baláž, 2005).

Smuggling, cross-border informal trade, and tourism are often connected, since these activities, besides other illegal or immoral motivations such as prostitution, abortion, or euthanasia, can be viewed as "camouflaged tourism"—a form of travel disguised as a holiday or business trip (Rátz et al., 2015).

Drug or narcotourism is based on legal and regulatory differences on opposite sides of a border (Hunt, in press). Year by year millions of people cross national or subnational borders with the intent of acquiring, consuming, and transporting narcotics: a clear association between tourism and drug consumption. Since selling, purchasing, and consuming drugs is forbidden in most countries (Grobe & Lüer, 2011), drug tourism targets destinations with relatively liberal drug regulations. In Europe, the Netherlands is one of the most popular destination for drug tourists, which is due to the fact that the sale of cannabis for personal consumption is tolerated in coffee shops. Since in neighbouring countries cannabis can only be obtained on illegal markets, many foreigners visit Dutch coffee shops especially in municipalities near the German and Belgian borders (van Ooyen-Houben, 2017).

Similarly, regulatory differences are the major driving forces behind marijuana tourism in the United States, which can be observed from states where cannabis is illegal to states where marijuana has been legalized. Marijuana tourism creates numerous business opportunities in the tourism industry and the recreational use of cannabis has become a top tourist attraction in some destinations (Kang et al., 2016). Drug tourism and smuggling are sometimes interrelated as tourists may try to transport drugs across borders illegally. Nevertheless, research results show that most tourists try to avoid carrying drugs during international border crossings, since they perceive this activity as particularly risky (Uriely & Belhassen, 2006).

Cigarettes are one of the most frequently targeted items in illicit cross-border trade (Allen, 2012; Lee & Timothy, 2016) because they are relatively easy to smuggle, and carriers can make substantial profits by exploiting cross-border price differentials that derive from different tax rates, some of which can be tremendous. Although cigarettes and other tobacco products are legal to purchase, they become illegal goods when suppliers or customers fail to pay taxes and tariffs at the point of sale, or when travellers try to get away with importing more than they are allowed (FATF, 2012). By evading taxes and import duties, consumers can buy tobacco products below the legal retail price and make substantial profits when they sell them (Von Lampe, 2011).

Similar to other informal cross-border activities, arms trafficking is also a basically profit-oriented transaction. Nevertheless, cultural, social, and political factors may also play a decisive role in this process, since possessing firearms is coupled with power, which involves the possibility of resolving disputes violently (Dube, Dube & García-Ponce, 2013; Panos & Jana, 2008). Illicit arms trade is only one aspect of a complex, multi-dimensional, and mostly unexplored range of activities that include the unlawful manufacture, acquisition, possession, use, and storage of firearms. Arms trafficking is a complex network with numerous participants including buyers, sellers, brokers, financiers, and traffickers (Greene, 2000; Rothe & Collins, 2011; UNODC, 2020).

## *Trade-oriented Specialized Border Business Travel*

A unique manifestation of the symbiosis of tourism and the retail sector is shopping for second-hand goods—a phenomenon that thrives in border areas, especially in cities (Gravari-Barbas & Jacquot, 2019; Hazlan et al., 2019). Cross-border shopping for second-hand goods usually entails leisure-driven visits to flea markets, antique shops, second-hand bookstores, garage sales, and charity shops in a touristic role. It may also include rummaging, collecting, and transporting home items placed on curb sides on council clean-up days. "Council clean-up tourism" entails people crossing a border into a wealthier region to rummage through other people's throwaway items for things that can be salvaged and sold back home. This activity and visiting garage sales are popular pursuits among Mexicans who cross into the United States to acquire items that can be sold in their home communities (Gauthier, 2012; Minter, 2019). In this case, these informal merchants drive their personal trucks across the frontier to US border cities, scavenge on council clean-up days and visit many garage sales, loading their trucks in the process. They return back to Mexico with a wide range of goods that can be sold as is or repaired to fetch a higher price. With proper visas, they can enter the United States for this purpose, and for the most part Mexican border officials wave them through on their return journeys or charge them a small fee to import their previously owned merchandise.

In Europe, most of these traders use vans or trucks, and address lists are obtained from the Internet or purchased at a high price. These council clean-up consumers ("tourists") collect gently used, well-maintained, and easily resellable items, but many of their acquisitions remain their own property for use at home. Council clean-up tourism and garage sale tourism are concentrated in border areas because profits will be reduced when greater travel distances are required, although longer-distance travel is known to occur if higher-end and more valuable treasures can be found. Since council clean-up rummaging can disturb the local population and create more mess, authorities in some countries have prohibited people from taking goods from the street sides. This does not always deter determined salvagers, whose informal cross-border businesses continue to flourish.

Seasonal workers form another unique type of tourism and labour flow in border regions (Joppe, 2012; Klein & Hood, 2015; Lundberg et al., 2009). Seasonal workers often cross an international frontier to work in borderland agricultural areas or in the services sector (e.g., cleaning hotel rooms) on a daily basis or on a short-term basis. They may travel by foot if their place of employment is very close to the border, or they may come by car or minibus, or by public transportation, contributing to the local economy by using fuel stations, paying tolls, dining out, or shopping. If they stay longer than a single day at a time, they will often use registered accommodation, supermarkets, catering services, and retail establishments. To satisfy the lodging and sustenance needs of seasonal cross-border workers, tourism infrastructure and services are used, even if workers are employed in the informal or shadow economy. Where seasonal workers are employed in the hospitality sector in border areas, the tourism aspects of production-oriented temporary mobility is even more pronounced.

Part of the hidden economy, from the viewpoint of the home state, is cross-border medical tourism, which is a form of trade and commerce. The rising costs of medicine and health care in many countries drives people to seek treatments away from home. Medical tourism is especially prominent in borderlands where more affluent countries with high medical premiums lie adjacent to countries where medical care is cheaper. Medical mobility takes place in many border regions but has been especially well studied along the USA–Mexico border, where Americans (and Canadians) visit Mexico on day trips for dental work, eye exams, chiropractic care, pharmaceutical purchases, and consultations with medical specialists, and stay longer in hospitals-cum-recovery resorts when inpatient surgeries are performed (Adams et al., 2018; Cuevas Contreras, 2015). The border advantage is primarily an economic one, although certain medical specializations (e.g., oncology or fertility treatments) might be more plentiful abroad than in a patient's home country. In 2020–2021, this gave rise to people travelling across national borders to receive COVID-19 vaccinations when they were unavailable in their own home regions (Espindola & Vaca, 2022).

In some cases, certain treatments are legal on one side of a border but not on the other, leading to a lopsided demand for certain medicines and healthcare services. Americans utilizing healthcare in the Mexican borderlands save thousands of dollars per treatment, and the Mexican medical industry has learned to capitalize on its well-regarded trade in health services (Villa-Zamorano et al., 2021). Even in parts of Europe, healthcare across the border is seen as a business transaction, less so for economic purposes, but more so for geographic proximity and other pragmatic reasons (Connell, 2016).

An unusual and informal trade-related phenomenon that is important in certain border areas is "postal tourism". This refers to people renting mailboxes or addresses from post offices in neighbouring countries and sending packages from the post offices abroad. For example, many Romans send packages and mass mailings from Vatican City post offices, because Vatican Post is perceived to be more efficient and dependable than the Italian postal service. Likewise, a large number of Canadians rent mailboxes/addresses in US border towns to capitalize on less expensive postal charges. Many Canadians purchase online orders from US merchants. Shipping fees are always less expensive if their purchases can be mailed to their US postbox or a rented address rather than across the border to Canada. Some small US post offices have far more mailboxes in use than their own populations can support, with the majority of boxes being leased by Canadians who visit regularly to pick up their mail, send international mail (cheaper than in Canada), and participate in other retail activities (Gelbman & Timothy, 2019).

Prior to the border shutting down due to the COVID-19 pandemic, postal tourism was a significant economic stimulus for many US border towns. For instance, Point Roberts and Blaine, both in Washington state, host a great deal of postal tourism from the city of Vancouver, Canada. Even though the items Canadians pick up at their US post office must still pass through Canadian customs inspections, it is a lucrative opportunity for Canadians and good business for Blaine, Point Roberts, and other US border communities. In the words of Samuel (2018, n.p.), "for these Canadians, Blaine is simply a mailing address: the nearest, cheapest, and most convenient way to order packages from Amazon".

Another unique form of transfrontier border business travel is so-called "electoral tourism", though it is not as prominent as seasonal work, medical mobility, or petty trade (Bauböck, 2010). The main idea behind electoral tourism is that borderlanders with dual citizenship travel to the other side of the border during elections to vote in national or municipal elections or participate in referenda on any number of issues. For this, they typically need an address of residence in the country where they vote as dual citizens. They arrive in the role of a "tourist" on the day of the vote (although they might arrive earlier and need accommodation), and their needs are satisfied by hospitality services in the destination.

Second-hand shoppers and scavengers, medical tourists, postal tourists, and electoral tourists all are part of the shadow border economy, and their activities involve economic and social rationales. Rubbish rummagers, medical tourists, and postal tourists cross borders to save money and skirt certain commercial or healthcare requirements (or prohibitions). Electoral tourists exercise their citizenship rights by participating in elections and referenda on the other side of the border, even if this is frowned upon by officials because they currently live abroad. All of these, and many other unique border tourisms, have three things in common: they all take place in a transnational context, they contribute to the local transborder economy, and they are "shadowed", meaning that they have developed in order to skirt certain regulations, avoid long waiting times, save or earn money, and may be undertaken surreptitiously to avoid conflict with official agents of the state.

## Conclusion

This chapter has examined the trade- and commerce-oriented elements of the economy of border regions. The topic was breached within the theoretical framework of the dichotomy of border regions and "non-conventional tourism" mobilities. We have argued that commercial activities, while not typically considered "traditional" or customary forms of tourism, do in fact manifest in many ways as tourist activities, not least because these cross-frontier mobilities require some level of tourism services (e.g., petrol stations, hotels, and restaurants) to meet the needs of traders and other business or commercial-oriented travellers. Besides, these travellers all leave their home environments, cross an international border, and partake of what the other side has to offer. Motivations for travelling are not part of the definition of who a tourist is. Thus, even if they do not meet the strict World Tourism Organization definition of a tourist—someone who travels away from home for more than 24 hours and is not remunerated financially from within the visited destination—they do in fact participate in a broadly conceived travel and tourism system. As Timothy and Teye (2005) contend, petty cross-border traders are the Global South's parallel to the business traveller of the Global North and are every bit a part of the global tourism system.

The theme of non-conventional cross-border mobilities, especially those of a trade and economic transactional nature, was discussed as part of the shadow or informal economy. We have placed significant emphasis on the phenomenon of petty trade and smuggling, which in most borderlands consists primarily of trafficking tobacco, drugs, and weapons illegally. Temporary labour flows in the agricultural and tourism/hospitality sectors, exporting merchandise for resale, the trade of second-hand goods, using postal services abroad, seeking medical treatment in a neighbouring country, and election-related transfrontier journeys by dual citizens also take place under the umbrella of border-induced business travel. With few exceptions, border business affairs and cross-frontier informal business transactions affect the socioeconomic conditions of the borderlands and take place within the legal, informal, or illegal auspices of the borderland economy. Taking place overwhelmingly on the margins of the state, state control is less effective in many cases so that illicit, dubious, and/or hidden socioeconomic transactions are enabled to thrive on national peripheries and flourish in the borderlands.

## Acknowledgement

This chapter was supported by the OTKA K134877 project.

## References

Adams, K., Snyder, J., Crooks, V.A., & Berry, N.S. (2018). A critical examination of empowerment discourse in medical tourism: The case of the dental tourism industry in Los Algodones, Mexico. *Globalization and Health*, 14(1), 1–10.

Afrika, J.G., & Ajumbo, G. (2012). Informal cross border trade in Africa: Implications and policy recommendations. *Africa Economic Brief*, 3(10), 1–13.

Allen, E. (2012). The illicit trade in tobacco products and how to tackle it. *World Customs Journal*, 6(2), 121–130.

Back, A., & Marjavaara, R. (2017). Mapping an invisible population: The uneven geography of second-home tourism. *Tourism Geographies*, 19(4), 595–611.

Bauböck, R. (ed) (2010). Dual citizenship for transborder minorities? How to respond to the Hungarian-Slovak tit-for-tat. *EUI Working Papers*. RSCAS 2010/75.

Bigo, D., & Guild, E. (eds) (2005). *Controlling frontiers: Free movement into and within Europe*. Burlington, VT: Ashgate.

Bowers, I., & Koh, S. (eds) (2019). *Grey and white hulls: An international analysis of the navy-coastguard nexus*. Singapore: Palgrave-Macmillan.

Bruns, B., Miggelbrink, J., & Müller, K. (2011). Smuggling and small-scale trade as part of informal economic practices: Empirical findings from the Eastern external EU border. *International Journal of Sociology and Social Policy*, 31(11/12), 664–680.

Butler, R. (2019). Overtourism and the Tourism Area Life Cycle. In. R. Dodds, & R. Butler (eds) *Overtourism: Issues, realities and solutions*, pp. 76–94. Berlin: De Gruyter.

Byrne, D. (2001). On passports and border controls. *Annals of Tourism Research*, 28(2), 399–416.

Cantens, T., Ireland, R., & Raballand, G. (2015). Introduction: Borders, informality, international trade and customs. *Journal of Borderlands Studies*, 30(3), 365–380.

Castells, M., & Portes, A. (1989). World underneath: The origins, dynamics, and effects of the informal economy. In A. Portes, M. Castells, & L.A. Benton (eds) *The informal economy: Studies in advanced and less developed countries*, pp. 11–37. Baltimore: Johns Hopkins University Press.

Chen, S., Jeevan, J., & Cahoon, S. (2016). Malaysian container seaport-hinterland connectivity: Status, challenges and strategies. *The Asian Journal of Shipping and Logistics*, 32(3), 127–137.

Chikanda, A., & Raimundo, I. (2017). Informal entrepreneurship and cross-border trade between Mozambique and South Africa. *African Human Mobility Review*, 3, 943–974.

Cohen, E., & Avieli, N. (2004). Food in tourism: Attraction and impediment. *Annals of Tourism Research*, 31(4), 755–778.

Connell, J. (2016). Reducing the scale? From global images to border crossings in medical tourism. *Global Networks*, 16(4), 531–550.

Cuevas Contreras, T. (2015). An approach to medical tourism on Mexico's northern border. *Eurasia Border Review*, 6(1), 45–62.

D'Amore, L. (1988). Tourism: The world's peace industry. *Journal of Travel Research*, 27(1), 35–40.

De Cantis, S., Parroco, A., Ferrante, M., & Vaccina, F. (2015). Unobserved tourism. *Annals of Tourism Research*, 50, 1–18.

Dedman, M. (1996). *The origins and development of the European Union, 1945–95*. London: Routledge.

Diener, A., & Hagen, J. (2009). Theorizing borders in a 'borderless world': Globalization, territory and identity. *Geography Compass*, 3(3), 1196–1216.

Dobruszkes, F. (2006). An analysis of European low-cost airlines and their networks. *Journal of Transport Geography*, 14(4), 249–264.

Dube, A., Dube, O., & García-Ponce, O. (2013). Cross-border spillover: U.S. gun laws and violence in Mexico. *The American Political Science Review*, 107(3), 397–417.

Egbert, H. (2006). Cross-border small-scale trading in south-eastern Europe: Do embeddedness and social capital explain enough? *International Journal of Urban and Regional Research*, 30(2), 346–361.

Espindola, J., & Vaca, M. (2022). On the morality of vaccination tourism. *Bioethics*. 36(1), 93–99.

FATF (2012). *Illicit tobacco trade*. Paris: Financial Action Task Force/Organisation for Economic Cooperation and Development.

Franch, M., Irimiás, A., & Buffa, F. (2017). Place identity and war heritage: Managerial challenges in tourism development in Trentino and Alto Adige/Südtirol. *Place Branding and Public Diplomacy*, 13(2), 119–135.

Furnham, A. (1984). Tourism and culture shock. *Annals of Tourism Research*, 11, 41–57.

Gallent, N., Mace, A., & Tewdwr-Jones, M. (2016). *Second homes: European perspectives and UK policies*. London: Routledge.

Gao, J., Ryan, C., Cave, J., & Zhang, C. (2019). Tourism border-making: A political economy of China's border tourism. *Annals of Tourism Research*, 76, 1–13.

Gauthier, M. (2012). Mexican 'ant traders' in the El Paso/Ciudad Juarez border region. In G. Matthews, G.L. Ribeiro, & C.A. Vega (eds) *Globalization from below: The world's other economy*, pp. 138–153. London: Routledge.

Gelbman, A. (2008). Border tourism in Israel: Conflict, peace, fear and hope. *Tourism Geographies*, 10(2), 193–213.

Gelbman, A., & Timothy, D.J. (2011). Border complexity, tourism and international exclaves: A case study. *Annals of Tourism Research*, 38(1), 110–131.

Gelbman, A., & Timothy, D.J. (2019). Differential tourism zones on the western Canada-US border. *Current Issues in Tourism*, 22(6), 682–704.

Gössling, S., Scott, D., & Hall, C.M. (2021). Pandemics, tourism and global change: A rapid assessment of COVID-19. *Journal of Sustainable Tourism*, 29(1), 1–20.

Gravari-Barbas, M., & Jacquot, S. (2019). Mechanisms, actors and impacts of the touristification of a tourism periphery: The Saint-Ouen Flea Market, Paris. *International Journal of Tourism Cities*, 5(3), 370–391.

Greene, O. (2000). Examining international responses to illicit arms trafficking. *Crime, Law & Social Change*, 33, 151–190.

Grobe, A., & Lüer, J. (2011). 'Drug tourism'. In A. Papathanassis (ed.) *The long tail of tourism: Holiday niches and their impact on mainstream tourism*, pp. 137–147. Wiesbaden: Gabler Springer.

Guo, R. (2018). *Cross-border resource management*. Amsterdam: Elsevier.

Hall, C.M. (2014). Second home tourism: An international review. *Tourism Review International*, 18(3), 115–135.

Hall, D. (ed.) (2017). *Tourism and geopolitics: Issues and concepts from Central and Eastern Europe*. Wallingford: CABI.

Hannonen, O., Tuulentie, S., & Pitkänen, K. (2015). Borders and second home tourism: Norwegian and Russian second home owners in Finnish border areas. *Journal of Borderlands Studies*, 30(1), 53–67.

Hazlan, H., Ismail, H., & Jaafar, S. (2019). Flea market tourism: A review of motivation and characteristics of specialised tourist segmentation. *International Journal of Built Environment & Sustainability*, 6(1–2), 55–61.

Heo, C. (2016). Sharing economy and prospects in tourism research. *Annals of Tourism Research*, 58, 166–170.

Heung-Ryel, K., Changhyo, Y., & Yoonjeung, J. (2019). Relationships among overseas travel, domestic travel, and day trips for latent tourists using longitudinal data. *Tourism Management*, 72, 159–169.

Higgins-Desbiolles, F., Carnicelli, S., Krolikowski, C., Wijesinghe, G., & Boluk, K. (2019). Degrowing tourism: Rethinking tourism. *Journal of Sustainable Tourism*, 27(12), 1926–1944.

Holešovský, V. (1965). Personal consumption in Czechoslovakia, Hungary, and Poland, 1950-1960: A comparison. *Slavic Review*, 24(4), 622–635.

Hunt, C. (in press). Narcotourism: A conceptual framework and research agenda. *Tourism Geographies*. https://doi.org/10.1080/14616688.2021.1953124

Irimiás, A. (2014). The Great War heritage site management in Trentino, northern Italy. *Journal of Heritage Tourism*, 9(4), 317–331.

Jansson, A. (2020). The transmedia tourist: A theory of how digitalization reinforces the de-differentiation of tourism and social life. *Tourist Studies*, 20(4), 391–408.

Joppe, M. (2012). Migrant workers: Challenges and opportunities in addressing tourism labour shortages. *Tourism Management*, 33(3), 662–671.

Kang, S.K., O'Leary, J., & Miller, J. (2016). From forbidden fruit to the goose that lays golden eggs: Marijuana tourism in Colorado. *Sage Open*, 6(4), 1–23.

Karrar, H.H. (2019). Between border and bazaar: Central Asia's informal economy. *Journal of Contemporary Asia*, 49(2), 272–293.

Klein, E., & Hood, N. (2015). The smoking ban next door: Do hospitality businesses in border areas have reduced sales after a statewide smoke-free policy? *Health Policy*, 119, 44–49.

Klemm, M. (2002). Tourism and ethnic minorities in Bradford: The invisible segment. *Journal of Travel Research*, 41, 85–91.

Kocsis, K., Molnár Sansum, J., Michalkó, G., Bottlik, Zs., Szabó, B., Balizs, D., & Varga, G. (2017). International migration into Europe – an old-new challenge from the Afro-Asian neighbourhood. *Eurolimes*, 23–24, 167–190.

Lee, W., & Timothy, D.J. (2016). Smuggling. In J. Jafari, & H. Xiao (eds) *Encyclopedia of tourism*, pp. 863–864. New York: Springer.

Lesser, C., & Moisé-Leeman, E. (2009). *Informal cross-border trade and trade facilitation reform in Sub-Saharan Africa*. Paris: OECD Publishing.

Litvin, S. (1998). Tourism: The world's peace industry? *Journal of Travel Research*, 37(1), 63–66.

Lundberg, C., Gudmundson, A., & Andresson, T. (2009). Herzberg's two-factor theory of work motivation tested empirically on seasonal workers in hospitality and tourism. *Tourism Management*, 30(6), 890–899.

McCrossen, A. (2009). Disrupting boundaries: Consumer capitalism and culture in the U.S.-Mexico borderlands, 1940–2008. In A. McCrossen (ed.) *Land of necessity: Consumer culture in the United States-Mexico borderlands*, pp. 48–79. Durham, NC: Duke University Press.

Michalkó, G., Rátz, T., Hinek, M., & Tömöri M. (2014). Shopping tourism in Hungary during the period of the economic crisis. *Tourism Economics*, 20(6), 1319–1336.

Michalkó, G., & Timothy, D.J. (2001). Cross-border shopping in Hungary: Causes and effects. *Visions in Leisure and Business*, 20(1), 4–22.

Minter, A. (2019). Inside Mexico's massive, hidden market for used American goods. November 15, 2019. Online at: https://www.linkedin.com/pulse/inside-mexicos-massive-hidden-market-used-american-goods-adam-minter/ Accessed August 3, 2021.

Nagy, E. (2001). Winners and losers in the transformation of city centre retailing in East Central Europe. *European Urban and Regional Studies*, 8(4), 340–348.

Nagy, E. (2017). New consumption spaces and cross-border mobilities. In D.R. Hall (ed.) *Tourism and geopolitics: Issues and concepts from Central and Eastern Europe*, pp. 142–157. Wallingford: CABI.

Ngo, T.W., & Hung, E.P. (2019). The political economy of border checkpoints in shadow exchanges. *Journal of Contemporary Asia*, 49(2), 178–192.

Novelli, M. (ed) (2005). *Niche tourism*. Oxford: Butterworth-Heinemann.

van Ooyen-Houben, M.M. (2017). The Dutch coffee shop system, tensions and benefits. *Michigan State International Law Review*, 25(3), 623–663.

Paasi, A. (2019). Borderless worlds and beyond: Challenging the state-centric cartographies. In A. Paasi, E-K. Prokkola, J. Saarinen, & K. Zimmerbauer (eds.) *Borderless worlds for whom? Ethics, moralities and mobilities*, pp. 21–36. London: Routledge.

Panos, K.A., & Jana, A. (2008). Illicit arms trafficking and the limits of rational choice theory: The case of the Balkans. *Trends in Organized Crime*, 11(4), 352–378.

Parker, B. (2006). Toward an understanding of borderland processes. *American Antiquity*, 71(1), 77–100.

Pearson, C. (2016). Canines and contraband: Dogs, nonhuman agency and the making of the Franco-Belgian border during the French Third Republic. *Journal of Historical Geography*, 54, 50–62.

Peberdy, S. (2000). Mobile entrepreneurship: Informal sector cross-border trade and street trade in South Africa. *Development Southern Africa*, 17(2), 201–219.

Pécsek, B. (2018). Working on holiday: The theory and practice of workcation. *Balkans Journal of Emerging Trends in Social Sciences*, 1(1), 1–13.

Portes, A., & Haller, W. (2005). The informal economy. In N.J. Smelser, & R. Swedberg (eds) *The handbook of economic sociology*, pp. 403–426. Princeton, NJ: Princeton University Press.

Raghuram, P. (2013). Theorising the spaces of student migration. *Population, Space and Place*, 19(2), 138–154.

Rátz, T., Kundi, V., & Michalkó, G. (2015). The hidden dimensions of cultural consumption within the framework of tourism mobility. In S. Sonnenburg, & D. Wee (eds) *Touring consumption*, pp. 285–302. Wiesbaden: Springer.

Rothe, D.L., & Collins, V. (2011). An exploration of applying system criminality to arms trafficking. *International Criminal Justice Review*, 21(1), 22–38.

Rumley, D., & Minghi, J. (eds.) (2014). *The geography of border landscapes*. London: Routledge.

Ryan, C., & Kinder, R. (1996). Sex, tourism and sex tourism: Fulfilling similar needs? *Tourism Management*, 17(7), 507–518.

Samuel, A. (2018). Welcome to Blaine: The town Amazon Prime built. Online at: https://www.theverge.com/2018/6/20/17484052/blaine-washington-amazon-prime-canada-us-mailbox-address Accessed August 1, 2021.

Sassen, S. (1994). The informal economy: Between new developments and old regulations. *Yale Law Journal*, 103(8), 2289–2304.

Schimmelfennig, F. (2021). Rebordering Europe: External boundaries and integration in the European Union. *Journal of European Public Policy*, 28(3), 311–330.

Seddighi, H., & Theocharous, A. (2002). A model of tourism destination choice: A theoretical and empirical analysis. *Tourism Management*, 23(5), 475–487.

Sik, E. (2012). Trust, network capital, and informality: Cross-border entrepreneurship in the first two decades of post-communism. *Review of Sociology*, 4, 53–72.

Smallbone, D., & Welter, F. (2012). Cross-border entrepreneurship. *Entrepreneurship & Regional Development*, 24(3–4), 95–104.

Smith, A. (2000). Employment restructuring and household survival in 'postcommunist transition': Rethinking economic practices in Eastern Europe. *Environment and Planning A*, 32, 1759–1780.

Soto Bermant, L. (2015). The myth of resistance: Rethinking the "Informal" economy in a Mediterranean border enclave. *Journal of Borderlands Studies*, 30(2), 263–278.

Szytniewski, B.B., Spierings, B., & Van Der Velde, M. (2020). Stretching the border: Shopping, petty trade and everyday life experiences in the Polish–Ukrainian borderland. *International Journal of Urban and Regional Research*, 44(3), 469–483.

Timothy, D.J. (2005). *Shopping tourism, retailing and leisure*. Clevedon: Channel View Publications.

Timothy, D.J., & Saarinen, J. (2013). Cross-border cooperation and tourism in Europe. In C. Costa, E. Panyik, & D. Buhalis (eds) *Trends in European tourism planning and organisation*, pp. 64–75. Bristol: Channel View Publications.

Timothy, D.J., & Teye, V.B. (2005). Informal sector business travellers in the developing world: A borderlands perspective. *Journal of Tourism Studies*, 16(1), 82–92.

Timothy, D.J., & Tosun, C. (2003). Tourists' perceptions of the Canada–USA border as a barrier to tourism at the International Peace Garden. *Tourism Management*, 24(4), 411–421.

Timothy, D.J., & Wall, G. (1997). Selling to tourists: Indonesian street vendors. *Annals of Tourism Research*, 24(2), 322–340.

Tomonori, S., Kazuto, I., Osamu, I., & Mika, M. (1994). A model for predicting the temporal distribution of one-day recreational travel. *Transportation Planning and Technology*, 18(3), 199–221.

Tömöri, M. (2010). Investigating shopping tourism along the borders of Hungary: A theoretical perspective. *GeoJournal of Tourism and Geosites*, 6(2), 202–210.

Tóth, G., Kincses, Á., Michalkó, G., & Tömöri, M. (2017). Characteristics of transit tourism in Hungary with a focus on expenditure. *Regional Statistics*, 6(2), 129–148.

UNODC (2020). *Global study on firearms trafficking*. Geneva: United Nations.
Uriely, N., & Belhassen, Y. (2006). Drugs and risk-taking in tourism. *Annals of Tourism Research*, 33(2), 339–359.
Villa-Zamorano, Z., Cuevas-Contreras, T., & Timothy, D.J. (2021). Paradoja de la competitividad en turismo frente al COVID-19: Ciudad Juárez como localidad fronteriza. (The paradox of competitiveness in tourism compared to COVID-19). *Cenário: Revista Interdisciplinar em Turismo e Território, Brasília*, 9(1), 68–84.
Von Lampe, K. (2011). The illegal cigarette trade. In M. Natarajan (ed.) *International criminal justice*, pp. 148–154. New York: Cambridge University Press.
Weiss, T. (2015). The United Nations: Before, during and after 1945. *International Affairs*, 91(6), 1221–1235.
Wessely, A. (2002). Travelling people, travelling objects. *Cultural Studies*, 16(1), 3–15.
Więckowski, M. (in press). How border tripoints offer opportunities for transboundary tourism development. *Tourism Geographies*, https://doi.org/10.1080/14616688.2021.1878268
Williams, A.M., & Baláž, V. (2002). International petty trading: Changing practices in trans–Carpathian Ukraine. *International Journal of Urban and Regional Research*, 26(2), 323–342.
Williams, A.M., & Baláž, V. (2005). Winning, then losing, the battle with globalization: Vietnamese petty traders in Slovakia. *International Journal of Urban and Regional Research*, 29(3), 533–549.
Xheneti, M., Smallbone, D., & Welter, F. (2013). EU enlargement effects on cross-border informal entrepreneurial activities. *European Urban and Regional Studies*, 20(3), 314–328.
Yalçın-Heckmann, L., & Aivazishvili, N. (2012). Scales of trade, informal economy and citizenship at Georgian-Azerbaijani borderlands. In B. Bruns, & J. Miggelbrink (eds.) *Subverting borders*, pp. 193–211. Berlin: VS Verlag für Sozialwissenschaften.
Zátori, A., Michalkó, G., Nagy, J.T., Kulcsár, N., & Balizs, D. (2019). The tourist experience of domestic VFR travellers: The case of Hungary. *Current Issues in Tourism*, 22(12), 1437–1459.

# PART V

# Contemporary Change: Transfrontier Cooperation and Collaboration

# 25
# PLANNING AND MANAGING TOURISM IN TRANSBORDER AREAS

*Arie Stoffelen*

## Introduction

The rapid increase in cross-border human mobility since the second half of the twentieth century has led to changes in academic and practical approaches to transnational borderlands. Traditionally, borders were seen as physical and symbolic boundaries that manifest the state's territoriality and sovereignty. Borderlands were seen to be suffering from a "double peripherality" consisting of economic disadvantages owing to their remote location combined with the barrier effect of the border (House, 1980). Nowadays, in the context of rapid globalization, borders are seen as much more complex entities and processes. They function as potential triggers rather than barriers to spatial development and as key processes and institutions for geopolitical and sociocultural meaning-making (Brambilla, 2015; Newman, 2006; Van Houtum, 2000). In practical policy-making, this shift in thinking has led to views that borders have become transition zones that facilitate rather than block communication. Borders do not just function as discontinuities for economic flows but provide opportunities for future collaboration and for spatial development (Konrad & Nicol, 2011; Newman, 2006; Van Houtum, 2000). Notions of "new regionalism", a regional development paradigm that emphasizes the central position of regions within multi-level governance and place-based innovation networks for economic competitiveness (Jones & Macleod, 1999), have challenged nation-state-centred views of international relations, territorial sovereignty, and socioeconomic and cultural regulation. Consequently, more relational and regionalized focuses have gained ground in many borderlands (Paasi & Zimmerbauer, 2016). State borders no longer automatically coincide with the boundaries of functional areas, in terms of economic development, but also regarding identity and resource management in its broadest sense, including tourism destination development and management.

With these societal changes, tourism has become targeted in many borderlands from the viewpoint of a simple visitor attraction, as well as with the aim of uncovering previously neglected opportunities for socioeconomic development. Because of the sector's perceived ease to develop across borders, its perceived political insensitivity compared to other sectors (Church & Reid, 1999; Deppisch, 2012; Stoffelen & Vanneste, 2017), as well as its symbolism for cross-border relations (Prokkola, 2007, 2011; Stoffelen & Vanneste, 2019; Vogel & Field, 2020), tourism has been highlighted by practitioners as a precursor to more intensive cross-border administrative contact and sociocultural relationship building. In recent times, tourism has become a key instrument for initiating cross-border collaboration and for its potential direct socioeconomic results.

However, despite relative optimism about the opportunities of cross-border tourism development, the mainstream tourism planning and governance literature continues to raise critical notes about the ease with which positive impacts could be achieved with tourism. Fragmentation of ownership structures, the uneven spatial distribution of tourism resources and stakeholders, unequal power relations, and the cross-sectoral nature of tourism policy make tourism planning very much needed but notoriously complicated (Adu-Ampong, 2017; Bramwell, 2011; Hall, 2000; Saarinen, 2007). These reflections have led to a consensus among tourism scholars that inclusive, participatory governance, planning, and management are needed to uncover the sector's potentials and to avoid inequalities sprouting from tourism development (Saarinen et al., 2017). Plenty of evidence exists that achieving this is anything but straightforward. Disappointing regional and community development results are commonplace, both in the Global North and in developing countries (e.g., Keyim, 2018; Rogerson, 2015; Stoffelen, Adiyia, Vanneste, & Kotze, 2020; Stoffelen & Vanneste, 2016).

An evident mismatch appears. If the sector's fragmentation makes inclusive tourism governance and planning necessary but very difficult, how could tourism be an "easy" sector to facilitate cross-border contact and lead to cross-border regional socioeconomic and cultural development? The need for systematic tourism cooperation and planning in borderlands has become increasingly apparent. It is needed to improve visitor management and tourists' experiences but also to distribute benefits and costs more equally among stakeholders and in spaces in these traditionally peripheral locations.

In this context, the purpose of this chapter is to look at the opportunities, challenges, and barriers to transfrontier destinations from the perspective of governance, planning, and management. The chapter's second section outlines the necessity of systematic transnational collaboration in tourism if higher-order objectives are to be met. Without aiming to provide a comprehensive review of the tourism governance and planning literature, this section also highlights key elements that make planning and managing tourism with the objectives of sustainability, equity, and stakeholder integration notoriously difficult, even without considering borderland contexts. In the third section, I briefly reflect on the cross-border planning literature to reflect on structural difficulties that cross-border tourism planning may encounter. The following part is about the implications for managing tourism in borderlands. The final section reflects on possible success factors for establishing integrative tourism planning and management in transboundary settings.

## Cross-border Tourism Development and the Need for Integrative Planning

In light of increasing global cross-border human mobility, border regions have been systematically studied as possible tourism attractions at least since the 1990s. Shared or complementary resources along and across the border, including the presence of the border itself, may lead to very attractive tourism products (Gelbman & Timothy, 2010; Timothy, 1995). For these reasons, tourism and cross-border collaboration coincide throughout the world, with a range of objectives. Cross-border tourism development in Europe has been strongly embedded in the European neoliberal economic venture, with the ultimate aims of breaking down economic and mental barriers as part of the European unification process (Stoffelen & Vanneste, 2019). Cross-border collaboration could unearth important but previously unrecognized opportunities of knowledge exchange and innovation (Trippl, 2010). The mobility fluxes related to tourism allow establishing relations between stakeholders and, consequently, the dispersal of new ideas, processes, products, or services (Weidenfeld, 2013). Tourism innovation in borderlands mostly refers to the diffusion of best practices, which could lead to improved competitiveness of tourism organizations (Makkonen et al., 2018). Whereas the permeability of borders influences the ease with which knowledge transfer could take place, a degree of contrast or unfamiliarity (Spierings & van der Velde, 2013) gives room for more radical innovation and learning (Makkonen et al., 2018).

In other places, for example sub-Saharan Africa (SSA), tourism has also been a key cross-border development tool but has been predominantly linked up with nature conservation, community development and, pro-poor intentions, for example in Transfrontier Conservation Areas (TFCAs) (Chaderopa, 2013; Chirozva, 2015; Doppelfeld, 2006; Duffy, 2006). Supported by NGOs and international financial organizations, TFCAs depart from the idea that borders in SSA do not necessarily delineate the most effective nature conservation and community development areas (Duffy, 2006). Considering the substantial natural resources in many of these places, community-based ecotourism across borders is seen as a way to provide the means for nature conservation, to strengthen social and cultural ties with communities on both sides, and to empower previously disadvantaged communities (Chirozva, 2015).

The fact that transnational borderlands remain the meeting point of different administrative systems and, in many cases, social and cultural characteristics could also have adverse effects on tourism planning. These include strong competition between tourism destinations on both sides, duplication of tourism investments, and limited proactive stances towards establishing integrated cross-border destinations (Ilbery & Saxena, 2011; Ioannides et al., 2006; Timothy, 1999, 2001). For example, borders may provide opportunities for knowledge exchange and innovation, but the barrier effect of borders may limit this exchange and lead to competitive disadvantages compared to other places. Moreover, Chaderopa (2013) shows with a case study of TFCAs between South Africa, Mozambique, and Zimbabwe that even though most borders in SSA have been artificially imposed by colonists, many borders have been strongly internalized by borderland inhabitants. This has led in some cases to "a sense of place that refuses to embrace a project that may interfere with the integrity of their identity" (Chaderopa, 2013, p. 58). Combined with external NGO involvement, such projects may lead to limited results, limited attention to internal dynamics within borderland communities, and inequalities due to different development levels on both sides of the border (Duffy, 2006).

The bottom line of these reflections is that cooperation and coordination across the border is needed for successful tourism project development but also, and even more pressingly, for reaching higher-order objectives such as integrative resource management and facilitating knowledge exchange and innovation. The classification of cross-border relations by Martínez (1994), updated by Timothy (1999), has proven influential in tourism studies to describe the level of planning alignment in borderlands. Martínez classified borderlands according to increasing levels of cooperation, starting from alienated borderlands at one end of the spectrum to integrated borderlands at the other. In alienated borderlands, there is little to no interaction between both sides of the border. At the other end of the scale, in integrated borderlands, boundaries hardly influence the contact between stakeholders anymore. While this classification has proven useful for describing general situations and for comparison between different areas, this scheme also has limitations for understanding bottlenecks and best-practices of cross-border tourism planning. For example, case study evidence shows that obstacles to regional cross-border development do not disappear even in cases where cross-border contact is well-developed. Ioannides et al. (2006) and Prokkola (2007) show for the Swedish–Finnish border that even in this case where the border is to a large extent "invisible" and cross-border (tourism) relations are highly integrated, political and cultural differences such as language and traditions still create mental barriers that increase the perceived distance between places. This example shows that "while distinction is often drawn between mental boundaries and material boundaries, the two are, in fact, integrated" (Sofield, 2006, p. 103). Moreover, cross-border cooperation may be characterized by a selective opening and closing, or a sectoral, social, temporal, and spatial bias (Timothy et al., 2016). This means that

> transboundary exchange could be relatively straightforward in one domain, for one set of stakeholders or for the region on one side of the border, but the border may concurrently be hermetically closed for other sectors, stakeholders or the region on the other side of the border.
>
> (Stoffelen, 2017, pp. 1–2)

These reflections show that the underlying processes that explain why a certain level of integration is reached remain implicit in Martínez's (1994) framework. Yet, exactly these underlying processes are key in tourism planning (Blasco et al., 2014).

Saarinen et al. (2017) describe the consensus among tourism geographers that tourism, being a growth-oriented sector, requires holistic and inclusive planning to avoid negative externalities and to transform growth into more qualitative development. Similarly, Bramwell (2011) argues that tourism policy needs governance and planning to facilitate coordination and cooperation between stakeholders to deal with power imbalances. The reason for these calls is that tourism planning with the goal of socioeconomic development is difficult. The tourism sector is characterized by many stakeholders with different goals and visions, but these stakeholders are simultaneously dependent on each other. There is a need to include different stakeholders in a participation process because of the diversity of involved actors, their inability to develop and manage tourism on their own, their mutual interdependencies, and the ideas of regional development that include notions of equity (Hall, 2000; Jamal & Getz, 1995; Timothy, 1998).

Since tourism as an economic activity is not self-regulating from an equity perspective, an active civil society and a regulatory framework are needed to guarantee equal opportunities for all stakeholders (Burns, 2004). Using the concept of adaptive co-management, Plummer and Fennell (2009) argue that tourism planning should be inclusive, flexible, and continuous rather than focusing on top-down, rigid master planning. Tourism planning should build on a network of affected stakeholders to facilitate dynamic learning, conflict mediation, innovation, and adaptation (Plummer & Fennell, 2009). Such characteristics increase the power of the network to deal with sudden changes in economic, social, or ecological conditions (Jamal & Getz, 1995).

Establishing these dynamics requires skills and capacities, mutual trust, legitimacy of conveners, and the ability of individual actors to collaborate on issues where they may disagree with each other but still require each other's contribution. Consequently, many implementation gaps exist in uncovering the potentials of tourism in reality (Stoffelen & Vanneste, 2017). In borderlands, material cross-border interdependencies of a social, economic, and environmental nature have to be addressed so that possible synergies could be created and negative externalities avoided (Prokkola, 2007). However, the processes needed to succeed with integrative networking and planning may be even more difficult to uncover due to the presence of political, natural, and/or cultural boundaries.

## The Complementarity of Tourism and Cross-border Planning Studies

In a study published in 1998, Dallen Timothy argued that four types of cooperation are needed to establish integrative tourism planning: cooperation between government agencies, between levels of administration, between public and private sectors, and between same-level polities (Timothy, 1998). In other words, some form of cross-territorial policy alignment, be it transnational collaboration or inter-municipal exchange, is needed to deal with the fragmentation of the tourism stakeholders, interests, and resources discussed above.

Despite the increased attention paid to cross-border tourism governance and planning since the publication of that paper, it remains striking that tourism scholars have only made tentative explorations of existing work in the academic field of (cross-border) spatial planning. In fact, cross-border spatial planning constitutes a relatively mature academic field and the few papers refering to this literature have improved our insights into the bottlenecks and success factors of integrative tourism planning in borderlands. For example, Stoffelen et al. (2017) presented an in-depth case study of tourism governance and planning obstacles in the borderlands of Germany and the Czech Republic. They found that "structural cross-border destination management does not exist because of (transnational) multi-scalar institutional alignment problems and (internal) tourism-specific destination-level power contestations" (Stoffelen et al., 2017, p. 126). Put differently, this study found that the tourism-specific complexities of inclusive participatory planning, discussed above, are compounded in borderlands by general border-related spatial planning complexities. Cross-pollination between the tourism planning and spatial planning literature is, thus, necessary to understand the difficulties that have led to suggestions that tourism governance in cross-border settings is generally disappointing (Blasco et al., 2014).

A key hindrance to establishing inclusive spatial planning in borderlands is asymmetry between institutions and multi-level governance arrangements on both sides of the border. This asymmetry refers to the contrasting scalar composition of administrative levels, as well as mismatches between decision-making cultures, identities, and official cross-border discourses on both sides. For example, García-Álvarez and Trillo-Santamaría (2013) describe how centralized decision-making structures in Portugal and more decentralized planning regimes in Spain complicate systematic planning between both sides (see Altinay and Bowen, 2006 for a similar case of tourism planning between North and South Cyprus). In particular, the jumping of scales required of regional policymakers in Galicia (Spain) to communicate on topics that are the responsibility of the national government in Portugal proves extremely difficult. Moreover, the authors identified a mismatch between Galician political discourses and the daily experiences of the inhabitants of this area. This situation complicates inclusivity in spatial planning in two ways: from the grassroots to regional planning on one side, and systematic alignment across the border from regional to national levels on the other side (García-Álvarez & Trillo-Santamaría, 2013).

Knippschild (2011) adds that since cross-border planning is mostly secondary to the within-country responsibilities of regional planners, lacking knowledge, motivation, and experience further inhibit systematic decision-making across the border. The result is often a patchwork of existing governmental levels and territories responsible for cross-border spatial planning (Fricke, 2015; Perkmann, 1999). Tölle (2013) argues that even in cases where the multi-level governance systems on both sides of the border seem very compatible, internal dynamics make spatial planning across national borders very complicated. These dynamics include contrasting visions of which topics should be covered with spatial planning, who has final responsibility, and when a plan is definitive and binding (Tölle, 2013).

These reflections directly apply to tourism. Case study evidence has shown that tourism planning and management remains embedded in national systems, even in integrated borderlands (Blasco et al., 2014; Ilbery & Saxena, 2011; Ioannides et al., 2006; Saxena & Ilbery, 2008; Shepherd & Ioannides, 2020). For example, Ilbery and Saxena (2011) present a case study of the English–Welsh borderlands where no long-term cross-border plans have been established despite similar administrative structures. Tourism activities remain strongly embedded in existing, nationally organized tourism structures that compete with each other for attracting the same tourists. Similarly, Woyo and Slabbert (2019) show how separate tourism marketing of one shared resource (Victoria Falls between Zambia and Zimbabwe) results in duplication of investments and limits opportunities to attract tourists.

Hence, regarding tourism, institutional asymmetry refers not just to a difficult alignment between public policy levels due to their different scalar organization. The concept also refers to the different centrality of existing cross-border tourism projects to the destinations on both sides. This includes different importance given to shared projects or resources in the respective tourism marketing on both sides and different possibilities of local stakeholders to tap into these sometimes high-profile tourism products (Stoffelen, 2018).

Ineffective and exclusive tourism planning on one side may lead to uneven development possibilities with tourism products that are shared across the border (Stoffelen & Vanneste, 2017). Moreover, changes over time in multi-level relations on one side may influence how cross-border tourism projects are planned by the stakeholders from that side. For example, Gao et al. (2019) show how practical cross-border tourism development activities in China follow from reactions of the national state and local stakeholders to each other's perspective on the border. For the national government "the border, whether open or closed, operates as a barrier to ensure state security as stability is the priority for Beijing, whereas, for local jurisdictions, a different discourse is premised on an open border as an economic resource" (ibid., p. 11). Changing relations between local and national levels on border issues influence the level of empowerment of local communities and tourism stakeholders and, hence, the benefits they obtain with cross-border tourism activities (Gao et al., 2019).

## Issues of Integrative Destination Management in Borderlands

Because of the processes and complexities of integrative tourism planning in transborder areas, as discussed above, tourism planning in these places is mostly about alignment rather than real destination development and management. Only a few academically recorded exceptions exist of situations where transboundary destination management has replaced existing bordered territorial tourism management (e.g., Hartmann, 2006; Stoffelen & Vanneste, 2018). Even Euroregions, which constitute European cross-border network organizations and contact brokers within a specific territory (Perkmann, 1999), complement rather than replace administrative levels on both sides of the border.

While it makes sense from a policy perspective to focus on alignment rather than new destination development considering the transaction costs involved, it does pose challenges from a management perspective. Supply and demand-oriented visitor management techniques will be split up between destination agencies. For example, spatial zoning mechanisms to regulate access and environmental impacts of tourism will inevitably differ when multiple jurisdictions are involved and different planning regulations apply. The same goes for providing uniform marketing, market research, and monitoring of visitors. For example, monitoring the use of tourism trails is already notoriously difficult within one destination (Meschik, 2012), let alone in cross-border settings where trails are popular tourism products. Similarly, Hartmann (2006) highlights the difficulty of dealing with incompatible booking systems in the otherwise highly integrated Lake Constance destination between Germany, Switzerland, and Austria. Solving such issues often means dealing with massive bureaucracy (Timothy, 1999; Yodsuwan et al., 2018). Finally, the financing of tourism projects is one of the main highlighted difficulties in tourism development and management resulting from the presence of administrative borders (e.g., Doppelfeld, 2006; Hartmann, 2006; Shepherd & Ioannides, 2020).

The danger exists that positive impacts of existing transboundary tourism activities are simply assumed. Yet, the possibility of uneven development in borderlands is very real. Socioeconomic contrasts between both sides could result in different investment opportunities and a different quality of tourism service provided. Furthermore, tourism resources are distributed unevenly throughout destinations and on both sides of the border. Tourists' imaginaries, cross-cultural expectations, and language contrasts may lead to preferences for one side over the other among the tourists with highest spending power. Finally, and most crucially, uneven levels of participation and stakeholder integration on both sides of the border could mean that the distribution of decision-making power and of benefits sprouting from tourism development may differ between areas.

In these situations, tourism projects could confirm and even worsen existing situations instead of alleviating inequality (Timothy, 2001), even when cross-border tourism projects are commercially viable. For example, the earlier described separation of tourism marketing and planning between Zimbabwe and Zambia regarding Victoria Falls promotes uneven development between the two countries. Zimbabwe benefits disproportionally more, partly due to better access from nature-based destinations in nearby Botswana (Woyo & Slabbert, 2019). The same situation emerged in the German–Czech borderlands, where despite the presence of many cross-border projects the stakeholders on the German side benefit more than their Czech counterparts owing to a much more inclusive, participatory tourism management system (Stoffelen et al., 2017).

These reflections show that transborder tourism planning and management should distinguish between tourism product development and more systematic tourism planning and management. For the former, local-level exchanges could suffice to create commercially viable tourism products. For the latter, higher-level integrative planning is needed. In other words, scale matters in transboundary tourism planning and management. Whereas individual contact and personal relations, such as between mayors of municipalities, could overcome border-related planning obstacles like different decision-making cultures, language contrasts, and unfamiliarity with the planning system on the other side (Ilbery & Saxena, 2011), higher-level alignment is often more sensitive to institutional asymmetry and boundary effects of the border (Perkmann, 1999). If tourism development in transboundary settings is to be planned in an integrative, holistic way, these key cooperation issues, as well as possible consequences, should already be considered in the very first planning phase, even before tourism projects are financed and developed (Burns, 2004), in the "problem-setting" rather than "direction-setting" or "implementation" stages of collaborative tourism planning (Jamal & Getz, 1995).

## Success Factors for Transborder Tourism Planning and Management

Even though establishing integrative transborder planning and destination management is simultaneously necessary and difficult, it is not impossible. Several studies have highlighted crucial success factors. Some of these are contextual elements that are hard to facilitate from a planning standpoint. For example, a shared language, good cross-border accessibility, a shared currency, and long histories of collaboration could help lower functional barriers for transboundary tourism cooperation. Consequently, Blasco et al. (2014) argue that serendipity should not be disregarded when explaining successful cases of cross-border tourism governance.

However, integrative cross-border planning relations do not only develop by chance. Blasco et al. (2014) found in the same study of tourism collaboration between Spain and France that social and cultural affinity could foster individual and organizational relationships across the border. Focusing on the "softer" elements of cross-border cooperation, such as establishing social interactions and trust relations, could facilitate transborder exchange more efficiently than focusing on "hard" projects like infrastructure development (Makkonen et al., 2018). Knowledge about the respective decision-making cultures could smooth cross-border negotiations and speed up planning processes (Stoffelen et al., 2017).

Moreover, culture and spatial identity could be obstacles but also policy tools for establishing integrative cross-border tourism planning and management. Chaderopa (2013) found for a TFCA between South Africa, Mozambique, and Zimbabwe that culture and spatial identity could function as a cooperation barrier when mismatching with cross-border tourism policies. The reverse also seems true. Stoffelen and Vanneste (2018) found with a case study of the Vogtland destination between two German federal states that shared histories were strategically used by policymakers in an internal marketing campaign to grow cross-border identities among residents. By doing so, the policymakers managed to create support for an ultimately financially driven cross-border destination merger. Cultural identity seems, at least to some degree, malleable for purposes of transboundary tourism planning.

A recurring success factor in many case studies is the presence of personal relations and mutual trust between individuals in key positions on both sides of the border.

Establishing formal administrative channels across the border is complex. Moreover, established formal transboundary exchange procedures are often inflexible and time-consuming (Timothy, 1999). Good individual contacts, based on trust, between stakeholders could advance the decision-making process. Informal arrangements could avoid red tape and establish a common sense approach regarding cross-border information exchange that is otherwise inhibited by inflexible or incompatible formal procedures (Princen et al., 2016). For example, Kozak and Buhalis (2019) find that linking seaside destinations between Greece and Turkey was seen by many tour operators as potentially bringing competitive advantages to the area. The practical linking happened on the basis of individual business decisions rather than through systematic organizational collaboration and public policy support. Practically, small ferry operators provided and promoted cross-border transport possibilities for tourists, partly but not completely filling the void left by local politics on both sides (Kozak & Buhalis, 2019).

However, dependency on individual contacts with limited institutionalized arrangements backing up these contacts makes it hard to deal with the tourism sector's fragmentation. It also makes tourism planning vulnerable to changes in personnel (Stokke & Haukeland, 2018). Hence, despite the undoubted value of individual relations in establishing cross-border tourism activities, several studies emphasize that systematic alignment and planning remain crucial to reach higher-order objectives with tourism in cross-border areas (e.g., Altinay & Bowen, 2006; Ilbery & Saxena, 2011; Kozak & Buhalis, 2019). Blasco et al. (2014) and Stoffelen and Vanneste (2017) both argue that institutionalized bridging actors could facilitate the upscaling of cross-border relations from individual contact to systematic and more durable organizational alignment. Furthermore, very practical discussions such as deciding on durable funding arrangements of cross-border projects could increase these projects' long-term viability and provide a stepping stone towards establishing more systematic planning agreements (Stoffelen, 2018).

On final reflection, Yodsuwan et al. (2018) point to the importance of recognizing cultural practices when dealing with these systematic complexities in cross-border tourism planning. Using a case study of the Thai side of the Golden Triangle between Thailand, Laos, and Myanmar, they argue that Thai cultural behaviour and expectations, valuing among other things hierarchy and individual relations over institutional efficiency, require culturally sensitive adaptations to the solutions discussed above. For example, they propose establishing collaborative groups comprised of participants of similar societal standing to encourage open dialogue. Such a solution would require a step-by-step participatory process instead of one continuous round-table forum.

## Conclusion

Planning and managing tourism in transborder areas is a double-edged sword. On the one hand, the tourism sector provides clear opportunities to reach higher-order spatial development objectives in borderlands. These objectives could include knowledge exchange, combined nature conservation and pro-poor effects, and socioeconomic and cultural region-building. On the other hand, inclusivity in tourism planning and management is difficult to achieve even without considering border-related cooperation barriers, let alone in cross-border contexts. Yet, systematic participatory planning is a prerequisite if one wants to move beyond individual tourism project development.

The general complexities of participatory tourism planning, which have been widely documented over the years, also apply to borderland settings. The cross-sectoral nature of tourism policy means that there are high transaction costs for coordinating between sectors, interests, land uses, and stakeholders with different power positions (Hooghe & Marks, 2003), and also in borderlands. Specifically, within cross-border tourism negotiations, interests and objectives may also differ between tourism-specific actors. For example, the objectives of cross-border knowledge exchange and innovation, focusing ultimately on economic competitiveness of (cross-border) tourism destinations, are not necessarily in line with combined pro-poor efforts and the environmental sustainability strived for in TFCAs.

Moreover, spatial planning in borderlands encounters structural complexities that also apply to the tourism sector. The review in this chapter has highlighted the necessity to reflect on the compatibility of multi-level tourism governance and planning systems on both sides as well as across the border. Even though local-level cross-border exchange is regularly relatively feasible, systematic and inclusive tourism planning requires institutional alignment also on higher scales where coordination complexities are often more pronounced.

Quick fix solutions seem insufficient to deal with structural tourism planning issues in borderlands. This makes achieving higher-level objectives with cross-border tourism difficult, particularly in places where cross-border relations are tense but also in less contested places such as those that could benefit from European cross-border co-funding arrangements like INTERREG. These funds are potentially very helpful to support policymakers cramped for time and finances. However, they could entice stakeholders to focus on short-term, local-level goals and individual projects rather than systematic, inclusive planning (Shepherd & Ioannides, 2020).

Tourism planners should explicitly reflect on stakeholder inclusivity as well as structural institutional compatibility and alignment across the border, irrespective of the position of their area in Martínez's (1994) continuum of cross-border relations. The identification of the multi-level institutional organization of tourism on both sides of the border, as well as across the border, should take place in the very earliest planning phase. This mantra particularly applies to areas where funding schemes are available or individual cross-border contacts have been made already: circumstances where individual tourism project development may seem relatively straightforward but where systematic planning often lags behind. In less integrative borderlands, attention to softer elements of cross-border collaboration such as social interactions between people should be emphasized in addition (Makkonen et al., 2018) to avoid structural institutional problems later on.

## References

Adu-Ampong, E. A. (2017). Divided we stand: Institutional collaboration in tourism planning and development in the Central Region of Ghana. *Current Issues in Tourism*, 20(3), 295–314.

Altinay, L., & Bowen, D. (2006). Politics and tourism interface: The case of Cyprus. *Annals of Tourism Research*, 33(4), 939–956.

Blasco, D., Guia, J., & Prats, L. (2014). Emergence of governance in cross-border destinations. *Annals of Tourism Research*, 49, 159–173.

Brambilla, C. (2015). Exploring the critical potential of the borderscapes concept. *Geopolitics*, 20(1), 14–34.

Bramwell, B. (2011). Governance, the state and sustainable tourism: A political economy approach. *Journal of Sustainable Tourism*, 19(4–5), 459–477.

Burns, P. (2004). Tourism planning: A third way? *Annals of Tourism Research*, 31(1), 24–43.

Chaderopa, C. (2013). Crossborder cooperation in transboundary conservation-development initiatives in southern Africa: The role of borders of the mind. *Tourism Management*, 39, 50–61.

Chirozva, C. (2015). Community agency and entrepreneurship in ecotourism planning and development in the Great Limpopo Transfrontier Conservation Area. *Journal of Ecotourism*, 14(2–3), 185–203.

Church, A., & Reid, P. (1999). Cross-border co-operation, institutionalization and political space across the English Channel. *Regional Studies*, 33(7), 643–655.

Deppisch, S. (2012). Governance processes in Euregios: Evidence from six cases across the Austrian–German border. *Planning Practice and Research*, 27(3), 315–332.

Doppelfeld, M. (2006). Collaborative stakeholder planning in cross-border regions: The case of the Great Limpopo Transfrontier Park in Southern Africa. In H. Wachowiak (Ed.), *Tourism and borders. Contemporary issues, policies and international research*, pp. 113–138. Aldershot: Ashgate.

Duffy, R. (2006). The potential and pitfalls of global environmental governance: The politics of transfrontier conservation areas in Southern Africa. *Political Geography*, 25(1), 89–112.

Fricke, C. (2015). Spatial governance across borders revisited: Organizational forms and spatial planning in metropolitan cross-border regions. *European Planning Studies*, 23(5), 849–870.

Gao, J., Ryan, C., Cave, J., & Zhang, C. (2019). Tourism border-making: A political economy of China's border T tourism. *Annals of Tourism Research*, 76, 1–13.

García-Álvarez, J., & Trillo-Santamaría, J.-M. (2013). Between regional spaces and spaces of regionalism: Cross-border region building in the Spanish 'State of the Autonomies'. *Regional Studies*, 47(1), 104–115.

Gelbman, A., & Timothy, D. J. (2010). From hostile boundaries to tourist attractions. *Current Issues in Tourism*, 13(3), 239–259.

Hall, C. M. (2000). *Tourism planning: Policies, processes and relationships*. London: Pearson.

Hartmann, K. (2006). Destination management in cross-border regions. In H. Wachowiak (ed.), *Tourism and borders: Contemporary issues, policies and international research*, pp. 89–109. Aldershot: Ashgate.

Hooghe, L., & Marks, G. (2003). Unraveling the central state, but how? Types of multi-level governance. *American Political Science Review*, 97(2), 233–243.

House, J. W. (1980). The frontier zone: A conceptual problem for policy makers. *International Political Science Review*, 1(4), 456–477.

Ilbery, B., & Saxena, G. (2011). Integrated rural tourism in the English–Welsh cross-border region: An analysis of strategic, administrative and personal challenges. *Regional Studies*, 45(8), 1139–1155.

Ioannides, D., Nielsen, P. Å., & Billing, P. (2006). Transboundary collaboration in tourism: The case of the Bothnian Arc. *Tourism Geographies*, 8(2), 122–142.

Jamal, T. B., & Getz, D. (1995). Collaboration theory and community tourism planning. *Annals of Tourism Research*, 22(1), 186–204.

Jones, M., & Macleod, G. (1999). Towards a regional renaissance? Reconfiguring and rescaling England's economic governance. *Transactions of the Institute of British Geographers*, 24(3), 295–313.

Keyim, P. (2018). Tourism collaborative governance and rural community development in Finland. *Journal of Travel Research*, 57(4), 483–494.

Knippschild, R. (2011). Cross-border spatial planning: Understanding, designing and managing cooperation processes in the German–Polish–Czech borderland. *European Planning Studies*, 19(4): 629–645.

Konrad, V., & Nicol, H. N. (2011). Border culture, the boundary between Canada and the United States of America, and the advancement of borderlands theory. *Geopolitics*, 16(1), 70–90.

Kozak, M., & Buhalis, D. (2019). Cross-border tourism destination marketing: Prerequisites and critical success factors. *Journal of Destination Marketing and Management*, 14, 1–9.

Makkonen, T., Williams, A. M., Weidenfeld, A., & Kaisto, V. (2018). Cross-border knowledge transfer and innovation in the European neighbourhood: Tourism cooperation at the Finnish-Russian border. *Tourism Management*, 68, 140–151.

Martínez, O. J. (1994). *Border people: Life and society in the U.S. - Mexico borderlands.* Tucson: University of Arizona Press.

Meschik, M. (2012). Sustainable cycle tourism along the Danube cycle route in Austria. *Tourism Planning & Development*, 9(1), 41–56.

Newman, D. (2006). The lines that continue to separate us: Borders in our "borderless" world. *Progress in Human Geography*, 30(2), 143–161.

Paasi, A., & Zimmerbauer, K. (2016). Penumbral borders and planning paradoxes: Relational thinking and the question of borders in spatial planning. *Environment and Planning A*, 48(1), 75–93.

Perkmann, M. (1999). Building governance institutions across European borders. *Regional Studies*, 33(7), 657–667.

Plummer, R., & Fennell, D. A. (2009). Managing protected areas for sustainable tourism: Prospects for adaptive co-management. *Journal of Sustainable Tourism*, 17(2), 149–168.

Princen, S., Geuijen, K., Candel, J., Folgerts, O., & Hooijer, R. (2016). Establishing cross-border co-operation between professional organizations: Police, fire brigades and emergency health services in Dutch border regions. *European Urban and Regional Studies*, 23(3), 497–512.

Prokkola, E.-K. (2007). Cross-border regionalization and tourism development at the Swedish-Finnish border: Destination Arctic Circle. *Scandinavian Journal of Hospitality and Tourism*, 7(2), 120–138.

Prokkola, E.-K. (2011). Regionalization, tourism development and partnership: The European Union's North Calotte sub-programme of INTERREG III A North. *Tourism Geographies*, 13(4), 507–530.

Rogerson, C.M. (2015). Tourism and regional development: The case of South Africa's distressed areas. *Development Southern Africa*, 32(3), 277–291.

Saarinen, J. (2007). Tourism in peripheries: The role of tourism in regional development in northern Finland. In D. K. Müller & B. Jansson (Eds.), *Tourism in peripheries: Perspectives from the far north and south*, pp. 41–52. Wallingford: CABI.

Saarinen, J., Rogerson, C. M., & Hall, C. M. (2017). Geographies of tourism development and planning. *Tourism Geographies*, 19(3), 307–317.

Saxena, G., & Ilbery, B. (2008). Integrated rural tourism: A border case study. *Annals of Tourism Research*, 35(1), 233–254.

Shepherd, J., & Ioannides, D. (2020). Useful funds, disappointing framework: Tourism stakeholder experiences of INTERREG. *Scandinavian Journal of Hospitality and Tourism*, 20(5), 485–502.

Sofield, T. H. B. (2006). Border Tourism and Border Communities: An overview. *Tourism Geographies*, 8(2), 102–121.

Spierings, B., & van der Velde, M. (2013). Cross-border mobility, Unfamiliarity and development policy in Europe. *European Planning Studies*, 21(1), 1–4.

Stoffelen, A. (2017). *Borders, a blessing in disguise? A structural analysis of tourism and regional development processes in European borderlands.* Doctoral dissertation, KU Leuven - University of Leuven, Belgium.

Stoffelen, A. (2018). Tourism trails as tools for cross-border integration: A best practice case study of the Vennbahn cycling route. *Annals of Tourism Research*, 73, 91–102.

Stoffelen, A., Adiyia, B., Vanneste, D., & Kotze, N. (2020). Post-apartheid local sustainable development through tourism: An analysis of policy perceptions among 'responsible' tourism stakeholders around Pilanesberg National Park, South Africa. *Journal of Sustainable Tourism*, 28(3), 414–432.

Stoffelen, A., Ioannides, D., & Vanneste, D. (2017). Obstacles to achieving cross-border tourism governance: A multi-scalar approach focusing on the German-Czech borderlands. *Annals of Tourism Research*, 64, 126–138.

Stoffelen, A., & Vanneste, D. (2016). Institutional (dis)integration and regional development implications of whisky tourism in Speyside, Scotland. *Scandinavian Journal of Hospitality and Tourism*, 16(1), 42–60.

Stoffelen, A., & Vanneste, D. (2017). Tourism and cross-border regional development: Insights in European contexts. *European Planning Studies*, 25(6), 1013–1033.

Stoffelen, A., & Vanneste, D. (2018). The role of history and identity discourses in cross-border tourism destination development: A Vogtland case study. *Journal of Destination Marketing and Management*, 8, 204–213.

Stoffelen, A., & Vanneste, D. (2019). Commodification of contested borderscapes for tourism development: Viability, community representation and equity of relic Iron Curtain and Sudetenland heritage tourism landscapes. In A. Paasi, E.-K. Prokkola, J. Saarinen, & K. Zimmerbauer (eds.), *Borderless worlds for whom? Ethics, moralities and mobilities*, pp. 139–153. London: Routledge.

Stokke, K. B., & Haukeland, J. V. (2018). Balancing between tourism development and nature protection across national park borders – a case study of a coastal protected area in Norway. *Journal of Environmental Planning and Management*, 61(12), 2151–2165.

Timothy, D. J. (1995). Political boundaries and tourism: Borders as tourist attractions. *Tourism Management*, 16(7), 525–532.

Timothy, D. J. (1998). Cooperative tourism planning in a developing destination. *Journal of Sustainable Tourism*, 6(1), 52–68.

Timothy, D. J. (1999). Cross-border partnership in tourism resource management: International parks along the US-Canada border. *Journal of Sustainable Tourism*, 7(3–4), 182–205.

Timothy, D. J. (2001). *Tourism and political boundaries*. London: Routledge.

Timothy, D. J., Saarinen, J., & Viken, A. (2016). Editorial: Tourism issues and international borders in the Nordic Region. *Scandinavian Journal of Hospitality and Tourism*, 16(1), 1–13.

Tölle, A. (2013). National planning systems between convergence and incongruity: Implications for cross-border cooperation from the German–Polish perspective. *European Planning Studies*, 21(4), 615–630.

Trippl, M. (2010). Developing cross-border regional innovation systems: Key factors and challenges. *Tijdschrift Voor Economische en Sociale Geografie*, 101(2), 150–160.

Van Houtum, H. (2000). An overview of European geographical research on borders and border regions. *Journal of Borderlands Studies*, 15(1), 57–83.

Vogel, B., & Field, J. (2020). (Re)constructing borders through the governance of tourism and trade in Ladakh, India. *Political Geography*, 82, 102226.

Weidenfeld, A. (2013). Tourism and cross border regional innovation systems. *Annals of Tourism Research*, 42, 191–213.

Woyo, E., & Slabbert, E. (2019). Cross-border destination marketing of attractions between borders: the case of Victoria Falls. *Journal of Hospitality and Tourism Insights*, 2(2), 145–165.

Yodsuwan, C., Pianluprasidh, P., & Butcher, K. (2018). Against the flow: Challenges in tourism development for a small-border town in Thailand. In Y. Wang, A. Shakeela, A. Kwek, & C. Khoo-Lattimore (eds.), *Managing asian destinations*, pp. 107–123. Singapore: Springer.

# 26
# CROSS-BORDER TOURISM INITIATIVES IN THE EUROPEAN UNION

*Eeva-Kaisa Prokkola*

## Introduction

Tourism is one of the biggest industries in the European Union (EU), bringing significant economic growth and employment to many regions. Tourism is an especially important part of the economy in many border regions that are often peripheral and lack opportunities for economic growth, employment, and cultural development, yet they are often rich in natural resources and heritage attractions (Timothy, 2001). European integration and the establishment of the Schengen area brought about a significant change in tourism development in the region's border areas. The idea of Schengen, the abolition of border controls between the member states of the European Community at that time (Germany, France, Belgium, the Netherlands, and Luxembourg), was introduced in 1984, and the agreement was signed in the town of Schengen, Luxembourg, in 1985. Ten years later, the Schengen system was implemented, in 1995 (Zaiotti, 2011). At that time, Jansen-Verbeke and Spee (1995, p. 73) wrote that "crossing national borders – being the definition of international tourism – has become rather irrelevant in the European context". With the European integration process, border withdrawals, and the renewal of regional policies, tourism became the focus of much economic development. Tourism development, clustering, and destination building were rolled out at the cross-border regional scale, not only at the national scale. The former borderscapes were transformed into open landscapes where borders were crossed almost unnoticed and frontier infrastructure, such as customs buildings and passport controls, were torn down or transformed into tourism information centres, small museums, bars, shops, or cafes (Lois, 2013; Prokkola, 2007; Timothy, 2001; Więckowski & Timothy, 2021). Borders became a resource for tourism development instead of merely barriers to tourism. As a result, the excitement and exoticism of border tourism diminished.

Growing academic interest in cross-border tourism development within the framework of the EU and its structural fund programmes arose in the early 2000s. Cross-border tourism initiatives and destination development have been of interdisciplinary interest, bridging scholars from the work of tourism studies and border studies, human geography, policy and governance, planning, and heritage and cultural studies, among other fields. Scholars have documented how European integration, border transitions, and new cross-border initiatives are interlinked with tourism development and destination building (Hartman, 2006; Ioannides et al., 2006;

Leimgruber, 1998; Prokkola, 2007). Within growing transfrontier regional integration, the financial support from the EU's structural funds has motivated tourism developers, communities, and other stakeholders to turn to cross-border regional tourism instead of being tied only to national development agendas (Ioannides et al., 2006; Leimgruber, 1998; Prokkola, 2007; Timothy, 2021; Wachowiak, 2006). Wachowiak (2006) describes how the removal of border restrictions, the easing of political divisions, and economic support for cross-border cooperation created new situations for politicians, regional tourism developers, and other stakeholders in former European peripheral borderlands: "managers and politicians subsequently face questions on whether a border region could be considered a destination itself, how to market it as a competitive destination unit, and what to consider in managing it in a sustainable way" (Wachowiak, 2006, p. 2). The collaborative mode of tourism planning and development in border regions reflects an effort to establish integrated economic areas and promote regional and social cohesion within and across the frontiers of Europe. Regional competitiveness and sustainability, both keywords in the current political vernacular, are understood to be better achieved through collaboration, clustering tourist attractions, greening transportation, innovation, and knowledge sharing. It is also suggested that in an open border context, in particular, cross-border destination development would offer a more consumer-friendly approach to tourism development and planning (Blasco, Guia & Prats, 2014).

Research on the EU's boundary-spanning tourism initiatives has provided knowledge of cross-border destination management and development in different border contexts, both internal and external to the EU. It has also provided an understanding of how regional and local tourism development relates to European regional policy and planning, as well as global and regional shifts and changes in cross-border dynamics. In this chapter, the examination of the EU's cross-border tourism initiatives is structured around the themes of its regional policy, integration and enlargement, multi-scaler governance and partnerships, stakeholder engagement, and cross-border heritage and natural attractions.

## EU Regional Policy and Tourism

Halkier (2010) argues that the role of the EU in tourism development is more significant than is often understood, underlining the significance of public policy beyond direct intervention, such as through tailored tourism development programmes. He notes that the strategic areas with extensive European intervention, including competition and regional development policies, have considerable impact on tourism development. The connection between supranational policies and tourism is not one-way but mutually symbiotic. On the one hand, tourism is understood to foster economic growth and employment in often peripheral border areas, while on the other hand, tourism and its collaborative development build new bridges and foster a common European identity across national frontiers and among European citizens. As the European Commissioner Elzbieta Bienkowska underscores, "Europeans need a strong tourism sector for economic reasons, but also to better know each other and better see what unites them" (European Commission, 2016, foreword).

Since the reformation of the EU's structural funds in 1988, regional and cohesion policies have increased in importance—today accounting for approximately thirty per cent of the EU budget—and have acquired a territorial dimension. The structural funds provide money for activities that involve national, regional, local, and private-sector actors in promoting sustainability and innovation in tourism and supporting access to EU funding for the development of regional tourism. In addition to tourism, the structural funds target other sectors and development arenas, including health, transport, education, labour mobility, and environmental protection. Owing to the diversity of the tourism sector and its needs, tourism has been supported by several EU programmes, such as the European Regional Development Fund (ERDF), the European Social Fund (ESDF), Horizon, and Erasmus+.

From the perspective of cross-border tourism development, the regional development fund Interreg (European Territorial Cooperation) is the most significant and most studied programme. The Interreg programme and its projects are financed by the ERDF, but national-level funding from each state involved is also required. Interreg is a cohesion policy mechanism and provides a framework for implementing joint actions and initiatives between national, regional, and local actors from different member states. To gain finance from the programme, initiatives must involve partners and actors from at least two EU countries (Faby, 2006). The first Interreg initiative in 1990 was developed as a community effort that was then extended to a transnational and interregional cooperative endeavour. According to the European Commission (2020), the objective of the Interreg initiative is to promote harmonious regional, economic, and social development. The scheme was built around three strands of cooperation that have different scalar dimensions and geographical scopes: cross-border (Interreg A), transnational (Interreg B), and interregional (Interreg C). Interreg A is the most extensive and influential from the perspective of cross-border tourism development, with a budget of €6.6 billion and 60 cooperative programmes along intra-EU borders (Interreg Europe 2021–2027, 2020). To date, five programme periods of Interreg have been implemented: Interreg I (1990–1993), Interreg II (1994–1999), Interreg III (2000–2006), Interreg IV (2007–2013), and Interreg V (2014–2020). The new 2021–2027 period will continue to provide support and funding for interregional cooperation. The current programme prioritizes area four: a more social Europe, "enhancing the role of culture and tourism in economic development, social inclusion and social innovation" (Interreg Europe, 2020, pp. 10, 16). Faby (2006) provides a useful introduction to the principles and challenges related to the tourism projects and shows how the EU's tourism policy tools and the Interreg initiative supports and institutionalizes cooperative tourism development in Europe's borderlands.

Cross-border tourism development and planning are recognized in the Interreg policy documents as something that provides possible solutions for dealing with regional socioeconomic issues such as low income, out-migration, and unemployment (Stoffelen et al., 2017)—all issues that are common in national peripheries and borderlands. Research shows that the Interreg initiative has had considerable impact on the transformation of Europe's internal border regions into international tourism destinations (Ioannides et al., 2006; Leimgruber, 1998; Prokkola 2007; Timothy, 2021; Wachowiak, 2006). The initiative has played a crucial role in the process of tourism development in border areas as it has supported tourism innovation and sustainability in frontier areas, as well as new joint tourism destinations and attractions (Więckowski, in press). Scholars have noted that Interreg initiatives are often utilized strategically to support local and regional tourism development and interest (Nilsson et al., 2010; Prokkola, Zimmerbauer & Jakola, 2015). The Interreg scheme operates at various scales, ranging from binational local projects to geographically wide-ranging initiatives that involve actors from several member states. There are also separate programmes that fund and encourage collaboration with neighbouring non-EU countries (Timothy, 2021).

The potential for cross-border tourism development in a specific frontier area cannot be predicted by any single factor. Instead, a set of variables needs to be evaluated, such as geographical distance from core population areas, political environments, economic conditions, means of communication, and sociocultural cohesion. Cross-border tourism development has proved to be a challenging undertaking even in well integrated regions where border permeability has been high for centuries (Hartman, 2006; Leimgruber, 1998). Spierings and van der Velde

(2013) analysed cross-border shopping in the Dutch–German Rhine-Waal Euroregion. Their study shows that even the old established and well-institutionalized European Euroregions are still characterized by mental barriers that hinder cross-border interaction and shopping tourism. In many cases, cross-border initiatives are simply a strategy for regional developers to obtain co-funding from the EU, ostensibly as a means to work toward sustainable tourism development. In their examination of the Bothnian Arc project, Ioannides and his colleagues (2006, p. 137) observed that the protection of national interests often eliminates the potential regional benefits to be achieved from cross-border cooperation.

## EU Enlargement in 2004 and 2007

Although cross-border tourism schemes are supported and steered by EU institutions and funding instruments, the processes of tourism management and destination development are often place-dependent, and there are considerable differences in various parts of the continent. EU integration and the adding of new member states is a dynamic process that influences cross-border cooperation and development in tourism. The 2004 enlargement, where ten new members states joined the union, increased the total number of members to 25, fundamentally changing its character. In 2007, the fifth wave of EU enlargement saw Bulgaria and Romania join. The 2004 and 2007 enlargements expanded the EU's outer borders eastward and have enabled new spaces of cross-border cooperation in tourism (Williams & van der Velde, 2005). The EU enlargement processes have opened new research avenues and increased interest in the historical development of east–west divisions in Europe and how the history of borders and political tensions might be eased with the help of cross-border tourism and tourism development initiatives.

Some researchers have traced the general regional and historical paths of development and the impact of political events and debordering while others have focused on specific Interreg programmes and regional tourism endeavours. Mayer et al. (2019) analyse the EU's cross-border development policies with a focus on Central and Eastern Europe after the fall of the Iron Curtain in 1989–1991 and provide an overview of the alliance's structural instruments, including the Interreg programme and Euroregions. Hall (2008) has provided a general overview of the major issues facing tourism development in Central and Eastern Europe. According to him, there is a need to better interrogate post-enlargement tourism development within the institutions of the EU.

Cross-border tourism initiatives between the older and newer member states, as well as the new members and their non-EU neighbours, are of increasing interest among scholars. The German boundary with Poland and the Czech Republic has been especially well studied. Stoffelen and Vanneste (2017) provide a comparison and institutional analysis between a newer and an older, well-institutionalized, internal, cross-border region: the German–Czech and German–Belgian border zones. They argue that there are no automatic causal relations between tourism development and regional development in cross-border contexts. According to the authors, successful local cross-border tourism efforts do not guarantee destination-wide positive development outcomes. Cross-border projects may sometimes even reinforce existing asymmetrical social and economic conditions between neighbouring borderlands. Stoffelen and Vanneste's (2017) research points out that Czech and German stakeholders regard the border location as an advantage for tourism development. Simultaneously, the impacts of the considerable institutional and cultural disparities between the two sides were well recognized.

Nilsson et al. (2010) focus on cross-border tourism development in the Baltic Sea area, involving both new and old EU member states in the context of the Interreg III programme (2000–2006). Their work shows how regional identities are re-presented and narrated in the process of developing the Baltic Sea area tourism destination and argue that in the development of cross-border tourism, economic rationales are always highlighted, whereas political issues are often silenced. The Baltic Sea region has also been of interest in the work of Cerić and Więckowski (2020; Więckowski & Cerić, 2016). Więckowski and Cerić (2016) examined the role of tourism development on Poland's Baltic Sea coast and what role transnational tourism has in the integration process and people's cross-border mobilities. They propose a sequential model for investigating tourist flows, cross-border tourism development, and partnerships. Cerić and Więckowski (2020) also looked at the development of transboundary tourism on the Baltic Sea, focusing on the role of the Interreg programme between 2007 and 2013. According to their research, transboundary tourism development in the region depends on EU co-financing, which determines the possible actions taken, such as transportation, tourism management, and product development, and a common regional identity. They found that collaborative tourism projects in the Baltic Sea region are often led by entities from the more developed "old" member states. This creates asymmetries in terms of funding and therefore may not effectively reduce regional disparities between the older and newer EU members.

Whereas cross-border tourism development on the EU's internal borders has received considerable attention, research on tourism development along the EU's external borders and within the framework of the EU neighbourhood initiatives has only recently started to gain academic attention. Bozhuk and Buchko (2018) analysed the Carpathian Euroregion, focusing on Ukrainian–Hungarian cross-border cooperation and changes in tourism flows. According to their analysis, the area's cross-border programmes have increased new cross-border services and produced more tourism infrastructure in the border area. Following the February 2022 Russian invasion of Ukraine, it remains to be seen how this programme might continue in the future. Rădoi (2020) examines the role of cultural cooperation between EU member state Romania and its non-EU neighbour Serbia, focusing on the European Capital of Culture brand for 2021. He emphasizes that cultural cross-border cooperation transforms "borders from barriers to bridges of cooperation" and strengthens ties between and within local communities (Rădoi, 2020, p. 11). Makkonen et al. (2018) scrutinize the Finnish–Russian cross-border region where European funding has played an important role in facilitating interactions and knowledge transfer. They highlight that, although remarkable differences in culture and administrative systems between Finland and Russia create barriers to cooperation, the cultural and technological disparities that collaborative partners need to resolve simultaneously contribute to knowledge transfer and innovation in the borderlands.

## Multi-scalar Governance and Partnerships

The EU's regional policy both decentralizes and centralizes. This means that cross-border regions have gained more authority relative to national centres and simultaneously are strongly connected to European institutions and modes of governance (Perkmann, 1999). The European Commission introduced a multi-level governance model to prevent the piggybacking of EU structural funds to finance fully national objectives (Harguindeguy, 2007, p. 318). A multi-scalar model of implementation distributes economic responsibilities among different actors and thus enforces dialogue between different interest groups.

An analysis of the multi-scalar institutions of governance provides an understanding of the opportunity structures and challenges of tourism destinations and their management in border areas (Stoffelen et al., 2017). Many scholars have highlighted the challenges and asymmetries inherent in the EU multilevel governance framework. In comparison to destinations that follow national administrative boundaries and where governance structures usually aim to bridge sectoral divides, in cross-border destinations the governance structures should transcend both sectoral and institutional divides (Blasco, Guia & Prats, 2014, p. 160). The importance of institutional factors is also emphasized by Stoffelen and Vanneste (2017), who argue that the key factors predicting the success of cross-border tourism development are the "thickness" of institutional arrangements, the involvement of actors at multiple scales, regional and tourism development strategies, and the informal networks of institutional brokers.

Stoffelen and his colleagues (2017) analyse the obstacles to establishing cross-border tourism destination governance in the German–Czech borderlands. Their research shows that both the German–Czech international border and domestic borders between German federal states pose challenges for establishing effective multi-scalar collaboration. They learned that local collaborative tourism projects are often successful at both international and subnational levels. According to their study, obstacles are caused by problems regarding the functioning of multi-scalar institutions. Similar border obstacles have been documented in other domestic border contexts, too. Ilbery and Saxena (2011) reveal how strategic, administrative, and personal-level challenges occur in rural tourism in the English–Welsh cross-border region. Thus, even within a country, in this case the United Kingdom, interregional and intersectoral cooperation can be contentious and problematic.

In examining the processes of cross-border destination-making and how transfrontier networks emerge, Blasco, Guia, and Prats (2014) identify factors that facilitate the self-governance of cross-border collaborative structures on the French–Spanish border in the Cerdanya Valley. Accordingly, institutional, cultural, and organizational similarities facilitate cross-border cooperation and networking, whereas "long periods of sociocultural separation favoured the emergence of mistrust, envy, rivalry, suspicion" (Blasco et al., 2014, p. 167). Likewise, entrepreneurial capacities and leadership have considerable influences in cross-border destination-making. Blasco, Guia, and Prats discovered that private sector-led grassroots effort were often more permanent than public-sector initiatives. Mutual trust was probably the most important and axiomatic factor explaining the success of cross-border destination-making and cross-border networking.

Prokkola (2011) likewise examined the multi-scalar governance of cross-border initiatives and how partnerships are established in tourism-related projects. Although the Interreg documents underline cooperation and partnerships between various actors and stakeholders, actual project implementation in the North Calotte Interreg programme (2000–2006) was organized in a highly selective manner between same-level regional organizations. According to Prokkola (2008), the significance of cross-border partnership and cooperation in tourism development cannot be measured only in pragmatic terms, for example by measuring direct investment and new jobs in the region. Instead, the substance of cross-border initiatives should be evaluated in the wider context of the EU's territorial coherence policies that aim to transition peripheral border regions into zones of economic growth.

Geographically wider programme areas and large-scale projects provide opportunities for bigger regional actors, whereas small-scale actors (e.g., small municipalities and associations) may find it difficult to have their voices heard. This is problematic because current research suggests that local-level cross-border cooperation is often more successful than large-scale projects that are often more complicated with complex multi-level governance structures and political contestations (Stoffelen et al. 2017, p. 136; Timothy & Saarinen, 2013). According to Stoffelen et al. (2017), geographically wide macro-regional tourism projects are unlikely to become central destination governance institutions because the decision-making bodies in these projects are usually located far away from the actual border localities where they occur. Research on cross-border tourism development should recognize the economic, political, and social environment and pay attention to the scale (global, regional, bilateral, or inter-local) of activities (Timothy, Saarinen & Viken 2016; Timothy & Teye, 2004).

An important part of Interreg initiatives and project implementation is the establishment of partnerships. Several studies have examined the potential and challenges in the formation and maintenance of partnerships in cross-border regional contexts. Greer (2002) has studied the development of interjurisdictional tourism partnerships in Ireland with the focus on the island's two tourist boards: the Northern Ireland Tourist Board and Bord Failte. According to Greer, cooperation can be successfully maintained by designing an integrated and inclusive tourism strategy, ensuring partnership balance, establishing local participative partnerships, and considering the political sensitivities of border regions. Efforts to improve the tourism sector are often backed by policy initiatives and new funding opportunities from the International Fund for Ireland and the European Union (Interreg), which together facilitate the development of tourism infrastructure and greater north–south collaboration. Yet, even if the tourist boards are motivated to work together in partnership, the Northern Ireland Tourist Board and Ireland's Bord Failte continue to perceive each other as competitors. The tourist boards have worked well together in marketing when promoting Ireland as a whole in the international marketplace, whereas marketing closer to home has been characterized by more tension, self-interest, and competition (Greer, 2002). The friction between cooperation and competition in partnership has created obstacles and divisions between the partners.

## The Challenge of Engaging Stakeholders

European policymakers (see EC, 2016) have underscored the potential of cross-border tourism activities in fostering a sense of togetherness and a pan-European identity. Accordingly, fostering partnerships between the public and private sectors is considered a way of extending social responsibility and the norms created by the EU to the workings of the private tourism sector. Likewise, Interreg co-funded tourism development projects are regional and development-centred, which means that they should broadly benefit a region's enterprises and residents. This explains why, regardless of some positive developments, cross-border practices are largely performed by a limited number of public-sector actors. Private-sector tourism stakeholders are rarely involved as primary project partners, but they are involved through networks and project-specific activities (Jakola & Prokkola, 2018). Research has shown that high inter-firm competition reduces the willingness of private-sector actors to commit themselves to collaborative cross-border tourism initiatives. Engaging community members in locally implemented cross-border tourism initiatives remains a significant challenge (Stoffelen et al., 2017).

Research has suggested, however, that national norms, divisions, and interests are highly persistent and resilient. There are often remarkable national differences between people's attitudes and commitment to cross-border cooperation. Prokkola (2011) argues that cross-border cooperation and stakeholder engagement is often rather superficial and more vulnerable to political changes and even local changes, such as changes in personnel, than inter-sectoral cooperation within a state's borders. Similar findings have been reported by Ioannides and his colleagues (2006) who examined tourism development in the Finnish–Swedish Bothnian Arc Project. Their investigation of the planning, development, and marketing of the coastal Bothnian Arc region concluded that, although the region is often considered an exemplar of cross-border collaboration, for many regional stakeholders it is still difficult to approach "borderless" tourism development in terms of realizing equal and mutual benefits to both sides.

The challenge of engaging other stakeholders does not only concern public–private partnerships. Shepherd and Ioannides (2020) examine regional stakeholders' perspectives in three Interreg co-funded projects between tourism destinations in the Swedish–Norwegian borderlands. The Swedish–Norwegian border is an external EU border; Norway is not part of the EU, but both countries are part of the Schengen free movement area. The study shows that stakeholders consider the Interreg project funding a useful resource that can "supplement sources of income from national actors" (Shepherd & Ioannides, 2020, p. 493), but they were not especially committed to cross-border collaboration. The authors also note differences in the experiences and perceptions of stakeholders. Interested parties on both sides did not all actively participate in development activities, and those actors who were committed to cross-border development were sometimes exhausted in their attempts to motivate the others. Blasco et al. (2014) describe a similar situation on the French–Spanish border. Shepherd and Ioannides (2020) stress that short-term funding schemes form a tenuous ground for achieving sustainable tourism development within the border region (see also Prokkola, 2008).

Recently, scholars have started to focus on the benefits of tourism and cross-border stakeholder engagement for knowledge transfer and innovation, which are considered crucial for regional growth and development. Weidenfeld (2013, pp. 208–209) analyses cross-border innovation systems and tourism, arguing that tourism should be prioritized in cross-border regions because of its ability to enable and facilitate cross-frontier interaction. Tourism supports engagement, knowledge transfer, and innovation among stakeholders and places. The knowledge transfer and creativity that result from tourism development fittingly illustrate how difficult it is to measure the benefits of tourism for regional development. In the long term, such indirect and more unpredictable effects of cross-border tourism may have a profound impact on the path of regional development.

## Cross-border Heritage and Natural Attractions

Cross-border tourist attractions and products, and destination development, have been analysed in many studies with a common focus on border culture and heritage, regional identity narratives, and nature and leisure attractions such as cycling routes and hiking paths. Internal border regions are often regarded as laboratories of territorial cohesion policies and the development of spatial identities in the EU. Hence, it is important to consider the utilization and communization of local and cross-border heritage in the production of tourist attractions.

Liberato et al. (2018) show how in Galicia, Spain, and northern Portugal, borderland tourism works as a strategic tool for growing interregional interaction, regional branding, and identity narrative formation. Their study notes that cooperation:

> is important and should be achieved through cooperation agreements between public actors, the private sector and society itself. Specifically referring to tourism, given its cross-cutting nature, it is important to promote collaboration between the business sector and economic agents and to develop natural, cultural and heritage resources.
> *(Liberato et al., 2018, p. 1360)*

Lois and Cairo (2015) explore the commodification of cross-border heritage and histories in EU co-funded tourism initiatives. They explain how

> the setting of the border as an experiential place for tourist encounters opens it up as a scene for the negotiation and performance of the different spatial border stories. Museums and interpretation centers provide a tour description of the borders, spatializing activities and telling stories about them.
> *(Lois & Cairo, 2015, p. 338)*

Similarly, Nilsson et al. (2010) and Prokkola and Lois (2016) provide examples of how regional heritage and histories have been used as tools to promote cross-border tourism destinations in the Nordic countries. The commercialization and marketing of borderland heritage as a tourist attraction require political sensitivity, however. Borderland stories are often utilized selectively because some regional histories and heritage remain politically sensitive and contested (Prokkola & Lois, 2016; Stoffelen & Vanneste, 2017). Tourism marketing, therefore, usually focuses strategically on unproblematic regional characteristics such as natural beauty, seaside resorts, and beautiful landscapes, instead of discussing contested regional histories and traumatic war memories, for example (Nilsson et al., 2010).

Prokkola (2007, 2010) examines the transformation of the Finnish–Swedish border landscape from the Cold War east–west frontier to an open EU internal boundary. Focusing on the EU Interreg programme "Destination Arctic Circle", she analyses the development and branding of destinations that seek a competitive advantage by emphasizing the political, temporal borders, and geometric border dimensions of the Arctic Circle and its environs. She shows that alongside the potential of local cross-border projects, many barriers still exist for further cross-border integration and regionalization. Prokkola and Lois (2016) examine and compare how cultural traditions and border-related historic events are memorialized at the Finnish–Swedish and Spanish–Portuguese borders. Their examination of various EU-funded tourism projects identifies many similarities and differences in the production of local heritage. National-scale heritage was more strongly present in tourism and historic sites in the Spanish–Portuguese border region than it was in the Finnish–Swedish borderlands.

Current and future trends in developing cross-border tourism within the framework of EU initiatives depend on the politically horizontal criteria determined by the European Commission. The increasingly important criterion of green growth will impact tourism development and what new tourism products and innovations may emerge. Sustainability and green growth are now at the centre of international and European institutional agendas. The introduction of the European Green Deal signals how sustainability, climate change, and environmental change are now key priorities of the EU, thus encouraging tourism, like other industries, to move towards more environmentally and socially sustainable solutions (Stoffelen, 2018; Tambovceva et al., 2020).

Tambovceva et al. (2020) examine the development of cross-border greenways in Western and Eastern Europe, including the Greenway (GW) Riga–Pskov; North Latvia and South Estonia; and the Latvia, Sweden, Finland, and Estonia greenways. Greenways provide an alternative tourism product that is usually initiated from the bottom-up by local communities. Greenways straddle across and connect several countries, highlighting their common histories, heritages, and natural values. The construction of greenway tourism trails has been supported by structural funds as part of the EU's thrust toward sustainable and green growth.

Hiking trails and cycling tourism routes provide fitting examples of green tourism development and cross-border regionalism (Timothy & Boyd, 2015). They have also received considerable amounts of funding from recent Interreg programmes throughout Europe. Stoffelen (2018) looks at how tourism trails contribute to cross-border integration processes with a focus on the Vennbahn rail-trail between Germany, Belgium, and Luxemburg, showing how the influence of cycling routes on cross-border integration depends on various factors, such as the degree of cross-border institutionalization, the nature of the destinations involved, and the geography of the trail itself. In some border regions like the Spanish–Portuguese border old smuggling routes have been transformed into walking paths (Cairo & Lois, 2017), illustrating how cross-border projects have contributed to green tourism and heritage tourism in innovative ways. Some cycling tourism routes like the EuroVelo Iron Curtain Trail follow the external borders of the EU in some areas where heritage-making is even more sensitive; as Stoffelen and Vanneste (2019, p. 142) put it, "relic border landscape tourism projects … may be sensitive for contestation and stakeholder alienation because of the projects' political role in EU regionalization processes". Research shows that tourism trail and cycling route projects have potential to contribute to cross-border communication and social cohesion in both European internal and external borderlands, but stronger initiatives are needed to overcome the real and perceived barriers to tourism development.

## Conclusion

In the era of more open borders—1990 to 2020—regional cross-border tourism organizations and partnerships have been established and institutionalized, and state boundaries have become a resource that fosters interaction and innovation between tourism stakeholders. European integration and debordering processes have opened new avenues for tourism development, and equally the tourism industry has furthered social cohesion and cross-border knowledge-sharing (Prokkola, 2007). In many border regions, tourism has been one of the few economic sectors to have shown growth in recent years (Saarinen, 2004). The Interreg cross-border cooperation programmes and initiatives are an important mediator of tourism development across national borders. The potential of cross-border tourism development within the Interreg framework has been discussed at great length and so have its weaknesses and challenges. Research shows that politically driven top-down tourism development in a transfrontier context is not always effective and sustainable. Regardless of the innovativeness of local and regional tourism initiatives, the challenges and "bottlenecks" of cross-border tourism—regarding governance, project management and partnership, barriers created by national competition and mistrust, reaching private sector actors and communities, as well as sustainable tourism development—have proved persistent. Interdisciplinary debate concerning cross-border destination development and its shortcomings is substantial between tourism studies and other research fields. Many topics would benefit from more in-depth dialogue and collaboration. For example, research on cross-border destination management and governance would benefit from more active dialogue between tourism planning research and studies of cross-border governance (Stoffelen et al., 2017).

Tourism planning initiatives are important for regional development, and their influence should be considered against wider politically driven institutionalization processes, not merely against the interest of local stakeholders and tourism industries (Prokkola, 2007; Stoffelen & Vanneste, 2017). The branding and creation of functional tourism regions across national borders is seen to contribute to the EU's efforts at regional coherence and a shared European identity (Prokkola, 2007), something that has been seriously emphasized in the past several years.

European integration and enlargement processes, state protectionism, Brexit, and the COVID-19 pandemic have challenged the functioning of and solidarity within the EU, impeding the implementation of many cross-border initiatives. Whereas Europe's tourism sector proved relatively resilient to the 2008 fiscal crisis (EC, 2016), COVID-19 border closures, travel restrictions, and social distancing have crippled the tourism industry especially hard. The new 2021–2027 Interreg programme recognizes the special needs of the tourism industry, stating that "regional economies dominated by sectors heavily affected in the COVID-19 crisis, such as tourism or the cultural sector, may experience more severe and prolonged negative impacts on their socioeconomic condition compared with regions with a more diversified economic structure" (Interreg, 2021–2017, p. 9). The recovery plans therefore need to pay particular attention to tourism development and how the structural fund initiatives are used and coordinated within multi-level governance frameworks that include European, national, and regional partnerships.

## References

Blasco, D., Guia, J., & Prats, L. (2014). Emergence of governance in cross-border destinations. *Annals of Tourism Research*, 49, 159–173.

Bozhuk, T.I., & Buchko, Z.I. (2018). Cross-border Ukrainian-Hungarian cooperation in the sphere of tourism. *Journal of Geology, Geography and Geoecology*, 27(1), 35–42.

Cairo, H., & Lois, M. (2017). Cross-border walking trails as a tourist experience in the Spanish-Portuguese border. In M.C. Hall, Y. Ram, & N. Shoval (eds) *The Routledge international handbook of walking*, pp. 215–222. London: Routledge.

Cerić, D., & Więckowski, M. (2020). Establishing transboundary tourist space in the Baltic Sea region. *Baltic Journal of Health and Physical Activity*, 12, 149–157.

European Commission (2016). Guide on EU funding for the tourism sector 2014–2020. https://drive.google.com/file/d/0B48Zk-0LhgX7LXlxRjUwVXY4Ukk/view?resourcekey=0-EWTPkAGxF-OY9kY44jyapA

European Commission (2020). Interreg: European Territorial Co-operation. https://ec.europa.eu/regional_policy/en/policy/cooperation/european-territorial/

Faby, H. (2006). Tourism policy tools applied by the European Union to support tourism. In H. Wachowiak (ed) *Tourism and borders: Contemporary issues, policies and international research*, pp. 19–30. Aldershot: Ashgate.

Greer, J. (2002). Developing trans-jurisdictional tourism partnerships - Insights from the Island of Ireland. *Tourism Management*, 23(4), 355–366.

Halkier, H. (2010). EU and tourism development: Bark or bite? *Scandinavian Journal of Hospitality and Tourism*, 10(2), 92–106.

Hall, D. (2008). From 'bricklaying' to '*bricolage*': Transition and tourism development in Central and Eastern Europe. *Tourism Geographies*, 10(4), 410–428.

Harguindeguy, J. (2007). Cross-border policy in Europe: Implementing INTERREG III-A, France–Spain. *Regional and Federal Studies*, 17, 317–334.

Hartman, K. (2006). Destination management in cross-border regions. In H. Wachowiak (ed). *Tourism and borders: Contemporary issues, policies and international research*, pp. 89–109. Aldershot: Ashgate.

Ilbery, B., & Saxena, G. (2011). Integrated rural tourism in the English-Welsh cross-border region: An analysis of strategic, administrative and Personal challenges. *Regional Studies*, 45(8), 1139–1155.

Interreg Europe 2021-2027 (2020, January 29). *European Union, European Regional Development Fund*. https://www.interregeurope.eu/

Ioannides, D., Nielsen, P.Å., & Billing, P. (2006). Transboundary collaboration in tourism: The case of the Bothnian Arc. *Tourism Geographies*, 8(2), 122–142.

Jakola, F., & Prokkola, E-K. (2018). Trust building or vested interest? Social capital processes of cross-border co-operation in the border towns of Tornio and Haparanda. *Tijdschrift voor Economische en Sociale Geografie*, 109(2), 224–238.

Jansen-Verbeke, M., & Spee, R. (1995). A regional analysis of tourist flows within Europe. *Tourism Management*, 16(1),73–80.

Leimgruber, W. (1998). Defying political boundaries: Transborder tourism in a regional context. *Visions in Leisure and Business*, 17(3), 8–29.

Liberato, D., Alen, E., Liberato, P., & Dominguez, T. (2018). Governance and cooperation in Euroregions: Border tourism between Spain and Portugal. *European Planning Studies*, 26(7), 1347–1365.

Lois, M. (2013). Re-significando la frontera: El caso de la eurociudad Chaves-Verín, *Boletín de la Asociación de Geógrafos Españoles*, 61, 309–327.

Lois, M., & Cairo, H. (2015). Heritage-ized places and spatial stories: B/Ordering practices at the Spanish-Portuguese *Raya/Raia*. *Territory, Politics, Governance*, 3(3), 321–343.

Makkonen, T., Williams, A.M., Weidenfeld, A., & Kaisto, V. (2018). Cross-border knowledge transfer and innovation in the European neighbourhood: Tourism cooperation at the Finnish-Russian border. *Tourism Management*, 68, 140–151.

Mayer, M., Zbaraszewski W., Pieńkowski D., Gach G., & Gernert J. (2019). *Cross-border tourism in protected areas: Potentials, pitfalls and perspectives*. Cham, Switzerland: Springer.

Nilsson, J.H., Eskilsson, L., & Richard, E. (2010). Creating cross-border destinations: Interreg programmes and regionalisation in the Baltic Sea area. *Scandinavian Journal of Hospitality and Tourism*, 10(2), 153–172.

Perkmann, M. (1999). Building governance institutions across European borders. *Regional Studies*, 33, 657–667.

Prokkola, E.K. (2007). Cross-border regionalization and tourism development at the Swedish-Finnish border: Destination Arctic Circle. *Scandinavian Journal of Hospitality and Tourism*, 7(2), 120–138.

Prokkola, E.K. (2011). Regionalization, tourism development and partnership: The European Union's North Calotte sub-programme of INTERREG III A North. *Tourism Geographies*, 13(4), 507–530.

Prokkola, E-K. (2008). Resources and barriers in tourism development: Cross-border cooperation, regionalization and destination building at the Finnish-Swedish border. *Fennia-International Journal of Geography*, 186(1), 31–46.

Prokkola, E.K., Lois, M. (2016). Scalar politics of border heritage: An examination of the EU's northern and southern border areas. *Scandinavian Journal of Hospitality and Tourism*, 16(1), 14–35.

Prokkola, E.K., Zimmerbauer, K., & Jakola, F. (2015). Performance of regional identity in the implementation of European cross-border initiatives. *European Urban and Regional Studies*, 22(1), 104–117.

Rădoi, I. (2020). European capital of culture, urban tourism and cross-border cooperation between Romania and Serbia. *Journal of Balkan and Near Eastern Studies*, 22(4), 547–559.

Saarinen, J. (2004). Tourism and touristic representations of nature. In A.A. Lew, C.M. Hall, & A.M. Williams (Eds.) *A companion to tourism*, pp. 438–449. Oxford: Blackwell.

Shepherd, J., & Ioannides, D. (2020). Useful funds, disappointing framework: Tourism stakeholder experiences of INTERREG. *Scandinavian Journal of Hospitality and Tourism*, 20(5), 485–502.

Spierings, B., & van der Velde, M. (2013). Cross-border differences and unfamiliarity: Shopping mobility in the Dutch-German Rhine-Waal Euroregion. *European Planning Studies*, 21(1), 5–23.

Stoffelen, A. (2018). Tourism trails as tools for cross-border integration: A best practice case study of the Vennbahn cycling route. *Annals of Tourism Research*, 73, 91–102.

Stoffelen, A., Ioannides, D., & Vanneste, D. (2017). Obstacles to achieving cross-border tourism governance: A multi-scalar approach focusing on the German-Czech borderlands. *Annals of Tourism Research*, 64, 126–138.

Stoffelen, A., & Vanneste, D. (2017). Tourism and cross-border regional development: Insights in European contexts. *European Planning Studies*, 25(6), 1013–1033.

Stoffelen, A., & Vanneste, D. (2019). Commodification of contested borderscapes for tourism development. In A. Paasi, E.K. Prokkola, J. Saarinen, & K. Zimmerbauer (eds) *Borderless worlds for whom? Ethics, moralities and mobilities*, pp. 139–153. London: Routledge.

Tambovceva, T., Atstaja, D., Tereshina, M., Uvarova, I., & Livina, A. (2020). Sustainability challenges and drivers of cross-border greenway tourism in rural areas. *Sustainability*, 12(15), 5927.

Timothy, D.J. (2001). *Tourism and political boundaries*. London: Routledge.

Timothy, D.J. (2021). *Tourism in European microstates and dependencies: Geopolitics, scale and resource limitations*. Wallingford: CABI.

Timothy, D.J., & Boyd, S.W. (2015). *Tourism and trails: Cultural, ecological and management issues*. Bristol: Channel View Publications.

Timothy, D.J., & Saarinen, J. (2013). Cross-border co-operation and tourism in Europe. In C. Costa, E. Panyik, & D. Buhalis (eds) *Trends in European tourism planning and organisation*, pp. 64–74. Bristol: Channel View Publications.

Timothy, D.J., Saarinen, J., & Viken, A. (2016). Tourism issues and international borders in the Nordic Region. *Scandinavian Journal of Hospitality and Tourism*, 16(1), 1–13.

Timothy, D.J., & Teye, V.B. (2004). Political boundaries and regional cooperation in tourism. In A.A. Lew, C.M. Hall, & A.M. Williams (eds) *A companion to tourism*, pp. 584–595. London: Blackwell.

Wachowiak. H. (2006). Introduction. In H. Wachowiak (ed). *Tourism and borders: Contemporary issues, policies and international research*, pp. 1–6. Aldershot: Ashgate.

Weidenfeld, A. (2013). Tourism and cross border regional innovation systems. *Annals of Tourism Research*, 42, 191–213.

Więckowski, M. (in press). How border tripoints offer opportunities for transboundary tourism development. *Tourism Geographies*. https://doi.org/10.1080/14616688.2021.1878268

Więckowski, M., & Cerić, D. (2016). Evolving tourism on the Baltic Sea coast: Perspectives on change in the Polish maritime borderland. *Scandinavian Journal of Hospitality and Tourism*, 16(1), 98–111.

Więckowski, M., & Timothy, D.J. (2021). Tourism and an evolving international boundary: Bordering, debordering and rebordering on Usedom Island, Poland-Germany. *Journal of Destination Marketing & Management*, 22, 100647.

Williams, E., & van der Velde, M. (2005). Borders for a new Europe: Between history and new challenges. *Journal of Borderlands Studies*, 20(2), 1–11.

Zaiotti, R. (2011). *Cultures of border control: Schengen and the evolution of European borders*. Chicago: University of Chicago Press.

# 27
# TOURISM IN PROTECTED AREAS AND TRANSBOUNDARY PARKS FOR PEACE

*Alon Gelbman and Rachel Schweitzer*

## Introduction

Rarely coinciding with biotic boundaries, geopolitical boundaries frequently divide ecosystems, partitioning the natural habitats of animal and plant species, and creating environmental problems. Environmental issues associated with geopolitical borders include biodiversity reduction, ecosystem fragmentation, and the destruction of habitat through human construction, road services, and military operations in border areas (Best, 2021; Cunningham, 2012; Pouya & Pouya, 2018). Ecosystems divided by man-made boundaries can be influenced by many different policies, legal and institutional structures, management and governance regimes, and various social, cultural, and economic systems, as well as by complex relations between countries. To overcome these differences, transboundary conservation is intended to encourage cooperative work across international frontiers to achieve shared conservation goals (Vasilijević et al., 2015).

The unrestrained nature of ecosystems encourages the development of transboundary protected areas. Conservation across borders manifests in several different ways and results in a number of institutional entities, including transboundary protected areas (TBPAs), transfrontier conservation areas (TFCAs), transfrontier parks (TFPs), and peace parks (Mearns, 2012), most of which share similar goals related to conservation and protecting biodiversity. We mostly use the term TBPAs when referring to transfrontier conservation areas. These conservation areas have been a significant element of nature-based tourism in many parts of the globe since the 1920s, with large expanses of land made available for this purpose (Hoogendoorn, Kelso & Sinthumule, 2019). Bi-national or multinational parks are established in many border areas to protect unique ecological and cultural heritage systems. Some of these parks are highly attractive to tourists, as is illustrated by a few outstanding examples, including the Waterton-Glacier International Peace Park (USA–Canada), Iguazu Falls (Argentina–Brazil), and Victoria Falls (Zambia–Zimbabwe). Some of these transborder parks are branded with UNESCO's World Heritage Site status, which adds an element of importance and global visibility and may increase their desirability among many potential tourists.

Although the first and foremost incentive for establishing TBPAs is ecological conservation, they fulfill additional roles. The benefits and objectives, beyond environmental protection, include enabling sustainable socioeconomic growth through ecotourism, strengthening cooperation and peace between countries, boosting political stability, facilitating sociocultural integration, and encouraging the economic and political empowerment of local communities (Hanks, 2003; Mearns, 2012; Sandwith et al., 2001; Trogisch & Fletcher, 2022; Vasilijević et al., 2015). Within this phenomenon the concept of "peace parks" (or parks for peace) has developed—transboundary biodiversity and wildlife conservation areas (and often cultural areas or monuments) that are jointly managed by two or more countries with the explicit aim of strengthening international relations and supporting the sustainable economic development of communities in the area (Van Amerom & Büscher, 2005; Walters, 2015).

This chapter details the terminology related to conservation areas that straddle two or more international borders and describes and analyzes two major aspects of TBPAs and tourism: borderland nature and community-based tourism, as well as the geopolitical context vis-à-vis the peace park function. The chapter also presents the development of the TBPA concept over time.

## The Development of Transboundary Protected Areas

Parks and nature preserves are often found adjacent to, or within, border areas because these frontier spaces are isolated, sparsely populated, located at the periphery of the state, and largely untouched by physical development and urbanization. In many borderlands, border tourism attractions develop because of their proximity to unique natural resources and the borderline, which provides many tourism advantages. The International Union for Conservation of Nature (IUCN) defines TBPAs as protected areas that span the boundaries of multiple countries in which all forms of physical boundaries are removed, ostensibly allowing the free movement of people and animals within the area, although most TBPAs still do not have completely open borders, even within their transnational contexts. In most cases, tourists must undergo border-crossing procedures in transfrontier protected areas (Albrecht, 2010; Danforth, 2020; Timothy, 2000), and international boundaries within parks and conservation areas are usually maintained to prevent unauthorized border crossings (Gelbman, 2010).

The first initiatives to establish TBPAs in North America and Europe date to the 1930s. In 1924, Poland and Czechoslovakia signed The Krakow Protocol; however, the agreement was only implemented in 1932, when Europe's first TBPA was established between the two countries (Więckowski, 2013, 2018). Earlier the same year, Waterton-Glacier International Peace Park, considered to be the first TPBA in the world, was established between two existing adjacent national parks in Canada and the United States to symbolize the peaceful relations between the two countries, to strengthen their friendship, and to protect natural ecosystems that spill across their common border (Gelbman, 2010; Timothy, 2000; Vasilijević et al., 2015).

In Africa, the origins of transboundary conservation can be traced to colonial times, when Albert National Park (now Virunga National Park) was created in 1925 to protect mountain gorilla populations in what was Belgian Congo (now the Democratic Republic of the Congo). Today the park is linked with protected areas across the border in Rwanda and Uganda to form the trinational Virunga Conservation Area (Trogisch & Fletcher, 2022). Since the official ending of apartheid in South Africa in 1994 and the warming of relations with neighboring countries, TBPAs have been recognized as a tool to promote economic and political cooperation in southern Africa (Mearns, 2012; Van Amerom, 2002). The Kgalagadi Transfrontier Park was launched in 2000 between Botswana and South Africa under a unified system of control and management, with the aim of protecting wildlife and facilitating the free movement of tourists within the boundaries of a single park (Hanks, 2003; Vasilijević et al., 2015). Once tourists clear border formalities on the edges of the park, they are generally permitted to wander back and forth across the international border within the limits of the TFP.

Since the 1980s there has been a rapid expansion of transboundary conservation entities throughout the world, spurred in large part by the Ramsar Convention, the World Wildlife Fund (WWF), and UNESCO's World Heritage program (Table 27.1). This growth also parallels a similar growth of designated protected areas at the national level. The trend can be attributed to people and governments recognizing the benefits of transboundary conservation and the monumentalization of remarkable natural areas by the organizations noted above. In 1988, the IUCN compiled the first global inventory of "border parks", identifying 59 TBPAs. By the start of the twenty-first century, this number had grown to 169, involving 666 individual protected areas (Sandwith et al., 2001). Today, there are more than 200 transboundary conservation initiatives and projects in which cooperation ranges from informal agreements to government-to-government treaties (Vasilijević et al., 2015) (Table 27.1).

*Table 27.1* Examples of Recently Established Nature-based Transboundary Protected Areas

| Protected Area | Borderland Location | Emphasis or Theme | Year Established |
|---|---|---|---|
| Bialowieza Forest | Poland & Belarus | UNESCO World Heritage Site. Home to the European bison and a large section of European Plain primeval forest. | 2014 |
| Lago Titicaca | Bolivia & Peru | Transborder Ramsar wetland. High-altitude lake with diverse aquatic species and home to a unique culture. | 1998 |
| East Carpathian Biosphere Reserve | Poland, Slovakia & Ukraine | Encompasses national parks in all three countries, focusing on the forested mountain landscapes in the Carpathian range. | 1992 |
| Maloti-Drakensberg Park | Lesotho & South Africa | Joins two national parks into a cross-boundary TBPA in the Drakensburg Mountains. Many endemic species and unique montane ecosystems. | 2001 |
| Volcán Tacaná Biosphere Reserve | Guatemala & Mexico | UNESCO Biosphere Reserve to protect biodiversity in the volcanic mountain environment. | 2006 |
| Great Limpopo Transfrontier Park | Mozambique, South Africa & Zimababwe | Connects national parks in all three countries. Is home to many animals such as giraffes, leopards, lions, hyenas, elephants, rhinos, and wildebeests. | 2000 |
| Landscapes of Dauria | Mongolia & Russia | A UNESCO World Heritage Site straddling the international boundary comprised of a biosphere reserve in Mongolia and a nature reserve in Russia. Both sides protect the steppe grasslands of the region. | 2017 |
| Danube Delta | Romania & Ukraine | UNESCO Biosphere Reserve to protect the Danube wetland and its unique ecosystem and species diversity. | 1998 |
| Kluane/Wrangell–St. Elias/Glacier Bay/Tatshenshini-Alsek | Canada & USA | UNESCO World Heritage Site comprised of a national park and a provincial park in Canada and two national parks in the US. Known for its glaciers, icefields, and animal species. | 1994 |

(*Continued*)

*Table 27.1* (Continued)

| Protected Area | Borderland Location | Emphasis or Theme | Year Established |
|---|---|---|---|
| Mount Nimba Strict Nature Reserve | Côte d'Ivoire & Guinea | A UNESCO site that covers much of the Nimba Mountains, which are home to a rich array of endemic species of flora and fauna. | 1981 |
| Sangha Trinational | Cameroon, Central African Republic, & Congo | A UNESCO World Heritage Site that connects three contiguous national parks in the tropical rainforest. Best known for its vast tropical biodiversity. | 2012 |
| Heart of Borneo | Brunei, Indonesia & Malaysia | A WWF-sponsored endeavor to connect protected areas and national parks in all three countries to draw attention to Borneo's endemic species. | 2007 |
| Caves of Aggtelek Karst and Slovak Karst | Hungary & Slovakia | A UNESCO World Heritage Site focused on a system of more than 700 karst caves along the Hungarian-Slovak border. | 1995 |
| Monte San Giorgio | Italy & Switzerland | A UNESCO World Heritage Site focused on fossilized marine life from the Triassic period. | 2003 |
| Kavango–Zambezi Transfrontier Conservation Area | Angola, Botswana, Namibia, Zambia & Zimbabwe | The effort aims to manage the Kavango Zambezi river ecosystem sustainably and to develop tourism to benefit the region's communities. | 2011 |

*Source:* compiled from multiple sources.

## Definitions of Transboundary Conservation Areas and Parks

Several terms are often used in the literature for discussing the phenomenon of conservation areas in the geopolitical borderlands of two or more countries. As noted earlier, these include TFCAs, TBPAs, TFPs, and peace parks. Although these terms are frequently used interchangeably, there are subtle differences between them (Wolmer, 2003). Timothy (2000, p. 265) used the term "international park" for parks that "require some degree of cross-border coordination, which is necessary for sustainable transfrontier management". International parks are in high demand as tourist attractions and their management must coordinate sustainable management practices, resource use and protection, and cross-frontier partnerships. The impacts of tourism development in international parks are economic, political, and cultural, with fundamental aspects of nature conservation included.

Timothy (1999) identifies three types of international parks based on their spatial relationship to the international boundary and their management structures (Figure 27.1). The first type includes parks that lie directly on the border itself and usually function as one entity. An example is the International Peace Garden on the USA–Canada boundary. The second type includes parks that lie entirely in one country but are adjacent to the border, like the Roosevelt Campobello International Park (USA–Canada). The third type is two contiguous protected areas lying adjacent to each other on opposite sides of the border and functioning as individual and separate entities, but usually with close communication and sometimes joint training, firefighting efforts, data sharing, and technology transfers. They can also be considered an international park if they are jointly managed and financed by both adjacent countries.

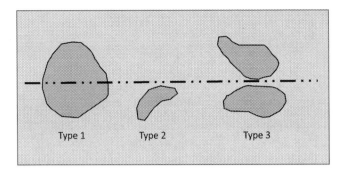

*Figure 27.1* Three spatial types of international parks (after Timothy, 1999).

Waterton-Glacier on the USA–Canada border is a commonly cited example of a type 3 international park, managed by each nation's park service but sharing common goals and collaborative efforts. This last type is typical of most international parks and TBPAs around the world.

The terminology used when referring to transboundary conservation areas can vary from region to region. For example, the Southern African Development Community (SADC) defines a transfrontier conservation area as "the area or component of a large ecological region that straddles the boundaries of two or more countries, encompassing one or more protected areas as well as multiple resource use areas" (Southern African Development Community, 1999, p. 4). Griffin et al. (1999), in their study of transboundary natural resource management areas in southern Africa, point out that TBCAs and TFCAs are both based on the concept of some aspect of shared environmental management between nations. The terms are used interchangeably in the region and in the literature, with little or no real distinction between them. On the other hand, Singh (1999) observes that while TBCAs relate to areas that span well-defined borders and are created to achieve the conservation of biodiversity and/or cultural heritage, and provide economic benefits, TFCAs span regions where the boundaries have not been agreed upon and, in addition to conservation, they are often created to heal tensions related to disputed borderlands. Van Amerom (2002) distinguishes between a "park" that fulfills one primary land-use, namely wildlife conservation, and an "area" that combines different components and multiple land-use areas (see also Van Amerom & Büscher, 2005).

In 2015, the Transboundary Conservation Specialist Group of IUCN's World Commission on Protected Areas (WCPA) prepared guidelines for approaches and best practices of transboundary conservation. The publication tried to standardize the terminology relating to transboundary conservation and proposed the following definitions of three types of such areas:

- Type 1: TBPA—a clearly defined geographical space which consists of protected areas that are ecologically connected across one or more international boundaries and involves some form of cooperation.
- Type 2: Transboundary Conservation Landscape and/or Seascape (TBCL/S)—an ecologically connected area that sustains ecological processes and crosses one or more international boundaries, and which includes both protected areas and multiple resource use areas, and involves some form of cooperation.
- Type 3: Transboundary Migration Conservation Area (TBMCA)—wildlife habitats in two or more countries that are necessary to sustain populations of migratory species and involve some form of cooperation (Vasilijević et al., 2015).

The WCPA proposes a special category that can be applied to any type of TBCA: "parks for peace", which is a special designation and dedicated to the promotion, celebration, and/or commemoration of peace and cooperation. The use of the term "parks for peace" rather than "peace park" emphasizes the international boundary context of the park, as opposed to urban parks or commemorative monuments and battlefields that may be labeled a "peace park" but are located away from the international borderlands. This definition of "parks for peace" includes their various purposes. They may celebrate the endurance and commemoration of peace in a region; they may help reinforce peace and cooperation and improve relationships between partners through cooperative work; and they can promote peace at some point in the future (Gelbman, 2019). The IUCN WCPA also noted that, in practice, there is no significant difference in meaning between the terms "transboundary", "transfrontier", or "transborder" (Vasilijević et al., 2015). These terms and the terms "peace park" and "park for peace" are used interchangeably in this chapter.

## Borderland Nature and Community-based Tourism Perspectives

Transboundary parks encompass a variety of conservation locations and land tenures, from communal lands to wildlife management areas, and multiple resource uses by the local communities. Their overall aim is to conserve biodiversity while promoting tourism, local economic opportunities, and regional cohesiveness through collaboration (Wynberg, 2002). Researchers have focused on the link between protected areas or peace parks and the economic development of rural communities in close proximity to them (Hanks, 2003; Mearns, 2012; Snyman, 2014).

One of the ways to implement this connection is through community-based tourism, which provides opportunities for the local communities to receive significant benefits for poverty relief and improves quality of life (Hanks, 2003; Mearns, 2012). Community-based tourism encourages poor and marginalized citizens to participate in decision-making, and managing and providing activities and services in their area (Mearns, 2012; Timothy, 2007). The advantages of community-based tourism include empowering local communities to take control over their land and resources, the acquisition of skills necessary for their own development, and providing incentives to ensure a respectful coexistence between the rural communities and conservation areas (Mearns, 2012). Thus, participatory community-based forms of tourism are especially suited to border regions, which tend to be less stable, more neglected by national governments, and less affluent than in national core areas (Bressan, 2017; Goodhand, 2018; House, 1980).

In this context, TBPAs and cross-border conservation provide the opportunity for community-based tourism as a way to utilize existing natural resources for the benefit of local communities, without depleting these resources (Mearns, 2012). Ecotourism can help reduce poverty by allowing local communities to receive economic benefits from conservation, both directly through employment, and indirectly as suppliers of goods and services (e.g., farm produce). It can also assist them in conserving their natural resources to maintain or enhance other livelihood options (Nyaupane & Poudel, 2011; Snyman, 2014). The potential of tourism to generate benefits for the poor in natural rural areas stems from four main conditions: participation of stakeholders and businesses, opportunities for innovation and entrepreneurship, dependence on natural capital such as wildlife and cultural capital such as heritage, and the creation of jobs (Spenceley & Goodwin, 2007). These benefits can be better assured through sustainable tourism management, considering the participation of local communities in decision-making processes (Hoogendoorn et al., 2019; Timothy, 2007).

The parks for peace initiative in Southern Africa links the prosperity of rural communities through tourism with the goals of biodiversity conservation (Ferreira, 2004; Mearns, 2012; Scovronick & Turpie, 2009). The Peace Park Foundation (PPF) was established in South

Africa in 1997 to help facilitate and ensure these principles. The foundation now has offices in several developed countries, including Germany, the Netherlands, Sweden, Switzerland, the United Kingdom, the United States, Australia, and New Zealand, whose main responsibilities are fundraising for PPF to help its conservation and community development goals in southern Africa. Mearns (2012) highlights a reciprocal connection between community-based tourism and international peace parks: peace parks and conservation areas have the potential to attract tourists, which in turn creates economic and social opportunities that benefit the local communities. In turn, existing community-based tourism ventures may incentivize the establishment of parks for peace by providing existing tourism infrastructure in close proximity to the proposed peace park (Spenceley & Goodwin, 2007).

Tourism has the potential to grow more effectively at jointly managed TBPAs than if each protected area continues to operate separately on its own side of the border. Sharing administrative resources across international boundaries may potentially reduce national budgets for conservation activities and free up funds for other purposes (Hanks, 2003; Timothy, 1999). Peace park advocates argue that these ventures can expand the national economy, especially in peripheral areas, thus improving the well-being of citizens and cooperation between governments in managing shared ecosystems. However, at times collaboration has led to increased competition, mistrust, and mutual denigration (Pisk, 2021; Trogisch & Fletcher, 2022).

The objectives of TBPAs attract the interest of many stakeholders, including national and provincial governments, local communities, NGOs, and the private sector. In most cases, all stakeholder interests are perceived as complementary, thereby creating a "win–win" situation and a unified social force. Yet in reality, the involvement of a wide range of actors and interests can lead to potential conflict, power struggles, competition, and mistrust between parties (Trogisch & Fletcher, 2022; Van Amerom, 2002). Likewise, differences in conservation laws and practices, as well as different administrative cultures on opposite sides of a border, often erect barriers to communication and collaboration, even when conservation is the primary goal—for conservation may mean different things to different people or organizations. Peace parks may also heighten inequalities between states and communities, giving preference to "higher political priorities" over the good of the local communities (Van Amerom & Büscher, 2005).

## Geopolitical Aspects and the Place of Peace Parks

Transboundary parks are protected areas that are artificially divided by national borders, thus creating environmental and geopolitical management challenges. Parks for peace are TBPAs or other monument areas that encourage cooperation between countries which once were, or still are, suffering from conflict or other types of contention (Trogisch & Fletcher, 2022). An example of this is the Island of Peace monument at the border of Israel and Jordan at Naharayim (Gelbman & Maoz, 2012). However, some peace parks are developed between benevolent neighbors in an effort to commemorate their long-term peaceful relations (e.g., the International Peace Garden and the Peace Arch Park, both on the USA–Canada border).

The official term "parks for peace" first came into use in the 1980s when the IUCN started to promote peace parks on international borders (Van Amerom & Büscher, 2005). The parks encourage regulated tourism, sustainable development, and goodwill between neighboring countries (Kliot, 2002; Van Amerom & Büscher, 2005; Więckowski, 2013). The promotion of tourism in shared conservation areas may provide an incentive for cooperation between formerly hostile neighboring countries (Trogisch & Fletcher, 2022). One of the conditions for sustainable tourism development in transboundary areas is the mutual interest of residents on either side of the border in cross-border attractions, regardless of the contentious politics or level of economic development (Manakov, Kondrateva & Terenina, 2020). The potential of TBPAs to promote and strengthen peace and cooperation between countries is necessary for sustainable economic development and foreign investment in the area (Hanks, 2003).

Since the establishment of the Waterton-Glacier International Peace Park (Canada–USA) in 1932, transboundary peace park initiatives have increased significantly (Vasilijević et al., 2015) (Table 27.2). TBPAs involve a unique level of international cooperation, especially with regard

*Table 27.2* Examples of international peace parks established to commemorate or encourage peaceful relations and nature conservation

| Peace Park* | Borderland Location | Emphasis or Theme | Year Established |
|---|---|---|---|
| International Peace Garden | Canada, USA | Continuing peaceful relations between the US and Canada; manicured botanical garden | 1932 |
| Greater Mapungubwe Transfrontier Conservation Area | Botswana, South Africa, Zimbabwe | Protecting wildlife, cultural landscapes, and promoting peace between neighbors. | 2006 |
| Island of Peace | Israel, Jordan | Jordanian sovereign territory on its side of the Jordan River but with free access to Israeli farmers and visitors until 2019. | 1994 |
| European Green Belt | Norway, Finland, Russia, Estonia, Latvia, Lithuania, Poland, Germany, Czechia, Slovakia, Austria, Hungary, Slovenia, Croatia, Italy, Serbia, Montenegro, Kosovo, Bulgaria, Romania, North Macedonia, Albania, Greece, Turkey | A peace park initiative for nature conservation and the protection of the relict border landscapes along the former Iron Curtain. Commemorates the collapse of communism and the opening of the Eastern Bloc countries. | 2003 |
| Waterton-Glacier International Peace Park | Canada-USA | A UNESCO World Heritage Site joins two national parks with a collaborative management framework. It works to protect the Rocky Mountain environment and commemorate peaceful relations between neighboring countries. | 1932 |
| Balkans Peace Park | Albania, Kosovo, Montenegro | A symbol of peace and collaboration between the three countries working to protect their environment and provide tourism economic development opportunities. | 2006 (proposed) |

*Source:* compiled from multiple sources.

* Several of the TBPAs in Table 1 are designated peace parks, and the term is sometimes used interchangeably with TBPA.

to the removal of physical barriers and the freer movement of tourists across international borders (Hanks, 2003). Mutually good political relations between neighboring countries have the advantage of easing border crossings and allowing communities on both sides to profit economically from income generated as tourists cross from the neighboring country or come from further afield and visit both sides. In addition, tourists can be exposed to the natural environment more holistically, and for some, the border crossing experience within the shared park may be a highlight of the visit (Gelbman, 2010).

The European Green Belt is a type of peace park that crosses Europe along the route of the former Iron Curtain (Figure 27.2). This is an example of transboundary cooperation in nature conservation, geopolitical peace, and sustainable tourism development. The shared cooperative management of the parks and green spaces along the corridor demonstrates harmony between human activities and the natural environment (Gelbman, 2017). These parks also symbolize the heritage and transformation of the former Iron Curtain border from one of hostility and separation to one of cooperation, friendship, and unity and are an expression of integration and the process of debordering (Gelbman, 2017; Timothy, 1999).

Peace parks have been identified as an important tool for promoting the African renaissance dream and cross-border cooperation, as well as contributing to the reduction of poverty in marginalized border regions through ecotourism (Hanks, 2003; Van Amerom & Büscher, 2005). Van Amerom and Büscher (2005) suggest offering conflict mediation if necessary to facilitate cooperation between neighboring countries in peace parks and to overcome political difficulties.

*Figure 27.2* An ecosystem exhibition of the Russian-Norwegian transboundary cooperation in the Barents region as part of the European Green Belt along the former Iron Curtain.

(Photo: A. Gelbman)

In 2000, an agreement was signed to establish the 35,000 km² Great Limpopo Transfrontier Park as a peace park and protected area that encompasses parts of Mozambique, South Africa, and Zimbabwe. The aims of the park are to renew ecological systems and ensure the free movement of wild animals, encourage the preservation and viable use of natural resources, and develop nature-based tourism to create employment and serve as an economic lever for the indigenous population. It also brings together different ethnic groups and helps them live as good neighbors in greater harmony. All this takes place despite the complex geopolitical realities of international conflicts in the region, with fears of political violence, refugees, arms smuggling, and the spread of diseases (Aeby, 2018; Derman & Kaarhus, 2013; Kliot, 2002). Some of the border fences within the Great Limpopo have been dismantled, allowing more freedom for animals to roam between countries, and a new border checkpoint has been established within the reserve on the Mozambique–South Africa border to facilitate better tourist access to other parts of the park (Büscher & Ramutsindela, 2016).

Peace parks may be an optimal example of environmental, social, and sustainable tourism cooperation in shared border areas. The actual process of initiating and planning peace parks and TBPAs requires strengthening transborder political ties as well as readiness on the part of governments and goodwill among stakeholders on both sides of the border. Unfortunately, these are often lacking in transnational contexts, which has been shown to be a major barrier to cross-border cooperation in tourism and environmental settings (Chaderopa, 2013; Gelbman & Timothy, 2019).

However, the fact that in recent years new peace parks have been declared and established in various parts of the world is proof of the success and relevance of TBPAs for introducing and implementing environmental and peace values as well as cooperation between neighboring countries, with sustainable tourism playing a central role (Gelbman, 2010) (Table 27.2). Scholars have referred to tourism's potential to upgrade low-level diplomacy in post-conflict environments so that governments can begin to rebuild international ties (Butler & Mao, 1996; Vitic & Ringer, 2008) as well as reinvigorate a nation's economy (Anson, 1999). Tourism has also been recognized as a tool for promoting people-to-people relations (Karki, 2020). The two tracks of diplomacy suggested by Kim and Crompton (1990) for North and South Korea's reunification reflect a parallel attitude. The first diplomatic track is described as the official level, government-to-government relations, while the second is an unofficial track of people-to-people relations through tourism.

## Conclusion

Transboundary protected areas are a phenomenon that combines aspects of nature conservation, sustainable economic development, and the promotion of peaceful relations (Hanks, 2003; Mearns, 2012; Sandwith et al., 2001; Trogisch & Fletcher, 2022; Vasilijević et al., 2015). Since the establishment of the first TBPAs in the 1920s, conservation areas and transboundary parks have become popular destinations within nature-based tourism (Chiutsi & Saarinen, 2017; Hoogendoorn et al., 2019; Lekgau & Tichaawa, 2021; Moswete, Thapa & Darley, 2020). Ongoing preoccupation with the subject has led to the coining of various terms pertaining to transboundary conservation such as TFCA, TBPA, TFP, international park, and peace park, yet researchers agree that there are no significant distinctions in meaning between these, although "parks for peace" and "peace parks" sometimes have a connotation of conflict resolution or commemorating a long history of cross-border benevolence (Ali, 2007). Almost all TBPAs are referred to as peace parks because of the efforts required to work between governments on an international level with compromises and collaboration on issues that affect multiple countries simultaneously.

*Figure 27.3* The interaction between sustainable tourism and community, environment and peace diplomacy.

The TBPA concept plays an important role in addressing both environmental and geopolitical conditions that challenge cross-border collaboration. The idea highlights the need for joint management and cooperation between adjacent states to address the needs of shared ecosystems and local populations by providing economic and social benefits and reducing poverty on national peripheries (Hanks, 2003; Mearns, 2012; Snyman, 2014; Wynberg, 2002). Tourism has a central and significant place in these processes for community-based development and for warming peaceful relations and cooperation (Figure 27.3).

Figure 27.3 demonstrates the interaction between tourism and the environment, the community, and peace diplomacy. Nature-based tourism may provide an incentive to preserve natural resources in a conservation area and to remove boundaries to ensure the free movement of wildlife and to ease the crossing procedures for tourists. Sustainable tourism can contribute to the prosperity of peripheral rural areas and indigenous people by strengthening the economic potential of TBPAs in providing employment opportunities and other benefits (Hanks, 2003; Mearns, 2012). Nature-based tourism can also attract new initiatives and entrepreneurs (Spenceley & Goodwin, 2007), which may be crucial in the socioeconomic development of borderlands. Joint management of TBPAs and shared interest in the economic advantages of tourism have the potential to encourage peaceful relations between neighboring countries (Kliot, 2002; Van Amerom & Büscher, 2005) and motivate cooperation between formerly hostile neighbors (Trogisch & Fletcher, 2022) by emphasizing their commonalities instead of their differences.

## References

Aeby, M. (2018). *Peace and security challenges in southern Africa: Governance deficits and lacklustre regional conflict management*. Uppsala, Sweden: Nordiska Afrikainstitutet.

Albrecht, M. (2010). Transboundary governance of the Curonian Spit World Heritage Site. *Journal of Environmental Planning and Management*, 53(6), 725–742.

Ali, S.H. (2007). *Peace parks: Conservation and conflict resolution*. Cambridge, MA: MIT Press.

Anson, C. (1999). Planning for peace: The role of tourism in the aftermath of violence. *Journal of Travel Research*, 38(1), 57–61.

Best, S. (2021). The costs of a wall: The impact of pseudo-security policies on communities, wildlife, and ecosystems on the US-Mexico border. In N. Khazaal & N. Almiron (eds) *Like an animal: Critical animal studies approaches to borders, displacement, and othering*, pp. 255–280. Leiden: Brill.

Bressan, G. (2017). Power, mobility and the economic vulnerability of borderlands. *Journal of Borderlands Studies*, 32(3), 361–377.

Büscher, B., & Ramutsindela, M. (2016). Green violence: Rhino poaching and the war to save southern Africa's peace parks. *African Affairs*, 115(458), 1–22.

Butler, R.W., & Mao, B. (1996). Conceptual and theoretical implications of tourism between partitioned states. *Asia Pacific Journal of Tourism Research*, 1(1), 25–34.

Chaderopa, C. (2013). Cross-border cooperation in transboundary conservation-development initiatives in southern Africa: The role of borders of the mind. *Tourism Management*, 39, 50–61.

Chiutsi, S., & Saarinen, J. (2017). Local participation in transfrontier tourism: Case of Sengwe community in Great Limpopo Transfrontier Conservation Area, Zimbabwe. *Development Southern Africa*, 34(3), 260–275.

Cunningham, H. (2012). Permeabilities, ecology and geopolitical boundaries. In T.M. Wilson & H. Donnan (eds) *A companion to border studies*, pp. 371–386. Chichester: Wiley.

Danforth, L.M. (2020). Three countries, two lakes, one future: The Prespa Lakes and the signing of the Prespa Agreement. In V.P. Neofotistos (ed.) *Macedonia and identity politics after the Prespa Agreement*, pp. 28–50. London: Routledge.

Derman, B., & Kaarhus, R. (eds) (2013). *In the shadow of a conflict: Crisis in Zimbabwe and its effects in Mozambique, South Africa and Zambia*. Harare: Weaver Press.

Ferreira, S. (2004). Problems associated with tourism development in southern Africa: The case of transfrontier conservation areas. *GeoJournal*, 60(3), 301–310.

Gelbman, A. (2010). Border tourism as a space of presenting and symbolizing peace. In O. Moufakkir & I. Kelly (eds) *Tourism progress and peace*, pp. 83–89. Wallingford: CABI.

Gelbman, A. (2017). The heritage of geopolitical borders as peace tourism attractions. In D. Walters, D. Laven, & P. Davis (eds) *Heritage and peacebuilding*, pp. 191–204. Woodbridge: The Boydell Press.

Gelbman, A. (2019). Tourism, peace, and global stability. In D.J. Timothy (ed) *Handbook of globalisation and tourism*, pp. 149–160. Cheltenham: Edward Elgar.

Gelbman, A., & Maoz, D.T. (2012). Island of peace or island of war: Tourist guiding. *Annals of Tourism Research*, 39(1), 108–133.

Gelbman, A., & Timothy, D.J. (2019). Differential tourism zones on the western Canada-US border. *Current Issues in Tourism*, 22(6), 682–704.

Goodhand, J. (2018). *The centrality of the margins: The political economy of conflict and development in borderlands*. Batticaloa, Sri Lanka: Borderlands Asia.

Griffin, J., Cumming, D., Metcalfe, S., t'Sas-Rolfes, M., Singh, J., Chonguiça, E., Rowan, M., & Oglethorpe, J. (1999). *Study on the development of transboundary natural resource management areas in southern Africa*. Washington, DC: Biodiversity Support Program.

Hanks, J. (2003). Transfrontier conservation areas (TFCAs) in southern Africa: Their role in conserving biodiversity, socioeconomic development and promoting a culture of peace. *Journal of Sustainable Forestry*, 17(1–2), 127–148.

Hoogendoorn, G., Kelso, C., & Sinthumule, I. (2019). Tourism in the Great Limpopo Transfrontier Park: A review. *African Journal of Hospitality, Tourism and Leisure*, 8(5), 1–15.

House, J.W. (1980). The frontier zone: A conceptual problem for policy makers. *International Political Science Review*, 1(4), 456–477.

Karki, N. (2020). Tourism: A tool for track-two diplomacy in promoting people-to-people relations between Nepal and China. *Journal of APF Command and Staff College*, 3(1), 49–71.

Kim, Y., & Crompton J. (1990). Role of tourism in unifying the two Koreas. *Annals of Tourism Research* 17, 353–366.

Kliot, N. (2002). Transborder peace parks: The political geography of cooperation and conflict in borderlands. In C. Schofield, D. Newman, A. Drysdale, & J. Allison-Brown (eds) *The razor's edge: International boundaries and political geography*, pp. 407–437. London: Kluwer.

Lekgau, R.J., & Tichaawa, T.M. (2021). Community participation in wildlife tourism in the Kgalagadi Transfrontier Park. *Tourism Review International*, 25(2–3), 139–155.

Manakov, A.G., Kondrateva, S.V., & Terenina, N.K. (2020). Development of cross-border tourist and recreational regions on the Karelian section of the Russian-Finnish border. *Baltic Region*, 12(3), 140–152.

Mearns, K. (2012). Community-based tourism and peace parks benefit local communities through conservation in southern Africa. *Acta Academica*, 44(2), 70–87.

Moswete, N., Thapa, B., & Darley, W.K. (2020). Local communities' attitudes and support towards the Kgalagadi Transfrontier Park in southwest Botswana. *Sustainability*, 12(4), 1524.

Nyaupane, G.P., & Poudel, S. (2011). Linkages among biodiversity, livelihood, and tourism. *Annals of Tourism Research*, 38(4), 1344–1366.

Pisk, M. (2021). Challenges of cross-border cooperation: The initiative of trilateral Goričko–Raab–Őrség Nature Park. *Acta Ethnographica Hungarica*, 65(2), 415–432.

Pouya, S., & Pouya, S. (2018). Planning for peace: Introduction of transboundary conservation areas. *Kocaeli Journal of Science and Engineering*, 1(2), 33–41.

Sandwith, T., Shine, C., Hamilton, L., & Sheppard, D. (2001). *Transboundary protected areas for peace and co-operation: Best practice protected area guidelines.* Gland, Switzerland: IUCN.

Scovronick, N.C., & Turpie, J.K. (2009). Is enhanced tourism a reasonable expectation for transboundary conservation? An evaluation of the Kgalagadi Transfrontier Park. *Environmental Conservation*, 36(2), 149–156.

Singh, J. (1999). *Study on the development of transboundary natural resource management areas in southern Africa - global review: Lessons learned.* Washington, DC: Biodiversity Support Program.

Snyman, S. (2014). Assessment of the main factors impacting community members' attitudes towards tourism and protected areas in six southern African countries. *Koedoe*, 56(2), 1–12.

Southern African Development Community (1999). *Protocol on wildlife conservation and law enforcement.* Gabarone: Southern African Development Community.

Spenceley, A., & Goodwin, H. (2007). Nature-based tourism and poverty alleviation: Impacts of private sector and parastatal enterprises in and around Kruger National Park, South Africa. *Current Issues in Tourism*, 10(2–3), 255–277.

Timothy, D.J. (1999). Cross-border partnership in tourism resource management: International parks along the US-Canada border. *Journal of Sustainable Tourism*, 7(3–4), 182–205.

Timothy, D.J. (2000). Tourism and international parks. In R.W. Butler & S.W. Boyd (eds) *Tourism and national parks: Issues and implications*, pp. 263–282. Chichester: Wiley.

Timothy, D.J. (2007). Empowerment and stakeholder participation in tourism destination communities. In A. Church & T. Coles (eds) *Tourism, power and space*, pp. 199–216. London: Routledge.

Trogisch, L., & Fletcher, R. (2022). Fortress tourism: Exploring dynamics of tourism, security and peace around the Virunga Transboundary Conservation Area. *Journal of Sustainable Tourism*, 30(2–3), 352–371.

Van Amerom, M. (2002). National sovereignty & transboundary protected areas in southern Africa. *GeoJournal*, 58(4), 265–273.

Van Amerom, M., & Büscher, B. (2005). Peace parks in southern Africa: Bringers of an African renaissance? *Journal of Modern African Studies*, 43(2), 159–182.

Vasilijević, M., Zunckel, K., McKinney, M., Erg, B., Schoon, M., & Rosen Michel, T. (2015). *Transboundary conservation: A systematic and integrated approach.* Gland, Switzerland: IUCN.

Vitic, A., & Ringer, G. (2008). Branding post-conflict destinations: Recreating Montenegro after the disintegration of Yugoslavia. *Journal of Travel & Tourism Marketing*, 23(2–4), 127–137.

Walters, J.T. (2015). A peace park in the Balkans: Cross-border cooperation and livelihood creation through coordinated environmental conservation. In H. Young & L. Goldman (eds) *Livelihoods, natural resources, and post-conflict peacebuilding*, pp. 179–190. London: Routledge.

Więckowski, M. (2013). Eco-frontier in the mountainous borderlands of Central Europe: The case of Polish border parks. *Journal of Alpine Research | Revue de géographie alpine*, 101(2), 1–13.

Więckowski, M. (2018). Political borders under ecological control on the Polish borderlands. *Geographia Polonica*, 91(1), 127–138.

Wolmer, W. (2003). Transboundary conservation: The politics of ecological integrity in the Great Limpopo Transfrontier Park. *Journal of Southern African Studies*, 29(1), 261–278.

Wynberg, R. (2002). A decade of biodiversity conservation and use in South Africa: Tracking progress from the Rio Earth Summit to the Johannesburg World Summit on Sustainable Development. *South African Journal of Science*, 98(5), 233–243.

# 28

# TRANSFRONTIER ROUTES AND TRAILS

## Cooperation and Scalar Considerations

*Arie Stoffelen*

### Introduction

Routes and trails, used interchangeably in this chapter to refer to circuits, corridors or spatial networks that interconnect certain natural or cultural features (Timothy & Boyd, 2015), have become increasingly popular tourism products throughout the world. They can take the form of themed heritage routes (Cheung, 1999; Hayes & Macleod, 2008; Miles, 2017; Snowball & Courtney, 2010), nature trails (Godtman Kling, Dahlberg, & Wall-Reinius, 2019; Kołodziejczyk, 2019), pilgrimage routes (Hitchner et al., 2019; Olsen & Trono, 2018), rail trails (Stoffelen, 2018; Taylor, 2015) or numerous other formats. They often centre around the use of one specific mode of transportation. Providing a systematic discussion of these tourism products has proven difficult because of the enormous diversity of routes and trails in terms of scale of operations, locations, organizational structures and adopted themes (Hayes & Macleod, 2008; Timothy & Boyd, 2015).

From a user perspective, the main attraction of tourism trails might be the mobility along the trail itself, for example in hiking paths and scenic trails (Quinlan Cutler, Carmichael, & Doherty, 2014; Sykes & Kelly, 2016), or it could be the central nodes where tourist flows concentrate. From a supplier perspective, these points of attraction are linked up in a supply network to reflect the coherence of the destination and the developed theme, to stimulate cross-selling and to increase consumers' length of stay. Food and beverage trails are excellent examples of tourism routes with such a networked organizational structure (e.g., Broadway, 2017; Del Chiappa, Bregoli, & Kim, 2019; Meyer, 2004; Plummer, Telfer, & Hashimoto, 2006; Stoffelen & Vanneste, 2016; Telfer, 2001).

In developing and managing tourism trails, borders almost inevitably come into play (Ryan, Fábos, & Allan, 2006; Więckowski, 2018). Cross-territorial cooperation, for example, between municipalities, is required even for many short-distance trails. While not often conceptualized in such terms, within-country inter-jurisdictional collaboration can and possibly should also be seen as a form of cross-border governance (Stoffelen, Ioannides, & Vanneste, 2017). Inter-jurisdictional collaboration often becomes more challenging for larger projects that cross international borders. Yet paradoxically, routes and trails have also become prime tourism products particularly in international borderlands. Trails are developed across borders but also along borders, with the border itself forming the main axis of the experience (Timothy & Boyd, 2015; Więckowski, in press). In many cases, transnational tourism trails even have the explicit aims of linking different areas and regional tourism products and destinations. This may ultimately lead to cross-border region-building, defined as "the symbolic breaking down of administrative obstacles, dissolving of mental borders and facilitating of shared mindsets" (Stoffelen, 2018, p. 92). With their organization as a spatial network and developed around particular themes, tourism trails increasingly function as a go-to tourism product in places searching for ways to increase cooperation between stakeholders or regions, or to establish a high-profile, place-based thematic offering.

However, there are several challenges to success in cross-border contexts. These include the enormous diversity of spatial scales at which trails are developed, themes, organizational frameworks, financial arrangements and their dependency on bilateral geopolitical relations and daily communications across the border. It is already difficult to succeed in achieving foreseen cross-border bridge-building in tourism in general, let alone in the context of a specific tourism product. There is also a knowledge gap in this regard. Researchers have struggled to build a solid body of knowledge on the operationalization of transfrontier tourism routes and trails, despite widespread practical applications. Little has changed since Timothy, Saarinen and Viken (2016) marked cross-border routes and trails as a topic with plenty of research potential (a call also made earlier by Timothy and Boyd, 2006). This is a field of study that to date remains rather small and fragmented.

The purpose of this chapter is to provide an overview of the scholarly attention to cross-border routes and trails. I pay particular attention to cooperation issues and scalar considerations pertinent to the socio-economic, cultural and geopolitical bridge-building role often strived for with transboundary tourism trails. The first part of the chapter sets the scene by providing a short reflection on the potential of tourism trails for achieving tourism-induced, place-based development, without aiming to provide an all-encompassing review of this literature. This section is followed by a discussion about the rich diversity of cross-border routes and trails. The final discussion focuses on the foreseen benefits of transboundary routes and trails but also the challenges in achieving their success.

## Tourism Trails and Their Development Potential

Considering the supply and demand characteristics outlined briefly in the introduction, tourism routes and trails are often seen as prime instruments for achieving tourism-induced, place-based development (Briedenhann & Wickens, 2004; Timothy, 2018). Several key characteristics comprise the foundations of this development potential. To start, routes and trails are spatially explicit tourism products. Developed as either linear (Lourens, 2007; Ryan et al., 2006; Taylor, 2015) or more interlinked (Cox, 2012; Kołodziejczyk, 2019) connections of suppliers and/or sites, tourism routes and trails provide a backbone along which the spatial behaviour and consumption paths of tourists can be steered. As such, tourism trails have the potential to lengthen the average time spent by tourists in an area and spread out economic benefits throughout the destination, particularly to places or individual sites that otherwise struggle to attract tourists on their own (Hall, 2005; Hayes & Macleod, 2008; Lennon & Harris, 2020; Meyer, 2004; Ritchie & Hall, 1999; Russo & Romagosa, 2010; Stoffelen & Vanneste, 2016). The linear spread of tourism may also be effective in diluting the potential negative effects of intensive tourism development over space and among stakeholders.

Meyer (2004) summarizes this potential of trails to contribute to regional development by referring to three interconnected benefits. Routes can reduce pressure from core areas; disperse income-generating activities into peripheral, under-developed parts of the destination; and increase the overall attractiveness of the destination by making "new" features available to tourists. Sites that might struggle as stand-alone attractions can reach a synergy when packaged into a themed trail (Russo & Romagosa, 2010). This can open up areas for future tourism consumption and economic development, as well as increase the efficiency of investments that are being made anyway. For these reasons, Meyer (2004) argues that tourist trails, while less prevalent in developing countries than in the developed world, could be particularly useful tourism assets in the developing world. This call has been heeded in South Africa, where several trails have been developed, even though important implementation difficulties have also been identified (Briedenhann & Wickens, 2004; Lourens, 2007; Rogerson, 2007).

Different providers and stakeholders need to communicate with each other in at least a basic formal cooperative structure for a tourism trail to be more than just a paper trail/a trail on paper (Rogerson, 2007; Ryan et al., 2006; Taylor, 2015). If organized well, the product lends itself to having an inclusive management structure. Involved stakeholders must cooperate to enable trail development in the first place. Particularly, but not exclusively, for tourism trails with a multi-nodal network structure, where the trail's main attractions consist of specific sites where tourists concentrate, trail development can facilitate information exchange between actors who otherwise would not cooperate and would consider one another as competitors, or as mentioned earlier, may not be commercially viable as tourist attractions on an individual basis (Meyer, 2004; Russo & Romagosa, 2010). If developed inclusively, these networks may provide a framework for local control of tourism development. They may strengthen local empowerment in decision-making and better ensure that tourism-related economic and socio-cultural benefits remain in the local area (Hardy, 2003; Timothy, 2018; Timothy & Boyd, 2015).

However, using a case study of outdoor trails in Sweden, Godtman Kling et al. (2019) found that this dependence on networking and trust in tourism trail development is a chicken and egg situation. On the one hand, trail development, and place-based development flowing from it, depends on cooperation and trust to avoid development and management problems. For example, Plummer et al. (2006) present a case study of an ale trail in Canada that was ultimately cancelled because of competing interests and a lack of trust between actors involved in the trail's supporting partnership. On the other hand, cooperating around trail development and management can also be a first step towards establishing this much-needed trust (Godtman Kling et al., 2019). In this sense, trail development could also facilitate one of the key elements often mentioned to make tourism work for area-inclusive development, namely inclusivity and participation.

Trails can be established utilizing existing or abandoned infrastructure such as disused railway lines (Mundet & Coenders, 2010; Taylor, 2015), towpaths along rivers and canals (Stoffelen, 2018) or historic trade routes and pilgrim paths (Timothy & Boyd, 2015). As such, tourism trail development often does not have to start from scratch, which reduces the complexity of the project and the investments required. By making use of existing infrastructure or historically built connections (labelled "organically evolved routes" by Timothy & Boyd, 2015), potential trail users include both tourists and local residents. Thus, trails contribute to general rural services, leisure activities, sense of place and heritage conservation (Mundet & Coenders, 2010; Snowball & Courtney, 2010; Stoffelen, 2018). Local use may also improve the legitimacy of the tourism project, lower barriers against cooperation and achieve the much-needed trust among involved actors.

*Arie Stoffelen*

# Transfrontier Tourism Routes and Trails: Development in Practice v. Academic Attention

Considering their spatial character and network organizational framework, tourism route and trail development almost always involves dealing with administrative and/or cultural boundaries at different scales. This situation is often approached as an unavoidable complexity (Ryan et al., 2006; Sykes & Kelly, 2016), but tourism routes and trails are regularly developed with explicit regional integration objectives in mind.

While present throughout the globe from local to transcontinental levels, it is not surprising that such purposive cross-border tourism trails (Timothy & Boyd, 2015) are most common in Europe. European cross-border trail development has flourished owing to the large number and high density of international borders, the free movement of people and goods within the Schengen area, and co-funding arrangements in the form of Interreg schemes from the European Union to stimulate cross-border collaboration. Table 28.1 shows that investments in tourism routes in the now finished Interreg IV-a (2007–2014) European co-funding programme are very significant indeed. On a more local level, Badulescu and Badulescu (2017) identify that 14 out of 30 rural tourism projects co-financed by Europe between 2003 and 2014 in the borderlands of Hungary and Romania included tourism trails, including the establishment of 12 new ones. In addition to these short-distance, small-scale, thematic routes that can be found throughout the continent, Europe also has a high density of transnational, long-distance, hiking and cycling trails (Figure 28.1). The most famous of these are: the EuroVelo cycling network, consisting of 17 routes with a combined distance of 45,000 kilometres (to be expanded to 70,000 kilometres) that collectively aim to facilitate and symbolize the European unification process (European Cyclists' Federation, 2020); the Grande Randonnée (GR) hiking network; and the European long-distance paths (E-paths). In parallel, the Council of Europe launched the Cultural Routes of the Council of Europe programme in 1987. This network has grown to 38 European-level routes in 2020. This programme aims to identify pan-European heritage and raise awareness of a European cultural identity, facilitate inter-cultural dialogue, protect the cultural past and use it as a tool for development towards the future, and develop tourism with the same objective (Council of Europe, 2020; Timothy & Saarinen, 2013).

North America also boasts an impressive array of transfrontier thematic recreational routes and trails, including the US National Trails System, the Canadian Heritage Rivers System and several long-distance rail trails and car routes (Timothy & Boyd, 2015). The most well-known international trail is the (International) Appalachian Trail between the United States and Canada. Yet, even this route consists of two separate trails: the Appalachian Trail in the USA and the International Appalachian Trail from the northern end in Maine onwards into Canada. In contrast to Europe, cross-border routes and trails in North America are mostly limited to domestic itineraries (Figure 28.1), owing largely to border security concerns. Examples of particularly iconic ones include Route 66 and the Pacific Crest Trail. However, despite this

*Table 28.1* Share of tourism investments and route and trail investments as part of the 2007-2014 INTERREG IV-a programme in Europe.

| Total programmes | Total budget (approx.) | Total tourism investments (approx.) | Share of tourism | Total route/trail investments (approx.) | Share of routes/trails in tourism investments |
|---|---|---|---|---|---|
| 53 | €7.695.500.000 | €1.050.000.000 | 13.6% | €372.600.000 | 35.5% |

Based on individual programme documents and EU databases.

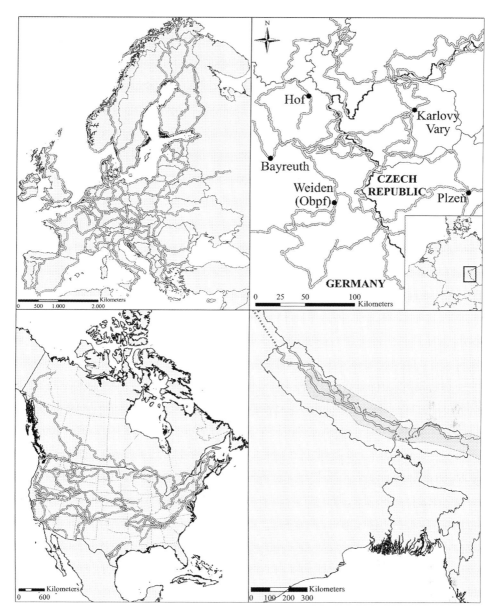

*Figure 28.1* Examples of existing transboundary trails on different continents and at different scales. Top left: EuroVelo cycling routes in Europe (EuroVelo, 2020). Top right: transboundary hiking and cycling trails in the borderlands between the states of Bavaria, Thuringia and Saxony in Germany, and the Czech Republic. Bottom left: interstate routes of the US National Trail System (National Park Service, 2021) and interstate recreational trails in Canada. Bottom right: Existing and proposed ecotourism and cultural tourism trails and corridors in the Himalayas by ICIMOD (2019). Note that these maps do not include all existing tourism routes and trails in the highlighted regions.

emphasis on subnational routes, domestic borders can be very obstructive for developing or managing tourism trails (Ruiz, Lamers, Bush, & Wells, 2019; Ryan et al., 2006; Stoffelen et al., 2017; Sykes & Kelly, 2016). Consequently, conceptualizing within-country trails in terms of borders and cross-border cooperation is beneficial, particularly when administrative areas with a level of autonomy in decision-making such as federal states or provinces are crossed.

Cross-border trails are more pervasive in the Global North than in the Global South. Timothy and Boyd (2015, p. 164) note that "the relative absence of policy analysis and planning documentation within the developing world is perhaps more a reflection that their wider policy actions do not consider routes and trails as part of their wider tourism planning and development strategies". For example, while cross-border tourism activities in Africa are quite intensive, particularly in transfrontier conservation areas where tourism development, livelihood support and nature conservation are all combined, there are still relatively few transnational routes and trails. South Africa serves as the main exception (Briedenhann & Wickens, 2004; Lourens, 2007; Rogerson, 2007). However, this absence is relative. Cross-border routes and trails are not absent in developing countries. In fact, as mentioned earlier, Meyer (2004) posited that transfrontier trail development has a large development potential in the developing world. This statement has been reiterated by Viljoen et al. (2010) and has resonated, for example, in a set of proposed transboundary nature and culture trails in the Himalayas by the International Centre for Integrated Mountain Development (ICIMOD) (2019) (Figure 28.1).

The section above indicates that the mere presence of transfrontier routes and trails, without even discussing their cross-border integrative effects, depends among other things on the presence of international boundaries, domestic administrative systems and tourism governance responsibilities, public sector capacities, the "hardness" of the border to be crossed, bilateral/cross-border (geopolitical) relations and, quite simply, physical accessibility. Yet despite these obvious complexities, and "while [tourism trails] have been recognized elements of human landscapes, the contribution they have brought to tourism and recreation has been understated" (Timothy & Boyd, 2015, p. 1). Currently, there still is remarkably little explicit attention to the topic, especially when compared to the prevalence of routes and trails as transfrontier (interregional and international) tourism products in practice. Reflections on transboundary tourism trails still feature predominantly as side notes in case study research rather than as objects of research in their own right. Whereas the literature on routes and trails has benefited from (overdue) attention with the publication of a key book by Timothy and Boyd (2015), and the cross-border tourism (cooperation) literature has grown over time to become part of the mainstream tourism literature, the combination of both fields remains limited.

## Transfrontier Routes and Trails, Bridge-building and Challenges

As described above, the limited scholarship on transfrontier tourism routes and trails should not be confused with their limited importance as instruments for breaking down administrative barriers. In a globalizing world of increasing transnational flows and mobilities, tourism is often seen by scholars and practitioners as a conducive sector for establishing cross-border contact, particularly when compared to other socio-economic spheres (Church & Reid, 1999; Deppisch, 2012; Stoffelen et al., 2017; Timothy, 2001). In practice, transfrontier trails have become key assets for achieving this aim. In this sense, borders are an inevitability in developing and managing tourism trails (Ryan et al., 2006; Taylor, 2015), and they provide settings where the potential of trail development can be realized. In addition to the place-based development potential of tourism trails described earlier, there are several practical advantages and potentials for trail development in transfrontier settings, including the following:

- Transboundary routes and trails are thematically flexible and have significant potential appeal for tourists. For example, transboundary routes may add to the mystique involved in crossing borders (Gelbman & Timothy, 2010; Timothy, 1995), or they may help connect complementary tourism products on both sides of the border. This is particularly the case for trails compared to other tourism products because they intrinsically involve linking different areas and stakeholders and require the transboundary mobility of tourists.
- Tourism trails and related infrastructure also aim to reach local residents, enriching their recreational opportunities and breaking down not just administrative barriers but also mental borders between people living in neighbouring, albeit foreign, areas (Stoffelen, 2018).
- Since trails are, in most cases, initiated or coordinated by public-sector agencies or social organizations (Hayes & Macleod, 2008), they provide a tool for increasing public sector alignment in cross-border settings. This situation may increase the compatibility and coherence of the cross-border tourism supply. Since trail development requires cross-sectoral planning (Hayes & Macleod, 2008), it may also facilitate information exchange in areas such as healthcare and emergency services (Stoffelen, 2018).
- Transnational tourism trails often underpin (sometimes implicit yet very much present) geopolitical interests and values. Considering that tourism is a major symbol of a global connector of peoples and cultures, transnational tourism trails can be symbolic products that reflect cultural/political bridge-building efforts between neighbouring countries, or even continent-wide.

One example that illustrates this combined potential is the Iron Curtain Trail (ICT) in Europe. As a route that is listed in both the EuroVelo network and the Cultural Routes of the Council of Europe, the ICT was developed to raise awareness about a historical memorial landscape through leisure and tourism. The pan-European project has multi-scalar intentions and organizing structures. Its underpinning objectives include strengthening European geopolitical bridge-building and symbolism, and hence a politically influenced and selective representation of memory (Harlov-Csortán, 2017). The sub-projects are managed by national chapters, and the executive levels are cross-border regional cooperation networks, which are supposed to facilitate cultural exchange between residents and create networks between towns on both sides of the borders along the trail (Havlick, 2014; Stoffelen & Vanneste, 2019).

One of the major advantages of trails in cross-border settings is that their spatial structure allows a wider distribution of socio-economic benefits and cross-border socio-cultural integration, the effects of which are not just felt along the trail but also in its bigger surroundings. For example, the Vennbahn rail trail between Belgium, Luxemburg and Germany forms a backbone along which different tourism products, including smaller trails within the respective destinations on both sides, are connected. Involved stakeholders described this particular trail's itinerary as "scar tissue". On the one hand, this metaphor reflects the historical significance in a borderland that has had a volatile past until World War II. On the other hand, it also signifies the trail's function to connect the respective borderlands into one integrative, continuous, socio-economic and socio-cultural entity (Stoffelen, 2018). In this sense, a relatively short trail of 125 kilometres in a narrow strip along the border reaches much higher scales in terms of both visitor recognition and region-building impacts.

The multi-functionality of cross-border tourism routes has made them prime tourism products in borderlands. However, borderland settings clearly add to the complexity since "without [partnerships] any trail development project is doomed to fail" (Timothy & Boyd, 2015, p. 188), and in most cases cross-frontier trail partnerships are difficult to initiate and maintain. Public participation and collaboration are widely identified as key to establishing the cohesive, area-inclusive networks that are needed to utilize the trail for region-building. This makes trails, particularly but not uniquely long-distance routes, vulnerable to the general complexity of developing tourism in cross-border settings, namely institutional asymmetry. This concept refers to the contrasting and possibly even conflicting multi-level governance system of tourism on both sides of the border (García-Álvarez & Trillo-Santamaría, 2013; Knippschild, 2011) but also the different institutionalization (acceptance, use, internalization and collaboration) of the trail on both sides. In a worst case scenario, such asymmetries could result in widening power imbalances between stakeholders on both sides (Stoffelen et al., 2017).

Moreover, the difficulty of cooperating in developing and managing trails with linear characteristics is that, in addition to crossing hard administrative or geopolitical borders, they also usually cross multiple smaller or "softer" boundaries. Localities through which part of a trail runs are dependent on the actions of destinations further along the trail. Destination management organizations often have no formal influence on the actions undertaken in other locations. In trail development, where administrative borders are almost always crossed, even for very small-scale trails that traverse property lines and municipalities, Timothy's (1998) argument that cooperation between same-level polities is crucial for inclusive and sustainable tourism planning gains even more importance. For example, Viljoen et al. (2010) found for the "Bush to Beach" trail between Kruger National Park, South Africa, and Mozambique that the long distance of the trail and, hence, the long distance between participants (nodal points) of the trail complicated cooperation across the border but also within the respective countries between the management units of different sections of the trail. Hence, the chicken or egg situation outlined before in relation to outdoor recreation trails in Sweden (Godtman Kling et al., 2019) also explicitly applies in cross-border settings where mutual exchange between actors on both sides is particularly tricky. Well-developed trails may stimulate mutual connections, further strengthening cross-border relations and systematic information exchange. Yet, without already strong cross-border relations, achieving broader region-building aims with trail development may be unlikely. In any case, borders add weight and tension to existing challenges in governing tourism route development.

The discussion above shows that the classic conceptualization of scale in transfrontier cooperation (global organizations, regional alliances, bilateral networks and international but inter-local collaboration) needs rethinking (Timothy & Saarinen, 2013). This new thinking needs to address inter-local collaboration in domestic settings, with cooperation between stakeholders along the trail corridor but also between stakeholders involved in parallel or other connected trails. Subnational inter-jurisdictional boundaries can also be challenging to navigate, especially when higher-order development goals are targeted. Even in subnational contexts, the rigidity of borders and degrees of administrative separation may differ strongly. This may be particular true in federations such as the United States or Germany, where regional states have high levels of self-governance. However, even among low-level municipalities, cooperation can be a challenge when administrative contrasts and budgets differ significantly and personal knowledge of cooperating partners is generally higher. For example, the Magaliesberg Trail in South Africa crosses the border between the Gauteng and North West provinces. Rogerson (2007) shows how low public sector involvement in both provinces led to limited concrete support for the private-sector-led trail network and limited development effects spreading into surrounding communities. Similarly, Stoffelen et al. (2017) found that the Rennsteig hiking trail between the German federal states of Bavaria and Thuringia suffered from severely hampered information exchange between stakeholders, despite very similar multi-level destination management structures on both sides. Some stakeholders in their studies even claimed that international cross-border trail development is sometimes easier than in domestic settings. Some of the reasons they identified include the presence of clearly visible socio-economic and socio-cultural differences in international borderlands, which creates a perception that collaboration is especially needed, and the availability of European cross-border cooperation funds in these places (Stoffelen et al., 2017). Sykes and Kelly (2016, p. 545) also write that county and state lines in the United States result in "a patchwork landscape of multiple jurisdictions, government agencies, varying land use, and public and private stakeholders". The authors argue that this complicated situation impedes the development of regional tourism organizations, which are needed to tap into the high potential of motorcycle tourism routes for rural economic development (Sykes & Kelly, 2016). Finally, Ruiz et al. (2019) even challenge the notion of bounded territorial management in a context of nature-based tourism routes. They argue that the hard administrative boundaries of protected areas simply mismatch with the realities of tourist mobilities. In a case study of Patagonia, Chile, they call for a more fluid, networked, management approach rather than one that is hard-bounded by national park borders. Rigid area management within the boundaries of the national park could have unwanted effects within, and outside of, the park's perimeter, including unwanted tourist behaviour and conflict between public and private landowners.

With borders adding weight to the existing challenges of inclusive trail development, there are clear difficulties in making use of the obvious potential that has convinced many practitioners to develop tourism routes and trails. In fact, cooperation challenges are present even in the internationally recognized best-practice example of the Vennbahn cycling route along and across the borders of Belgium, Luxemburg and Germany. These challenges exist due to the different centralities of the trail in the respective countries, in terms of geographical location, considering the contrasting size of the territory covered and scalar responsibilities of the destination management organizations on both sides of the border, but also in terms of contrasting product placement and prioritization of the trail in the respective destinations (Stoffelen, 2018). Challenges may also occur in regions with many local trails, such as the German–Czech borderlands where local cross-boundary trails have mushroomed with the support of European co-financing (see Figure 28.1).

Hayes and Macleod (2008) suggest that the absence of strategic thinking in route development in the United Kingdom means that many trails do not contribute to a broader cross-border strategy, do not cooperate in shared marketing and are not managed to integrate the existing tourism supply on both sides of a given border (Stoffelen et al., 2017). These examples show that the difficulties in coordinating between actors in cross-border settings due to institutional asymmetry could lead to half-hearted project developments with only short-term objectives, which undermine the ultimate objectives of cross-border integration and region-building. The combination of high trail densities in Europe's borderlands combined with the observed difficulties in making these work for broader integrative purposes led Stoffelen (2018, p. 91) to conclude that "there is an unfulfilled potential of tourism trails in their contribution to cross-border communication and social cohesion in many European borderlands". Therefore, it can be expected that achieving the development potential of tourism trails will be an uphill battle, even more so in areas with weaker public-sector capacities and polarized power relations among tourism stakeholders.

## Conclusion

Reviewing the literature on transfrontier tourism trails and trail development in practice unearths two important mismatches. The first one is the limited academic attention to tourism routes in borderlands, even basic case studies, given the intensity of tourism trail development in cross-border settings and the fact that borderlands are frequently ideal spaces for trail development owing to their natural settings in peripheral locations and their often-interesting histories. This mismatch is striking considering the now vibrant array of scholarship on tourism trails in general and the mainstreaming of cross-border research in tourism studies. Even long-overdue tentative explorations of tourism research in the domain of border studies are on the rise. Nevertheless, the academic cross-fertilization between tourism trails and cross-border tourism so far remains superficial.

The second mismatch is one between the potential of tourism routes for cross-border development and region-building on one hand and, on the other hand, the limited evidence of cases where this potential is realized. This situation reflects the complications that cross-border settings add, at least when the goal is to move beyond simple project development to reach higher-order, cross-border objectives using tourism trails. While routes and trails have all the intrinsic characteristics to connect separated stakeholders and places into one functional cross-border entity, the barrier effects of local and international borders are very real even in our increasingly globalized, networked world.

This review has drawn attention to two key elements that should be taken into consideration when studying the transfrontier, integrative role of tourism trails: the geographical area covered and connected, directly by the trail itself and indirectly through linking the existing tourism supply on both sides of the border to the trail, and the actors with multi-scalar actions on both sides that should be included to make the cross-border trails as integrative as possible. Research needs to engage better with the intersection of the geography and institutional framework of transfrontier tourism route development. More studies are required to develop theoretical perspectives and empirical knowledge through case studies, not least in the developing world, to mature our insights on these prevalent and multi-dimensional tourism products that have the potential to unite rather than to divide.

# References

Badulescu, D., & Badulescu, A. (2017). Rural tourism development through cross-border cooperation: The case of Romanian-Hungarian cross-border area. *Eastern European Countryside*, 23(1), 191–208.

Briedenhann, J., & Wickens, E. (2004). Tourism routes as a tool for the economic development of rural areas - vibrant hope or impossible dream? *Tourism Management*, 25(1), 71–79.

Broadway, M. J. (2017). "Putting Place on a Plate" along the West Cork Food Trail. *Tourism Geographies*, 19(3), 467–482.

Cheung, S. C. H. (1999). The meanings of a heritage trail in Hong Kong. *Annals of Tourism Research*, 26(3), 570–588.

Church, A., & Reid, P. (1999). Cross-border co-operation, institutionalization and political space across the English Channel. *Regional Studies*, 33(7), 643–655.

Council of Europe. (2020). Cultural Routes of the Council of Europe. Retrieved July 1, 2020, from https://pjp-eu.coe.int/en/web/cultural-routes-and-regional-development/coe-cultural-routes#:~:-text=The Cultural Routes of the,understanding of European shared heritage.

Cox, P. (2012). Strategies promoting cycle tourism in Belgium: Practices and implications. *Tourism Planning and Development*, 9(1), 25–39.

Del Chiappa, G., Bregoli, I., & Kim, A. K. (2019). Inter-sectoral collaboration in networks: A boundary object approach to wine routes. *Tourism Planning & Development*, 16(6), 591–611.

Deppisch, S. (2012). Governance processes in Euregios: Evidence from six cases across the Austrian–German border. *Planning Practice and Research*, 27(3), 315–332.

European Cyclists' Federation (2020). Eurovelo. Retrieved June 23, 2020, from https://ecf.com/projects/eurovelo

EuroVelo. (2020). Routes and countries. Retrieved January 9, 2020, from https://en.eurovelo.com/#routes-and-countries

García-Álvarez, J., & Trillo-Santamaría, J.-M. (2013). Between regional spaces and spaces of regionalism: Cross-border region building in the Spanish 'State of the Autonomies'. *Regional Studies*, 47(1), 104–115.

Gelbman, A., & Timothy, D. J. (2010). From hostile boundaries to tourist attractions. *Current Issues in Tourism*, 13(3), 239–259.

Godtman Kling, K., Dahlberg, A., & Wall-Reinius, S. (2019). Negotiating improved multifunctional landscape use: Trails as facilitators of collaboration among stakeholders. *Sustainability*, 11, 3511.

Hall, C. M. (2005). *Tourism: Rethinking the social science of mobility*. Harlow: Pearson.

Hardy, A. (2003). An investigation into the key factors necessary for the development of iconic touring routes. *Journal of Vacation Marketing*, 9(4), 314–330.

Harlov-Csortán, M. (2017). From the borderland of the Iron Curtain to European and world cultural heritage. *Folklore*, 70, 193–224.

Havlick, D. G. (2014). The Iron Curtain Trail's landscapes of memory, meaning, and recovery. *Focus on Geography*, 57(3), 126–133.

Hayes, D., & Macleod, N. (2008). Putting down routes: An examination of local government cultural policy shaping the development of heritage trails. *Managing Leisure*, 13, 57–73.

Hitchner, S., Schelhas, J., Brosius, P., & Nibbelink, N. (2019). Thru-hiking the John Muir Trail as a modern pilgrimage: Implications for natural resource management. *Journal of Ecotourism*, 18(1), 82–99.

ICIMOD (2019). *Transboundary ecotourism in the Kangchenjunga Landscape: Opportunities for sustainable development through regional cooperation*. Kathmandu: ICIMOD.

Knippschild, R. (2011). Cross-border spatial planning: Understanding, designing and managing cooperation processes in the German–Polish–Czech borderland. *European Planning Studies*, 19(4), 629–645.

Kołodziejczyk, K. (2019). Networks of hiking tourist trails in the Krkonoše (Czech Republic) and Peneda-Gerês (Portugal) national parks – comparative analysis. *Journal of Mountain Science*, 16, 725–743.

Lennon, J. J., & Harris, J. (2020). The North Coast 500: Developing tourism in the northern Scottish Highlands. *Scottish Affairs*, 29(2), 223–253.

Lourens, M. (2007). Route tourism: A roadmap for successful destinations and local economic development. *Development Southern Africa*, 24(3), 475–490.

Meyer, D. (2004). *Tourism routes and gateways: key issues for the development of tourism routes and gateways and their potential for pro-poor Tourism*. London: Overseas Development Institute.

Miles, S. (2017). Remembrance trails of the Great Western Front: Routes of heritage and memory. *Journal of Heritage Tourism*, 12(5), 441–451.

Mundet, L., & Coenders, G. (2010). Greenways: A sustainable leisure experience concept for both communities and tourists. *Journal of Sustainable Tourism*, 18(5), 657–674.

National Park Service (2021). National Trails System. Retreived May 29, 2021, from https://www.nps.gov/subjects/nationaltrailssystem/index.htm

Olsen, D. H., & Trono, A. (Eds.). (2018). *Religious pilgrimage routes and trails: Sustainable development and management*. Wallingford: CABI.

Plummer, R., Telfer, D., & Hashimoto, A. (2006). The rise and fall of the Waterloo-Wellington Ale Trail: A study of collaboration within the tourism industry. *Current Issues in Tourism*, 9(3), 191–205.

Quinlan Cutler, S., Carmichael, B., & Doherty, S. (2014). The Inca Trail experience: Does the journey matter? *Annals of Tourism Research*, 45, 152–166.

Ritchie, B. W., & Hall, C. M. (1999). Bicycle tourism and regional development: A New Zealand case study. *Anatolia*, 10(2), 89–112.

Rogerson, C. M. (2007). Tourism routes as vehicles for local economic development in South Africa: The example of the Magaliesberg Meander. *Urban Forum*, 18(2), 49–68.

Ruiz, J. B., Lamers, M., Bush, S., & Wells, G. B. (2019). Governing nature-based tourism mobility in National Park Torres del Paine, Chilean Southern Patagonia. *Mobilities*, 14(6), 745–761.

Russo, A. P., & Romagosa, F. (2010). The network of Spanish Jewries: In praise of connecting and sharing heritage. *Journal of Heritage Tourism*, 5(2), 141–157.

Ryan, R. L., Fábos, J. G., & Allan, J. J. (2006). Understanding opportunities and challenges for collaborative greenway planning in New England. *Landscape and Urban Planning*, 76(1–4), 172–191.

Snowball, J. D., & Courtney, S. (2010). Cultural heritage routes in South Africa: Effective tools for heritage conservation and local economic development? *Development Southern Africa*, 27(4), 563–576.

Stoffelen, A. (2018). Tourism trails as tools for cross-border integration: A best practice case study of the Vennbahn cycling route. *Annals of Tourism Research*, 73, 91–102.

Stoffelen, A., Ioannides, D., & Vanneste, D. (2017). Obstacles to achieving cross-border tourism governance: A multi-scalar approach focusing on the German-Czech borderlands. *Annals of Tourism Research*, 64, 126–138.

Stoffelen, A., & Vanneste, D. (2016). Institutional (dis)integration and regional development implications of whisky tourism in Speyside, Scotland. *Scandinavian Journal of Hospitality and Tourism*, 16(1), 42–60.

Stoffelen, A., & Vanneste, D. (2019). Commodification of contested borderscapes for tourism development: Viability, community representation and equity of relic Iron Curtain and Sudetenland heritage tourism landscapes. In A. Paasi, E.-K. Prokkola, J. Saarinen, & K. Zimmerbauer (Eds.), *Borderless worlds for whom? Ethics, moralities and mobilities*, pp. 139–153. London: Routledge.

Sykes, D., & Kelly, K. G. (2016). Motorcycle drive tourism leading to rural tourism opportunities. *Tourism Economics*, 22(3), 543–557.

Taylor, P. (2015). What factors make rail trails successful as tourism attractions? Developing a conceptual framework from relevant literature. *Journal of Outdoor Recreation and Tourism*, 12, 89–98.

Telfer, D. J. (2001). Strategic alliances along the Niagara Wine Route. *Tourism Management*, 22, 21–30.

Timothy, D. J. (1995). Political boundaries and tourism: Borders as tourist attractions. *Tourism Management*, 16(7), 525–532.

Timothy, D. J. (1998). Cooperative tourism planning in a developing destination. *Journal of Sustainable Tourism*, 6(1), 52–68.

Timothy, D. J. (2001). *Tourism and political boundaries*. London: Routledge.

Timothy, D. J. (2018). Cultural routes: Tourist destinations and tools for development. In D.H. Olsen, & A. Trono (eds) *Religious pilgrimage routes and trails: Sustainable development and management*, pp. 27–37. Wallingford: CABI.

Timothy, D. J., & Boyd, S. W. (2006). Heritage tourism in the 21st Century: Valued traditions and new perspectives. *Journal of Heritage Tourism*, 1(1), 1–16.

Timothy, D. J., & Boyd, S. W. (2015). *Tourism and trails: Cultural, ecological and management issues*. Bristol: Channel View Publications.

Timothy, D. J., & Saarinen, J. (2013). Cross-border cooperation and tourism in Europe. In C. Costa, E. Panyik, & D. Buhalis (Eds.), *Trends in European tourism planning and organisation*, pp. 64–74. Bristol: Channel View Publications.

Timothy, D. J., Saarinen, J., & Viken, A. (2016). Tourism issues and international borders in the Nordic region. *Scandinavian Journal of Hospitality and Tourism*, 16(Sup.1), 1–13.

Viljoen, J., Viljoen, F., & Struwig, J. (2010). Pro-poor tourism routes: The Open Africa experience. *Acta Academica*, 42(4), 65–90.

Więckowski, M. (2018). From periphery and the doubled national trails to the cross-border thematic trails: New cross-border tourism in Poland. In D. Müller, & W. Więckowski (eds), *Tourism in Transitions: Recovering decline, managing change*, pp. 173–186. Cham, Switzerland: Springer.

Więckowski, M. (in press). How border tripoints offer opportunities for transboundary tourism development. *Tourism Geographies*.

# 29
# TOURISM CLUSTER MANAGEMENT IN CROSS-BORDER DESTINATIONS
## Blind Spots and Invisible Lines

*Jaume Guia, Dani Blasco, and Natàlia Ferrer-Roca*

### Introduction

Tourism clusters are a complex form of tourism organization with a structure of various systems, the members of which retain their legal subjectivity and economic independence while, at same time, stay connected through a flexible form of economic integration aimed at achieving a common goal (Kachniewska, 2013). They have also been widely identified as effective tools for tourism growth in destinations (Jackson & Murphy, 2002, 2006; Melisidou et al., 2014; Michael, 2003).

In border regions, cross-border tourism clusters have also been referred to as cross-border partnerships (Ferrer-Roca et al., 2022), or simply cross-border destinations, and have been proposed as promising instruments for achieving an integrated governance of transfrontier tourism destinations (Blasco et al., 2014a). However, the literature on cross-border regions has elucidated the many obstacles that this potential integration may face, such as peripherality (Blasco et al., 2014b; Medeiros, 2020; Prokkola, 2010), methodological nationalism (Agnew, 2013; Ferrer-Roca et al., 2022), the asymmetrical development of neighbouring borderlands (Dodescu & Botezat, 2018), and a lack of cross-border tourism planning and policy-making (Liberato et al., 2018; Lovelock & Boyd, 2006).

Because of these obstacles, effective and integrated cross-border partnerships and clusters in border regions rarely last very long (Hills, 2016), and thus opportunities for tourism development are often missed. Therefore, in the face of obstacles to integration, attempts to create cross-border partnerships and clusters often fail. However, when these obstacles are overcome, cross-border clusters can be created, and opportunities for tourism growth and sustainable development are multiplied. The literature on cross-border tourism has paid only limited attention to the evolution of regional integration over time. Thus, we know little about the actual integrated managerial processes of cross-border destinations once cross-border networks have been achieved, and the problematic of the effectiveness of cross-border tourism clusters as managerial frameworks remains unsolved (Beritelli et al., 2014; Ferrer-Roca et al., 2022; Stoffelen et al., 2017). This chapter explores the reasons why integrated cross-border tourism clusters often fail to be sustainable over time and, therefore, we focus more on the effective tourism management of cross-border destinations.

As an illustrative case of this exploration, the history of recent tourism partnering and clustering in the transboundary Cerdanya Valley in the Catalan Pyrenees is showcased. Results highlight the importance of paying attention to cluster management practices, instead of only on cluster development, if attempts to develop cross-border partnerships and clusters should go beyond prolonged impasses and dissolutions. From an evolutionary perspective, this can be summarized in two phases or moments. First, in the development phase of transfrontier integration, emphasis is placed on the management and involvement of cross-border stakeholders to achieve and create integrated governance structures, and in overcoming whatever specific types of obstacles there may be. Second, in the consolidation phase of cross-border integration, once the integrated structure has been created, emphasis should be given to the traditional functions and tasks of destination management organizations, with particular attention to product, branding, and marketing strategies. However, as the case illustrates, this move is not necessarily straightforward and new hurdles may jeopardize the achievements made in the cluster development phase (Beritelli et al., 2014; Hills, 2016; Stoffelen & Vanneste, 2017).

## Cross-border Tourism Cluster Development and Evolution

The interest in researching tourism development in cross-border areas has increased considerably in the last couple of decades, with contributions in a wide range of tourism research domains, such as: geography (e.g., Ioannides, 2006; Timothy, 1995, 2001, 2006; Timothy et al., 2016; Wachowiak, 2006); sociology (e.g., Stoffelen & Vanneste, 2018); economy (e.g., Gao et al., 2019; Jackson, 2006); marketing (e.g., Kozak & Buhalis, 2019; Tosun et al., 2005; Vitner Marković & Šerić, 2011); and management (e.g., Hartman, 2006; Hills, 2016; Valente et al., 2015).

In the cross-border tourism literature, there is a growing body of research that looks at the creation and development of management and governance structures, such as cross-border tourism clusters. These structures may vary depending on their configuration and temporality (Beaumont & Dredge, 2010; Selin & Chavez, 1995), the diversity of the stakeholders involved (Greer, 2001; Timothy, 1998), and the intensity of their collaboration (Martinez, 1994; Timothy, 1999; Zhang & Blasco, 2022). They may be led by public administrations across the border, or they may be business- and community-led cross-border configurations (see Blasco et al., 2014b). In particular, when led by businesses, these networks are referred to as business clusters (Go & Williams, 1993; Jackson, 2006).

Cross-border tourism development initiatives and projects are strongly influenced by the specific dimensions and characteristics of the borders involved (Lovelock & Boyd, 2006; Saarinen, 2017; Stoffelen et al., 2017). Border histories, identities, and social and cultural discourses are important factors that either foster or hinder integration (Stoffelen & Vanneste, 2018). The issue of peripherality has also been acknowledged as being a relevant tourism development issue in some border areas (Medeiros, 2020; Prokkola, 2010). In these instances, there is generally a lack of cross-border tourism planning and policy-making (Liberato et al., 2018; Lovelock & Boyd, 2006). Indeed, "small populations and being located long distances from the centres of power and decision-making usually mean chronic deficits in infrastructure and investments, which hinders the region's achievement of economies of scale" (Ferrer-Roca et al., 2022, p. 2414). Consequently, there also needs to be consideration of the levels of similarities and complementarities and the symmetrical/asymmetrical (or uneven) development of neighbouring borderlands that make up a cross-border destination (Dodescu & Botezat, 2018), which sometimes includes different levels of experience with partnerships (Stoffelen & Vanneste, 2017).

There is a simple assumption that states exhibit institutional homogeneity, cultural similarity, and geographical unity, and that they differ from other states in these regards (Amelina et al., 2012). This discourse reinforces the notion of methodological nationalism (Agnew, 2013), which implicitly neglects the realities of many borderlands where the socioeconomic activity and environmental reality of both sides of the border are functionally entangled (Ferrer-Roca et al., 2022). As a consequence of these obstacles, long-lasting, effective, and integrated cross-border partnerships and clusters in border regions rarely occur (Hills, 2016).

In some cases, informal networks and institutional brokers act as facilitators to increase cross-border tourism collaboration (Stoffelen & Vanneste, 2017). Moreover, scholars have recognized the value of clusters as dynamic structures, with a number of important benefits for transfrontier destinations, such as: integrated destination governance frameworks (Blasco et al., 2014a; Hartman, 2006; Ioannides et al., 2006; Prokkola, 2010; Sofield, 2006); increasing levels of innovation (Blasco et al., 2016; Makkonen et al., 2018; Novelli et al., 2006; Weidenfeld, 2013); and shared marketing strategies and actions (Kozak & Buhalis, 2019; Tosun et al., 2005; Vitner Marković & Šerić, 2011).

Creating and maintaining governance structures is among the main concerns of both practitioners and researchers in tourism destination management. The concept of governance refers to self-organizing inter-organizational networks, characterized by interdependence, resource exchange, rules of the game, and autonomy from the state (Rhodes, 1996, 1997), and has been studied intensively in the last two decades in the field of tourism (Bramwell & Lane, 2011; Dos Anjos & Kennell, 2019; Hall, 2004; Ruhanen et al., 2010; Volgger & Pechlaner, 2015). Pechlaner, Volgger, and Herntrei (2012) define destination governance as the union of networked stakeholders aiming at improving competitiveness by eliciting and steering common action and inter-organizational cooperation.

In border regions, dedicated funding programmes have been identified as crucial catalysts for cross-border destination development by promoting the creation and development of relationships across the line. Some of these funding programmes have been analysed and claimed to be successful tools in the short term (Faby, 2006; Makkonen et al., 2018; Nilsson et al., 2010; Studzieniecki & Meyer, 2017). However, most of these newly created networks fail to be sustained once the funding period has ended (Hills, 2016; Prokkola, 2008). Once the transboundary governance structures are created, the focus must move from network building to network management, or for the case here at hand, from cross-border destination partnership building to cross-border destination management.

There is, nevertheless, much less literature dealing with cross-border tourism management (Sialverstava et al., 2019) and the sustainability of the management structures over time in cross-border settings. The concept of "destination management" has been discussed widely (Reinhold et al., 2019; Saraniemi & Kylänen, 2011). As stated by Beritelli et al. (2014), destination management implies the effective coordination of three reference frameworks, each one with its corresponding (and rarely matching) logics: the territorial logic, the business logic, and the experiential logic. Unfortunately,

> public institutions often fail to effectively participate in the business logic; private businesses fail to effectively translate their needs in the territorial logic of the public sector or to adapt to the requirements of the experiential logic of the tourist …. It is in this trap of multiple frameworks that destination management and DMOs regularly fail to achieve long-term plans and sustainable strategies.
>
> *(Beritelli et al., 2014, p. 406)*

To prevent these failures, Beritelli and Laesser (2017) and Baggio, Scott, and Cooper (2010) suggest that tourism destinations must be understood as dynamic and complex environments, with high rates of multiplicity, diversity, and variability. This requires a shift in the understanding of tourism destinations from one territorial area to multiple strategic business areas (Beritelli et al., 2014).

Implicitly, this is a call for the adoption of new mindsets in the management of tourism destinations, both in non-transfrontier settings and in cross-border settings. It also points out a need to increase the scale and connections across transboundary destination, and for "open cluster" participation where membership goes beyond territorial limits, including for instance stakeholders from the main source markets (Kachniewska, 2013). To achieve this, Bieger, Beritelli, and Laesser (2009) suggest that destinations need to extend their products and markets to be more competitive and meet globalizing tourism markets and increasing marketing costs, which translates into an increase in size and budget, and a continuous revision of the tourism destination's boundaries.

However, effective cross-border tourism management is not a natural consequence of cross-border tourism development, where in some cases transfrontier tourism activities and initiatives may instead reinforce existing asymmetries in the social and economic space in both countries (Stoffelen & Vanneste, 2017). Effective management principles and practices are more likely to derive from process-based aspects, such as "the presence of 'thick' institutional arrangements, multi-scalar representation of tourism stakeholders in decision-making processes and a transversal position of tourism in regional development strategies" (Stoffelen & Vanneste, 2017, p. 1013), and this is even more difficult to achieve in cross-border settings.

Figure 29.1 represents our attempt to synthesize the different moments or stages through which cross-border tourism clusters may evolve. We suggest that the creation and development of a cross-border tourism cluster is only the first stage of a more complex and non-linear process. After this initial stage, some of these structures may become successfully consolidated; some others may get trapped into a halt in their activity, and most of them may be struggling to survive until they finally get dissolved after some time. Due to the non-linearity, cross-border cluster structures may jump backward and forward from one stage to the other, re-emerging as different arrangements but finding it difficult to reach a final stage of solid consolidation.

We argue that effective cross-border tourist destinations require governance structures, such as partnerships and clusters, which need to be both created and managed sustainably. After all,

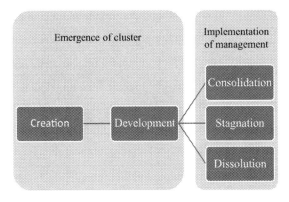

*Figure 29.1* Phases in cross-border tourism cluster evolution.

as Zahra (2011) argues, a lack of governance can lead to unstable tourism destination management organizations. We go beyond that statement and add that a lack of management can lead to the unsustainability and dissolution of governance structures.

## An Empirical Case: La Cerdanya

The Cerdanya Valley (La Cerdanya), divided by the French–Spanish border, was chosen as a case to study the creation and management of cross-border tourism structures over time. The reason for selecting this location is the pattern of sustained attempts at cross-border partnerships over a long period of time. This makes this cross-border area a suitable laboratory for analysing transfrontier tourism collaboration and governance. We have been conducting research in this region over a period of nine years (2012–2020) through observations, participation, and interviews with the main stakeholders involved, including tourism entrepreneurs and representatives of the governments and the communities on both sides of the border, which has proved valuable in ascertaining information from a broad, transfrontier perspective as advocated by Czernek (2013). Based on years of fieldwork, the following narrative reveals the challenges and opportunities in establishing transfrontier networks in La Cerdanya, from which other cross-border destinations can learn valuable lessons.

### *The Cross-border Cerdanya Valley Destination in the Pyrenees Mountains*

The Pyrenees are a 400-km mountain range in south-western Europe. The range reaches a height of 3,400 m and is about 10 km wide. The Pyrenees are a part of the Alpine chain of Western Europe "which runs from the northern Iberian margin in the West to the Alps in the East" (Choukroune, 1992, p. 143), forming a natural border between France and Spain. Regarding tourism planning, development, management, and promotion, it is relevant to highlight that "the Pyrenees region is divided into 13 different regions from 3 countries, which fully coincide with existing administrative divisions of the territory" (Blasco et al., 2014a, p. 6). The three countries that are home to the Pyrenees are France, Spain, and Andorra.

The Cerdanya Valley (La Cerdanya) region is a traditional mountain tourism destination in the Pyrenees. Its main towns are Puigcerdà (9,486 inhabitants), Font-Romeu (1,992), and the enclave of Llívia (1,431). Since the 1950s the destination has become increasingly popular, attracting residents from nearby cities such as Barcelona (150 km), Perpignan (100 km), and Toulouse (170 km). As Figure 29.2 shows, the Cerdanya Valley is currently divided into two administrative regions, one within French Catalonia and the other in Spanish Catalonia. They still share features such as history, culture, language, and traditions, as a reminiscence of the medieval ages where the entire valley functioned as an administrative unity and the current border had not yet been established. Today there are over 10 ski resorts in a 30 km catchment area from Puigcerdà, alongside cultural and heritage sites. From the tourism infrastructure perspective, the number of accommodation units has increased moderately during the last few decades, and a number of restaurants specializing in mountain cuisine have also been established. The whole Cerdanya region can be considered a single tourism destination because, for instance, accommodation on the Spanish Catalonian side also serves the ski resorts on the French Catalonia side (Blasco et al., 2014b), and their natural and cultural environments are very similar.

La Cerdanya is a montane valley ecosystem with no obvious physical border, where animals and people walk back and forth from one country to another. It has indeed a very special

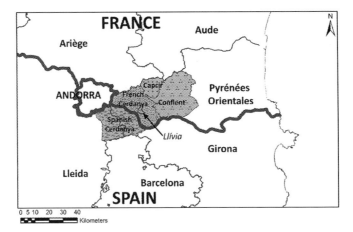

*Figure 29.2* The cross-border Cerdanya Valley region, including the enclave Llívia (Blasco et al., 2014a).

landscape, as described by an anonymous but proud inhabitant of Cerdanya in the early seventeenth century (Sahlins, 1989, p. 10):

> Its shape is in the form of a ship, with its prow to the east and its stern to the west, although it turns a bit south in the form of a half-moon, but without losing its shape. The oars can be likened to the many valleys on all sides. Its length is seven large leagues, from the Tet bridge where the Cerdanya ends and the Conflent begins, to a little below the Arsèguel bridge, a league and a half from the Seu d'Urgell. By that point, it is much less wide, with high mountains which can be likened to the sides of the ship.

## *The Evolution of the Cerdanya Valley Cross-border Cluster*

The initial introduction and fast growth of tourism in the Cerdanya Valley in the 1950s motivated the emergence of many individual operators whose business behaviours were largely individualistic and who pursued their own economic growth as the main objective. Without a conscious effort to build cross-border partnerships, it is not surprising that initial cross-border activity was absent or nearly non-existent.

In 2011, the cross-border region was able to gather key stakeholders and start working together towards an integrated structure as a first attempt, but when the public funding used for that purpose ended, the initiative entered a stagnation phase. The lack of an adequate managerial structure limited the scope of the actions that could be finally implemented. The focus had been put in product development with no or little concern on market development. Therefore, the new tourism products that were developed ended up only being sold to the same markets that the destination already had. These markets did not change their habits and behaviour and, consequently, no real impact was achieved. The potential for a long-term commitment to develop and attract new tourism markets was thus lost.

In the face of a potential stagnation and consequent possible future dissolution of the cluster, some prominent actors in the region, who had been active participants in the first partnership, decided to revamp the cross-border cluster and reconfigure its structure, adopting a new vision and strategy. The new more exclusive business-led cross-border cluster partnership focused on enhancing product innovation and economic sustainability in the region. The prominent role tourism had in the first structure was attenuated, becoming one among several other economic activities identified as strategic for the economy of the valley, which included healthcare, sport, food, and environment. The previously sought engagement of local public administrators was also abandoned, instead adopting a more lobbying role. The number of participants diminished considerably, due to the limited achievements of the first partnership in terms of business for the participants and the uncertainty around the new direction. This, however, resulted in close and trusting relationships between the members. The geographical composition of the cluster was unbalanced in favour of more members from the Spanish side of the valley than from the French side. Attempts were made to grow the number of members and to achieve a better transfrontier balance, but with no significant results.

Moreover, this cluster partnership, where both tourism and non-tourism businesses interact and innovate together without the need to have the tourism industry leading the process, was expected to lead to more ground-breaking innovations than the first attempt at the partnership, and thus open the door to potential new markets.

For instance, in the area of health, the business cluster partnership pioneered one of the innovations. On the French side of the valley, there are several medical facilities to cater for patients with pulmonary diseases. The quality of the air, the high altitude, and the long hours of daylight in the valley make it a world-class environment for these types of services. These medical services were provided exclusively to the French market and particularly to the public health services in that country. New demand from Barcelona was identified, a new world-class specialist was about to move to the region, and one of the medical clinics was opening to the private market, thus introducing medical tourism in the region. Moreover, some of the patients that do not need permanent medical assistance could stay in certain hotels, thereby easing the pressures of seasonality that these lodging establishments suffer most of the year outside the ski season. Relatives of the patients would also be attracted to visit La Cerdanya, thus contributing to the economic sustainability of the region. Further medical tourism services were expected to be added, drawing from the already developed medical tourism market in nearby Barcelona. Medical staff would move to the region, new talent would arrive, and higher-quality jobs would be introduced. Furthermore, the new medical practitioners would also be able to offer their services in the valley's public hospital, which due to the peripherality of the region is still understaffed, thus benefiting the whole community.

As a result, this new cross-border business cluster partnership with socially responsible private operators as members, belonging to both the tourism sector and other fields such as health, education/culture, and nature, and which have the capacity to expand and connect to other networks, seemed to be particularly suited to develop innovative forms of tourism. And in the case of transboundary areas, when institutional differences are seen as opportunities for innovation and where there are central actors that can bridge institutional and relational gaps, a cluster like this has the potential to be even more innovative and effective.

However, after some time, this innovative cross-border cluster structure entered a second phase of stagnation. The design and creation of new products was slow, and when the health tourism innovation described above was finally ready to enter the market, the COVID-19 pandemic arrived and hope of the promised impact of the cross-border cluster was jeopardized. As a result, fresh discussions among the members of the cluster took place, facing the potential dissolution of the cluster and the abandonment of the longstanding attempts at development. Instead, they decided to stay with the cross-border cluster structure and introduce changes in the strategy that would contemplate the lessons learned after the first previous two attempts at transboundary partnering for tourism and economic sustainable development in the Cerdanya Valley. The ultimate effectiveness will depend on the ability of the cluster to expand the network and embed it in larger extra-territorial innovative networks that will support further innovation and help to provide essential funding opportunities.

Thus, it seems that without strong and effective partnerships, cross-border integration cannot be implemented. The Cerdanya case evidences the difficulties of moving from initial developmental stages of integrated cross-border governance structures to the stage of effective management of these same structures.

## Discussion and Conclusions

We have described how the different cross-border governance structures in the Cerdanya Valley managed to develop a strategic vision (Blasco et al., 2014a). However, the implemented strategies were misaligned with that vision. The lack of managerial structures and the absence of a sound business plan, a clear conception of a business model, and a clear value proposition for the region as a cross-border destination resulted in ineffectiveness, poor results, and loss of hope for transformative change.

First, no new tourism markets were attracted because the new products were not designed with these markets in mind (Kozak & Buhalis, 2019; Tosun et al., 2005). With regard to existing markets in the Cerdanya Valley, they are mostly made up of proximal self-organizing visitors instead of visitors that purchase package tours and, therefore, the potential value added by cross-border integrated packages becomes irrelevant in this case. Also, the difficulty for, or slowness of, change in the existing patterns of visitors was not considered, particularly when those existing markets are largely comprised of loyal repeat visitors, as is the case for the region. Moreover, high border permeability makes transborder destinations function as natural extensions of each "local" market on either side of the frontier (Stoffelen & Vanneste, 2017), particularly for the purpose of cross-border shopping, or when the complementarity of attractions, products, and services is high (Dodescu & Botezat, 2018). Therefore, considering its markets and patterns of visitation, a cross-boundary tourism structure in this region would bring the most value for the purpose of attracting new markets, but in none of the three attempts to consolidate the transfrontier governance structure was partnering with representatives of potential new markets accomplished. Because of the lack of managerial structure and capacity in the different cross-border partnerships developed, no proper consideration of the requirements or needs of potential new markets (e.g., guide and interpretation service availability) was ever given. We contend that representatives of the potential new markets need to be part of the partnership and thus achieve a broader and more accurate vision about the opportunity, promise, and adequacy of the strategies designed. This implies the need for developing governance and managerial structures that go beyond local interests/conflicts and closed territorial identities.

Likewise, local governments were not fully engaged in the partnerships. They are natural players in tourism destination management and marketing, and without them the destination will develop distorted and incompatible tourism strategies (Beaumont & Dredge, 2010). Moreover, the financial and political capacity of local administrations across the border, particularly in peripheral and sparsely populated regions, is usually limited. Consequently, partnerships that can attract regional or national administrations as partners or collaborators will more likely have the financial capacity and political support needed for consolidation. Universities and other knowledge enterprises were also marginally included or not at all in the attempted transfrontier governance structures developed in La Cerdanya, thus missing the opportunities and benefits that knowledge-based actors can bring to a potential partnership. These findings call for cross-border tourism (regional/territorial) clusters to adopt instead an "industrial cluster" logic. This means that, while still being bounded by specific territorial limits, these clusters should, as much as possible, become extraterritorial following an industrial clustering logic which prioritizes and privileges a business-modelling of the cluster, and consequently the cross-border tourism destination, instead of focusing on territorial limitations. In the words of Beritelli et al. (2014), the industrial cluster logic would prioritize the experiential and business logics for destination management over territorial limits and logics. Territorial clusters may be influenced too much by pre-existing territorial (bordered) needs and conflicts, and therefore might relegate the managerial dimension required for the adoption of business and experiential logics for tourism destination management, both in general and in cross-border settings.

Another lesson learned is that most traditional obstacles or "invisible walls" identified by the literature for the development and consolidation of tourism cross-border governance structures were found in the different attempts described above (see Blasco et al., 2014a; Ferrer-Roca et al., 2022; Stoffelen et al., 2017). The first partnering attempt made progress and managed to overcome some of these invisible walls through the organization of events, training programmes, and other networking opportunities for operators and other actors from both sides of the border to meet and interact. This was lost with the strategic changes brought about by the business cluster development as a second attempt at cross-border partnering. In the new third attempt, this is being corrected by developing and organizing dedicated cross-border gatherings and co-working spaces to facilitate cross-border interaction. Finally, in this new phase, even if the equal prominence of different economic sectors is maintained, the strong weight of tourism in the regional economy is highlighted and, therefore, tourism is expected to play a critical role in most new product development initiatives. What has been lost compared to the first attempt is the aim of developing a complete transfrontier tourism destination that targets new and foreign markets.

To conclude, some additional blind spots and invisible lines have been identified beyond the already well-known obstacles for cross-border tourism partnership development that the literature has identified so far, and which hinder and often dissolve attempts to consolidate transboundary governance structures for tourism development and integrated destination management (Beritelli et al., 2014; Hills, 2016; Stoffelen & Vanneste, 2017). First, new tourism product development aimed at existing visitors or markets may not be effective when visitation patterns are entrenched, when visitors are mostly proximal self-organizing tourists, and when the border is highly porous. Second, the potential for attracting new markets—both close and distant—is high, but this potential must be addressed with a clear strategic vision, and with transborder destination managerial structures capable of developing proper business models and value propositions for the cross-border destination, including representatives of those markets in the partnerships. Third, this "market-induced" extra-territoriality needs to be complemented with the characteristic of the "industrial cluster" logic—that is, an extra-territoriality based on partnering with regional and national tourism administrations, and regional universities and other knowledge-based organizations. This shall be particularly so in cases of regional peripherality and small populations. Fourth, the local administration's role in tourism destination management should leave parochialisms behind and coordinate their actions with those that are part of the cross-border governance structure. Finally, networking events and co-working spaces must be developed, organized, and promoted to attenuate the intrinsic obstacles that have long hindered cross-border collaboration.

## References

Agnew, J. (2013). Territory, politics, governance. *Territory, Politics, Governance*, 1(1), 1–4.
Amelina, A., Nergiz, D.D., Faist, T., & Schiller, N.G. (2012). *Research methodologies for cross-border studies*. London: Routledge.
Baggio, R., Scott, N., & Cooper, C. (2010). Improving tourism destination governance: A complexity science approach. *Tourism Review*, 65(4), 51–60.
Beaumont, N., & Dredge, D. (2010). Local tourism governance: A comparison of three network approaches. *Journal of Sustainable Tourism*, 18(1), 7–28.
Beritelli, P., Bieger, T., & Laesser, C. (2014). The new frontiers of destination management: Applying variable geometry as a function-based approach. *Journal of Travel Research*, 53(4), 403–417.
Beritelli, P., & Laesser, C. (2017). The dynamics of destinations and tourism development. In D.R. Fesenmaier, & Z. Xiang (eds) *Design science in tourism*, pp. 195–214. Cham, Switzerland: Springer.
Bieger, T., Beritelli, P., & Laesser, C. (2009). Size matters! Increasing DMO effectiveness and extending tourist destination boundaries. *Tourism*, 57(3), 309–327.
Blasco, D., Guia, J., & Prats, L. (2014a). Emergence of governance in cross-border destinations. *Annals of Tourism Research*, 49, 159–173.
Blasco, D., Guia, J., & Prats, L. (2014b). Tourism destination zoning in mountain regions: A consumer-based approach. *Tourism Geographies*, 16(3), 512–528.
Blasco, D., Guia, J., & Prats, L. (2016). Mountain tourism supply chain networks in cross-border settings: The case of Intercerdanya. In H. Richins, & J.S. Hull (eds) *Mountain tourism: Experiences, communities, environments and sustainable Futures*, pp. 235–245. Wallingford: CABI.
Bramwell, B., & Lane, B. (2011). Critical research on the governance of tourism and sustainability. *Journal of Sustainable Tourism*, 19(4–5), 411–421.
Choukroune, P. (1992). Tectonic evolution of the Pyrenees. *Annual Review of Earth and Planetary Sciences*, 20(1), 143–158.
Czernek, K. (2013). Determinants of cooperation in a tourist region. *Annals of Tourism Research*, 40, 83–104.
Dodescu, A., & Botezat, E. (2018). Similarity and complementarity in tourism development in a cross-border region: The case of Bihor-Hajdu Bihar. *Transylvanian Review*, 27, 143–159.
Dos Anjos, F.A., & Kennell, J. (2019). Tourism, governance and sustainable development. *Sustainability*, 11, 4257.
Faby, H. (2006). Tourism policy tools applied by the European Union to support cross-bordered tourism. In H. Wachowiak (ed) *Tourism and borders: Contemporary issues, policies and international research*, pp. 19–31. Aldershot: Ashgate.
Ferrer-Roca, N., Guia, J., & Blasco, D. (2022). Partnerships and the SDGs in a cross-border destination: The case of the Cerdanya Valley. *Journal of Sustainable Tourism*, 30(10), 2410–2427.
Gao, J., Ryan, C., Cave, J., & Zhang, C. (2019). Tourism border-making: A political economy of China's border tourism. *Annals of Tourism Research*, 76, 1–13.
Go, F.M., & Williams, A.P. (1993). Competing and cooperating in the changing tourism channel system. *Journal of Travel and Tourism Marketing*, 2(2/3), 229–248.
Greer, J. (2001). Whither partnership governance in Northern Ireland? *Environment and Planning C: Government and Policy*, 19, 751–770.
Hall, D. (2004). *Tourism and transition: Governance, transformation and development*. Wallingford: CABI.
Hartman, K. (2006). Destination management in cross border regions. In H. Wachowiak (ed) *Tourism and borders: Contemporary issues, policies and international research*, pp. 19–31. Aldershot: Ashgate.
Hills, J.R. (2016). *Tourism management and subnational borders under Australian federalism: Cross-border tourism management episodes in the Australian central east coast border region*. Lismore: Southern Cross University.
Ioannides, D. (2006). Editorial: Tourism in borderlands. *Tourism Geographies*, 8(2), 99–101.
Ioannides, D., Nielsen, P., & Billing, P. (2006). Transboundary collaboration in tourism: The case of the Bothnian Arc. *Tourism Geographies*, 8(2), 122–142.
Jackson, J. (2006). Developing regional tourism in China: The potential for activating business clusters in a socialist market economy. *Tourism Management*, 27(4), 695–706.
Jackson, J., & Murphy, P. (2002). Tourism destinations as clusters: Analytical experiences from the New World. *Tourism and Hospitality Research*, 4(1), 36–52.
Jackson, J., & Murphy, P. (2006). Clusters in regional tourism: An Australian case. *Annals of Tourism Research*, 33, 1018–1035.

Kachniewska, M. (2013). Towards the definition of a tourism cluster. *Journal of Entrepreneurship Management and Innovation (JEMI)*, 9(1), 33–56.

Kozak, M., & Buhalis, D. (2019). Cross–border tourism destination marketing: Prerequisites and critical success factors. *Journal of Destination Marketing & Management*, 14, 1–9.

Liberato, D., Alén, E., Liberato, P., & Domínguez, T. (2018). Governance and cooperation in Euroregions: Border tourism between Spain and Portugal. *European Planning Studies*, 26(7), 1347–1365.

Lovelock, B., & Boyd, S. (2006). Impediments to a cross-border collaborative model of destination management in the Catlins, New Zealand. *Tourism Geographies*, 8(2), 143–161.

Makkonen, T., Williams, A.M., Weidenfeld, A., & Kaistoe, V. (2018). Cross-border knowledge transfer and innovation in the European neighbourhood: Tourism cooperation at the Finnish-Russian border. *Tourism Management*, 68, 140–151.

Martinez, O. (1994). The dynamics of border interaction: New approaches to border analysis. In C. Schofield (ed), *Global Boundaries*, pp. 1–15. London: Routledge.

Medeiros, E. (2020). Delimiting cross-border areas for policy implementation: A multi-factor proposal. *European Planning Studies*, 28(1), 125–145.

Melisidou, S., Papageorgiou, A., Papayiannis, D., & Varvaressos, S. (2014). Tourism clusters as a potentially effective tool for local development and sustainability. *Journal of Tourism Research*, 9, 218–232.

Michael, E.J. (2003). Tourism micro-clusters. *Tourism Economics*, 9(2), 133–145.

Nilsson, J.K., Eskilsson, L., & Ek, R. (2010). Creating cross-border destinations: Interreg programmes and regionalization in the Baltic Sea Area. *Scandinavian Journal of Hospitality and Tourism*, 10(2), 153–172.

Novelli, M., Schmitz, B., & Spencer, T. (2006). Networks, clusters and innovation in tourism: A UK experience. *Tourism Management*, 27(6), 1141–1152.

Pechlaner, H., Volgger, M., & Herntrei, M. (2012). Destination management organizations as interface between destination governance and corporate governance. *Anatolia*, 23(2), 151–168.

Prokkola, E-K. (2008). Resources and barriers in tourism development: Cross-border cooperation, regionalization and destination building at the Finnish-Swedish border. *Fennia*, 186(1), 31–46.

Prokkola, E-K. (2010). Borders in tourism: The transformation of the Swedish-Finnish border landscape. *Current Issues in Tourism*, 13, 223–238.

Reinhold, S., Beritelli, P., & Grünig, R. (2019). A business model typology for destination management organizations. *Tourism Review*, 74(4), 1135–1152.

Rhodes, R.A.W. (1996). The new governance: Governing without government. *Political Studies*, 44(4), 652–667.

Rhodes, R.A.W. (1997). *Understanding governance: Policy networks, governance, reflexivity and accountability*. Buckingham: Open University Press.

Ruhanen, L., Scott, N., Ritchie, B., & Tkaczynski, A. (2010). Governance: A review and synthesis of the literature. *Tourism Review*, 65, 1–13.

Saarinen, J. (2017). Enclavic tourism spaces territorialization and bordering in tourism destination development and planning. *Tourism Geographies*, 19(3), 425–437.

Sahlins, P. (1989). *The making of France and Spain in the Pyrenees*. Oxford: University of California Press.

Saraniemi, S., & Kylänen, M. (2011). Problematizing the concept of tourism destination: An analysis of different theoretical approaches. *Journal of Travel Research*, 50(2), 133–143.

Selin, S., & Chavez, D. (1995). Developing an evolutionary tourism partnership model. *Annals of Tourism Research*, 22(4), 844–856.

Sialverstava, S., Hanchar, A., & Jalinik, M. (2019). Current issues of cross-border tourism management-Bibliometric analysis of research directions. *Studia Periegetica*, 28, 73–85.

Sofield, T. (2006). Border tourism and border communities: An overview. *Tourism Geographies*, 8(2), 102–121.

Stoffelen, A., Ioannides, D., & Vanneste, D. (2017). Obstacles to achieving cross-border tourism governance: A multi-scalar approach focusing on the German-Czech borderlands. *Annals of Tourism Research*, 64, 126–138.

Stoffelen, A., & Vanneste, D. (2017). Tourism and cross-border regional development: Insights in European contexts. *European Planning Studies*, 25(6), 1013–1033.

Stoffelen, A., & Vanneste, D. (2018). The role of history and identity discourses in cross-border tourism destination development: A Vogtland case study. *Journal of Destination Marketing and Management*, 8, 204–213.

Studzieniecki, T., & Meyer, B. (2017). The programming of tourism development in Polish cross-border areas during the 2007-2013 period. *6th Central European Conference in Regional Science – CERS*.

Timothy, D.J. (1995). Political boundaries and tourism: Borders as tourist attractions. *Tourism Management*, 16(7), 525–532.

Timothy, D.J. (1998). Cooperative tourism planning in a developing destination. *Journal of Sustainable Tourism*, 6(1), 52–68.

Timothy, D.J. (1999). Cross-border partnership in tourism resource management: International parks along the US-Canada border. *Journal of Sustainable Tourism*, 7(3–4), 182–205.

Timothy, D.J. (2001). *Tourism and political boundaries*. London: Routledge.

Timothy, D.J. (2006). Relationships between tourism and international boundaries. In H. Wachowiak (ed) *Tourism and borders: Contemporary issues, policies and international research*, pp. 9–18. Aldershot: Ashgate.

Timothy, D.J., Saarinen, J., & Viken, A. (2016). Tourism issues and international borders in the Nordic region. *Scandinavian Journal of Hospitality and Tourism*, 16(1), 1–13.

Tosun, C., Timothy, D.J., Parpairis, A., & MacDonald, D. (2005). Cross-border cooperation in tourism marketing growth strategies. *Journal of Travel & Tourism Marketing*, 18(1), 5–23.

Valente, F.J., Dredge, D., & Lohmann, G. (2015). Leadership and governance in regional tourism. *Journal of Destination Marketing & Management*, 4(2), 127–136.

Vitner Marković, S., & Šerić, N. (2011). Managing brand of cross-border tourist destinations: Case study cross-border cooperation Karlovac County (CRO) – Southeast Slovenia (SLO). *Proceedings of 8th International Conference 'Economic Integration, Competition and Cooperation'*, Opatija, University of Rijeka – Faculty of Economics.

Volgger, M., & Pechlaner, H. (2015). Governing networks in tourism: What have we achieved, what is still to be done and learned? *Tourism Review*, 70(4), 298–312.

Wachowiak, H. (2006). *Tourism and borders: Contemporary issues, policies and international research*. Aldershot: Ashgate.

Weidenfeld, A. (2013). Tourism and cross border regional innovation systems. *Annals of Tourism Research*, 42, 191–213.

Zahra, A.L. (2011). Rethinking regional tourism governance: The principle of subsidiarity. *Journal of Sustainable Tourism*, 19(4–5), 535–552.

Zhang, Y., & Blasco, D. (2022). Destination management amid COVID-19: A case study in La Cerdanya, Spain. *Anatolia*, 33(1), 116–127.

# 30
# TOURISM AND POLITICAL BORDERS

## Past–present Dynamics and the Age of Globalization

*Dallen J. Timothy and Alon Gelbman*

### Introduction

This book has provided an updated and comprehensive examination of the traditional relationships between borders and tourism—attractions, barriers, transit spaces, and modifiers of tourism landscapes, as well as deeper insight into the manifold recent geopolitical and cultural changes that are taking place throughout the world in this era of globalization, neoliberalism, exclusion and inclusion, mobility and immobility, and growing international tourism. This concluding chapter builds upon these traditions and the contents of this book by examining several issues that need further elaboration and research in border and tourism studies.

Although traditionally international boundaries and borderlands were largely neglected by state agents, they are today becoming increasingly recognized as an important part of national territory with considerable social and economic development potential. Throughout modern history, tourism in most borderlands has grown organically as locational conditions and border policies have stimulated the establishment of cross-border activities such as retail and shopping, prostitution, drug use, smuggling and petty trade, and gambling (Gao et al., 2019; Timothy, 1995a, 1995b, 2001; Zhang et al., 2019). However, today we see that tourism is being more intentionally planned at national borders to draw people across, as well as to draw domestic consumers to the same borderland services that appeal to people on the other side. Shopping centers, entertainment complexes (e.g., water parks and theme parks), resorts and golf courses, nature preserves and ecotourism centers, and heritage areas play an increasingly prominent role in countries' borderland tourism development plans. Likewise, many of the illicit activities that once plagued authorities in border areas have now been legitimized through official channels. For example, to quell illegal gambling, casinos have been built (Figure 30.1). Similarly, the establishment of free trade commercial zones in some borderlands is seen as a way to curtail illegal trade and smuggling, while simultaneously capturing more expenditures and taxes. The purposive planning of medical and healthcare facilities in close proximity to national boundaries draws large numbers of medical tourists to a highly lucrative service cluster that is becoming increasingly common at borders in North America, Europe, and Asia.

Regardless of their appeal, borders traditionally have been significant obstacles to human mobility in many ways, not least of which have included physical, administrative, and perceived barriers, despite prevailing discussions on the human right to travel (Bianchi et al., 2020;

*Figure 30.1* This Egyptian casino only 150 meters from the Israeli border was built at this site to capitalize on its close proximity to Israel.

(Photo: D.J. Timothy)

Timothy & Michalkó, 2016). Many of these impediments are intentional, enacted by the state to thwart undesirable forces or to provide opportunities to vet people and products. Heavy border fortifications and strict crossing regulations (e.g., visas and permits) are intentional, whereas people's perceptions about life on the other side, whether correct or incorrect, typically develop organically through stories, media exposure, and personal prejudices. These perceived constraints may in fact be a more significant barrier to crossing than are fences and heavy visa regulations.

In recent years, various debordering processes have diminished the obstructive role of borders. Increased levels of cross-border cooperation and growing transfrontier networks have alleviated many of the traditional obstacles to transboundary tourism development to the point now that communities and regions on opposite sides plan co-sponsored events, build joint-use infrastructure, and develop tourism co-marketing strategies with increased frequency (Michniak & Więckowski, 2021; Tosun et al., 2005; Timothy, 2019a; Timothy & Saarinen, 2013). With widespread debordering processes in Europe and elsewhere, these collaborative efforts have become ever present and have benefited many marginal communities whose action spaces have now extended abroad.

For many tourists, borders are simple nuisances that must be crossed to get to their intended destination. Thus, borders hold little meaning for many international travelers, but for the transit communities and merchants involved, "transit tourism" is an important economic mainstay. When border communities are tourist destinations or when they serve as points of transit, unique landscapes are created that reflect a complex relationship between urban morphology and tourism servicescapes. This is true for land and sea borders, as well as airport entry points.

The tourism landscapes of border destinations and transit areas are characterized by the prevalence of services that reflect different rules, regulations, or other elements of "otherness". All border spaces are home to government agencies that carry out their responsibilities related to passport and visa controls, customs inspections, tax authorities, security, and agricultural inspections. In addition to government regulatory agencies, border towns often have a distinct look about them. Service clusters tend to grow very near ports of entry, with highly taxed merchandise concentrating on retail establishments on the less-expensive side (Borzooie et al., 2021; Cuevas et al., 2016). Petrol stations, tobacconists, and alcohol shops often cluster against the border on the side with lower gas, tobacco, and alcohol taxes. Border-specific services also cluster near ports of entry, including insurance sales, currency exchange offices and banks, tax refund stations, and tourist information offices. In addition, much of the urban morphology may be altered depending on the role of the community in providing services and the types of tourism that develop there. Because of the early growth of prostitution- and alcohol-based tourism in Mexico's northern border towns, many of the cities physically developed with alcohol/bar zones and houses of prostitution in what Curtis and Arreola (1991; Arreola & Curtis, 1993) called "tolerance zones", or *zonas de tolerancia*, which physically demonstrate distance-decay patterns with regard to the intensity of service clusters in relation to the international border.

Most of these traditional patterns of border-tourism relationships still exist, but with rapid changes in globalization, debordering, rebordering, transfrontier networking, and other geopolitical forces, deeper perspectives on borders and tourism should be examined.

## Borders and Tourism: Concepts to Consider

The contributors to this volume have valiantly examined a wide range of concepts and theories pertaining to the development of tourism in borderlands and the interrelationships between borders and tourism, touching upon geopolitical, sociocultural, environmental, and economic perspectives. Many of the key issues, theories, and concepts related to borders and tourism raised in the book can be encapsulated in several themes. We have chosen to focus on the following: past–present relationships, conflict–peace processes, the dynamics of debordering and rebordering/borderlessness, transfrontier cooperation and collaboration, marginality and peripherality, and the age of the global pandemic. Each of these will be examined briefly in the sections that follow.

### *Past-present Relationships*

Border areas engaged in disputes and wars are paradoxically places fraught with danger, death, and darkness, yet they are also spaces of touristic intrigue and tourism development (Gelbman, 2019; Timothy, 2019c). In the past, such situations would have dissuaded the majority of visitors and severely curtailed tourism development, catering only to a small number of intrepid "danger tourists" (Butler & Suntikul, 2013). War tourism, a type of dark tourism, draws people interested in visiting authentic places where dangerous events occurred in the recent or distant past, or where conflict is ongoing. These types of attractions and visitation are part of the growing market niche of dark tourism, with battlefield tourism, war tourism, and heritage tourism surrounding sites of former wars, and danger zone tourism, extreme tourism, shock tourism, solidarity tourism, and political tourism being expressions of a desire to visit ongoing conflicts (Mahrouse, 2016).

Throughout history, border regions have been one of the most common theaters of war, where a closed and fortified border meant no tourism development and little, if any, tourist access to the border area for security and political reasons. Sometimes one-sided border attractions developed, allowing tourists in one country to gaze into the adversarial "other side" (e.g., the Israel–Syria, East–West Germany, North–South Cyprus, and South Korea–North Korea borders). These are popular because of the contrasting socio-political systems and the sharp distinctions between "here" and "there", magnified by intense propaganda that demonized the visible, albeit safely distant, "Other".

Although functioning as salient barriers to human mobility, these situations were, nonetheless, important tourist spectacles that were economically and politically lucrative. With geopolitical changes, transformative debordering often occurs, so that closed, militarized borders open to greater mobility and commerce. In these cases, the boundary line may become a tourist attraction that focuses primarily on the history and heritage of the place but also offers the possibility of developing more varied tourism products in the formerly closed border area in which it develops (Gelbman & Timothy, 2010; Hunter, 2015). Today, most of these tourism changes focus on retail and shopping, although there are many examples of beach tourism, ecotourism, and heritage tourism also opening with the debordering of once-restrictive border areas (Chhabra, 2018; Felsenstein & Freeman, 2001; Jury et al., 2011; Su & Li, 2021; Timothy, 2001, 2019c).

In addition to the development of tourism directly linked to a history of conflict and war, other models have also emerged, including cultural heritage-based tourism related to borderland communities. The hybridized lives of borderlanders have become a focus of tourism attention in recent years, but we still know relatively little about their lived experiences in the shadows of the border and how it has shaped their sense of identity and what they might want to share with outsiders (i.e., tourists). State peripheries often constitute the living spaces of ethnic minorities, who might have been marginalized socioeconomically and politically because of their minority status. Living on the state frontier has compounded the marginality of many such groups, and so they frequently seek tourism as a means of developing their livelihoods and as a theater for showcasing their living cultures (Chan, 2013; Marsico, 2016; Martínez, 1994). Research needs to address questions such as how ethnic minorities on the physical margins of the state see their own role in the state and the ways in which the border has affected their lives. These conditions have salient implications for the development of nature-based tourism, heritage tourism, and other tourisms (e.g., solidarity tourism) that might help elevate their status within the state and their economic wellbeing.

Perhaps no other concepts illustrate the past–present relationships in frontier areas like the notions of bordering, debordering, and rebordering. Bordering has the contradictory and multidextrous ability to repel and attract tourism simultaneously. Debordering tends to increase tourism flows and therefore cross-border management through networks and development clusters (Blasco et al., 2014; Makkonen et al., 2018), whereas rebordering inherently repels mobility and re-establishes the attractiveness that borders exuded early through the bordering process (Więckowski & Timothy, 2021).

An interesting perspective on debordering and rebordering is the idea that tourism is a powerful enough force to warrant changes in sovereign territory and the redrawing of state boundaries. Although this might seem highly unlikely, there are several examples where this has happened, including the shift of the Andorra–France border in 2001 for tourism purposes to accommodate the construction of the Envalira Tunnel to ensure that all of the new infrastructure would be on Andorran territory (Timothy et al., 2014). Likewise, in the 1960s, land was exchanged between France and Switzerland to ensure that the Geneva Airport would be built entirely on Swiss territory. In other locations, tourism is used as a justification to support legal claims to sovereign territory or boundary positioning (e.g., the Spratley Islands and

Antarctica) (Timothy, 2010, 2019c). Other examples of the geopolitical power of tourism to effect changes in state sovereignty and border alignments exist and should be examined from the perspective of sovereign rights and tourism.

Another phenomenon linking the past to the present is the dynamic nature of nationhood, statehood, territory, and borders. This dynamic nature is reflected in various secessionist movements throughout the world, most notably in Europe. There are strong and fervent movements in Spain (e.g., Catalonia) and the United Kingdom (e.g., Scotland), as well as less fervent movements in other countries, that embrace the idea of independence for parts of the current state. If these and other secession actions are eventually successful, they will have major implications for bordering and territorial change, which raises many questions about membership in supranational alliances, citizenship, economic development and asset allocation, government health care and pensions, and many other critical parts of everyday life that will be affected. Tourism, too, will see major impacts from these independence movements, along with bordering implications, just as the United Kingdom's break (Brexit) from the European Union did in 2020–2021 (Hall, 2020; Wilson, 2020).

## *Conflict-peace Process*

Borders between countries can be characterized by peaceful or conflictual relations in the past or present, as well as by transformational processes from one type of reality to another. In this way, the existing or past situation is reflected significantly in the area's characteristics and potential for tourism development. Many border regions are associated with geopolitical conflicts, disagreements, disputes, and political sensitivities (Coyle, 2017; Lal, 2006; Gelbman & Timothy, 2010; Timothy, 2019c). This type of border is known to be a barrier to tourism because it makes people feel unsafe and it thwarts cooperative development. Frontier regions tend to suffer from peripherality, which may be compounded by security problems and by their being regarded as unimportant in anything but strategic terms (Butler, 1996). While the potential for actual danger in frontier regions has little allure for most tourists, the excitement of visiting a politically controversial area does appeal to certain tourist market segments (Gelbman & Timothy, 2010; Isaac et al., 2019; Mansfeld & Korman, 2015; Perera, 2016; Timothy, 2001, 2019c). Many tourists who visit borders around the world that have undergone the transformation from a closed and hostile border to an open border where tourism dominates can remember or learn from the hostile past of the place (Gelbman & Timothy, 2010).

Unlike the tourism characteristics identified in the study of conflictual border tourism areas (Gelbman, 2008; Timothy, 2001), other studies address the varied characteristics of border and peace tourism (Gelbman, 2010) with their mostly non-existent barriers to cross-border tourism. Many different attractions (such as shopping, gambling, heritage, and nature preserves) develop along such borders, some of which may attract tourists from the other side (Timothy, 2001). Peace as a theme is especially prominent in border areas that formerly suffered from wars and confrontations, and tourism may serve as one of the strategies for warming or strengthening ties or symbolizing peaceful relations between bordering countries. Such elements can be seen for example in transfrontier nature preserves that straddle two or more boundaries, where physical barriers are removed and the area enjoys tourism-induced economic development.

## *Border(lessness) Dynamics*

On the heels of ongoing debate about the possible effects of globalization on the need for geopolitical borderlines, some scholars describe a debordering process that leads to a "borderless and deterritorialised world" (Caney, 2005; Kuper, 2004; Timothy, 1999). Newman (2006), however, argues that despite globalization, it is not feasible to expect a world that is entirely borderless or deterritorialized. Additional studies emphasize the continued need for borderlines, as even in a globalized world, the basic order of society must be preserved, and one of the functions of borders is to create order (Albert et al., 2001). Borders are political, and tourism is especially sensitive to the political effects of cross-border cooperation and the opening of borders, or conversely, to their closure to human movement. The effects of international terror activities are to arouse fear and tension, leading to caution and a hardening of cross-border tourism policies as part of a government's efforts to protect its citizens. Thus, we are witness to more and more border closings. Similar consequences develop as a result of international health crises and the spread of diseases such as SARS or avian flu, which restore borders to their traditional role as barriers (Sofield, 2006). This was emphasized recently with the global impact of COVID-19 on cross-border barriers to human movement (Hall et al., 2020; Zenker & Kock, 2020). While the opening of boundaries is viewed as a positive factor that encourages good relationships between neighboring countries, the recent global epidemic has shown how easily these bridges can be destroyed and barriers reconstructed. This issue will be discussed in greater detail in a later section.

A unique perspective related to borderlessness is the notion of placelessness (Relph, 1976). Space becomes place as humans imprint their cultures, values, and perspectives. Home, campus, grandma's farm, a tourist destination—are all places because of the values associated with them. Bordering is a process in which geopolitical values create place from space. Yet, on an individual level and commonly from a tourist perspective, borders are essentially placeless spaces. For most travelers, visiting border communities briefly or transiting an airport or train station would not constitute "having been there". Relatively few people would probably consider themselves having visited Qatar if their only presence in the country was changing flights at Hamad International Airport, yet they were physically in Qatar. Similarly, many people crossing a boundary only to visit a border community for a short time might not consider themselves having been in a country. For the first author (Dallen Timothy), this has been a matter of deep contemplation for many years. Years ago, a friend mentioned that he and his family had visited Tijuana on a day trip from San Diego. Timothy responded, "You told me you have never been to Mexico", to which his friend quipped, "Well, that's not *really* Mexico, and we were only there for a few hours". This leads us to think that perhaps borders and transit spaces for many people are non-places. Visiting just over the border for a brief day-trip or transiting through an airport do not represent having "been there". What then constitutes having been there? Is the act of leaving the airport and going into town essential? At borderlines, what constitutes an actual visit? At what geographic point do people consider themselves to be "abroad"? More research is needed, but the answers likely entail elements of distance, time, spending, and participating in common "touristic" activities.

Relatedly, in contemporary society, spaces of placelessness are increasing in their reach and extent. The widespread use of cyberspace as the new action space of the twenty-first century illustrates this point well (Kellerman, 2012). Gaming, virtual tours, visiting friends and relatives through video chatting platforms, and online shopping have essentially erased many borders that constrained physical mobility for centuries. Virtual living has hastened the globalization process and enabled access to places, products, and experiences many people only dreamed of. There is a growing literature on virtual travel and leisure e-shopping (e.g., Ankomah & Larson, 2019; Lu et al., 2022; Michalkó & Rátz, 2006; Régi et al., 2016), but understanding these opportunities from a debordering and deterritorializing perspective has yet to be well explored (Timothy, 2019b). Despite how it seems on the surface, even cyberspace has bordered limitations, such as people's inaccess to certain social media platforms or search engines in China and North Korea (e.g., Google and Facebook), which also restricts tourists' abilities to use these tools (Fu & Timothy, 2021). In cases of embargoes, such as the curtailing of social media access in Russia (by foreign companies and the Russian government) as a result of Russia's invasion of Ukraine in 2022, cyberspace may also be bordered and rebordered.

With regard to borderlessness, souvenirs no longer have to be purchased in situ as mementos of places dreamt of by would-be tourists (Swanson, 2014; Yuan et al., 2022). Souvenirs from even faraway places such as Pitcairn Island or Easter Island, mystical places where few tourists visit, can now be purchased online through those places' efforts at e-commerce. An added benefit of online souvenir sales is a reduction in remorse among former visitors. Often, tourists miss opportunities to buy certain souvenirs while in the destination, causing angst and regret among many visitors. Online souvenir sales provide opportunities for people to purchase the items they might have missed buying in the destination (Abendroth, 2011; Swanson, 2014). The online souvenir buying experience may provide exciting leisure opportunities, and the chance to purchase handicrafts or other souvenirs of unvisited places deterritorializes some aspects of the travel experience, rendering boundaries almost meaningless from an e-commerce perspective.

There is limited scholarly attention to the notion of borderless virtual travel and leisure consumption (e.g., Akhtar et al., 2021; Hassan, 2022; Kellerman, 2012; Leotta, 2021), but more work is needed to understand fully the implications of the deterritorialized spaces of tourism (cyberspace) which may allow people to "visit" desirable or curious destinations without having to cross political boundaries, even though as previously noted, cyberspace also has bounded limits. The growing presence of online shopping and cyber-travel deterritorializes and deborders consumption spaces dramatically and may have salient implications for the right to mobility and travel (Bianchi et al., 2020).

The COVID-19 pandemic and the shutting of borders to prevent its spread has received particular attention by scholars who have assessed the value of virtual, borderless travel (Akhtar et al., 2021; Leotta, 2021; Lu et al., 2022; Sarkady et al., 2021). The widespread outbreak of the coronavirus in early 2020 grounded thousands of flights, shuttered thousands of restaurants and lodging establishments, closed down many tourist attractions, and caused many service-sector employees to lose their livelihoods. Online journeys in cyberspace appear to have gained popularity during the pandemic, as these overcame the limits of physical borders in a virtual sense. People have been able to "visit" famous museums and archaeological sites through virtual tours and webcam technology. These situations raise many questions that have yet to be answered. How might cyber-travel convert into corporeal travel once the pandemic subsides and international travel resumes? Will the bounded online spaces that people have been forced to navigate translate into visiting physical places they learned about or watched online?

## *Transfrontier Cooperation and Collaboration*

Cooperative tourism development projects from both sides of the border are common in many frontier areas, especially where friendly relations exist between parties or when they wish to encourage good ties in places that have suffered in the past from conflicts. Evidence of this is especially prominent in academic research pertaining to transborder parks, in which neighboring countries come together to manage natural spaces jointly to preserve specific ecosystems where tourism almost always plays an important role. Transfrontier parks are territories encompassing parts of at least two countries and managed by a joint authority established for conservation purposes without regard to political boundaries. This does not mean, however, that the border is irrelevant. In nearly all cases, crossing formalities and procedures must still take place (Moswete et al., 2012; Timothy, 1999, 2000). Such parks bear various names: transfrontier protected areas, transboundary parks, transborder protected areas, conservation areas, or peace parks (Gelbman, 2010). Unique border areas of protected ecological and cultural heritage systems often become highly attractive to tourists (Więckowski, 2013, 2018). Prominent examples include Waterton-Glacier International Peace Park (USA–Canada), Iguazu Falls (Argentina–Brazil), and Victoria Falls (Zambia–Zimbabwe).

Other areas in tourism have benefited from the spread of transboundary collaboration, including regional marketing, product development, transportation, and joint visa policies. Common visa and passport areas now exist in Europe and Central America, and there is talk of other supranational alliances in Africa and Asia adopting common visa policies to ensure easier cross-border travel for citizens and tourists. There is a long history of cooperation in developing transportation and infrastructure astride borders or parallel to them for use by people on both sides. A recent example is the Cross Border Xpress, which was built across the USA–Mexico boundary to connect California with Tijuana's international airport, which enables pedestrians to walk to the airport without having to drive in Mexico or queue at customs and immigration stations. Basel airport is another example of close collaboration between Switzerland and France. Although the airport is in France, it services both countries and has separate customs offices for each one depending on where passengers are going. Along the Tornio River, which forms part of the Finland–Sweden border, the twin towns of Haparanda (Sweden) and Tornio (Finland) work closely in areas of education, emergency services, and particularly tourism development as the broader transboundary region is promoted holistically as a single destination. Thousands of examples of cross-border cooperation in nature protection, cultural conservation, and tourism exist and should be studied more to provide an understanding of how different contexts require different border waivers or levels of cooperation. It should also be important to understand the different constraints to cross-border collaboration, because these invariably differ by location, neighborly relations, and current degrees of integration.

## *Marginality and Peripherality*

By definition, political borders are located at the periphery of the state, often, but not always, far from more densely populated and economically advantaged core areas. As a result, they are often regarded as inferior to central areas, and many experience significant difficulties in developing economically and socially. Where few other socioeconomic activities have a chance to thrive, tourism is often looked favorably upon as a means of developing borderlands, not least because of these places' often-pristine natural environments and open areas, unique cultural heritages, and the potential opportunity to create closer ties with a neighboring country, which may lead to tourism growth opportunities, such as shopping and retail.

In most of the world's borderlands, however, tourism looks different from other areas. Of particular fascination is the idea of unconventional tourism, which alludes to tourism that is not measured or enumerated because it is either small in scale, does not involve overnight stays, or is of dubious legality. Smuggling and petty trade are two of the most common manifestations of unconventional tourism in border areas, and even though the smugglers and traders may not spend the night abroad, they are in fact participating in the broader phenomenon of tourism as they cross borders, buy, sell, and consume border spaces in other ways. Many border people earn a living selling their homemade or homegrown products across the frontier in marketplaces or to prepaying customers. Because these unofficial traders cross boundaries for their livelihoods, Timothy and Teye (2005) argue that they ought to be regarded as one manifestation of the Global South's version of business tourists. Such economic activities exist in many border areas, if not most, and have significant socioeconomic value and cultural salience, including intergenerational commercial activities in the borderlands. Thus, although these day visits and sometimes illicit activities are not conventionally counted in official tourism statistics, they assuredly are a part of the global tourism system (Michalkó & Timothy, 2001; Szytniewski et al., 2020; Timothy & Teye, 2005). Additional research is needed to understand their transfrontier networks, their economic impacts, and the social capital they create in undertaking their "business tourism" ventures. Such research would also expand our knowledge base about human "tourist" mobility beyond the normative tourism experience that features in most scholarly research.

An issue that was mentioned but not examined deeply in the volume is the notion of cross-border action space, which is an important consideration on the margins of the state with regard to mobility and debordering. In some places the lived experience of people's ordinary action space extends across national boundaries (Brandell, 2006). This occurs in borderlands where both sides of a border are culturally and economically integrated and where few barriers exist for transboundary interaction. A good example of this is the twin cities of Leticia, Colombia, and Tabatinga, Brazil, on the Amazon River at the tripoint between Colombia, Brazil, and Peru. This transfrontier agglomeration is essentially a functioning urban ecosystem with few connections to the rest of Brazil or Colombia, owing to the towns' peripheral location and lack of road-based access. The action space of residents of both municipalities is truly transfrontier; the border here is open, and personal and commercial activities occur freely despite their separation by an international boundary (Figure 30.2).

In other border areas, where societies have been separated longer, where borders are tighter, and where border settlements are better connected to the national core, people's action space may be reduced to their own side of the boundary. In these cases, borders usually create functional distances, where even though geographic distance is short, perceived distance is great, often with very little transfrontier interaction.

## *From a Security Agenda to a Pandemic Agenda*

In times of security crises states harden their border infrastructure and their transboundary mobility policies in an effort to protect their citizens (Newman, 2006; Scuzzarello & Kinnvall, 2013; Sofield, 2006). The Twin Towers tragedy in New York on September 11, 2001, saw an immediate closure of the USA's borders and enhanced the world's security agenda, adding considerable scrutiny to international cross-border activity in every corner of the globe (Hale, 2011; Mitchell, 2018; Nail, 2020). Many countries invested in security apparatuses everywhere but were particularly vigilant in securitizing national borders on land, at sea, and in airports. This rebordering process has affected human mobility in many ways, including changes in visa and passport regulations, increased security scrutiny at airports and border crossings, and increased vigilance in all tourism settings.

From March 2020, many countries began to tighten border controls and re-erect frontier fortifications in an effort to quell the spread of the coronavirus. This was particularly poignant in Europe, where the Schengen Agreement ensures open borders between signatory states, except in emergency conditions. Countries were fast to erect additional frontier barriers, and images abounded in the media in 2020 and 2021 of family members and friends, unable to cross or even touch one another across borderlines, facing each other on either side of the line. Border beaches, border villages, bisected heritage areas, hiking trails, and other tourism assets were fenced off and truncated to prevent people from crossing or coming into contact with

*Figure 30.2* Though clearly demarcated, the Colombia-Brazil border at Tabatinga and Leticia is open and facilitates a truly transfrontier lived action space for borderlanders and tourists.

(Photo: D.J. Timothy)

one another. In May 2021, the Chinese government even proposed building a border barrier on the summit of Mount Everest—an area of only around 8–10 m², depending on snow pack and ice—to limit contact between those who scaled from the Tibetan side and those who climbed from the Nepalese side (Reuters, 2021). This never came to fruition, but the fact that China had seriously considered doing it reveals the depth of seriousness and the scale at which border closures were considered and how microscopically human (im)mobility can be managed.

Frontier towns and villages were rebordered throughout the world. Main streets, residential avenues, and even rural farm roads were truncated with metal barriers, rock piles, gates, and police checkpoints. In some communities, buildings that straddle an international boundary were physically partitioned with barriers being erected indoors. In the Baarle-Hertog/Baarle-Nassau enclave community, a handful of shops and buildings lie astride the Dutch–Belgian border. In March 2020, the Belgian government ordered all non-essential stores to close, whereas the Dutch government did not. In the shops that overlie the borderline, only the Dutch portions remained open, creating some unique commercial and mobility challenges. Owing to the different national policies, a Zeeman store on the borderline only opened its Dutch portion, closing off the Belgian end of the store with caution tape. Accordingly, one Dutch customer quoted in Chini's (2020, n.p.) report lamented, "I needed underwear, but that's in the Belgian part of the store, so I could not get it".

Likewise, since the outbreak of the COVID-19 pandemic at the end of 2019 and the subsequent closing of many national borders in 2020, the global health agenda has gained a prominent position, along with other security measures, at international border crossings (Mallapaty, 2021; Więckowski & Timothy, 2021). Many international boundaries were closed early in 2020 with only periodic openings that year and in 2021. As of early 2022, many borders have reopened to increased trade and human traffic, including tourism. New regulations pertaining to health tests before and after crossing the border, quarantines, forms and health declarations, and various limitations instituted as part of the safety measures taken to prevent the spread of the coronavirus, have become the accepted standard (Pitkänen et al., 2020; Ryu et al., 2020). Policies regarding tourists and travel are constantly changing, sometimes from day to day, according to the level of coronavirus-related cases in a country. This new reality dramatically affects the scope of transborder tourism movement, as well as tourists' decision-making and travel patterns.

The COVID-19 pandemic also effected other types of bordering, namely in the form of "travel bubbles". The Baltic Bubble was a restricted travel zone that was formed on April 29, 2020. This area included Estonia, Latvia, and Lithuania, and enabled unrestricted travel within and between the three countries without the need for quarantines. The area's outer boundaries with Russia, Poland, and Belarus were closed to cross-border traffic. The Baltic Bubble lasted only until November the same year when COVID-19 cases began to resurge, solidifying the need for each state to close its own borders to human movement. Similarly, on April 19, 2021, a New Zealand and Australia travel bubble was initiated, allowing people to travel freely between the two neighbors for the first time in over a year (Frost, 2021). This non-quarantined travel zone was suspended only three months later due to severe outbreaks in Australia.

The effects of the global pandemic were largely overshadowed by the February 2022 Russian invasion of Ukraine. This was a clear example of the salience of state borders but also an illustration of how fallible they are. Although the Russian incursion at its essence is about the territorial integrity of a sovereign state (Ukraine) and the perceived territorial claims to a greater Russia, it also has major implications for human mobility beyond the borders of Russia and Ukraine. At the time this book went to press, over three million Ukrainian refugees had fled into Poland, Romania, Moldova, Slovakia, and Hungary, as well as further in Europe and North America, to escape the war. This has added another layer of frontier security, not just between the states that border Ukraine, but throughout Europe, especially in the countries that border Russia and which used to be part of the Soviet Union or in its communist-centered sphere of influence. In countries such as Poland, Lithuania, Latvia, and Estonia, borders and territorial integrity have moved to the forefront of concern among citizens, governments, and international agencies. The Russian aggression across Ukraine's borders U-turned the world's emphasis from COVID-19 back to the former security agenda with implications far beyond the borders of Eastern Europe.

## Final Word

Borders are around us everywhere, including the social boundaries that affect ordinary life, many of which are also political in nature and require careful navigation. Without discounting the importance of social, racial, gender, and other barriers, the focus of this book is tangible geopolitical borders, how they manifest on the ground, and how they affect tourism and ordinary life. Borders provide a wide range of opportunities for, and constraints to, tourism. They are simultaneously lines of exclusion and lines of inclusion, with both roles having salient implications for tourism, particularly as tourist attractions and destinations, constraints to travel and tourism development, as meaningless or meaningful transit spaces, and as co-creators of tourism and cultural landscapes.

Perhaps the most constant feature of political boundaries is their continuous state of change, in real, physical terms, as well as with regard to laws and policies that affect human mobility and economic development (Timothy & Michalkó, 2016). Bordering processes bring into existence state frontiers that mark limits of sovereign control and national territory, and perform security functions. This process and its outcomes demonstrate clear past–present relationships, marginality of borderlands and borderlanders, and are the foundations of border tourism, which has now been well documented in the literature. Debordering is a process that entails increased transfrontier cooperation, joint planning, cross-border networks, treaties, and other sorts of supranationalism and globalization that reduce the obstructive effects that have traditionally been the province of borders. This has given way to greater tourism growth, freer mobility, increased cooperation for common interests, more peaceful relations between neighbors, and a growing sense of borderlessness. Rebordering, the term *de jour*, has come about in particular in recent decades with the increased securitization of national frontiers in light of threats of terrorism, biosecurity, human trafficking, and drug and arms smuggling. These dynamic processes are nowadays in a constant state of flux, with global borders debordering and rebordering almost simultaneously at a dizzying pace.

Throughout history, borders have shifted, creating nations of people who lack a cohesive identity, while separating others that should rightfully belong together. This has resulted in

*Figure 30.3* The editors agreeing to edit this book together across the Dutch-Belgian border! (Photo: A. Gelbman)

many border conflicts and secessionist movements that have devastated regions, destabilized state governments, and slowed economic growth. It has also created certain socioeconomic competitive advantages in borderlands that do not exist elsewhere. These contradictions are what drive tourism in some border areas and repel its growth potential in others.

This book makes perfectly clear that borders are not simply lines on a map. In legal terms, they are the linear interfaces where two (or more) sovereign entities meet; they have no width or physical depth, but they extend to the center of the earth and upward into the atmosphere. In practice, however, borders do have depth, meaning, and value as places of inclusion or spaces of exclusion. To be successful, tourism requires both inclusion and exclusion, making borders and borderlands an ideal laboratory for understanding the political, social, and economic intricacies of tourism. The crossover between tourism and political boundaries is one of both editors' deepest academic passions, and we have pursued this line of inquiry for nearly 30 years (Figure 30.3). It is our sincerest hope that others will find this tome of value and carry on studying the multitudinous ways in which borders manifest in place and how they influence the human experience.

# References

Abendroth, L.J. (2011). The souvenir purchase decision: Effects of online availability. *International Journal of Culture, Tourism and Hospitality Research*, 5(2), 173–183.

Akhtar, N., Khan, N., Mahroof Khan, M., Ashraf, S., Hashmi, M.S., Khan, M.M., & Hishan, S.S. (2021). Post-COVID 19 tourism: Will digital tourism replace mass tourism? *Sustainability*, 13(10), 5352.

Albert, M., Jacobson, D., & Lapid, Y. (Eds.) (2001). *Identities, borders, orders: New directions in international relations theory*. Minneapolis: University of Minnesota Press.

Ankomah, P., & Larson, T. (2019). Virtual tourism and its potential for tourism development in sub-Saharan Africa. In M. Khosrow-Pour (Ed.), *Advanced methodologies and technologies in digital marketing and entrepreneurship*, pp. 584–595. Hershey, PA: IGI Global.

Arreola, D.D., & Curtis, J.R. (1993). *The Mexican border cities: Landscape anatomy and place personality*. Tucson: University of Arizona Press.

Bianchi, R.V., Stephenson, M.L., & Hannam, K. (2020). The contradictory politics of the right to travel: Mobilities, borders and tourism. *Mobilities*, 15(2), 290–306.

Blasco, D., Guia, J., & Prats, L. (2014). Emergence of governance in cross-border destinations. *Annals of Tourism Research*, 49, 159–173.

Borzooie, P., Lak, A., & Timothy, D.J. (2021). Designing urban customs and border marketplaces: A model and case study from Lotfabad, Iran. *Journal of Borderlands Studies*, 36(3), 469–486.

Brandell, I. (2006). *State frontiers: Borders and boundaries in the Middle East*. New York: Bloomsbury.

Butler, R.W. (1996). The development of tourism in frontier regions: Issues and approaches. In Y. Gradus, & H. Lithwick (Eds) *Frontiers in regional development*, pp. 213–229. Lanham, MD: Rowman & Littlefield.

Butler, R.W., & Suntikul, W. (Eds.). (2013). *Tourism and war*. London: Routledge.

Caney, S. (2005). *Justice beyond borders: A global political theory*. Oxford: Oxford University Press.

Chan, Y.W. (2013). *Vietnamese-Chinese relationships at the borderlands: Trade, tourism and cultural politics*. London: Routledge.

Chhabra, D. (2018). Soft power analysis in alienated borderline tourism. *Journal of Heritage Tourism*, 13(4), 289–304.

Chini, M. (2020). Coronavirus: Only half a store opens on Dutch/Belgian border. *The Brussels Times*, 25 March, 2020. Online: https://www.brusselstimes.com/102653/coronavirus-only-half-a-store-opens-on-the-dutch-belgian-border Accessed December 22, 2021.

Coyle, J.J. (2017). *Russia's border wars and frozen conflicts*. Cham, Switzerland: Springer.

Cuevas, T., Blasco, D., & Timothy, D.J. (2016). The Pink Store: A unique tourism enterprise at the US-Mexico border. *European Journal of Tourism Research*, 13, 122–131.

Curtis, J.R., & Arreola, D.D. (1991). Zonas de tolerancia on the northern Mexican border. *Geographical Review*, 81(3), 333–346.

Felsenstein, D., & Freeman, D. (2001). Estimating the impacts of crossborder competition: The case of gambling in Israel and Egypt. *Tourism Management*, 22(5), 511–521.

Frost, N. (2021). Families are reunited as Australia and New Zealand begin their travel bubble. *New York Times*, April 19, 2021. Online: https://www.nytimes.com/2021/04/19/world/australia-new-zealand-travel-bubble.html

Fu, Y., & Timothy, D.J. (2021). Social media constraints and destination images: The potential of barrier-free internet access for foreign tourists in an internet-restricted destination. *Tourism Management Perspectives*, 37, 100771.

Gao, J., Ryan, C., Cave, J., & Zhang, C. (2019). Tourism border-making: A political economy of China's border tourism. *Annals of Tourism Research*, 76, 1–13.

Gelbman, A. (2008). Border tourism in Israel: Conflict, peace, fear and hope. *Tourism Geographies*, 10(2), 193–213.

Gelbman, A. (2010). Border tourism as a space of presenting and symbolizing peace. In O. Moufakkir, & I. Kelly (Eds.), *Tourism, progress and peace*, pp. 83–98. Wallingford: CABI.

Gelbman, A. (2019). Tourism, peace, and global stability. In D.J. Timothy (ed.), *Handbook of globalisation and tourism*, pp. 149–160. Cheltenham: Edward Elgar.

Gelbman, A., & Timothy, D. J. (2010). From hostile boundaries to tourist attractions. *Current Issues in Tourism*, 13(3), 239–259.

Hale, G. (2011). Politics, people and passports: Contesting security, travel and trade on the US-Canada border. *Geopolitics*, 16(1), 27–69.

Hall, C.M., Scott, D., & Gössling, S. (2020). Pandemics, transformations and tourism: Be careful what you wish for. *Tourism Geographies*, 22(3), 577–598.

Hall, D. (2020). *Brexit and tourism: Process, impacts and non-policy*. Bristol: Channel View Publications.

Hassan, A. (Ed.) (2022). *Technology application in tourism in Asia: Innovations, theories and practices*. Singapore: Springer.

Hunter, W.C. (2015). The visual representation of border tourism: Demilitarized zone (DMZ) and Dokdo in South Korea. *International Journal of Tourism Research*, 17(2), 151–160.

Isaac, R.K., Çakmak, E., & Butler, R. (Eds.). (2019). *Tourism and hospitality in conflict-ridden destinations*. London: Routledge.

Jury, M.R., Cuamba, P., & Rubuluza, P. (2011). Development strategies for a coastal resort in Southern Mozambique. *African Journal of Business Management*, 5(2), 481–504.

Kellerman, A. (2012). *Daily spatial mobilities: Physical and virtual*. London: Routledge.

Kuper, A. (2004). *Democracy beyond borders: Justice and representation in global institutions*. Oxford: Oxford University Press.

Lal, C.K. (2006). The complexities of border conflicts in South Asia. *South Asian Survey*, 13(2), 253–263.

Leotta, A. (2021). Virtual tourism in the age of COVID-19: A case study of the Faroe Islands 'Remote Tourism' campaign. In D. Bonelli, & A. Leotta (Eds.), *Audiovisual tourism promotion: A critical overview*, pp. 107–125. Singapore: Palgrave Macmillan.

Lu, J., Xiao, X., Xu, Z., Wang, C., Zhang, M., & Zhou, Y. (2022). The potential of virtual tourism in the recovery of tourism industry during the COVID-19 pandemic. *Current Issues in Tourism*, 25(3), 441–457.

Mahrouse, G. (2016). War-zone tourism: Thinking beyond voyeurism and danger. *ACME: An International Journal for Critical Geographies*, 15(2), 330–345.

Makkonen, T., Hokkanen, T. J., Morozova, T., & Suharev, M. (2018). A social network analysis of cooperation in forest, mining and tourism industries in the Finnish–Russian cross-border region: Connectivity, hubs and robustness. *Eurasian Geography and Economics*, 59(5–6), 685–707.

Mallapaty, S. (2021). What the data say about border closures and COVID spread. *Nature*, 589(7841), 185–186.

Mansfeld, Y., & Korman, T. (2015). Between war and peace: Conflict heritage tourism along three Israeli border areas. *Tourism Geographies*, 17(3), 437–460.

Marsico, G. (2016). The borderland. *Culture & Psychology*, 22(2), 206–215.

Martínez, O.J. (1994). The dynamics of border interaction: New approaches to border analysis. In C.H. Schofield (ed), *World boundaries Vol. 1: Global boundaries*, pp. 1–15. London: Routledge.

Michalkó, G., & Rátz, T. (2006). Typically female features in Hungarian shopping tourism. *Migracijske i Etničke Teme*, 22(1–2), 79–93.

Michalkó, G., & Timothy, D.J. (2001). Cross-border shopping in Hungary: Causes and effects. *Visions in Leisure and Business*, 20(1), 4–22.

Michniak, D., & Więckowski, M. (2021). Changes of transport in cross-border tourist regions in the Polish–Slovak borderland: An (Un)sustainable development? In L. Zamparini (Ed.), *Sustainable transport and tourism destinations*, pp. 11–25. Bingley: Emerald.

Mitchell, C. (2018). An ever-closer union: Communitarization of the European Union's border security. *Mapping Politics*, 8, 77–89.

Moswete, N.N., Thapa, B., & Child, B. (2012). Attitudes and opinions of local and national public sector stakeholders towards Kgalagadi Transfrontier Park, Botswana. *International Journal of Sustainable Development & World Ecology*, 19(1), 67–80.

Nail, T. (2020). The politics of borders: Sovereignty, security, and the citizen after 9/11. *Contemporary Political Theory*, 19(3), 206–209.

Newman, D. (2006). The lines that continue to separate us: Borders in our 'borderless' world. *Progress in Human Geography*, 30(2), 143–161.

Perera, S. (2016). *Warzone tourism in Sri Lanka: Tales from darker places in paradise*. Los Angeles: SAGE.

Pitkänen, K., Hannonen, O., Toso, S., Gallent, N., Hamiduddin, I., Halseth, G., Hall, C.M., Müller, D.K., Treivish, A., & Nefedova, T. (2020). Second homes during corona – safe or unsafe haven and for whom? Reflections from researchers around the world. *Finnish Journal of Tourism Studies*, 16(2), 20–39.

Régi, T., Rátz, T., & Michalkó, G. (2016). Anti-shopping tourism: A new concept in the field of consumption. *Journal of Tourism and Cultural Change*, 14(1), 62–79.

Relph, E. (1976). *Place and placelessness*. London: Pion.

Reuters (2021). China to create 'line of separation' at Everest summit on COVID fears. Retrieved May 9, 2021, from www.reuters.com/world/asia-pacific/china-create-line-separation-everest-summit-covid-fears-2021-05-09/

Ryu, S., Gao, H., Wong, J.Y., Shiu, E.Y.C., Xiao, J., Fong, M.W., & Cowling, B.J. (2020). Nonpharmaceutical measures for pandemic influenza in nonhealthcare settings – international travel-related measures. *Emerging Infectious Diseases*, 26(5), 961–966.

Sarkady, D., Neuburger, L., & Egger, R. (2021). Virtual reality as a travel substitution tool during COVID-19. In L. Wörndl, C. Koo, & J.L. Stienmetz (Eds.), *Information and communication technologies in tourism 2021*, pp. 452–463. Cham, Switzerland: Springer.

Scuzzarello, S., & Kinnvall, C. (2013). Rebordering France and Denmark narratives and practices of border-construction in two European countries. *Mobilities*, 8(1), 90–106.

Sofield, T.H.B. (2006). Border tourism and border communities: An overview. *Tourism Geographies*, 8(2), 102–121.

Su, X., & Li, C. (2021). Bordering dynamics and the geopolitics of cross-border tourism between China and Myanmar. *Political Geography*, 86, 102372.

Swanson, K. (2014). Souvenirs, tourists, and tourism. In A.A. Lew, C.M. Hall, & A.M. Williams (Eds.), *The Wiley Blackwell companion to tourism*, pp. 179–188. Chichester: Wiley.

Szytniewski, B.B., Spierings, B., & Van Der Velde, M. (2020). Stretching the border: Shopping, petty trade and everyday life experiences in the Polish–Ukrainian borderland. *International Journal of Urban and Regional Research*, 44(3), 469–483.

Timothy, D.J. (1995a). International boundaries: new frontiers for tourism research. *Progress in Tourism and Hospitality Research*, 1(2), 141–152.

Timothy, D.J. (1995b). Political boundaries and tourism: Borders as tourist attractions. *Tourism Management*, 16(7), 525–532.

Timothy, D.J. (1999). Cross-border partnership in tourism resource management: International parks along the US–Canada border. *Journal of Sustainable Tourism*, 7(3/4), 182–205.

Timothy, D.J. (2000). Tourism and international parks. In R.W. Butler, & S.W. Boyd (Eds.), *Tourism and national parks: Issues and implications*, pp. 263–282. Chichester: Wiley.

Timothy, D.J. (2001). *Tourism and political boundaries*. London: Routledge.

Timothy, D.J. (2010). Contested place and the legitimization of sovereignty claims through tourism in Polar regions. In C.M. Hall, & J. Saarinen (Eds.), *Tourism and change in Polar regions: Climate, environment and experience*, pp. 288–300. London: Routledge.

Timothy, D.J. (2019a). Cooperation, border tourism, and policy implications. In K. Andriotis, D. Stylidis, & A. Weidenfeld (Eds.), *Tourism policy and planning implementation: Issues and challenges*, pp. 155–171. London: Routledge.

Timothy, D.J. (2019b) Introduction to the Handbook of Globalisation and Tourism. In D.J. Timothy (ed.) *Handbook of Globalisation and Tourism*, pp. 2–11. Cheltenham: Edward Elgar.

Timothy, D.J. (2019c). Tourism, border disputes and claims to territorial sovereignty. In R.K. Isaac, E. Çakmak, & R. Butler (eds) *Tourism and hospitality in conflict-ridden destinations*, pp. 25–38. London: Routledge.

Timothy, D.J., Guia, J., & Berthet, N. (2014). Tourism as a catalyst for changing boundaries and territorial sovereignty at an international border. *Current Issues in Tourism*, 17(1), 21–27.

Timothy, D.J., & Michalkó, G. (2016). European trends in spatial mobility. *Hungarian Geographical Bulletin*, 65(4), 317–320.

Timothy, D.J., & Saarinen, J. (2013). Cross-border co-operation and tourism in Europe. In C. Costa, E. Panyik, & D. Buhalis (Eds.), *Trends in European tourism planning and organisation*, pp. 64–74. Bristol: Channel View Publications.

Timothy, D.J., & Teye, V.B. (2005). Informal sector business travelers in the developing world: A borderlands perspective. *Journal of Tourism Studies*, 16(1), 82–92.

Tosun, C., Timothy, D.J., Parpairis, A., & McDonald, D. (2005). Cross-border cooperation in tourism marketing growth strategies. *Journal of Travel and Tourism Marketing*, 18(1), 5–23.

Więckowski, M. (2013). Eco-frontier in the mountainous borderlands of Central Europe: The case of Polish border parks. *Journal of Alpine Research*, 101(2), 1–13.

Więckowski, M. (2018). Political borders under ecological control in the Polish borderlands. *Geographia Polonica*, 91(1), 127–138.

Więckowski, M., & Timothy, D.J. (2021). Tourism and an evolving international boundary: Bordering, debordering and rebordering on Usedom Island, Poland-Germany. *Journal of Destination Marketing & Management*, 22, 100647.

Wilson, T.M. (2020). Fearing Brexit: The changing face of Europeanization in the borderlands of Northern Ireland. *Ethnologia Europaea*, 50(2), 32–48.

Yuan, X., Xie, Y., Li, S., & Shen, Y. (2022). When souvenirs meet online shopping–the effect of food souvenir types on online sales. *International Journal of Tourism Research*, 24(1), 58–70.

Zenker, S., & Kock, F. (2020). The coronavirus pandemic–A critical discussion of a tourism research agenda. *Tourism Management*, 81, 1–4.

Zhang, S., Zhong, L., Ju, H., & Wang, Y. (2019). Land border tourism resources in China: Spatial patterns and tourism management. *Sustainability*, 11(1), 236.

# INDEX

Afghanistan 196, 211, 260
airports 5, 114, 135, 139, 179, 404, 406, 408, 410
Albania 151, 152–153
alcohol consumption 5, 32, 225–226, 253, 271, 272, 288, 405
Andorra 179, 227, 230, 253, 395, 406
Angola 179
anthropology 36–37, 40, 43, 51, 112, 162
Antonine Walls 177, 184, 188
Approved Destination List (China) 138
Arctic Circle 180, 189, 253–262, 361
Argentina 366, 410
Armenia 2, 153, 197
asymmetrical development 318, 329, 345–347, 356–357, 386, 391, 394, 406
attractions, borders as 47, 50, 112, 117, 119, 177–191, 195–202, 205–214, 241–250, 254, 298, 310, 342, 403, 406, 414
attractions, border-themed 180, 184–187
attractions, divided by a border 179–180, 184–187
Australia 3, 88, 126, 154, 161, 320, 372, 413
Austria 3, 136, 185, 188, 220–221, 226, 330, 347
authenticity 166–167, 196, 241, 257, 260, 273
Azerbaijan 2, 153, 197, 224, 231, 235

backpacker tourism 126–131, 140–141
Bahrain 141
Baltic Bubble 126, 413
Bangladesh 2, 54, 103, 231
barriers 1, 3, 47, 69, 112–121, 162–163, 177–178, 182–184, 196–197, 200, 206, 209, 220, 244, 269, 271, 275, 310–311, 317, 329, 342, 372, 374, 384, 403–404, 406, 407, 408, 413

Belarus 2, 3, 66, 90–91, 112, 221, 413
Belgium 2, 181, 184, 185–186, 188, 222, 226–229, 331, 356, 361, 385, 387, 412, 414
Belize 327
Benelux 2, 313
Berlin Wall 50, 77, 106, 112, 117, 177, 184, 188, 195, 200–201, 211, 219, 223–225, 226–228, 249
biodiversity 48, 87–95, 366–367, 370
biometric surveillance 116
border closures *see* rebordering
border controls 101, 107, 112–113, 114, 119, 134–142, 178, 180, 182–183, 185, 229, 254, 271, 275, 315, 326, 367, 375, 404–405, 410
border identities 177, 199, 221, 225, 228, 254, 310, 341, 348, 354, 392, 406
bordering 4, 7, 18, 35, 55–56, 78, 113, 118–119, 169, 183, 195, 220, 222, 260, 406, 408–409
border markers 178, 180–181, 196–197, 226, 228, 230, 244, 253, 256–258
borderscapes/landscapes 5, 53, 112, 114, 117, 119, 178–179, 181, 182, 185, 221–222, 228, 230, 253, 256, 353
borderlessness 49, 52, 54–55, 65–66, 136, 141, 324, 359, 405, 407–409, 414
border-making *see* bordering
borderwork 2, 4, 53
Bosnia and Herzegovina 249
Botswana 220, 347, 367
boycotts *see* sanctions
Brazil 284, 366, 410, 411–412
Brexit 32–33, 42–43, 62, 161, 271, 314, 362, 407
Brunei 220
Bulgaria 112, 221, 318, 356
business travel 140–141, 270–271, 325, 331–334, 411

# Index

Cambodia 224
Canada 3, 54, 88, 91, 92, 103, 104, 105, 118, 154, 181, 185, 187–188, 226, 227, 230, 231, 256–257, 274, 284–285, 289, 313, 333, 366–367, 369–370, 382, 410
capitalism 49, 69, 73, 74–75, 77, 81, 82, 169
casinos 126–131, 403–404; *see also* gambling
Checkpoint Charlie 177, 182–183, 195, 219
Chile 387
China 23, 90, 102, 103, 116, 134, 137–138, 145–146, 152, 161, 163–164, 166, 177, 219, 223, 272, 274, 284, 304, 311, 313, 318–319, 346, 409, 412
citizenship 4, 53, 73–82, 101–102, 117, 136, 141, 297, 407
climate change 57, 62, 121, 361
clusters, cross-border 67, 230, 253, 391–399, 405, 406
Cold War 115, 177, 180, 197, 200, 361
collaboration *see* cooperation
Colombia 214, 411–412
colonialism 2, 24, 27, 66, 73–74, 297–298, 343
common pool resources 62–63
conflict 118, 145, 181, 187, 195–202, 206–209, 212, 241–250, 375, 405–407, 409
conservation 87–89, 92–95, 186–187, 221, 343, 366–376, 409–410
constraints *see* barriers
cooperation, cross-border 2, 6, 40, 61–69, 94–95, 101, 119, 120, 165, 178, 179, 181, 220–221, 225–227, 231, 249, 325, 341–342, 344–345, 347, 353–359, 366–376, 379–388, 391–399, 404–405, 407–408, 409–410, 414
core-periphery relationships 1, 177, 179, 371, 381, 407, 410–411
COVID-19 3, 47, 62, 66, 69, 73, 77, 79, 80–82, 104, 113, 116–117, 121, 126, 129, 134–135, 137–140, 209, 220, 269, 271, 275, 282, 290, 325, 332–333, 362, 397, 408–409, 411, 413
crime 130, 207, 215, 225, 328
crossing points *see* border controls
Croatia 3, 119, 120, 221
cruises 126–131, 154, 298
Cuba 114–115, 138, 190, 284
cultural boundaries 161–169
cultural differences 178–180, 310, 318, 329, 356, 372, 387
currency 6, 114, 153–154, 271, 347, 405
customs controls 112, 182, 185, 197, 228, 271, 275, 326, 333, 405; *see also* border controls
customs union 2, 161
cyberspace 52, 408–409
Cyprus 5, 120, 146, 149, 154, 182–183, 184, 195, 205–206, 212–213, 223–224, 345, 406
Czechia 120, 187, 226–227, 313, 345, 347, 356, 358, 387
Czechoslovakia 178–179, 367

danger zone tourism 196, 205
dark tourism 9, 184, 196–201, 205–215, 220, 223–225, 244–245, 248, 277, 405
day trips 1, 246, 270–271, 274, 281, 288, 325, 327, 408, 411
debordering 2–3, 4, 7, 47, 50, 52, 56, 121, 161, 179, 220–221, 229, 244, 312, 324, 356, 374, 404–408, 411, 414
defense *see* security
demarcation 52, 114, 117, 127, 178, 179, 185, 187, 220, 223, 228, 254, 315, 324
Denmark 80, 90, 92, 94–95, 271, 313
diasporas 106–107
distance decay 90, 92, 94, 272, 405
DR Congo 367
drugs 3, 214, 220, 225, 296, 326, 329–330, 403, 414
duty-free *see* tax-free

economic development/tourism development 1, 2–3, 4, 120, 135, 153, 177–179, 187, 200, 253, 297, 341, 353, 355–358, 372–373, 380, 386, 393, 403, 405, 407, 410, 414
economic leakage 129, 274
economy of scale 271–272
ecosystems 119, 366, 409; *see also* biodiversity
ecotourism 4, 87, 88–89, 94–95, 343, 347, 366, 371–372, 374–376, 387, 403, 406
Ecuador 253, 259
Egypt 151–152, 225, 404
embargos *see* sanctions
enclaved spaces *see* tourist bubbles
enclaves 41
England 88
Equator 180, 189, 253, 257, 259–260
Estonia 74, 80, 90, 126, 138, 361, 413
ethnicity 4, 161–169, 406
ethnography 19, 20, 32–44
European Coal and Steel Community 2
European Economic Community *see* European Union
European Union 2, 3, 4, 32–33, 53, 63–65, 67, 80, 95, 102, 104, 107, 112, 114, 116, 118–120, 137, 140–141, 146, 154–155, 162–163, 185–186, 187, 188, 220–221, 227, 229, 254, 273, 276, 313–314, 318, 324–325, 329–330, 353–362, 382, 407
exchange rates 114, 272, 274, 286; *see also* currency
exclaves *see* enclaves

fences *see* walls
Finland 80, 115, 117, 119, 120, 138, 178–179, 181, 185, 186, 189, 230, 253–260, 269, 271, 275, 311, 313–319, 344, 357, 359, 361, 410
First World War 228–229
fortifications *see* walls

France 2, 80, 105, 136, 138–139, 168, 179, 181, 184, 185, 188, 223, 226, 227, 228, 230, 231, 235, 253, 313–314, 316, 319, 358, 395–399, 406, 410
freedom of movement *see* human mobility
free trade area *see* customs union
Frontex 104

gambling 4, 6, 41, 178, 179, 225, 226, 253, 288, 296, 311, 326, 403; *see also* casinos
gender 4, 118, 283, 297–300, 303, 413
geodetic lines 189–190, 253, 260
geography 48, 51, 61, 282, 289, 344, 353, 361, 392
Georgia 50, 224, 231, 235
Germany 2, 47, 50, 77, 80, 94–95, 103, 105–106, 120, 136, 137, 139, 177, 178–179, 180–181, 184–186, 187–188, 195, 200, 219, 222, 223, 226, 228, 331, 345, 347, 356, 358, 361, 372, 385, 386–387, 406
Ghana 92, 230
global citizenship *see* citizenship
globalization 2, 37, 47–56, 61–62, 75–76, 130, 134–142, 166, 168–169, 220–221, 281–282, 287, 297–298, 300, 312, 329–330, 384, 394, 403–414; *see also* cooperation, cross-border
governance *see* cooperation; management
Great Wall of China 177, 184, 219, 223
Greece 18–22, 104, 106, 112, 152–153, 348
Guatemala 230
guest workers 36, 81, 103, 106, 138, 141, 332

Hadrian's Wall 177, 184
healthcare *see* medical tourism
heritage 4, 40, 56, 117, 152–153, 165–167, 177, 179–188, 195–201, 205–214, 241, 243, 249, 253, 273, 282, 288, 319, 353, 360–362, 367, 370, 374, 379, 381, 395, 403, 406, 410–411
Hong Kong 137–138, 272, 274, 311, 316, 318–319
human mobility 2, 6, 17, 37, 47–56, 73–82, 102, 112–121, 134–142, 155, 164–165, 182–183, 220, 253–254, 271, 274, 277, 310, 312, 315, 324, 329, 341–342, 354–355, 357, 374, 382, 403, 406, 408, 414
human rights 73–83, 101, 116, 134–136, 282, 315, 403
human trafficking 186, 220, 225, 296, 329, 414
Hungary 3, 50, 112, 221, 226, 313, 330, 357, 382, 413

Iliad and Odyssey 18, 21–22
illicit trade 40, 220, 324–334, 403; *see also* petty trade
immigration *see* migrants
India 2, 5, 21, 54, 102, 103, 107, 114, 180, 181, 183, 184, 196, 210, 223, 231, 285
Indigenous people 52, 163, 166, 168, 281

Indonesia 106, 302
Industrial Revolution 49
informal economy/trade *see* petty trade
infrastructure 120, 182, 228–230, 271, 275, 296–297, 326–327, 381, 404, 410; *see also* walls
integration 40, 65–67, 114, 161–162, 221, 314, 342–343, 346, 353–354, 356, 361, 367, 391–392, 410
international law 55, 146, 178, 184
International Peace Garden 185, 226, 372
Interreg 64, 231, 349, 355–359, 382
Iraq 105, 153
Ireland 2, 32–33, 200
Iron Curtain 5, 117, 177, 184, 188–189, 195–196, 224–225, 226–227, 255, 356, 362, 374, 385; *see also* Berlin Wall
Israel 5, 54, 106, 114, 115, 117–118, 120, 146–157, 184, 196–198, 207, 225, 246–249, 372, 404, 406
Italy 2, 3, 80, 103, 136, 148, 150, 152–153, 185, 187

Japan 149, 152, 154, 161, 284–285
Jordan 152, 154–155, 225, 246–247, 249, 372

Kenya 88, 211
Korean Demilitarized Zone 5, 163, 177, 180, 196–199, 201, 207, 212, 223, 229–230, 246
Korean War 149
Kuwait 138, 141

landscapes, border *see* borderscapes
language barriers 117–119, 263, 315, 347
Laos 181–182, 214, 348–349
Latvia 126, 361, 413
Lebanon 114, 149, 184, 197–198, 225
leisure travel 1, 37, 149, 152, 178, 269, 271, 274, 276, 282, 325, 331
Liberation Tigers of Tamil Eelam 105
Libya 150, 152–153
lifestyle migration 312–313
liminality 37, 39–40, 297
Lithuania 2, 50, 112, 126, 182, 413
low-cost carriers (airlines) 135, 139–140
Luxembourg 2, 181, 188, 226, 273, 361, 385, 387

Macau 137–138, 272, 274
Maginot Line 184, 228
Malaysia 166, 220, 227, 284, 301, 313, 316, 320
Maldives 81
Malta 320
management, border 1, 55, 63, 65, 82, 341–349, 356, 367, 372, 379–388, 384, 391–399
marketing 68, 120, 130–131, 179, 187, 191, 226, 269–270, 276–277, 346–347, 392–394, 404, 410

## Index

medical tourism 1, 4, 5–6, 178, 226, 253, 281–291, 326, 332, 397, 403
mental barriers *see* barriers
Mexico 6, 29, 54, 62, 88, 92, 104, 105, 106–107, 113, 114, 118, 119, 146, 162–163, 186, 187–188, 207, 210, 213–214, 220, 226, 228, 230, 284, 288–290, 298, 301, 313, 316, 329, 331–332, 405, 408, 410
microstates 230, 261, 326
migrants 36–37, 48, 52, 53–55, 101–107, 141, 165, 220, 225, 226, 254, 319, 325
migration *see* migrants
mobility of borders 53, 55
mobility rights *see* human rights
Moldova 155, 413
Montenegro 119, 120
Morocco 107, 146–147, 150–151, 155, 220
Mozambique 343, 348, 375, 386
museums *see* heritage
Myanmar 103, 181–182, 214, 348–349
myths/mythology 19–24, 244

Namibia 179
narcotourism *see* drugs
nationalism 47, 52, 56, 67, 73, 168, 222–224, 230, 303, 393
nation-building *see* nationalism
national identity *see* nationalism
national parks *see* parks
natural areas 47, 68, 81, 87, 92, 113, 119, 135, 179, 186, 188, 226, 241, 343, 371–372, 379, 397, 403, 407, 409–410
nature-based tourism *see* ecotourism
neoliberalism 50, 69, 75–78, 301, 305, 342, 403
Nepal 412
Netherlands 2, 94–95, 105, 181, 185–186, 227–229, 330, 356, 372, 412, 414
networks *see* cooperation
New Zealand 126, 161, 260, 372, 413
Northern Ireland 32–33, 41–43, 146, 211–212, 246–247
North Korea 114, 115, 138, 163, 177, 184, 196–199, 207, 223, 229–230, 246, 260, 375, 406, 409
Norway 115, 257, 359, 374

occupied regions 145–158
Oman 220
Orientalism 24, 27
overtourism 48, 135, 324–325

Pakistan 5, 103, 114, 180, 181, 183, 184, 196, 211, 223, 284
Palestine 106, 117–118, 120, 145–157, 225, 246, 248
Papua New Guinea 304

parks 47, 68, 88, 89–90, 177, 181–182, 185–187, 226, 343, 366–376, 387, 409
partitioned states 120, 195
partnerships *see* cooperation
passports 2, 53, 74, 103, 115–116, 135, 149, 229, 260–262, 271, 325, 353, 405, 410
peace 10, 67, 74, 107, 158, 180, 199, 211–212, 226, 244, 249, 324, 366–376, 405, 407, 414
Peace Arch Park 181, 185, 226, 372
Peace of Westphalia 101, 184, 221–222, 291, 324
peace parks *see* parks
performing borders 1–5, 117, 162, 253–263
peripherality 33, 68, 120, 163, 166, 178, 297, 341–342, 353–354, 392, 404–406, 410–411
permeability 61, 112–121, 197, 271, 275–276, 355
Peru 411
petty trade 4, 164, 324–334, 403, 410; *see also* illicit trade
physical barriers *see* barriers
pilgrimage 4, 24–26, 152, 154–155, 209, 282, 379
placelessness 141, 408
planning 7–8, 10, 63, 64, 68, 119, 179, 231, 302, 320, 341–349, 375, 384, 392, 403–404, 414
Poland 3, 50, 90–91, 181–182, 187, 188, 190, 221, 222, 225, 226–227, 228, 273, 356–357, 367, 413
political geography *see* geography
political science 51
ports of entry *see* border controls
Portugal 345, 360
poverty tourism 213
prostitution 4–5, 6, 148, 178, 225, 226, 253, 296–306, 326, 403, 405
protected areas *see* parks
psychological constraints 5

Qatar 141, 408

recreational travel *see* leisure tourism
rebordering 3, 7, 47, 50–51, 52, 56, 161, 210, 220, 222, 324–325, 405, 409, 411, 414
refugees 36–37, 48, 102, 103, 325, 375
relict boundaries 47, 177, 180–182, 200–201, 222–236
remittances 105–106, 306
resorts 126–131, 141, 149, 287, 298, 332, 361, 403
retail tourism *see* shopping
return visits 106; *see also* diasporas
right of access/mobility *see* human rights
Roman limes 1, 177, 184, 222
Romania 116, 356, 382, 413
routes *see* trails

Russia 50, 103, 115, 117, 134, 137, 149–150, 154, 155, 181, 186, 222, 235, 254–256, 260, 269, 271, 275, 316, 318, 357, 374, 409, 413
Russian invasion of Ukraine 69, 155, 269, 275, 357, 409, 413
Rwanda 208, 210, 367

sanctions 113, 114–115, 116, 120, 154, 301, 409
Saudi Arabia 103, 138, 141, 213
scale 48, 51, 61, 67, 94, 219–220, 345, 353, 357–359, 379–388, 394, 412
Schengen 3, 66, 118, 137, 140, 181, 185–188, 220–221, 229, 271, 314, 324, 330, 353, 360, 382, 411
secession 1, 225, 407
second-home tourism 117, 119, 310–320, 325
Second World War 2, 53, 65–66, 74, 102, 136, 138–139, 145–146, 147–152, 187, 220, 228, 324, 385
security 2, 4, 32, 78, 80, 127, 130, 135, 178, 184, 201, 225, 228, 254, 315, 325, 326, 382, 405–406, 414
sense of place 7, 177, 343, 381
September 11 terror attacks 3, 53–54, 271
Serbia 221, 357
sex tourism *see* prostitution
shadow economy *see* petty trade
shopping 2, 4, 5, 35, 40–41, 114, 121, 128, 178, 179, 181, 226, 230, 235–236, 253, 269–277, 287, 288, 311, 326–327, 332, 353, 355–356, 403, 405–406, 408–410
Singapore 284–285, 301, 302, 316
Slovakia 188, 225, 413
Slovenia 3, 112, 220–221, 313
smuggling 4, 5, 55, 187–188, 225, 226, 227–228, 230, 296, 324–334, 361, 375, 403, 410, 414
social capital 62, 63, 68–69, 127, 329, 411
social media 62, 135, 254, 258, 261–263, 287, 409
sociology 51, 392
solidarity tourism 106–107, 150, 406
Somalia 211
South Africa 103, 190, 343, 348, 367, 371–372, 375, 381, 386
South Korea 80, 114, 161, 163, 177, 184, 196–199, 207, 223, 229–230, 246, 302, 375, 406
sovereignty 1, 35, 38, 51–52, 54–55, 56, 73–75, 101, 121, 178, 179, 181, 184, 220–222, 226, 228–229, 324, 341, 406–407, 414
Soviet Union 2, 74–76, 115, 138, 181, 200, 223, 318, 413
Spain 92, 106, 168, 184, 188, 220, 226, 227, 230, 231, 235, 253, 273, 313, 315, 319, 345, 358, 360, 395–399, 407

Sri Lanka 105
stereotypes 80, 104, 117, 119, 187, 302
supranationalism 2, 62, 66–67, 95, 102–103, 135, 162, 179, 220, 276, 319, 324, 407, 414; *see also* European Union
sustainability 47, 119, 354, 367, 372, 374, 376, 391
Sweden 120–121, 181, 185, 230, 269, 271, 314, 318, 344, 359, 361, 372, 381, 386, 410
Switzerland 136, 179, 181, 185, 187, 347, 372, 406, 410
symbolism, borders 51, 118, 180–181, 221, 226, 228, 341
Syria 62, 103, 152–153, 155, 184, 196–198, 225, 260, 406

Taiwan 80, 116, 316
Tanzania 88
taxes 1, 113, 153–154, 178, 230, 319, 328, 331, 403
tax-free 35, 182, 230, 271, 326
terrorism 54, 141, 414
territorial change 2, 225, 407
territoriality 48, 51, 52–53, 61–62, 341
Thailand 181–182, 214, 224, 227, 284, 285, 301, 302, 348–349
theme parks 126–131, 166, 403
tobacco 5, 253, 272, 331, 334, 404
Togo 230
tour guides 241–250
tourism landscapes 177, 181, 244, 288, 310, 320, 403–405, 414
tourist bubbles 126–131, 141, 413
tour operators 199, 282
trails 178–179, 181, 184, 187, 188–189, 201, 226, 346–347, 360–361, 379–388, 411
transboundary protected areas *see* parks
transit spaces 2, 5, 139, 178, 190, 326–327, 403–405, 408, 414
transit tourism *see* transit spaces
transportation 134–142, 182, 275, 282, 332, 348, 354, 379, 410
travel bans *see* sanctions
travel restrictions *see* barriers
Treaty of Versailles 181, 228
tripoint 181–182, 186–188, 226
Tunisia 78, 285
Turkey 104, 105, 154, 205, 221, 348

Uganda 367
Ukraine 155, 357
UNESCO World Heritage 184, 223, 231, 366, 368
United Arab Emirates 138–139, 141, 151, 220
United Kingdom 2, 32, 81, 103, 105, 138, 155, 223, 319, 346, 358, 372, 387, 407

*Index*

United Nations 55, 74, 102, 103, 108, 136, 146, 151, 205, 324
United States 3, 47, 53, 62, 74, 79, 88, 91, 92, 103, 104, 105, 107, 113, 114–115, 116, 118, 119, 134, 137, 140, 154, 162–163, 181, 185, 187, 190, 200, 207, 213–214, 220, 222, 223, 226–227, 228, 230, 231, 255–256, 274, 285, 288–290, 298, 301, 316, 329, 331–333, 366–367, 369–370, 372, 382, 386, 410

vaccines 3–4, 81, 116, 134
VFR (visiting friends and relatives) tourism 1, 226, 281, 325, 408
Vietnam 54, 163–164, 166, 168, 245–246, 248–249, 302, 304
violence *see* security war
visa-free access 116, 140, 155
visas 2, 53, 74, 103, 113, 115–117, 120, 135, 137–138, 271, 275, 319, 325, 404–405, 410

walls, border 48, 53–54, 104, 112–113, 117, 119, 127, 152, 153, 177–178, 180, 183–184, 196, 220, 223, 225–226, 230, 246–247; *see also* barriers
wanderlust 17
wars 53, 62, 114–115, 145, 151, 180, 184, 195–196, 199, 220, 221, 224, 246, 361, 405–406
war on terror 53–54, 116; *see also* conflict
Western Sahara 146, 150–151, 155
World Tourism Organization 1, 75, 138, 270, 333

xenophobia 35, 80, 118, 165

Yemen 151, 213
Yugoslavia 50

Zambia 346–347, 366, 410
Zimbabwe 220, 343, 346, 347–348, 366, 375, 410